THE ROAD TO DIEN BIEN PHU

THE ROAD TO DIEN BIEN PHU

A HISTORY OF THE FIRST WAR FOR VIETNAM

CHRISTOPHER GOSCHA

PRINCETON UNIVERSITY PRESS

PRINCETON & OXFORD

Published by Princeton University Press
41 William Street, Princeton, New Jersey 08540
6 Oxford Street, Woodstock, Oxfordshire OX20 1TR

press.princeton.edu   .

All Rights Reserved

Library of Congress Cataloging-in-Publication Data

Names: Goscha, Christopher E., author.
Title: The road to Dien Bien Phu : a history of the first war for Vietnam /
    Christopher Goscha.
Description: Princeton : Princeton University Press, 2022. | Includes bibliographical
    references and index.
Identifiers: LCCN 2021010045 (print) | LCCN 2021010046 (ebook) |
    ISBN 9780691180168 (hardback) | ISBN 9780691228655 (ebook)
Subjects: LCSH: Indochinese War, 1946–1954. | Communism—Vietnam—
    History—20th century. | Decolonization—Vietnam—History. | Vietnam—
    History, Military—20th century.
Classification: LCC DS556.54 .G67 2022 (print) | LCC DS556.54 (ebook) |
    DDC 959.704/1–dc23
LC record available at https://lccn.loc.gov/2021010045
LC ebook record available at https://lccn.loc.gov/2021010046

British Library Cataloging-in-Publication Data is available

Editorial: Priya Nelson, Thalia Leaf, and Barbara Shi
Production Editorial: Kathleen Cioffi
Text Design: Karl Spurzem
Jacket Design: Faceout Studio
Production: Danielle Amatucci
Publicity: Alyssa Sanford and Carmen Jimenez

Jacket image: Werner Bischof, "Vietnamese women walking along the road in front of the grave of a French soldier killed during the war," 1952, Tonkin / Magnum Photo

This book has been composed in Arno with Herchey Serif and DIN Next display

Printed on acid-free paper. ∞

Printed in the United States of America

10 9 8 7 6 5 4 3 2 1

CONTENTS

A link to the online bibliography with Vietnamese diacritics can be found at www.cgoscha.uqam.ca

ACKNOWLEDGMENTS

I never realized when I first set out to write this book how difficult the task would be. Things were rarely what they appeared to be at the start. What I thought was a simple war of decolonization turned out to be a series of conflicts wrapped into one very complicated conflagration. Where I thought there were only two main actors, the French and their Vietnamese opponents led by Ho Chi Minh, there were many more. And even the Vietnam whose statecraft I thought I knew best, Ho's, was not what I had initially thought it to be. To help me find my way, a group of friends, colleagues, scholars, and editors were always there to help me. Although they may not agree with the path I ended up taking to get through the forest of the first war for Vietnam, also known as the Indochina War (1945–54), I am deeply indebted to each of them. They took the time out of their busy schedules to read and comment on my draft chapters, shared references and ideas with me, and made invaluable suggestions for improving the book. They are: Nasir Abdoul-Carime, Pierre Asselin, Andrew Barros, Madame Bernard (chi Son), Michel Bonin, Pascal Bordeaux, the late Georges Boudarel, Mark Bradley, Raphaëlle Branche, Pierre Brocheux, Ivan Cadeau, Nayan Chanda, Chen Jian, Haydon Cherry, Gareth Curless, Do Kien, Doan Cam Thi Poisson, Olga Dror, Duong Van Mai Elliot, David Elliot, Max Friedman, Martin Grossheim, François Guillemot, Andrew Hardy, Steve Heder, Daniel Hémery, Judith Henchey, Alec Holcombe, Jim House, Talbot Imlay, Jérémy Jammes, Charles Keith, Liam Kelly, Agathe Larcher, Mark Lawrence, Antoine Le, Yuxi Liu, Henri Locard, Bruce Lockhart, Fredrik Logevall, Lorenz Lüthi, Neils Macmaster, Edward Marolda, Alexis Mathé, Ariane Mathieu, Shawn McHale, Mark Moyar, Jeremy Murray,

Nguyen Lan Binh, Nguyen Manh Hung, Phi-Van Nguyen, Nguyen Quoc Thanh, Nguyen Tung, Philippe Papin, Vatthana Pholsena, Emmanuel Poisson, Merle Pribbenow, Qiang Zhai, Sophie Quinn-Judge, Martin Rathi, Brett Reilly, Félix Rhéaume, Brigitta van Rheinberg, Véronique Sales, Gerard Sasges, Ronald Spector, Balazs Szalontai, Elie Tenenbaum, Sylvie Thénault, Claire Tran Thi Lien, William Turley, Maurice Vaïsse, Dominique Vesin, Paul and Marie-Catherine Villatoux, Alex-Thai D. Vo, and Peter Zinoman. A special thank you to those who generously went through (or rather suffered through) all or almost all of the manuscript: Pierre Grosser, François Guillemot, Mark Lawrence, David Marr, Edward Miller, Edwin Moise, Martin Thomas, Stein Tonnesson, George (Jay) Veith, Tuong Vu, Edward (Ted) Walters, and Arne Westad. I also owe a special thanks to two anonymous readers who carefully went through my draft manuscript and provided incredibly helpful comments. On the equally important production side, Jeff Edwards did a brilliant job on the maps. My thanks at Princeton University Press to Eric Crahan, Thalia Leaf, Kathleen Cioffi, David Campbell, Karl Spurzem, and Priya Nelson for their excellent work in bringing this project to fruition and for putting up with me along the way. I am particularly grateful to Louisa Sladen Watson for her excellent copyediting. Her watchful eye and excellent suggestions made this a better book.

All errors, factual or interpretative, are mine alone.

Christopher Goscha
Université du Québec à Montréal

A WORD ABOUT WORDS

In the pages that follow, I will only use one name for the Vietnamese state that went to war against the French (and then against the Americans). It is the "Democratic Republic of Vietnam," abbreviated as the DRV. In Vietnamese it is: Viet Nam Dan Chu Cong Hoa. This term refers to the state Ho Chi Minh declared independent on 2 September 1945 and which he led as President until an armistice was signed in Geneva on 21 July 1954, ending the fighting and my book. I do not use the term "Viet Minh" or the "Viet Minh regime" to describe this state or its activities. For one, the Viet Minh ceased to exist in early 1951, intentionally dissolved by its communist makers. That is reason enough not to use it after that date. Second, the "Viet Minh" was a nationalist front created in 1941, briefly a political party in 1945 and 1946, but it was never a state. To treat it as if it were is not only inaccurate; but it also prevents us from seeing a more complicated and, I believe, more interesting story of statecraft during the Indochina War, the subject of this book.

We also need to agree on the terms we use to describe what the French and their Vietnamese partners were doing. First, I use the terms "French Indochina" or the "Indochinese federation" to refer to the colonial state the French stitched back together in one form or another between 1945 and 1954. The French folded their Indochinese federation into a larger colonial entity known as the French Union, which was created in October 1946 and based out of Paris.[1] To this, we need to add the "Associated State of Vietnam." It came to life when the French finally allowed their noncommunist Vietnamese partners lined up behind the former Emperor Bao Dai to combine Cochinchina, Annam, and Tonkin (for the colonial south, center, and north) into a unified territorial state the French agreed to call "Vietnam." This Vietnamese state was nevertheless part of an Indochinese ensemble known officially as the Etats associés de l'Indochine or the "Associated States of Indochina." It included Bao Dai's Vietnam, King Sisavang Vong's Laos, and King Norodom Sihanouk's Cambodia. All three states were by "association" part of an Indochinese federal state run by the French. It was not the "State of Vietnam." It was the "Associated State of Vietnam." Collectively, the "Associated States of Indochina" were, in turn, part of this larger imperial body administered from Paris, the French Union. The Vietnamese allied with the French knew that "Association" at both the Indochinese and French Union levels bound them legally to the French republic.

A further word on Bao Dai's Vietnam is necessary here. Official historians in communist Vietnam today, the one Ho declared independent in 1945, have preferred to banish the Associated State of Vietnam from their historical memory.[2] Starting in 1949, Ho Chi Minh's disciples dismissed it as a "puppet regime" (*che do bu nhin* or *nguy*) and its leaders as the "lackeys" (*tay sai*) of the French, not least of all its head of state, the ex-emperor Bao Dai. The problem is that Bao Dai's Associated State of Vietnam existed at the time. It is not because it was not fully sovereign that it does not matter. Bao Dai's Vietnam and the French Indochinese federation standing behind it were actors with whom Ho Chi Minh had to contend in order to build the Democratic Republic of Vietnam. The same is true of the two sister states Ho Chi Minh brought to life in Laos and Cambodia during the second half of the Indochina conflict, discussed later in this book. Although they were not sovereign states, free of Vietnamese control, that does not mean that they do not matter. They run Laos and Cambodia to this day.

Words count, and by using them precisely and carefully they can help us to shed new light on the complexity of the Democratic Republic of Vietnam, as well as the other states involved in the Indochina War. Having said all of this, there will admittedly be times when I use the words "Vietnam" and "the Vietnamese" to refer in general terms to Ho Chi Minh's Vietnam or to the one Bao Dai led in association with the French. Readers should not interpret this as political bias, but rather as a desire to keep the narrative moving. I do not want to burden my readers with all sorts of qualifications. For similar reasons, I will also speak from time to time of "Vietnamese communists" and "French colonialists." I justify this usage on the following grounds: at the core of the Democratic Republic of Vietnam was the Communist Party and its founder, Ho Chi Minh. No matter how anticolonialist Ho and his entourage most certainly were, they were also dedicated communists. Similarly, those in charge of the French republic during the Indochina War, with the possible exception of the communists from 1948, wanted to keep Vietnam French, in the French Union, and this straight through until the Geneva Conference. Again, no matter how anticommunist many French leaders were, they were the colonizers during the Indochina War. It was no accident that the French went to war in Algeria a few months after Dien Bien Phu fell in May 1954. It was not to stop communists.

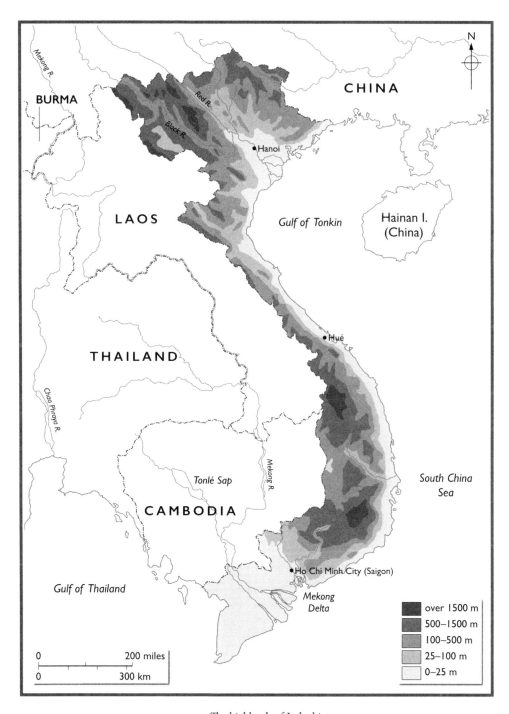

MAP 1. The highlands of Indochina.

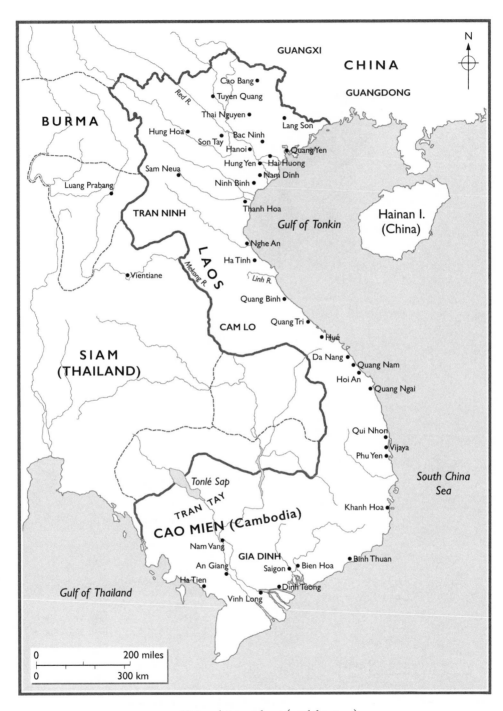

MAP 2. Vietnam's imperial past (until the 1840s).

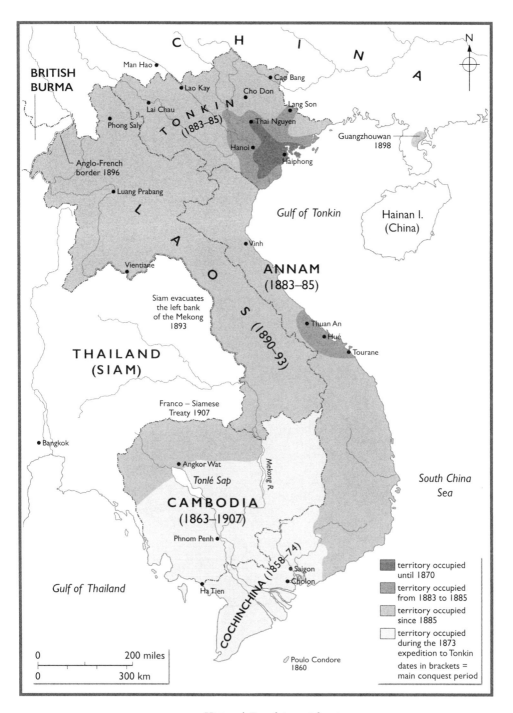

C　H　I　N　A

BRITISH
BURMA

Man Hao

Cao Bang

Lao Kay

Cho Don

Lai Chau

Lang Son

T O N K I N
(1883–85)

Thai Nguyen

Phong Saly

Hanoi

Guangzhouwan
1898

Haiphong

Anglo-French
border 1896

Gulf of Tonkin

Hainan I.
(China)

Luang Prabang

L

Vinh

A

ANNAM
(1883–85)

O

Siam evacuates
the left bank
of the Mekong
1893

S

(1890–93)

Thuan An

Hué

Tourane

THAILAND
(SIAM)

Franco – Siamese
Treaty 1907

Bangkok

Angkor Wat

Mekong R.

South China
Sea

Tonlé Sap

CAMBODIA
(1863–1907)

Phnom Penh

Gulf of Thailand

Ha Tien

COCHINCHINA (1858–74)

Saigon

Cholon

0   200 miles

0   300 km

Poulo Condore
1860

territory occupied
until 1870

territory occupied
from 1883 to 1885

territory occupied
since 1885

territory occupied
during the 1873
expedition to Tonkin

dates in brackets =
main conquest period

MAP 3. Vietnam's French imperial past.

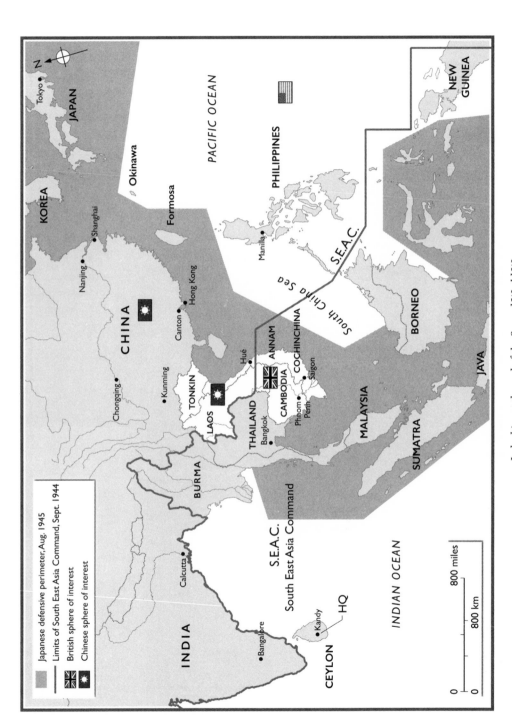

MAP 4. Indochina at the end of the Second World War.

Japanese defensive perimeter, Aug. 1945
Limits of South East Asia Command, Sept. 1944
British sphere of interest
Chinese sphere of interest

JAPAN
Tokyo
KOREA
Okinawa
Shanghai
Nanjing
Formosa
CHINA
Hong Kong
Canton
PACIFIC OCEAN
Chongqing
Kunming
TONKIN
PHILIPPINES
Manila
LAOS
Hué
ANNAM
S.E.A.C.
BURMA
THAILAND
COCHINCHINA
Saigon
South China Sea
Bangkok
CAMBODIA
Phnom
Penh
BORNEO
S.E.A.C.
South East Asia Command
MALAYSIA
SUMATRA
JAVA
NEW
GUINEA
INDIA
Calcutta
Bangalore
CEYLON
Kandy
HQ
INDIAN OCEAN

800 miles
800 km
0
0

MAP 5. Allied occupation of Indochina (1945–6).

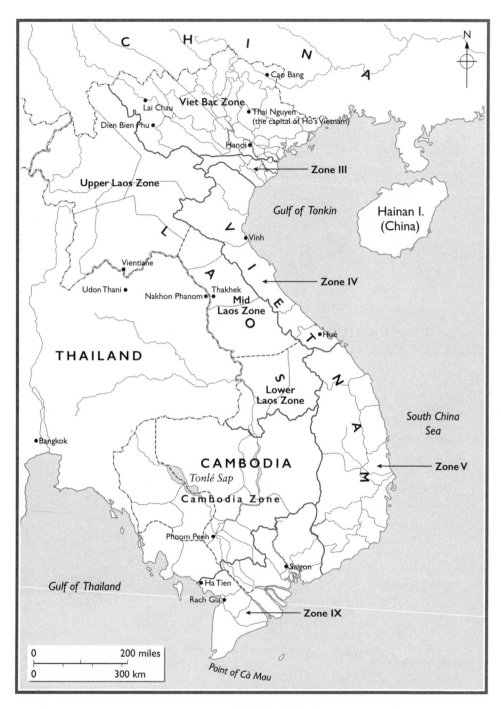

MAP 6. The main DRV zones.

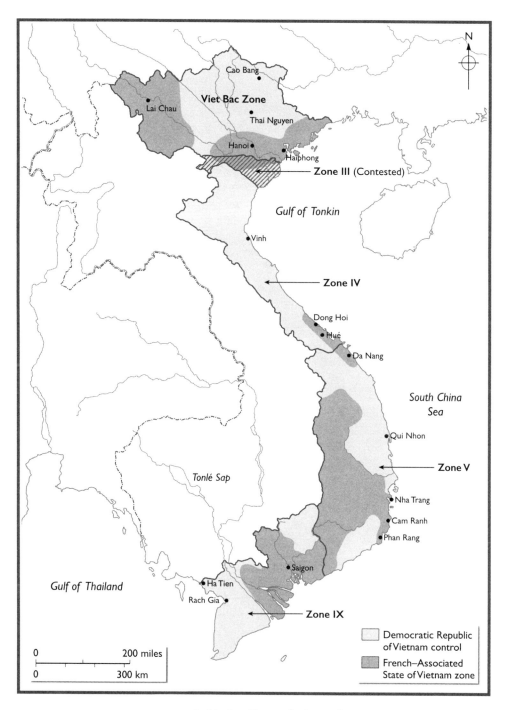

N

Cao Bang

Viet Bac Zone

Lai Chau

Thai Nguyen

Hanoi

Haiphong

——— Zone III (Contested)

Gulf of Tonkin

Vinh

Zone IV

Dong Hoi

Hué

Da Nang

*South China
Sea*

Qui Nhon

Zone V

Nha Trang

Cam Ranh

Phan Rang

Tonlé Sap

Saigon

Gulf of Thailand

Ha Tien

Rach Gia

Zone IX

Democratic Republic
of Vietnam control

French–Associated
State of Vietnam zone

| 0 | | 200 miles |
| 0 | | 300 km |

MAP 7. Archipelago Vietnam (early 1950s).

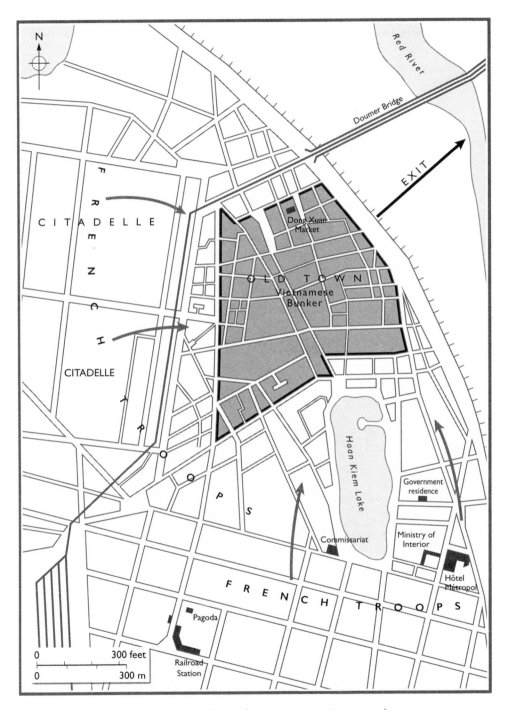

MAP 8. The Battle of Hanoi (December 1946–February 1947).

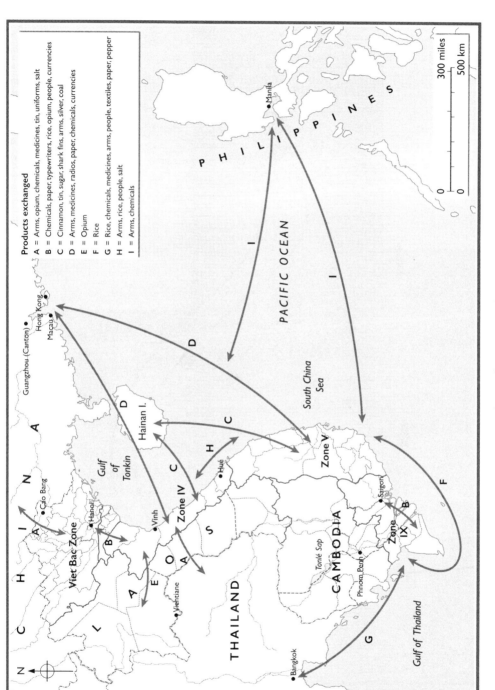

Products exchanged

A = Arms, opium, chemicals, medicines, tin, uniforms, salt
B = Chemicals, paper, typewriters, rice, opium, people, currencies
C = Cinnamon, tin, sugar, shark fins, arms, silver, coal
D = Arms, medicines, radios, paper, chemicals, currencies
E = Opium
F = Rice
G = Rice, chemicals, medicines, arms, people, textiles, paper, pepper
H = Arms, rice, people, salt
I = Arms, chemicals

MAP 9. The DRV's economic exchanges.

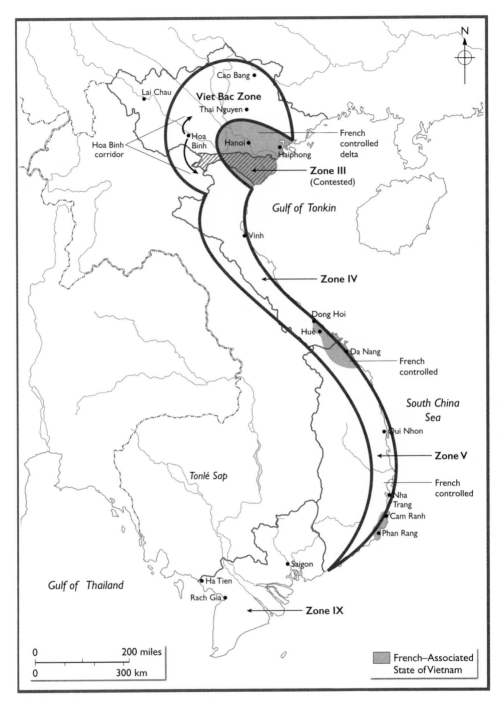

MAP 10. The DRV's "sickle shape" (1950–54).

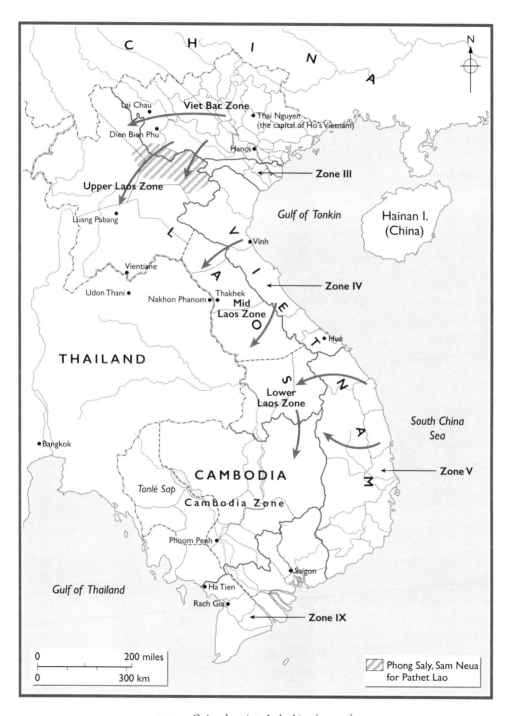

MAP 11. Going deep into Indochina (1952–4).

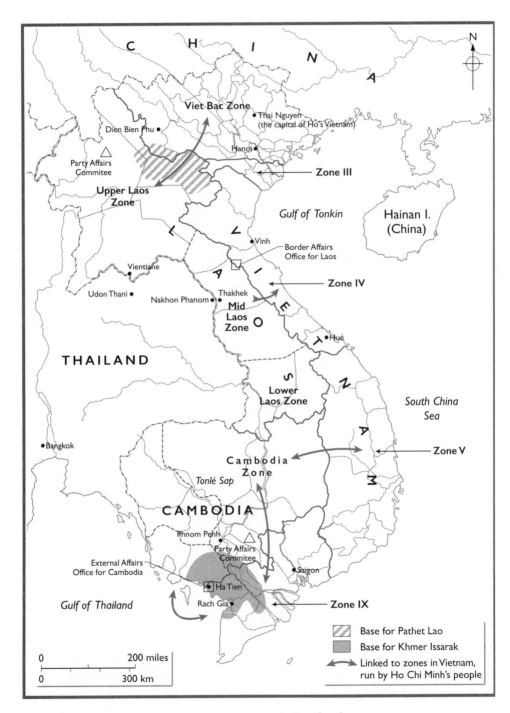

MAP 12. Communist Indochina (1952).

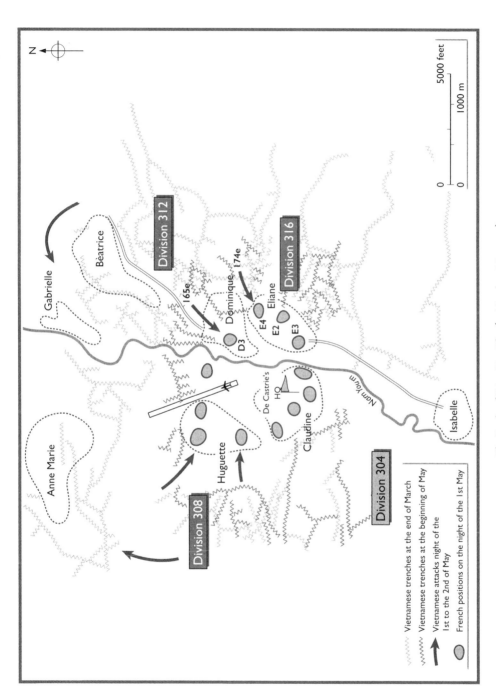

MAP 13. The Battle of Dien Bien Phu (13 March–7 May 1954).

N

5000 feet

1000 m

0

0

Gabrielle

Béatrice

Division 312

Anne Marie

165e

Dominique

174e

D3

Eliane

E4

E2

E3

Division 316

De Castries's

HQ

Claudine

Nam Youm

Huguette

Division 308

Division 304

Isabelle

Vietnamese trenches at the end of March

Vietnamese trenches at the beginning of May

Vietnamese attacks night of the 1st to the 2nd of May

French positions on the night of the 1st May

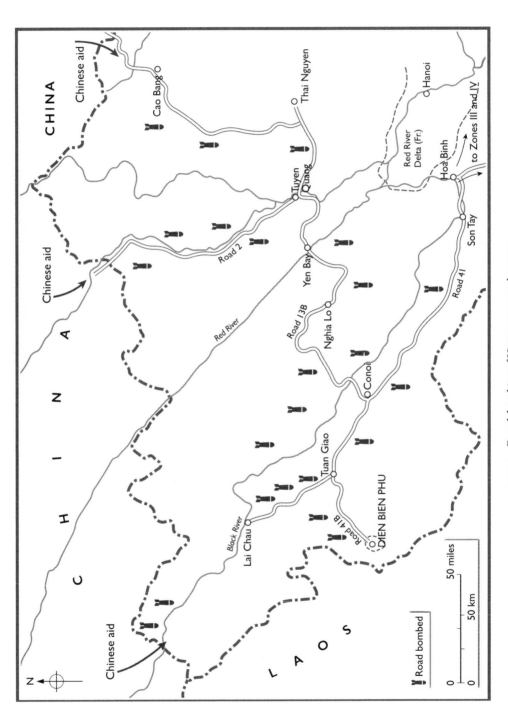

MAP 14. French bombing of Vietnamese supply routes.

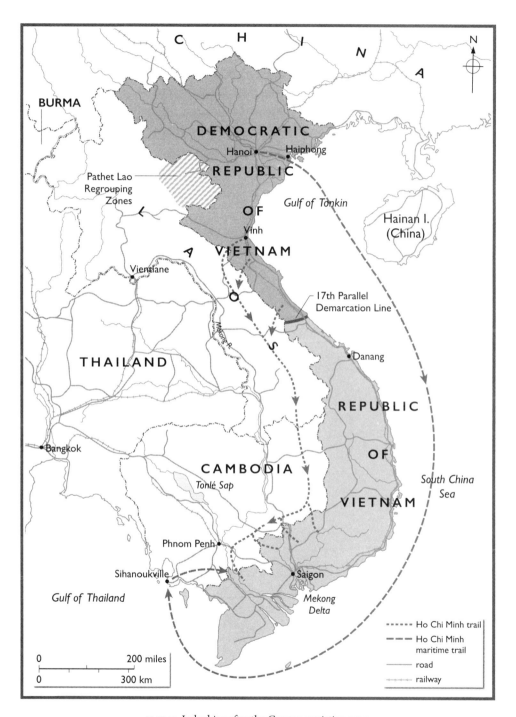

MAP 15. Indochina after the Geneva armistice, 1954.

THE ROAD TO DIEN BIEN PHU

States of War

On 11 September 1946, as negotiations between the French and the Vietnamese broke down in Paris over the question of Vietnam's independence, the president of the one-year-old Democratic Republic of Vietnam, Ho Chi Minh, met with a recently demobilized American army reporter named David Schoenbrun. When Ho informed his sympathetic listener that the Vietnamese had no choice but to fight to ensure their national independence from the French, Schoenbrun was incredulous. How, he asked, could the Vietnamese expect to win against a professional Western army equipped with modern arms? Ho responded that he too had a powerful weapon at his disposal—"Vietnamese nationalism."[1] Still skeptical, Schoenbrun gently reminded the Vietnamese president that he himself had recently conceded that Vietnam's forces were ill prepared to go to war against the French. Ho agreed, but the war in Indochina would be different. "It would be," he predicted:

> a war between an elephant and a tiger. If the tiger ever stands still the elephant will crush him with his mighty tusks. But the tiger does not stand still. He lurks in the jungle by day and emerges by night. He will leap upon the back of the elephant, tearing huge chunks from his hide, and then he will leap back into the dark jungle. And slowly the elephant will bleed to death. That will be the war of Indochina.[2]

Eight years later, Ho's prophecy seemed to come true when the Vietnamese handed the French a humiliating defeat on a remote valley floor in northwestern Vietnam called Dien Bien Phu. On 7 May 1954, after two months of intense fighting, the tiger bested the elephant in a clash that led the French to abandon Vietnam. Ho, it seemed, had been right after all: small independence movements running on high levels of nationalism could triumph over Western military giants in the twentieth century.

Vietnam: The Power of the Nation-in-Arms

Two of the best-known French veterans of the Battle of Dien Bien Phu agreed—or at least would come to do so. In his account of this epic showdown published in 1963, as the French relinquished their hold over Algeria after another long colonial conflict, the legendary commander Pierre Langlais insisted that Ho's army won because it had fought for an ideal, its own national liberation. "The Indochina War," he wrote, "was a war of independence against the French. And if the instrument of combat was forged by Marxist methods, it is no less true that the Viet Minh soldier who mounted the assault against our positions at Dien Bien Phu—and with what courage—did so in a struggle to run us out of his country, not ours."[3] Langlais' brother-in-arms in this epic battle, Marcel Bigeard, also marveled at what the Vietnamese army led by Vo Nguyen Giap had achieved in a decade of war: "Although these men of extraordinary morale had started out with nothing but a hodgepodge of weapons in 1945, they had an ideal, a goal: to drive out the French. In nine years, Giap had indisputably defeated our Expeditionary Corps."[4] For these highly decorated warriors of France's lost colonial wars writing as the historical reality of decolonization finally sank in, it no longer mattered that Ho's state was of communist design. The power of nationalism explained everything.

News of what this Vietnamese David had done in the remote highlands of Southeast Asia quickly reverberated across the French empire as it began to crack. In North Africa, Ferhat Abbas, the first president of the newly independent Algerian Republic, cast the Vietnamese victory at Dien Bien Phu in epoch-changing terms as significant as those created by the French revolutionary army's victory over the Prussians during the historic battle of Valmy in 1792:

Dien Bien Phu was more than just a military victory. This battle is a symbol. It's the "Valmy" of the colonized peoples. It's the affirmation of the Asian and African vis-à-vis the European. It is the confirmation of the universality of human rights. At Dien Bien Phu, the French lost the only source of "legitimation" on which their presence turned, that is the right of the strongest [to rule the weakest].[5]

Frantz Fanon, the Martiniquais doctor, intellectual, and member of the Algerian Front de libération nationale (FLN), agreed. Working inside the Algerian nationalist movement, like Abbas, he had followed the war in Indochina closely. But it was the Vietnamese military victory at Dien Bien Phu that caught his eye. How, he wondered, could the FLN duplicate this remarkable feat on the Algerian battlefield? As he put it in his famous denunciation of colonialism, *The Wretched of the Earth*, published in 1961: "The great victory of the Vietnamese people at Dien-Bien-Phu is no longer, strictly speaking, a Vietnamese victory. From July 1954, the question for colonized peoples was now: 'What must we do in order to realize a Dien Bien Phu? How do we go about doing it?'"[6]

Fanon never had the time to craft a response. (He passed away shortly before the FLN attained Algeria's independence through a negotiated settlement in 1962.) David Schoenbrun, however, was convinced now more than ever of the answer: nationalism, Ho's "secret weapon."[7] And as the Americans expanded their involvement in Vietnam in the hope that the internationally brokered division of the country at the Geneva Conference of 1954 would allow them to protect its southern half from the communist north Ho now ruled, Schoenbrun started telling the parable of the tiger and the elephant to American audiences. He did so in a carefully scripted appearance before the camera in a 1962 documentary hosted by CBS's Walter Cronkite on the end of the French empire in Indochina.[8] He made his case again in a book he published in 1968 as massive US firepower and half a million American troops tried to stop Ho's forces from reuniting the country the Vietnamese president had first declared independent in September 1945. Scholars and journalists have turned to Ho's fable of the tiger and the elephant to remind readers that the Americans, despite their superior army and modern weapons, were doomed to failure in Vietnam—just like the French before them—because they were fighting against a nation-in-arms, Ho's.[9]

Vietnam: The Myth of the Nation-in-Arms

But does nationalism alone explain everything? We now know that the French revolutionary army also won at Valmy because its commanding officers unleashed state-of-the-art artillery on the adversary and relied on professional soldiers from the *ancien régime* to lead.[10] Moreover, the armies of the first French republic and then those of Napoleon Bonaparte owed their success more to the introduction of compulsory military service initiated in 1793 in the form of the *levée en masse* or "mass mobilization" than to patriotic volunteers. The American War of Independence is also instructive. While patriotism certainly motivated many Americans to take up arms against the British, French military assistance and European advisers also helped transform militia-styled "Minutemen" into an increasingly effective fighting force, the ancestor of the United States Army today. In short, the armies emerging from these Atlantic revolutionary wars in the late eighteenth century were very different from what they had been going in.

Unfortunately, as seductive as it is, Ho Chi Minh's parable of the tiger and the elephant leaves little room for understanding the complexity of the Vietnamese revolutionary war and how it and the state running it adapted and changed over the course of almost a decade of war, the subject of this book. Consider the following: on 13 March 1954, the day the battle of Dien Bien Phu commenced in northwest Vietnam, Vietnamese soldiers did exactly the opposite of what Ho had predicted to Schoenbrun in 1946: they descended from the surrounding hills to attack the French troops waiting to crush them in the open. After a bloody fifty-six-day siege, soldiers of the People's Army of Vietnam, better known to the Americans during the Vietnam War as the PAVN, overran the French Union forces in the entrenched camp on the valley floor and hoisted their red flag in victory against the clear blue sky that day. This had clearly not been a hit-and-run guerrilla skirmish. The army's commanding general, Vo Nguyen Giap, operated a professional army of seven armed divisions, equipped with intelligence, communications, medical, and logistical services. The general's cannons had rained down shells on the French camp for almost two months, turning the valley floor into a lunar landscape strangely reminiscent of the Western Front during the First World War. Meanwhile, Vietnamese antiaircraft guns lit up the skies with flak not seen since the Second World War. Little wonder Langlais and Bigeard were in awe as PAVN troops marched them off to a prisoner-of-war camp in mid-1954: the Vietnamese tiger had fought like an elephant and won. Ho Chi Minh's parable was wrong.

Frantz Fanon must have known as his *Wretched of the Earth* went to press that the Algerian army, despite running on equally high levels of nationalism, was nowhere near being able to engineer such a military revolution against the same French army. For Fanon, the FLN remained a "tiger," its struggle a guerrilla one. Algerian nationalists were not alone in their inability to transition to conventional warfare. In fact, no other twentieth-century war of decolonization ever reproduced a "PAVN" or a "Dien Bien Phu." The Indonesian republicans fighting the Dutch in the late 1940s and the Kenyans at war with the British a decade later did not. Nor have recent, religiously fired insurgencies led by Al-Qaeda and the Islamic State (ISIS) succeeded in designing forces capable of executing a modern, pitched battle on the scale of Dien Bien Phu. Only Ho Chi Minh's Vietnam did.

Why? If nationalism alone cannot explain Dien Bien Phu and this Vietnamese tiger fighting like a French elephant in the open, then what else allowed this Vietnamese guerrilla army to transform itself into this redoubtable fighting machine? What was it about the nature of the Vietnamese war state that had allowed it to engineer such a historic victory on the battlefield? How had Ho and his followers gone about creating an army of seven divisions in the middle of a full-blown war of decolonization? How did they mobilize hundreds of thousands of people to join in such a Herculean task? And if the French had helped American revolutionaries to prevail against superior British forces in the 1770s, then to what extent did Chinese communist military support and advice help Ho to build a new type of state capable of wielding military force in ways unmatched by anticolonialist polities elsewhere?

No one denies that tens of thousands of Vietnamese patriots closed ranks behind Ho's republic when full-scale war broke out in Hanoi in

1946 (they did),[11] just as so many French men and women rushed to the defense of their embattled republic at Valmy in 1792. Nationalism was an important factor, as many pages in this book will show. The problem is that the notion of the "nation-in-arms" or "people's war" poses problems when it is advanced as the sole explanation for "Valmy" or "Dien Bien Phu." Serious students of the French Revolution know this. They recognize, for example, that the famous *levée en masse* of 1793 may have been couched in terms glorifying the nation, but, in reality, it imposed military conscription on young men and required civilians of both sexes to participate in the war effort whether they wanted to or not. These scholars know, too, that there was resistance to the *levée en masse*, and not just from counterrevolutionary, pro-monarchist elites opposed to republican government, but also from exhausted peasants who wanted nothing to do with war or revolution. Desertion occurred during the French revolutionary war and the American one. It occurred during the Vietnamese ones too.[12]

Specialists of the Vietnamese revolutionary wars have overlooked the fact that Ho's government also introduced obligatory military service (*nghia vu quan su*) and decreed mass mobilization of the population (*tong dong vien*) in 1949–50 in order to generate the military and civilian manpower needed to win at Dien Bien Phu.[13] By imposing the draft and mobilization laws in the middle of the Indochina War, Vietnamese revolutionaries acknowledged what their French predecessors had discovered in the early 1790s: namely, that nationalism alone could never move enough people to ensure victory on the battlefields against powerful foreign enemies. Whether wrapped in a French, American, or Vietnamese flag, the "nation-in-arms" or "people's war" is a state-sponsored myth designed in part to legitimate the coercive side of mass mobilization.

The Two States of the Vietnamese Revolutionary War

In this book, I would like to move beyond the myth of the Vietnamese nation-in-arms without necessarily denying the importance of nationalism. It was one factor, an important one, but it did not alone determine the outcome of the war in 1954. In the following chapters, I would like to look more closely at the nature of this Vietnamese revolutionary state forged from almost a decade of war against the French between September 1945, when Ho Chi Minh declared modern Vietnam's birth, and May 1954, when Vo Nguyen Giap's army defeated the French in pitched battle at Dien Bien Phu. Two interconnected arguments run through this book about the dual nature of the state of the Democratic Republic of Vietnam led by Ho Chi Minh. The first concerns the development and operation of a decentralized guerrilla polity during the Indochina War. The second analyzes how a communist-driven, single-party state arose from this very entity thanks to Chinese communist backing during the second half of the conflict. Let me explain what I mean a little further.

The Archipelago State

The first argument seeks to explain how Ho and his followers built an operational yet territorially incomplete guerrilla state in the countryside that was strong enough to weather French attacks in order to still be "there" in 1950 to receive communist bloc aid and turn itself into something else. Here I explore the contingent, fragmented, and decentralized nature of the Democratic Republic of Vietnam during the Indochina War. Despite the support the two main belligerents would eventually receive from their respective American and Chinese allies, neither the French nor the Vietnamese were ever able to impose undisputed control over people, territory, and resources. The French may have controlled Hanoi, Hue, and Saigon, parts of the Mekong and Red River deltas, as well as a handful of provincial towns and roads connecting them. But they never had enough troops, administrators, or money to be everywhere all the time. As a result, they ended up ceding large swaths of territory to their adversaries in central Vietnam, parts of the northern highlands, and, to a lesser extent, in secluded areas of the Mekong Delta in the south.

In 1949, to complicate matters further, a third political entity entered the picture when the French presided over the creation of the "Associated State of Vietnam" under the leadership of the ex-emperor Bao Dai.

"Association" was the legally binding term that kept this new Vietnamese state (along with its Laotian and Cambodian counterparts) within the confines of an Indochinese colonial federation, itself part of a larger French Union directed from Paris. Inside Indochina, this second Vietnam possessed its own administration, army, and security forces. Its leaders claimed sovereignty over all of Vietnam, including the areas controlled by Ho's government. The French and their Vietnamese partners joined hands to administer people, territory, and resources as well as to fight a common adversary. They shared one common colonial currency with the Laotians and the Cambodians: the Indochinese piaster.[14]

These "two-and-a-half" competing sovereignties—the French Indochinese federation, the Democratic Republic of Vietnam, and this less-than-fully independent Associated State of Vietnam—gave rise to archipelago-like territorial formations fanning out from core centers like islands in a stream. Despite denying the existence of the other and declaring sovereignty over all of Vietnam for themselves, leaders on each side knew that their claims were exaggerated. On the ground, territorial control was fragmented. The war dragged on precisely because no one side exercised the military force or possessed the political infrastructure needed to control people, territory, and resources completely. As a result, these island-like domains were in a constant state of competitive flux. Each bumped up against the other, expanding and contracting like sponges being squeezed in and out as their soldiers, security officials, and civil servants moved into an area while their adversaries pulled back—and vice versa. For the French and their Vietnamese allies, political control was anchored in the urban centers and stretched out from there. Ho Chi Minh presided over a rural constellation in which smaller territories revolved around larger clusters in northern, central, and, to a lesser extent, southern Vietnam.

In this contingent, fragmented, and makeshift world where political power was diffuse and military control incomplete, territorial sovereignties could overlap. People and resources could be shared. One state's administrators could exercise sovereignty during the day and then turn it over to the other side's people during the night. Sovereignties touched up against each other or even intertwined along roads, jungle trails, coastlines, rivers, and canals. In certain, revealing instances, civil servants, security officials, and customs agents from opposing sides could coexist in the same villages, relying on family ties, prewar friendships, and, beneath it all, the diluted nature of power in order to operate. As the interim head of the Communist Party, Truong Chinh, had described it as early as 1947: "This war has the characteristic of two combs whose teeth are interlocked."[15]

This Vietnamese archipelago state was, by its nature, weak. The main strategic goal for its architects was always to expand it, to spread its control over as much territory and as many people as it could, whenever and wherever possible. The idea was to push the available streams of sovereignty, no matter how small, into every possible nook and cranny left unguarded by the enemy, even poking feelers into the colonial cities. The success of the archipelago state, its ability to expand and hold itself together despite its incomplete territorial constitution, owed much to nationalism to be sure, but it turned on other things too—the use of wireless radios and hand couriers; the collection, analysis, and circulation of information; the expansion of police control and intelligence services; the movement of civil servants and their paperwork; and the administration of a war economy and clandestine commercial networks running into the colonial cities and surrounding Asian markets. Together, these things made up the nervous system that connected, supplied, and accorded operational coherence to what was, again, a highly fragmented and rudimentary state of war. As seemingly unimportant as these "connective tissues" might appear at first glance, they were, in fact, vital to the war state's survival, the object of several of the thematic chapters in this book. The French and their Vietnamese allies understood what their enemy was doing with these things. In fact, they were trying to do similar "things" in order to operate their own states and hold them together in this highly volatile and ever-shifting wartime constellation that was, when taken together, "Vietnam" between 1945 and 1954.[16]

Vietnamese War Communism and the Rise of a Single-Party State

That was one kind of state the Vietnamese revolutionary war carried within it. The second type arose from its upper half because of the favorable conditions created by the Chinese communist victory in 1949 and Mao Zedong's decision to back his Vietnamese allies in their bid to take the war to the French and remake their state in communist ways at the same time. With Mao's support, from 1950 Ho Chi Minh and his communist core used war—in fact, they ramped it up—to create a postcolonial state very different from the ones Sukarno and Ferhat Abbas were building in Indonesia and Algeria in their national liberation struggles. Indeed, the state Ho started building was very different from the republican-minded, national union government he had himself declared independent in 1945. Ho and his lieutenants now saw in communist bloc support and in the simultaneous intensification of the war the chance to transform their guerrilla archipelago of a coalition kind into a single-party state under the Communist Party's sole control.

Backed by the Chinese, Ho began transforming the Democratic Republic of Vietnam in communist ways. In 1951, for example, he presided over the creation of the Vietnamese Workers Party, replacing the one he had first established in Hong Kong two decades earlier. The Vietnamese communists aligned this new party ideologically with its bigger brothers in Moscow and Beijing. They streamlined and purged it of unwanted elements in order to expand the party center's control over the state. The communists did something similar by creating the People's Army of Vietnam in 1950. The party would now run the armed forces and the state. To do both, Ho and his entourage implemented a series of Sino-Soviet methods of revolutionary statecraft: rectification campaigns, struggle sessions, emulation movements, new hero worship, intensive cadre training, a personality cult for Ho, central planning, state banking, food requisitioning, and land reform. Combined, this war-driven process allowed Ho to forge a new type of revolutionary state in the crucible of war—a communist one. It did not replace the preexisting archipelago entity. It arose from within it. It was an embedded process of statecraft.

The advent of this second type of revolutionary state is the product of what I call "Vietnamese War Communism." At a broad level, I use this term as a heuristic device to explain the "rise" of the single-party Vietnamese communist state in wartime between 1945 and 1954. Used in this way, the phrase allows me to describe how the Communist Party, at the helm of the Democratic Republic of Vietnam, worked to expand its fragile hold over a sprawling archipelago state that was not all that communist at the start. At a more specific level, though, "War Communism" refers to a process which started in 1950 when the Vietnamese communists used Soviet and Chinese communist advice, support, and models to intensify the war in conventional ways and, through the massive mobilization this required, expand their control over the preexisting coalition state to the detriment of their noncommunist allies in their own ranks. Again, this included the application of specific tools of communist design (rectification, emulation campaigns, the cult of personality, food requisitioning, and land reform). Like the Chinese, the Vietnamese did not wait for the hostilities to end before using these instruments to push through the creation of a single-party state. They used war to do it. This process of War Communism generated during the second half of the conflict what was, in effect, a slow-burning coup d'état of historic proportions, largely imperceptible to outsiders at the time, but from which the Vietnam we know today first emerged, a communist Vietnam with nationalist characteristics.

This second type of "War Communist state" was not a Vietnamese or Chinese invention. It was part of a bigger process. War Communism had first emerged as part of the struggle that brought to life the first communist-run nation-state in world history, the Soviet Union (1922). The Bolsheviks under Vladimir Lenin had first conceived and implemented this war-driven form of communist statecraft in Russia after the First World War. No sooner had communist leaders withdrawn Russia from the Great War than they found themselves mired in a civil conflict against anticommunist forces, the "Whites," and engaged in a war of national salvation against Allied intervention forces opposed to the

October Revolution of 1917. At the helm of the embattled revolutionary state, Lenin applied a policy of "War Communism" (Военный коммунизм) between 1918 and 1921 that saw the Bolsheviks extend their control over the army, the state, and the economy as part of an effort to mobilize everyone and everything for war. At a purely pragmatic level, War Communism authorized the revolutionary state to mobilize the majority rural population to procure much-needed food for the cities and to recruit essential manpower for the army. The young regime's survival depended on it.

Of course, imperiled states do this everywhere in wartime. But there was also an ideological component to it in the Bolshevik case—followed by the Chinese and the Vietnamese. Many in the leadership, including Lenin, saw in "war" and the mobilization it required the chance, indeed the favorable conditions, for implementing revolutionary policies in the countryside essential to transforming social and political relations in communist ways (increased central management by the party, the nationalization of industry and trade, and the requisition of labor and food in the countryside, among other things). War and communist statecraft could advance hand in hand, one feeding off the other. And like their successors in East Asia, the Bolsheviks did not wait for the hostilities to end before embarking upon the communist transformation of state and society. They used war to do it.[17]

Vietnamese War Communism, however, was never designed to wage war on the peasantry in the way that the Bolsheviks ended up doing during the civil war and later under Stalin. It would have been suicidal in a country where, as in China, around 90 percent of the Vietnamese population lived in the countryside and the French controlled most of Indochina's cities and working class. Vietnamese communists looked more to the peasant-mobilizing methods developed by Mao during two decades of war, first against Chiang Kai-shek's Republic of China in civil war (1928–36), next against the Japanese (1937–45), then in a new round of civil war against Chiang Kai-shek that ended in communist victory (1946–9). Using Maoist methods, Vietnamese communists based in the countryside sought to politicize their majority peasant population in order to control and mobilize this rural force for fighting war, procuring food and labor, and building a communist state. Like the Chinese, the Vietnamese made land reform a central part of their War Communism. They could incentivize peasants to fight by giving them land, all the while breaking the "feudal" bonds of the landowning class, thereby allowing the party to take control of social and political relations in the countryside. It was no accident that Ho Chi Minh finally unleashed full-scale land reform in late 1953 as he and his party went for broke against the colonialists in the set-piece battle at Dien Bien Phu just as Mao was doing as he fought the Americans to a draw in Korea in 1953.[18]

In short, in revolutionary Russia, China, and Vietnam, war served as an accelerator in the crafting of statecraft of a communist kind. I am not saying that Vietnamese "War Communism" is a replica of the Bolshevik model or the Chinese one. What I am saying is that from 1950 the Vietnamese, like the Chinese and the Soviets, practiced a unique type of warfare, a communist one, with the dual goals of generating a modern military force and a single-party state to direct it at the same time. This type of Vietnamese communist warfare was part of a wider Eurasian revolutionary arc that adapted and changed as its practitioners in China and Indochina tailored it to their local needs. Revolutionary Algeria and Indonesia never went down this road because neither had a Communist Party at the helm of their archipelago states. All wars of decolonization are not alike, and it is time we stop treating them as if they were.[19]

Some readers will jump ship on me here. This may not be the story they were expecting to hear about Vietnam, especially Ho's. Admittedly, the narrative I am laying out here is more complicated than the myth of the "nation-in-arms," "people's war," and the parable of the "tiger and the elephant." I ask readers to stay on board, for I would like to think that the story I am about to tell, as complicated as it may be, can serve as an alternative narrative, capable of explaining in more historical and less polemical ways the making of modern Vietnam and the nature of the wars fought over it during the second half of the twentieth century. Although this book focuses on the "first war," the one against the French between 1945 and 1954, I would also like to think that those seeking a better understanding of the "making of America's Vietnam" might find something of interest in the pages that follow. I say this too, because Ho Chi Minh and his communist disciples would resurrect and turn their states of war, both of them, on the Americans and their Vietnamese allies with a vengeance after the French left. But more than anything else, I hope that this book might respond to Fanon's question above—"What must we do in order to realize a Dien Bien Phu?" The answer is perhaps not what we have long thought. To understand why, let us follow the Vietnamese "tiger" from 1945 as it moved to turn itself into something very different a decade later—and not necessarily an "elephant."

1

The Rise of the Archipelago State

On 7 July 1949, a heated exchange occurred deep in the Mekong Delta between the Communist Party's newly arrived delegate to the south, Le Duc Tho, and noncommunist members of the nationalist organization called the Lien Viet. Created in 1946, the Lien Viet regrouped noncommunist anticolonialists into the Democratic Republic of Vietnam. It served as an alternative to the Viet Minh front, created by Ho Chi Minh in 1941, but shunned by many patriots because of its communist core. Things became tense when Le Duc Tho told his audience that the time had come to combine the Viet Minh with the Lien Viet under the Communist Party's guidance. One front was enough, he said. Not everyone in the room agreed, though. One brave soul suggested that Le Duc Tho close the Viet Minh instead and leave the Lien Viet to the noncommunist nationalists. This unexpected challenge to his party's primacy from within the resistance blindsided Le Duc Tho. If we can believe an informant reporting to the French about what happened next, the party's man became red with rage until he finally exploded: "To oppose communism is tantamount to opposing the resistance; it's treason." His words reportedly created an uproar in the audience. In the following days, the communists tried to downplay what had happened. But the damage had been done. Everyone in the room that day knew that Le Duc Tho had meant exactly what he had said—one party stood above the rest in the national coalition fighting the French: his.[1]

For anticommunist nationalists, Le Duc Tho's words only confirmed what they had always said—that the communists ran the show, the "resistance," the state. Those who thought otherwise were naïve. Official historians in communist Vietnam today would agree, though for very different reasons: It was only because of the Communist Party and its farsighted control every step of the way that the Vietnamese were able to defeat the French and then the Americans during thirty years of war. The problem was that, at the time, on the ground, deep in the Mekong Delta in mid-1949, things were not so clear. That would start to change within a few months when the Chinese communists came to power and threw their weight behind Ho Chi Minh's Vietnam. But until 1950, even later in many areas, the Democratic Republic of Vietnam (DRV) was not a single-party communist state. It was a compromise creation, a coalition state uniting communist and noncommunist anticolonialists. It was also a highly decentralized polity that was particularly weak in the south. Le Duc Tho knew this. That was why he was there.

The Compromise State

A Nation-State Is Born

The communists were not the first to try to stitch Vietnam together in a time of war. In 1802, the leader of the Nguyen dynasty, Gia Long, emerged victorious from a civil war that had divided the country for a good thirty years. For the first time in Vietnam's history, this battle-hardened emperor had finally unified the country in its current shape, running from the border with China in the north to the tip of the Ca Mau peninsula in the far south (see maps 1 and 2). Over the next fifty years, he and his successors did their best to hold the country together by endowing it with a strong monarchy and accompanying bureaucracy. Gia Long's son, Minh Mang, led the way with a number of administrative reforms in the 1820s and 1830s. He introduced a Chinese-inspired civil service based on merit, promulgated a state-sponsored ideology founded on Confucianism, and imposed tight royal control over competing ideas, religious groups, and diverse peoples.

Unfortunately, the Nguyen monarchs never had the time to realize their dream before the French moved in, looking to expand their empire into Asia and their trade into southern China. Starting in the late 1850s, they attacked the Empire of Vietnam in the south, the area over which the Nguyen had the least control, before moving northwards by force over the next two decades. Having conquered all of the country by 1885, the French divided it into two protectorates, one in the north, Tonkin, the other in the center, Annam, and a colony in the south they called Cochinchina. They shackled the monarchy all the while using its emperors, bureaucracy, and mandarins to rule indirectly. In 1888, together with Laos and Cambodia, Vietnam entered the Indochinese Union, better known as French Indochina. By the turn of the twentieth century, young French and Vietnamese schoolchildren could locate Indochina on the world maps hanging on their classroom walls, shaded in with the same color as Paris and France's other colonial possessions in Asia and Africa. "Vietnam" was no more. (See Map 3.)

It was an idea, to be sure, and an increasingly powerful one by the early 1930s. However, Vietnam did not reemerge as a possible political reality until the Second World War radically changed the balance of power inside Indochina. Three specific events deserve mention: firstly, the Japanese occupation of Vietnam after the fall of France to the Germans in mid-1940 left no doubt that the French were no longer in full control of their colony. The leaders of the new French government that had collaborated with the Axis powers during the war, better known as Vichy, understood this. Secondly, the Japanese decision to overthrow their Vichy partner on 9 March 1945 put an end to almost a century of French colonial rule in Indochina. Lastly, the Japanese capitulation to the Allies on 15 August 1945 after the American nuclear blasts over Hiroshima and Nagasaki left the Indochinese political field wide open.

The Vietnamese lost no time in making their moves in this fluid situation. Two days after the 9 March coup, backed by the Japanese, Emperor Bao Dai declared the independence of Vietnam in the form of a resurrected "Empire of Vietnam" and abrogated the treaties binding it to France. The emperor named a respected educator and nationalist, Tran Trong Kim, to form a government and to serve as prime minister. For the first time in over eighty years, the Vietnamese operated their institutions free of the French. It was a liberating experience, although the Japanese were still there. The new government unified the country territorially by combining the Cochinchinese colony with the protectorates of Annam and Tonkin and started crafting a Vietnamese national identity to accompany it. Tran Trong Kim's cabinet introduced a national anthem and flag, began reappropriating the country's history, and renamed colonial streets after patriotic heroes.

However, the Japanese capitulation in mid-August opened up at the same time the real possibility that the French would try to retake their lost colony. The Vietnamese emperor immediately fired off letters to the Allies and France's new leaders urging them to respect the country's newly recovered independence. In one to Charles de Gaulle, Bao Dai implored the man who had just liberated the French from Germany's imperial hold to refrain from reimposing a colonial order on the Vietnamese with the Japanese now defeated: "I would ask that you understand that the only way to maintain French interests and spiritual influence in Indochina is to recognize Vietnamese independence openly and to renounce all thoughts of re-establishing French sovereignty or an administration of any kind or form here." De Gaulle never responded. He searched instead for a more pliant royal and ordered his officers leaving for Indochina to retake the former colony by force, if need be, in order to restore French sovereignty.[2]

The Empire of Vietnam led by the Emperor Bao Dai could have survived the fall of the Japanese and reconfigured itself in national ways. After all, Cambodia's king, Norodom Sihanouk, would consolidate his power after the Second World War and lead a famous Royalist Independence Crusade against the French in 1953. The monarchy exists in Cambodia to this day. But Bao Dai saw things differently at the time: on 25 August 1945, he formally abdicated his throne without naming a successor. He abandoned his dynastic name, Bao Dai, the "Great Protector," to become a simple "citizen." French colonial administrators looking on from Japanese internment camps were shocked: How could the docile emperor they had programmed so carefully in their colonial thinking do away with the very monarchy they had used to rule the country for so long? But he did.

Vietnamese nationalists coalescing around Ho Chi Minh were just as incredulous, but did not ask questions. With the stroke of a pen, Bao Dai had eliminated what could have been a serious royalist challenge to the embryonic nation-state Ho was nurturing in the wings since his nationalist front, the Viet Minh had taken power in Hanoi on 19 August. Moving fast, on 27 August, Ho and his inner circle presided over the birth of a provisional government that would take over from the vanishing monarchy as if it were in line with the natural order of things. The transfer officially occurred three days later, when Bao Dai relinquished his family's dynastic seal in a solemn ceremony and turned it over to the delegate Ho had rushed to the imperial capital of Hue to receive it. As an eyewitness to the abdication ceremony in Hue later remembered this historic event: "The members of the Royal Family were weeping. The people cried out and applauded. Then the emperor could be seen picking up the royal seal, which was wrapped in a yellow brocade, and also his huge sword to display to the crowd for the last time before handing them over to the Viet Minh functionaries."[3]

It is difficult to exaggerate the significance of what had happened that day in Hue. Bao Dai had effectively thrown his political weight and symbolism behind the fledgling national government. When some mandarins tried to stop the Viet Minh's officials from taking over in the provinces, their ruler ordered them to stand down. Bao Dai then traveled to Hanoi, the new national capital, where he joined President Ho Chi Minh as a "supreme adviser." Although the emperor's decision thrilled many, one does not have to be a monarchist to understand why some in the royal family cried bitter tears in late August. Without spilling a drop of blood, the emperor, acting of his own volition, had dealt the deathblow to a centuries-old monarchical regime from which it would never recover.[4]

The Japanese coup de force and Bao Dai's coup de grâce provided Ho with the clean slate and political legitimacy he needed to create a new nation-state delinked from its colonial and monarchical molds. Ho seized the moment with arresting confidence. Nowhere was this on better display than in Ba Dinh Square on 2 September 1945 in downtown Hanoi, when he formally announced the independence of the

Democratic Republic of Vietnam. The scene was an impressive one on that sunny afternoon when this middle-aged man, who had spent thirty years abroad, mounted the stairs of the podium to read aloud the country's formal declaration of independence. With his cabinet members standing solemnly behind him, he gazed upon the sea of people standing before him as they looked up at him. Unfurled before the balustrade were banners heralding Vietnam's independence and the end of colonialism. The band played. Young scouts saluted the new president. Soldiers stood at attention.

It was a carefully choreographed event to be sure, complete with all the required pomp and circumstance. But there was nothing artificial about the pride and joy the Vietnamese felt that day. Rich and poor, young and old, men and women of all ages were there. The nationalism that had been in the making for decades now burst into the open for all to see. A young Ngo Van Chieu, who had just slipped on a new uniform to begin a career in the army, described it memorably: "On this occasion, the provisional government of the Democratic Republic of Vietnam presented itself to the nation. A square grandstand, crowned with the new national flag (red with a yellow star on it), had been prepared. The rostrum itself was draped with an immense flag. The entire government was there, everyone."[5] And then silence as Ho approached the microphone and began to read the Declaration of Independence in his recognizable Nghe An accent. At one point, he paused and asked his fellow countrymen if they could hear him clearly. A roaring "Yes!" came thundering back in reply. Standing on the stage that day, Vo Nguyen Giap later wrote that it was at that moment that Ho and the people became one.[6]

Perhaps, but things were not quite as spontaneous or as natural as the future victor of Dien Bien Phu would have us believe. For one, Ho Chi Minh and his team knew how to use modern means of communication to spread the nationalist message faster and better than anyone else. They had been doing it since taking power in mid-August. Photos of Independence Day celebrations, the huge crowds, and President Ho appeared on the front pages of the country's papers. He was everywhere: artists painted his portrait, the first national banknotes and stamps soon carried his determined face, and wall pictures of him were already on sale. The Voice of Vietnam rebroadcast his reading of the declaration of independence so that the whole country could share in the national moment. A total stranger upon arriving in Hanoi in mid-August 1945, Ho Chi Minh had rapidly become a remarkably familiar face. Even a future enemy of Ho's Vietnam remembered how proud he was as a boy of his country's first president:

> In the beginning of September 1945, Ho Chi Minh's portraits, printed in black-and-white and in various sizes, were sold everywhere. Each of us schoolboys tried to buy one to hang in the best places of our homes if the adults had not [already] done so. We were hungry to have a national hero to worship.[7]

Ho intentionally positioned himself at the center of this creative process. He carefully cast himself as the culturally familiar Confucian sage and benevolent ruler. He dressed and lived simply, let his beard grow to a silvery wisp, wore modest sandals, and made a point of speaking in plain, parable-like terms. Celibate, wise, and grandfatherly, he stressed virtuous action, moral cultivation, rectitude, and selflessness in his public pronouncements. He addressed the Vietnamese as his children and invited them to refer to him as *Bac* or "Uncle." Until his death in 1969, he welcomed "brothers" and "sisters" from southern, central, and northern Vietnam into the same national family and embraced ethnic minorities as equal members in this new national community. His entourage carefully choreographed and photographed his visits to schools, hospitals, and state functions. He moved among "the people," reached out to them and let them approach him, talk to him, and touch him. As president (*Ho chu tich*) and father figure (*bac Ho*), he not only aimed to set the new nationalist example; Ho simultaneously moved to embody the nation. Gone was any mention of Ho's first wife, a Chinese woman from Guangzhou (formerly Canton). The Vietnamese nation was now his family, and Ho was its father.

Things were, again, more complicated than this rather official version would have it. Ho may have been casting himself as the "father of the Vietnamese nation" in 1945, but he was also the "father of Vietnamese communism." Ho, more than anyone else in his entourage, had founded the party in Hong Kong in 1930 with the help of the Moscow-based "Communist International" or the "Comintern" in order to help diffuse communism across the globe. He had himself spread the communist word well beyond Vietnam's borders during the interwar period. Working with Comintern agents and Chinese communists, he helped establish communist parties in Thailand and British Malaya. Like Mao Zedong in China and Kim Il-sung in Korea, Ho Chi Minh believed in the Marxist-Leninist creed, including its Stalinist and Maoist gospels, and the salvation it would one day bring to his country and others.

Vietnamese anticommunists knew much of this and did their best to paint Ho as red as possible. They warned that this man would one day sell out the nation to another set of imperialists based out of Moscow and Beijing as well as unleash Vietnamese classes against each other. And yet Ho's detractors had little success in stopping him at the outset. Why? For one, Ho's people controlled the press and the airwaves in the crucial early days. Outmaneuvered, the nationalists had little else to fall back on to spread their message except for two or three independent papers. The bigger problem, though, was that the noncommunist parties failed to offer up a charismatic man or woman of prowess capable of competing with Ho on the national stage at this crucial point in time. Shy and introverted, Bao Dai had already abdicated. So had Tran Trong Kim. The leader of the Alliance Party, Nguyen Hai Than (discussed in more detail later), was certainly an authentic nationalist who had left the country in his youth to free Vietnam, like Ho. The problem was that, unlike Ho, he had lost his fluency in Vietnamese after living abroad for so long. Upon his return to Hanoi in September 1945, he found it much harder to appeal to the Vietnamese public in a language they could understand—theirs.

Vietnamese communists had no problems with Ho Chi Minh's personification of the nation. They fully backed it. Ho was one of them. He weighed in on party matters of the highest order. They agreed too, that the creation of a cult around this engaging man would help the people to associate Ho with the state they sought to build, the war of national liberation they would soon fight, and the communist order they wanted to impose on the country one day. Everyone in the party would have been aware of Stalin's personality cult and the political function it served in expanding communist power in the Soviet Union. Ho certainly was: he had been in Moscow when Stalin became the "father of the nation" there (and was famous for surrounding himself with adoring children years before Ho followed his lead). And Ho was very astute in the way in which he singled himself out from others upon his return to Vietnam in 1941. It was during that year that he decided to change his name to Ho Chi Minh, meaning "Ho the Enlightened One." Upon taking power in 1945, the communists deliberately went further when, to refer to Ho, they began to give the first letter of the Vietnamese word for "he" or "person" a capital: *Nguoi*. In so doing, the party intentionally set him above the rest as the "Chosen One." Through Ho Chi Minh, with him and in him, the Vietnamese communist inner circle added a powerful cultural weapon to its political repertoire. Ho may be venerated or despised, but the success this world-class communist achieved in becoming the charismatic father of the Vietnamese nation is undeniable.[8]

Colonial Grafts

As new as the nation appeared in the heady days of late 1945, there was much administrative continuity between this independent Vietnam and its colonial predecessor, and even the earlier monarchical regime (which had never completely disappeared under French rule). This interface was most prominent in central and northern Vietnam, thanks in large part to the Allied occupation of Indochina at the end of the Second World War. In a nutshell, because of decisions taken by the Allies in a faraway conference in Potsdam, Germany, on the eve of Tokyo's capitulation in mid-1945, the British received the task of accepting the Japanese surrender in areas of Vietnam located below the 16th parallel, while Chiang Kai-shek's Republic of China was in charge of the territory above that line. The French, led by de Gaulle, were not considered to be one of the Allies in Asia and were thus excluded from the occupation. (See maps 4 and 5.)

British and Chinese troops landed in their respective zones by mid-September 1945. Events quickly took a turn for the worse in the south, when, on 23 September, the British allowed Japanese-interned Vichy troops to take over in Saigon, and, in so doing, dislodge Ho's fragile government. Although the British commander General Douglas Gracey thought this would bring stability, it ignited war instead. Things got so unruly in Saigon that he had to reconfine the 1,500 French colonial troops and put (defeated) Japanese ones on duty until General Philippe Leclerc's Expeditionary Corps arrived in early October, pushed the Vietnamese out of Saigon, and started attacking into the countryside up to the 16th parallel, just south of Da Nang. What would turn out to be a thirty years' war for Vietnam started in Saigon in 1945 and would end there in 1975.

Things worked out very differently in areas above that line. Unwilling to allow a destabilizing colonial conflict to erupt on their watch, the Chinese refused to let the French rush back in. Ho was grateful for this decision, because it allowed him to consolidate his hold over the colonial state until December 1946, when, after the Chinese withdrawal a few months earlier, war finally came to the rest of the country. Nowhere was this graft above the 16th parallel more visible than in the pages of the Journal officiel de l'Indochine as it imperceptibly became the Viet Nam Dan Quoc Cong Bao (Administrative Record of Vietnam).[9] A veritable gold mine of information, this national gazette provides a day-by-day, ministry-by-ministry, decree-by-decree account of how the young republic in its central and northern parts assumed the operation of the colonial state's civil servants, offices, services, materials, even its stamps and stationery—and then went about transforming them in national ways. Starting in late August 1945, scores of decrees instructed bureaucrats to remain in their positions to ensure the continued functioning of the administration. Internal and external trade resumed, transport systems reopened, and telegraph, postal, and customs services carried on as if nothing all that dramatic had occurred. Rather than create a new police service, on 24 September the minister of the interior, Vo Nguyen Giap, told his subordinates that they should take over the colonial force, get rid of any bad apples, but keep the good ones. These people could help the republic consolidate its hold over this vital instrument of state power. Other ministries did similar things.[10] This should come as no surprise: revolutionary states always owe more to their anciens régimes after taking power than their leaders would have us believe later.

Ho Chi Minh's officials also took possession of colonial materials essential to running their new state in central and northern Vietnam. Decrees authorized the requisition of colonial laboratories, hospitals, power and light companies, libraries, schools, and the Indochinese University, including its medical, law, veterinarian, and fine arts faculties. High on the acquisitions list too, were printing presses, ink, newspapers, radios, medicines, and typewriters. Vo Nguyen Giap authorized the confiscation of wireless radios from Air France's downtown Hanoi office. Paper was in high demand from the beginning and always would be. Without it, the bureaucracy would have ground to a halt along with the state it supported. Other edicts established the national anthem and flag while street names changed again.[11]

The new government immediately passed legislation to protect itself from internal and external enemies. On 1 September 1945, authorities imposed a curfew in Hanoi. They strictly prohibited abetting the French. The sale and possession of firearms came under government control. Decrees criminalized a host of political parties, some of whose leaders had cooperated with the Japanese or threatened to move against the fledgling republic. The leadership used law to define proper nationalist behavior, its opposite, treason, and meted out punishment for those who threatened national security. Ho sanctioned the creation of a military court on 13 September, Article 2 of which legally authorized the court to put on trial any person who might harm the Democratic Republic of Vietnam's independence. It is hard to believe that the timing was unrelated to the arrival of anticommunist nationalists in Hanoi with their Chinese backers. Meanwhile, the Ministry of the Interior did an impressive job of controlling the press, so that public opinion remained supportive.[12]

Some Vietnamese civil servants left their posts upon Bao Dai's dissolution of the Empire of Vietnam and the advent of the Democratic Republic of Vietnam. The majority, however, stayed put. Patriotism certainly moved them; but just as many hedged their bets for personal and family reasons until they could gauge better what the future held in store for them. For some it was a question of putting food on the table and paying the bills. Others continued to go to work because that was all they knew how to do. A veteran of the Indochina War later recalled how his father, a colonial-trained railroad operator, remained on the job in August 1945: "He worked for the revolution, still as a civil servant. He did not work for the sake of ideology, but just out of the diligent, conscientious devotion of a civil servant. He just continued to follow his profession and to do his job." This bureaucratic continuity helped Ho's people latch on to the colonial state in central and northern Vietnam until full-scale war broke out in December 1946. Nothing of the kind occurred in the south.[13]

New Instruments and Institutions of Governance

Of course, all of this was not a simple graft. First of all, this Vietnamese nation-state required a new legal definition for those belonging to it: whereas the French had created a hodgepodge of legal identities for their colonial subjects residing in Indochina's protectorates, colonies, military territories, and cities, the new republic established one inclusive definition of citizenship in a decree issued in October 1945. This law transformed almost all of those residing within northern, central, and southern Vietnam into "Vietnamese citizens." Gone were separate legal categories for the "Cochinchinese," "Annamese," or "Tonkinese." Referred to as "colonial subjects" (*sujets*) under the French, they now became "national citizens" (*công dân*). A Democratic Republic of Vietnam passport soon replaced the French Indochinese one.[14]

This decree also turned "ethnic minorities" living within Vietnam into DRV citizens. Following the Second World War, minority populations in the northern and central highlands numbered over a million. A large ethnic Khmer community of several hundred thousand lived in the Mekong Delta along the Cambodian border. Having operated clandestinely in the highlands for years, the communists knew how important these areas were to consolidating Vietnam territorially. They also understood how important it was to keep them out of French hands. In September 1946, the Ministry of the Interior established the National Minorities Office and began dispatching teachers, bureaucrats, and soldiers into the highlands to help administer these areas as well as to turn these ethnically and culturally distinct peoples into Vietnamese "nationals." The only exception to this rule—and it was an important one—was made for the Chinese, who could keep their passports *or* become Vietnamese citizens. And when the Chinese communists came to power in late 1949, their Vietnamese counterparts went out of their way to be as flexible as possible when it came to dealing with the large number of overseas Chinese living inside the DRV. They never required them to adopt Vietnamese citizenship during the Indochina conflict.[15]

Vietnamese fears that the French wanted to break the non-Viet peoples off from the fledgling republic were well founded. They did. The French moved first in the central highlands below the 16th parallel in mid-1946, when they created the Populations montagnardes du Sud-Indochinois or the "Highland peoples of Southern Indochina." Building on initiatives dating from the interwar period, they accorded a special legal status to the "Highland peoples" and promoted indigenous languages, cultures, and identities in opposition to the inclusive Vietnamese one DRV authorities were promoting. In the far northwest of the country, the French did the same thing in 1948 when they created the "Tai federation" in Lai Chau province and neighboring areas. Both autonomous zones were part of a wider colonial coalition the French were assembling to counter Ho's Vietnam. Unsurprisingly, clashes between the French and the Vietnamese for control of the highlands first broke out in 1946 on the bureaucratic front. And things only got worse over the next thirty years, as governments and armies vied for control over this ethnically diverse strategic corridor running up Indochina's highland spine.[16]

Regardless of ethnicity, the government required all Vietnamese aged eighteen and over to carry citizenship cards. On them appeared the individual's picture, name, date and place of birth, thumbprint, and profession. These cards helped authorities incorporate populations into the DRV's political realm, provided decision-makers with essential information on the population, and allowed agents of the state to conduct the census, tax, monitor, and mobilize people for a variety of tasks, including the military draft and labor service discussed later in this book. Similar cards existed for mass organizations such as the Viet Minh and the Lien Viet. The Indochinese Communist Party issued formal membership cards and later required personal histories (*ly lich*) from its members for quality control purposes and to protect against enemy infiltration. While people always found ways to get around the "state" in their daily lives, the leaders of the Democratic Republic of Vietnam were determined to expand their political control over people and territory whenever and wherever they could.[17]

Meanwhile, on high, Vietnamese authorities could not wait for the approval of a constitution to begin building new political institutions and administrative zones. From its inception, the provisional government consisted of a presidency, a cabinet, twelve ministries, and, from March 1946, an elected national assembly. Territorially, the government divided the country into three main administrative regions—Bac Bo for Tonkin in the north, Trung Bo for Annam in the center, and Nam Bo for Cochinchina in the south. These regional divisions were not French administrative creations; they dated from Minh Mang's reforms of the 1830s. Over a century later, Ho's people now divided them into a series of politico-military zones designed for war. Each one possessed an "administrative and resistance committee" in charge of running day-to-day governmental matters down to the village level by way of provincial and district committees. This hierarchy of state governance (region, zone, province, district, and village) constituted the administrative backbone through which instructions, decisions, and information flowed. Through it, government ministries authorized agents to collect taxes, judges to hold court, postal workers to deliver the mail, policemen to maintain order, and teachers to hold class. When Le Duc Tho spoke of the "resistance" at the opening of this chapter, he meant the "resistance administration," the "state."[18]

Theoretically, power flowed up and down this resistance column. Zonal leaders across the country took their orders from the government headquarters in the north and expected lower echelons of their respective chains to do the same. However, Vietnamese state-builders also wanted to give the grassroots level a voice in governance. Starting at the bottom rung, people of voting age elected "people's councils." Through them, they could choose the executive committees of their village resistance committee. These councils were deliberative bodies that set local agendas and communicated desiderata to resistance leaders at village and district levels. The latter were expected to represent their constituencies to those higher up the ladder. This was not an entirely revolutionary creation, though. Such village councils had long existed as part of the monarchical state which the French had preserved in order to rule indirectly. Ho Chi Minh did not destroy them so much as he tried to co-opt them.

All kinds of compromises like this occurred at the local level in order to get the new republic off the ground as it went to war. Young Viet Minh activists might have spoken eloquently of revolution and independence, they may have blamed the French for all the evils of the world, and they may have promised a glorious future under Ho's benevolent rule. But for all that, villagers still tended to elect people for their local councils whom they knew and trusted. Sometimes it was the village chief who had guided them through hard times—famine in central and northern Vietnam for example—and acted fairly and honestly in daily affairs. There were "bad mandarins" to be sure; but the idea that all "mandarins" were corrupt, obsequious colonial creatures is inaccurate.[19] A range of local experiences as well as social and kinship ties continued to connect many "good mandarins" from the ancien régime to their constituencies in the "revolutionary state." Communist Party members were there too, and some had gained local respect for similar reasons. Not all communists were "bad" either, but they were still few and far between in the early years.

As a result, Ho and his team left the majority of the good officials in place as long as they did their jobs and were loyal to the new government. Villagers even elected noncommunist nationalists whom they had known for years. Nguyen Cong Luan, a young boy who grew up in Nam Dinh province south of Hanoi, recalled how his father, a member

of the anticommunist Vietnamese Nationalist Party (VNQDD), remained in his village to serve Ho's government on patriotic grounds:
"In the village election, my father became chairman of the village Administrative and Resistance Committee, a village chief with a new title.
More than 90 percent of voters wanted him to have the job. The job was
too low for him, but he accepted it as a tacit compromise with the Viet
Minh provincial government. Later, he was elected vice-chairman of the
district Lien Viet front." All sorts of bargains like this occurred at the
grassroots level, without which the "resistance state" would have collapsed early on. Nor should we be surprised to learn that many DRV
village councils and resistance committees often operated out of old
colonial offices or preexisting village councils of royalist heritage.[20]

Like their Chinese counterparts, Vietnamese communists relied on
a united front to help them take hold of, administer, and mobilize
people, the overwhelming majority of whom were not communists. Ho
Chi Minh led the way in introducing this important instrument of communist political control to Vietnam. In 1937, as Japanese troops invaded
China in full force, Ho left Moscow, bound for China and his ultimate
destination—Vietnam. During his trip, he passed through the Chinese
communist capital of Yan'an in northern China, where Mao Zedong and
his Communist Party had regrouped after barely escaping destruction
by Chiang Kai-shek's army during the Long March (1934–5).[21] There,
Ho observed the broad united front Mao was busy building to fight the
Japanese and strengthen and expand the Chinese Communist Party's
territorial base.

Determined to do the same, Ho moved to the Vietnamese side of the
northern border with China, where, in May 1941, he created a large patriotic front focused on securing independence (and put talk of radical
revolution such as land reform on the back burner). It was called the
Vietnamese Independence League (Viet Nam Doc Lap Dong Minh) or
the Viet Minh for short. It served the communists well at the outset.
Out of patriotism or because their family or friends belonged to it,
people of all walks of life joined this nationalist front as it spread from
the north southwards. Its composition was an impressive collection of
patriotic associations, federations, and unions based on religious affili-

ation (Catholic, Buddhist, Hoa Hao, and Cao Dai faiths), gender and age (women, elderly, and youth federations), ethnicity (overseas Chinese, Cambodians in the Mekong Delta, highland peoples), and various professions (peasants, workers, civil servants, artists, merchants). As in China and the Soviet Union, the list was long since the Communist Party sought to bring "everyone" into this front and, by extension, its political realm.

However, the Viet Minh was not quite the success Ho had hoped for. The problem was that as the communists moved from taking power to creating the Democratic Republic of Vietnam in late August 1945, they also went from using the Viet Minh as a national front to transforming it into a de facto political party through which to govern. This caused immediate problems. While the communists viewed this metamorphosis as a natural thing (they had created the Viet Minh; it was theirs), many noncommunist nationalists were less sanguine. The latter realized within weeks that many of those hailing from the Viet Minh party in Ho's newly formed provisional government were in fact members of the Indochinese Communist Party. Ho, the president of the provisional government, certainly was. He had created the communist party in Hong Kong in 1930. So were many of his cabinet members and advisers, several of whom were well known to the public eye. Vo Nguyen Giap, Pham Van Dong, Le Van Hien, and Truong Chinh, among others, had all operated openly as communists during the Left-wing Popular Front period in Indochina during the late 1930s. For many noncommunist anticolonialists, supporting a communist-led Viet Minh to win national independence was one thing; but joining it as a national political party was quite another.

Anticommunist groups arriving with the Chinese occupying forces in September 1945 wanted nothing to do with the Viet Minh. Their leaders, united in the triumvirate of the Vietnamese Nationalist Party (Viet Nam Quoc Dan Dang, or VNQDD for short), the Alliance Group (Dong Minh Hoi), and the Greater Vietnam Party (Dai Viet), had suffered under the French for their anticolonialism. Some had ended up in colonial prisons with communists while others competed against them for Chiang Kai-shek's support in southern China during the Second

World War. Several had known Ho Chi Minh since the 1920s. Upon their return to Vietnam, the leaders of these three parties did everything in their power to paint Ho and the Viet Minh as "red" as possible. For them, it was nothing more than a communist front organization. This fierce opposition to the Viet Minh only made it harder for the communists to expand their national front after taking power. Things got so bad in November 1945 that Ho announced the "dissolution" of the Indochinese Communist Party with great patriotic fanfare. The idea was to avoid giving Chiang Kai-shek's nationalist troops (who had accepted the Japanese surrender in Vietnam) a pretext to move against Ho's party at a crucial point in the DRV's fragile existence by putting their anticommunist Vietnamese allies in charge of it.

If the Indochinese Communist Party continued to operate clandestinely (and it did),[22] the communists had to accept that their national front, the Viet Minh, was compromised. The problem was that the national front as an instrument of political control was too important to be left to others. The communists did not want to allow a potentially large bloc of noncommunist anticolonialists to become a political force operating outside their guidance. They certainly did not want them to join the anticommunist triumvirate or fall into the French colonial orbit. A front separate from the Viet Minh but remotely controlled by the communists would help Ho bring on board reluctant patriotic civil servants, merchants, intellectuals, and landowners, all of whom he badly needed to man his republic in its hour of greatest need.[23]

The communists made their move in May 1946 as Chinese troops prepared to withdraw and the French began assembling a separate government for Vietnam. This second front was known as the Association of the United Vietnamese People (Hoi Lien Hiep Quoc Dan Viet Nam), widely known in its abbreviated form, Lien Viet. It included the noncommunist socialist and democrat parties, influential members of southern religious faiths who had not rallied to the French, a host of patriotic merchants and landowners, and well-known scholar-patriots like Huynh Thuc Khang and Nguyen Van To. For those who could not countenance another front of communist design, most notably the triumvirate parties, the communists destroyed them during the civil war that followed the main Chinese withdrawal during the summer of 1946 discussed later in this book. Ho Chi Minh did not enjoy the support of everyone. His communism was a problem.[24]

Another new institution that deserves mention here is the National Assembly. Although the French had created a colonial council for Cochinchina at the turn of the twentieth century, they never introduced a representative institution to operate in all of French Indochina or Vietnam, one which nationalists could have made their own after 1945. The French Cochinchinese Council had opened its doors to a small minority of wealthy southern Vietnamese men by the early 1920s but refused to go much further. This was in contrast to the Americans who, during the interwar period, had allowed for the creation of a bicameral congress for the Philippines in the form of a commonwealth and the British who had created legislatures and constitutions for the indigenous populations in colonial India and Burma. Of course, the British and Americans had done this in order to hold on to their empires or decolonize on favorable terms. The French Third Republic could never bring itself to do either.

This is why the creation of Vietnam's first national assembly fell to the leaders of the Democratic Republic of Vietnam. In September, Vo Nguyen Giap signed into law universal suffrage for men and women aged eighteen years and older and called for national elections to be held to form a constituent assembly. Its main job would be to elaborate the country's first constitution, the legal foundation on which the DRV would turn and from which it would draw its legitimacy. Lively debates occurred in 1945–6 in favor of the creation of a constitutional democracy led by such noncommunist luminaries as Nguyen Van To. Though the communists did their best to control the course of the debate (they dominated the assembly's standing committee), they did not stand in the way of the elaboration of a republican form of government. In fact, they accepted sharing power for several reasons. Firstly, with only a few thousand party members in September 1945, the communists depended on overwhelming noncommunist cooperation to run the administration and the army. As the French prepared for war in late 1946, Ho would only be able to keep his newly born state alive by accepting to rule as part of a coalition with noncommunist nationalists. He did. Secondly, the Vietnamese communists had to show themselves as politically liberal in order to counter French promises to grant the people greater representation within the framework of a new Indochinese federation and projected assembly. Thirdly, Ho and his communist entourage had to convince the victorious Americans pushing for a liberal economic and political order in the postwar Asia-Pacific region that he and his followers were not out to create a dictatorship of the proletariat.[25]

Lastly, no one in the communist core, not even Ho Chi Minh, the "Enlightened One," could foresee that the Chinese communists would take power in 1949 and throw their weight behind their Vietnamese counterparts. Indeed, the presence of Chiang Kai-shek's troops in northern Vietnam until September 1946 put pressure on the Vietnamese communists to share power in a coalition form of government or risk the possibility of a hostile takeover. Until their withdrawal, Chinese commanders supported their Vietnamese anticommunist partners in forcing Ho to share power. The president obliged, postponing elections until January 1946, in order to give the opposition more time to prepare.[26]

Elections occurred and, as flawed as they were, gave rise to the first democratically constituted government in Vietnam's history in March 1946. Ho Chi Minh became the country's first popularly elected president. One of Vietnam's earliest republican minds, Huynh Thuc Khang, became the leader of the National Assembly. Six months later, after vigorous debates about the nature of postcolonial Vietnam's political system, the National Assembly approved the country's first constitution making Vietnam a representative democracy. Thousands of noncommunist patriots joined the Democratic Republic of Vietnam, convinced that the communists were serious about the "Republic" in the state's name and that the "Democratic Republic" (meaning communist) part could be contained via a multiparty democracy now formally guaranteed by a constitution and a national assembly. This was a huge gamble, and, as we now know, one which they would ultimately lose. But, at the time, true republicans had no way of knowing this.[27]

Significantly, most of the noncommunist democrats working inside the government with Ho looked the other way as the communists crushed anticommunist opposition in mid-1946. Republicans like Huynh Thuc Khang and Nguyen Van To considered Ho and his communist allies better suited to leading the fight against the French than those in charge of the anticommunist triumvirate. As interim president of the government during Ho Chi Minh's absence in France during the summer of 1946 and as chairman of the Lien Viet, Huynh Thuc Khang fully backed the destruction of the anticommunist patriotic parties. He knew many of those who had been urging him to do so since the 1930s, most notably, Vo Nguyen Giap. By the end of the year, what was left of the VNQDD, Alliance, and Dai Viet parties were languishing in government prisons or had fled to southern China, gone into hiding, crossed over to the French, or joined the Lien Viet and kept their heads down. When the National Assembly met for the second time on 28 October 1946, of the total number of 444 deputies, only 291 were present (the distances were long; fighting raged in the south). Of this number, the opposition parties hostile to the communists counted only thirty-seven delegates. Continued communist-directed operations against them were such that on 8 November, the day the National Assembly voted to approve the constitution, only two members of the opposition were present out of the total number of 240 delegates there.[28]

And yet, as significant as the destruction of the anticommunist opposition was to the communist ability to consolidate its hold on power, Ho was still not the president of a single-party communist state in late 1946. More than anything else, the Democratic Republic of Vietnam remained a compromise, a coalition state. Again, the communists accepted the creation of a constitutional democracy, not because they believed in it (they did not, as we shall see), but in exchange for widespread noncommunist support against an imminent colonial assault upon the whole country. They had no choice. It was the only way for them to hold on to power. It was war.

The Archipelago State

Shattered Sovereignties

The outbreak of armed conflict, first in the south in September 1945, then in central and northern Vietnam in late 1946, shattered the Democratic Republic of Vietnam's territorial hold over all of the country and immediately gave rise to a highly decentralized state. In the south, the French Expeditionary Corps landed in early October 1945 and began occupying areas below the 16th parallel, the main towns, roads, and bridges. In 1947, the Hoa Hao and Cao Dai religious groups (discussed more fully in Chapter 6) joined the French in opposing the embattled Vietnamese republic. In exchange for their cooperation, the French allowed both groups to administer large domains in the western Mekong Delta. Meanwhile, communist leaders did their best to hold things together from their jungle bases. Chief among them were three powerful men who would later run the war against the Americans—Le Duan, Nguyen Van Linh, and Pham Hung. They had all done hard time together in the colonial prison of Poulo Condor, an island located off the southern coast of Vietnam. They joined forces with another former inmate whom Ho Chi Minh had sent south to run the armed forces, Nguyen Binh. Together, these men kept the Democratic Republic of Vietnam alive against all odds as the French army went on the attack. It was an extremely difficult time. The best they could do on the ground was to hang on to pockets of territory, most notably in My Tho province, and a strip running across the tip of the Ca Mau peninsula in Zone IX. Ho's military commander for the south, Nguyen Binh, built up an army in Zone VII, west of Saigon.[29] The Hoa Hoa, Cao Dai, and, from 1948 onwards, the Binh Xuyen ruled the rest of the south in association with the French.

Things were very different in central Vietnam after full-scale war broke out in late 1946. There, the French army seized the highland town of Dalat and the main coastal cities of Da Nang and Hue. However, the Expeditionary Corps left large swaths of land in the upper and lower halves of central Vietnam in the hands of its adversary in order to focus on holding on to the country's northern and southern deltas. Ho's government referred to the upper half of central Vietnam it controlled as Zone IV, which was located south of Hanoi. The latter zone included the densely populated provinces stretching from Thanh Hoa and Nghe An down to Quang Tri and Thua Thien. This zone was a major source of labor, recruits, and food as hostilities intensified. Further down the coast from there was Zone V. It included provinces such as Quang Nam, Quang Ngai and Binh Dinh and competed with the French for control of the central highlands running down Indochina's midsection. Ho Chi Minh dispatched Nguyen Son to run Zone IV while Pham Van Dong served as the party's special delegate to Zone V. Both were experienced party men. Nguyen Son had made the Long March with Mao Zedong's Red Army in the 1930s, and Pham Van Dong was one of Ho's closest lieutenants. As the DRV strengthened, thanks to Chinese communist aid, Vietnamese communists increasingly challenged the French for control over a corridor of provinces sandwiched between Zone IV's northern border and the colonial Red River Delta, in particular Hoa Binh, Nam Dinh, and Thai Binh provinces. This was Zone III.[30] (See maps 6 and 7.)

In the north, following the outbreak of full-scale war in Hanoi in late 1946, the government evacuated to an upland expanse of territory concentrated in Thai Nguyen, Tuyen Quang, Bac Can, and Cao Bang provinces. This resistance corridor looked over the Red River Delta from its southern tip and reached northwards towards the Chinese border from the other end. The government set up its capital in a "secure zone" in Thai Nguyen province. Carefully camouflaged huts housed the main ministries, the army's General Staff, and the Communist Party's standing committee. From this upland capital, the DRV pushed its administrative units into the northern delta whenever it could and, as the army strengthened, into the surrounding highlands in what would become the "Viet Bac" or northern zone in 1949. The French, however, held the main roads and towns, Hanoi and Haiphong in particular, the northwest Tai highlands in Lai Chau province, the border with China until 1950, and much, but not all, of the Red River plains between the capital and the coast running to Haiphong (see Map 7).

Although both sides claimed sovereignty over all of Vietnam through-out the conflagration, each belligerent knew that their territorial control on the ground was partial. The fragmentary nature of power even al-lowed for autonomous or semi-autonomous entities to emerge within the interstices. Allied with the French politically and militarily, the Hoa Hao and Cao Dai religious congregations in the south were a semi-autonomous example. In exchange for their cooperation against the Democratic Republic of Vietnam, the French accorded the leaders of these southern faiths considerable leeway in running their religious do-mains locally. They were not independent states, however. They were part of a French Indochinese state. And if their leaders acted too inde-pendently, the French used force to bring them back in line.

Sandwiched between French Hanoi and the DRV's Zone IV, Viet-namese Catholics living in the dioceses of Bui Chu and Phat Diem ad-ministered a much more independent religious realm under the leader-ship of a feisty bishop named Le Huu Tu. Although this man had left Ho's government, distrustful of its communist core, he refused to cross over to the French on anticolonialist grounds. His opposition to the "communists" and to the "colonialists" and the relative weakness of Vietnamese and French power provided Le Huu Tu with the in-between space he needed to administer a religious estate with its own civil ser-vants, militia, customs officials, and border checkpoints. The DRV cur-rency, the dong, and the colonial piaster served as its dual legal tender. Only in 1951, when Ho's Chinese-primed people's army finally threat-ened to impose the DRV's control by force did this rogue bishop finally join the French in search of military protection. In exchange, the Catho-lics had to accept, like the southern religious groups before them, po-litical association with the French colonial state and the loss of indepen-dence that came with it. They did.[31]

To further complicate things, during the late 1940s the French en-tered into negotiations with noncommunist Vietnamese who continued to push the French to accord them what they had refused Ho Chi Minh—territorial unity and national independence. Many of these nationalists coalesced around the former Emperor Bao Dai who had left the DRV in 1946, wary of the communists running it. He had gone into voluntary exile in southern China. After discussions with noncommunist nationalists inside and outside the country, in September 1947 the former emperor agreed to enter into negotiations with the French to create a second, noncommunist Vietnam, allied with but eventually independent of the French. Intense exchanges between the former emperor and the French followed throughout 1948. In 1949, the French finally agreed to the unification of Vietnam (meaning no more Cochinchina, Annam, or Tonkin), but they insisted that this new Vietnam had to remain in an "Association" with France, federated with neighboring Laos and Cambodia, and, together, part of the French Union. Bao Dai grudgingly agreed, pushed by the Americans and the British, who needed help containing the communists. The ex-emperor was nonetheless convinced that he could force the French to grant full independence and even use the Americans to help him do that (Washington was pushing the Dutch to grant independence to noncommunist Indonesians at this time). On 2 July 1949, the Associated State of Vietnam officially came to life, and Bao Dai returned to run it.[32]

Based out of Saigon, this second Vietnam operated its own ministries, civil service, schools, and soon an army, police force, and intelligence service. Despite their deep differences over how long "association" should last, both sides saw in this new Vietnamese state a powerful bureaucratic instrument for peeling off noncommunist nationalists from the Democratic Republic of Vietnam. The idea was that the French army would take territories from Ho's Vietnam wherever it could by force. The Associated State of Vietnam would then immediately move in its civil servants, police, and militias to administer the "liberated" territories and their populations. Of course this was also known as good old-fashioned "pacification," the kind its French godfathers like Joseph Galliéni and Herbert Lyautey had "theorized" in nineteenth-century Tonkin and elsewhere. The French liked to call it the "oil spot strategy" or *tâche d'huile*—administrative control spread with military power from village to village. The difference after the Second World War was that the Vietnamese anticolonialists lined up behind Ho Chi Minh did not stand by idly this time and let the enemy "oil spots" expand colonial sovereignty without a fight. They pushed back against this second French colonial conquest. During the Indochina War, state building cut both ways.[33]

The Badlands

The result of all of this was that territorial sovereignty shattered into pieces for all involved. Working from their core "islands" in northern and central Vietnam and pockets in the south, Ho Chi Minh's officials pushed their control out in streams from one craggy, atoll-like territory to another. Thanks to militias, security officers, and civil servants, they built up a sprawling national polity that expanded and contracted like a sponge being squeezed as enemies pushed into it and then pulled out. Viewed from above, the Democratic Republic of Vietnam resembled an archipelago. It was a highly decentralized, vulnerable, and weak constellation of power concentrated around island cores. But it functioned. Radios connected its various parts through the air while messengers and itinerant traders did so on the ground, by foot, in boats, or on horseback.[34]

Arrayed against this Vietnamese archipelago stood the French-led Indochinese federation of associated regimes—the Associated State of Vietnam, the affiliated religious estates of the Hoa Hao, Cao Dai, and Catholics, the highlander federations, the Binh Xuyen, and even French plantation fiefdoms. Unable to defeat the Democratic Republic of Vietnam militarily, this colonial coalition morphed early on into a parallel constellation interlocking with the enemy one as leaders on each side tried to push their respective sovereignties as far as they could into and against the other. This is why there was no such thing before 1954 as "one S-like Vietnam." There was certainly no "North Vietnam" or "South Vietnam." All that came later. There were only intertwined states locked in a perpetual state of motion and competition for people, territories, and things. There was nothing necessarily new or "Vietnamese" about this: similar examples of intertwining sovereignties in times of war riddle world history from antiquity to the present, in Syria, Afghanistan, and the Ukraine as I write. To put it another way, the (actual) state and the (imagined) nation rarely coincide on the ground in wartime.

This is also why soldiers were not the only ones doing the fighting during the Indochina War. Civil servants were deeply involved in expanding each side's bureaucratic hold over the other. Since the outbreak of hostilities in the south in 1945, the French had initiated an effort to coordinate military operations against the Democratic Republic of Vietnam with a simultaneous administrative assault designed to win over and use local leaders and village councils to expand their colonial grip. After the outbreak of full-scale war in late 1946, the French launched a concerted "pacification" effort in the Red River Delta: once colonial soldiers had cleared this territory of enemy DRV forces, French and Vietnamese civil servants moved in to run it via a new committee called the "Provisional Committee for Administrative and Social Action." In reaction, Ho Chi Minh's government ordered its own administrators to hold their line and push back against this colonial subversion of the Vietnamese republic at the village level. Orders went out to expand their administrative and resistance committees and grow their own people's councils in order to win over people and secure territory. Local civil servants received instructions to increase the visibility of the government's presence through robust propaganda drives, intensive literacy and hygiene campaigns, as well as all sorts of governmental ceremonies and meetings. The leadership counseled persuasion and discussions with village and district chiefs tempted by the French so that they would not defect. Commands went out to build up trust at local level and to rein in young Viet Minh hotheads whom villagers avoided. Cadres received instructions to destroy intruding bureaucratic structures if need be, including enemy village councils; but they also had the authorization to *maintain* them and to *use* them for their own state building, especially if they could help the government expand administratively there. If village chiefs did not fall into line, however, then local authorities could issue strong warnings, make arrests, and even execute the most recalcitrant in order to protect, expand, or consolidate administrative control.[35]

This battle of the administrations turned particularly violent, not in their secure centers, but in areas where the archipelagos touched up against each other. The struggle almost always started when one side attempted to land its civil servants on the adversary's shores in order to create a "new organization" or, more likely, to win over the enemy's village councils and local leaders through persuasion and promises of protection and good jobs if they defected. And as in any battle, before moving out, each side needed detailed and accurate information on the other side's village administration, councils, and the people working in both—not their weapons but rather their professional backgrounds, political résumés, work colleagues, kinship ties, friends, and how to get to them. The Vietnamese turned to their intelligence and security services to provide this vital information, just as the French and their Vietnamese associates did. And as the intelligence reports piled up on each side, archiving local knowledge became essential to waging this type of war, a civil as much as a colonial one, and the aggressive state-building it was designed to generate.

The Vietnamese have left us invaluable accounts of the war of the village councils and resistance administrations. Having grown up in the DRV borderlands, Nguyen Cong Luan describes in his memoirs how the French attacked the lower levels of the DRV civil service, where his father, we know, was a noncommunist nationalist administrator elected to lead the village administrative committee and its Lien Viet front. In late 1949, as the Associated State of Vietnam took off and with it the French strategy to use it to detach noncommunists from Ho's Vietnam, the war for village control naturally intensified. The opening salvo that would forever change young Luan's life came through a letter delivered to his father from the French via a trusted friend sometime in 1949:

The French officer who signed the letter promised my father a job as district chief or provincial deputy chief if he left the Viet Minh and moved to the French controlled territory. If my father accepted the proposal, a small-scale operation would be conducted in our village area to bring my whole family to the city. . . . At that time the French were looking for a political solution and they needed a Vietnamese administrative system to assist them in various civil affairs.[36]

Despite pleas from family members to accept the offer and get them out of "there," his father refused, and the family remained in the DRV on the grounds that the French had to grant full independence first. Friends of his father who had received similar letters left their administrative posts in the DRV to join the French-backed State of Vietnam as district chiefs, often located just across from where they had previously worked in Ho's Vietnam. This is where their knowledge and contacts would be most useful to expanding the French Indochinese federation and its associated Vietnamese state. For his home province of Nam Dinh alone, Nguyen Cong Luan estimated that 1,000 nationalists left the Democratic Republic of Vietnam in 1949, hoping that Bao Dai would make good on his promise to force the French to grant his Vietnam full independence. The DRV's security services quickly picked up on what was going on—they had to stop this internal administrative hemorrhaging—and arrested Luan's father and sent him to prison. He died there, never formally charged with any crime.[37]

This sustained bureaucratic war in the countryside sowed distrust up and down the DRV's borderlands, swallowing up people like Luan's father, not because he was guilty of anything, certainly not treason, but rather because government and military authorities wanted to make sure the French never got their administrative hands on him (or others like him). Often highly educated and well-connected, these noncommunist civil servants were, in the eyes of the French, the administrative equivalent of taking modern weapons away from the enemy's army. Meanwhile, just like their adversaries, Ho's intelligence and security services were firing off letters to administrators on the Franco-Vietnamese side, promising them attractive positions in the DRV in exchange for their collaboration.

Although the French and their Vietnamese partners agreed that the best way to take on their common adversary was at administrative level, the French refusal to decolonize made it harder for those defecting to the Associated State of Vietnam to do so with a clean patriotic

conscience. When Tran Ngoc Chau, another noncommunist patriot
working in Ho's army, slipped into the French-occupied zone in a nerve-
wracking boat ride taking him from one shore to the other, he
immediately told his Vietnamese captors that he would only turn himself in to the newly formed State of Vietnam led by Bao Dai. Tran Ngoc
Chau was woefully if understandably naïve if he thought that would
happen. Indeed, he learned within hours what "association" was and
who was really in charge when a French security agent speaking flawless
Vietnamese took over his case to find out about the enemy's administration. Following him came another Frenchman from Army Intelligence.
He wanted to know about the enemy's order of battle.[38] Tensions certainly
existed between the French and their Vietnamese partners over the
question of independence, even over who had the right to interrogate
defectors in the field first. But as long as the French refused to decolonize
and the DRV continued to hold out, the "State of Vietnam" remained
precisely that, "a state," without a "nation," a bureaucratic machine, a
French colonial weapon, a thinly veiled protectorate. Even in these borderlands, the State of Vietnam remained "Associated," part of a colonial
constellation.

As these competing polities led by the French "colonialists" and the
Vietnamese "communists" expanded and contracted upon contact
with each other, as armies and bureaucrats extended territorial control
and then lost it again, people living on the edges got caught in the
cross fire or in no-man's-lands, in eerie, open territorial waters where
no one state exercised full control. Nguyen Cong Luan learned this as
a child, because he had grown up in this shattered Vietnam: "Babies
were born, young men and women got married, and people died without being registered," he tells us. "We had no ID cards from the French
or from the Viet Minh, children had no school to go to, and wounded
and sick people were treated with herbal medicines."[39] And like the
ocean's tide, sovereignty could rise in favor of one side at night and
then recede during the day in favor of the other: "Every night," Luan
continues, "from 7 p.m. to 6 a.m. was the time of fear during which I
had to speak softly and make no loud noises. My gate to the road outside the bamboo hedge was closed at 7 p.m., and it seemed to be the

boundary between safety and danger. The darkness outside the hedge was full of risks that frightened me whenever I had something to do near the gate." Decades later, as an old man, the memory of this world still haunted him as it must have countless villagers who had lived through "it," too.[40]

Accounts like Nguyen Cong Luan's provide us with a rare glimpse into how so many nameless Vietnamese navigated these dangerous waters, individually and collectively, day in and day out, night after night. Communist Party documents and French intelligence reports we read in the archives rarely speak of emotions like "fear," "sorrow," "revenge," and "hate." They tell us little about how people had to make choices on the ground, in a split second, often in unfathomable circumstances. There was little that was black-and-white in these areas where the competing archipelago states touched up against each other. If loyalties were obscure, it was because "things" were often blurred. As a result, people living in these places operated their daily lives in something of a perpetual state of instability. Local people had no choice but to come up with strategies to protect themselves and their loved ones. Consider how important this plan of action described by Nguyen Cong Luan must have been at the time, and how it was undoubtedly repeated elsewhere in war-ravaged Vietnam well into the 1970s:

> In every village, there were some people who worked as spies for either side. In my village, a man of thirty years volunteered to play a double agent to protect the village from both French and Viet Minh terrorism. With help from some villagers, he regularly reported military intelligence information to the French by a "secret letter box," an intermediary, in the adjacent village. At the same time, he provided the Viet Minh intelligence service with what he collected in the French controlled area. . . . I was sure that my village had some others who worked for both sides. Owing to those spies, my village was not terrorized in the second half of 1949.[41]

That last line about "terror" and the village's six-month respite from it is important. For it was also in these borderlands, where French military and political control was weakest, but the power of heavily armed local commanders greatest, that some of the darkest violence of the Indochina War occurred. Before Nguyen Cong Luan had even turned sixteen, he tells us in disturbing and often graphic detail, how he had somehow survived French arrest, ferocious beatings, and near execution as his village flipped from one side to the other—and then back again (the worst possible combination). Luan witnessed horrible civilian massacres, including torture, rape, and summary executions. As he and others make clear, entire villages—hundreds of human beings—could get wiped out in a matter of minutes in these contested areas when French patrols moved in. This was especially the case when a partisan attack—a booby trap, a kidnapping, or a sniper's bullet—set off a surge of cruelty. Everyone knows what American soldiers did to a village called My Lai in 1968. But unknown to this day in France are the massacres its army committed in My Trach in 1947 (300 civilians, women and children—killed) and My Thuy a year later (over 500 civilians, young and old—all dead). In his moving account of his father's life, Andrew Pham describes the Franco-Algerian monster of a sergeant who inflicted unspeakable violence on innocent civilians located precisely in another one of these areas where sovereignties "flipped," the state was weak, and heavily armed commanders roamed with impunity, like medieval lords.[42]

The effects of this violence even spilled into the afterlife for thousands of Vietnamese souls caught in the open. On 12 August 1948, French troops arrived in Thanh Khe village near the provincial capital of Nam Dinh. When local officials came out to welcome them, the patrol shot them dead. As the soldiers fanned out into the village, they also killed the grandmother of Tuong Vu, now a renowned political scientist at the University of Oregon. She had been trying to bury money in a hole in the bank of a pond. Although survivors recovered her body and buried her in a casket donated by friends, they could not get her soul out of the water. Villagers soon heard her voice in their dreams, bad ones, "crying about being cold." "Eventually," as Professor Vu explained to me, "the villagers had to hold a special ritual in which they made a bridge from fabric [reaching] from the pond to the house and invited

monks to come and chant in order to guide her soul out of the pond."
Only then did the nightmares among her friends and family stop as
Le Thi Bong finally made it to the other side and got out of the water
and the war.[43]

Walking through this land of sorrow was another emotion, just as
profound—hate. It did more than any communist propaganda campaign to send scores of Vietnamese straight into the arms of Ho Chi
Minh. Ngo Van Chieu writes in awe in his memoirs of the political com-
missar in his company, a simple man from the countryside, who had led
a band of brothers into ferocious combat against the French during the
battle of Cao Bang in late 1950. What drove this peasant communist to
fight, Chieu tells us, was not Marx or Lenin, not Ho or even the promise
of land. It was the memory of the faceless French Union troops who had
burned down his village during his absence, including the thatched hut
in which his handicapped mother had perished on that fateful day.
Things could have been different, the fiercely anticommunist Nguyen
Cong Luan confided to his memoirs: the French could have "won the
hearts and minds of the population," if they had prohibited "their soldiers from committing war crimes and treating the Vietnamese so sav-
agely."[44] One thing is sure, though: if ever a map of the dead during the
Indochina War is drawn, I suspect that the reddest stains will cover the
badlands running down the outer banks of the Vietnamese archipelago,
not on the battlefields of Cao Bang or Dien Bien Phu, but rather in
borderland places like My Trach, My Thuy, and Nam Dinh. In all, between 1945 and 1954, as many as one million Vietnamese perished, civilians and combatants, the former in much greater numbers than the latter.[45] (See plates 3, 4, 5, and 6.)

The Unbearable Weakness of Communist Control

The communists at the center of the embattled Democratic Republic of
Vietnam may have wanted to protect their citizens against this colonial
violence.[46] They may have hoped that a single-party state of Marxist-
Leninist design would allow them to do so. But in the late 1940s, even

later in many areas, communist control over the state was remarkably weak. In September 1945, the Indochinese Communist Party counted only 5,000 members out of a total Vietnamese population of over 20 million people. When full-scale war broke out a year and a half later, the party had 15,000 members, all of whom had been recruited hastily and most of whom were inexperienced. As a result, the communists had no choice but to rely on the collaboration of tens of thousands of noncommunist colonial-era civil servants, merchants, professionals of all kinds, and landowners to keep their state up and running as the French attacked.

Ho Chi Minh, Truong Chinh, and other high-ranking communist leaders repeatedly called upon the patriotic bourgeoisie and the landowning classes in the countryside to continue trading and producing as well as participating in local government, mass organizations, militias, and the armed forces. The communist core kept its plans for radical land reform and class struggle under lock and key. Pragmatism trumped radical revolution. Ho and Truong Chinh only redistributed land taken from French plantation owners and absent Vietnamese landowning "traitors" (*Viet gian*). They imposed rent reductions of 25 percent and approved lower borrowing rates for peasants. None of which was very radical.[47] Duong Van Mai Elliot has explained in her memoirs how the government approached her uncle at this time, a fairly well-off property holder in the northern zone. He farmed 260 acres on which he had built a prosperous orange grove and cultivated rice with the help of hired hands. He rented the rest of his land in exchange for 10 percent of the crop.

> At this time, the Viet Minh were preaching unity and trying to recruit anyone who was willing to join their movement, regardless of class origin. In time, the communists would turn the old social order upside down, destroying the traditional elite and the middle class to put the workers and poor peasants on top. But for now, they could not afford to alienate people like my uncle. So, in spite of his background as a big landowner and a mandarin, the Viet Minh approached him. They invited him to serve as a vice chairman of the province committee of the Lien Viet, an organization they had set up to attract middle class people and intellectuals into their ranks.[48]

The hardest years for the communists were 1947 and 1948. During this time, the party, the government, and the army were on the run in the north and even fearful that the French would debark in central Vietnam and destroy their large safe bases there. Ho and his entourage only set up their wartime capital in the remote northern area of Thai Nguyen province in mid-1947, but even then, it remained vulnerable to attack. A few months later, in a bid to destroy Ho's Vietnam by striking at its "head," the French launched their surprise paratrooper attack, *Operation Léa*. French soldiers fanned into northern republican areas running from Thai Nguyen to the Chinese border. They did not capture Ho, the party center, or ministers; but they came close and sowed chaos as they went on the offensive.

That said, the communists were not newcomers to operating in such difficult conditions. They could draw upon years of experience in organizing their party clandestinely. Against all odds, the center had survived colonial repression in the early 1930s and combined Franco–Japanese surveillance during the Second World War. No other anticolonialist group could rival the communists when it came to operating under extreme police surveillance. The French seemed to have forgotten this after 1945, when they hastily claimed that they would deal with the "rebels" in a matter of months. They should have known better. Upon coming to power in August 1945, top-ranking communists immediately put decades of clandestine experience to good use by reestablishing contact with recently released political prisoners, resurrecting sleeper cells, remobilizing a coterie of messengers and liaison agents, reopening safe houses, and stockpiling communications equipment whenever they could. All of this was part of a concerted effort, initiated before 1945, to reconstruct the Indochinese Communist Party's hierarchy as rapidly as possible so that it could guide this newly independent Vietnam, its bureaucracy, army, mass organizations, and national fronts. The communists were not in a position of strength in 1945, but they knew that the rapid building of their party—not just the core leadership, but its internal administration and civil service—was essential to controlling the direction of the Democratic Republic of Vietnam and the course of the war on their terms.[49]

The communists lined up behind Ho Chi Minh and Truong Chinh went to work immediately upon taking power in August 1945. At the top of the territorial pyramid they designed for the Indochinese Communist Party stood its central committee, what I call the "center" (*trung uong*) or the core communist leadership. Because colonial war had broken out so rapidly in the south before spreading to the north a year later, the communists had never had the time to organize a national congress to elect an official central committee, politburo, and general secretary. (The previous party congress had taken place before the war, in Portuguese Macau, in 1935.) For the time being, Truong Chinh served as the party's interim leader. Ho Chi Minh served as its gatekeeper, in addition to being the president of the government. Under Ho's personal guidance, rule by consensus prevailed within the Communist Party during the Indochina War, a "roundtable" if you will, similar to the one Mao Zedong had established upon arriving at Yan'an after the disastrous Long March of the mid-1930s.[50]

Following the outbreak of full-scale war, the party's political center operated from the resistance capital in Thai Nguyen. Directly below the standing committee were the party's "territorial committees" for the north, the center, and the south, respectively, as well as for Laos and Cambodia. Prison-tested, loyal, and veteran communists ran them in Vietnam: Le Duc Tho in the north, Nguyen Chi Thanh in central Vietnam, and Le Duan in the south. Each of the five territorial committees was in effect a specialized Communist Party office, in charge of all political matters, ideological instruction, propaganda, finances, and intelligence work. Each territory, in turn, broke down into zones along the lines explained above for the resistance administration. Hierarchically organized, the party headquarters in each zone operated communist affairs via its provincial, district, and village committees. Some of this communist infrastructure built on preexisting networks and contacts. Most of it was created from scratch after 1945, and always in fits and starts.

Horizontally, each party office in the communist hierarchy (again: territorial office, zone, province, district, and village) interfaced with their respective counterparts in the resistance and administrative committees, and in the mass associations and fronts (Viet Minh, Lien Viet, and so on). The idea was that the communist hierarchy would connect with each of its sister state structures in order to watch over and eventually run them. The communists operated this administrative interface through a special party committee (*cap uy*), an essential administrative link, which an eminent communist would describe as the "chord" or the "threads" binding party to state. Its members—always communists—had the job of following, advising, and controlling what was going on in the parallel pillars running the army, resistance administration, and national fronts. The godfather of French counterinsurgency theory during the Indochina War, Charles Lacheroy, was thus right to speak of "parallel hierarchies" to describe how the Communist Party's pillar interacted cross-sectionally with the army and the state.[51] He was wrong, however, to conclude that because the communists said they ruled through these parallel hierarchies that they actually did so. He erred too, in thinking that because the communists had "parallel hierarchies," they therefore exercised "totalitarian control." That is what Ho and his entourage *wanted*; but wanting something and actually having it are two very different things.[52]

The center encountered several problems in expanding its authority during the first half of the conflict and even later. For one, the disarray caused by war naturally complicated efforts to expand communist control as the archipelago expanded and contracted unpredictably, rapidly, and often violently. Second, there were problems of quantity and quality, again two very different things. With only 5,000 members in September 1945, expanding party membership was a priority and, at the outset, the center had opened its doors to welcome as many new members in as possible. Although membership grew rapidly, party expansion was regionally uneven. If central and northern Vietnam counted over 100,000 members by 1948, the embattled southern Mekong Delta counted only 10,000, Laos and Cambodia even less. Moreover, as the leadership lowered admission standards to increase numbers, the quality of the new recruits predictably declined. Many people joined the party to secure good jobs in a new civil service. Some did so because their friends or a sibling did. Others acted out of revenge against heavy-handed French patrols—not necessarily because they believed in the Marxist-Leninist gospel. Bourgeois, notables, and landowners signed up to protect themselves and their interests, leading Truong Chinh to point out that this might make it harder to collect taxes, reduce rents, and implement land reform one day. He had a point. In some areas, things were so bad that many members did not even know what the party was. In 1948, officials lamented that "there are places where propaganda for the party's doctrine seems to have been abolished and the training of new comrades seems to have stopped." Elsewhere "there reigns an atmosphere of doubt as to this group's role. The group's [Communist Party] influence has as a result diminished in part."[53] Equally alarming were statistics showing that women had not joined the party in large numbers. They only constituted 8 percent of the party's total membership in 1948.[54]

No one was more aware of these weaknesses than the party's rapidly emerging organizational czar, Le Duc Tho, and the acting general secretary, Truong Chinh. They made their case in meetings in 1948, most notably during an important party plenum held in August of that year. Both men criticized the poor training members had received in Marxist-Leninist thought, the careless recruiting of incompetent, unmotivated, and individualistic people; the resulting lack of cohesion within the party organization; and a serious shortage of qualified cadres capable of keeping tabs on what often very educated noncommunist professionals were doing in the areas of education, the economy, communications, medicine, and law. One clear message emerged from these top-level communist reports in 1948: the center's control was unbearably weak.[55]

Again, the problem was not one of numbers. By early 1950, the party would have around 450,000 members on file. It was a question of quality. Too many of them were, in Le Duc Tho's words, "unmotivated, undisciplined, and degenerate."[56] He agreed that many should be expelled. But what Le Duc Tho and Truong Chinh wanted most was not more "communist members" (*dang vien*) but more and better-trained "communist cadres" (*can bo*). A Catholic or Buddhist Church can have many believers, but without enough priests or monks it is hard to operate effectively. To expand the center's control, the communists needed trusted and competent Party civil servants to interface with the non-communists in the resistance administration, the army, and on the patriotic fronts. The training of an elite communist bureaucratic caste was, Le Duc Tho explained, the sine qua non for expanding communist control over the state. Truong Chinh agreed, adding that the party had to "unify ideology and action" among its own members and train much-needed cadres in order to establish "the party's leadership in every area: the military, administration, economics, finances, culture." In September 1950, the party leadership would go so far as to suspend the induction of new party members in order to maintain discipline and quality control within its own ranks.[57]

Probably one of the most important results of all of this was the creation of the Nguyen Ai Quoc Party Academy in the north in April 1949. Its mission was to train a new bureaucratic communist elite, the "cadres." Based in Thai Nguyen province, carefully selected students studied under the party's top leaders, including Pham Van Dong, Truong Chinh, and Ho Chi Minh. Pupils carefully memorized the Marxist-Leninist creed, the Vietnamese Communist Party's history, and learned how it operated and interacted administratively with the rest of the Democratic Republic of Vietnam and the armed forces. To this day, as in communist China and the former Soviet Union, this academy trains the elite bureaucratic class that fulfills civil service type roles within the party and for its center in the state, the armed forces, and mass organizations. During the Indochina War, it probably trained an elite of around 4,000 communist cadres to fill top party positions.[58]

Closer to the ground, Le Duc Tho made a number of suggestions to make the "parallel hierarchies" work. For a start, the party needed to be more "scientific" in its ability to gather information, build statistics and analyze them to craft better policy, training, and control. Information had to move up the chain of command, and orders had to be implemented in a timely fashion from the top down. "Investigation and research" became buzz words, as did instructions to avoid generalities in favor of solving problems concretely.[59] Next, for Le Duc Tho, much depended on imposing stricter admissions standards. Not only did aspiring candidates have to fill out the famous personal history forms, but the center also had to verify carefully that it was accurate. Background checks were de rigueur. He recommended better surveillance of the party's internal ranks, and the introduction of disciplinary measures to ensure quality control. Last of all, he issued orders to improve communications vertically down the chain of command and horizontally between different regions and zones.

But if things were bad in northern and central Vietnam, they were even worse in the south. Party numbers were lowest there, as was the quality of the membership. The nationalist front, the Lien Viet, and the army operated free of communist control in many cases. The commander-in-chief of the southern armed forces, Nguyen Binh, only became a communist in 1947. To turn things around, the Indochinese Communist Party dispatched Le Duc Tho to the south to bring organizational and ideological order. He left in the fall of 1948, travelling first to areas in zones IV and V to share party instructions. He arrived in the Mekong Delta in April 1949 as the Chinese Red Army crossed the Yangzi River into southern China. He joined forces with the communists in charge in the south, Le Duan, Nguyen Van Linh, and Pham Hung. They presided over the creation of the Truong Chinh Party Academy in the Mekong Delta, the sister-school to the Nguyen Ai Quoc Academy in the north. This elite party academy in the south would create a new communist clergy of cadres capable of taking things in hand. The names these two academies carried made it clear who was in charge of the communist establishment—Ho Chi Minh and Truong Chinh.[60] (Nguyen Ai Quoc was one of Ho's aliases.)

Of particular concern for Le Duc Tho and his new party allies in the south was the need to bring the southern section of the Lien Viet back into line. Many noncommunist nationalists had taken the communists at their word in 1946 and joined the Lien Viet in large numbers to fight the French as part of the coalition state. This nationalist front included anticolonialist traders, entrepreneurs, and landowners as well as noncommunist republicans and socialists. The problem was that the party lacked sufficiently trained cadres to keep tabs on their noncommunist counterparts. And the fact that the communists had retained most of their members in the Viet Minh had, paradoxically, strengthened the hand of the noncommunists in the Lien Viet.

The rise of a noncommunist, anticolonialist bloc within the party's own Lien Viet, to some extent free of communist control, troubled Le Duc Tho (and it was apparently cause for concern elsewhere in the archipelago as well). To ensure his party's hold over this mass organization, the communists came up with the idea of folding the Viet Minh into the Lien Viet so as to create a single national front. In so doing, the communists would be in a better position to reestablish control over the Lien Viet by slowly marginalizing the noncommunist leaders who had pried this mass organization from the fingers of its communist architects. The party's Second Congress held in early 1951 (examined further in Chapter 8) formally dissolved the Viet Minh and collapsed it into the Lien Viet. The Lien Viet would operate until the end of the Indochina War under increasing communist control while the Viet Minh ceased to exist. The communists would resurrect the Lien Viet in the form of the National Liberation Front (NLF) in 1960 in order to expand, once again, their hold over people and territory during the Vietnam War. But we should keep in mind that, although the communists secretly ran the NLF like the Lien Viet before it, in both cases they had to concede considerable power to noncommunists in exchange for their cooperation in running the coalition state at its lower, less communist albeit vital levels in wartime. It is not because you create something that it necessarily remains yours.[61]

This is what Le Duc Tho had forgotten in July 1949 when he stepped in front of the noncommunists in the Lien Viet, deep in the Mekong Delta. The party's special envoy to the south had reason to be worried, for three days before he had shouted that anyone who opposed the communists was a traitor, and the Associated State of Vietnam had officially come to life under the leadership of the former emperor of Vietnam, Bao Dai. It was part of a French (and, increasingly, an American) grand strategy designed to cause a hemorrhage inside the Democratic Republic of Vietnam, by breaking off the very nationalists whom the communists were having a hard time controlling from within. It was also a colonial recipe for ramping up civil war among the Vietnamese.

2

Building Military Force

In early February 1954, *Le Monde*'s veteran war correspondent, Robert Guillain, toured the fortress the French had built in the valley of Dien Bien Phu in preparation for an imminent showdown with Vo Nguyen Giap's soldiers. What struck him most as he toured the site was the strange disconnect between the soldiers' confidence heading into the battle and the military force their adversaries were busy building up around them. "We'll show them," soldiers repeated, "We are going to show them." "Show them what?" Guillain asked. "We're going to break the Vietnamese." *Casser du Viet* was the French expression—it meant to destroy Vo Nguyen Giap's regular army in set-piece battle. Having seen this picture recently in Korea, Guillain was less than convinced. And when French commandos probed into the hills above Dien Bien Phu in February 1954, he noted, the Vietnamese drove them back down in a hail of fire. Something was clearly out there. Guillain wrote that the French fortress was dangling in the "mouth of a wolf."[1]

What stepped out of the jungle when the battle finally commenced on 13 March was the People's Army of Vietnam. However, it had not always been there. Military force of this magnitude did not just appear out of thin air. It had to be carefully crafted over time. Officers had to be schooled, infantrymen had to be disciplined, and scores of intelligence, radio, and artillery specialists trained. That Chinese communist aid allowed the Vietnamese to take military force to a new level from 1950, there can be no debate. It did. But had the Vietnamese state Ho Chi Minh declared independent in 1945 not begun early on building a regular army, command structure, and officer corps capable of handling such modern weapons, then artillery pieces and antiaircraft guns would have rusted at the border. There would have been no Dien Bien Phu, because there would have been no regular army. It is important to start at the beginning to understand how the Vietnamese accumulated military force of this impressive caliber.

An Army Is Born

Creating Force

As the Allies closed in on the Germans in Europe in late 1944 and focused their undivided attention on defeating the Japanese in Asia, Vietnamese communists led by Ho Chi Minh knew that they would need more than the national front created in 1941, the Viet Minh, to take power when the Axis inevitably collapsed. In December 1944, in jungle areas located near the Chinese border, Ho Chi Minh presided over the creation of the "Armed Propaganda Brigade for the Liberation of Vietnam," renamed the "Vietnamese Liberation Army" a few months later. Vo Nguyen Giap served as its first commander, seconded by a close communist confidant, Hoang Van Thai. At the start, this "brigade" consisted of a few dozen people. They led small-scale propaganda campaigns to garner local support in the north and initiated minor hit-and-run operations against isolated Japanese outposts. As miniscule as it was, this was the kernel from which modern Vietnamese military force would grow.

Although these guerrilla units protected Viet Minh leaders as they took power in Hanoi on 19 August 1945, they did not liberate Hanoi, Hue, or Saigon. They did not have to. The Japanese had already incarcerated French colonial troops during their 9 March coup before surrendering themselves to the Allies on 15 August. Instead of stopping the Viet Minh from taking power (which they could have easily done), in most cases the Japanese looked the other way as Ho's officials and supporters took over Hanoi on the 19th and the rest of the country during the following weeks in what is known in Vietnam today as the "August

Revolution." To Ho's relief, the Japanese refused to liberate colonial troops and ignored orders coming from Charles de Gaulle's emissaries to do so. Given that de Gaulle had not been privy to the Allied conference held in Potsdam in early August assigning zones for accepting the surrender of Japanese troops strewn across the region, the Japanese did not consider the French, Gaullist or not, to be part of the Allied camp in Asia. In accordance with the Potsdam decision, the Japanese surrendered to the British below the 16th parallel and to Chiang Kai-shek's Chinese troops above that line.

Ho knew, though, that the absence of the French would not last. The Japanese would soon be gone, and the Gaullists were already maneuvering their way back in. The Vietnamese president would need to build up his military forces fast to protect his government's fragile hold on power. And he was right: on 23 September, hardly two weeks after the declaration of Vietnam's independence, war broke out in Saigon when the British allowed previously interned Vichy troops to take over in this southern city. The fighting intensified rapidly in the following weeks when de Gaulle's Expeditionary Corps landed and fanned out into the countryside. In the northern half of the country, however, the situation was very different, thanks to the Chinese decision not to let the French attack as the British had in the south. On account of this Chinese protective shield, the Vietnamese were able to train officers and troops in central and northern parts of the country free of colonial molestation for over a year. The government recruited, trained, and armed as best it could thousands of young Vietnamese to form the backbone of the Vietnamese National Army (Quan Doi Quoc Gia Viet Nam) formally announced in May of 1946. (Ho Chi Minh's national army of 1946 is not to be confused with the one the French created for the Associated State of Vietnam in 1949 bearing the same name and discussed further in Chapter 9.)

For the communists at the helm of the Democratic Republic of Vietnam, controlling the army was as important as running the security services. And no one knew this better than Vo Nguyen Giap: he commanded both of these instruments of state power from the start. In September 1945, he became minister of the interior, in charge of the police and internal security. The following year, the Indochinese Communist Party also put him in charge of its newly created Central Military Commission. As in the Soviet Union and communist China, the Central Military Commission in Vietnam was the office through which the communist party ran the armed forces from the top down. Members of this commission, all senior communists, devised military strategy and plans such as major campaigns and troop build-ups. Led by Vo Nguyen Giap during the Indochina War, this commission, in turn, implemented its policies through the General Staff, the department in charge of running the armed forces on a daily basis. Hoang Van Thai led the General Staff until the end of the war, working closely with Giap. In short, the communists were in charge of all military matters.[2]

The General Staff was the instrument through which the Vietnamese forged a modern army during the Indochina War. Based on a European model at the start, it consisted of a group of mainly military personnel who tended to the day-to-day operations of the armed forces. The General Staff consisted of offices in charge of logistics, intelligence, communications, and training. During the first half of the war, when guerrilla warfare dominated, work focused mainly on officer and troop training, improving radio communications, and basic field operations. While the Communist Party ran the General Staff, noncommunist officers and civilians held important positions at mid- and lower levels. That would change in 1950, when Chinese communist advice and support transformed the nature of the war and of the army fighting it. But until then (and even after), Giap needed all the help he could get.[3]

Teaching Force

Essential to building an effective army was the creation of an officer corps trained in modern military science.[4] Leaders, from Vo Nguyen Giap and Hoang Van Thai down to company commanders, had to know what war was, how it was fought, and what command entailed concretely in the field. Some of the earliest instruction occurred via the makeshift academy the communists had created at the close of the

Second World War: the Anti-Japanese Political-Military Academy. American intelligence officers in the Office of Strategic Studies (OSS) probably gave a few lessons there in commando and radio operations in exchange for information which Ho Chi Minh's agents provided on Japanese military installations and for returning downed US pilots. The common struggle against the Japanese also explains why the leader of the Republic of China at the time, Chiang Kai-shek, allowed Vietnamese communists to train in his military academy in Liuzhou (located near the northern Vietnamese border). Hoang Van Thai had been one of them. Upon his return to Vietnam in the early 1940s, he joined Giap in creating the Viet Minh's liberation army. He would have shared his knowledge of military matters with young cadets joining them at that time as well.[5]

Such training naturally accelerated upon the creation of the Democratic Republic of Vietnam. The General Staff recruited Vietnamese soldiers from the defunct colonial army. As long as these men in it passed a background check and pledged loyalty to Ho's Vietnam, the Ministry of Defense welcomed them into its ranks and the best of them into its classrooms to help teach a flood of new recruits.[6] The same was true of dozens of Japanese soldiers and a handful of their officers who crossed over to the DRV at the close of the Pacific War. The government granted them citizenship, making them "New Vietnamese," in exchange for their help in developing and running officer-training camps. A handful of European soldiers in the French colonial army also crossed over to Ho's Vietnam (most had volunteered in the late 1930s, thinking they would be fighting the Nazis, maybe the Japanese, but not the Vietnamese). All of these instructors instilled discipline, taught the basics of handling arms, and drilled cadets on how to organize and carry out combat missions. A select few also advised Vo Nguyen Giap and other top-level commanders on the finer points of command, intelligence, and communications.[7]

The Vietnamese created several officer-training schools in the safer areas above the 16th parallel. In April 1946, for example, the General Staff opened the Tran Quoc Tuan Military Academy in Son Tay. It had initially been a colonial military base. Dozens of its first graduates came from the pre-war scouting movement and youth groups. In fact, the academy's first director until 1948, Hoang Dao Thuy, had been the head of the Vietnamese scouting movement in Indochina during the interwar period. Instruction focused on the fundamentals again—the handling of weapons, military discipline, troop formation, and maneuvering. Hoang Dao Thuy also taught his specialty—radio communications. The DRV established two other important training centers—the Infantry Academy of Quang Ngai in central Vietnam and another in Bac Son in the far north. More schools opened their doors as the war continued. Even today, Vietnam's National Military Academy is the direct descendant of the Tran Quoc Tuan one.

Significantly, modern military science arrived in postcolonial Vietnam through mainly Asian channels. Distrustful of Vietnamese anticolonialism, the French had always balked at training Vietnamese officers and only allowed a few naturalized ones to do so. It may have seemed like safe politics at the time, but in doing so they failed to co-opt potential opponents by making them officers in a colonial army and part of Vietnam's future. One of the unintended but far-reaching results of this was that during the interwar period an increasing number of young Vietnamese anticolonialists applied to study the art of war in military academies which Chinese nationalists and communists were opening just to the north in places like Guangzhou. (In 1923, both Chinese sides had briefly joined hands in a united front with Sun Yat-sen, the father of modern China, to create a Chinese republic.) Founded in 1924, the Huangpu Military Academy located near Guangzhou taught modern military science to many of the Chinese who would go on to command the nationalist and communist armies. It also attracted more than 200 Vietnamese to its classrooms by 1930.

One such graduate was none other than Le Thiet Hung, who ran the Tran Quoc Tuan Military Academy between 1948 and 1954. Nguyen Son was another alumnus. After leaving the Huangpu Academy following the violent break between Chinese communists and nationalists in the late 1920s, he made the Long March with Mao Zedong in 1934–5 and joined in the fight against the Japanese during the Second World War. Fluent in Chinese, he joined the Chinese Communist Party and became an officer in their army. Upon his return to Vietnam, Ho put him in charge of the Quang Ngai Military Academy and made him a general in Zone IV. Vuong Thua Vu is a third example. He had first served in Chiang Kai-shek's army during the Japanese invasion of Manchuria in 1931. A graduate of Huangpu too, he returned to Vietnam a decade later, converted to communism in a colonial jail cell following his arrest, and, upon liberation in 1945, joined Ho Chi Minh's army to lead the Battle of Hanoi a year later. He became the commander of the mighty 308th division and led his men into battle at Dien Bien Phu in 1954. The Vietnamese national army established by Ho in 1946 was not a postcolonial phenomenon. It was very much a transnational one, deeply connected to the surrounding Asian region.

This is why the future victor at Dien Bien Phu, Vo Nguyen Giap, did not simply walk into a colonial library in Hanoi, learn the Western canon of military science by reading Clausewitz, and then lead the army to victory single-handedly in 1954 as some sort of "Red Napoleon" of European design.[8] In fact, Vo Nguyen Giap would have been the first to admit how much he owed to this impressive collection of Chinese-trained Vietnamese officers the Huangpu Military Academy in Guangzhou and the experience of the Second World War in Asia had placed at his doorstep in Hanoi in 1945. This also helps to explain why so many of the commanding officers in the Vietnamese army were more at ease speaking in Chinese than they were in French. That year, Giap himself was probably as familiar with Maoist thinking on the art of war as he was with that of Clausewitz, thanks to the access he had to Vietnamese translations of Mao Zedong's essays on war published legally in Indochina during the liberal French Popular Front period of the late 1930s. In 1939, Giap himself published a booklet on Maoist military strategy. The commander-in-chief also had access to military texts translated by his own officers, such as Nguyen Son.[9]

This brings us to the power of the written word. From its creation, the General Staff did its best to obtain the classics in military science, training manuals, and specialized journal articles. Agents abroad received orders to purchase a host of such books and manuals in Chinese, French, English, and other languages. The bookshelves in colonial libraries in

Hanoi and Saigon and abandoned colonial military installations surrendered many valuable texts on the art of war, including Clausewitz's
On War. The DRV General Staff soon ran its own translation services
to render the military classics in the Vietnamese national script, *quoc
ngu*, as well as a host of other essays and books on the finer points of
military command, tactics, communications, intelligence, and cryptol-
ogy. Army presses produced specialized journals and manuals used for
training purposes until the end of the conflict. All of this knowledge
and the infrastructure supporting it contributed directly to the Vietnamese ability to assemble military force early on and to take it to a
new level when the Chinese communists arrived on the northern border in 1950.[10]

The early growth of the army also owed a great deal to the outpouring
of patriotic support for Vietnamese independence. This profound joy
was no less real than the elation so many French had experienced a year
earlier upon the Allied liberation of their country from Nazi occupation.
Thousands of elated Vietnamese turned out to listen to Ho Chi Minh
declare the independence of Vietnam on 2 September 1945. The French
attack on this independence two weeks later in Saigon turned this nationalist pride into moral outrage, as well as providing a spike in enlistments. Young Vietnamese, already running on high levels of nationalism, were soon jumping on to trains in Haiphong, Hanoi, and Vinh to
go and fight in the south. Peasants and workers volunteered in droves,
to the wonder of urbanites like Tran Ngoc Chau, who, in the past, had
often ridiculed them as country bumpkins: "We felt guilty, remember-
ing that we had often looked down on the peasants in the past like so
many of the educated Vietnamese did." Crowds greeted them all enthusiastically at stations as they made their way southwards. Fighting the
invaders never seemed so right, Chau wrote, galvanizing the rich and
the poor into one common endeavor.[11]

Vietnamese nationalism was real. The problem was what happened
once these enthusiastic Vietnamese soldiers got off the train, crossed
the 16th parallel, and moved into the areas the invading army was reoc-
cupying with tanks, artillery, and machine guns. Holding positions,
returning fire, and moving as a combat unit in a coordinated fashion

against such force required serious training, discipline, and nerve. If not properly prepared, a company caught in the open could be wiped out in a matter of minutes by superior enemy firepower and air attacks. Having fought during the entire Indochina War, Ngo Van Chieu provides us with vivid examples of this in his memoirs, *Diary of a Viet Minh Soldier.* Filled with the ardent patriotism that moved so many to action in 1945, Chieu enlisted with a couple of friends in the heady days when Ho first declared Vietnam's independence. His commanding officer assigned him to a training camp led by former officers in the Japanese army and told him to learn from them fast in order to lead a company himself: "Quiz them, observe them, and good luck. You will then be in charge of a new group of arrivals." Looking back from 1955, having barely survived some of the bloodiest clashes of the Indochina War, Chieu painted a realistic picture of his unit and the early years of the army in his memoirs.

Ngo Van Chieu's 1945 class was a disparate collection of men of all ages and backgrounds, he tells us candidly, badly armed and with little or no discipline. "To be honest," he wrote, "we looked more like a gang than an organized army." When Chieu went into combat for one of the first times, instinct and pure luck served him better than his military training because, he conceded, he had little. A botched operation in mid-1946 cost his unit tremendous losses because he and his men "did not know how to react with sufficient coordination." They failed to hold under fire and attacked as if they were "in a riot." Everyone, he wrote, fought without any idea of what the other was doing: "In short, it was one big mess." And though Ngo Van Chieu may have despised the colonial-trained Vietnamese sergeant he had suffered under in boot camp in late 1945, he had to admit a decade later that this man might have been right after all when he had sternly warned his headstrong pupils: "It's only by being harsh, and harsher, and ever more relentless that I feel I can transform peasant children and these more or less trou- blemaking bourgeois kids into officers and soldiers in our army." (Ngo Van Chieu and his "bourgeois" comrades had tried (unsuccessfully) to have their sergeant courtmartialed in late 1945!)[12]

More charismatic leaders could instil discipline without alienating their young volunteers. In central Vietnam, another newly minted officer

in his twenties later recalled just how important Nguyen Son's explanations had been to his understanding of the art of war. He learned the
most from lively group discussions this Maoist-trained general had organized to analyze operations: "These reviews gave us valuable insights
into what had happened during actual field operations. Since most of us
had had only six months or less of military experience, such analyses
were especially useful. They provided sound theoretical training."[13]
These impressions are precious, as they demonstrate that building military force, even at the guerrilla level, required organization, coordination, and brains. Mistakes were made, some of them paid for in blood;
but lessons were also learned and many of them then consigned to training manuals. Nationalism was indeed important and helped fire the
Vietnamese war state to victory; but it provided no magical shield on
the modern battlefield against death or injury.

Organizing Force

Organization was as necessary as instruction when it came to building
force. To operate and coordinate the army, the General Staff divided the
country into three administrative units responsible for the north, the
center, and the south. Each regional entity broke down into zones—VII,
VIII, and IX in the south, III, IV, and V in the center, and a northern one
for the Red River Delta and the surrounding highlands (which, by 1949,
was generally referred to as the Viet Bac zone). Within each zone, the
General Staff assigned high-ranking officers to each headquarters in
charge of military affairs, running down to the local level. They did so
in close collaboration with their counterparts working on the resistance
committees, the Viet Minh and Lien Viet fronts, and the Communist
Party's own administrative hierarchy. Based out of the resistance center
in Thai Nguyen province, the General Staff and the party's Central Military Commission directed the armed forces. The communists were in
charge of this vital arm of state power; but the majority of its enlisted
men and even its officer class were not all party members during the late
1940s.[14]

While tens of thousands of young Vietnamese men joined the army in the early years, such a volunteer system could not generate the large standing army Vo Nguyen Giap needed to engage the French Expeditionary Corps in conventional battle. That came later. For the time being, there was no draft. Guerrilla warfare ruled.[15] The strategic goal during the first half of the conflict was to organize an army of a modest size, a volunteer one, capable of bogging the enemy down in small-scale operations of an organized and coordinated kind. On the eve of the outbreak of full-scale war with the French in late 1946, the regular army counted around 85,000 troops, with the majority of them located in safe areas above the 16th parallel. In August 1947, the regular army had grown to around 100,000 men, with 60,000 located in the northern half of the country while the rest operated in the south. This number remained constant until late 1949, when the DRV imposed obligatory military service and the army's size took off.[16]

Despite its smaller size and guerrilla configuration, the Vietnamese National Army operated as a regular force (*quan chinh quy*). When volunteers signed up (and were later drafted), they wore the uniform, trained as an integrated combat unit, and were deployed. This was not a reserve or a national guard. The General Staff coordinated its operations, administered a network of radios, devised battle plans, and organized combat groups carefully into battalions, companies, and platoons. By early 1949, a handful of regiments were in operation. Although there were no divisions yet, this careful organization laid the groundwork for moving rapidly in such a direction when the time came. Having learned from past mistakes, by late 1948 local commanders going out on missions had a better handle, though far from perfect, on what they were doing. They gathered and received intelligence, analyzed it, knew the lay of the land, the size of enemy units, and increasingly coordinated their moves with those of their counterparts conducting missions elsewhere. Things could go wrong, and did, but it was not the chaos Ngo Van Chieu had encountered at the start.

In addition to the regular army, the General Staff built up guerrilla forces based on two types of partisan fighters. For the first kind, local commanders received instructions to organize people into combined village militias (*tu ve*) and people's guerrilla units (*dan quan du kich*). Rural civilians mainly filled their ranks, men and women, young and old, and sometimes even fairly well-off landowners joined in. They were always poorly armed. The guerrilla/militia's main roles were defensive—to protect villages as best they could in the absence of the army, to provide regular troops with food, salt, and potable water when they passed through on operations, to take care of wounded soldiers, and to provide "volunteers" whenever possible. Village partisans warned of enemy movements, served as guides and messengers, and provided intelligence. The General Staff organized these people in collaboration with the resistance administration, the Communist Party's parallel hierarchy if there was one, and especially the Lien Viet and Viet Minh mass organizations through which it did most of its recruiting.

The second type of guerrilla force was the "regional troop" (*bo doi dia phuong*). These semi-regular units operated at the zonal level, mainly in central Vietnam where the resistance population was largest and recruiting, as a result, easiest. They had better military training than the militias/guerrillas, were slightly better armed, and could eventually be mobilized to second the regular army in combat operations. Like the militias, however, they were *not* full-time, professional soldiers, at least not before 1950. They were partisans; they lived in their villages and mobilized accordingly. They had much in common with the Minute Men of the American War of Independence. They employed hit-and-run tactics, usually operating under the cover of night, but they always avoided direct engagement with the enemy on the battlefield. When the ambush was over, they went home, whereas the regular troops did not necessarily do so.

It is hard to know for sure how many guerrillas the DRV controlled through its grassroots organizations. The numbers could change dramatically over time and space, especially if one counts partisans operating in enemy-occupied territories (which often changed administrative hands repeatedly). A conservative estimate of the number of those enrolled in DRV territories, as of early 1950, would be a maximum of

400,000 men and women out of a total potential DRV population of 10 million in that year. This does not include the regional guerrillas. They numbered around 50,000 and were mainly men. The regular army did not exceed 100,000 all-male troops before 1950.

The strategic goal for all three forces was the same: to protect and grow the administration, disperse and bog down the enemy in a drawn-out conflict which would sap the enemy army's morale, turn the tide of French public opinion against the politicians, and convince the French and their army that there was no military solution to what was essentially a political problem—that of Vietnam's independence. Until Mao Zedong threw his weight behind Ho Chi Minh in 1950, the communist core of the Democratic Republic of Vietnam was unwilling to build a larger standing army and make the transition to conventional operations. Logistically, the General Staff could not provide the transport, the food, and the arms such an army would need to fight over long distances and for extended periods of time. Until 1950, regular troops operating mainly in companies (of 100–200 men) and battalions (of 500–800 men) remained tied to specific areas which they knew and where local villages provided them with the food and lodging they required. There was no mobile, maneuverable type of warfare in which armies went up against each other in a series of pitched battles. That came later.

This was why orders went out to troops to help villagers with the planting and the harvest. This basically meant providing free labor for working fields and repairing dikes. They did so because these people—not the state—were the ones effectively feeding the regular army. It meant treating villagers, their livestock, and granaries with careful respect. Such action generated legitimacy and, alongside it, facilitated territorial control. This is one reason why the army severely sanctioned any abuse of civilian populations. Supplied from elsewhere, French Union troops, followed by the Americans later, were less concerned about the welfare of the civilian population. They even tried to destroy the enemy civilian population's dikes, harvests, and livestock in an economic assault on Vietnamese military force.

Lastly, during the first half of the Indochina War, these two armies, again, one regular, the other guerrilla, were highly decentralized affairs like the state they served and the archipelago-like terrain they patrolled. The party's Central Military Commission and the General Staff it directed might have created a seemingly centralized war bureaucracy of a zonal kind for all of Vietnam—but only on paper. In reality, the communists just attended to certain parts of what was a very fragmented state. Located far from the resistance capital in Thai Nguyen, local commanders in central and, especially, southern Vietnam had considerable leeway and discretionary powers. What worked in one zone might not apply in another. The north was not the south, where party control over the army was weakest. Free of the French, zones IV and V in a wide swath of central Vietnam stood apart militarily from the more hotly contested deltas. And communications were always difficult—everywhere. Radios may have connected the archipelago through the air, but on the ground only trusted party people could deliver the secret documents regional commanders needed to remain in synch with the General Staff's grand strategy. The special envoy the Indochinese Communist Party dispatched from the north in 1948 to deliver instructions to leaders in central and southern Vietnam, Le Duc Tho, needed almost a year to make it to the Mekong Delta. A lot can change in a year. (See Plate 7.)[17]

Manufacturing Force

Weapons are, of course, essential to creating military force, and the quality and quantity of available weaponry necessarily influence it a great deal. Vietnam was no exception to this rule. Although the regular army was better equipped than the guerrilla forces, it never possessed arms in sufficient numbers or quality to engage in conventional battles before 1950. For all of their ingenuity, the Vietnamese could not produce machine guns, artillery cannons, antiaircraft guns, or the bullets and shells each weapon devoured in enormous quantities. Only communist bloc assistance could provide this and, with it, the possibility to change the course of the war on the battlefield.

Until then, the Vietnamese had to make do as best they could. The Viet Minh nationalist front had acquired some small-scale weapons from the Allies during the Second World War and, upon taking power, had seized others from colonial stockpiles. They also imported weapons via regional black markets (discussed in Chapter 3). A handful of sympathetic or cash-strapped Japanese soldiers with access to caches of army equipment provided some arms to the nascent Vietnamese army, including sub-machine guns, small artillery (howitzers) and mortars (muzzle-load weapons that shot shells). The Ministry of Defense purchased "two entire trainloads of weapons" of this kind from Chinese soldiers shortly after their arrival in northern Vietnam. And, like resistance groups fighting the Germans and Japanese during the Second World War, the Vietnamese turned the stealing of weapons from the enemy into an art form.[18]

The General Staff did, however, create an impressive small weapons industry. A couple of dozen main sites produced homemade grenades, mines, and small rockets. Although the quality of these weapons left much to be desired, they served their purpose well in the context of the guerrilla conflict. The idea was not to blast French positions with carefully calibrated artillery fire before sending in troops, but rather to harass the enemy with small arms fire via hit-and-run attacks. Whether or not homemade mortars fired in the middle of the night hit their targets or not was less important than maintaining a climate of fear and reminding the enemy of the republic's presence no matter how weak it actually was on the battlefield.

But that does not mean that the Vietnamese did not try to build weapons of a more lethal kind. In 1947, for example, the General Staff's small arms industry started producing a shoulder-fired bazooka whose projectiles could penetrate enemy blockhouses, watchtowers, and some light tanks. The French war correspondent, Lucien Bodard, wrote in admiration of what the makeshift partisan war industry could do: "One can only imagine what went into this effort since they only had a hundred 'factories'—huts in the jungle where they succeeded, without specialized steel, almost without any equipment, to make mortars and even bazookas that they called SKZ. What could they not have come up with?"[19]

The man who was the moving force in Vietnam's weapons research and development deserves a detour here, as his trajectory tells us something important about the brain power into which Ho Chi Minh tapped in order to create a new level of force without the communist bloc's help. His name was Tran Dai Nghia, and he was one of the rare southerners to rise to the highest ranks of the General Staff. He did so thanks to his hard work as a schoolboy and a colonial scholarship that allowed him to escape his family's crushing poverty to study engineering, science, and mathematics in France during the 1930s. A brilliant mind by all accounts, Tran Dai Nghia graduated from the most prestigious engineering schools in the metropolis, the Ecole des mines and Polytechnique, the combined equivalents of America's MIT or Japan's Todai. He remained in France after graduation to take a job in the booming aerospace industry in Toulouse (the home of Airbus today). When the Germans occupied the lower half of France in late 1942, they recognized what they had in this young man and hustled him off to Germany to work for them in a weapons research laboratory.[20]

At the war's end, Tran Dai Nghia returned to France to resume a promising career in the aerospace industry. Those plans changed suddenly though when he met Ho Chi Minh in France during the latter's negotiations with the French government during the summer of 1946. Putting all of his persuasive powers to work, Ho convinced dozens of French-trained Vietnamese engineers, doctors, and students, some of the best and the brightest at the time, to return to Vietnam to help the country in its hour of greatest need.[21] Tran Dai Nghia was one of them. Upon his return to Hanoi in late 1946, he put his unrivalled knowledge of European wartime science to work fabricating weapons to secure Vietnam's independence. In December 1946, he headed up the Bureau of Armaments Production and continued to do so from the northern *maquis* where he relocated after the outbreak of full-scale war. By 1948, his workshops produced hand grenades, shells, and even went a step beyond the bazooka to produce a recoilless rifle based on an American model that shot rockets of German design at the enemy. The Vietnamese, followed by the French, referred to this improved rocket launcher as the "SKZ" (for *sung khong giat* or a "recoilless rifle.")[22] Once again, the Second World War had fed into Vietnamese military science in the strangest of ways, this time from the European side. This was the weapon that had so impressed Bodard and many other officers in the French army. Tran Dai Nghia's rocket launcher may have been the one that slammed into the colonial watchtower in Graham Greene's *The Quiet American* when the American secret agent, Pyle, saves the cynical British journalist, Fowler, from certain death. In any case, between 1946 and 1951, the Vietnamese defense industry produced 785 bazookas, 486 SKZs, and thousands of shells.[23]

Tran Dai Nghia's colonial education in engineering and wartime experience in weapons production saw his military career take off. In exchange for his services, the Ministry of Defense made him a general in 1948. A year later, he assumed the direction of the Office of Artillery and became deputy director of the General Technical Bureau as the General Staff started to develop the army and take it in the direction of conventional warfare. From 1950, it is true, the DRV started importing the majority of its heavy arms from communist China. But, far from remaining idle, Tran Dai Nghia focused his time on training dozens of young Vietnamese artillery officers in how to use modern weapons systems like artillery cannons and antiaircraft guns. He supervised the armaments section until the end of the conflict.

This is also how Tran Dai Nghia and several others like him helped the General Staff become an instrument of war which was capable of taking Chinese communist assistance in hand (quite literally) to generate a new sort of army and a new kind of force needed to fight a new type of war. Hoang Dao Thuy did something similar in the communications field. Had the Vietnamese not already done this groundwork (and harnessed this brainpower of European, Asian, and colonial design) before 1950, then they would have found it impossible to transform their military force in modern ways once the Chinese communists started sending them large-scale military aid. Modern military hardware is useless if you don't know how to use it.[24]

Communist China and the Rise of
Modern Military Force

Chinese Communist Assistance and the Birth of the PAVN

The victory of the Chinese communists in October 1949 and their decision to assist Ho Chi Minh against the French by providing military aid, training, and advisers allowed the Vietnamese to transform their military force in record time. Between April and September 1950 alone, in order to prepare their counterparts for the border battle at Cao Bang, the Chinese communists provided their Vietnamese counterparts with over 14,000 guns, 1,700 machine guns, 150 pieces of various types of cannons, not to mention communications equipment, uniforms, and medicines. More Chinese transport trucks arrived at the border in August to deliver tens of thousands of machine-gun cartridges, mortars, grenades, and mines.

Mao Zedong's decision to send Chinese troops to fight the Americans in Korea in October 1950 in no way changed his commitment to helping the Vietnamese against the French. Sino-Vietnamese communist relations were at their zenith in 1950. As we know, both revolutionary movements had intertwined since the 1920s in southern China. The Chinese also saw in the Vietnamese armed struggle against the French a second front in their wider struggle against the Americans in Korea, while the Vietnamese understood that the Korean War protected them from the full brunt of a potential all-out American assault on Indochina.[25] What is sure is that until the end of the Indochina War, the Chinese supplied the Vietnamese with as many weapons as they could in light of their own needs in Korea (and increased the supplies following the armistice ending the Korean War in mid-1953). In all, the Vietnamese have acknowledged, this included 21,517 tons of military assistance between May 1950 and July 1954. The Chinese claim that for that same period they provided the Vietnamese with 155,000 guns, 58 million bullets, 3,692 artillery pieces, 840,000 hand grenades, 1,231 vehicles, and 1.4 million uniforms. Of that, the Soviet Union provided seventy-six 37mm anti-aircraft guns, twelve H6 multi-tube rocket launchers

(*Katyusha*), a large number of K50 sub-machine guns, and 685 of the total 745 vehicles sent to the DRV towards the end of the war.[26]

Although this list is admittedly long, one does not have to be a military historian to grasp that little of it was destined for fighting a guerrilla war. Indonesian republicans fighting the Dutch in 1949 never received heavy artillery and anti-aircraft guns in such large amounts from an outside power. Nor did Algerian nationalists fighting the French in the form of the Front de libération nationale. The Vietnamese did and it mattered. And if the Chinese communists delivered so much modern weaponry to their Vietnamese counterparts so rapidly, it was because they felt that Ho Chi Minh's state, army, and Communist Party could use it effectively not as a "guerrilla tiger" but as a "modern elephant" fighting the French head-on.

To their credit, the Vietnamese communists lined up behind Ho had anticipated the changes they would have to make in order to handle such large amounts of modern weaponry. Starting as early as mid-1949—as the Chinese Red Army crossed into southern China—the Vietnamese began expanding their General Staff accordingly. This meant increasing personnel across the board in logistics, intelligence, and military instruction. It required training more officers and soldiers for fighting pitched, coordinated, and complex battles. It necessitated the creation of what was soon to become a professional army consisting of regiments and, a first, modern divisions of 10,000 to 15,000 men each. To do this, the party implemented military conscription in November 1949, decreed the general mobilization of the population three months later, and officially approved the transition to conventional warfare as defined by Mao as the "General Counteroffensive." By late 1949, the Vietnamese General Staff had assembled its first modern division, the 308th. Commanding it was none other than Vuong Thua Vu, the man who had led the Battle of Hanoi against the French in early 1947.

Although the Chinese did not intervene directly in the Indochina War as they did in Korea, they dispatched a Chinese Military Advisers Group to Vietnam to oversee military assistance and to help Vo Nguyen Giap create a professional army. The team leaders, Luo Guibo and

Chen Geng, arrived in the resistance capital of Thai Nguyen in mid-1950 at the head of a 200-strong delegation. Advisers worked directly with Ho Chi Minh, the Indochinese Communist Party's standing committee members, and the leaders of the Central Military Commission and General Staff, most notably Vo Nguyen Giap and Hoang Van Thai. Chen Geng focused on military matters in his advisory role. This high-ranking general had studied military science at the Huangpu Military Academy in Guangzhou in the mid-1920s, where he had first befriended Ho Chi Minh. Chen Geng then went on to command troops against the Japanese during the Second World War and helped defeat Chiang Kai-shek's Republic of China in the civil war of the late 1940s. Luo Guibo had made the Long March in the 1930s and served on the Chinese Communist Party's Central Military Commission. In Vietnam, he tended to more political matters in military training. Another important military adviser was Wei Guoqing. This Chinese officer had also commanded troops against the Japanese and Chiang Kai-shek. He would run the military advisory group from late 1950, following Chen Geng's transfer to the Korean front, until the end of the Indochina War.

Like the Americans standing behind the French in the form of the Military Assistance Advisory Group (MAAG) created in September 1950, the Chinese military advisory team helped the Vietnamese equip and train a divisional army, improve logistics and radio communications, develop an operational intelligence branch, flesh out a strategy capable of beating the French on the battlefield, and, more generally, share the military experiences which had just allowed the Chinese communists to take power. They did this through special classes in military science organized for Vietnamese General Staff members as well as for commanders at divisional and regimental levels. As we saw above, the infrastructure for teaching military science was already in place (academies, instructors, manuals, and translation services). It was now a question of expanding it. Training in the Chinese language took off. Interpreters were in hot demand. Although Giap was not a Chinese-speaker himself, he drew on a small but important pool of officers in his ranks who had served in China during the Second World War. Hoang Van Thai, Le Thiet Hung, and Vuong Thua Vu were all fluent in Chinese.

They had little difficulty following military science courses dispensed in Chinese. And like Ho Chi Minh, they could translate on the spot and be trusted to keep the contents secret.[27]

The Chinese Military Advisory Group's main aim was not to teach Maoist guerrilla warfare. The Vietnamese already had a good handle on that both in theory and practice. Rather, as Mao reminded his advisers upon their departure for Vietnam, the goal was to help the Vietnamese build a professional army without which there could be no General Counter-offensive:

> While the French control the big cities, transportation routes and coastal towns, the [Vietnamese] revolutionaries must establish themselves in the countryside. The situation is similar to what we had experienced during the anti-Japanese war period. However, your duty is not only to teach the Vietnamese about guerrilla warfare, but also to help [them] to fight a modern war against the French. You must teach them how to organize a professional army, use modern weapons, and provide military aid.[28]

This training occurred on both sides of the Sino-Vietnamese border. The Chinese advisory group helped the Vietnamese create and train a professional army from remote northern areas in the Democratic Republic of Vietnam. They also dispatched Vietnamese cadets and officers to southern China to train in bases safe from French attack (especially bombing raids). As Chinese weapons and advisers entered Vietnam from mid-1950, thousands of Vietnamese soldiers and officers went in the other direction, crossing into southern China to study military science. Two months before the Korean War broke out, in April 1950, the Ministry of Defense transferred the entire Tran Quoc Tuan Military Academy, personnel, and cadets to safe havens in southern China. There, they underwent intensive training, studying and drilling for hours on end, free of colonial molestation. Fluent in Chinese and a graduate himself of the Huangpu Military Academy in the 1920s, General Le Thiet Hung directed Vietnam's military academy during its operations in China. He and others also tended to a host of smaller, specialized schools the Vietnamese transferred to southern China for the training of artillery, radio, encryption, intelligence, and logistics specialists. Ho Chi Minh, the man who had helped so many Vietnamese anticolonialists to enter the Huangpu Military Academy in the 1920s, must have experienced a moment of déjà vu as he sent an even bigger cohort to southern China to study modern military science in Yunnan province two decades later. In a possibly related move, in 1951 the Chinese authorized the Vietnamese Ministry of Education to set up a central campus in Nanning (known as the Khu Hoc Xa Trung Uong) in order to allow the Vietnamese to train technicians, scientists, and interpreters.

Young soldiers and officers learned what they would need to operate in a professional army deploying modern firepower and battle tactics. Cadets studied the organization and direction of coordinated combat units on the battlefield, the calibration and use of artillery in pitched battle, the operation of anti-aircraft guns, and how to carry out wave attacks against fortified enemy positions (including intensive indoctrination programs). Military intelligence, communications, and logistics would now be important in ways they never had been before. In 1950, 3,100 Vietnamese cadre-officers received advanced military training—producing, among others, 1,200 officers for the infantry, 400 for artillery tasks, 150 in communications, 200 for cryptography, 300 for the (future) air force, and 200 for the navy. Without this specialized personnel, the Vietnamese could never have taken Cao Bang by force later that year. The French estimated that around 30,000 soldiers in all trained in southern China in the early 1950s. This is how the Chinese—not the French—helped the Vietnamese train most of their elite officer class, many of whom would go on to fight the Americans. Meanwhile, the Americans welcomed French officers to South Korean and US military academies to study the new types of wars they were fighting in the Far East.[29]

Thanks to Chinese military assistance and advisers, instruction in modern military science, and the introduction of the draft and mobilization laws discussed later, the Vietnamese communists presided over a military revolution unknown in any other war of decolonization in the twentieth century. Between August 1949 and March 1951, the Chinese and the Vietnamese communists transformed their preexisting "Vietnamese

National Army" of 1946 into a professional army of a divisional kind. The creation of seven divisions and their combined birthdates marked the emergence of a new type of modern force, what the Vietnamese still call the People's Army of Vietnam (Quan Doi Nhan Dan Viet Nam, or PAVN): the 304th (March 1950), the 308th (August 1949), 312th (December 1950), the 316th (May 1951), the 320th (January 1951), the 325th (March 1951), and the 351st, an artillery division (March 1951). This PAVN "elephant" generated a new level of force in terms of the firepower it could deploy, the sophistication and coordination its handlers could bring to the battlefield, the number of troops it held in its ranks, and the distances it could cover to take the battle to the French. Although the communists in charge of this revolutionary transformation would often continue to refer to this new force with its old name, the seven dates above marked the birth of the People's Army of Vietnam. By late 1950, it numbered 166,452 men.[30]

This new army did not arise uniformly across the archipelago state, however: the PAVN rose first in the far north, on both sides of the Sino-Vietnamese border. This is where communist bloc military assistance arrived first, troops trained, and this is where the supply of modern weapons and instruction connected with a preexisting military infrastructure that could turn it into something usable and deadly in record time. This force then spread southwards from the Sino-Vietnamese border to central Vietnam via an overland corridor wrapped around the western side of the Red River Delta. However, the PAVN never emerged as much of a force in the southern part of the Democratic Republic of Vietnam. The military science and equally high levels of nationalism were there, but not the modern weapons, the artillery, and machine guns needed to make the transition. Two parallel attempts at modern battle in 1950 demonstrate the success and the failure of this military revolution—the PAVN victory over the French on the Sino-Vietnamese border, at Cao Bang, and the French pummeling of Vietnamese efforts to create such a modern army in the Mekong Delta. Let us start in the south, for the story of how southerners built up a surprisingly professionalized army on their own, tried to turn it on the French without modern weapons, and then lost, is important to understanding the limits to the building of force. It also sheds new light on the war the Americans would encounter there in the 1960s.

1950: The Southern Failure to Create a Modern Military Force

From the beginning to the end of the Indochina War, military force was always weaker in the south. The British (unlike the Chinese in central and northern Vietnam), contributed to this early on when they allowed the French to return by force to areas below the 16th parallel. Since southern Vietnamese had hardly had the time to put any serious army together before the French attacked on 23 September 1945 (and those in central and northern Vietnam had eighteen months to do so), they turned to the Hanoi-based government to send weapons and troops to help. The first to leave northern areas did so as young volunteers in the Southern Advance (or Nam Tien units). Six contingents left areas above the 16th parallel in late September; five others followed over the next year. In all, 10,000 young recruits marched south until war lit up the entire country in late December 1946. To the west, several thousand volunteers from the Vietnamese diaspora in Thailand marched to the Mekong Delta. As in the north at the time, the training for all of these groups was cursory at best. Weapons were in short supply. Patriotism moved them more than anything else, but few carried party cards.[31]

Even Nguyen Binh, the commander of the southern army, was not a party man, at least not at the outset. Born into a poor northern family, he had first ventured to Saigon in the 1920s in his youth in search of work. He found a job cleaning laundry and unloading the ships which visited this bustling port city. He also became involved in nationalist politics and helped the Vietnamese Nationalist Party expand into the south. His political activities soon attracted the attention of the colonial police, who, in 1930, sentenced him to hard time on the island penitentiary of Poulo Condor. There, Binh rubbed shoulders with some of the future leaders of the Vietnamese Communist Party, but he did not convert to communism. He regained his liberty in 1934 and dropped out of sight until he resurfaced in the north during the Second World War.

There he organized miners to fight the Japanese in guerrilla hit-and-run attacks. News of this, his charismatic bravado, and knowledge of the south quickly came to the attention of President Ho Chi Minh not long after he declared the country's independence. Within a few weeks, Nguyen Binh arrived in the capital with a Japanese sword dangling from his side. Convinced that he had the right man, communist or not, Ho dispatched Nguyen Binh to the Mekong Delta to incorporate disparate armed groups there into the national army and to assert and maintain the Democratic Republic of Vietnam's sovereignty below the 16th parallel.

Nguyen Binh arrived in the south in November 1945 and immediately went to work. He entered into contact with old friends, workers in and around Saigon, and the leaders of different religious and paramilitary groups scattered across the delta. Religious congregations, such as the Hoa Hao and the Cao Dai, had operated their own militias and pursued their own political agendas under the leadership of Huynh Phu So and Pham Cong Tac respectively. The Binh Xuyen, a group of semi-brigands from Saigon-Cholon turned patriots in 1945, did the same. Nguyen Binh played on their patriotism and went out of his way to respect their interests and sensibilities in exchange for their cooperation against the French. He made Bay Vien, the chief of the Binh Xuyen, his deputy for Zone VII (the area west of Saigon). The possibility of achieving national union seemed promising in 1946, when Nguyen Binh, the Hoa Hao, Cao Dai, and Binh Xuyen leaders gathered a dozen independent detachments of 1,000 soldiers each into the young republic's national army.[32]

Of course, the French did everything they could to break up this anticolonialist coalition. Following the outbreak of full-scale war in late 1946, they immediately accelerated their efforts to detach the religious groups from the Democratic Republic of Vietnam, even if it meant turning the Vietnamese on each other in civil war. The leaders of the Hoa Hao and Cao Dai were increasingly open to a deal, suspicious that the communists were working behind the scenes (they were) and reluctant to join a nation-state in which they would have to give up a great deal of their territorial autonomy (they would). In early January 1947, Pham

Cong Tac signed a military convention in which he brought his Cao Dai followers in the western Mekong Delta over to the French. Furious, Nguyen Binh interpreted this as treason and ordered his men to attack. To the southwest, similar violence broke out with the Hoa Hao. Nguyen Binh suspected the leader of this church, Huynh Phu So, of opening similar discussions with the French (which was indeed true). Government officials authorized the execution of Huynh Phu So in April for treason. A year later, things deteriorated further when the Binh Xuyen's Bay Vien broke with Nguyen Binh, left his position in Zone VII, and rallied to the French standard with his loyal units.

Although the defection of these three groups slowed efforts to build a united southern military force—and would do so well into the 1960s—it nonetheless allowed Nguyen Binh to create a separate military force on his own terms, with his people, in areas he controlled. Working feverishly from mid-1948 onwards, he established a dozen battalions over the next year, the backbone of the national army in the south. Access to Voice of Vietnam broadcasts and wireless radios allowed his people to follow events across Indochina and permitted contact with the General Staff in the north. Nguyen Binh's entourage relied on local weapons factories, captured weapons, and impressive imports from Thailand to outfit his combat units. Officer training schools opened their doors, basic training camps received young volunteers, and schools in intelligence and communications accepted applications. In 1948, the General Staff in the north sent specialists to the south to help improve the command structure, communications, and intelligence-gathering capabilities there. In late 1948, the creation of a new military intelligence branch and a "high command for the south" in charge of it confirmed such improvements. Nguyen Binh officially served as the commander-in-chief of southern forces. Although he had apparently only joined the Communist Party sometime since 1947, the sine qua non for holding such an important position, he knew little of the Marxist-Leninist creed and probably gave it little thought. Nor did the communists when they named him a general in 1948.

What counted most was defeating the French, and the communists clearly thought Nguyen Binh was the best man for this job. From mid-1949, he prepared, like his counterparts in central and northern Vietnam, for the "General Counter-offensive." That this occurred in the south should not surprise: firstly, southerners knew from radio communications and delegates arriving from the north that the General Staff in Thai Nguyen had decided on the counter-offensive, at least in principle, earlier on that same year. Nguyen Binh and the communists shadowing him realized that they had to keep in step by transforming the existing national army in the south into something new. Secondly, since 1948, the southern commander had done a remarkable job of building and training a modest but effective regular army. By late 1949, it was much more than a band of guerrillas. In early 1950, our southern general commanded 25,516 regular troops backed up by 6,000 regional ones. His regular forces were organized into battalions and, perhaps, one or two regiments, each of which could operate over fairly long distances and maneuver in coordinated fashion. Something new was in the works.[33]

This is also why Nguyen Binh's head-on attack on the French in the Mekong Delta in 1950 was not a rogue move. It was part of a coordinated offensive for all of Vietnam. Nguyen Binh's offensive in 1950 paralleled the one his counterpart in central Vietnam, Nguyen Son, launched against the French-held city and military base at Dong Hoi, and the famous one Vo Nguyen Giap executed at Cao Bang later that same year. Nguyen Binh struck first in April 1950, when 3,000 of his regulars attacked enemy forces at Soc Trang and Sa Dec in the southern delta. Shortly thereafter, in a move possibly designed to divert French attention from the assault on Cao Bang, he launched frontal attacks on strongly fortified enemy positions in Tra Vinh, Tri Ton, and Ben Tre. He launched a sustained and audacious attack on Ben Cat in October and November 1950. As one eminent military historian has rightly stated: "For the first time the Vietnamese were not refusing to fight. On the contrary, they were trying to start it."[34] If true, then the first part of the "General Counter-offensive" began in the Mekong Delta in early 1950 and not on the Chinese border later that year.[35]

But as impressive as their southern offensive was, Nguyen Binh and his commander, General Vo Nguyen Giap, badly overplayed their hands. The French commander for the south, General Charles Chanson, admired his opponent's bravado and welcomed his adversary's decision to fight in the open. It provided this colonial officer with the opportunity to break the Vietnamese regular army before it grew into something new and more dangerous. In destroying it, he also wanted to secure the south for the newly created Associated State of Vietnam. And smash it he did. Chanson was an artilleryman by training and unleashed his cannons with devastating effect on attacking soldiers. Nguyen Binh had nothing to protect his men from a barrage of artillery fire. Nor did he have his own cannons to "soften up" enemy positions before he sent his men over the top to attack. Worse still, the French air force bombed attacking soldiers who were caught in the open. Equally problematic, southern logistics were still in no position to support conventional warfare of this type. Nguyen Binh had no trucks nor the manpower he needed to transport the food and weapons his near regiment-sized units required to fight over a sustained period of time and far from sources of food. And the much smaller size of the southern archipelago meant a smaller population to tap for rice and recruits. The result was not pretty. Chanson left the corpses of hundreds of young Vietnamese piled on the ground, many hanging from barbed-wire perimeters they had never penetrated. Within weeks, the French turned the southern attempt at conventional war into one massive failure. Nguyen Binh's failed assault on the south foreshadowed the even more spectacular Tet Offensive of 1968 (itself anything but a military victory).[36]

So why? The most likely explanation is the blind application of counter-offensive warfare to an unready south. The party's leader in the south, Le Duan, severely criticized this premature shift to conventional warfare there. He immediately ordered the dissolution of Nguyen Binh's regiments and a return to guerrilla tactics. Another explanation is that strategists in the General Staff and the Communist Party running it had extended the offensive to include the south based on the assumption that *two* supply lines would be pushed into the Democratic Republic of Vietnam from communist China: one across the border at Cao Bang (it was), the other into central and southern Vietnam from Hainan Island (it was not, as we shall see in the next chapter). Had that second maritime supply route gone through as planned and, with it, heavy artillery, machine guns, and anti-aircraft cannons, the modern weapons constituting the second prerequisite for fighting conventional war, then things could have taken a very different turn.

It was not to be. Following Nguyen Binh's defeat, the Ministry of Defence recalled its general to the north. Nguyen Binh left in 1951, but never made it to his final destination: a French-led commando unit killed him during a firefight in the jungles of northeastern Cambodia.[37] On his body, the French recovered his Colt, his diary, and a long report he had prepared for the Ministry of Defence. In the latter, Nguyen Binh urged his superiors to start work immediately on creating an overland supply route from the north to channel Chinese military assistance to the south. Although he did not put it in writing as such, this was a prerequisite for transitioning to conventional warfare. It was not enough to have a regular army. Troops had to have modern weapons to succeed, and that remained true all the way through the war against the Americans.

1950: The Rise of Northern Military Force

Something very different occurred on the far northern side of the archipelago state. There, for the first time, the Vietnamese finally achieved stunning battlefield success of a conventional kind. Starting in mid-1950, the Chinese communists began shipping the modern weapons described above to areas bordering the Vietnamese provinces of Cao Bang and Lang Son. From there, the Vietnamese moved them carefully into secret pockets of land which they controlled in order to outfit their new army and begin preparing the counter-offensive's second showdown at Cao Bang, the Vietnamese provincial capital situated very close to the country's northern border with China. The Chinese and Vietnamese had agreed upon Cao Bang as the best place to strike first: a successful attack there against the French would allow the Vietnamese to take this strategic part of the border, secure a direct supply route to southern China in so doing, and, what was equally important, seize the opportunity to consolidate a wider territorial triangle, thanks to roads connecting Cao Bang and Lang Son provinces to the resistance capital in Thai Nguyen.

Like Nguyen Binh, Vo Nguyen Giap had an army which was potentially capable of waging modern war; but unlike his counterpart in the far south, Giap also had direct access to modern firepower and Chinese advisers to help him make this revolutionary transition work. Even better, his French opponents handed the Vietnamese commander-in-chief on a platter exactly the type of battle he needed to succeed. Rather than consolidating their hold on the northern border, as some had urged, the high commissioner for Indochina, Léon Pignon, and military commanders such as Georges Revers and Marcel Carpentier decided it was best to pull their troops back from Cao Bang in order to avoid giving the Chinese communists nearby a reason to intervene in the Franco-Vietnamese war (the Chinese Red Army had entered Korea in mid-October 1950). Instead, Carpentier ordered his men to attack the enemy's capital in Thai Nguyen. They did so and duly captured it in early October without any fighting, for the simple reason that Ho's government had already evacuated the area and were fully focused on destroying the now vulnerable French troops starting to withdraw from the border. When Carpentier realized what he had done by focusing on Thai Nguyen and tried to compensate by rushing troops from Lang Son to link up with those leaving Cao Bang, he provided his adversaries with a battle in the border highlands that they could win. If the Vietnamese could destroy French troops moving towards midway posts at That Khe and Dong Khe, the Cao Bang capital would be theirs to attack from a position of strength.

This is exactly what they did. During the first week of October 1950, Vo Nguyen Giap's machine-gunners and artillerymen opened up on enemy convoys moving along the road leading to Dong Khe and That Khe. Although caught by surprise, French Union troops did not give up without a fight. Ngo Van Chieu, whom we first met in Hanoi in 1945 as a new recruit, was there. He was now an experienced company commander in the very regiment that attacked first at That Khe. He describes in detail how the radios around him buzzed with orders. As officers gave their final instructions and patriotic pep talks, he and his men grouped in a ravine below the road as the enemy columns approached. Then the order to attack came: "We leapt upon them like madmen. Hell broke loose on the road above. We ran. Men fell under a hail of bullets and grenades. Behind us, our mortars opened fire, hitting the road, and then at the bend in a grove I saw khaki uniforms fleeing with a machine gun." No sooner had Ngo Van Chieu's men taken the road, thinking victory was theirs, then those "khaki uniforms" counter-attacked, driving the Vietnamese back down the hill. After a second equally brutal attack right back up the same slope, Chieu's company finally overran the French. The enemy had been destroyed, he confided in his memoirs, but the battle "had been so ferocious." "Why," he wrote, "did the French fight so well for such a bad cause?"[38]

The answer to that question was not that complicated, and Chieu probably knew it. Two professional armies had clashed on the northern border in October 1950—the People's Army of Vietnam and the French Expeditionary Corps. They did so at the same time that Chinese and Korean communist divisions went up against American-led brigades in Korea. If the Far East became the scene of the most violent wars during the Cold War, they were so in part because Chinese, Vietnamese, and Korean communists were able to field professional armies and fight in the open, not like tigers, but like the elephants they were determined to be. Vo Nguyen Giap won the border battle. His men marched off hundreds of French Union prisoners of war.

Even if Chanson had crushed Nguyen Binh's army earlier that year in the south and consolidated the French colonial hold over the south for the rest of the Indochina War, Carpentier and Pignon had allowed their adversary to field a veritable army just inside the Vietnamese border. Moreover, following the Cao Bang defeat, these two men withdrew the colonial army from along the entire northern border, except for the far northwest corner in Lai Chau province and areas around Haiphong on the eastern side. By pulling back into the delta, the French allowed their enemies to establish a direct supply line to China and consolidate their territorial hold over a large triangle of land consisting of the Cao Bang, Langson, and Thai Nguyen provinces and the routes connecting them. It was into this "triangle" that communist bloc aid poured from late 1950, largely unhindered, until the war's end. And it was from here that this new People's Army of Vietnam would expand the archipelago state's territorial control over the next four years. The question now was whether that expansion should occur via a direct assault on the Red River Delta located just off this triangle's southern side. Or perhaps the PAVN should move the government's territorial control around the western side of the Tonkin Delta, through the highlands running to Laos, and thereby link up with the archipelago's central islands in zones IV and V? One thing was sure, though: the deep south, what the Vietnamese increasingly referred to as Nam Bo, was on its own. And it would be so for the rest of the Indochina War.[39] (See Plate 8.)

3

The Asian Routes of War

In September 1948, General Vo Nguyen Giap dispatched a special delegate to Thailand named Nguyen Nhu Kim. He was a former colonial scout, a physics graduate, a talented radio operator, as well as a freshly minted Communist Party member. His mission was to take command of a 50-ton vessel which government agents in Bangkok had purchased to supply the Democratic Republic of Vietnam with what it needed via the sea. The ship flew a Thai flag, but it had secretly been renamed the *Song Lo*, so called for a river in northern Vietnam. Kim's team carefully loaded the ship's hull with 10 tons of supplies—radios, electronics, cameras, paper, medicines, an X-ray machine, propaganda materials, and scientific textbooks. The boat would also make a stopover in southern Vietnam to pick up rice to feed hungry mouths in central Vietnam, the mission's final destination. By June 1949, the *Song Lo*, its crew, and cargo were ready to go. A "remarkable radio system" allowed the ship to communicate with the government's diplomatic delegation in Bangkok, Zone IV's commander, and the Ministry of Defense monitoring the operation from its jungle redoubt in the hills of northern Vietnam. "Nothing was left to chance," is how a French intelligence report later described it. The Vietnamese established codes and changed them meticulously as French signals specialists kept on breaking them in a feverish race to keep up. On the night of 15 June 1949, after almost a year of preparations, the Vietnamese vessel quietly slipped out of Bangkok's harbor.

From the Thai capital, the *Song Lo* headed east across the Gulf of Thailand to Ca Mau, the southernmost tip of Vietnam jutting into the South China Sea. There, the crew spent a week repairing one of the boat's three outboard motors in a makeshift marina hidden in the marshes and loaded several tons of rice. On 17 July, the vessel shoved off again to make its way around the island prison of Poulo Condor and then head northwards towards Zone IV. That was the plan, and French code breakers relayed this information to their navy. The air force may have been tipped off too, for when Kim saw a reconnaissance plane flying overhead, he immediately took the *Song Lo* to China's Hainan Island opposite central Vietnam. He and his crew remained there, hoping to establish contact with local Chinese communist cells (Mao Zedong's armies had not yet liberated the island). But the pressure to make a run for Zone IV's coast proved too great as a typhoon approached, and fears arose that the republican Chinese, presumably notified by the French, would ambush them. Whatever the reasons, on the night of 28 August 1949, Nguyen Nhu Kim radioed that he would take his chances. Duly apprised, the French navy moved into position. Outrun and outgunned, the *Song Lo* was hit as it neared a cove near Zone IV's coast, sending a ball of fire dancing above the water, but not before the crew had raised Vietnam's national flag in an angry gesture of defiance. Of the initial crew of twenty-two men, all but one was recovered, including Kim. Everything else was lost to the sea. The French had just blocked one of the young republic's most audacious attempts to supply Vietnam by the sea, not from China, but from Thailand.[1]

That the *Song Lo*'s mission failed, there can be no debate. It did. However, this carefully organized, top-secret, radio-guided operation is significant because it tells us several things about the Vietnamese revolutionary war. Firstly, the Vietnamese did not fight the French independently from the rest of the surrounding Asian region. Secondly, the origin of the *Song Lo* mission in Bangkok, and not in southern China, means that Southeast Asia was as important as East Asia to the Vietnamese in keeping their sprawling state alive in its different extensions. Thirdly, the Vietnamese had clearly decided with the *Song Lo* that they were willing to use the sea and not solely overland routes to supply their sprawling state. Lastly, there were few, if any, weapons on the *Song Lo*. It carried food, medicines, radios, and paper—the things which the government's archipelagic system needed to hang on to, so that it could still be "there" in 1950 when the Chinese communists started injecting massive military aid, changing the nature of the conflict and of the state fighting it.

Northern Vietnam's Overland Trade with Southern China

Between East and Southeast Asia: Vietnam and the Asian Region in the Past

Vietnam has always been connected to its surrounding Asian context and the site of imperial competition. If Vietnam is recognizable to so many today, it is largely because this small country is located in one of those coveted parts of the world where empires go. Lest we forget, the French, the Japanese, and the Americans were not the first to intervene in Vietnam. The Chinese were. For almost a thousand years, until the tenth century, today's Red River Delta was part of the Chinese empire. As China's southernmost province, Vietnam served as the opening for the Middle Kingdom's trade with the Southeast Asian Spice Islands and markets located deeper in the Indian Ocean. Independence in no way changed this geopolitical reality. In the thirteenth century, the Vietnamese had to fend off Mongol invaders, who, having conquered China, tried to pass through the northern Vietnamese delta to reach Southeast Asia. The Vietnamese briefly lost their independence to the Chinese again in the early fifteenth century when the Ming dynasty, having thrown off the Mongols, tried to expand its influence into the Indian Ocean. Vietnam was China's preferred gateway for doing that. The Vietnamese realized how important their geographical niche was and, upon regaining their independence in 1427, started growing it southwards themselves. Vietnam was (and is) the product of its own imperial expansion too.

But holding that expanding territorial form together was no mean feat, as competing military families effectively divided the country into northern and southern halves from the mid-seventeenth century onwards. In the Red River basin, northerners turned to southern China to operate their exchanges. Southerners set up their capital in Hue. From there, they developed commercial and diplomatic ties with neighboring Thailand and Burma. The outbreak of a thirty-year civil war in Vietnam in the late eighteenth century only intensified hostile exchanges with the surrounding region. It started in 1771, when a band of angry brothers descended from an area in the central highlands called Tay Son. Opposed to the northern and southern military houses, the Tay Son brothers wanted all of Vietnam for themselves. As they marched down the Vietnamese coast, a remarkable leader of the southern Nguyen dynasty named Gia Long resisted. Pushed out of Hue, he established guerrilla bases in jungle areas of the Mekong Delta and, from there, built up local alliances, an army, and began operating a wartime government. He turned to the Thais for support. He nurtured relations with overseas Chinese and Western merchants plying the South China Seas. In the end, Gia Long outdid all of his rivals in securing aid from the surrounding region. If Ho Chi Minh's troops would take Vietnam in 1975 by marching from the north to the south, Gia Long's armed forces rolled their way northwards to victory from the south, unifying Vietnam in its current form for the first time in 1802.[2]

Although the French conquered the Nguyen dynasty and severed Vietnam's tributary relationship with China in the late nineteenth century, this did not mean that they isolated their new colony from the Asian region and the world. By the turn of the twentieth century, the French had created a railway running from Hanoi to Kunming, the capital of southern China's Yunnan province. They dredged and widened Saigon's harbor and created a deepwater port in Cam Ranh Bay, making it France's preeminent forward base in Asia. A host of shipping companies transported goods to and from Tokyo, Hong Kong, Shanghai, Bangkok, Singapore, as well as Paris and Marseille. Haiphong became a vibrant regional port as Chinese junks continued to move up and down the Vietnamese coast carrying rice from the Mekong Delta to northern Vietnam and on to southern China. Little wonder then that Ho Chi Minh, upon coming to power at the head of a newly independent Vietnam in mid-1945, had every intention of connecting his country to the surrounding Asian region. Others had done it. And so would he.

The Northern Networks

When Ho Chi Minh and his advisers met in the government's first cabinet meetings to discuss foreign trade in late 1945, we can be sure that they had maps in the room. We can be confident too that each of them brought different sets of geographical knowledge to the table. This was particularly true of the communist core at the helm of the nascent republic. Several in the party had learned their Marxism in France, had studied and lived there, and were at ease in French. They knew France and Western Europe best. A handful had studied in Moscow. Some had honed their communism to a creed in the cell blocks of Poulo Condor and Son La, while others had been active in urban radicalism in Saigon and Hanoi during the 1930s. Ho Chi Minh's trajectory was in a class of its own, though: he had left Saigon on a colonial steamship in 1911 and walked back into Vietnam from southern China thirty years later. He was a revolutionary globe-trotter like few others at the time, having moved between Paris, London, and New York before joining the Comintern in Moscow in 1923.

He knew Asia just as well. In fact, when it came to knowing this part of the world, Ho and a closely knit group of communists recruited by him possessed an unrivalled knowledge of the region's geography, peoples, cultures, languages, and lines of communications. This knowledge flowed directly from their clandestine movements in Asia during the interwar period. Upon arriving in Guangzhou from Moscow in 1924, Ho went to work building up a Vietnamese revolutionary organization in this southern Chinese port city (which had been connected to Vietnam by a myriad of maritime routes since the first century BCE). He recruited young Vietnamese from inside Vietnam. He introduced dozens of them into the Huangpu Military Academy outside Guangzhou. Others, he left among the Vietnamese diaspora in Thailand to build up bases there. He dispatched a handful to Moscow. Ho also joined hands with Chinese and Comintern advisers in Bangkok, Singapore, and Hong Kong to create communist parties for Thailand, Malaya, and his own Vietnam. All of this came less than a decade after the Comintern had helped the Chinese to create their party in Shanghai. Ho knew from his own revolutionary movements that Asian communism was initially a very maritime phenomenon. His party, like the others, had first emerged along an arc of port cities running from Singapore to Shanghai by way of Bangkok and Guangzhou. While Ho may not have articulated it as such in cabinet discussions in Hanoi, he carried this mental map of the region with him when he became Vietnam's first president. So too did a core group of "Asia hands," experienced specialists of the region he and his Communist Party counted on to run their clandestine trading operations during the Indochina War. Like Ho, they spoke Thai, Chinese, and English.

Southern China was the priority for those meeting in Hanoi in late 1945 to discuss foreign trade. Many knew from their activities there during the Second World War that this global conflagration had flooded the region with arms and supplies. This was certainly true for southwestern China's Sichuan and Yunnan provinces, to which Chiang Kai-shek had transferred his embattled republic following the Japanese onslaught in 1937. His government received large amounts of military, economic, and medical assistance from the United States through the Lend-Lease Program: until 1945, the Americans flew or trucked over 600,000 tons of weapons, vehicles, medicines, and supplies of all kinds into southwestern China. Ho and many in his entourage knew from experience how important these provinces were. Yunnan bordered northern Vietnam. Several in Ho's entourage had moved in and out of republican Chongqing and Kunming during the war. Others had lived and worked among the large Vietnamese communities the French had brought in to run the Yunnanese railway in a string of towns extending from Kunming to Hanoi.[3]

The arrival of Chiang Kai-shek's troops in northern Vietnam in September 1945 to accept the Japanese surrender reminded everyone of just how close China was. While many might have lamented the negative effects of Chinese occupation (and they were real), there were also reasons to be thankful. Most importantly, unlike the British in the south, Chiang Kai-shek's commanders refused to allow the French to overthrow Ho's newly formed government above the 16th parallel. As a result, officials in central and northern Vietnam were able to expand their trading relations with the Republic of China largely free of colonial interference for over a year. (Southern Vietnamese never benefitted from such favorable circumstances; colonial war broke out there almost immediately.)

Northerners looked to southern China for the arms they needed to outfit the government's fledgling army and to send to units fighting the French in the south. Agents immediately explored all sorts of ways to buy army surplus and weapons either legally from the Republic of China or via the black market. In mid-1946, the government approved the importation from China of hundreds of tons of guns, bullets, grenades, and gunpowder. A few weeks later, officials signed a contract with a private trader to procure weapons, chemicals, medicines, and fabric for making uniforms. In exchange, the Vietnamese agreed to provide the Chinese with coal and cement, authorizing the export of 50 tons of the latter. This contract symbolized one of the first independent Vietnamese commercial transactions with China since the nineteenth century.[4]

The outbreak of full-scale hostilities between the French and the Vietnamese in December 1946 dashed any hopes of resuming normal patterns of trade. However, as in earlier chapters of Vietnamese history, war still required continued exchanges with the region. To administer wartime commerce, in early 1947, the government established the Bureau of External Trade. This office initially operated from Cao Bang, the northern Vietnamese province located opposite the Chinese border. This state-run trading house focused on exchanges between northern Vietnam and southern China—Yunnan, Guangxi, and Guangdong provinces. The bureau started off with 20 million Bank of Indochinese piasters to purchase imports. One of Ho's best Asia specialists oversaw it, Nguyen Duc Thuy. Fluent in Chinese, this veteran communist hailed from the Indochinese Communist Party's prewar Asian network. He knew Chinese communist and nationalist leaders from years of having operated in southern China and navigated its political waters. He now put his impressive array of contacts in the service of the DRV by organizing meetings with both influential members of the Republic of China and an array of traders operating across the border. He handled orders, approved deals, and monitored the importing and distribution of weapons and supplies purchased in China. By mid-1947, Nguyen Duc Thuy's office operated agencies in several towns strung along both sides of the northern border. (Focused for the time being on taking control of the Red River Delta, the French army could do little to stop these northern Vietnamese exchanges with southern China.)[5]

The government's main purchases in 1947 included weapons and ammunition as well as petroleum products, chemicals, medicines, radio equipment, and uniforms. In exchange, the Vietnamese exported opium, gold, and natural resources. Nguyen Duc Thuy's office relied heavily on Chinese traders across the border and overseas Chinese merchants living in northern Vietnam to serve as intermediaries. That Nguyen Duc Thuy personally directed the Foreign Ministry's office in charge of the overseas Chinese in Vietnam must have helped. In a personal letter to one of his subordinates, he recommended two such merchants "who would be able to buy special goods" the resistance needed. He vouched for other Chinese go-betweens, including the vice-president of the Chinese community of the provincial capital of Cao Bang and a former officer in Chiang Kai-shek's army. Thanks to such contacts, the northern trade office rapidly expanded its networks into Yunnan, Guangxi, and Guangdong provinces in China.[6]

All of this was well timed. On the run, the Vietnamese had not yet had the chance to set up local arms factories. They had not even finished establishing a new capital in the northern hills of Thai Nguyen province. Many things had been lost to enemy attacks during the government's "Long March" from Hanoi, which had started in late 1946. Troops needed weapons and uniforms. Paper was always in short supply. In February 1947, as the Vietnamese withdrew from Hanoi, Nguyen Duc Thuy crossed into the province of Guangdong to meet the well-known General Zhang Fakui of the Republic of China. Nguyen Duc Thuy asked him to approve the establishment of a special Vietnamese trading bureau in China to oversee the export of natural resources and rice from northern Vietnam in exchange for weapons and supplies. Backed by Zhang Fakui, Nguyen Duc Thuy flew to the Chinese republican capital in Nanjing, where he met with officials there before returning to the border in March. On the way back, he received business offers and prototypes from Chinese and American businessmen interested in the emerging Vietnamese market.[7]

While it is unclear whether such a Vietnamese office ever got off the ground (as civil war would soon consume China), these early efforts bore some fruit. In April 1947, Chinese officers possessing large amounts of arms were negotiating with Vietnamese representatives in southern China. One Chinese officer agreed to sell the DRV a stock of around a million cartridges and 300 rifles to accompany them, 100 machine guns and 50 mortars, all coming from Allied army surplus. This deal was sealed, and the majority of the arms moved to the border. In another instance, Ho's people purchased large amounts of war material across the border in Longzhou, including machine guns, mortars, radios, and rifles. Statistics for the month of May 1947 (captured a few months later by the French) show that Nguyen Duc Thuy's office imported over 50 tons of gunpowder and explosives, plus 10 tons of acid, as well as large amounts of pharmaceutical products and petrol from China. Modern Vietnam's China trade had clearly begun with Chiang Kai-shek's republic and not with Mao Zedong's, still located far to the north.[8]

It was an eye-opening experience for some, especially those in the Communist Party who had been strangers to Asia during the colonial period. The minister of finance, Le Van Hien, was one of them. As he confided to his diary during a visit to the Chinese border in 1947:

> We opened a map to consider our routes running to China. After our trip, we realized clearly the importance of our terrain in relation to the southwestern provinces of China, such as Yunnan. Our situation is very advantageous thanks to the estuaries, especially that of Hai Phong. Thanks to that advantage and our organized transportation later on, we will definitely hold the key in terms of economy and distribution of essential food to the Chinese people in this region.

We thus realized that China would serve as our communications line, taking [our] goods to the outside and bringing goods [to us] on the inside.[9]

Ideology counted for little in running these commercial networks. The fact that Nguyen Duc Thuy was one of the Communist Party's foremost authorities on Maoist thought in no way stopped him or others like him from doing business with Chinese republican officials, merchants, and a mosaic of smugglers who cared little for Marx or Lenin. What mattered most was the deep geographical knowledge, language skills, unflinching loyalty, and reliable contacts these experienced Asia hands provided to the government in its hour of greatest need. Assisting the director of the northern trading office was a handful of tightly knit communists who knew each other and China well from years of having operated there during the interwar period. Hunkered down in the northern highlands of Vietnam in 1947, the Vietnamese leadership needed these people to keep the gateway to southern China open at all costs.

The French knew this too, General Raoul Salan in particular. Between 1945 and 1947, he was the commander of the Expeditionary Corps for northern Vietnam and the official representative in charge of negotiations with the Republic of China. This feisty officer, who would turn on the French republic during the Algerian War, had first served in Indochina's northern borderlands in the 1930s. He immediately understood the dangers of letting his adversaries expand their trading networks along the Sino-Vietnamese border. Starting in early 1947, he presided over the organization of a major offensive in the northern borderlands called Operation Léa.[10] Besides destroying Ho's government, Salan also wanted to deny his enemy access to China. Airborne raids began in October of that year, followed by vigorous sweeps across the northern borderlands. If paratroopers failed to destroy the government in their first surprise attacks (though they came very close in a place called Bac Can), Salan did largely achieve his strategic goal of severing his adversary's trading routes running into China. His men dealt a serious blow to Nguyen Duc Thuy's import-export office in Cao Bang:

they captured several of its agents, as well as much of its funds, documents, and some opium. Colonial troops also took control of the main routes, the railway, and ports of entry along the northern border, forcing the Vietnamese to use much more difficult lines of communication.

It was only three years later, having retaken Cao Bang and its surrounding roads with Chinese communist backing, that Ho Chi Minh regained direct access to southern China and with it large-scale communist bloc aid. Vo Nguyen Giap used the word "encircled" (*vong vay*) in his memoirs to describe the DRV's isolated position until then.[11] It was, to be sure, a difficult period. To hang on, northerners had to tighten their belts, increase internal weapons production, and reorient their foreign trade towards the colonial-controlled zones and cities. Capturing enemy weapons in ambushes became a priority. But intense encirclement did not mean complete isolation. The French could never seal off their enemy entirely from the outside. Small-scale exchanges continued through local markets on each side of the Sino-Vietnamese border, less in arms than in textiles, salt, medicines, ink, radio equipment, chemicals, and opium. Of course, the Vietnamese could never outfit a modern division from such basics—that came later; but they could maintain the paper trail, keep civil servants healthy enough to push their pencils, and arm guerrilla fighters with small weapons. In 1948, Ho Duc Thanh, a Vietnamese educated in Chinese circles in the 1930s and married to a Chinese woman, procured "important quantities" of weapons, bicycles, and petroleum products in southern China. He paid in opium and tin exported to Guangxi (thanks to Chinese merchants serving as brokers). Such small-scale smuggling continued throughout the conflict, sustaining the embattled state in its fragmented form.[12]

Opium helped. Northerners relied on Chinese go-betweens to obtain raw opium from highland areas in northwest Vietnam and Laos. They also negotiated its export and sale abroad. Although upon coming to power the Vietnamese government had outlawed the distribution of this drug to its citizens, it allowed local Chinese users to continue using this narcotic and dealing in the opium trade on the condition that the government could tax and control this important source of revenue. In practice, Vietnamese nationalists never really abolished the colonial opium monopoly; they assumed it discreetly, including for Laos. As early as 1946, customs officials authorized Chinese merchants to carry arms to protect themselves when traveling to buy raw opium in Laos' Sam Neua province. The government shipped opium produced there to neighboring Zone IV, again thanks to the collaboration of Chinese traders long involved in this business.[13]

It is hard to say how much opium the Democratic Republic of Vietnam collected annually from growing areas in northern Indochina. During the colonial period, upland zones in Laos had annually provided 14 tons of opium to the colonial state. In 1947, the French only collected a fraction of that. Some of it ended up in DRV hands. In mid-1947, for example, the French air force destroyed an enemy depot containing over 4 tons of opium—that is, more than 28 million piasters (at a 7,000 piasters-per-kilogram price) went up in smoke that day. Two years later, the finance minister, Le Van Hien, had 600 kg of opium stashed somewhere in Cao Bang province for financing imports. And one of the highest-ranking members of the Indochinese Communist Party, Nguyen Luong Bang, dealt in this commodity via a special unit called the "Northern Victory Company." Given the stakes involved, the opium trade remained in party hands throughout the conflict. The British estimated that the DRV had successfully exported 15 tons of opium from Laos in the spring of 1953, that is, 150 million piasters at the 10,000 piasters-per-kilogram price for that year. The French army was also involved in the opium trade in the Tai federation they administered in nearby Lai Chau Province. Revenues were such that some have suggested that the French decision to take a stand at Dien Bien Phu was driven by a desire to control the nearby opium harvests.[14]

Not quite. That the "communists" and the "colonialists" wanted to monopolize the opium trade in Indochina, there can be no question. Opium was easily transportable, and its value was such that it could buy just about anything if managed correctly. When once Nguyen Duc Thuy was detained in southern China, he was carrying a stash of opium with him, "a sort of traveler's check," as an informant nicely put it to his American handler. But does that mean that the Vietnamese relied solely on this "hard currency" to finance their greatest battle feats? No. Did it help? Of course, it did. But the opium trade was only one part of a bigger Asian constellation of commercial opportunities that helped the guer- rilla state to hang on until a new northern route opened unhindered access to communist China and large-scale communist bloc assistance. Trade with the colonial cities was particularly important, as was the internal production of small-scale weapons, paper, and medicines. Were the Vietnamese communists drug traffickers because of their involve- ment in the opium trade? No, at least not any more than were French intelligence officers who used this drug during the second half of the conflict to help finance their guerrilla operations against Vo Nguyen Giap's divisions in the run-up to Dien Bien Phu. More than anything else, opium allows cash-strapped states to run their wars on the cheap. This includes paying for covert operations when governments prefer not to pay themselves. That the American Central Intelligence Agency or CIA was alleged to have been involved in this drug trade during the Vietnam War should come as no surprise.[15]

Central Vietnam's Seaborne Trade with Southern China

If overland routes helped northerners reach southern China, the South China Sea allowed the Democratic Republic of Vietnam's authorities in central Vietnam to reach Chinese port cities. Like their counterparts in the north, in 1946 central Vietnamese officials created an import-export company called the Viet Thang or the "Vietnamese Victory Company." It received start-up funds of around 5 million Indochinese piasters and was fittingly based in the ancient trading post of Hoi An. Until the out- break of full-scale war in late 1946, the Viet Thang operated subsidiaries in Hanoi, Hue, Da Nang, and Vinh. With the French occupation of these towns in 1947 (except for Vinh), the company's headquarters moved to Zone V in lower central Vietnam. From there, the Viet Thang presided over exchanges with southern Chinese ports in Guangdong Province—Beihai (Pakhoi), Macau, Hong Kong, Guangzhou, and Hainan Island. To conduct these exchanges, Vietnamese officials relied on overseas Chinese traders and skippers, Vietnamese fishermen and sailors, Republic of China merchants and officials, and their own agents.[16]

Working through local antennas scattered throughout the country-side, these people located, purchased, and stockpiled merchandise for export to China. Using carefully camouflaged depots, they stored cin-namon, sugar, opium, shark fins, silk, tin, areca, and a variety of delica-cies appreciated in Chinese markets. Chinese merchants working for the company possessed large stocks of tin extracted from the mines of Bangka in Indonesia. They had recovered it from a Japanese transport ship the Allies had sunk off Zone V's coast during the Pacific War. In September 1949, authorities in Zone V used a 70-ton junk to export 40 tons of tin to the Chinese coast. A year later, the French navy inter-cepted a junk carrying 4 tons of cinnamon and another loaded with 20 tons of this spice as well as 3 tons of tin. With the sale of these exports, traders purchased what the government required and then transported it back to Vietnam. They also did their own business.[17]

The government had no choice but to rely on private traders to con-duct much of its trade. If the authorities bought two-thirds of the com-pany's merchandise at the official price from local traders, they allowed them to sell the remaining third of their goods at the higher, unfixed market price. (We may assume that a similar policy applied along the Sino-Vietnamese land border.) Viet Thang merchants were happy to have local authorities allocate them the lion's share of the trade in cen-tral Vietnam. In 1949, a French naval intelligence officer reported that the company operated a near-monopoly in the area. Moreover, because the French never reoccupied much of central Vietnam, the Viet Thang traders found it easier to operate than their northern counterparts did in areas along the Chinese frontier always subject to enemy attacks (like Operation Léa).[18]

Chinese junk traders played the dominant role in running the gov-ernment's seaborne exchanges to and from central Vietnam, including Zone IV, nestled just south of Hanoi and which shared a southern bor-der with Zone V. According to the French, "twenty or so important Chinese traders, with perfect knowledge of Tonkin and northern

Annam" dominated "almost all of the traffic" with Zone IV. The former president of the Chinese community of Cat Ba (a small island in the Gulf of Tonkin) used several of his 20-to-40-ton junks to smuggle goods from Beihai to this colonial-free zone. Vietnamese customs agents carefully monitored these commercial exchanges. They issued departure and arrival lists, seized undeclared goods, and always required receipts. Clandestine or not, this was official trade. Opium coming via its western border with Laos may explain how Zone IV financed its imports from China with little government capital. In 1948, a Vietnamese informant reported that opium arriving from Laos helped pay for purchases occurring in this zone. Thanh Hoa, his report continued, had become a vibrant trading post selling all sorts of things: "It is about the only place in the Viet Minh zones where American cigarettes are available; the last outpost of the foreign world before entering the austerity zones."[19]

That the Vietnamese turned to southern Chinese port-cities is hardly surprising. Again, all across the Asia-Pacific region, the Second World War had left behind large stocks of weapons and supplies. Guangzhou, Macau, and Hong Kong had rapidly become important sites for smugglers to stock such things before shipping them on by boat to emerging war markets in Indochina and Indonesia. Moreover, the free-port status of Macau and Hong Kong in the late 1940s made these ports attractive destinations for buying medicines, chemicals, petroleum products, radios, and replacement parts at competitive prices. Additionally, DRV agents opened secret bank accounts in these financial centers in southern China and conducted part of the government's trafficking in Indochinese piasters there. Lastly, Guangzhou, Macau, Beihai, and even Hong Kong were often the home bases for Chinese traders dealing with the DRV in central Vietnam.[20]

The availability of army surplus material on the Macau black market was at its height from late 1946 to the end of 1947, precisely the period during which Ho Chi Minh was scrambling to keep his state alive. In early 1948, Vietnamese agents traveled to Macau to take possession of a large quantity of mercury and arms coming from the Pacific region worth a total of 5 million Hong Kong dollars. A Chinese crew was to deliver it to the region of Vinh in Zone IV. Motorized junks left Macau two times a month to deliver small amounts of American army surplus and Chinese and Western medicines to areas further south. In return, the Vietnamese exported opium, cinnamon, sugar, textiles, and sunken tin from Bangka. The French estimated that their navy only intercepted half of this contraband. Macau was important enough that central Vietnam's Viet Thang set up a branch office there. Vietnamese communists running these operations were certainly no strangers to this part of the Chinese coast. They had created their party in Hong Kong in 1930 and secretly held their initial congress in this nearby Portuguese port city five years later.[21]

Hainan Island formed another link in central Vietnam's seaborne operations. For centuries, Hainanese traders had purchased central Vietnamese forest products, precious stones, cinnamon, opium, tiger pelts, and elephant tusks from as far inland as central Laos. As elsewhere, Ho Chi Minh's people tapped into these preexisting Asian networks. A Hainanese trader, one Cao Vinh Sanh, ran trading missions for the central Vietnamese authorities. He was a well-known cinnamon trader in the area. In August 1950, another Chinese merchant told colonial authorities that he had participated in this traffic between Hainan and central Vietnam because of the "important profits" to be made. The French had just confiscated six and a half tons of sugar and three and a half tons of cinnamon he was exporting for Vietnamese officials in Quang Ngai. In exchange, he had imported medical equipment. For the French navy, there was no question about it: a "regular" trade existed between Hainan and central Vietnam. This ocean trade helped different parts of the Vietnamese archipelago to hold out from their respective "islands," all the while forcing the French to invest huge sums of money and resources to stop them. This was quagmire writ large.[22]

The Southeast Asia Networks of the Vietnamese Revolutionary War

And what about areas located farther down the Vietnamese coast?[23] If northern and central Vietnamese leaders looked to southern China to maintain an opening to Asia, those on the southern end of the Vietnamese guerrilla archipelago turned to Thailand. In fact, between 1945 and 1951, overland and maritime routes originating from there channeled impressive amounts of weapons, radio equipment, paper, printers, chemicals, and medicines to lower parts of the DRV. As elsewhere in the region, the Second World War had left large amounts of arms and supplies scattered across Southeast Asia. Most of the Lend-Lease aid the Americans shipped to Chiang Kai-shek's government in southwestern China had in fact gone through British India and Burma via the Indian Ocean, on the western side of mainland Southeast Asia. Much of it, however, did *not* make it over the Himalayan "hump" to Chiang Kai-shek's government before the war's end. And at least some of it remained bottlenecked in northern Burma, which, of course, shares a long border with Thailand. Meanwhile, hundreds of thousands of surrendering Japanese troops in Burma, Thailand, southern Indochina, and Indonesia began turning their weapons over to the British in charge of their surrender and disarmament.

The problem was that British forces in charge of the Japanese surrender in most of Southeast Asia were far too small to keep tabs on all these leaking Japanese and Lend-Lease stockpiles. When the British tried to dispose of Japanese weapons quickly in Thailand by dumping many of them into the Gulf of Thailand, enterprising smugglers always found ways to recover, repair, and sell them. And although the Royal Thai Army demobilized upon the defeat of its Japanese ally, senior officers held on to large caches of weapons and supplies in northeastern areas near the Mekong river. So did the leaders of the "Seri" or "Free Thai" movement. This underground guerrilla force had run covert operations against the Japanese and received almost 200 tons of weapons from the Allies in order to do so. In short, Thailand was awash with arms following the end of the Second World War.

If the Europeans returning to reclaim their colonies bemoaned this sad state of affairs, Southeast Asian anticolonialists welcomed it. Located at the center of the region, connected by land and sea routes to much of the area around it, and free of colonial control, Thailand was a magnet for the Vietnamese and Indonesians as they went to war with the French and the Dutch. While it is true that the Thais had avoided the colonial fate of their neighbors, they had their own problems with the Europeans, above all, with the French. Thai leaders were particularly reluctant to return territories in Laos and Cambodia to the French which they had seized from them with the support of the Japanese during the Second World War. Thai leaders of all political colors felt that the French had unjustly taken these lands from them in the nineteenth century when they created colonial Indochina. But the French now wanted these "lost territories" back from the Thais as much as they did Vietnam from Ho Chi Minh. This immediately drove the Vietnamese and Thais together.

The Thais were happy to make life as difficult as possible for the French by supporting independence movements in Vietnam, Laos, and Cambodia discreetly. They did this in three ways, for which Ho Chi Minh was personally grateful: by allowing his people to buy arms and supplies in Thailand and ship them home unhindered; by permitting them to run a diplomatic office out of Bangkok; and by granting them the opportunity to operate a busy news agency there. Until the Cold War finally arrived in Thailand in 1951, when anticommunism finally trumped anticolonialism in Bangkok politics, Thai sympathy and support for the Vietnamese fighting against the French ran high. Despite repeated French protests, Ho Chi Minh's officials operated freely in Thailand for the duration of six years.

Given that war broke out almost immediately in Saigon in September 1945, southerners were fortunate to have access to such a sympathetic Thai officialdom and this vibrant arms market. One of the Vietnamese government's first representatives to hit the ground running in Bangkok after the war, Tran Van Giau, told me years later in an interview that "purchasing arms in Thailand was as easy as buying a beer." Upon his arrival in the Thai capital in mid-1946 as a special government emissary, he immediately met with Pridi Phanomyong, the former head of the Seri Thai who was now the Thai prime minister. He and Giau had first met during their student days in France. Pridi allowed Ho Chi Minh's government to establish a secret supply committee for southern Vietnam in Bangkok to transport arms and supplies there. Agents brought Indochinese piasters and gold to finance purchases. Like the Viet Thang in central Vietnam and the Bureau of External Trade in the far north, this Bangkok-based, government-backed trading house took care of southern Vietnam. It did so through branches it established inside Thailand to procure weapons and to organize their shipment back home.

To assist them, the leadership recruited heavily from among the 50,000-strong overseas Vietnamese concentrated in northeast Thailand, scattered along the coast of the Gulf of Thailand, and in the Bangkok area. Although many in the diaspora had lived in Thailand for decades, if not longer, they were overwhelmingly supportive of Vietnamese independence. Anticolonialists had moved among them since the turn of the century, including President Ho himself. Many of the Vietnamese in Thailand worked in construction. Others held lower-level positions in the government. Some were fishermen, others local merchants. Always fluent in Thai, several became invaluable go-betweens for government delegates debarking in Bangkok or crossing the Mekong in the northeast. Tran Van Giau and others like him needed them to translate, broker deals, and enter into contact with Thai officials and merchants. The Supply Committee for Southern Vietnam relied on a coterie of agents from the diaspora to organize the safe shipment of arms and supplies to the country. They served as invaluable guides, escorts, messengers, informants, porters, sailors, and radio operators.

Two individuals stand out in this network, one in northeast Thailand, the other in Bangkok. The first is Vu Huu Binh. During the 1930s, this young man rose through the ranks of the French colonial army in Laos. He also became involved in radical politics and secretly joined the Indochinese Communist Party in Laos. With the outbreak of the Second World War, Binh deserted the colonial army, crossed into northeast Thailand, and became an officer in the Royal Thai Army. His anticolonialism and knowledge of French Indochina immediately attracted the attention of top-rank Thai officers, who were in command of areas bordering Indochina as they went to war briefly with the French in 1941 and annexed territories in Laos and Cambodia. Vu Huu Binh's importance was such that even Phibul Songkram, the leader of wartime Thailand, received him. While the latter receded temporarily from the political scene at the war's end, Vu Huu Binh maintained his contacts with the

Thai military as he rapidly became one of the Vietnamese government's indispensable intermediaries for doing business in Thailand. Fluent in Lao and Thai, he put Tran Van Giau and others in contact with a broad section of Thai officialdom. He helped negotiate the creation of the DRV's diplomatic mission office in Bangkok. Like Nguyen Duc Thuy's overtures to General Zhang Fakui in southern China, Vu Huu Binh contacted his former Thai commander, General Phin Chunhawan, the deputy commander of the northeastern army, in order to secure the delivery of 10,000 rifles to the Vietnamese in 1946. (Later on, this same man's son would normalize Thailand's relations with Vietnam at the end of the Cold War). Vu Huu Binh could also count on the support of the Seri Thai, whose leaders in the northeast he also knew well. Thanks to him, Free Thai officials allowed the DRV to use boxcars to ship weapons and supplies from Bangkok to the Lao border by train.

A Buddhist monk, Bao An, was the government's go-to man for smuggling guns and supplies out of Bangkok. Born in Sa Dec, an area of southern Vietnam populated by ethnic Buddhist Khmers, Bao An grew up speaking Khmer and Vietnamese. He moved to Cambodia during the interwar period and traveled extensively in the country. He became involved in nationalist politics of a religious kind there and eventually sought refuge in Thailand in the late 1930s to avoid colonial surveillance. Like Vu Huu Binh, Bao An's hostility towards French colonialism won him immediate sympathy among the Thais. Fluent in Thai by this time, he became heavily involved in Buddhist politics in Bangkok (strongly supported by the Thai government as a way of promoting the government's influence in Laos and Cambodia). After the Japanese capitulation, this tireless monk put his contacts and language skills in the service of the Vietnamese nationalist movement. He directed liaisons and transactions with Thai and Chinese arms dealers from his unofficial headquarters in the temple at Nang Loern. Tran Van Giau used him, as did others in the DRV. He and five other monks worked out of the DRV's diplomatic delegation doing deals until its closure in 1951. For this period, the French considered this monk's network to be one of the "best organized and the strongest in Thailand."[24]

What the Vietnamese could not find in Thailand they located else-where in the region, thanks to their ability to operate freely in Bangkok. From the Thai capital, DRV agents traveled to the Philippines, Malaya, and Burma to make deals. One of Vietnam's legendary spies during the war against the Americans, Pham Ngoc Thao, allegedly organized a deal with Filipino traders to ship arms to southern Vietnam in ex-change for rice, shrimp, pork, and, above all, gold and Indochinese bank notes. In early 1947, the Vietnamese received a large arms ship-ment from the Malayan Communist Party in the British-held Malayan straits. The man in charge of this country's Communist Party was in fact the same man Ho Chi Minh had left behind in Singapore in 1930 to build communism there. His name was Lai Tek. He came from southern Vietnam. Yet again, Vietnamese communists had effectively tapped into this active revolutionary arc, which had been established before the Second World War and which ran from Singapore to Guang-zhou, thanks in no small part to the man now in charge of the country, Ho Chi Minh.[25]

Albeit relative newcomers, at the end of the Pacific War several American intelligence officers used their wartime contacts, experience, and knowledge of Asia to make money. Some of them also played roles in moving arms to and from Southeast Asia via Bangkok. James Thomp-son was one of them. Educated at Princeton, he had served in the Office of Strategic Services in Thailand during the Second World War. Rather than staying in intelligence as the OSS turned into the CIA, he went into business for himself in Southeast Asia. Thanks to his friendship with such Free Thai luminaries as Pridi Phanomyong, he started a famous silk business and joined the board of what would become the renowned Oriental Hotel in Bangkok. Sympathetic to independence movements in Indochina and elsewhere, he built up a wide range of contacts with Vietnamese, Laotian, and Cambodian anticolonialists, helping them locate and negotiate arms deals. He was not alone in this line of busi-ness. As in postwar Europe, the Second World War left a motley crew of merchants, smugglers, and "specialists" of all nationalities in its wake in the Asian theater. As one French officer trying to make sense of the smuggling going on through Thailand described it in 1950:

At the head of these firms are an ever-growing number of American adventurers, often former OSS officers [like James Thompson]. They scouted out the market during their service and returned there at the end of the war, along with people of every European nationality and officials from Southeast Asia, from the highest-ranking to the simple policeman. As such, Bangkok has become the market, the nerve center, where all kinds of traffickers operate fake businesses which act as cover for their illegal activities. Important shipping companies created with the sole aim of trafficking, air transport enterprises, and a fluid junk trade feed a Thai market already supplied with large stocks of well-camouflaged wartime arms ready for trafficking.[26]

The Vietnamese operated two major supply lines out of Thailand. A lower Indochinese route followed the Cambodian coast along the Gulf of Thailand to supply Zone IX nestled in the Ca Mau peninsula, the southernmost tip of the Vietnamese resistance state. The second was an upper Indochinese road that ran from northeast Thailand to Zone IV's backdoor through central Laos. The coastal route crossing the Gulf of Thailand was by far the most important.[27]

A handful of colonial-trained navigators placed their seafaring knowledge in the service of the nationalist cause. Nguyen Y Net was a former colonial skipper who had worked for the French during the interwar period. He now headed the Vietnamese government's overseas maritime transport service running between Bangkok and the Ca Mau peninsula. Nguyen Y Net became something of a legend for operating a string of missions to southern Vietnam from Thailand as the skipper of a 14-meter-long motorized vessel called the *Doc Lap* (meaning "Independence" in Vietnamese). In September 1947, the *Doc Lap* successfully transported 8 tons of weapons and explosives across the Gulf of Thailand to southern Vietnam. In May 1948, his team brought 4 tons of medicines and some arms back to Zone IX. A third voyage, in December 1948, delivered an impressive 4 tons of sheet metal, 1 ton of copper bars, sulfuric acid, and 20 cases of radio material to the south. In May 1949, it delivered 4 tons of paper, a printing press, and chemicals. Finally, a fifth trip to the south shortly thereafter delivered 2 tons of paper, diverse equipment, and acids for making explosives. It seems likely that he was on the *Song Lo* when the French sank it off the coast of central Vietnam later that year.[28]

Bending the Maritime Arc
The Western Route and the Hainan Trail

A failure though it was, the *Song Lo* symbolized the degree to which the Vietnamese in charge of these Asian routes believed in the connective power of the sea. If much ink has been spilt—and rightly so—telling the story of the Ho Chi Minh Trail used against the Americans during the Vietnam War, this overland focus has prevented us from fully appreciating the degree to which the Vietnamese communists initially sought to supply their sprawling state via the sea. Starting in 1948, Ho Chi Minh turned to his Asia specialists to find ways of bending this maritime arc they knew so well from the interwar period, so that it could supply central and southern Vietnam from each of its ends. The sea, they were willing to venture, was perhaps the best way of providing the largest amounts of weapons and supplies in the shortest periods of time at the most competitive price to the lower islands of this archipelago that was wartime Vietnam. What Fernand Braudel wrote of the connective power of the Mediterranean for the sixteenth century could have easily been applied to the South China Sea hugging Vietnam's long coastline in the middle of the twentieth: "Water does everything people say it does: It is a source of union, it is transport, it is exchange and it brings things together; but it only does this on the condition that people work at it and that they accept to pay the price for using it."[29]

Three of Ho Chi Minh's best Asia specialists ran this top-secret maritime project—Cao Hong Lanh, Hoang Van Hoan, and Nguyen Thanh Son. All three men "knew the arc" and its connecting port cities like the back of their hands—Hong Kong, Macau, Guangzhou, Saigon, and Bangkok. They had worked with Ho Chi Minh in southern China and Thailand during the interwar period. In the late 1920s, Ho Chi Minh had left Hoang Van Hoan in Thailand (where he had joined hands with

Chinese revolutionaries building communist networks in the region).
He helped organize the large Vietnamese diaspora in northeast Thailand, all the while working with the Indochinese Communist Party's
agents in southern China, where he transferred to in the mid-1930s.
Based in southern China, Cao Hong Lanh did many of the same things
that Hoang Van Hoan did in Thailand. He also moved back and forth
along shipping lines between Guangzhou in southern China and Bangkok in Thailand. Nguyen Thanh Son returned from Guangzhou to
southern Vietnam where he nurtured communism in the Mekong
Delta. Upon the outbreak of the Indochina War, he operated deep in
the Ca Mau peninsula, the heart of Zone IX. From the ports of Ha Tien
and Rach Gia, he directed a powerful External Affairs Committee in
charge of the south's commercial exchanges with East and Southeast
Asia. All three of these men spoke Chinese almost as well as their native
Vietnamese. The first two were fluent in Thai. In 1948, they returned to
southern China and Thailand where they reactivated a host of deep contacts and networks among the Vietnamese and Chinese communities
in Thailand, Cambodia, and southern China.[30]

Their mission was to find ways to supply central and southern Vietnam from both ends of this long coastline running from Guangzhou to
Bangkok. Cao Hong Lanh traveled to Hong Kong, Macau, Guangzhou,
and even stopped over in Saigon to meet with trusted contacts. Hoang
Van Hoan concentrated his work among the overseas Vietnamese in
northeast Thailand and Bangkok, where Nguyen Thanh Son joined him.
Together, they mapped out ways to provision central and southern Vietnam with weapons and supplies. To do this, they divided the maritime
arc into two main routes—one running horizontally from Bangkok to
southern and central Vietnam, the other dropping vertically down from
the southern Chinese coast to the same destinations. The strategic goal
was not only to supply the lower half of the DRV via these two avenues,
but also to ensure that these routes would be ready to go in the event
the Chinese communists took control of the mainland.[31]

The one running from Bangkok to Zone IX was known as the "western route." In reality, it was something of a graft on to the preexisting
Southeast Asian operations discussed above. Hoang Van Hoan and

Nguyen Thanh Son operated it and the *Doc Lap* missions which ran so successfully between Bangkok and Ca Mau's ports in Ha Tien and Rach Gia as well. It should thus come as no surprise that the *Song Lo* mission described in the opening to this chapter was the brainchild of the Asia operatives. Nguyen Thanh Son had personally christened this vessel. They overplayed their hands, though, when, in 1949, they tried to push the western route out of the Gulf of Thailand into the South China Sea and then bend it back into central Vietnam. The *Song Lo*'s sinking was a stinging setback for Ho Chi Minh's attempt to use the sea. It was the "price" of using the sea's connective power, as Braudel had warned. The Vietnamese realized too that the French navy was stronger in the South China Sea than it was in the Gulf of Thailand. In the end, what the western route did best was to provide for the southern tip of the Vietnamese archipelago at Ca Mau. That said, the Vietnamese would use the maritime knowledge they had built up during the Indochina War to take on the Americans later. In fact, two of the men who ran the western route's overseas operations from Bangkok would, in the early 1960s, organize secret seaborne missions running from Haiphong to the Mekong Delta.[32]

As the western route faded in importance and the Chinese Red Army crossed the Yangzi River into southern China, all eyes immediately turned to the northern end of the arc and the possibility of projecting a seaborne route south towards central Vietnam from China. The Chinese communist victory in October 1949 and the Red Army's liberation of Hainan in early May 1950 emboldened Ho's Asia hands in their efforts to curve a supply line through this large island just off Vietnam's entire coastline, jutting into the Gulf of Tonkin. Days after Mao's junks had successfully seized Hainan, Le Van Hien, the minister of finance, wrote in his diary that Hainan and the Paracel islands could serve as the stepping stones for supplying central and southern Vietnam by sea.[33]

This route, however, was part of a wider shift within the party to use the ocean to provide central and southern Vietnamese forces with the weapons and supplies they would need to make the transition towards conventional warfare in the event the Chinese communists came to power on the continent. In September 1949, as Mao Zedong's Red Army raced southwards down the coast, the Vietnamese General Staff created a "Naval Studies Section." Its main tasks were to begin training officers in coastal and astronomical navigation as a first step in creating a larger maritime supply operation. In 1950, a special naval unit, secretly referred to as "Company 71," traveled to now communist China for training. Initially, Vietnamese military strategists counted on the maritime route to outfit one division and an anti-aircraft battalion in central Vietnam. In August 1950, the DRV authorities in Zone V were busy making preparations to receive Chinese military aid coming from Hainan, including the creation of an airbase to receive arms shipments by plane. This was why hundreds of Vietnamese naval and air force cadets had been sent to China for training. Meanwhile, Cao Hong Lanh received authorization to open talks in Guangzhou with the Chinese on running an ocean-going route to Vietnam via Hainan.[34]

This maritime connection for central and southern Vietnam was clearly as important as the overland one being discussed for the north. Excitement ran so high in Zone V that communist officials there independently dispatched a special delegation to Hainan to discuss the creation of such a sea route. That mission went to a certain Vo Bam. Few readers outside Vietnam will recognize this man's name. Inside Vietnam, however, he is considered to be one of the main architects of the Ho Chi Minh Trail during the war against the Americans. His trip to Hainan in mid-1950 deserves a detour here, because it allows us to understand better why Vietnamese communists initially designed their supply lines to operate along two trajectories, an overland route running into northern Vietnam across the Chinese land border at Cao Bang and an oceangoing one running to central and southern Vietnam across the South China Sea from Hainan Island.

The instructions to Vo Bam in May 1950 were simple: he was to lead a half dozen 5-ton junks to Hainan as a commercial cover, contact Chinese communists taking over there, and, his real mission, help find a way to supply central Vietnam by sea. On 1 August 1950, after weeks of careful preparation, Vo Bam and his crew finally set sail. Within days, if not hours, however, Vo Bam realized what the *Song Lo*'s commander,

Nguyen Kim Nhu, had learned a year earlier—the French navy was good. Their vessels intercepted three of Vo Bam's junks before they could even get away from the coast. Their capture allowed the others to slip away with Vo Bam still on board one of them, but not before a violent storm knocked them off course and left them adrift without drinking water. Just when things started to look very grim, they chanced upon a Chinese nationalist vessel fleeing Hainan Island. Unaware of who the thirsty Vietnamese asking him for directions to Hainan really were, the nationalist skipper gave them some fresh water and pointed them the right way, but with a warning: "Continue straight ahead, it's not far, but there are communists there." More thankful than the Chinese captain would ever know, Vo Bam headed straight for communist Hainan as one Chinese political sovereignty gave way to another in the middle of the Gulf of Tonkin, this one particularly favorable to the Vietnamese at the helm of the Democratic Republic of Vietnam and its three intrepid junks.[35]

Vo Bam and his crew arrived safely on Hainan Island a day or two later. After some rest, the mission chief met the island's new communist leaders. This included an audience with none other than Feng Baiju, the legendary Chinese communist whose column had resisted the Japanese and then the Chinese republicans on the island for years. Feng informed his Vietnamese visitor that he had known Ho Chi Minh from their days together in southern China, confirming yet again the importance of the interwar Sino-Vietnamese contacts Ho had forged. But this Chinese communist could do little without approval from his superiors. So, Feng sent the Vietnamese delegation on its way to Guangzhou. Once there, Vo Bam learned that his mission was, in fact, part of the wider reconfiguration engineered by the Asia hands since 1948. Cao Hong Lanh personally explained that the plan was to channel Chinese communist assistance to the Vietnamese via an overland route running into northern Vietnam while a seaborne one would supply central and southern Vietnam. This means that the initial goal, in mid-1950, was to inject the *entire* Vietnamese archipelago with massive Chinese aid, not just the northern tier by land, but also the central and southern parts of the country, thanks to the ocean's connective power.[36]

The Korean War and the End of the Maritime Routes

And yet, despite all of these prescient efforts to bend the maritime arc towards central and southern Vietnam, in the end it was not to be. Sometime in September 1950, as Chinese and Vietnamese communists prepared to open a land route through Cao Bang by force, they concluded that running a maritime route at the same time was too risky. There were several reasons for this, and they are essential to understanding the transformation of the archipelago state and subsequent course of the war for Vietnam well into the 1960s. Firstly, everyone knew that the French were watching and listening closely to what was going on off the coast. Their navy had easily sunk the *Song Lo* on its run from Hainan to Zone IV a year earlier; their signals people were reading Vietnamese radio traffic with remarkable ease; and somehow their security services had obtained copies of Cao Hong Lanh's letters about the ocean-going plan.

Secondly, the Americans were watching. True, they did not intervene to stop the Chinese communists from taking Hainan on 1 May 1950; however, on that same day, President Harry S. Truman signed legislation initiating large-scale American military assistance to the French. And during the first week of May, as Vo Bam headed for communist Hainan, the US Seventh Fleet commander visited Saigon with two destroyers in a clear sign that the United States stood behind the French, determinedly opposed to any communist thrust further southwards by land or sea. Fighter planes flew over Saigon to reiterate the warning. Equally important, the American Military Assistance Advisory Group began operations in September 1950 to supply military and economic assistance to the French and their Associated States. This included the supply of naval vessels, planes, and refurbished ports in Indochina.[37]

Thirdly, and probably the most important factor convincing Chinese and Vietnamese communist strategists to put the Hainan route on hold, there was the outbreak of the Korean War on 25 June 1950. In response to communist North Korea's invasion of the south, Truman rushed troops to the Korean peninsula while American destroyers moved into the Straits of Taiwan. The Americans immediately expanded their surveillance of the entire Chinese coast and assisted the French in monitoring the South China Sea as the United States Navy began to extend a line of containment running from their bases in South Korea and Japan to Thailand and Singapore by way of the Philippines. Similarly, Mao Zedong's decision to send combat troops into Korea to fight mainly American troops a few months later mitigated Chinese support for the Hainan project. (Beijing probably did not want to risk triggering an American attack against them in the Gulf of Tonkin by supporting a large-scale seaborne supply operation against the French in Indochina via Hainan.) And while the Chinese communists had used thousands of junks to take Hainan, they had no modern navy capable of battling against American destroyers and aircraft carriers which would have certainly backed up the French navy had they been needed. Ironically then, by invading South Korea, North Korea's Kim Il-sung indirectly killed the "Hainan project," pushing his Chinese and Vietnamese counterparts to focus on opening a single, overland route to supply the Democratic Republic of Vietnam via Cao Bang province.[38]

Vietnamese sources confirm the closing of the Hainan route on the eve of the Battle of Cao Bang. In mid-September 1950, Nguyen Luong Bang, a high-ranking party leader, informed Vo Bam that the Chinese and Vietnamese sides had finally decided to focus on the creation of one main overland supply line going from southern China into northern Vietnam via Cao Bang. Weapons and trucks in Guangzhou earmarked for the Vietnamese would not go via Hainan or on to Zone V from there. Cao Bang was their new destination. When Vo Bam and no doubt others asked what would happen to areas located far from the Chinese land border, Nguyen Luong Bang responded that the strategic goal was to push this landline from Cao Bang southwards through the highlands to reach zones IV and V from the rear side of the Tonkin Delta. Admittedly, this would be a more arduous and costly endeavor but, he insisted, it would also be a safer one.[39]

The expanding American presence in the Pacific only reinforced the Vietnamese communist focus on this overland route. In early November 1950, authorities in Zone IV told their counterparts in the Mekong

Delta that they had received word that the time had not come to send junks to Hainan. As they explained in a cable, "the assistance the Chinese must provide to [North] Korea took precedence and the situation there would influence the aid provided by the Chinese to the Vietnamese." The strategic goal now was to connect the northern and central cores of the Vietnamese state via a land route.[40]

Meanwhile, the Americans began spinning a web of containment off the long coastline running from Taiwan to Thailand. Mao's support of Ho Chi Minh's Vietnam and Kim Il-sung's North Korea led the Americans to increase their military and diplomatic commitment, not only to the French in Indochina in the form of the MAAG in September 1950, but also to the Thais. In that same year, Washington established a similar military assistance advisory group for Thailand in Bangkok, and the same program began in Taiwan in 1951. The Americans ramped up the pressure on the Thai ruling class to shut down Ho Chi Minh's activities in their country once and for all. They expected the Thais to get behind Washington's efforts to prevent Indochina and South Korea from "falling" to the communists.

If the Thais had been able to ignore the French, they now duly followed American orders. In February 1950, Thai Prime Minister Phibul Songkhram recognized the Associated State of Vietnam led by Bao Dai. A year later, Phibul expelled the DRV's diplomatic mission from Bangkok and cracked down on Vietnamese trading activities in the capital, along the Mekong river, and across the Gulf of Thailand. The Americans stepped up their combined support of the Thai and Taiwanese armed forces just as they did the French forces in Indochina and their associated armies in Laos, Cambodia, and Vietnam. The Gulf of Thailand, the South China Sea, and their coastal borders now came under unprecedented levels of surveillance. In 1952, the Vietnamese in Ca Mau reported that the western road to Thailand, for all intents and purposes, had ceased to operate.[41] This, then, is how international events, the arrival of the Cold War to Asia, directly affected the Vietnamese ability to supply their archipelagic state via the sea, from southern China to the Gulf of Thailand. (See Plate 9.)

A Ho Chi Minh or an Indochinese Trail?

Before concluding, we should keep in mind the dangers the internation-alization of the Indochina War represented for the army's leaders holed up on the far southern side of the Democratic Republic of Vietnam's archipelago. Until 1950, the commander-in-chief of the government's army in southern Vietnam, Nguyen Binh, had done a surprisingly good job of creating regular battalions with supplies coming clandestinely from Thailand and French colonial cities. He even relied on a collection of sampans, little junks, and fishermen who had been shuttling small amounts of arms and supplies up and down the eastern coastline. Nguyen Binh referred to it as the "Ho Chi Minh liaison road" (*Duong lien lac Ho Chi Minh*).[42] However, none of these sources provided him with the modern weapons he needed to arm, outfit, and supply regi-ments and divisions. Southerners had no heavy artillery and no anti-aircraft guns. As we know, without a direct line to China through, say, Hainan, Nguyen Binh's army was in no position to take on the French in conventional battle in 1950 and win.

Faced with the near-destruction of their armed forces and the inten-sification of American interference as the Cold War spread into Asia, by 1951 southern strategists had begun to turn their attention towards the inside of Indochina in the hope of connecting with the overland trail dropping from Cao Bang to the central zones (IV and V). In an internal study General Nguyen Binh penned shortly before his death in 1951, he argued in favor of the creation of what he called the "Indochinese Trail" (*duong mon Dong Duong*). In this report addressed to the Ministry of Defense, he left no doubt that the creation of this new overland "route crossing all of Indochina" from north to south via Zone IV, southern Laos, and northeastern Cambodia would be the only way to supply southerners along the eastern coastline "once the Ho Chi Minh liaison route presently doubling route no. 1 is blocked." This interior land route was all the more important, he argued, given that the Chinese commu-nist victory had increased the probability of stepped-up American in-tervention in the Indochina War via southern Vietnam and overland through Thailand and Cambodia. If the Americans entered the war directly against the Vietnamese in Indochina, he predicted, then they would come in the same way they had in Korea—through the south and, of course, via the sea. This would place southerners in an extraordinarily difficult position.[43]

> We must find the means to deal with the situation in which the French enemies increase their armed forces in order to consolidate their hold over the southern zone. We must take defensive measures in preparation for the outbreak of the Third World War and when Indochina will become the principal front in Southeast Asia. French forces could isolate the northern zone from the southern one.[44]

Viewed over the *longue durée*, it's possible to see how the Asian routes of the Indochina War would lead to the later development of the Ho Chi Minh Trail. However, this land route coming from the eastern side of communist Eurasia wouldn't reach southern Vietnam before the end of the conflict in 1954. It only got as far as the area west of colonial Hue, petering out somewhere in the central highlands by the war's end. Although orders went out in 1951 to push this route further south, it didn't happen. Southerners never received the supplies, modern weapons, or Chinese advisers with their new models of war which would be needed to create a conventional army and a single-party state to run it. The south was to remain in its archipelago form until the very end of the war.[45]

4

The City at War

In 1966, the Italian filmmaker Gillo Pontecorvo produced something of a cult film with *The Battle of Algiers*. For many, this docudrama encapsulated brilliantly the Algerian fight for independence against the French. For others, it symbolized the wider struggle of national liberation movements across the globe as the reality of decolonization finally sank into colonial minds. Starting in 1954, with the creation of the Front de libération nationale (FLN), Pontecorvo shows how the nationalists led by Saâdi Yacef finally took the battle to the French in the Algerian capital in 1957. We follow Yacef and his agents as they organize revolutionary networks and turn to people of all kinds to do so—men and women, young and old, rich and poor. Unable to cope, the French government brings in the paratroopers. As these elite soldiers march down the main street of Algiers, throngs of ecstatic settlers come out to greet them, relieved that the army will keep Algeria French. At the head of the parade walks one Colonel Mathieu. We follow him and his soldiers as they track down and torture FLN operatives and methodically dismantle their urban cells. Mathieu wins the battle of Algiers; Yacef goes to prison. But Pontecorvo leaves no doubt as to who will win in the end: the film closes with the "people" rising up from the Casbah, the Algerian soul of the nation-in-arms.

It is a masterpiece, filmed in grainy black-and-white shots that give it a powerful realism. But the story Pontecorvo tells of urban warfare in a time of decolonization was anything but a new one. Over a decade before the FLN set off bombs in Algiers, the Vietnamese had already fought major battles in Saigon, Haiphong, and Hanoi. And they were brutal affairs. The French used tanks, artillery, and bombers to blast Vietnamese urban positions. From the port outside Haiphong in November 1946, warships shelled the city with their guns. As the French turned their attention to Hanoi, Ho Chi Minh ordered civilians out of the city, but asked his armed forces to hold the capital for as long as they could when full-scale war broke out a few weeks later. They did, for two months in Hanoi, longer still in Nam Dinh, located south of there. House by house, street by street, Vietnamese partisans fought French commandos. By the end of the battle, Hanoi's "Casbah," the Old Quarter (Khu pho co in Vietnamese), lay in ruins. What is striking is that the Battle of Hanoi remains largely unknown outside Vietnam. Although everyone knows the story of how the Vietnamese ended the war in Indochina by defeating the French on an open valley floor in Dien Bien Phu in 1954, few realize that this conflict started in the cities, precisely where it would end when Saigon fell in 1975.[1]

The Battle of Hanoi

On 2 September 1945, in Hanoi, Ho Chi Minh declared the independence of Vietnam and the birth of the Democratic Republic of Vietnam. Celebrations of this historic event occurred in Saigon in the south and in the imperial capital of Hue in central Vietnam. With French colonial troops and administrators still languishing in camps where the Japanese had put them in March and with the Japanese now having surrendered to the Allies in August, the Vietnamese took control of all their cities for the first time since the nineteenth century. (Nothing of the sort occurred in Algeria where the French had remained in charge of their North African empire during the Second World War.) Nationalist leaders in Vietnam were thus in a better position to get started building a new nation-state and lost no time in assuming the levers of power. Working from the former governor general's palace in Hanoi, President Ho Chi Minh focused on solving the country's most pressing problems—the arrival of the Allies to accept the Japanese surrender; negotiations with the French who were determined to recover their empire;

and ending a deadly famine in the countryside. The new government took charge of ministries, radio stations, printing presses, power plants, hospitals, and schools in urban centers across the country. Meanwhile, some 30,000 French settlers, concentrated mainly in the southern commercial hub of Saigon and, to a lesser extent, the capital of Hanoi, could only hope that the arrival of the Allies and the French Expeditionary Corps would restore the colonial order to its prewar hierarchy with them back on top. For the time being though, they watched from their windows and balconies as the unthinkable unfolded around them— the colonized were administering their own country without the colonizers.

The Allies did arrive, but they did so with very different effects on northern, central, and southern cities. In the south, we know, British troops began debarking in Saigon in early September with orders to free Allied prisoners of war and to accept the Japanese surrender in Indochina below the 16th parallel. Spread thinly, British troops did their best to keep order as relations between the large French settler community and the Vietnamese deteriorated. On 22–3 September, the British commander, General Douglas Gracey, freed Japanese-interned French colonial troops and authorized them to retake Saigon from officials of the Democratic Republic of Vietnam. Gracey did this thinking that these troops would help him reestablish order. But things turned immediately ugly when French settlers joined colonial troops to vent months of pent-up frustration and humiliation on the "natives." They seized upon the Vietnamese in the streets of Saigon, hauling many off, vigilante-style, to shocked British authorities.[2]

Vietnamese forces immediately retaliated with violent attacks on colonial troops, Allied positions, and the settler community in and around Saigon. Partisans committed a horrible massacre in the Cité Hérault quarter of Saigon, killing around a hundred French settlers and Eurasians and carrying off dozens of others. "Saigon was in flames," is how one Dutch war correspondent described the situation as she flew out of the city in late September.[3] Gracey ordered the colonial troops back to their barracks and turned to his Indian Gurkas and Japanese soldiers to help him maintain order in their place. Two weeks later, the French

Expeditionary Corps led by General Philippe Leclerc landed its first troops in Saigon and began to repel the Vietnamese attackers away from Saigon before fanning out into the countryside to take control of roads, railways, bridges, and provincial towns. Unlike in North Africa, the French had to reconquer Indochina after the Second World War, and that meant retaking the urban centers in a strange replay of what they had done in the nineteenth century. (See Plate 10.)

The situation was different in cities located above the 16th parallel. There, Chiang Kai-shek's troops had begun arriving on 8 September. Unlike their British counterparts, Chinese officers blocked French efforts to return by force. Having seen the chaos Gracey had unleashed in the south by rearming the French, the Chinese commander, Lou Han, was reluctant to trigger such a destabilizing colonial war on his watch. He refused to free French colonial troops from their Japanese camps in the north until an accord had been reached with Paris. As a result, Ho Chi Minh's Republic continued to administer the cities and towns in central and northern Vietnam free of colonial molestation. While the Sino-French and Franco-Vietnamese accords signed in February and March 1946 respectively allowed the French to secure the eventual withdrawal of the Chinese and begin stationing a limited number of their troops in their place, the French could not attack the DRV directly above the 16th parallel until all the Chinese troops had left.

With the Chinese gone by September 1946, that changed. In November, they moved on their first city in the north when they claimed the right to collect customs duties in the port of Haiphong. The Vietnamese refused, insisting it was an encroachment on their national sovereignty. Convinced that force would solve the problem, the head of the French government, Georges Bidault, had already authorized the navy to shell Haiphong to bring the Vietnamese to heel (*faire tirer le canon*). In a show of gunboat diplomacy that would have been unthinkable in Algiers a decade later, on 23–4 November 1946 colonial warships fired shells into the Vietnamese and Chinese quarters of Haiphong. Armored units then went in with French infantry units behind them while aircraft strafed from above. French troops easily dislodged badly organized militias but did so with little regard for the safety of civilians. The colonial seizure of this port city and outlying areas was a violent affair. When refugees fled the city seeking shelter in nearby Kien An, the French shelled them too. In all, the mayor of Haiphong later told an American journalist, at least 1,000 Vietnamese died, mostly civilians. Others have put the number of dead well above that.[4]

Having secured Haiphong, the French then focused their attention on the capital, Hanoi, and the remaining cities located above the 16th parallel like Nam Dinh, Hue, and Da Nang. That the capital was the site where a full-scale war for Vietnam began should come as no surprise. Nationalist leaders were as determined to hold on to Hanoi as their colonial opponents were to recover it. It held obvious political value for both sides. There were other reasons, though. For one, the heavy-handed French occupation of Haiphong in November had left the impression that the Vietnamese government could not or would not do much concretely to protect its citizens. The leadership wanted to send a clear message to its people that it was willing to fight. The last thing Ho wanted was to lose popular support at this critical juncture in the republic's fragile existence. Secondly, the Vietnamese knew that they would be unable to hold the capital indefinitely in the event of war. Taking a stand in Hanoi would serve to pin down the enemy while the leadership would make its own "Long March" to bases in the jungles of northern and central Vietnam. Thirdly, an urban battle would draw international attention to the struggle of the Vietnamese people against old-fashioned colonial conquest. Foreign diplomats and correspondents from such major newspapers as the *New York Times* and *Le Monde* were covering events in Vietnam and had been meeting with Ho Chi Minh in Hanoi. From the start, the Vietnamese were keenly aware of the importance of influencing international opinion through the modern media. Lastly, intimate knowledge of the capital emboldened the communist core of the young republic to take a stand. The Indochinese Communist Party had run underground networks in colonial cities since its creation in 1930. The interim head of the Communist Party, Truong Chinh, had grown up near the capital and had been active there since the 1930s. He organized the party's clandestine activities in Hanoi during the Second World War. Working with him were such important leaders as Tran Quoc Hoan, "Vietnam's Saâdi Yacef" if you will. This powerful communist ran the party's secret services in Hanoi during the Battle of Hanoi and for most of the Indochina War.[5]

It is true that Ho Chi Minh did not want war; but, backed into a corner by the French, he and his Communist Party prepared for it.[6] The result was that while the president did everything he could to reach a negotiated settlement with the French government, he and his entourage developed battle plans for holding Hanoi against a probable French assault on the capital like that of Saigon. Starting in mid-1946, Vietnamese leaders studied what they knew of how the Soviets had fought at Stalingrad. They noted how southerners had created and used barricades during their clashes with the French a year earlier. They analyzed what had gone wrong in Saigon in 1945 and in Haiphong more recently. The General Staff put Vuong Thua Vu—a seasoned military man trained in the Chinese republican army, a native of Hanoi, and now a trusted communist—in charge of devising a battle plan for the capital. He went to work immediately, inspecting the city, recruiting a range of agents, and training militias. Tran Quoc Hoan assisted him from behind the scenes. All of this was well timed, as relations between the French and the Vietnamese deteriorated rapidly after Ho's return from France, empty-handed, in the fall of 1946. The French had balked at moving forward with the unification of Vietnam, as had been promised, and insisted on rebuilding the Indochinese federation instead of recognizing Vietnamese aspirations for independence. By mid-October 1946, the party concluded that "sooner or later" the French would attack and the Vietnamese had to be ready to adopt an armed line, not just in the south, but throughout Vietnam.[7]

All the same, the situation was complicated. Since the signature of the March Accords of 1946, and an accompanying military annex a few weeks later, the French had acquired the right to station 15,000 troops above the 16th parallel to replace the departing Chinese contingent, which, of course, they then did. This meant that one government, the Democratic Republic of Vietnam, and two armies, its own and the French one, operated in a delicate balancing act in central and northern Vietnam, with the French directing their troops from the high commissioner's office in Saigon. Both sides agreed to maintain order through the creation of joint military commissions in the main cities and towns until their governments could resolve their outstanding political issues. On the ground, the Vietnamese army had around 2,500 regular troops on active duty in Hanoi, backed by a 10,000-strong militia force. The rest of the DRV's regular army was spread around the country, stationed in larger cities like Hue, Nam Dinh, and Haiphong. In all, it numbered about 80,000 troops. The French meanwhile could count on 6,000 well-armed and trained Expeditionary Corps—crack troops—to take up positions in Hanoi. Ten thousand more were scattered thinly across the rest of upper Vietnam, mainly in the towns and at strategic points on the roads connecting them. Armored vehicles, tanks, artillery, and machine-gun-equipped Spitfire planes backed them up. From the port of Haiphong, the French navy patrolled the Gulf of Tonkin coastline. Commanders also armed the French community in Hanoi and allowed them to run small militias. The same was true in other towns with French populations.[8]

Hanoi proper and its outlying villages covered about 150 square kilometers. Residing in the suburbs were over 200,000 overwhelmingly Vietnamese inhabitants. Around 40,000 people lived in Hanoi proper. Besides the Vietnamese majority, there were around 10,000 Chinese, 2,000 French settlers, and perhaps a hundred (British) Indians. The downtown area was home to government buildings, factories, shops, and several markets. On the northeastern side of the city was the bustling Vietnamese Old Quarter centered around the Dong Xuan Market. The neighborhood was and remains famous for its narrow, winding streets lined with a host of boutiques, shops, small restaurants, and street vendors. The Old Quarter's streets had long specialized in one specific type of manufacturing or commerce (silk, dyes, etc.). This is also where the bulk of the Vietnamese and Chinese populations resided at the time.[9] (See Map 8.)

The government's militia forces patrolled Hanoi and its suburbs. Since taking power in August 1945, the DRV had created three main militia groups in Hanoi: the Hoang Dieu Fighting Militia Force, the Hoang Dieu City Militia, and the Industrial Workers Militia. In August 1946, the government combined these three elements into the Hanoi Youth Militia Corps, which operated in the city and numbered about 9,000 individuals in all. In the outlying areas, the government counted on the Suburban People's Armed Militia for support. In all, in December 1946, the militia inside Hanoi numbered around 10,000 individuals. Backing them up were around 1,000–2,000 regular troops consisting of a couple of battalions, no more. Equipped with a few colonial-era artillery guns, light machine guns, bazookas, and mortars, the regular troops had orders to stop the French from rushing reinforcements into the city. All of these forces, the militias and regular troops, answered to Vuong Thua Vu.[10]

But could the Vietnamese pin down the French in Hanoi long enough to allow the government to get away and send a convincing message of defiance at the same time? The loss of Haiphong a month earlier was hardly encouraging. Young militiamen and women ran on high levels of patriotism. On that everyone agreed. But those in charge knew that they were also poorly trained and woefully underarmed. Discipline was lacking. Few had any combat experience. During a meeting held in mid-December, Ho Chi Minh, Truong Chinh, Vo Nguyen Giap, and the army's chief of staff, Hoang Van Thai, discussed this matter at length. The president pointedly asked his colleagues: "If war were to break out, for how long could we hold Hanoi?" A wall of silence apparently met his question. So, he repeated it, no doubt wondering whether republican forces could even hold the capital for more than a few days. His men consulted each other before finally promising the president that they could do it. But there was no real guarantee that they would do any better than their counterparts had in Haiphong or Saigon before them. They knew that the Expeditionary Corps, whatever its problems were on coming out of the Second World War, was no pushover. And the French use of massive firepower at Haiphong must have been on the minds of those attending that meeting. It certainly explains why the government had already ordered civilians to begin evacuating the capital by early December.[11]

Following the French conquest of Haiphong, tensions spread rapidly to Hanoi and the other northern towns, where French and Vietnamese sentries now eyed each other warily from opposite sides of the streets. Commanding officers meeting in the mixed commissions struggled to rein in their troops as violent incidents multiplied, tempers flared, and mutual confidence hit new lows. It was in this tense atmosphere that, on 13 December 1946, Vuong Thua Vu's final battle plan received the leadership's approval. He posted people to defend the government buildings, industrial plants, and thoroughfares that the French army would try to seize first if hostilities broke out. As the enemy advanced, the plan went, the militia would then fall back to the Old Quarter, while the regular army would do its best to stop the French from bringing in reinforcements from the Gia Lam Airfield (a military base located on the opposite side of the Red River) and from further up the road in Haiphong. The militia would then exploit the maze of narrow streets and alleys of the Old Quarter to bog the enemy down for as long as possible before withdrawing across the Red River themselves.

Like the Casbah in Algiers, the Old Quarter was Ground Zero for the Battle of Hanoi. (A heroic monument dedicated to the event marks the entry into the old town at Dinh Tien Hoang Street today.) In the weeks leading up to full-scale hostilities, Vuong Thua Vu's team had organized a labyrinth of relays and safe houses in the Old Quarter, stashed supplies and arms underneath floors, and recruited messengers and guides who knew the neighborhood by heart. They made openings in house and shop walls to connect one unit to another so that partisans could move along streets without actually entering them and thereby exposing themselves to enemy fire. They placed barricades in the narrow streets of the Old Quarter to prevent tanks, armored vehicles, and enemy troops from advancing easily. The government requisitioned houses and emptied their contents into the streets. Mountains of furniture, felled trees, and debris were strewn across the city in the days leading up to war. French and Vietnamese snipers took up their positions. When the lights finally went out on the evening of the 19th December,[12] the signal for the Vietnamese to attack, some 2,000 fighters, men, women, and children, scurried into this rabbit warren of interconnected houses, shops, back alleys, and buildings. This "barricading of the streets" (*chien luy duong pho*) and cat-and-mouse tactics would encumber the French as the Vietnamese General Staff officers sought to make good on their pledge to hold the capital's Old Quarter for at least a month. Meanwhile, orders had already gone out to authorities elsewhere above the 16th parallel to hold urban centers for as long as possible, most notably in Hue, Vinh, Da Nang, and Nam Dinh.[13]

Urban warfare was hardly a Vietnamese invention. Only a few years earlier, Soviet militias and troops had tied down the Nazis in ferocious fighting for Stalingrad. In Shanghai in 1937, Chinese republican soldiers had fought a bloody urban battle against the invading Japanese army. Many of the French soldiers in the Expeditionary Corps had themselves dislodged the Nazis holed up in French and German towns in house-to-house warfare only a couple of years earlier (and, in fact, some in the French Foreign Legion were ex-Nazis). What was novel in Indochina was that the Vietnamese were now using the model to fight a war of decolonization. The French complained that by barricading the roads and evacuating civilians, the Vietnamese were preparing for war. Of course they were. And any French military commander worth his mettle would have done exactly the same thing had he found himself in the Vietnamese position during the Second World War in charge of, say, defending Paris or Lyon against foreign invasion. With their backs against the wall since Haiphong, the Vietnamese moved to attack the French in Hanoi on the evening of 19 December 1946. Unlike in the nineteenth century, there would be no capitulation this time. "*Non, mon commandant*," Ho Chi Minh's chief diplomat had said a few days earlier to his French counterpart, "It is no longer possible."[14] The Vietnamese were going to make the French pay for retaking the capital and other towns in a way which they had not in the 1880s.

That said, things hardly went as planned once the shooting started that evening. Many in the militias scattered and ran. Of the estimated 10,000 enrolled in its ranks, probably only 2,000 individuals actually participated in the battle. That number would dwindle to a couple of hundred towards the end of the fighting. Vietnamese demolitionists failed to sabotage the Paul Doumer Bridge to stop the French from rushing in troops from across the Red River. Nor did their commandos succeed in taking over the Gia Lam military airbase or destroying any of the Spitfire planes sitting on its tarmac (despite later propaganda spouting the contrary). While they did their best, regular troops were no match for the French army and its air force once the firing of Vietnamese artillery guns had given away their positions. The French quickly took control of the main routes connecting Hanoi to the outside, hustling soldiers to the capital from Haiphong and Langson. Unfettered control of the Gia Lam Airbase allowed the French to fly in troops, arms, and supplies from Saigon. It also allowed them to bomb and shell Vietnamese positions in Hanoi with impunity.[15] The Expeditionary Corps rapidly secured the French quarter in Hanoi and took control of the main arteries and administrative buildings of the capital, including the presidential palace. But not before Vietnamese partisans, with or without government approval, had massacred dozens of French civilians in Hanoi in horrific ways all too reminiscent of what had happened in Saigon a year earlier. Michel L'Herpinière, a young French settler sympathetic to Vietnamese independence aspirations, was never the same after finding his friends, including their young children, lying dead in pools of blood. A few days earlier, French soldiers had killed twenty Vietnamese civilians, including women and children, on Yen Ninh Street.[16]

Powerful and profound emotions began to blow through the city—fear, grief, and most destructive of all, vengeance. The latter quickly allowed war to start doing its dirty work by dehumanizing the "other" and casting hate in racialized terms. As one French settler in Hanoi reported to *Le Monde* in the heat of the moment:

> Morale remains very high and, after the humiliation of 9 March 1945, the French have even greater amounts of courage needed to smash an organized banditry . . . which has been able to fool the entire world with a mask of loyal collaboration but was at the same time slowly and surely organizing the extermination not only of the French but of all the whites in general.[17]

The Vietnamese were no longer a people; they were "bandits." And the Vietnamese used a remarkably similar term to dehumanize the French—*giac* or "pirates," which can also mean "bandits." In translation, it is hard to capture the feelings swirling behind these words and their use at the time; but at the core meaning of each was one common denominator—seething hate. One young French soldier who had lost a friend in the fighting in Hanoi declared to a confidant what he wanted to do to the "Vietnamese": "We have to destroy all of them, without any pity for them; they're real savages . . ."[18] And this is how very bad things can happen, committed by people who, in peacetime, whether Vietnamese or French, had been perfectly good souls. A young left-wing French officer who had fought against the Nazis during the Second World War could not believe his eyes when his comrades took a captured Vietnamese militiaman to a hangar at the Gia Lam Airbase. There his French and Vietnamese captors attached him to the "*gégène*" (the military slang term for the radio "*gen*erators" torturers rewired during the Indochina War) to administer "shock therapy" to this man (via his penis) and to too many others after him. Torture got way out of control in the French army years before paratroopers ever set foot in Algiers.[19]

Convinced they could reestablish order quickly, the French wanted to reoccupy Hanoi and the rest of Vietnam fast, starting with the cities. In accordance with laws passed in 1849 to suppress "internal disorders" of a revolutionary kind in France, the government declared an *Etat de siège* as the army went on the offensive in Hanoi.[20] This legally binding state of siege effectively authorized the conquering forces to bring the remainder of Indochina under French sovereignty and administer it until civilian authorities could take over. The siege included the implementation of martial law, the arrest of "rebels," and the organization of military tribunals. The French government had already ceded increased policing and judiciary powers to its military officers in southern Indochina. Settlers welcomed all of this and turned out in droves to welcome the soldiers liberating them from "native" rule in Saigon, Hanoi, Hue, and elsewhere. It was also the start of a process that would repeat itself in Algeria as the French army came to play an increasingly political role in France's long "Indo-Algerian War of Decolonization" (1945–62) and joined in a closer alliance with settler communities in Indochina and North Africa.[21]

By early January 1947, the French army had taken control of most of the capital, except for the maze of streets, houses, and shops making up the Old Quarter of Hanoi with the Dong Xuan Market nestled at its center. Pinned down in this part of town were 20,000 Vietnamese civilians and 10,000 Chinese. Joining them were hundreds of the republic's militiamen and women, who were not coming out without a fight. On 27 December 1946 the French had attempted to penetrate this area but failed at the price of fifteen dead and thirty injured. The commander-in-chief of the Expeditionary Corps in Indochina, General Jean Valluy, called for a demonstration of force along the lines Bidault had approved for Haiphong. Valluy instructed his officer in charge of Hanoi, General Louis-Constant Morlière, to "hit them hard with the cannon and the bomb . . . in order to put an end to [the resistance] and to prove to our adversary the overwhelming superiority of our capabilities." Morlière saw things differently. Rather than level the Old Quarter at the cost of hundreds of civilian lives, he imposed a blockade around it, intentionally leaving an outlet for people to escape.[22]

More than anything though, it was the decision taken by the head of the Republic of China's consul in Hanoi, Yuan Zi Jian, to protect the Chinese community caught in the crossfire that allowed the Vietnamese to hold the city long enough for Ho and his entourage to get away. Having been directly involved in trying to protect the large Chinese community in Haiphong a few weeks earlier, the consul knew that the French army had no qualms about using massive firepower to take a city. He immediately called for a pause in the fighting, so that he could evacuate his nationals before things took a turn for the worse. Trevor Wilson and James O'Sullivan, his British and American counterparts respectively, agreed. On 15 January 1947, thanks to a truce brokered by these three consuls, thousands of civilians—Chinese, Vietnamese, and a handful of British Indian nationals—evacuated the besieged Old Quarter. On the 15th alone 6,000 women, children, and elderly Vietnamese, as well as around 500 Chinese, left the city. About a week later, an additional 3,000 Chinese and 200 more elderly and sick Vietnamese left the town.[23]

Meanwhile, the Vietnamese General Staff attempted to unite the disparate forces holed up there under the command of Vuong Thua Vu. The "capital regiment," as it was grandiosely called, came to life in the

Old Quarter on 12 January under this man's command. In all, it numbered over 1,000 male and female militia fighters, badly armed, but committed to bogging down the French until the order to evacuate came. A few regular combatants might have been mixed in. As for the others, several hundred had perished. Just as many had slipped away with refugees during the truce, while the remainder melded into the population or escaped through Morlière's humane back-door exit and across the Red River.[24]

The reprieve in the fighting ended around 1 February 1947, as did Morlière's command. Replacing him was none other than Colonel Pierre Debès, the man who had commanded the seizure of Haiphong. Like his superiors, Debès' preferred method in this second colonial conquest of Hanoi was to use a lot of force. In early February, he sent his troops into the old town's maze of streets behind armored carriers to destroy the resistance. He called in artillery and air strikes and sent in tanks and bulldozers to clear the historic center—something which the French would carefully refrain from doing during the Battle of Algiers. Whereas Colonel Mathieu in Pontecorvo's fictive Battle of Algiers would plead with the last "rebel," Ali La Pointe, to give himself up before he dynamited the room in which the young Algerian bandit-turned-patriot was hiding in the Casbah, Debès and Valluy shelled the old town in Hanoi, leaving much of it in a pile of rubble. It was not a movie. If anything, it came straight out of the playbook of the Second World War's destruction. Of the capital's 13,191 houses, 2,837 were destroyed.[25] (See Plate 11.)

Although the fighting during the Battle of Hanoi was sporadic, combat was often intense as French soldiers had to go house by house to eliminate all resistance. Belligerents caught glimpses of each other as they darted back and forth across the barricades lining many of the Old Quarter's narrow streets. The fighting for the Dong Xuan Market was apparently ferocious. Meanwhile, French planes bombed Vietnamese positions while artillery fired shells into the city. Duong Van Mai Elliott, a child at the time, described later in her memoirs how her two older brothers, militiamen, first encountered combat during the Battle of Hanoi:

Suddenly, being in the militia was no longer just fun and games for my brothers Giu and Xuong, no longer just marches and drills with spears. Their militia unit buried its first casualty when French snipers shot a squad leader as he climbed up a flagpole to display the Viet Minh banner. Right after that incident, a messenger arrived with the news that French troops stationed in the Lanessan hospital near our house were getting ready for an assault, supported with lots of tanks. The messenger told the militia unit to withdraw that night, under the cover of darkness. But the French attack came before nightfall, with airplanes and tanks strafing the Viet Minh troops' barracks near the dike. After the bombardment, French paratroopers advanced into the neighborhood from three directions, with fierce shouts of *"En avant!"* There was no return fire from the Viet Minh regulars, who had secretly and hastily withdrawn, leaving the militiamen to fend for themselves. . . . That night, the Viet Minh sneaked back and opened fire on French positions. No damage was done, but the attack angered the French. The next day, they stormed back with German shepherds to search the neighborhood. The streets echoed with the furious barking of the dogs, the crunching of French boots, and the angry voices of the soldiers, who were spoiling for retaliation.[26]

By early February, bulldozers were clearing the barricades and the rubble blocking their way. French troops advanced slowly but surely as the militia forces retreated to areas near the Red River, waiting for the order to evacuate. The order finally came on 18 February 1947. Under the cover of night, the men and women of the capital regiment crossed under the Doumer Bridge and left Hanoi.[27]

In his call to resistance on 20 December 1946, Ho Chi Minh had exhorted young and old, men and women, to pick up whatever they had to fight the invading forces: "Those who have rifles will use their rifles; those who have swords will use their swords; those who have no swords will use spades, hoes, or sticks. Everyone must endeavor to oppose the French colonialists and save his country!"[28] Given that the DRV withdrew most of its regular troops early in the battle and pinned its hopes on the militia forces, combat necessarily fell on the shoulders of those who had the least preparation for it—civilians. Like so many others before them during the Second World War, the Vietnamese relied on people with little or no military training to help delay the forces bearing down upon them all.

During the Battle of Hanoi, Vietnamese authorities expanded the use of civilians for wartime purposes to include children. Nowhere was this more evident than in the creation of the "Children's Guard" (*Ve Ut*). It consisted of 175 children, many of whom the famine of 1944–5 orphaned. The army did not recruit them to fight as combatants per se. It was their knowledge of the urban topography (backstreets, alleys, markets, and bridges) that made them invaluable guides, messengers, and scouts. As a result, they were integrated into the regular army and militia's operations. Aged between eight and fourteen, a dozen or so worked for the capital regiment. Among these, one, Vu Trong Phung, was ten years old and another, Nguyen Van Phuc, was eight. Huong Van Ba joined the army in Hanoi when he was just thirteen.[29] In 1988, the writer, Phung Quan, opened up this universe to his readers in a popular patriotic, semi-autobiographical novel, *A Fierce Childhood* (*Thoi tho du doi*). In it, he follows a group of twelve-year-olds whose baptism in fire during the Battle of Hue of 1946–7 was only the beginning of their memorable childhoods. Phung Quan joined the army as a child scout in Hue in 1945. He was thirteen.[30] Of course, using children in wartime was not a "Vietnamese" or an "Asian" phenomenon. One has only to think of the dangers drummer boys and young messengers endured during the American Civil War (the youngest in the Union army was nine).[31]

The problem, whether in Vietnam in the late 1940s or the United States in the early 1860s, is that these children often ended up in the line of fire. In Hanoi, most hustled messages into and out of the city. A few administered basic first aid to the wounded. Some lobbed a few grenades in front of unsuspecting tank drivers entering narrow Hanoi streets. Several got killed when enemy soldiers took no chances. In all, the Children's Guard lost over twenty young ones when the capital regiment finally pulled out of Hanoi in February 1947. Vietnamese studies confirm that during the battle of Hanoi children "accompanied" troops and militia "during assaults to destroy secret enemy pockets of resistance." As one official history reads: "One member of a unit, a child named Luong, died heroically during a battle to defend the liquor-making factory on Sergent Larivée Street."[32]

No one should question little Luong's courage, but the death of children in battle was not such a glorious thing. Recalling her attempt to escape Hue with a schoolmate on 20 December 1946, as the French opened fire on the imperial capital of Vietnam, a then seventeen-year-old Xuan Phuong captured poignantly the tragedy of children who got caught in the line of fire:

> We had to ford a river in order to get to the school located on the other side, climbed a bank, and then crossed a road before getting to the hedge. The French controlled the road from buildings that they were occupying. Once we had struggled up the bank, we were to wait for them to fire before crossing the road. I held hands with Le Khac Tinh, a boy in my class. He murmured: 'At the count of three, go!' Together, we crossed the road and jumped into the hedge. I saw him double over and fall down. 'Are you hurt?' He didn't answer. Something slimy began to drip on my hand and I understood that he had been killed. This death marked the end of my adolescence.[33]

There is no reason to doubt her words. And there is no reason to think that this type of traumatic experience did not sow the seeds of hate as destructive and as psychologically transformative as the one expressed by the terrified French settler above who described the Vietnamese as "real savages." This then too was the Vietnamese war state as it took off for the countryside. Powerful emotions would blow through it from start to finish. In all, the French colonial reconquest of Vietnamese urban centers between September 1945 and April 1947 cost the lives of at least 5,000 Vietnamese and probably 1,000 French, civilians and combatants combined.

The City in the Countryside

If the line between civilians and combatants was never a clear-cut one during the Battle of Hanoi, the distinction between the city and the surrounding countryside was just as blurred. Even before full-scale war broke out this was the case. The presence of the Republic of China's troops in central and northern Vietnam had not only allowed the Democratic Republic of Vietnam to operate freely in cities above the 16th parallel for over a year, it had also allowed the leadership to begin transferring the government, its ministries, civil servants, and files to the countryside before the French had actually attacked (something which southerners were largely unable to do). In northern and central cities, during the summer of 1946, as war with the French became increasingly likely, republican authorities began emptying the cities of the things which they would need to operate from the countryside—radios, telephones, generators, motors, spare parts, and fuel. They confiscated vaccines, medicines, and equipment from the Pasteur Institute and a host of colonial hospitals, clinics, and pharmacies. They drafted as many doctors and nurses to the army as possible and even transferred much of the French medical school (the Faculté de medicine at the University of Hanoi) to the countryside. Agents secretly removed Dr. Ton That Tung's medical library from Hanoi. Evacuated too were printing presses, paper, and ink, without which there would have been no circulation of information, no functional bureaucracy, no real education system, or propaganda. At the outset, even the armaments industry operating in the maquis during the conflict depended largely on seized machinery, spare parts, and chemicals of urban origin. As the French moved in on Hanoi, the Vietnamese trucked off the Voice of Vietnam transmitter. In short, nationalists took with them as much of the colonial city as they could carry. In all, one study says, the Vietnamese evacuated around 40,000 tons of machinery and materials from the cities.[34]

Of course, this symbiotic relationship between the city and the countryside did not cease with the colonial reoccupation of Hanoi, Hue, or Saigon. The rural-based republic would always need the colonial city: medicines ran out quickly in wartime, ink dried up, paper supplies dwindled, machines broke, and more than one bureaucrat, soldier, or worker lost heart and went home. Things and people had to be replaced. Holed up in the hills of northern Vietnam, cut off in central Vietnam's plains, and bogged down in the insalubrious marshes of the Mekong Delta, officials were constantly on the lookout for radios, paper, and medicines. Clandestine trade with Asian markets helped provide such things, as we know, but it was never enough. This only changed in northern Vietnam from 1950 onwards, when the Chinese and, to a lesser degree, the Soviets began supplying the Vietnamese with such necessary materials via southern China. But this communist foreign assistance only trickled into central zones, and it never reached the south, making continued access to the colonial enemy's cities a top priority for authorities in central and southern Vietnam until 1954—and right through the war against the Americans for the southerners.[35]

This is why we should be careful not to accept at face value claims that the Vietnamese systematically practiced scorched-earth tactics (*vuong khong, nha trong*) upon evacuating the cities throughout the conflict until its end in 1954. The Communist Party gave orders to this effect, and the leadership did indeed have things razed to the ground so as to deny them to the enemy, especially when withdrawing from cities above the 16th parallel in early 1947. But in war, theory and practice are always two different things, and few rules are "systematically" applied over long periods of time. The interim head of the Communist Party, Truong Chinh, issued orders in late 1946 that scorched-earth tactics had to be used carefully and methodically so as not to destroy things that would be useful to keeping the republic up and running.[36]

As a result, urban soldiers quickly learned how to target their terrorist attacks with laser-like precision. General Nguyen Binh may have authorized the sabotage of enemy military installations in Saigon and had no qualms about ordering the assassination of French and Vietnamese adversaries. But southerners, like their counterparts elsewhere in Vietnam, intentionally excluded colonial pharmacies, hospitals, printing shops, and paper mills from their hit lists. Soft intimidation and hard cash were often more effective in securing market access than brute force or spectacular explosions. Protection money generated in the form of government taxes on urban-based traders provided hard currency to purchase imports for the rural-based war state. During 1948 alone, such taxes in Saigon-Cholon generated a tidy 340,000 French Indochinese piasters for the southern resistance.[37]

Undercover operatives received orders early on to cultivate relations with Western, Asian, and Vietnamese businessmen and women. Deals were cut with Chinese merchants in urban centers like Cholon and Haiphong. They helped the Democratic Republic of Vietnam run its clandestine rice trade with the colonial cities and the surrounding Asian region. Vietnamese authorities reached agreements with the owners of the biggest gambling casino in Saigon at the time, Le Grand Monde. Ideology counted for little in these urban interstices. If these people paid their "patriotic dues" on time, then everyone could get along just fine. Lucien Bodard, a longtime French war correspondent during the Indochina War and fine observer of Saigon's rougher sides, was convinced of it:

> Capitalism is so important to the Vietnamese that they are careful not to destroy it. To do so would be a terrible blow to them! Nothing is currently stopping them from burning all the trucks on the road, killing more of the French in Saigon, and placing mines and bombs anywhere they want. It would be easy for them to paralyze [Saigon's] economic life. And yet they do not do it. They have even gone as far as to organize self-criticism sessions on the "incorrect solution" of wide-scale destruction.[38]

One Saigon-based undercover agent even went so far as to claim that he operated in the city because his government "need[ed] French colonialism." There was a grain of truth in this. Indeed, the colonial cities remained essential to the Democratic Republic of Vietnam's foreign trade throughout the entire Indochina War. Vietnamese agents were constantly on the lookout for the paper and ink required to ensure the continued operation of printing presses; the medicine and antibiotics needed to keep the war state's personnel, leadership, and troops healthy; the hard-to-find radio parts to guarantee real time communications; and the typewriters essential to putting words on paper. The functioning of the bureaucracy depended on it. Sick soldiers cannot fight. Colonial security services reported that between June and August 1948, 9 million units of penicillin, 200,000 packets of Dagenan (an antibiotic) and 60,000 pills of premaline and quinacrine (both antimalaria medicines) disappeared from Saigon-Cholon drugstore shelves.

Another report concluded in mid-1947 that "most" Vietnamese pharmacists in the Saigon-Cholon region were "supplying the rebels in pharmaceuticals either out of sympathy for the Viet Minh or in fear of them."[39] Even footwear for civil servants and soldiers was high on the DRV's export list. In 1952, a French intelligence officer complained to his superiors:

> For several months now traffic in sandals is going on between Tourane [Da Nang] and the rebel zone. Made of used tires, these sandals are identical to those used by Viet Minh troops. Almost everyday, on the borders of the [French] controlled zones, our patrols arrest Vietnamese transporting relatively important quantities of these sandals. Lately, a stock of 600 pairs of sandals was discovered in Tourane itself, while the owner was preparing to send them into the non-controlled zone [meaning the DRV].[40]

The government operated special "supply sections" called *tiep lieu*. Located just outside the colonial cities, agents in these offices took orders from the armed forces and the resistance administration authorities. The supply section for Hue, for example, received orders from its delegates in nearby DRV zones. Women itinerant traders transported goods such as pharmaceutical products, office supplies, and clothing out of the city to the supply sections. They carried orders back in to trusted intermediaries working in the cities. In 1951, far from the Chinese communist aid flowing into the north, Pham Van Dong authorized provincial officials in central Vietnam to organize special zones bordering the enemy ones to better administer the government's foreign trade. He urged local authorities to increase exports as much as possible in order to lower the government's chronic trade deficit with French Indochina.[41]

Authorities also exported people from the cities who could help them run the state from the countryside. From start to finish, Ho Chi Minh needed a host of literate civil servants, officers, medical personnel, and specialized workers. They pushed paper in the ministries, commanded battalions, manned radios, and worked in weapons workshops, clinics, and hospitals. This was particularly the case in the south, where leaders never had the time to recruit such essential personnel before the war started. From the beginning, southerners organized elaborate networks to bring people out of the city to the maquis. By 1947, the government in the south had welcomed more than 5,000 patriotic civil servants and intellectuals and 1,000 skilled workers into its ranks. Child scouts went into the cities to deliver letters to nationalist elites urging them to join the resistance. The rallying to the DRV of the engineer Dang Phuc Thong, the surgeon Dr. Nguyen Van Huong, and Bao Dai's former royal secretary, Pham Khac Hoe, were not only propaganda coups. These noncommunist patriots also provided badly needed technical expertise, services, and legitimacy to the fledgling state. Young guides carefully escorted them into the Vietnamese archipelago along secure resistance pathways few others knew.[42]

That said, patriotism never mobilized a sufficient number of civil servants. Upon abandoning the cities between 1945 and 1947, the government forcibly transferred dozens of specialists and technicians to rural zones in central Vietnam. These included the well-known merchant Pham Le Bong and the colonially trained civil servant Nguyen Tien Lang. The latter's services were so important that the Vietnamese authorities finally freed him from jail in 1948 and put him to work translating French military manuals into Vietnamese for training new cadets in Zone IV. His experience in administrative matters was such that Nguyen Tien Lang even worked as a personal secretary to the military commander of central Vietnam, General Nguyen Son, until he (and Pham Le Bong) defected to the French in 1950.[43]

In the north, the heavy-handed French reoccupation of urban centers sent thousands of city dwellers flooding into the countryside, where the authorities could easily recruit them. And those powerful emotions of revenge discussed elsewhere in this book must have only increased their success rate. How many people left the cities as the French moved in? It is hard to say for sure. Until as late as 1948–9, Hanoi's population may have remained as low as 10,000. If this number represents the fall in the population of Hanoi from a total of around 40,000 people in 1946, this would mean that 30,000 people had fled the capital and had yet to return two years later. Thousands of refugees also streamed out of Saigon, Haiphong, Hue, and Nam Dinh when the French attacked. This was not the last time violence would drive people from the cities into the sur-rounding countryside and even further away.[44]

All of these urbanites brought with them new ideas, styles, and ways of speaking and living to rural villages. Exchanges occurred as displaced city folk had to earn their keep helping those lodging them, whether they were friends, family, or strangers. Everyone had to lend a hand during the planting and harvest seasons. "The Peasant Question," the title of a famous essay written by Vo Nguyen Giap and Truong Chinh in 1938 on the plight of the rural poor, was no longer as abstract as it had been for so many of its urban readers a decade earlier. In fact, war pro-vided urban nationalists at the helm of the rural war state with a close-up, often eye-opening view of what life was like for around 90 percent of the Vietnamese population, the heart and soul of the nation. For some it was an edifying experience. For others it could be a disturbing one. For the patriotic daughter of a Hue mandarin, it was too much. As she confided to a friend in a resistance area located 50 kilometers from the ancient capital: "I can't stand seeing the peasants living like this anymore. I'm going to return to the city. I beg you to come with me."[45] She returned; her friend and confidante, Xuan Phuong, carried on. We met her above and we will meet her again.

Tensions may have also arisen within the countryside as Ho's resis-tance administration and people expanded into rural areas in which male mandarins had run the show for centuries. While I know of no study of the question, it is hard to believe that social and gender prob-lems did not arise as younger urbanites, including women, challenged a male-dominated village mandarin system the French had largely left intact during the colonial period in northern and central Vietnam. What is sure is that knowledge of the Vietnamese Romanized national lan-guage, *quoc ngu*, facilitated the upward mobility of younger urbanites within this rapidly expanding rural-based bureaucracy and army that depended on people literate in Vietnamese, and not classical Chinese or French. Most of the civil servants working in the new DRV capital in Thai Nguyen province in the late 1940s had left Hanoi and other towns upon the outbreak of war in late 1946 and early 1947. They were always highly literate.[46]

The colonial cities provided the rural resistance state with something else it needed badly—information. Modern means of communication and transportation had long connected Hanoi, Hue, and Saigon to the surrounding Asian region, France, and the world. One could buy French, Vietnamese, and international newspapers in these cities. Libraries reopened their doors after the Second World War, including new ones run by the American and British consulates. International newspapers like the *New York Times* and *Le Monde* sent foreign correspondents to Indochina to cover the conflict. The famous British novelist Graham Greene wrote for several British newspapers from his bureau in Saigon before penning his bestselling novel on the Indochina War, *The Quiet American*. Hanoi and Saigon also constituted the locus of colonial power in Indochina. The French high command organized its military operations there. The country's most important air bases were located near Hanoi (at Gia Lam) and Saigon (at Tan Son Nhat). The elaboration of political projects to counter Ho Chi Minh's Vietnam, such as the "Bao Dai solution" and the "Associated State of Vietnam," all emerged in the colonial cities.

Engaged in a war of national liberation with increasingly important international dimensions, Ho Chi Minh and his entourage had to keep abreast of the activities of their French and Vietnamese enemies, the Americans, newly decolonizing countries like Indonesia and India, and international allies, most importantly the Soviets and Chinese communists. Access to information was essential to formulating good diplomacy, devising effective military strategies, and calibrating propaganda to the finest degree. Agents wove a web of relationships with a range of urbanites, ranging from the down-and-out to the well-to-do, doing their best to infiltrate labor unions, student groups, and cultural associations all the while. They recruited a host of "assets" to help them do this. Undercover analysts in Hanoi, Saigon, and elsewhere carefully established reports on the attitudes of the local populations. They bought French, Vietnamese, and foreign newspapers, clipped relevant articles and statistics from them, summarized them, commented on them, and then discreetly sent reports to the government. As one Vietnamese study put it:

> The city's precinct-level public security elements sent hundreds of reports about enemy military activities, political activities, enemy spies, and reactionary political parties back to the city public security headquarters in our base area. Many of these reports contained valuable information that helped us to counter the enemy's efforts to hunt down and arrest our agents and organizations inside the city. Books, magazines, and newspapers that the enemy published inside the city were sent regularly out to the base area. These published materials helped us to analyze and uncover a great deal of valuable information about enemy activities of all kinds, information that directly supported our counter-espionage operations and our efforts to monitor the overall situation.[47]

But to do all of this, the government had to maintain its presence in the French cities. No sooner had the Vietnamese communists in charge evacuated Hanoi and Saigon than the party sent trusted people back in to build up a parallel "underground city," better known in Vietnamese as "special urban zones." One of the first teams the party sent back into Hanoi to begin building its secret services consisted of five children from the "Young Boys Surveillance Squad." Trusted agents followed. Under strict and exclusive communist control, these clandestine cities consisted of a phalanx of loyal cadres who secretly organized information-gathering networks, espionage and counter-espionage operations, trade, and tax services. Working from secure cells, the communists sectored off Hanoi, Hue, Saigon, and other towns into quarters staffed by its people. Trusted party security officials, like Tran Quoc Hoan in Hanoi and Pham Hung in Saigon, directed and expanded these cells through the creation of safe houses; the recruiting of trusted cadres, spies, and scouts; the identification of reliable families and loyal shop and restaurant owners; and by using secure routes.

Although membership in the Communist Party and fierce nationalism were prerequisites for advancement in the underground city, cadres relied on a variety of social relations and people to move things into and

out of the enemy urban zones. Trusted family members, close friendships, and trusted schoolmates bound the party's "special zones" together at their base. In 1947, young radio technicians working in the
southern countryside renewed their contact with their former professor
of electronics, who was living in Saigon. The latter helped them export
the parts they needed to build the Voice of the South transmitter from
scratch. Prewar friendships also explained why, on several occasions,
pharmacists smuggled medicines out of the city and doctors provided
medical treatment to wounded or sick underground cadres, regardless
of their politics.[48] The authors of a detailed history of the DRV's urban
militia in Saigon during the Indochina War wrote that the "fulcrum" for
building neighborhood bases revolved around each cadre's ability to
win the support of fathers, mothers, sisters, brothers, and close neighbors. These were the ties that bound together the underground city and
allowed it to operate over long periods of time.[49]

These carefully camouflaged urban enclaves were, at another level,
the extremities of the DRV archipelago state as it poked, like an antenna,
into the enemy's territory, watching the other side as if it were holding
up a periscope. The underground cities in Hanoi and Saigon were the
eyes and ears of the party too. It was the space in which the leadership
organized its most sensitive and important espionage and commercial
operations. No other nationalist party before 1945 or after ever matched
the communists when it came to organizing the city clandestinely, first
against the French, then against the Americans. Pham Xuan An, the
communist superspy to whom the Americans became so endeared during the Vietnam War, and Nguyen Tai, the one the CIA tried to break,
were both products of the prewar-1954 underground cities in Hanoi and
Saigon. Indeed, the communist spy networks that worked so well
against the Americans and their Vietnamese allies began during the Indochina War. We can be sure that Pham Xuan An knew Tran Quoc Hoan,
the man who presided over the party's espionage operations against the
French and the Americans.[50]

The French colonial police had always followed revolutionary activities in the cities closely. They continued to do so after 1945. What was
new in the Indochina conflict was that the French security services, the

Sûreté fédérale, could now rely on the army's intelligence service, the Deuxième bureau, and a host of newly created secret services to help them in gathering information, policing, and even carrying out political work. In the cities, for example, soldiers subjected buses and cars entering and exiting the cities to routine searches. The French military set up armed checkpoints along the main thoroughfares. The Deuxième Bureau opened files on Saigon, Hanoi, and Hue, dispatched a phalanx of their own informants and moles into each city, and remained as involved in monitoring the cities as it was in military operations focused on the countryside. Deuxième bureau officers joined the colonial security services in helping former bandits like Bay Vien and his armed forces (known as the Binh Xuyen) recover their old stomping grounds in and around Saigon. In exchange, they were expected to help the French root out the enemy there. They did, and by the end of the war oversaw policing Saigon in exchange for their collaboration. This too was how the French army, through its intelligence services, became ever more deeply involved in political matters, first in Indochina and then in Algeria.

One thing is sure: colonial cities like Saigon, Hanoi, and Hue came under unprecedented levels of surveillance from both sides early on during the Indochina War. This, in turn, contributed to the increasing regimentation of city life and the militarization of urban centers. Citizens carried obligatory identity cards with them and grew accustomed to showing their papers to security officials, undergoing frisks, and passing through military checkpoints. Police sweeps were common. The sale of large amounts of products like radios, medicines, and sandals needed approval. Curfews were de rigueur. French Union soldiers patrolling the streets of Saigon and Hanoi with rifles in their hands became part and parcel of the urban landscape. Less visible, but no less real, were the informers both sides deployed throughout the cities. For some, moving through the city became a nerve-wracking experience. As one undercover communist agent recalled of his time in Hanoi in the early 1950s:

When one moves about, one must do so with calm and it is particularly important not to look over one's shoulder. An anxious look, a scared face or an abnormal demeanor is enough to give you away and get you nabbed. To know if you are being followed or not, the best thing is to pedal slowly in front of a department store window and, by pretending to be interested in something on display, use a practiced eye to look into the reflection [from the glass] to peer into the street.[51]

Working from their clandestine spaces in the archipelago's urban enclaves, DRV security officers mirrored the activities of their French adversaries. They opened files on French and Vietnamese political leaders, army officers, sympathetic and dangerous civil servants, trusted and traitorous families, enemy moles, informers, and so on. They assigned their people to tail a variety of enemy personnel, noting their itineraries, frequentations, and habits. French officials were, indeed, being watched, and they had every reason to travel with security details and change their itineraries regularly. In 1950, after carefully studying the movements of Marcel Bazin, the redoubtable French head of the Sûreté in the south since the 1930s, a DRV special unit shot this colonial spymaster dead as he was walking to work. The official communist history later claimed that only then could "[t]he internal bases in the city . . . be reconsolidated and developed again, our cadres could move about the city more freely [than before]." While this conclusion is highly debatable, this event reveals nonetheless one of the important uses of the security and intelligence services in urban warfare—targeted assassination of a political and strategic kind.[52]

Those Vietnamese working with the French also had to be careful: there was a good chance that the DRV's secret services would catch up with them. In 1948, they eliminated the noncommunist nationalist Nguyen Van Sam, who had threatened to join the Vietnamese state the French were putting together with the former emperor of Vietnam, Bao Dai. Others killed during the late 1940s included noncommunist politicians and journalists hostile to Ho's Vietnam, men such as Tran Tan Phat, Duong Hien Su, and Nguyen Van Thach.[53] If we can believe the official history of the security services, agents in Hanoi in the late 1940s "executed a Deuxième Bureau agent at Lu Market at a time when the market was crowded with people." Another team "took a Deuxième Bureau agent prisoner in Dong Phu hamlet, capturing him in broad daylight right in front of armed enemy soldiers." As a recent Vietnamese account described another incident of this kind:

> These operations excited the people of Hanoi and made them trust us, but they drove the French military commanders crazy and made them take action. After young Hoang Xuan Tue, a member of the Bat Sat [the all-children "Iron Bowl"] unit, killed French Sûreté officer Paquet right in his home on Chanceulme Street, they stepped up their obtrusive searches and checks inside the city's center, continuously conducted search operations all around the city's outskirts, and laid ambushes on the routes we used to enter the city.[54]

How "excited" the people were about these events or how "trustful" of the party they were as a result is, again, open to debate. What is not is the unprecedented level of surveillance spreading over Vietnamese cities as each side shadowed the other.[55]

Movements into and out of major urban centers also came under heavy surveillance. It is true that Vietnam's legendary spymaster, Tran Quoc Hoan, ran the party's urban networks for Hanoi and that Nguyen Binh's entrance into Saigon under the noses of the French in 1947 became the stuff of legends. On closer examination, however, it is also true that all of these officials relied on a host of intermediaries to get them into and out of the "occupied cities." These mainly nameless people gathered information, secured routes, organized surveillance networks, operated commando teams on high-risk missions, and moved people, medicines, chemicals, radio parts, and documents across enemy lines. They came from all walks of life—merchants, rickshaw drivers, street vendors, civil servants, rich and poor, young and old. Students from the bourgeoisie, driven by the patriotism flowing during the exciting days of 1945–7, were certainly active, especially at the outset, as were intellectuals, teachers, lawyers, and merchants. The underground cities could never have operated had it not been for all these men and women moving the goods and information to and fro on the ground, often at extraordinary personal risk.[56]

Dr. Nguyen Thi Ngoc Toan, a member of the Vietnamese royal family, is a case in point. She began her revolutionary career in Hue as a teenager in the heady days of 1945. After the outbreak of full-scale war and the French reoccupation of the imperial capital in early 1947, she secretly carried documents and medicines out of the city and handed out propaganda pamphlets in Hue and Saigon for the DRV. "I was just so excited, so I followed the others," she later recalled, "we enjoyed it very much," because "these kinds of activities were very well suited to that age, when one enjoys adventure and danger." Toan's elite education in a French-run girl's school before the war and high social standing served her well in her forays around the city, providing her a degree of protection from the colonial security services denied to partisans of more modest social backgrounds. Indeed, her royal status and connections helped her to get out of jail on several occasions. Her French captors (as well as her worried mother) told her that a member of the royal family, and a woman at that, should not be involved in these subversive activities reserved "for the poor and the downtrodden." This did not stop Toan or other educated and well-off youth. In 1948, exasperated, the Sûreté finally expelled her from Hue. Her student group leader was less fortunate though; the colonial security services executed him.[57]

Of equal importance was the phalanx of itinerant women traders, street vendors, and hawkers who plied their trade daily between the city and its outlying areas, moving from village to village, market to market, street by street, step by step. The mobile nature of their jobs dovetailed nicely with the government's need to move materials in small amounts, documents, and people into and out of the city. These women, mainly in their teens and twenties, covered the urban landscape with two baskets connected by a pole they carried on their shoulders. They also offered the resistance detailed, reliable knowledge of the major arteries, backstreets, and the social underside of Hanoi, Saigon, and Hue. Male nationalist leaders betted heavily that their gender (female) and class (poor) would shield them, and thus the goods they carried, from enemy attention, body searches, and above all confiscation. The French were not dupes, of course: they body-searched when they had to and ran their own networks also using such women. They referred to these intermediaries as *passeuses*; the Vietnamese knew them as *nguoi giao lien*.[58]

It is hard to say for sure how many female intermediaries worked for Vietnam's underground cities, but probably no more than thirty or forty for each one.[59] This select, tightly knit, and trusted group of women moved small quantities of things across enemy checkpoints, through no-man's-lands, and then into the DRV's borderlands, where they met their handlers. While they could never carry much at one time (a packet of messages, a vial of antibiotics, or a couple of revolvers), over time it added up. These women were essential to bringing out new recruits from the cities and infiltrating seasoned cadres to administer the underground city as well. In their memoirs, very senior communists often mention their female guides. Reflecting on his entry into Hanoi in 1951, Nguyen Bac could still marvel thirty years later at the impressive knowledge his female guide had marshaled that day she took him to the "occupied city":

> My liaison agent, that is the person charged with taking me [into Hanoi], was a solid young woman with a sun-tanned complexion who knew the area perfectly. There was nothing that escaped her when it came to her work. She warned me immediately that in the event of a police check or even if someone asked indiscreet questions, we were to answer that we were a couple returning to Hanoi after spending several days in our native village to take part in a ceremony in honor of a deceased parent. She gave me the name of the imaginary village, that of the hamlet, and the complete family lineage of the members of our supposed rural family, as well as the kinship ties uniting our families for generations. And she made it clear to me in all seriousness that I had to be able to repeat all of this without hesitation and do so with a straight face![60]

And she was right. The knowledge—*real or invented*—these young women mastered was priceless, situated at that very real intersection where the rural-based war state's sovereignty touched up against that of the French colonial city. These were the people, on the ground, running the outer islands of the archipelago state, connecting it to the underground cities nestled within the French colonial regime. And these were extremely dangerous places to be. Suspicions always ran high at border checkpoints manned by gun-toting French or Associated State of Vietnam soldiers. ID was mandatory. Body searches were expected. Demeanor, diction, brains, and pure cool counted for more than brawn or bravado. Ngo Van Chieu, whom we have already met, owed everything to his young female guide for smuggling him back into the capital safely to see his wife and children in 1951. He describes in his memoirs how everything was going just fine during a routine police inspection of the bus carrying him and his "little sister" into the capital until Chieu forgot where he was, after so many years as a soldier in the DRV, and disingenuously used the word "comrade" (*dong chi*) when responding to the Associated State of Vietnam soldier questioning him at the checkpoint. "Why did you call me comrade?" the officer asked as he approached Chieu. "I was speechless," he later recalled, but, in the flash of an eye, "the young girl took over" the conversation. In fact, the "young girl" did *all* the talking, and she did *all* the thinking in that one crowded hour during which things could have gone terribly wrong. She provided the enemy officer with a detailed and convincing account of Chieu's life as a poor Catholic peasant suffering under communist tyranny and thus a believable alibi for using the term "comrade." As she concluded brilliantly to the soldier standing right before her, never missing a beat, according to Chieu:

> Honorable officer, she said, the rebels invaded our village not long ago and my brother was injured by them when he tried to repair our church. . . . Honorable officer, my brother is a very good bricklayer but he's not that intelligent. We are but poor peasants. Please be so kind as to forgive us. We are coming to place ourselves under your protection in Hanoi.
>
> OFFICER: OK, that's fine, get going. But don't call people here comrades. . . . You could come across less understanding policemen.
>
> THE LIAISON AGENT: Yes, honorable officer, thank you, sir. [To Chieu:] Quick . . . we will go to my godmother, who lives near here.[61]

Ngo Van Chieu, who had distinguished himself in hand-to-hand combat a year earlier in the Battle of Cao Bang, owed his freedom, perhaps his life, to this coolheaded young Catholic woman whom he apparently never met again. It would be good to know her name because she deserves to be known for her heroism. Indeed, crossing the lines into the colonial federation had to be one of most dangerous assignments of the Indochina War, short of going into battle. Women did it— in the thousands and, again, straight through the war with the Americans too.[62]

So did children. As we saw during the Battle of Hanoi, their knowledge of the terrain was such that they helped circulate cadres, information, and orders in the heat of battle. The communists continued to use them to build up and run their underground cities once the fighting had ended. Children, boys and girls, moved cadres back and forth between the free zones and the occupied city in the same way that Ngo Van Chieu's "little sister" just demonstrated. They delivered letters from the resistance government to cadres in the cities and even to the French. They also smuggled supplies and weapons out of the cities. One children's unit operating in northern Vietnam obtained 4,350 grenades, one wireless radio, 250 boxes of batteries, several hundred liters of gasoline, and much-needed clothing and canvas and exported it all to the maquis over five years.[63] Le Van Tra was nine when he started stealing from the French: "My job was to steal ammunition, grenades, anything I could get. I say it was my job, but all the kids did it. We'd hang around at the marketplace and watch the French soldiers as they came along, waiting for a chance to grab something and run. The next day on the way to school we'd brag to each other about what we had managed to get."[64] (See Plate 13.)

The Failed Battle of Saigon, 1946–9

Two decades before the famous Tet Offensive on southern cities in 1968, General Nguyen Binh, commander-in-chief of the southern forces, launched a campaign of terror, sabotage, and intimidation in Saigon. While it would be wrong to see this as a sustained or even a true battle, for Nguyen Binh the occupied city constituted a legitimate site for military operations (similar to those undertaken by the FLN in Algiers in 1957). In early 1947, as battles raged in Hanoi and Hue, he secretly entered Saigon and its Chinese sister city of Cholon to identify enemy targets and prepare his underground networks for urban warfare. Again, his targets were not the manufactured products his government needed to import clandestinely from this "foreign" market. They were colonial companies that helped finance the war in some way, or military sites such as naval shipyards, or radio stations which spewed out anti-DRV propaganda. He also fingered for assassination those French and Vietnamese who threatened the government's legitimacy—administrators, officers, spies, pro-French newspaper editors, and colonial-minded radio announcers. On 20 May 1947, Binh explained to his urban soldiers why they had to take the battle to the French and their Vietnamese allies in Saigon:

> Destroying Saigon is a legitimate and humane action. It is regrettable that scorched-earth policies were not applied from the start of hostilities. In the history of the southern resistance, this serves as a lesson, a painful experience. It was both a political and military error to simply ask people not to collaborate, to evacuate government buildings without destroying them as was done in Hanoi. The broadcasting station Radio Saigon continues daily with its counter propaganda, calling our fighters rebels. The electricity station in Saigon continues to power the enemy. The [French naval] arsenal[65] and the FACI [naval shipbuilders][66] are still repairing boats and weapons for French colonial troops who kill thousands and thousands of Vietnamese. The Bank of Indochina continues to hold in its hands the economic destiny of Cochinchina . . . If I remind you of this painful past, it's so that you can learn from its lessons.[67]

Nguyen Binh's background lent itself to this type of warfare. In his youth, we know he had worked on the Saigon docks before being arrested and sent to the rough-and-tumble world of the colonial prison for his nationalist activities. After being released from Poulo Condor in 1934, he resurfaced in the early 1940s, working briefly among miners and sailors in northeastern Vietnam before Ho sent him back to the south in late 1945 to create an army there. As the head of Zone VII located in the jungles outside Saigon, he personally organized terror and sabotage operations against enemy military and political installations and Franco-Vietnamese representatives in the city. If he could not win over Vietnamese political elites to the national cause, he would strike fear into their hearts to keep them on the fence and use lethal force against those who persisted in their collaboration with the enemy.

To do this, Nguyen Binh turned to a wide range of social relations ranging from lawyer friends who protected him during his personal tour of the city to a trusted coterie of dockers, workers, house servants, drivers, laborers, and students he recruited into his urban militias. He joined hands with the communist-run security services in the city, assigning agents to the eighteen quarters into which colonial Saigon had been divided by his intelligence people. The legendary Catholic spy Pham Ngoc Thao began his espionage career serving as Nguyen Binh's personal chief of military special operations in Saigon before going on to work full-time running espionage and counterespionage operations against the Americans during the Vietnam War.[68]

Of the dozen urban operational squads (called *ban cong tac*) in Saigon which Nguyen Binh assembled from 1947, workers were the main social component. Most came from unions in Saigon-Cholon; others worked on nearby rubber plantations. At the height of the violence in Saigon, during 1948–9, Nguyen Binh's teams probably counted around 2,500 people in all. From Zone VII, Nguyen Binh and his staff ran these squads and even administered a special academy for training them in urban warfare. (These networks would also come in handy later during the war against the Americans.)[69]

As in the north, southerners also turned to civilian women and children to serve as transporters, guides, and information-gatherers. In 1947, an all-female "Minh Khai Platoon" came to life in this way, named after the communist heroine the French executed outside Saigon in 1941, Nguyen Thi Minh Khai. This platoon numbered thirty young women aged between eighteen and twenty-two. Most of them came from poor urban or semi-rural families and usually worked as street hawkers. Also created was the "pip-squeak" class. It supplied boys and girls to serve as scouts, guides, and messengers in Saigon-Cholon. As in the north, most were orphans, aged between eleven and sixteen. Together, women, teenagers, and children passed into and out of the city carrying directives, money, mail, small arms, grenades, and explosives.[70]

Although women could not serve in the regular army, they were on the front lines of the battle for Saigon. In March 1947, DRV authorities recruited a Vietnamese woman and a newly arrived Cantonese immigrant to infiltrate the famous Chinese-run casino, Le Grand Monde. Outfitted in Chinese clothes, the Chinese woman talked herself and her companion through the front door and then into the heart of the casino. A short while later their grenades went off, creating panic in the club. Later on in that same year, Chinese owners and the DRV reached a deal, whereby Le Grand monde paid protection money to avoid the repetition of such events. According to French intelligence, the owners had secretly agreed to make a 2-million-piaster down payment and thereafter deposited between 5,000 and 10,000 piasters to DRV agents from daily gambling takes.[71]

The famous bombing of the Majestic Cinema on the Rue Catinat in 1948 is another example. Soldiers, officials, and wealthy Vietnamese allied with the French frequented this popular theater, making it a prime target. Having learned that a group of twenty French officers would be attending a showing of *Adieu chérie* (*Goodbye My Love*) on 10 June 1948, the DRV turned to the all-female Minh Khai Unit. Of the four women entrusted with this mission, the oldest was twenty-four, the three others aged between fifteen and sixteen. Because of their "soft-mannered" nature, "cool-headedness," and "physical beauty," they successfully crossed through the security checkpoints. Once inside, they waited until 8 p.m. when the feature film started and the lights dimmed. It was their cue to lob their grenades to where the French officers were sitting. Three devices went off, killing several sailors and naval officers and wounding innocent bystanders. In the commotion that followed all but one of the female assassins escaped capture. The news made the papers and unnerved an already anxious city. Nguyen Binh had attained his objectives. Women had allowed him to do it.[72] One of Vietnam's greatest heroines from this period, Vo Thi Sau, was a liaison agent the French captured in 1949, charged with murder, and executed in 1952. She was eighteen.[73]

While this "grenading" of the city that started in earnest in 1948 never shut down Saigon or Cholon, it did affect the way people went about their daily lives. Curfews were the rule. Checkpoints appeared across the city as body searches became commonplace. In 1949, according to Lucien Bodard, dozens of small grenades could go off in one night, usually around dusk, and mainly in the European quarters, along the Rue Catinat in Saigon and the Rue des Marins in Cholon. Shopkeepers responded accordingly as protective fencing and iron mesh went up around their establishments. "All of Saigon has shut itself up behind bars," Bodard wrote. "It was then that Saigon became something of a prison. It wrapped itself in wire netting—boutiques, bistros and dancing halls enrobed themselves in a veil of metal. Safe on the inside, the French could hear the detonations as they ate and drank." One Chinese restaurant owner serving settlers in the city finally decided to "enclose his establishment in a thick wall of iron." One dined in peace, Bodard observed, but one did so "in a cage."[74]

The psychological impact of this urban experience reverberated further than we might think. In 1951, then congressman John F. Kennedy and his brother Robert visited Saigon. While they remarked upon the bustling shops and pleasant restaurants lining the famous Rue Catinat, they also observed that the anti-grenade netting meant that all was not well. An outbreak of small-arms fire only reinforced their apprehensions and fuelled their doubts about the French war. "Cannot go outside city because of guerrillas," Robert confided to his diary. "Could hear shooting as evening wore on."[75]

Although this climate of fear is exactly what Nguyen Binh and his followers wanted to create, urban terrorism also reflected military weakness. Vietnamese communists running the Democratic Republic of Vietnam were never able to impose a siege on Saigon like Mao Zedong's Red Army was doing to republican-controlled Chinese cities. The Vietnamese army did not have the numbers, and the French army was much stronger than that of Mao's opponent, Chiang Kai-shek. Nor were Vietnamese communists willing to destroy the colonial city to force their opponent's hand. It was one of the government's most important trading partners until the end of the conflict. It is not even clear that the climate of fear Nguyen Binh created during the "Battle of Saigon" did much to inspire urban Vietnamese confidence in the resistance government or rally fence-sitting Vietnamese to its cause. In contrast to what Pontecorvo portrays at the end of his fictive *Battle of Algiers,* the Vietnamese attacks on Saigon-Cholon in the late 1940s never triggered a "general uprising" of a nationalist kind, any more than the Tet Offensive did in 1968. In fact, when the French finally shut down the urban terrorist networks and dismantled Nguyen Binh's combat units in 1951, most of the urban population welcomed the return to peace. Even after the start of set-piece battles in the north, from 1950 onwards, there is no evidence indicating that the people of Saigon, Hue, or Hanoi were ever thinking of rising up against the colonialists. And, in the end, there would be no siege of Hanoi in 1954 either. The final showdown in the Indochina War would occur in a remote valley in northwestern Vietnam called Dien Bien Phu.

5

Wiring War

Shortly after the fall of Dien Bien Phu on 7 May 1954, Vietnamese intelligence officers asked the commanding general of the French side, Christian de Castries, what his impressions were of the battle that had just ended in his capture. One of the Vietnamese officers present during the exchange recalled the French general telling them wryly, "Did you know that in French 'Dien Bien Phu' is pronounced 'Devienfou' [(Je) deviens fou], which means 'I have gone mad'?"

> We all laughed out loud, because before de Castries surrendered, our technical reconnaissance team had intercepted the following radio conversation between Cogny, the commander of the French forces in Tonkin, and de Castries, who was in charge of the Dien Bien Phu camp:
> COGNY: "Tiens bien." ["Hang in there."]
> DE CASTRIES: "Fou!" ["That's mad!"][1]

What de Castries did not know was that the Vietnamese intelligence officer standing before him that day had already heard this one—from him, in real time, as the enemy's artillery shells rained down on his bunker, sending him just as crazy as those last three words of conversation spoken between Cogny and himself: "Tiens," "bien," "[f]ou," ("I have gone mad") for Dien Bien Phu.[2]

On the technical front, the Vietnamese had been doing a lot more than simply intercepting enemy radio transmissions. During this epic showdown, de Castries' nemesis, the commanding general of the

People's Army of Vietnam, Vo Nguyen Giap, had never been far from his wireless radio set and field telephone. He read telegrams on what the enemy was doing from as nearby as the valley below him and as far away as central Vietnam. The Vietnamese technician who wired the battlefield was there too. His name was Hoang Dao Thuy. Tourists walking through the Vietnamese camp above the town of Dien Bien Phu today can visit the office from which this unsung hero directed communications during this epic battle. A former colonial scout, Hoang Dao Thuy had been there from the outbreak of the Indochina War. He had first helped Giap create a communications system during the Battle of Hanoi in late 1946. He had also provided the government with the radios and technicians it needed to hold itself together in its fragmented, archipelagic shape. It's impossible to understand the victory of Dien Bien Phu or the nature of the state standing behind it without considering how the Vietnamese wired decolonization and their state of war from the start.

Communications in a Time of Decolonization

Turning Colonial Modernity on the Colonizer

In many ways, the Vietnamese listening in on the French at Dien Bien Phu in 1954 owed a great deal to the colonizers for introducing modern communications. Since conquering all of Vietnam by the late nineteenth century, the French had established a network of radios, telephones, telegraphs, and postal services. On the eve of the Second World War, thousands of kilometers of telephone and telegraph wires crisscrossed Vietnam and the wider Indochinese realm into which the French had inserted it. The Postes, Télégraphes et Téléphones, better known in French as the PTT for the post office, operated centers throughout all of Vietnam, Laos, and Cambodia. The colonial postal service allowed civil servants, military officers, and merchants to dispatch telegrams, place calls, and send letters. In addition to the PTT, the Agence radiotélégraphique de l'Indochine et du Pacifique (ARIP) provided radio and telegraph services to customers and broadcast up-to-date political, administrative, and financial information to listeners.

French and Vietnamese newspaper editors relied heavily on the ARIP as well as other wire services like Reuters and Havas (later known as the Agence France-Presse, or AFP) to keep their readers apprised of world events. Two broadcasting stations, Radio Saigon and Radio Hanoi, beamed news and music to listeners across the colony. By the 1930s, most French settlers and well-off urban Vietnamese had grown accustomed to reading the paper, listening to the radio, and sending letters from one end of Indochina to the other. They could do so thanks to several thousand Vietnamese technicians running the colonial post office and various wire services in Indochina. They dispatched telegrams, connected calls on switchboards, and repaired equipment. Many of them possessed some of the finest technical educations available at the time. The post office's fleet of bikes, trucks, and boats allowed mail carriers to circulate letters and parcels across Indochina. Colonial stamps carried the portraits of famous French conquerors, leaders, and administrators.[3]

Of course, communications technology and the people running it served to consolidate and protect the colonial state as well. Good governance depended on the flow of information in a timely, orderly, and secure manner. The PTT circulated the official instructions, reports, and statistics civil servants needed to do their jobs. Every week, for example, officials across the colony received the Journal officiel de l'Indochine (the Official Gazette of Indochina) detailing new laws, decrees, and guidelines. The governor-general in Hanoi could speak by phone or telegraph his administrators all the way down to the provincial level (perhaps even further in some places). Modern communications also helped the colonial security services to improve their surveillance of the population and identify potential troublemakers. Upon receiving urgent telegrams warning of revolts in the provinces, the governor-general and military commanders in Hanoi used the telegraph to dispatch the police and soldiers to the area. This was the case during uprisings that broke out in northern and central Vietnam in the early 1930s and in the south about a decade later.

In the wider world, colonial authorities tracked anticolonialists as they moved across the Asian region and beyond. Diplomats and intelligence officers stationed in places like Hong Kong, Bangkok, and Singapore synthesized information arriving from their in-country sources (conversations, the local press, and informants). They then forwarded reports on to the governor general in Hanoi, the minister of the colonies in Paris, or shared them with other station chiefs via the telegraph and diplomatic pouches. Telegrams allowed Euro-American intelligence services to combine their forces with great rapidity against those who would threaten their imperial domination in the region. That the French knew who Ho Chi Minh was in 1945, long before his compatriots, should come as no surprise. They had been tracking him from one end of Eurasia to the other for years.[4]

To avoid French surveillance, Vietnamese communists became uncannily good at combining the use of modern radio communications alongside the deployment of a coterie of couriers who carried important documents by hand. From the mid-1930s onwards, they turned the use of their hand-carried means of communication into an art form, in the colonial cities in particular, all the while strengthening safe bases in the countryside wherever they could. Of course, the French security services were not always easily duped and crushed southern communists when they attempted an uprising at the start of the Second World War. In the north, however, some of the Indochina War's most important leaders like Truong Chinh (later head of the Communist Party) and Tran Quoc Hoan (head of the security services) carried on. They carefully rebuilt and administered a communist network in Hanoi throughout the war years. The future head of modern Vietnam's military intelligence, Hoang Minh Dao, began his revolutionary career as a communist liaison agent and base builder in Haiphong and Hanoi. He distinguished himself in Hanoi, helping Tran Quoc Hoan build the foundations of the underground city there in the early 1940s. A legendary spy in Saigon during the Vietnam War, Hoang Minh Dao was to die in an enemy ambush in 1969 deep in the Mekong Delta.[5]

Communist nationalists were unique for another reason too: they plugged their anticolonialism into a wider revolutionary network established in Moscow in the form of the Comintern (short for the

Communist International). Founded in 1919 by Vladimir Lenin, the Comintern sought to assist and coordinate the establishment of communist parties across the globe. In Asia, this transnational organization helped the Chinese create their party in Shanghai in 1921 and the Vietnamese one in Hong Kong nine years later. To administer their operations, the Comintern relied on communications technology—wireless radios, telegraphs, and cipher devices. It also organized a phalanx of hand-carriers to circulate messages, instructions, and agents. Sailors, ship hands, and dockworkers were particularly important in the making of an Asian maritime communism that stretched from the port cities of Shanghai to Singapore by way of Guangzhou and Bangkok.[6]

No one knew this better than Ho Chi Minh. He had left Saigon in 1911 on a steamship bound for western Europe, where he lived and worked in a variety of places. After the First World War, he joined the communist movement in France, left for Moscow a year after the Soviet Union officially came to life in 1922, and then traveled to southern China. With Comintern help, he created the Vietnamese Communist Party in Hong Kong in 1930 (renamed the Indochinese Communist Party later on that same year). As a member of the Comintern, Ho diligently studied and professed the works of Marx and Lenin. He also learned the finer points of clandestine movements, the basics of espionage and counter-espionage, and above all the importance of secrecy and how to keep it (he and many others like him used dozens of covers and code-names for a reason). Ho studied how to use wireless radios, write short and concise telegrams, and cipher his messages carefully. When he returned to southern China from Moscow for the second time in the late 1930s, he not only lectured Chinese communists on peasant mobilization techniques, but also earned his keep working as a radio operator in the Chinese Red Army. And thanks to his movements in Asia for the Comintern, he built up an impressive list of trusted hand couriers, a motley crew of sailors in particular.[7]

Upon arriving in southern China, Ho Chi Minh also obtained what may have been his most cherished possession short of national independence—a state-of-the-art Hermes Featherweight typewriter. He apparently carried this machine with him wherever he went, tucked into its small case much as one would slip a laptop or an iPad into a backpack today. As the Japanese marched across Southeast Asia, we can safely assume that Ho used his Featherweight to type up one of the foundational texts of the Vietnamese nationalist canon, *The History of Our Country from 2879 BC to 1942*, and the inaugural documents of the Viet Minh nationalist front created in 1941. Ho would become the father of the Vietnamese nation we know today. But he was also a master organizer, a firm believer in modern communications and clandestine liaisons, and something of a tech geek. And he was not the only one of this kind in the Communist Party. Those operating legally and underground in the colonial cities of Hanoi and Saigon during the 1930s were just as tech-savvy. Vo Nguyen Giap and Truong Chinh were journalists during this time. The communists who linked up with Ho at the Chinese border in 1941 and then in the Viet Minh's mountain base at Tan Trao north of Hanoi did not need anyone to tell them why communications mattered. This embrace of technology and aptitude for tight-knit liaisons so evident at Dien Bien Phu in 1954 has a more complicated and interesting history than we might think. It is no accident that curators have put "revolutionary" and "wartime" typewriters on display in museums in Vietnam today.[8] (See Plate 14.)

The Second World War opened up another communications link for the Viet Minh. Allied intelligence officers working in southern China's Yunnan province, where Chiang Kai-shek had moved his wartime government, turned to people like Ho to help them gather information on the Japanese. At ease in English and Chinese, Ho saw an opening and immediately offered his services to the Allies. After all, if Stalin could join the capitalists in a Grand Alliance against the Axis, then so could the Vietnamese communists at the helm of the Viet Minh. The American wartime intelligence service, the OSS, agreed. So did the Chinese and British intelligence services. (The French, whether "Free" or "Vichy," refused.) The Americans provided Ho and his team with a few radio sets so that they could send back reports on Japanese troop movements and military installations inside Indochina. They also needed help in locating and retrieving their downed pilots. Relying on his agents inside Vietnam, a wireless radio or two, and his typewriter, Ho obliged on both counts. Meanwhile, American commandos infiltrating northern Vietnam for similar reasons gave Vietnamese technicians in Ho's entourage a crash course in radio communications. Those same technicians may have lectured in the first training class Vo Nguyen Giap started in June 1945 to train Viet Minh radio operators from the Tan Trao base. Britain's MI6 also instructed a handful of Vietnamese communists, including the future head of Ho Chi Minh's police service—Le Gian. The British parachuted him into northern Vietnam before the war's end. He reported on Japanese movements and military installations. He also linked up with Ho's Viet Minh and put his MK2 transceiver in the service of the revolution they were all so feverishly planning. Joining them was another British-trained agent, Tran Hieu. Parachuted into northern Vietnam with Le Gian, he would go on to run the DRV's Strategic Intelligence Service against the Americans during the Vietnam War. He had also received six months of intensive intelligence training from their OSS towards the end of the Second World War.[9]

However, as long as the French and the Japanese remained at the helm of Indochina, with their transmissions and intelligence services intact, anticolonialists were in no position to take over. Things began to change in March 1945, when the Japanese overthrew their Axis-cum-Vichy partners in Indochina for fear that they would defect to the Allied side as Nazi power crumbled in Europe. The Japanese removed most of the French from their positions in the PTT and replaced them with Vietnamese technicians (they needed to keep things running smoothly as they focused on fighting the Allies). This long-awaited fracture of the French colonial order created an opening for Vietnamese communists working underground in and around Hanoi. They had already cultivated relationships with Vietnamese civil servants working in the colonial administration. The communists appealed to their patriotism and relied on friendships and family connections to win them over to their cause. After the coup in March 1945, underground leaders in Hanoi like Truong Chinh and Tran Quoc Hoan stepped up their networking. They knew that even a handful of clerks and telegraph operators could help them seize power and spread the national word through the postal system, via its mail service, telegraphs, and telephones when the right time came. An important undercover agent working for the communists in the Hanoi postal service, Nguyen Thi Bich Thuan, helped the Viet Minh take command of the central office when the Japanese capitulated. Her handler was none other than Tran Quoc Hoan. He had carefully maneuvered from behind the scenes to keep the post office in the party's sights, and then captured it.[10]

Communists working clandestinely in Hanoi also targeted the colonial scouting movement in search of a potential pool of tech-savvy recruits. A notable catch had occurred in 1943, when Tran Quoc Hoan, again, recruited the best-known scoutmaster of the time, in fact one of the architects of Vietnam's scouting movement, Hoang Dao Thuy. Patriotic, well-connected, and very much at ease with the fundamentals of radio communications, this middle-aged man helped the communists in Hanoi to bring over some of the best and the brightest of the scouts. This included the mathematician and future foreign minister, Ta Quang Buu (who was also Hoang Dao Thuy's son-in-law). In early August 1945, the communists smuggled colonial Indochina's scoutmaster into Tan Trao in the nearby hills, where he met Ho and Giap, and then put his knowledge of the capital, the scouting movement, and radio communications in the service of the coming revolution.[11]

While radios alone do not explain the Viet Minh's seizure of power on 19 August 1945, they helped the communist core in Tan Trao to follow events in real time and identify the right moment at which to act. An American OSS team operating with the Viet Minh at this time allowed Ho to listen to radio reports on world events, including the bombing of Hiroshima and Nagasaki on 6 and 9 August 1945. A week later, the communists gathered in Tan Trao one last time to plan how they would imminently take power. They made their move on the day the Japanese emperor announced his country's capitulation—15 August 1945. Four days later, Ho's national front, the Viet Minh, took power in Hanoi and in the following weeks throughout the rest of the country too. While the famine of 1944–5 had created a groundswell of peasant hunger lifting the Viet Minh to power across the countryside, its communist core seized Hanoi, thanks to a tightly knit underground urban network dating from the 1930s and access to real-time information.[12]

In the capital, Viet Minh officials, guided by the communists who had been active there for years, took control of the main post office, its radios and telephones, and the broadcasting station at Bach Mai. They immediately began telephoning, cabling, radioing, and broadcasting instructions to civil servants in most of Vietnam's provincial towns. By late August, the post office switchboard in Hanoi buzzed with news arriving from around the country of the Viet Minh's expansion. The newly created provisional government of the Democratic Republic of Vietnam issued orders requiring those with radios to turn up the volume, so that those without them could hear the "good news." As a report to the French captured it: "They got the Bach Mai radio station up and running. At every street corner, they installed speakers and ordered all those with radios to make them available to the public."[13] Vietnamese technicians broadcasting the news of the birth of a new Vietnam were ecstatic when they learned that Radio Ceylon had reported that it "could clearly hear emissions coming from Bach Mai" and "would spread the news to the world."[14] This was not what the French wanted to hear, and they had every reason to be worried: Radio Ceylon was the oldest radio station in Asia, reaching tens of thousands of listeners at the time. That this Asian broadcasting station passed on this news while it was still under control of the British South East Asia Command only reminded new French leaders of how badly out of touch they were with their own messaging.[15]

Meanwhile, in radio broadcasts, telegrams, and newspaper articles, the leaders of the provisional government of Vietnam urged provincial administrators to remain in their jobs. While some left, many in the PTT, now renamed the Buu Chinh (Postal Service), stayed put. Some did so out of patriotism, others simply for lack of better options. Most continued dispatching and receiving cables and telegrams for the new Vietnamese state as if nothing all that revolutionary had occurred. However, southerners found it much harder to take control of colonial communications. A large French community of around 20,000 people had become concentrated in Saigon during the war. Settlers hotly contested Vietnamese efforts to seize colonial communications equipment and succeeded in convincing the British to block such attempts (as it was the British who accepted the Japanese surrender south of the 16th parallel). To my knowledge, the southern Vietnamese never seized Radio Saigon before war broke out with the French in late September 1945.[16]

Like their colonial predecessors, Vietnamese nationalists used the telegraph, the radio, telephones, and the postal service to consolidate and strengthen the nation-state Ho declared independent on 2 September 1945. Having been cut off from "the people" for so long, Ho used the airwaves to spread the nationalist word as widely and as rapidly as possible. The government also confiscated radios and telegraph apparatus so that they could further disseminate their message. Ho appealed to the patriotic sentiments of some 6,000 Vietnamese working in the postal service, urging them to continue serving their country. His government telegrammed orders to provincial chief administrators, while mail trucks delivered thick reports, statistics, and charts. In the heady days of late 1945, no one ever thought twice about turning colonial modernity on the colonizer, even if it meant plugging the new nation into the preexisting colonial grid to get it off the ground.[17]

The colonial print media was also of national interest. The fledgling republic immediately seized colonial printing presses, purchased private ones, and acquired a few as patriotic donations. This was particularly true in areas above the 16th parallel, where high-ranking communists like Truong Chinh and Vo Nguyen Giap had been well connected since their journalism days. They helped recruit printers and typesetters as the national government began to operate the prominent *Taupin* and *Imprimerie d'Extrême-Orient* presses. Within weeks of the Japanese defeat, dozens of Vietnamese-language papers were rolling off these presses and others, almost all of them controlled by and supportive of the Viet Minh, the Democratic Republic of Vietnam, and its new president, Ho Chi Minh. The government acquired, for example, the circular known as the *Northern Central News* (*Trung Bac Tan Van*). It controlled many others. No one could have imagined in early 1945 that by the end of the year newspapers would be carrying front-page portraits of Ho, cartoons ridiculing French colonialists, and celebrations of Vietnamese history, heroes, and national unity. Meanwhile, the Viet Nam Dan Quoc Cong Bao, the government's "national gazette," quietly replaced the Journal officiel de l'Indochine. It issued official decrees and instructions and provided information and statistics needed to operate the national state just as it had for the colonial one until a few days earlier.[18]

The graft, however, was not without its glitches. Stamps are a case in point and deserve a special mention here. For any country, stamps do several things. Firstly, they provide an important source of steady revenue. Secondly, they serve as the markers of territorial sovereignty: you cannot send a letter from Montreal to Vancouver with an American stamp; only a Canadian one will do. Lastly, they are signifiers of national identity. Governments issue stamps carrying the portraits of their national heroes, symbols, and historical moments and monuments. The problem was that in the early days Vietnamese officials did not have the materials to produce their own stamps straightaway. In order to continue collecting the postal tax without losing national face, authorities simply overlaid the portrait of President Ho and the words "Democratic Republic of Vietnam" on top of existing colonial stamps bearing the portraits of Vichy France's chief of state, Philippe Pétain, the former governor-general of Indochina, Paul Doumer, and the missionary, Alexandre de Rhodes, among others.

Nationalists building new countries from the ruins of the Second World War were doing similar things right across Eurasia. In fact, Charles de Gaulle's "Free French" officials landing in Indochina in late 1945 would have understood what the Vietnamese were doing with Vichy stamps very easily, as they had recently done it themselves. Upon the Allied liberation of France from the Germans in 1944, de Gaulle's newly formed provisional government overprinted the Free French resistance symbol, La Croix de Lorraine, on Vichy stamps carrying the picture of France's wartime leader, Philippe Pétain. The new French government stamped the two letters RF (République française, or the "French Republic") on top of other occupation government-stamps, including those bearing the picture of Hitler. In so doing, the "Free

French," like the "Free Vietnamese" or the "Viet Minh," affirmed the existence of a new national order over a preexisting one, each now considered to be illegitimate. These overprinted stamps provide a glimpse into that moment at which one sovereignty moves in on the other—but not without encroaching upon each other's status, quite literally, in the form of "overprints."[19]

The problem in Vietnam in 1945–6 was that two new republics born at the end of the Second World War, one French and the other Vietnamese, now vied for sovereign control of the country. In 1946, Vietnamese authorities began printing fully decolonized stamps proudly proclaiming the Democratic Republic of Vietnam—Viet Nam Dan Chu Cong Hoa—and carrying the portrait of a solemn, determined President Ho. These and others of this kind circulated until the end of the Indochina War. Meanwhile, the French issued stamps for Vietnamese territories as they came under their expanding military control. The idea was to contest the Vietnamese republic's sovereignty at every turn. In 1949, this philatelic battle expanded still further when the "Associated State of Vietnam" began issuing its own stamps. And where one stamp's territorial traction stopped on the ground and the other's started is where the borders of the archipelago states discussed in this book were to be found. In fact, Ho's entourage would only completely win the postal battle in 1975, when the communists took the south by force and created the Socialist Republic of Vietnam a year later.[20]

Not all Vietnamese supported the communist creation of the Democratic Republic of Vietnam, and these people challenged the government's hold on technology and information. This was particularly true of the anticolonialist and anticommunist Vietnamese Nationalist Party. Like the communists, these nationalists had engineered revolts in the early 1930s, and those leaders who did not end up in jail or executed fled to safe bases in southern China. There, they enjoyed the support of Chiang Kai-shek's Republic of China and were confident that with the arrival of his troops in Hanoi to accept the Japanese surrender they would also be able to roll back communist control of Vietnam. Although the Chinese refused to overthrow Ho's republic, they did provide protection to their Vietnamese anticommunist partners until they withdrew from Indochina in mid-1946. As a result, the Vietnamese Nationalist Party operated its own independent paper and printing press in Hanoi during this period. These nationalists hotly contested the position of communists at the head of the new republic and their right to call the shots. Highly gifted writers and journalists like Nhat Linh and Khai Hung ran the opposition's main paper, *Viet Nam*. They and others in their entourage published scores of articles critical of the government. Joining them in the battle for Vietnamese hearts and minds was the Dai Viet (Greater Vietnam) Party. They all painted the Viet Minh as red as possible—a favorite approach was to call it a band of ruthless communists bent on enslaving the country. Acrimonious exchanges occurred between the opposition press and the papers controlled by Ho's people. It was only when the Chinese started to pull out in mid-1946 that the communists could finally move against the nationalist opposition, their papers, and presses. In July 1946, the communist-controlled police seized the nationalist printing presses, papers, and offices in a civil war explored in the next chapter. But to make sure that everyone understood who had won the war of the words, the communists placed on the front page of the "reformed" nationalist paper, *Viet Nam*, a full-page picture of president Ho Chi Minh. Meanwhile, sympathetic postal workers in Hanoi and elsewhere kept an eye out for enemy saboteurs. Nguyen Cong Hoan, another famous writer from the 1930s, joined the communists to serve as the national government's first censor (he entered the party in 1948). For all sides—and this until the end in 1975—broadcasting stations, radios, stamps, newspapers, and censorship were all weapons in the struggle for Vietnam.[21]

Early Wiring, 1945–7

Wireless radios played an important role in consolidating and protecting the new postcolonial state.[22] On 2 September 1945, the day Ho proclaimed the independence of Vietnam in Hanoi, Vo Nguyen Giap, the new minister of defense, met with our former scoutmaster, Hoang Dao Thuy. The object of their meeting was the need to create a national communications service for the nascent army and state. Giap explained that the General Staff needed a proper radio transmissions service to direct and coordinate military operations in the event that hostilities broke out. Despite the joyful celebrations going on outside their window on that autumn day, things did not look good: Chinese troops were preparing to move into northern Indochina, down to the 16th parallel, while British forces were about to accept the Japanese surrender below that line. Gaullist agents were trying to find seats on Allied planes flying into Hanoi. Others had already begun parachuting into Indochina secretly. Meanwhile, in the south, opposition to Ho's fragile hold on power there began to surface.

The communists at the helm of the DRV needed a communications system to circulate up-to-date information on these potentially hostile groups. They also needed to get orders to their administrators and officers taking up posts across the country. Vietnam stretched for over 3,000 kilometers from north to south, including its rugged highland spine running down its middle. As Vo Nguyen Giap put it at the time: "While we have many troops, we must rapidly coordinate the different units from Lao Cai to Ca Mau." Only a wireless radio and telephone network could do this, he told Hoang Dao Thuy. In mid-September, a week before war broke out in Saigon, the Ministry of Defense assumed control of the central post office's wireless radio network in Hanoi and assigned its operations to a newly created Communications and Liaisons Office. Led by Hoang Dao Thuy, this entity served as the clearinghouse for circulating orders, information, and intelligence for the Ministry of Defense as well as for the government and, to some extent, the party. There was much overlap in the early years.

Hoang Dao Thuy dispatched most of the messages through a special subsection called the "Wireless Radio Service." It housed the main radios taken from the post office. It also operated an embryonic ciphering bureau for encrypting and decrypting messages.[23] Once again, the Chinese decision not to overthrow Ho's republic allowed the Vietnamese to develop a communications system largely free of colonial interference for nearly fifteen months. During this time, Hoang Dao Thuy recruited a handful of reliable radio specialists, many of whom had been scouts. Most had good math skills, knew their Morse code, and ran on high levels of patriotism. Besides the colonial material they confiscated, in late 1945 Hoang Dao Thuy's technicians also received two more Allied-trained Vietnamese radio operators, a 20-watt wireless radio transmitter, and an MK2 transceiver. The latter, a portable unit, had been developed and used by the Allies during the Second World War. It was powerful enough to communicate with radio sets scattered widely across upper Vietnam. Another MK2 unit operated near the 16th parallel, known as the intermediary transmitter. It bridged radio communications between the north and the south until at least 1950. Although Hoang Dao Thuy was not a communist at the start, his wartime collaboration with top party leaders like Tran Quoc Hoan and Ho Chi Minh shows how this former colonial scoutmaster assumed such a sensitive post. Hoang Dao Thuy could call on the communist leadership whenever he needed something. In exchange though, the communist leadership expected him to join the Indochinese Communist Party, which he did, in 1947.[24]

Things were always more difficult in the south due to the rapid French return, the relative weakness of the republic and the Communist Party there, and the growing dissension between the government and armed religious groups. On 23 September, with a green light from the British, the French ousted Ho's officials from Saigon and began taking over provincial towns and roads. The early attack on the south left the government with little time to evacuate much radio equipment or personnel from urban centers. The most southern authorities could do was to transform as many of their radios as they could into portable ones and move their main transmitter to a secret location in My Tho province south of Saigon. From there, on 23 September, the party's southern leaders radioed Hanoi that they were under attack and had no choice but to fight. Apprised of this, the party leadership approved armed struggle for the area below the 16th parallel while Ho tried to negotiate a peaceful path to decolonization before hostilities consumed the upper half of the country.[25]

The importance of radio communications between the north and south was clear to all reading the copy Hoang Dao Thuy's team was feeding them. The lack of communications that had separated both regions since the early 1930s, and especially after southerners had launched a failed uprising in 1940, could not be allowed to reoccur as the French sought to conquer Vietnam a second time. The party immediately ordered the dispatch of more wireless sets to the south. When Nguyen Binh arrived to take command of southern forces in November 1945, he brought a set with him and immediately opened a channel to the General Staff in Hanoi and commanders in neighboring zones. These wireless units, numbering no more than a dozen below the 16th parallel in 1946, nevertheless provided southerners with a real-time connection to the leadership in the north as well as an invaluable source of information about what was going on locally, nationally, and internationally. However, southerners had not had the time to evacuate or destroy Radio Saigon before surrendering the city. They had to build their own broadcast station, the Voice of the South, from scratch, exporting radio equipment out of French Saigon piece by piece to do so. Northerners learned from this and, as the country slid towards war above the 16th parallel in late 1946, they began evacuating radio equipment and technicians before hauling off the Voice of Vietnam transmitter to the countryside, where it would operate from during the entire Indochina War.[26]

Given the importance of communications, the Vietnamese opened primitive but functional academies to train a new generation of communications specialists who would serve during the rest of the conflict. The government desperately needed them to man the radios and telephones, repair equipment, and make and break codes. A handful of French-trained instructors dispensed courses when they could. In November 1945, in Hanoi, Hoang Dao Thuy's team organized the DRV's first formal training class. After four months of intensive training, students took up assignments operating radio sets in the provinces, emerging war zones, and combat units located mainly above the 16th parallel. Colonial-era and Allied training manuals figured in the curriculum. Given the communist core of Ho's government, Comintern and Maoist techniques and experiences were probably taught too. In any case, by the time the Battle of Dien Bien Phu started, Thuy's office had trained perhaps 3,000 specialists in the upper half of Vietnam. Starting a bit later, in 1947 or 1948, southerners had probably trained about 1,000 such technicians by the war's end. In both areas, these technicians were essential to ensuring military and bureaucratic communications during the Indochina War.[27]

Unlike the Algerians fighting the French a few years later, the Vietnamese used their national language in their wireless correspondence. Communications specialists were fluent in Vietnamese and fully at ease in using the Romanized national alphabet known as *quoc ngu* to write messages. There was never a need to "Vietnamize" the DRV's communications service, as that process had already occurred during the colonial period thanks, paradoxically, to the colonizers. Indeed, since conquering the south in the 1860s, the French had promoted the study of the Romanized script in the colonial education system. It was considered to be one of the best ways to sever the precolonial Vietnamese administration from its historical ties to China and the use of Chinese characters in its own bureaucratic system. In addition, the French correctly concluded, the Romanized alphabet would be easier to learn for the Vietnamese than the Chinese characters. The French, to be sure, promoted their own language within the bureaucracy, but they in no way sidelined the Vietnamese one. They saw in its Romanization a tool for consolidating colonial rule.

What the French could not fathom at the time was how much help this colonial transformation of the Vietnamese writing system would be to anticolonialists consolidating national rule. When Ho declared Vietnam independent, the vast majority of civil servants had no trouble switching over to Vietnamese full-time in crafting their telegrams, messages, and reports. They had learned French, of course; but they had also mastered *quoc ngu* as youngsters and had probably read more books and papers in that form than in the colonial language. Moreover, typewriters with French keyboards could produce the Latin letters and most of the tone markers needed to produce a readable paper trail in *quoc ngu*. Once they had finished typing up a report, officials could easily add any remaining accents by hand. The same was true for sending telegrams and radio messages. By the end of the conflict, Vietnamese cryptologists had no trouble writing codes in *quoc ngu*. But had the Vietnamese maintained their traditional Chinese-based character system known as *chu nom*, the work of Hoang Dao Thuy and his team would have been much more complicated and time-consuming.[28]

The necessities of war only reinforced this linguistic turn. Pushed into the countryside from September 1945 in the south and from January 1947 in upper Vietnam, the national government operated among a rural population that had never been exposed to very much of the French language. Rural children might have learned a few words in the language of Molière about "our ancestors the Gaul" (and even that is highly debatable) during the short time they were in school. But what they retained most were the basics of reading and writing in *quoc ngu*. Their teachers, moreover, were almost always Vietnamese. Pushed into the countryside and seeing their pool of tech-savvy, urban-trained technicians dry up quickly, the government embraced *quoc ngu* as the best and fastest way to train and recruit future communications specialists from the countryside as well as for every other branch of the republic. War thus ensured that the Vietnamese language in its Romanized form would reign supreme in communications from this point on. Paradoxically, the colonial Romanization of the Vietnamese language facilitated the wiring of the very nation-state the French now sought to destroy.[29]

The Vietnamese designed their postcolonial education system to ensure that this remained the case. Teaching people to read was at the top of the list. Between September 1945 and July 1954, the education system taught millions of people to read, young and old, girls and boys, ethnic Vietnamese (*kinh*) as well as "ethnic minorities" in the highlands the DRV controlled. A general education system provided instruction to young Vietnamese (up to the ninth grade), where they learned the basics of math and *quoc ngu* as well as a good dose of nationalist history. Over 700,000 youngsters had gone through the system by 1954, especially in zones IV and V in central Vietnam and in and around the provincial capital of Thai Nguyen. Following the Chinese communist victory and Mao Zedong's support of Ho Chi Minh, in 1951, the communist leadership implemented a major reform of the educational system to align it ideologically with the communist creed. The use and expansion of *quoc ngu* was essential to this revolutionary process as well.[30]

Things could have been different on the linguistic front. In 1945–6, in exchange for independence, Ho had offered the French the right to maintain their language in Vietnam's postcolonial education system and cultural activities. Paradoxically, by going to war over Vietnam in 1945–6, rather than negotiating its peaceful decolonization, the French torpedoed any chance they had of rooting their own language in Vietnam. Things worked out very differently in Algeria, where nationalists only truly shifted over from French to Arabic in 1962 once the war had ended there.

Propaganda and Diplomacy

Communications were essential to operating the new republic's diplomacy and winning over support for it abroad. Radios allowed decision-makers to stay abreast of changes taking place at both national and international levels. During the 1945–6 period, when the Vietnamese negotiated with the Chinese, the Americans, the British, and the French, the leadership required rapid updates on any meetings with these groups or decisions these powers made that could affect the government's well-being. From 1946 onwards, diplomats stationed in Bangkok provided leaders in Hanoi (and then in the countryside) with information and analyses of changes occurring in Asia and the world. More diplomatic delegations soon opened their doors in Rangoon, New Delhi, Singapore, Paris, and Prague. The communist bloc's recognition of the Democratic Republic of Vietnam in 1950 expanded the government's diplomatic representation to Moscow and Beijing. Equipped with wireless radios, diplomats reported on their meetings with Western and Asian officials, received instructions from their government, and, inversely, provided information which could be of use to policy-makers inside Vietnam. Officials in Thailand and India, for example, helped to organize the Vietnamese government's participation in the 1947 Asian Relations Conference in the recently independent Indian capital, New Delhi. When time was of the essence, as it so often was, delegates could send their messages without scrambling the signal, knowing that the French would be able to intercept them. It didn't matter.

On the propaganda front, the French left the Vietnamese a gift in the form of Radio Hanoi. By taking over the Bach Mai wireless transmission station in mid-1945, Vietnamese nationalists acquired a powerful technical means for reaching the Vietnamese people in their mother tongue. On 7 September, at 1:30 p.m., the speaker Madame Duong Thi Ngan announced via the airwaves the birth of Vietnam: "This is the Voice of Vietnam, broadcasting from Hanoi, the capital of the Democratic Republic of Vietnam." Hoang Dao Thuy's office ran the station and put a talented French-trained engineer from the south in charge of it, Nguyen Van Tinh. The Voice of Vietnam's main task was simple: counter colonial propaganda and promote that of the Democratic Republic of Vietnam in its daily broadcasts.

Determining how many Vietnamese actually had radios during the Indochina War is harder. Based on circumstantial evidence, a specialist of the period estimates there were 2,000–3,000 receivers in Vietnam in September 1945. In early 1951, one CIA study concluded: "Most of the Vietnamese in the French-controlled cities have radios, but there are very few among the people in the countryside." This was probably accurate, since radios were relatively expensive and the French tightly controlled their export to the maquis during the conflict. The Vietnamese government also kept everything it could to operate its own communications. The young republic probably enjoyed the largest Vietnamese audience between September 1945 and December 1946, when it operated independently from the cities above the 16th parallel. After the outbreak of full-scale war and the transfer of the central government to the countryside in 1947, the Voice of Vietnam concentrated less on maintaining a wide national audience at all costs. It focused instead on transmitting non-secret but essential information to radio-equipped bureaucrats running this decentralized, archipelagic state.[31]

The government communicated its point of view through the creation of another broadcasting service, the Vietnam News Agency (or VNA). Created in Hanoi in 1946, it transmitted the government's policies to the international community in English and French (and later in other languages too). The republic appealed on several occasions to the Americans, Soviets, and British to support the cause of Vietnamese independence. The VNA responded tit-for-tat to French provocations and accusations. It was vital to get the Vietnamese message out "there," "on the air," as quickly as possible. The VNA beamed information abroad, including Ho Chi Minh's declaration of independence and explanations of how French actions in 1945–6 had led to war. This agency operated throughout the Indochina War, and it functions to this day.

Over the years, the VNA set up a handful of offices abroad. The diplomatic delegation in Bangkok was particularly helpful in communicating the government's messages to the world and its newly decolonizing parts in Asia and then Africa. Many of the interviews foreign correspondents secured with Ho Chi Minh were prearranged through the Bangkok office. This included the important interview Ho gave to the Swedish newspaper, *Expressen*, in late 1953 during which the Vietnamese president signaled his desire to open serious diplomatic negotiations to end the war. In 1950, the CIA reported that the quality of information coming out of the VNA had "improved so greatly in journalistic aspects as to overtake and perhaps surpass that of the AFP [Agence France-Presse] file out of Saigon." That was a patent exaggeration, but the Voice of Vietnam and the VNA ensured that the second French colonial conquest, unlike the nineteenth-century one, would be challenged not just inside Vietnam but at an international level too. This was astute, and completely new.[32]

The French badly wanted to eliminate this challenge to their colonial control over the airwaves. They tried to locate radio source points through triangulation and asked the Americans for the latest scientific tools to jam their enemy's broadcasts. It is unclear whether the US obliged, but it is certainly true that the French never disabled Vietnamese voice broadcasting during the Indochina War.[33] Meanwhile, the Americans were already listening in to what was going on in Indochina, thanks to their monitoring of the region's airwaves. The first American intercept of the Democratic Republic of Vietnam's broadcasting apparently occurred on 23 September 1945—the day the Indochina War broke out in Saigon. On that day, according to the National Security Agency's history of the Vietnam War, the Americans picked up the message Ho sent without encryption to Joseph Stalin, pleading for assistance. This was the first of what would become an avalanche of messages that American code-breaking services would intercept over the next thirty years, most of which are still held under lock and key.[34]

The Vietnamese also used wireless radios to conduct diplomacy, though with mixed results. In April 1946, the central government dispatched cables to the commander-in-chief of the south, Nguyen Binh, ordering him to stop shooting in light of the signing of the 6 March provisional accords between the French and the Vietnamese. A few months later, in late September, he received instructions to implement the ceasefire Ho had just brokered in France. The fighting duly ceased in the south on both occasions. The Vietnamese president was in charge, thanks to radio communications.[35]

The Vietnamese government would use the radio to direct its diplomats during high-stakes talks over the country's destiny in other negotiations. For example, during heated sessions with the French in Dalat, in April 1946, the Vietnamese leadership instructed its communications people to provide the government's diplomatic team going there with a wireless radio set so that its members could keep the leadership in Hanoi abreast of negotiations as they proceeded (as the French controlled Dalat's telephone network). Nguyen Van Tinh oversaw radio transmissions for the young republic's negotiating team. He brought another MK2 transmitter and a handful of trusted cipher specialists with him to Dalat. Thanks to the opening of a direct channel, diplomats in Dalat provided reports on the state of negotiations to leaders in Hanoi and received back instructions as to how to proceed. The government also attached a special communications team to its delegation at the follow-up conference held outside Paris in Fontainebleau a few months later. With the help of the French Communist Party and Vietnamese sympathizers living in the metropolis, technicians opened radio contact with Hanoi from a secret location to report on the negotiations and to receive cabled instructions. Two decades later they would do the same thing when covert negotiations opened with the Americans to end the Vietnam War.[36]

As useful as real-time radio communications were for conducting diplomacy, it came with risks. The French had decades of experience in

intercepting enemy communications. They would now begin listening
in on those challenging their colonial right to rule in Asia and Africa.
They immediately hustled some of their best code-breakers to Indochina so they could inform their decision-makers on what the other side
was thinking. From late 1945, French signals specialists began cracking
Vietnamese cipher codes quite easily. In the early years, inexperienced
Vietnamese radio operators used codes which were too basic. Some
grew frustrated and simply sent their messages uncoded. Such careless-
ness opened the doors to the colonial code-breakers, and early Vietnamese diplomatic efforts suffered as a result. During the Dalat Conference,
for example, the French apparently read much of their enemy's cable
traffic. The Vietnamese realized something was wrong when Vo Nguyen
Giap ordered a halt to the MK2 dispatches. The same thing may have
occurred during follow-up negotiations in Fontainebleau. The balance
would change during the second half of the Indochina War, as the Vietnamese obtained the experience and equipment they needed from the
communist bloc to encode and even to begin intercepting French communications, first during the battle of Cao Bang in late 1950 and again
later, at Dien Bien Phu. But until 1950, and even for some time afterwards, the nationalist encryption services were no match for colonial
code-breakers.[37]

Wiring the Battle of Hanoi

Just as Hoang Dao Thuy would handle radio communications for the
Vietnamese army during the clash that ended the Indochina War at
Dien Bien Phu on 7 May 1954, he also wired the one that set it all off on
19 December 1946 in Hanoi. From mid-1946, as the French and the Vietnamese slid towards conflict, this former scoutmaster and his entourage
worked closely with Vo Nguyen Giap to prepare for full-scale war. As
head of the Communications and Liaisons Office, Hoang Dao Thuy
provided decision-makers with the latest incoming information on
enemy military movements in urban areas like Haiphong, Langson,
Hanoi, and Hue. The 6 March Accords and a subsequent annex to them
had allowed the French to post 15,000 troops above the 16th parallel,

most of whom set up camp in the cities. With the withdrawal of the last remaining Chinese soldiers in September 1946, tensions rapidly mounted as colonial authorities began to challenge the national government's autonomy at every turn. In October, Thuy's communications team organized a meeting in Hanoi, bringing technicians in from areas above the 16th parallel. After discussions, all agreed to consolidate and increase the effectiveness of radio and telephone transmissions in light of the coming storm.

To this end, the Ministry of Defense took control of the phone system for all of upper Vietnam, the fastest and most reliable means of communication. It ordered the immediate evacuation of valuable electronics, wire, and radio equipment from the cities.[38] On 17 December, two days before the war started, the Ministry of Defense created a Special Communications Committee under Vo Nguyen Giap's supervision. Its task was to transmit critical information on the enemy's movements via telephone, radio, and telegraph directly to the General Staff, as well as to the central government, the party, war zones, and provincial offices. Giap and his team outside Hanoi communicated directly by radio and hand-courier with the man in charge of the battle for the capital, Vuong Thua Vu.[39] But the person at the center of these crucial communications in Hanoi in December 1946 was Hoang Dao Thuy. According to Vietnamese sources, Thuy's special communications team transmitted the "ultra-urgent" message ordering troops in Hanoi to attack the French at 20:01 p.m. on 19 December. Significantly, Vo Nguyen Giap not only instructed his soldiers and militias to strike in the city, but he also radioed commanders across the country to launch simultaneous and coordinated attacks in other cities they held. Nguyen Binh, commanding general for southern forces, received a message to this effect and acted accordingly. Similar telegrams went out to commanders in Dalat, Hue, and Nam Dinh. Full-scale war in Vietnam broke out in something close to real time across the entire country.[40]

Of course, the use of technology never worked as smoothly as official accounts would have us believe. For example, during the French conquest of the port city of Haiphong in November 1946 the military leadership couldn't get enough information about what was happening there—for the embarrassing reason that they had no telephone connection.[41] Similar communication breakdowns occurred in the hours following the eruption of hostilities in Hanoi and elsewhere. Nevertheless, that the Vietnamese went to such lengths to use radios during the Battle of Hanoi left no doubt that they had every intention of deploying technology as a fundamental part of their armed struggle. And as rudimentary as all of it most certainly was, Ho Chi Minh and his officials were once again putting into place the infrastructure they would need to take in more sophisticated communications technology when it began arriving from the communist bloc in 1950.

Communications in Wartime

Communications technology was equally important for the architects of the Democratic Republic of Vietnam as they fled to the countryside in 1947 and began building and operating their state of war there. Pushed into the highlands of northern Vietnam and the marshes of the south, leaders no longer enjoyed the advantages of colonial-built infrastructure and means of transportation. They now traveled by foot, on horseback or in small boats. Meanwhile, the French did everything in their power to destroy the Vietnamese republic before it could build itself up in the countryside. For the whole of 1947, and well into 1948, the Expeditionary Corps had Ho and his state on the run. The surprise French airborne attack on the government's hideout in Cao Bang in northern Vietnam in late 1947, codenamed Operation Léa, almost ended in the capture of several senior communist leaders. This offensive and others like it, across much of northern Vietnam, caused the government enormous hardships in the maintenance of its radio transmissions and lines of communication. The Voice of Vietnam went off the air for several months at a time. The situation was no better in southern Vietnam, where French operations continued to force people to operate from some of the least accessible parts of the southern delta. Officials had intermittent contact with each other during these two difficult years. Only in central Vietnam, in zones IV and V, which ran from areas south of Hanoi to those near Qui Nhon, did the government postal system and communications continue to operate with little colonial interference.

Given the incomplete territorial control the Vietnamese government exercised and the constant enemy challenges to it, the embattled republic's administrators and military officers relied heavily on the wireless radio to hold their archipelago state together and assert its national sovereignty at every turn. In March 1947, the Ministry of Defense instructed officers across the country to maintain wireless radio communications at all costs with the central command. Each zonal leader had to have at least one radio at his disposal. Copy was to remain short and to the point. "Radio communications," Vo Nguyen Giap explained in 1948, "are always important and serve as the arteries of our military system. If transmissions shut down or are delayed, the entire system can stagnate, causing us to lose favorable opportunities or even turning them into defeats. At a time when the situation is changing and the enemy is attacking violently, the need for communications is urgent."[42]

The same was true for governmental affairs. Officials went to extraordinary lengths to maintain and expand communications channels between the central government ministries located in the north and the thousands of civil servants working in district and provincial offices scattered across this now fragmented war state. In 1948, when the government divided its territory into larger administrative units and corresponding military zones, it provided wireless radios to each. Bureaucrats and officers at the interzonal level could communicate with each other by radio as well as with the central government setting up its capital in Thai Nguyen province in the north.

Wireless radios allowed administrators to tend to such mundane but essential matters as ordering medicines, typewriters, chemicals, paper, batteries, books, and manuals from the overseas diplomatic delegation in Bangkok, for example, or from the underground cities in Hanoi, Hue, and Saigon (each one had radios by the late 1940s). Radios made it possible to circulate orders and instructions from the zonal and provincial levels to district offices as well as to neighboring administrative and military offices. Orders went out over the airwaves to transfer civil servants, technicians, and nurses from one post to another and to organize countless meetings essential to the everyday functioning of the state and its armed forces. Financial and agricultural officials used radios to order the transfer of foodstuffs (rice and salt, for example) from one zone to another. This was especially important when colonial blockades led to famine in parts of southern Vietnam in the late 1940s and in the north in the early 1950s. In September 1947, a perceptive French intelligence officer described the importance of radio communication to the Vietnamese nationalists very well: "In the current circumstances, wireless radio constitutes the surest and most rapid method of command. It seems obvious that without it the Viet Minh government and command would rapidly lose all authority, all prestige, and all its coordinating powers. Overland and maritime liaisons are slow and hardly safe. . . . Wireless transmissions remain the most efficient and rapid [line of communication], and this explains the considerable effort the [DRV] authorities exert to conceive and operate this important organization."[43]

Finally, once full-scale war began in late 1946, communications teams did everything in their power to keep the daily broadcasts of the Voice of Vietnam and the Voice of Southern Vietnam on the air. Each served to affirm the government's national reality in the battle of the airwaves. Equally important, each broadcasting station disseminated non-sensitive yet vitally important information concerning the everyday functioning of the state over long distances—instructions, decrees, personnel transfers, and announcements. Administrators across the country tuned in to its daily broadcasts for guidance. It was something like the equivalent of the "on the air" version of the official government gazette. The French recorded these daily broadcasts in the form of the "Le bulletin des écoutes Viet Minh." They would sometimes use the intelligence gleaned from them to send in special operations teams to arrest high-value enemy bureaucrats or dispatch bombers to destroy stockpiles of rice, medicines, or weapons. But the French never had the financial, logistical, or human resources to shut down the enemy's bureaucracy or confiscate the growing number of radios in its myriad of offices holding this sprawling state together. Those reading the Democratic Republic of Vietnam's cable traffic often could do little more than update their files, generating, as they did so, a goldmine of information for scholars like me. In short, radio communications streaking through the air allowed the embattled Vietnamese republic to assert its sovereignty and maintain a degree of administrative coherence and functionality that otherwise would have been dangerously lacking.[44]

The Hand-Courier System

However, we should not exaggerate the importance of modern communications in a time of war.[45] As essential as the hard-wiring of the state was at the time, radios could not transmit the lengthy documents the bureaucracy and General Staff needed in order to operate—party directives, thick government reports, lengthy military instructions and battle plans, pages of statistics and charts, photos, maps, voluminous tax records, to say nothing of wads of Indochinese piasters and vials of medicines and antibiotics. Again, other than in zones IV and V in central Vietnam and in the Thai Nguyen capital area in the north, the government could not rely on the preexisting postal system to deliver such things. Between 1945 and 1948, the French had conquered most of the provincial capitals in the deltas and pushed their opponents into some of the most inhospitable parts of the country. These jungle pockets certainly provided protection against colonial assaults, but they rarely lent themselves to easy and secure ground communications. And of course, the Vietnamese knew that the French were capable of reading just about anything they sent through the air.

To solve these problems and others, early on the Vietnamese developed a courier system which circulated documents by hand, with the couriers traveling on foot, bicycle, boat, and even horseback. The "Central Administrative Committee for Resistance Communications" operated this new mail distribution system from 1947–8 onwards. Some seventy cadres worked away diligently in this unit headquartered in the Thai Nguyen capital. Working in the service of the government's ministries and national fronts, the army's General Staff, and the Communist Party's standing committee, they prepared and dispatched mailbags and pouches containing instructions, orders, statistics, reports, newspapers, journals, propaganda, and photos. They collected, sorted, and distributed incoming mail and materials. The communists' secret courier system also organized and administered the routes used to move information from zone to zone. They knew from decades of experience how important a reliable courier system was to keeping the party and its now embattled state up and running.[46]

The government's regular postal service functioned mainly in free zones in and around the resistance capital in Thai Nguyen and areas of central Vietnam (IV and V). In these territories, thanks to hundreds of postal workers, the government circulated all sorts of information and documents it needed to operate without the French stopping them. Between 1950 and 1953, as Vietnamese military power expanded territorial control, the postal service in central and northern Vietnam operated forty provincial branches in charge of 370 district-level post offices and 2,657 smaller branches. In all, during the second half of the Indochina War, it circulated 15,239,000 documents, letters, and telegrams over an area of about 13,500 square kilometers. The service exploited 7,654 kilometers of telegraph and telephone lines and operated twenty-one wireless radios. Each year liaison agents covered some 6,000 kilometers in the delta and 5,000 in the highlands.[47]

Wartime postal officials recruited Vietnamese workers quite different from their colonial predecessors. For one, they had to know the terrain that they would cover more or less on their own. To do this, party and government recruiters tended to turn to young men and women who were quick on their feet both physically and mentally. They were usually in their teens or twenties. They were always carefully vetted. Those responsible for carrying particularly sensitive information required communist approval and even more extensive background checks.

Postal workers moving inside the core islands of the Vietnamese archipelago state had it easiest. They could move from one point to another with little fear of enemy surveillance or interception. Safest of all was the territorial cluster of zones IV and V in central Vietnam. It was also the case in areas in and around the resistance capital of Thai Nguyen as well as in zone IX in the southern Ca Mau peninsula. Things were very different, however, for those who moved among the Vietnamese archipelago state's "islands." They often had to cross into the borderlands, where very bad things could happen, as Nguyen Cong Luan describes poignantly in his memoirs (see chapter 1 of this volume). Others ventured into colonial-controlled Vietnam, where competing postal officials, soldiers, and security officials were always on the lookout for strangers and strange movements. Little wonder, then, that recruiters looked for individuals with nerves of steel, people who could keep their cool in the face of enemy surveillance and never talk if they were captured. Healthy individuals were needed too, because of other dangers lurking in the insalubrious areas they crossed—sickness, disease, and injury. Contracting malaria, cholera, or typhoid probably took as many postal workers' lives as the enemy did. A fall in the forest when travelling alone could end in tragedy. Tigers were still known to attack humans at the time.[48]

The terrain these people covered was often arduous. On average, in safe zones, a courier moving on foot carried several kilograms of mail a day over a distance of 20 kilometers. Those delivering on bikes could carry more, sometimes covering up to 150 kilometers in a day. Of course, distances varied depending on the nature of the terrain, the weather, and the level of enemy surveillance. A carrier's route ran between two or more way stations, normally located within a zone or even smaller blocks of territory. Upon arrival at their final destination, an official handler would empty their pouches, verify the contents, and then turn it all over to another worker who would either distribute it to the intended recipient or move it further along down the line on its route. On highly sensitive missions, messengers probably carried only a few documents or one special letter, and they usually delivered the message or merchandise personally.[49]

These foot soldiers rarely appear in the history of the Indochina War, and yet they were vital in keeping the war state running, as they did the underground cities. They asserted their government's sovereignty by their very movements. Deeply touched by the stories of those he had encountered during his four years working inside the Democratic Republic of Vietnam, Georges Boudarel provided the following description of these modest people moving across the ground, part of the connective tissue of the Vietnamese state in wartime, its human wiring, if you will:

> Every day, throughout Vietnam, they left their homes to maintain the contacts without which the resistance would never have been able to survive. Moving along impassable trails, very often barefoot, they took part in a real race against the clock, with only a simple bowl of rice and some dried fish for food. During the night, others passed by [enemy] posts, often traveling without a weapon on them. They advanced along paths where a trap might be hiding behind any bush. No sooner would they arrive at their destination than they would take off again, if the mission required it. And they walked on like this without stopping, alone in the forests and the rice fields, with the enemy watching out for them. And each day, there were those who died. Some ended up in the hands of an intelligence officer and that meant torture. Torture so terrible that it's too dreadful to describe— out of shame for those who administered it. And yet they did not talk. The resistance was, for many, the footprints of thousands of these agents, who guided a group, carried pouches full of mail or just one urgent letter, whether they managed to walk just 2 kilometers into a dangerous zone or went into the heart of the occupied zones, covering 60 kilometers in a day. They often died alone and in great suffering. And yet they were never alone. They were the human link, the blood that ran through the veins of the people. And had they not been deeply aware of the community they held up and which they had very largely nourished, then they never would have been able to surmount such hardships.[50]

French security officers may not have shared Boudarel's nationalist celebration of these messengers and the cause they served, but they would have agreed entirely with him that these brave liaison agents were vital to keeping their adversary's fragmented state up and running. And unsurprisingly, they did their best to stop them *en route* whenever they could. French intelligence services also tried to recruit these people to work for them in order to infiltrate the enemy's state.[51]

Postal liaisons with and within southern Vietnam were extremely difficult to operate during the war. In October 1947, as the French went on the attack above the 16th parallel, a high-level party delegation left for the south to create a secret line of communication to handle vital communications between the northern and southern halves of the Vietnamese archipelago state. This delegation recruited trustworthy personnel to run way stations and operate safe houses, which were essential to transmitting sensitive information and things that could not be sent over the heavily monitored airwaves. The party put two high-ranking communists in charge of this north-south link—Pham Van Dong as the Communist Party's special delegate to central Vietnam's Zone V and Le Duan as the head of the party's organization in the south. At some point in 1948, a secret, though extremely rudimentary, overland route started carrying mail and personnel to the south. This was the route Le Duc Tho used when he left the north in 1948 to make his way to the south about a year later. He carried with him top-secret party, government, and military documents for officials in central and southern parts of the republic.[52] That the French never seriously attacked zones IV and V before early 1954 remains one of the mysteries of the Indochina War for this author. In failing to do so, they allowed their enemy to connect the north and south of their sprawling state at its vital midsection.

6

Policing War

The eviction of the French and the Japanese from Indochina at the end of the Second World War opened the doors of the colonially established security services to those whom it had been tracking for so long. Nguyen Van Ngoc, the Democratic Republic of Vietnam's first chief of police for central Vietnam, was one of them. Sometime shortly after the Japanese capitulated on 15 August 1945, he walked into the colonial police station in downtown Hue to start his new job. While he does not tell us exactly what he discovered that day, his visit must have given him a close-up glimpse into what had made the colonial police tick—fingerprinting, criminal laboratories, filing systems with a great deal of information on different individuals, and a host of spies and informers. He does tell us that it was a satisfying feeling to stand behind the now vacant desk of Léon Sogny, the colonial police chief who had spied on anticolonialists from Hue for years. Nguyen Van Ngoc was now taking over that same position in the service of the nation-state. While there was no love lost for Sogny, Nguyen Van Ngoc had every intention of learning from French policing methods and knowledge. The new police chief even kept many good Vietnamese officers who had originally been trained by the French in their jobs: "I once again realized that they were an invaluable resource that the revolution had to know how to use."[1]

Policing the New Vietnamese State

The Colonial Origins of Early Vietnamese Policing

Nguyen Van Ngoc was right that Vietnam's intelligence and security services did not emerge in 1945 without any connection to the colonial past. Upon conquering Vietnam in the late nineteenth century, French admirals and then civilians created a host of security and intelligence services to keep tabs on the peoples they administered. As the Indochinese colonial state developed, so did its need for information on enemies both inside and outside Indochina. Worried by repeated revolts within Vietnam and troubled by the possibility that the Germans might help the anticolonialists outside the colony during the First World War, in 1917 the governor-general of Indochina consolidated a modern Indochinese-wide security apparatus known as the Sûreté générale. With the defeat of the Germans in 1918, the Sûreté rapidly shifted its attention to the potential threat the newly created Soviet Union might pose to the colonial order. The fear was that those running this first communist state in world history would make good on Lenin's promise to spread communist parties across the globe, including in its colonial parts. Security services in Indochina and elsewhere tracked the Communist International (often known as the Comintern) which Lenin had created in 1919 to spread communism around the world. During the interwar period, the authorities in Indochina expanded the Sûreté's political section, its staff, and technology to trace every kind of anticolonialist. Communist or not, they all represented a threat to the colonial order. The police also monitored Vietnam's vibrant religious world, the Catholics, Protestants, Buddhists and offshoots of the latter, like the Hoa Hao and Cao Dai faiths. Security officers compiled thick dossiers on all of these groups.[2]

Although French officials in Vietnam held the top posts in the Sûreté, they could never keep track of all these moving parts by themselves. Early on, the French relied on a host of Vietnamese civil servants, informants, and technicians to assist them in their work. These Vietnamese had the language skills and local knowledge essential to collecting information effectively over long periods of time. Until the Japanese overthrew the French and closed the Sûreté in March 1945, thousands of Vietnamese had worked in the Sûreté's offices inside and outside Indochina. They learned and mastered modern policing methods, such as fingerprinting, photography, and forensics. They used telegraphs to relay information from one post to another. Some combed the Vietnamese and Chinese language press, searching for signs of sedition, while others used their knowledge to plant informers within the highest reaches of the communist and nationalist ranks. Surveillance was at its apogee by the early 1930s, when the police smashed anticolonialist revolts in central and northern Vietnam. Proud of their record in doing so, the colonial authorities allowed a Left-leaning journalist, Andrée Viollis, to visit the Sûreté's headquarters in Hanoi at the time. Her description of the neatly arranged dossiers lining office walls is a memorable one:

> They are considerable and perfectly organized. 20,000 political files and 50,000 catalogue cards are kept there in perfect order in a vast library. Employes work away, as numerous as they are zealous. Others have the task of decoding telegrams coming in from China and beyond, monitoring letters (opening, photographing and then resealing them) while swarms of informers come and go moving about as they perform their foul work.[3]

We can be sure that Nguyen Van Ngoc discovered something like this during his visit to the colonial police headquarters in Hue in the fall of 1945. He certainly realized that he would need this colonial knowledge and these Vietnamese security specialists, who would turn their "foul work" into something noble by putting it in the service of the national cause.

There is another twist on this colonial connection, which deserves mention here: the colonial prison. When it came to staffing the highest and most sensitive positions in the Democratic Republic of Vietnam's security apparatus, there were two unwritten prerequisites: membership in the Communist Party and the experience of colonial imprisonment. In many ways, the "Colonial Bastille," to borrow one scholar's provocative term,[4] served as the elite police academy from which almost all of the DRV's top security chiefs and spymasters graduated. This should come as no surprise. Just as several German communists put behind bars by the Nazis during the Second World War returned from captivity to run East Germany's Stasi, so too did a tight-knit group of Vietnamese communists emerge from French prisons to run the post-colonial security apparatus.[5]

The two most important Vietnamese communist "police academies" were the colonial cellblocks on Poulo Condor Island located off the southern coast of Vietnam and in Son La province in the northwestern highlands. The latter had produced the likes of Nguyen Van Ngoc, whom we met above, and Le Gian, the man who served as director of the national security services between 1945 and 1953. Also spending time there were such important communists as Tran Dang Ninh, Le Duc Tho, and Tran Quoc Hoan. In 1945, Tran Dang Ninh, a powerful but highly discreet man, became the chief of the Communist Party's internal security services. Tran Quoc Hoan had worked as a printer in Hanoi during the 1930s. He ran the party's underground city in Hanoi until 1953, when he took over the national security services from Le Gian and ran them for another three decades. A man of steel, Le Duc Tho, would hammer out the Paris Peace Accord of 1973 with Henry Kissinger. In the south, Poulo Condor produced one of the most powerful bands of communist brothers in twentieth-century Vietnamese history: Le Duan, Nguyen Van Linh, Mai Chi Tho, and Pham Hung. The latter two ruled the southern police for almost half a century. Le Duan and Nguyen Van Linh, backed by Le Duc Tho, ran the party in the south during the Indochina conflict and then for the entire country during the war against the Americans. That was how important the colonial prison "education" was to running postcolonial Vietnam's security services, indeed the country itself.

Incarceration provided a common, formative experience to those who experienced it. For one, the prison brought communists together from all over the country and placed them together in one shared location. Crackdowns on a series of revolts in northern Vietnam and central Vietnam in 1930–31, and then in the south at the start of the Second World War, filled places like Poulo Condor and Son La with Vietnamese communists from all over the country. For another, many began to imagine an independent, future Vietnam from the microcosm of their prison experience. Even a famous bandit turned patriot in 1945, Bay Vien, recalled later that he first learned of the nationalist power of the word "Vietnam" (instead of the earlier term, "Annam"), from other inmates serving time in Poulo Condor. Communist prisoners also improved their mastery of the Marxist-Leninist canon behind bars. When they were not breaking rocks, literate and well-educated militants organized study sessions on communism. They discussed texts and ideas, memorized and recited party mantras, and exchanged books and pamphlets which had been smuggled in. Communists also converted fellow prisoners to the revolutionary faith whenever they could. To facilitate this process, they taught illiterate cellmates how to read the Romanized Vietnamese script, *quoc ngu*. The French helped them do this by mixing political prisoners with criminal detainees.[6]

These prisoners experienced the heavy hand of colonial power too. Some had endured torture of a medieval type and witnessed colonial atrocities. Political prisoners shared the punishing experience of living for long periods of time behind bars, hour after hour, day after day, and, for many, year after year. Monotony could be mind-wrecking. Living quarters were cramped and squalid. Work was often grueling. Sickness was all too common and medicines far too rare. Physical violence and verbal abuse were part and parcel of this universe. Many banded together to make it through. Some did not. "In prison," one of modern Vietnam's greatest minds wrote in the 1930s, "one either cracks or turns to steel."[7] The man who wrote this, Nguyen An Ninh, never made it out. The prison authorities let him die of disease in Poulo Condor in 1943.[8]

What is clear is that by the time the Japanese overthrew the French in March 1945, and, upon their capitulation, opened the gates of Son La and Poulo Condor, a handful of hardened party men stepped out of the "colonial Bastille" committed not only to winning national independence, but also to building the revolutionary Vietnam they had so long and carefully imagined in captivity—a Marxist-Leninist one. And having sacrificed so much of their freedom for so long, these people were not about to throw in the towel easily, succumb to enemy persuasion, or be intimidated by force during the Indochina War that soon followed. Little wonder that the communists at the helm of the Democratic Republic of Vietnam relied on these men to run their police and intelligence services during the thirty years of war that were to come until complete sovereignty was won.[9]

Something else happened in the colonial jail, and it bled directly into the newly created security services of 1945: the start of a long Vietnamese civil war. While the French Sûreté may have lumped Vietnamese communists and noncommunists together into the same anticolonialist bag, not all Vietnamese nationalists were imagining the "same Vietnam" as their communist colleagues inside or outside the colonial prison. They were, in fact, deeply divided ideologically as to who would define and, one day, control the soul of postcolonial Vietnam: would the future state be of a communist kind or one of a purely nationalist design? Political prisoners from the Vietnamese Nationalist Party embraced nationalism and Vietnamese independence as fiercely as the communists did. But they rejected the applicability of Marxism-Leninism and the creation of the single-party communist state it posited in the form of a dictatorship of the proletariat. They wanted a fully independent republic of a nationalist kind. They studied Sun Yat-sen's republican writings in prison, not Lenin's or Mao Zedong's.

However, by placing anticolonialists together in places like Poulo Condor, the French telescoped the ideological differences between these two groups. Political debates began in earnest within this microcosmic Vietnam the French had unwittingly created. It sometimes degenerated into physical violence between "nationalists" and "communists." This low-intensity clash occurring in colonial cellblocks among Vietnamese prisoners there paralleled the larger civil war that had broken out in southern Chinese cities in 1927 when Chiang Kai-shek, the head of the Chinese Nationalist Party, attacked the Chinese communists and established the Republic of China a year later in Nanjing. Although the Vietnamese civil war would only emerge for all to see following the Second World War, it had begun in the early 1930s in out-of-sight places like Poulo Condor.

Nationalism, communism, anticommunism, and hard jail time all combined to constitute the early cognitive lens through which communist security bosses and spymasters would later define enemies, interpret threats, and enforce correct social behavior. After taking power in mid-1945, communist "graduates" of Poulo Condor and Son La communicated this message to their students in lectures, training manuals, and one-on-one conversations. They made sure that their recruits knew that they had *two* enemies: the French colonialists *and* the Vietnamese anticommunists. This, in turn, gave rise to a deep mistrust of "noncommunism" within the Indochinese Communist Party's ranks and an almost existential hate of "anticommunism," one which the Vietnamese Nationalist and the Greater Vietnam parties came to symbolize in communist eyes. Nguyen Tai, a legendary spy who went up against the American Central Intelligence Agency during the Vietnam War, explains in his memoirs that during the late 1940s while training under Tran Quoc Hoan, the latter repeatedly drew upon his colonial prison experiences to impart vital lessons as to who were the enemies of the state (both real and imagined). In an internal address to police cadets in 1968, as the war against the Americans raged, Tran Quoc Hoan, now head of the national security services, told his listeners that they had to be on the constant lookout for "reactionary political parties," most importantly the Vietnamese Nationalist and Greater Vietnam ones. "These groups are extremely dangerous," he insisted, "the latter, the most reactionary, and the most recalcitrant remnants of the ruling class, of the landlords, of the feudalists, and of the capitalists." Imagining final victory, the chief of police concluded that the "struggle against them will be complex, difficult, and ferocious."[10]

There could be no concessions to those who would contest the communist right to rule. And there was an equally important corollary to this: an authentic nationalist could be nothing but a communist, the only form of national identity for the party at the helm of the Democratic Republic of Vietnam, and its security services in particular. Of course, anticommunist nationalists saw it in the opposite terms: a true Vietnamese could not be a communist. The war for Vietnam's postcolonial soul would be a civil one as much as it would be one of national liberation. And the security services would be on the front lines of both.

The Birth of the National Security Forces

This colonial detour helps to explain why, upon taking power in 1945, the Vietnamese communists did not need anyone to tell them why they needed a security service or spell out the inner workings of policing and information gathering to them. Veterans of the colonial "Bastille" were well versed in both modern and not-so-modern identification techniques and interrogation methods. They had no trouble grasping why policing was so important to building power. Holding on to it was the real challenge for the communists, as they knew when Ho Chi Minh declared Vietnam independent on 2 September 1945. Hostilities, we know, erupted within weeks in the south when the British allowed the French to dislodge Ho's officials from Saigon and other towns in the Mekong Delta. Meanwhile, from late September 1945, Chinese troops began arriving in central and northern Vietnam. Accompanying them were Vietnamese anticommunist nationalists who had resided in southern Chinese cities since fleeing French colonial repression years earlier. They were betting that their shared anticommunism alongside Chiang Kai-shek's occupying forces would unite them all in an effort to overthrow Ho Chi Minh and put their brand of nationalism at the helm of an independent Vietnam.

To protect and expand their power, the communists moved immediately to create a police force which would stay firmly under their control. Working from behind the scenes and drawing on prison contacts and local party networks, Tran Dang Ninh and Tran Quoc Hoan took the lead. In September 1945, they helped the government create the "Bureau of Security Services for North Vietnam." Le Gian served as its first director; Tran Hieu, a former prison-mate and fellow communist, was his deputy. In central Vietnam, as we know, Nguyen Van Ngoc was in charge. In the south, there were Mai Chi Tho and Pham

Hung. In all three regions, security officials did their best to vet experienced people coming from the Sûreté and recruit trustworthy new personnel, communists if possible; dispatch informants to monitor enemy troop movements; and collect information on any hostile threats to state power, foreign or domestic. On 21 February 1946, a week before the signing of the Franco-Chinese accord which opened the way for the French to replace the Chinese in the north, the communists at the helm of the government created the Public Security Department, better known as the Cong An (or security services). Housed in the Ministry of the Interior, it consisted of three regional services for northern, central, and southern Vietnam. Each one administered a provincial office and, depending on the local circumstances, operated at the lower levels too. The Cong An's main responsibility was, of course, to protect and consolidate the Democratic Republic of Vietnam. The security services maintained law and order, monitored Chinese, British, and French movements, kept tabs on the French settler population, combatted any anticommunist forms of trouble, and collected intelligence vital to protecting the state. (A specialized internal unit, the Central Espionage Service, did much of the information gathering.) The security services had a mandate to collect intelligence outside Vietnam as well, although little was to come of it in the early years.[11]

The communists directed the government's security services as best they could from on high. Although the head of the police, Le Gian, reported directly to the Ministry of the Interior led by Vo Nguyen Giap until early 1946, ultimately everyone answered to the party's security czars, Tran Quoc Hoan and Tran Dang Ninh. The latter was particularly powerful. Not only did the party put Tran Dang Ninh in charge of overseeing the activities of the government's security services, but it also entrusted him to police the internal functioning of the party itself. Tran Quoc Hoan implemented the party's security operations closer to the ground. He recruited and trained pivotal intelligence officers and established espionage and counterespionage networks in Hanoi which would operate throughout the Indochina and Vietnam wars, gathering information and running spies, informants, and moles. He took over the

party's security matters from Tran Dang Ninh with the creation of the
Ministry for the Security Services in 1953. Tran Quoc Hoan ruled it well
into the 1970s.[12]

In southern Vietnam, communist control was more precarious for
several reasons. Firstly, a failed communist uprising there in 1940 had
resulted in the decimation of the Indochinese Communist Party's networks, and party members there were in no position to dominate local
politics. Secondly, they had stiff competition from wary religious groups
like the Hoa Hao and Cao Dai. Thirdly, the rapid outbreak of war with
the French in late September 1945 had dispersed southern communists
into some of the most insalubrious and remote parts of the Mekong
Delta. During the conflict, communications with the party center in the
north and even across the south itself were poor. Leaders responsible
for policing in the south only heard about the formation of the new
security department in the north in February 1946, when they tuned
into a radio broadcast from Hanoi. In contrast, Ho Chi Minh's officials
in central and northern Vietnam had benefited from over a year to consolidate their security forces before full-scale war engulfed areas above
the 16th parallel.[13]

Nonetheless, when a tightly knit group of communists departed
Poulo Condor Island by boat after the Japanese capitulation and landed
in the south on the day war broke out with the French in September 1945, things were set to improve. We met these men in prison
above: Le Duan, Pham Hung, Mai Chi Tho, and Nguyen Van Linh. Led
by Le Duan, they rapidly took control of the party's southern leadership, began rebuilding party networks and membership, ended divisive internal feuds, and established contact with the north. Pham
Hung and Mai Chi Tho reorganized the security services in the south
along the lines outlined above for upper Vietnam. In May 1946, Pham
Hung became deputy director of the southern Cong An bureau. Like
Tran Quoc Hoan in the north, he operated from behind the scenes,
building up contacts and expanding his information-gathering networks in and around Saigon. He and Mai Chi Tho were in charge of
the security services in the south for the entire course of the Indochina War.[14]

The outbreak of full-scale war in late 1946 in Hanoi forced the central and northern security services into the countryside. The security service's main headquarters moved to Thai Nguyen province, while the police in central Vietnam pulled back into zones IV and V. My Tho province served as the main base for the southern security services. Working from all of these areas, the DRV expanded the Cong An's control throughout government-controlled territories. They organized the reception of information about internal and external threats, plus its classification, analysis, and exploitation. This included the monitoring of religious and ethnic groups, "counterrevolutionary" parties, and the Vietnamese population residing under their control, as well as those living in contiguous enemy territories. They updated card catalogues and subject files. They kept extensive biographical profiles of enemy leaders, agents, and operatives. Security officials read the press, listened to local and international broadcasts, and provided reports on all of this to decision-makers who needed to know what their adversaries were doing.

Security directors carefully recruited agents and informants inside the cities, along lines of communication, in enemy-controlled territories, and within their own zones. They exploited any colonial knowledge that could serve their cause, including part of the Sûreté's archives, which they went through meticulously after taking power. In the early 1950s, the French were shocked to learn that the enemy police force's identification unit in the southern maquis was modeled on their own. Even worse, the enemy was still trying to recruit specialists from inside the colonial ranks.[15] Of course, none of this ever worked smoothly. Leaks occurred, agents defected, enemy moles and double-agents existed, and mistakes were made; but by and large it worked. Within a few years, the leaders of the Democratic Republic of Vietnam were in a position to gather information essential to decision-making, protecting the state, expanding communist control, and monitoring society more systematically.[16]

Early on, the security services kept tabs as best they could on civil servants and soldiers in their respective zones. Officials opened investigations into any suspicious activities, interrogated suspects, and studied their files rigorously. Defections from the party were always a cause for concern: why did this person actually leave? Was he a spy? Did she have accomplices? Were the French involved? What about those pesky anticommunist parties? In the late 1940s, for example, the security services in central Vietnam's Zone IV brought in a young partisan, Xuan Phuong, and questioned her about her close friend who had recently left the resistance. As we saw in an earlier chapter, her well-off companion from Hue had left the resistance, unable to stomach the difficult conditions. The Cong An was not so sure about that and continued to question her. Why, the investigating officer repeatedly asked her, had her friend really disappeared? Did she work for the French? As the accused later related the experience: "I had to reiterate my answer at least five times and then write it down. Two days later, I was called in again. 'Write down what you said.' Then two days later, again: 'Write.'" Finally, several months later, the local head of security called her back in for the final verdict:

> "Brave Phuong," he said to me, "We now know that you had nothing to do with what happened. I interrogated you because I couldn't do otherwise. As of now, the case is closed. Reassure yourself."
>
> "I had told you the truth. Why did you order me to write it down?"
>
> "In a similar situation, even I would have had to do it. You were with someone who escaped, so it was normal procedure to interrogate you."[17]

This example is important for another reason: by way of this meticulous investigation, the security services also confirmed Xuan's patriotism and dedication to national independence. Reassured by what they saw in her now-thickened file, Xuan's minders asked her to go one step further by joining the Communist Party. They reminded her that membership would open new doors for her professionally, socially, and politically. Xuan declined the offer. When she told her uncle, a party member himself, he reprimanded her: "Are you an imbecile, or what? In the Party, you would have a lot of advantages. First of all, they would trust you much more. Then you would ascend the hierarchy. Your future would be all arranged."[18]

She was not the only ardent anticolonialist to balk at becoming a communist. Tran Ngoc Chau had also served Ho Chi Minh's Vietnam as an officer during the Indochina War. His conduct, leadership, and bravery in battle were such that the communist political minder in his zone offered Chau the chance to join the party. As Chau remembered a friend putting the offer to him in 1948:

> He thinks you are an excellent cadre and a good example for the troops, and he wants to know if you are willing to join the Communist Party. The party will make you an even better man and cadre to serve the country and the people with much greater efficiency, he said.[19]

Tran Ngoc Chau turned down the offer. Two years afterwards, in 1950, he left the resistance to join Bao Dai's emerging army and later still he became a counterinsurgency specialist in its successor state, the Republic of Vietnam, during the Vietnam War. Others, however, accepted the communist invitation and usually saw their careers take off. Tran Ngoc Chau's brother, in fact, had already joined the party and served as deputy, then as chief of intelligence and counterespionage in Zone V in southern central Vietnam—a position which only a communist member could have held. In extending these discreet yet well-planned invitations to join the party, the security services played an indirect though important role in recruiting and building a bureaucratic communist elite to help the party center expand its control throughout the archipelago.

Many a Vietnamese family today can tell both stories: how one member accepted the party's offer while the other did not. It was a choice that changed lives forever and set different members of the same family along very different roads. Tran Ngoc Chau recently passed away in California. His brother stayed in Vietnam where he is buried today. Xuan Phuong remained part of the communist resistance on anticolonialist grounds; but she saw her "no" to the party's invitation set a limit on how high she could go within the Marxist-Leninist state they were determined to build.

The Security Services: On the Front Lines of Civil War

Obviously, the French were not the only ones to challenge Ho Chi Minh's right to run an independent Vietnam. Noncommunist nationalist parties and religious groups opposed what they saw as the Communist Party's monopolization of power in postcolonial Vietnam. Several leaders of these noncommunist groups knew their competitors very well from the time they had spent together behind colonial prison bars or in exile. Their opposition to the communists at the head of the Democratic Republic of Vietnam brought this civil war that had been brewing since the early 1930s among prisoners in Poulo Condor and political exiles in the backstreets of southern Chinese cities into the open. And the security services were on the front lines.[20]

The Security Services and Civil War in
Upper Vietnam (1945–6)

The anticommunist Vietnamese parties contesting the communist core of the Democratic Republic of Vietnam after the Second World War consisted of three main groups: the Vietnamese Nationalist Party (VNQDD) led by Vu Hong Khanh, the Dai Viet or Greater Vietnam under Truong Tu Anh's leadership, and the Alliance Group marshaled by Nguyen Hai Than. None of them were pro-French; all of them were nationalist; and each was fiercely anticommunist. Created in 1927, the VNQDD had launched a famous "general uprising" in 1930, but the French smashed it. Some of its leaders fled; others were sent to jail in Poulo Condor or marched to the guillotine, including the party's legendary founder, Nguyen Thai Hoc. Vu Hong Khanh replaced the latter, having escaped to southern China and kept the party alive in places like Kunming, thanks to overseas Vietnamese residing there and Chinese republican support.

The Alliance Group was a collection of Vietnamese patriots based in southern China. The party dated back to the time of Phan Boi Chau, one of Vietnam's best-known anticolonialists. One of his top lieutenants, Nguyen Hai Than, ran the party in southern China after Phan Boi Chau returned to Vietnam in 1925. Like Ho Chi Minh, Nguyen Hai

Than had spent most of his revolutionary life outside Vietnam. Unlike Ho, however, he had rejected communism as the only way to achieve national salvation. He believed in creating some form of republican government similar to the one Sun Yat-sen and Chiang Kai-shek were in the process of establishing in China and worked closely with Chinese republican leaders in China until his return to Vietnam in 1945.

Created in 1939, the Dai Viet was a noncommunist coalition of younger, urban, mainly northern nationalists. This party had emerged inside Vietnam with vigor during the Left-wing Popular Front period in France and its empire. But once the Second World War began, renewed French repression sent its important figures underground or into exile. Its main leader was a charismatic law student named Truong Tu Anh. He was convinced that the very existence of Vietnam was in peril and advocated the creation of a strong state capable of unifying the country and ensuring its survival against colonialism and communism.[21]

The communists in control of the DRV had no love lost for this anticommunist triumvirate, these three nationalist opposition parties—the VNQDD, the Dai Viet, and the Alliance. And the feeling was most assuredly mutual. In the days following the communist seizure of power in August 1945, before the Chinese arrived, Ho's security officials jailed dozens of noncommunist nationalists who had collaborated with the French or the Japanese or worked against the communists in the past. The chief of the government's newly created security service in the north, Le Gian, recounts in his memoirs how he toured a jail near Hanoi at the time and viewed with great satisfaction the incarceration of several dangerous "traitors" who, as he saw it, "had blood debts" towards the people and the party. A certain Nguyen Ngoc Son was one of them. In the colonial prison, Le Gian wrote, this man had taunted communists and worked against their efforts to recruit members from among the prison population. The northern security service executed him. They also arrested those who had been political notables in Hue before the war, such as Ngo Dinh Khoi, his brother Ngo Dinh Diem, and Pham Quynh, for fear that they would help the French return to power via the monarchy they had always controlled. Ngo Dinh Khoi and Pham Quynh perished in September 1945. Only Ho's personal intervention saved Diem, known for his anticolonialism, from a similar fate. In all, several thousand people arrested during the first few months of the republic's existence were executed or died in custody.[22]

The arrival of Chinese republican troops to Vietnam above the 16th parallel put a brake on the executions and delayed the start of a full-blown civil war that fall. The communists realized that they could not authorize their security forces to attack—at least, not directly—the Vietnamese nationalists without risking Chinese intervention in their domestic politics. Determined to deny the Chinese any such pretext, the communists lined up behind Ho Chi Minh swallowed hard and allowed the triumvirate parties to organize propaganda drives, operate two or three opposition newspapers, and even to publish political cartoons satirizing the communists and the president himself. Thanks to this Chinese security umbrella, noncommunist parties widened their memberships, organized meetings, mobilized youth groups, and recruited their own militias, something that would have been unthinkable under the French, but which the communists had to accept. The opposition parties organized anti-Viet Minh demonstrations, criticized the government openly, and gave free rein to their anticommunism. They called for the creation of a wider governing coalition, with noncommunists holding key positions. Some called for even more.

The differences that had first divided communists and noncommunists during the interwar period now boiled over in the streets of Hanoi, Haiphong, and Hue in the form of verbal exchanges and political violence which fell just shy of outright conflict—kidnappings, assaults, skirmishes, and assassinations. Things got so bad that in mid-November 1945 the communists decided to "dissolve" their party as a sign of their patriotism and willingness to put the nation before party. More than anything else though, their move was designed to deny the Chinese occupying forces any excuse for overthrowing the Democratic Republic of Vietnam or putting an anticommunist coalition more to its liking in charge of it. Although the Indochinese Communist Party continued to exist, a party that has to fake its "dissolution" in order to survive is hardly in a strong position. The communists knew it, and their anger at the noncommunists burned red-hot as a result. In his memoirs,

Le Gian recalls the fury that overcame him every time he heard the VNQDD call on the "people" to oppose the communists or accuse Ho Chi Minh of being "pro French."[23] For the time being, though, the head of the police and his party had to accept that the presence of the Chinese was needed to protect the fledgling Vietnamese republic from an immediate attack by the French.

Civil war finally broke out unmistakably in June 1946, when the Chinese (having signed an agreement with the French a few months earlier) began withdrawing the bulk of their troops from northern Indochina. A few weeks later, the communists' security services turned on the anticommunists in Hanoi while Vo Nguyen Giap ordered the army to attack the VNQDD's troops located north of the capital. We will probably never know what, exactly, sparked the outbreak of civil war in Hanoi, but the incendiary event occurred sometime in early July 1946. According to official communist histories published long after the events, the Cong An got wind of a Dai Viet "plot" to join the "colonialists" in provoking Ho's militias into attacking a French parade scheduled for 14 July, Bastille Day, in downtown Hanoi. If the communists could be made to fire on the procession, the Dai Viet would have provided the French with the pretext they needed to overthrow Ho's government and, in exchange, to install them in power instead. It would also give the French an excuse to halt negotiations underway with Ho Chi Minh in Paris. The author of this alleged coup d'état was Truong Tu Anh, leader of the Dai Viet. Le Gian reported all of this to the minister of the interior and acting president, Huynh Thuc Khang, and the Communist Party's security chief, Tran Dang Ninh.[24]

As the communist version has the story,[25] before signing off on Le Gian's plans for a preemptive assault, Huynh Thuc Khang wanted proof. Ho had instructed him to maintain order at all costs during his absence in France. On 11 July, Huynh Thuc Khang authorized the police to enter the Dai Viet's headquarters in downtown Hanoi and search the premises. The search occurred the next day when the police allegedly found the abovementioned plan to overthrow the government. On seeing this document, Khang reportedly blurted out in anger, "Kill them! Wipe out this band of traitors to the country." With this "proof," the security forces immediately descended upon the opposition's headquarters, offices, and presses in Hanoi. Security forces arrested dozens of leaders and smaller fry. Some nationalists died in brief firefights while others miraculously escaped, including Truong Tu Anh. The Ministry of the Interior then confiscated all the opposition newspapers.[26]

In the countryside, the government dispatched its army to the north to recover provinces held by the opposition as their Chinese protectors retired across the border. Ngo Van Chieu, one of the commanding officers in the DRV's army dispatched to break up the Vietnamese Nationalist Party's troops in the Yen Bay area north of Hanoi, later recalled: "Until then the only Vietnamese troops stationed in this region were those of the VNQDD political militia. They had arrived with the Chinese and hardly recognized the government's authority. As the Chinese pulled out, we advanced with their withdrawal and took control of the evacuated villages and cities." Later, Ngo Van Chieu described a firefight he survived while taking a northern town from the nationalists: "On the right side of the building, a man emerged with a gun in his hand, a bayonet attached to it. He's three meters from me and has me in his sights. I throw myself to the ground and shoot. He froze there, still looking at me, his gun held high, then he collapsed."[27] Vietnamese were now killing Vietnamese. The security services' raid on the opposition parties in Hanoi in July 1946 and the army's simultaneous attacks on their bases in the countryside marked the first in a series of civil wars which would last well into the 1970s.[28]

The Cong An and Religious Strife in the South

Shocked by the Democratic Republic of Vietnam's elimination of the opposition parties in the north in 1946, French advisers to the high commissioner in Saigon were decidedly loath to deal one-on-one with the Democratic Republic of Vietnam and its president, Ho Chi Minh. The chief political adviser to the high commissioner of Saigon, Léon Pignon, was outraged when he learned that some French military commanders had actually *helped* Vo Nguyen Giap's army to eliminate the noncommunist nationalist parties in northern Vietnam during the summer of

1946 (he conveniently forgot that French officers had done so because of the strong anticolonialist sentiments of these nationalists). Machiavellian to a fault, Pignon was convinced that he could exploit the triumvirate's military weakness and hostility for Ho's government and win them over to the French colonial cause. On 4 January 1947, as the Battle of Hanoi raged, Pignon told his superiors that the French policy should be to "transpose the quarrel we have with the Viet Minh party on to a strictly Vietnamese playing field while we ourselves take part as little as possible in the campaigns and reprisals which should be the work of the native adversaries of this party."[29] The strategy Pignon advised—and which the French applied during the Indochina War—was of course classic divide and rule, but now it came in the guise of Vietnamese civil war. In order to hold on to their colonial state, the French did what colonizers always do: they played one side off against the other. They stoked up civil wars and made them still more deadly by arming one side against the other.[30]

The French targeted two religious groups first—the Cao Dai and the Hoa Hao. Early on, each had posed problems for Ho Chi Minh's officials in the south. The Cao Dai was a syncretic, monotheistic religion, combining elements of Taoism, Buddhism, Confucianism, Christianity, and Humanism. The Cao Dai faith emerged following the First World War, thanks to the initiative of a group of civil servants, landowners, and peasants attracted by the messianic message of the religion in a time of rapid socioeconomic change. One of the prime movers in this new religion was Pham Cong Tac. A colonial civil servant, he resigned from his post in the 1920s and went to Tay Ninh province in the western Mekong, where he became the movement's supreme spiritual leader. During the 1930s, he set it on an increasingly political trajectory, which drew the immediate attention of the Sûreté. During the Second World War, the colonial police arrested him because of his links to the Japanese and his attempts to create an autonomous religious state and militia free of colonial control. The French Vichy authorities sent this inspiring leader off to a prison cell in Madagascar. (Once there, he served time with none other than the future architects of the communist security services, Tran Hieu and Le Gian.)

The Hoa Hao faith followed a similar track. It had emerged in the late 1930s in the Mekong Delta. Its messianic leader, the young and dashing Huynh Phu So, drew heavily upon local Buddhist beliefs to build this millenarian religious movement into a considerable sociopolitical force. Uniquely charismatic, he soon attracted a large following among poor peasants looking for a saviour and the promise of a better world to help them make it through the difficult economic times the Depression had created. By the time the Japanese started moving into Indochina in 1940, Huynh Phu So had several thousands of his followers concentrated in large swaths of the western Mekong Delta. During the Second World War, the Japanese supported him and, when the French arrested this religious leader, they forced the Sûreté to release him. With the defeat of his Japanese backers in August 1945, Huynh Phu So temporarily aligned his followers with the Democratic Republic of Vietnam, as did local Cao Dai forces.[31]

However, this cooperation did not last for long. Religious leaders of both groups were wary of the nationalist government's communist nucleus and opposed to the idea of subordinating their forces to any state control other than their own. Determined to detach the Cao Dai from the DRV's territorial hold, the French flew Pham Cong Tac back to the Mekong Delta in mid-1946 on the condition that he rally his church to the French cause. In exchange, they offered his congregation more autonomy within the framework of the Indochinese federation and, in 1949, the Associated State of Vietnam too. Pham Cong Tac agreed. And on 8 January 1947, as the Expeditionary Corps took Hanoi by force, Pham Cong Tac signed an accord with the French along these lines. Within a few weeks, thousands of his followers began to leave the DRV and cross over to the French side.

The DRV's southern security services were aware of what the French were doing and authorized their representatives to contact the Cao Dai leadership secretly in a bid to stop their colonial adversaries. Talks took place, but to no avail. The Cao Dai asked Ho's officials to pull out of Tay Ninh, their home base. The government refused. Ho's representatives duly explained that the Democratic Republic of Vietnam was the sole and sovereign state representing all of Vietnam. The Cao Dai disagreed and, of course, so did the French. Things rapidly went from bad to worse. In February 1947, the chief of the south's Cong An, Pham Hung, authorized a crackdown on the Cao Dai "reactionaries."[32] By June 1947, most of this religious group's forces had crossed over to the French side, but not without leaving behind a trail of blood as Vietnamese went to war against each other in the south. Pignon's plan to sow civil war on colonial terms seemed to be working.[33]

Things further deteriorated when the Hoa Hao and the national government clashed. At the outset, Huynh Phu So was a special delegate in Ho Chi Minh's southern administration. However, when this Hoa Hao leader began to ally his followers with a political party independent of the government's control (the Dan Xa Dang), relations between the two sides unraveled. Like Pham Cong Tac, Huynh Phu So was loath to submit his military forces to national control. And his religious antipathy for communism was no secret. When, in early 1947, the southern security agents learned that he had entered into secret negotiations with the French secret services, the DRV's leaders reacted with force. In April 1947, the government authorized the execution of Huynh Phu So for "the crime of treason towards the Nation and for having fomented a civil war in the Western [part of southern Vietnam] at a time when all the energy of the people must be unified for the resistance."[34]

In the government's eyes, this may have seemed fully justified; they were, after all, at war with the French. However, tens of thousands of Hoa Hao believers saw it differently and started abandoning Ho Chi Minh in droves. Even though the French and Bao Dai would find it just as difficult to integrate these religious groups into their own state-building projects, the DRV's hard-handed policies contributed to alienating two major religious hierarchies and many thousands of their believers. This, in turn, made it particularly difficult for Ho Chi Minh to extend his state's territorial control over resources and people in the south. Recruitment of civil servants and solidiers became especially difficult in these strategically important areas of southern Vietnam. Hundreds, perhaps thousands, died in civil violence. Moreover, the hatred many Cao Dai and Hoa Hao believers now felt for the Democratic

Republic of Vietnam and the communists in charge of it only made it easier for the French to win them over. Such repression, no matter how imperative it may have seemed, undermined the coalition government the communists were trying to hold together.[35]

To be fair, the communists were asking the impossible of their security officials on the ground in the south. It would never be easy to adopt such a tolerant policy towards these groups when the Franco-Vietnamese side was determined to arm and use them against Ho's Vietnam. To make matters worse, in mid-1948, the French successfully rallied yet another southern group to the Franco-Vietnamese side, the brigands turned patriots known as the Binh Xuyen. Led by Bay Vien, this militia group broke off violently with the DRV in 1948, as the French Deuxième Bureau, the military intelligence branch of the army, adroitly brought them into the colonial federation. That the Binh Xuyen might well have been the group behind the massacre of Europeans in Saigon in September 1945 mattered little to the French authorities. But thwarting the Democratic Republic of Vietnam's nation state-building project did. Once Hoa Hao, Cao Dai, and Binh Xuyen leaders formally signed their "acts of submission" to the French in carefully organized ceremonies, Léon Pignon and Bao Dai pinned medals on their chests in exchange for their loyalty. (DRV authorities did much the same when they rallied splinter groups to their side.)

Together with the French, the Hoa Hao, Cao Dai, and Binh Xuyen rolled back the DRV's territorial hold on the ground bit by bit.[36] However, by agreeing to rely on the French for protection and military assistance, each group had now agreed to join the Indochinese colonial state the French were rebuilding in the form of the Associated State of Vietnam in 1949. This also included the Vietnamese Nationalist Party and the Dai Viet. Instead of remaining in exile in southern China or setting up a guerrilla state in the Vietnamese countryside to oppose both the "French colonialists" and the "Vietnamese communists," these anticommunist parties chose to work with the French. They all thought they could pressure the French to accord them full independence. But what would they do if the French used them for their colonial purposes without granting it?[37]

The Weakness of Early Military Intelligence

The Birth of Military Intelligence

Armies require intelligence to function, and postcolonial ones are no exception to this rule. Five days after Ho Chi Minh declared the independence of Vietnam on 2 September 1945, his two main military leaders, Vo Nguyen Giap and Hoang Van Thai, established the Office of Military Intelligence. Operating via the communist-controlled General Staff, its main tasks included the collection, processing, and distribution of information needed for establishing orders of battle, organizing military operations, and conceptualizing military strategy. Vo Nguyen Giap and Hoang Van Thai entrusted the direction of this new intelligence branch to Hoang Minh Dao. He was a trusted communist, a veteran of the colonial prison, as well as an experienced underground liaison agent in Haiphong and Hanoi. At the outset, the Office of Military Intelligence's operations focused on areas above the 16th parallel—keeping a close eye on the Chinese occupation army, then the 15,000 French troops who arrived to replace it in mid-1946, and, of course, the anti-communists building up their own armed forces as well.

With the outbreak of full-scale war in late 1946, military intelligence moved to Thai Nguyen province, alongside the General Staff, the central government, and the Communist Party's Military Commission led by Vo Nguyen Giap. A series of changes during 1947 and 1948 consolidated military intelligence in the form of a new body called the Bureau of Intelligence. Hoang Minh Dao transferred to the south, where he helped to create a military intelligence branch for the commander of the southern forces, General Nguyen Binh. Tran Hieu took over as the head of this new intelligence bureau for the army.[38]

But establishing a consolidated military intelligence service in the late 1940s was one thing. Getting it to work efficiently on the ground was another. In August 1947, Vo Nguyen Giap leveled a severe critique at his intelligence people as the army, on the run, regrouped in the northern hills. An intelligence service was "absolutely essential," he wrote, to the army's ability to "know and defeat the enemy." However, Giap lamented that his intelligence officers were badly trained and others were even suspected of being enemy spies. Moreover, having been concentrated in the cities until late 1946, the army's intelligence officers had little contact with the Vietnamese "masses" who were concentrated in the countryside. In a time of guerrilla warfare, Giap stressed, the people were the obvious source of information on enemy troops' movements and strength. Surely, he asked, it would be easier for the Vietnamese to win their support than the French?

But this was apparently not the case. Nowhere was this more evident than in the surprise French attack on senior party officials in their government hideout in the northern province of Cao Bang near the Chinese border. In late 1947, Operation Léa caught the Vietnamese armed forces off guard and came very close to capturing many of the government's leaders. A recent communist study claims that operatives in Hanoi only learned of the date of the attack two days before it was to occur. However, because of communication problems, this vital intelligence only reached Giap in the north as colonial paratroopers were making their raid.[39] More than anything else, the near-miss at Cao Bang taught the Vietnamese that intelligence gathering and sharing had to be improved fast. Shortly thereafter, in November 1947, delegates of the Ministry of the Interior's Public Security Department and the Ministry of Defense's Bureau of Military Intelligence met to improve cooperation between these two services. Given that the security services were already in a position to obtain intelligence of military value in the cities, a way had to be found so that it could be relayed rapidly to the army's decision-makers. It was decided that Le Gian, the head of the Public Security Department, would work with Tran Hieu in charge of the Bureau of Military Intelligence. (The fact that both men knew each other from prison in Madagascar helped.) The result was that the security services began sharing information gleaned from the underground cities with the military intelligence bureau, so that the military authorities had what they needed to devise policy accordingly.[40]

Despite these efforts at improvement, until 1950 military intelligence remained weak. Several factors explain this. Firstly, whereas the security services had latched on to the preexisting colonial infrastructure and civil servants to build an effective police force, the Vietnamese General Staff never confiscated the French colonial army's military archives or recruited many Vietnamese from its prewar staff. This was probably because there weren't many; the French Sûreté had monopolized most information gathering of any type before 1945. Secondly, the guerrilla nature of the first half of the Indochina conflict meant that the army's demand for detailed military intelligence on the enemy remained relatively low. Of course, guerrilla commanders needed to know where the enemy was, where he intended to go, and how well armed an intruding French force was, but detailed reports were not truly imperative during this early phase of the hostilities. In fact, the security services, rather than the military intelligence bureau, probably served as the most important source of intelligence for the army until 1950. The Cong An's agents counted troops entering and leaving the cities, planted moles in the enemy's military ranks, and religiously collected and circulated information and statistics on the French Union's forces to their counterparts in military intelligence.[41]

Things improved following the Chinese communist victory in 1950. In 1951, the Chinese would help their Vietnamese counterparts to modernize their military intelligence and communications services still further. This would be essential to running a professional army and providing it with the information and analysis it needed to conduct much more sophisticated set-piece battles over long distances and for extended periods of time. But even so, the collaborative nature of intelligence gathering between the security services and the military bureau continued during the second half of the war. When the Vietnamese remodeled their military intelligence in 1950, its new format still consisted of a service called the Liaison Directorate. It worked with the civilian security services to provide the General Staff's intelligence people with the information they needed to organize large military campaigns until 1954.[42]

Analytical Minds: The H122 Affair

The French secret services were clearly aware of the urban origins of their enemy's information gathering operations. In fact, French military intelligence, the Deuxième Bureau, took advantage of their adversary's reliance on the Cong An to execute one of the most effective deception operations of the Indochina War. It would sow panic within the army and even briefly divide the leadership against itself. In Vietnamese circles this event has gone down in history as the "H122 Incident."

Trouble apparently began in March 1948, when the security services in Hanoi obtained and forwarded to their superiors an enemy document entitled: "Report by an Agent Codenamed H122." The Cong An immediately transferred this information to the army's General Staff. Not only did agent H122's report reveal the General Staff's military plans for the upcoming Fall–Winter offensive, but the information it contained was also judged by the DRV's military branch to be "extremely accurate and reliable." After intense discussions, Vietnamese analysts and decision-makers concluded that a mole had to be working in the upper reaches of the DRV's military command for the French to know such details. Orders immediately went out to security services and the military intelligence bureau to locate the traitor. Arrests and interrogations multiplied within the army as investigators went to work. Within one month, "several hundred military cadres and officers at the regimental level were arrested and interrogated." Intelligence services resorted to the use of torture in several cases to try to flush out the mole. Some 200 cadres and military personnel and over 100 civilians underwent strong-armed interrogations. Under psychological and physical pressure, many admitted to being in the pay of the Deuxième Bureau or members of anticommunist nationalist parties. [43]

Things deteriorated further as accusations and counteraccusations spread from one office to another, sweeping through combat units, and even spilling into the party ranks, as people tried to save their skins. Paranoia morphed into hysteria. To prevent a complete meltdown, the Communist Party called in its security chief, Tran Dang Ninh, to help. It was a smart move. Tran Dang Ninh was known to be coolheaded, analytically minded, highly intelligent, and fair. He scrupulously and systematically investigated the affair with his security and intelligence officials. He apparently interviewed dozens of prisoners, questioning them carefully and respectfully, comparing and crosschecking their "confessions." He put a brake on the use of torture. After thorough reflection and consultation with his investigating teams and others in the party leadership, he concluded—and carefully explained—that this was a French-mounted deception plan designed to sow internal divisions— as it had been doing quite successfully. There was, he concluded, no mole behind codename "H122."[44]

This intelligence fiasco is important for several reasons. On the one hand, this toxic French document did indeed sow paranoia within the party and military leadership. The DRV interrogators not only saw the hand of the Deuxième Bureau, but also imagined the faces of their counterrevolutionary bogeymen, the VNQDD, Alliance Group, and the Dai Viet. What was still worse, these fears of subversion had led officials to apply torture in counterproductive ways. On the other hand, in the end, the Communist Party avoided a debilitating and potentially divisive breakdown. The leadership clearly had access to highly educated and analytical people like Tran Dang Ninh. He had the authority and trust needed to carry out an in-depth investigation into such a sensitive matter and ensure that his conclusions were accepted. This was essential to maintaining unity at a crucial point in the war.

Given the weakness of military intelligence, it is tempting to conclude here that the security services were an all-powerful party institution allowing communists to control, protect, and build the state, but that would be going too far. The communists controlled the upper levels of the Cong An from the start. But as with so many other areas of the DRV, they had to rely on a host of noncommunists to operate it at its lower levels. As late as 1950, Pham Van Dong lamented that the Communist Party still did not completely control the Cong An: "With regards to one branch of particular importance, the security services, we do not fully control it from top to bottom."[45] And that was a problem Pham Van Dong and the rest of his party could only begin to fix in 1950: once Mao Zedong had thrown his weight behind Ho Chi Minh.

7

Trickle Economics

In the early hours of 20 November 1946, a Chinese junk arrived in the northern port of Haiphong, docked, and began unloading a stock of petrol. A French patrol boat arrived shortly thereafter and took the junk in tow, while three security officers on the quay confiscated the fuel. Tensions mounted when government officials suddenly appeared on the scene. The French told them that this customs matter did not concern them; it was a Franco-Chinese affair. The Vietnamese disagreed and took the Frenchmen into custody. Upon learning of this, the French military commander stationed in Haiphong rushed troops downtown to free his men. After a brief firefight outside the police station costing the life of a French soldier, the Vietnamese released the three officials. Things could have ended there, but over the next two days the French issued two ultimatums calling on Ho Chi Minh's government to surrender control of Haiphong and its port. When the Vietnamese refused, on 23 November, four warships anchored in the harbor opened their cannons on the city and a nearby village, killing at least 1,000 Vietnamese in a hail of artillery fire. Nineteenth-century-French gunboat diplomacy was alive and well in the twentieth.[1]

This clash over customs control in Haiphong in November 1946 was anything but an economic sideshow in the events leading up to the outbreak of full-scale war a month later. It was at the center of the march towards full-scale war. Indeed, by seizing that Chinese junk filled with petrol and then by using the resulting violence as a pretext to seize Haiphong, the French lit the match that set off the first Vietnamese revolutionary war. Students of British and American colonial history will find nothing surprising about this. After all, the American War of Independence got its start in Boston harbor in 1773 when the British and their colonial subjects clashed over the taxation of imports of tea coming from China. Of course, behind each fiscal showdown lurked the real issue at hand—sovereignty.[2] Who had the right to tax in the two colonies? The colonized or the colonizers? What no one could know as the French and the Vietnamese went to war to answer that question was the degree to which economics would remain at the heart of the Indochina War until its bitter end.

War Economics

Before Haiphong

The Allied decision to divide Indochina at the 16th parallel into two zones to receive the Japanese surrender had enormous consequences for the Vietnamese economy. Below that line, the British set off a limited colonial conflict in Saigon on 23 September 1946 when they allowed the French to attack the Democratic Republic of Vietnam. Economically, Ho's officials in the south never really had the time to do much before the French struck. One month was not a long time. There was one notable exception, however: during those four weeks the Vietnamese shipped as much Japanese and French-stockpiled rice as they could from the Mekong Delta to areas north of the 16th parallel. Thanks to this food and a better than usual rice harvest in central and northern areas in 1946, Ho's government ended the famine of 1944–5 and in so doing solved one of the young republic's most pressing economic problems.[3]

In areas above the 16th parallel, Chiang Kai-shek's commanding officers sent to accept the Japanese surrender were loath to allow such a destabilizing conflagration to break out on their yearlong watch. In fact, by blocking any immediate French takeover, the Chinese allowed Ho Chi Minh's people to expand their hold over the colonial state's economic, financial, and fiscal offices as well as the Vietnamese agents in charge of them. French officials could do little. Still sitting in camps where the Japanese had confined them a few months earlier, they watched as the new national government abolished taxes and state monopolies. People cheered the elimination of the poll tax and the salt and alcohol monopolies long symbolic of oppressive colonial power. However, Ho could not do away with taxes entirely, and he reprimanded local firebrands who had tried to do so. The fledgling government had to pay civil servants, purchase imports, and finance a new army. As a result, a host of colonial permits and taxes on land, transport, business, trade, and building continued in national form. New ones appeared. The government had no choice. It had to tax to survive.[4]

Donations were another source of funds. Shortly after declaring the country's independence, Ho urged people to contribute rice, money, labor, and even land to an Independence Fund. That same month, the government organized a "Gold Week" throughout the country.[5] Appealing to people's patriotism, the president and his entourage urged the well-off to contribute gold to help the country in its hour of greatest need. Many gave out of patriotic fervor. Some donated, looking to curry favor. Others hoped that their contributions would help them secure official assistance in recovering property or materials lost during the war years. In the south, contributions in gold in Zone VII produced an impressive 32 kg, which was exfiltrated to the north to purchase arms for soldiers already at war in the Mekong Delta. In all, the Gold and Independence fund-raising drives of late 1945 generated 370 kg of gold and 20 million piasters.[6]

Of course, the state could be more persuasive if required. No sooner had a young Ngo Van Chieu joined the army in September than he had received instructions to bring in recalcitrant wealthy individuals and help them "donate" their fair share to the patriotic cause:

As I stand up, I tell him: "Compatriot, you are being taxed today [between 1,000 and 100,000 piasters] which you can pay in gold or American dollars. Do you have them at home?" A good deal of play-acting then followed, but it always ended the same way: "Will you contribute voluntarily that which you are capable of giving to the defense of the country, yes or no?"

They almost always did, though some, Chieu admits, got away. They packed their bags and headed for the south in a trickle that would turn into a steady stream a decade later when Ho's army returned to reclaim the capital it had to give up in early 1947.[7]

The young republic had less success appropriating the colony's financial sector. It is true that defeated Japanese soldiers had received orders to stand down as Ho and his nationalist front, the Viet Minh, took power in Hanoi in August 1945. But they received orders not to let the Vietnamese seize the Bank of Indochina, its reserves, or its mint. And they did not. Since its creation in 1875, the Bank of Indochina had provided much of the investment capital for the development of the colony. It minted the country's sole currency, *la piastre indochinoise* (the Indochinese piaster), and it did so right through the Second World War. In fact, unsure who was in charge when the Japanese capitulated in mid-August, bank officials provided an initial payment of 22 million piasters to Ho's provisional government (this may have been the sum counted in the "Gold Week" mentioned above). French officials arriving in Saigon in October immediately put an end to this and assumed control over the bank's policies and money supply. In so doing, French officials in Saigon recovered an important economic lever of colonial power in Hanoi and established a financial beachhead within the heart of the Democratic Republic of Vietnam. Meanwhile, Chinese officers arriving to accept the Japanese surrender preferred to keep the French in control of the bank in Hanoi while their government negotiated who would pay the wages for the 200,000 Republic of China soldiers now spreading out across upper Indochina.

Unable to attack Ho Chi Minh's government in the north because of the Chinese, the French authorities did their best to destabilize the Democratic Republic of Vietnam indirectly—on the economic front. Working from the newly created office of the high commissioner of Indochina in Saigon, they immediately tried to take control over rice production in the Mekong Delta and its distribution to areas above the 16th parallel (surplus rice in the south had always helped cover deficits elsewhere in Vietnam). While the French supplied rice that helped alleviate the famine, they also controlled food and its distribution to northern areas as a form of political pressure and a way of reasserting colonial control. For similar reasons, the high commissioner limited the amount of consumer products entering DRV Vietnam in what amounted to an economic blockade, as one colonial official put it at the time.[8]

The French also realized early on that the currency the two states still shared—the Indochinese piaster—provided them with a weapon. Upon coming to power in mid-1945, Vietnamese nationalists had continued to use the colonial piaster as the legal tender of their new nation-state. They had little choice: they had no national bank, no mint, or gold reserves to back up a new currency. Patriotism may have burned red hot across the country, but the fragility of the economy coming out of the war and the terrible famine it had unleashed was such that the government feared that the immediate introduction of a new currency could set off rampant inflation and, as a result, weaken public confidence in the republic. That was the last thing the leadership wanted.

The problem, of course, was that by using the colonial currency without controlling its value or supply, the Democratic Republic of Vietnam left itself vulnerable to enemy action. The Vietnamese got a bitter taste of this on 17 November 1945, when the high commissioner decreed the cancellation of large quantities of 500-piaster bills issued after the Japanese coup de force of March 1945. He did so on the grounds that the absence of a legitimate French authority during the summer of 1945 (until 23 September) rendered these notes null and void. People had a week to exchange any 500-piaster bills that had been issued before the coup, but it came at the price of a 30 percent devaluation. Although there were legitimate financial reasons for doing this, the colonial authorities also wanted to undermine popular confidence in the young republic. Well-off and middle-class Vietnamese families had tended to hold onto these big bills, including civil servants whom Ho needed to keep on board. The French hit them all hard in their pockets with this action, and the Vietnamese government could do nothing about it. Many middle- and upper-class people never forgot it.[9]

To make matters worse, Chinese commanding officers in Hanoi pressured the French to sell their army large quantities of piasters at a very favorable exchange rate for their currency, the yuan. The Bank of Indochina complied. The Chinese even secured the right to use the yuan to make purchases in Indochina above the 16th parallel. The French and Vietnamese acquiesced because each was hoping to play the Chinese off against the other. The Vietnamese people, though, bore the brunt of these financial machinations and the vertiginous inflation they so often unleashed. Little wonder Vietnamese households would stash away gold, silver, and precious stones whenever they could for the next thirty years. Many had already begun doing so during the Second World War.

These colonial manipulations of the piaster in late 1945 convinced Ho and his team that they had no choice: they had to issue their own national currency. It would protect the government from unilateral colonial action on the monetary front. It would put Vietnamese authorities in control of their own money supply and with it, they hoped, inflation. Stabilizing prices would always be a priority during the Indochina War. And, of course, a Vietnamese legal tender would be a powerful symbol of national independence as Ho negotiated with the French. By January 1946, the government had begun printing its own money, the dong, in areas of lower central Vietnam which were free of French troops but above the 16th parallel. They started with coins and then issued bills, always in small denominations. They stepped up the (dong) monetization of the economy when the Franco-Vietnamese accords of March 1946 seemed to authorize the Democratic Republic of Vietnam—as a "free state" (*état libre*) within the Indochinese federation—to administer "its own finances." During the summer of 1946, authorities began printing and distributing the dong in larger quantities. The portrait of President Ho Chi Minh graced the new bills as the Vietnamese used confiscated colonial presses to issue tens of thousands of banknotes. As a result, two currencies—one national, the other colonial—now circulated above the 16th parallel. Significantly, the Vietnamese refrained from using the dong below that line for the time being, not wanting to undermine delicate negotiations over the country's independence and the unification of lower Vietnam with its upper half.[10]

Negotiations held in France during the summer of 1946 went nowhere. The French commitment to colonial federalism was rock solid.

As they saw it, Vietnam was part of the Indochinese federation under reconstruction, together with Laos and Cambodia. In turn, all three countries would be part of the French Union, the new word for the empire enshrined in the Fourth Republic's October 1946 constitution. The French would run the Union and the Indochinese federation's diplomacy, army, currency, and customs from Paris. Unlike the commonwealth model, which allowed the British to accommodate the independence of Australia, Canada, and, in 1947, India, French federalism subordinated Vietnam, Laos, and Cambodia as well as Tunisia, Morocco, and Algeria to control from Paris. As Ho joked to a sympathetic American journalist in Paris after a grueling day of negotiations in mid-September 1946: "Well, I made progress today. The French are willing to grant me the street-cleaning detail in Hanoi." But the president's quip could hardly hide the gravity of the situation and the French refusal to recognize his government's sovereignty. In his next breath, he told his listener that he thought war with the French was now "inevitable."[11] That said, Ho did not want war, and he signed a last-minute modus vivendi on 14 September to keep the dialogue going in the hope that the worst could still be averted. But as he left Paris to return to Hanoi, he must have known that the French, on both the political Right and Left, in Paris and in Saigon, were committed to colonial federalism of a reformist design—not to decolonization of a British Commonwealth kind. For the French, by signing the modus vivendi, Ho, like his Cambodian and the Laotian counterparts, had agreed to join their federation.

Now at an impasse, things could only get worse unless one side accepted the primacy of the other's sovereignty. As politicians in Paris continued to call for peace without providing a political blueprint and concessions for achieving it, the colonial authorities in Saigon shifted their attention to the north in an attempt on the economic front to expand their control above the 16th parallel. The French economic thrust northwards began as the Chinese withdrew their last troops from upper Indochina and talks in France broke down. On 9 September, Saigon officials authorized the creation of an Indochinese customs service and began to challenge the Vietnamese republic's economic sovereignty above that line for the first time. Strengthening the high commissioner's hand was the fact that French negotiators in Paris had successfully negotiated a clause requiring the creation of a customs union to be included in the modus vivendi agreement and thus applicable to Ho's Vietnam. They added another clause, making the Indochinese piaster the sole currency for the federal state they were expanding northwards. In short, the French had weaponized federalism on the economic front by effectively outlawing the Vietnamese republic's national currency, the dong, and its right to control trade and collect customs duties.

Vietnamese of all political colors understood that the French were effectively rolling back their national sovereignty above the 16th parallel in this way. Angry, members of the Vietnamese National Assembly instructed the government not to negotiate on customs matters—"at any price." On 11 November, Ho warned the high commissioner's office not to create a colonial customs service for Haiphong at the expense of the DRV's. The French went ahead anyway, hoping to absorb Ho's Vietnam into their federation or to provoke a violent incident which they could use as a pretext to destroy this independent state whose continued existence undermined the reality of French Indochina. Although Ho signed the modus vivendi holding him to one currency and a federal customs service, he had done it to buy time more than anything else. He already knew in September that if he could not convince the French to let go of Indochinese federalism, then it was soon to be war.[12]

The primacy of the colonial piaster was obviously a problem. In early November 1946, the National Assembly authorized the distribution of the Vietnamese national currency to areas below the 16th parallel. If the French were going to challenge the young republic's sovereignty from within its northern half by affirming that only the piaster could serve as the legal tender there, then the Vietnamese would circulate the dong below the 16th parallel where the French had already created in June a piaster-powered "Cochinchinese Republic." Meanwhile, the high commissioner's political adviser, Léon Pignon, advised his boss to attack the dong with everything he had. "If the Ho Chi Minh currency were to collapse," he wrote, "the whole system would fall with it, since the government would be unable to procure the foreign curency it needs in any other way."[13] While it remains unclear how exactly Pignon intended to do this, he signed his memo on the day French gunboats opened fire on Haiphong. This, too, is how full-scale war commenced in Vietnam in late 1946: in a harbor over the collection of customs duties. The core issue in Haiphong was political sovereignty. It was certainly not 'communism'. Had Ho Chi Minh been a virulent anticommunist like his anticolonialist nemesis during the Vietnam War, Ngo Dinh Diem, the French still would have attacked him and his right to collect customs in the port of Haiphong on that November day in 1946.[14]

Island Economics

When the French and the Vietnamese finally began shooting at each other throughout the country a month later, government officials rushed their financial operations to safe places in the countryside. They evacuated printing presses, molds, paper, ink, acids, and as many specialists as they could to safe areas in northern and upper central Vietnam.[15] From the start, the Vietnamese war economy was, like the embattled state it served, a highly decentralized affair. Hostilities rapidly broke the Vietnamese republic into a series of regional economies strung from north to south. Roughly speaking, a northern economy operated in and around the resistance capital in Thai Nguyen province. Later, from 1950 onwards, as Chinese aid allowed the army to liberate more territory throughout the upper highlands, the economy's reach grew with it. Until then, the French controlled the border towns with China and large swaths of the Red River Delta concentrated around and between Hanoi and Haiphong. In the south, the Ca Mau peninsula was home to a vigorous Vietnamese economy based on rice and fishing.[16] A more modest economy operated to the west of Saigon in an area known as the Plain of Reeds. As we know, because the French focused strategically on holding the northern and southern deltas, the Democratic Republic of Vietnam ran most of central Vietnam extending from south of Hanoi to lower central Vietnam, except for areas in and around major coastal cities like Hue (see Map 10). A vibrant economy developed in Zone IV, thanks to its large population of around 5 million people, numerous cottage industries, good communications, and intensive rice production. In all, the republic administered around 10 million people by 1950 out of a total population of 23 million (the other 13 million lived in colonial Vietnam).[17] Based in the northern capital in Thai Nguyen, the Finance Ministry operated through administrative committees extending down to district level. The finance minister, Le Van Hien, traveled tirelessly on horseback and foot across northern and central parts of republican territory delivering directives, presiding over meetings, and supplying Ho Chi Minh banknotes to the local authorities. Reading his memoirs gives one a real feel for the decentralized nature of wartime Vietnam and its economic exchanges.

The Vietnamese war economy never possessed an armaments industry capable of rolling out large quantities of machine guns, artillery, and shells. The communist bloc would provide those things later. Until then, Vietnamese authorities did what so many other guerrilla movements denied access to modern weapons had just done across Eurasia during the Second World War—they created small-arms industries to keep the resistance armed. The French-trained engineer, Tran Dai Nghia, and a handful of other colonially educated scientists (discussed in Chapter 2) combined forces to manufacture grenades, mines, and small arms, including a surprisingly effective homemade bazooka. In 1949, around 150 national defense workshops operated. They employed around 30,000 workers in republican territory. They were almost always state-run entities answering to the Ministry of Defense.[18]

The government presided over the extraction and distribution of the natural resources this small-scale armaments industry needed to function. While the Vietnamese lost control of large coalfields in the northeast when the French reconquered most of the area close to the Chinese border by late 1947, DRV authorities held on to smaller ones and continued to extract silver, wolfram, tungsten, zinc, and lead from modest mines in free zones in central Vietnam and the northern highlands. The

Vietnamese recovered several coalfields in late 1950 when Chinese communist support helped them retake much of their land near the northern border. The Tinh Tuc Mine in liberated Cao Bang province produced tin and a little gold. Between 1950 and 1952, the Bac Son mines east of there churned out 43 tons of lead. Others in central and northern parts of the DRV produced coke for use in smelting furnaces. Meanwhile, chemical workshops produced the acids needed to produce a variety of explosives. Thanh Hoa factories produced over 20,000 kg of acids during the conflict.[19]

The government imported machines and chemicals from abroad to compensate for that which they could not produce or extract locally. In 1948, the French discovered 30 tons of potassium chlorate hidden in three different locations in Hanoi awaiting secret shipment into the DRV. It had arrived from the United States via Hong Kong.[20] That same year, officials in the Ca Mau peninsula ordered large quantities of acids needed for manufacturing explosives.[21] Equally important was the infiltration of designs for weapons, engineering manuals, and chemistry books. Lest we forget, Tran Dai Nghia had worked in French and German armaments plants during the Second World War before smuggling all sorts of designs and books back to Vietnam upon his return in 1946. By 1950, this cottage defense industry running on imports, locally extracted natural resources, and serious Vietnamese brainpower had produced an estimated 7,000 tons of small arms. To be sure, this was not a large number of weapons. It did not turn the tide of the war on the battlefield. But it was sufficient to keep the guerrilla army fed, in dribs and drabs, just enough so that Ho's Vietnam would still be "there" when large-scale communist bloc aid began pouring into the north in mid-1950.[22]

Producing paper was as important as small weapons when it came to keeping bureaucrats and their typewriters banging away. From the start, DRV authorities took over colonial-era paper mills concentrated mainly in the northern and central zones. Most were located near heavily forested areas where they could easily harvest wood to make pulp. The government ran some mills of its own, but it had no qualms about letting profit-motivated entrepreneurs run the show if they paid their taxes and could do it better. The Dong Minh and Dong Quang paper factories did the job in Zone IV. The government imported essential inputs which the mills needed, chemicals in particular. Later in the war, the Finance Ministry imported a glossy, highly resistant type of paper to produce crisper Ho Chi Minh banknotes that could last and which people would trust. In Zone V, officials acquired two sturdy presses from nearby Catholic missions and recruited workers from them to help design and print clean notes and bonds. Meanwhile, agents were always on the lookout for printers, molds, film, cameras, and all the sorts of things needed to supply the administration as well as the press, propaganda, and cultural services. In all, zones IV and V were home to 136 small paper mills. Despite the rather poor quality of the paper, they supplied around 70 percent of the government's needs, again, the trickles needed to keep the bureaucracy running and the propaganda flying off the presses.[23]

The most important cottage industries generally operated in central and northern parts of Vietnam. During the Second World War, Japanese, French, and Vietnamese officials and entrepreneurs had begun producing locally that which they could no longer import from abroad. This local demand for manufactured products facilitated the growth of small-scale cottage industries in Vietnam in the early 1940s. Paper mills, machine shops, textile workshops, pharmaceutical labs, soap factories, and small metal foundries popped up to supply Indochinese markets. Japanese- and French-run mines produced coal, iron, magnesium, wolfram, zinc, tin, and lead. Coal-fired local furnaces smelted metals to make a variety of domestic wares (tools, wire, simple machine parts, and the like). Many Vietnamese miners and specialized workers emerged from this earlier cottage-level "industrialization" to work for the Democratic Republic of Vietnam during the Indochina conflict.[24]

Although things would change in different parts of the DRV as the war intensified from 1950, until then the resistance economy was largely successful in providing its populations, soldiers, and civil servants with the basics they needed to carry on—fresh water, rice, salt, fish, fish sauce, and, to a lesser extent, meat. An abundance of rivers, streams, and colonially constructed canals, dikes, and reservoirs provided fresh water for irrigating rice. The French development of the rice economy in the Mekong Delta during the colonial period—the opening of new land to production, the construction of new dikes and canals, and the introduction of fertilizer—helped the fledgling republic feed its populations when it took over in 1945. A network of colonially expanded canals in the Ca Mau peninsula, for example, circulated rice from storehouses in Rach Gia and Ha Tien to neighboring areas in the southern delta. The Vietnamese in this area also taxed pepper plantations next door in Cambodia's Kampot province.[25]

Zone IV in upper central Vietnam was largely self-sufficient in rice production, thanks to the colonial construction of dikes for flood protection and canals and reservoirs needed for the irrigation that made double-cropping possible. Good weather and steady harvests helped greatly during the first half of the conflict. This zone sent rice to areas in the highlands where there was a deficit and later on to the northwest as Ho's Vietnam expanded its hold over areas running up to the border with Laos. Working from the resistance capital in Thai Nguyen province, authorities relied on areas they controlled in the Red River Delta to provide them with rice, or they imported it clandestinely from French-controlled zones. What the rather rice-poor Zone V in lower central Vietnam could not produce it imported from the neighboring Zone IV to the north or from Zone IX in the far south.

Salt was as important as rice to ensuring the minimum welfare of the population. Besides the fact that the human body cannot function for long without it, salt also served to preserve meat and fish and is a vital part of Vietnam's famous fish sauce, *nuoc mam*. (In 1950, 1 kg of salt was needed to conserve 3 kg of fish and 2 kg of salt to make 3 kg of nuoc mam.)[26] Until the war's end, the DRV was largely self-sufficient in salt production. At the outset, the government controlled important salt pits in the south in Bac Lieu and Baria, for example. Central Vietnam was home to several coastal pits, many of which supplied neighboring highland peoples. The north obtained salt from an important Catholic-controlled pit in Van Ly located on the coast south of Hanoi. In central and southern areas, thanks to easy access to salt, private fish sauce makers met wartime demand. Zone IV alone produced a respectable 450,000 liters of fish sauce annually.[27]

The government kept close tabs on livestock and poultry and did its best to promote animal husbandry. Officials encouraged villagers to raise water buffalos, oxen, and cows for working in the rice fields, pulling carts, and consumption. Pigs and poultry were also a vital part of the rural economy. The government relied on the local village economies to increase food, meat, and salt production to feed guerrilla fighters and soldiers when they came through. This also meant protecting animals from the enemy. Local militias had instructions to hustle animals to safe places in the event of things going wrong during enemy operations.[28] And they did. A child of the countryside during the war, Nguyen Cong Luan remembered vividly the strange symbiosis that developed between villagers and animals united in their desire to survive when enemy patrols passed through their villages:

> Even the animals knew how to get out of the way of French-led patrols. Whenever the French soldiers came, all kinds of sounds subsided. Even domestic animals—beasts of burden, pigs, and dogs—seemed to try to make the least noise. All kept quiet and acted frantically as if they could apprehend [the] fear conveyed by the behavior of panic-stricken villagers. Most dogs ran about to find a nook of safety in dense bamboo groves. Some pigs sneaked into concealed holes when their owners yelled, "French coming!" Two of the dozen buffaloes in my village would act accordingly to the shout "Lie down!" when they were under fire while fleeing the village. When the French soldiers were gone and the villagers returned to their normal activities, all those animals became lively again and made their usual noises and sounds.[29]

In coastal areas, fishermen continued to ply their trade as they had for generations. In 1930, fishing along the Indochinese coasts had produced 350,000 tons of fish annually. Some of the best fishing areas were located off Zone IV's coast in upper central Vietnam. Around 20,000 fishermen worked the coast of Thanh Hoa before the Second World

War and continued to do so under the Democratic Republic of Vietnam during the Indochina one. Thanks to them, the French reported in 1952, the government had succeeded in exporting dried fish to other areas of the state, including the north. During the first half of the Indochina War, when it came to rice, salt, poultry, meat, and fish, the government met its key goal of being self-sufficient. Its legitimacy depended on feeding its population, and it largely succeeded in that endeavor. Local village economies, not the central government and its supply networks, fed what was still a relatively small guerrilla army.[30]

Resistance Revenues

Rents and taxes provided a fairly reliable source of revenue for the government in the early years. Officials confiscated colonial plantations in the territories they controlled as well as the fields abandoned by Vietnamese landowners. A 1948 law authorized the government to rent these plots to landless peasants for certain periods of time. Landowners who remained and supported the new republic got to keep their rice fields, fruit farms, and plantations—at least until the last years of the conflict. The government required them to pay property taxes in cash (27 dong per hectare in the north, 50 in Zone IV, and 10 in the south) or in kind (rice, coffee, sugarcane, and so on).[31] In Zone IV, property taxes alone generated almost 12 million dong in revenue for 1947 and half of that for the first seven months of 1948. That said, tax revenues only provided for a quarter of the national budget annually before 1950. The government made up for the rest by printing money—over a dozen times during this period—at the cost of higher levels of inflation.[32]

Additional government revenue came from taxing local agricultural production, private trade, non-state cottage industries, and transport of all kinds (boats, ferries, buses, and trains). Many of these taxes were holdovers from the colonial era. In Thai Binh province, the northern administration collected a range of duties on transportation, trade, and local handicrafts. Taxes on the sale and transport of rice going clandestinely from farmers deep in the Mekong Delta to merchants in Saigon-

Cholon generated millions of Vietnamese dong and Indochinese piasters over the course of the conflict. For the rice-rich provinces of Soc Trang, Bac Lieu, and Can Tho, between November 1947 and March 1948 the southern administration collected taxes to the tune of more than 21 million piasters. Again, this patchwork economy never balanced budgets or tamed inflation, but it generated the financial minimum needed to keep a relatively small army and civil service operational in classic guerrilla style.[33]

Less effective was the sale of government resistance bonds. Like so many other embattled countries before it, the Vietnamese issued war bonds with great fanfare. Patriotic posters, newspapers, and radio announcers urged people to buy government-issued bonds to help the nation in its hour of greatest need. In theory, those who purchased them would be reimbursed at a later date, in say five or ten years, once the war was over. In practice, however, people were skeptical. They tended to see these "bonds" as just another word for "donation" or "taxes" and doubted the government's ability to repay them. Of course, this never stopped the government from going ahead anyway. Indeed, during almost a decade of war, there was no shortage of patriotic moneymaking drives, and a mind-boggling array of fundraising events. But as the war dragged on, day after day, month after month, year after year, people found it harder and harder to give, and the propaganda became ever less effective. (See Plate 15.)

During the first half of the Indochina War the Vietnamese could get away with printing money and relying on the local village economy to keep their war state running. But as we shall see soon, printing money and borrowing led to inflation and debt, which became a dangerous problem by 1950, when the communist leadership decided to create a large standing army and an expanded bureaucratic state. From then on, the government had to secure greater amounts of rice in order to feed a larger number of soldiers, civil servants, workers, and porters, who could no longer live off the village economy. If the question of food was never a dire problem in the late 1940s, it became a pressing one during the second half of the Indochina War, and arguably the single most important issue by its close at Dien Bien Phu.

Routes and Transport

An economy that cannot circulate its goods and services will not survive. This is true in peacetime, and it is equally true in times of war. The Vietnamese economy was no exception to this rule. Getting surplus rice stockpiled on the far side of the Ca Mau peninsula to hungry mouths in central Vietnam's Zone V was as important as ensuring that troops going into battle at Dien Bien Phu in 1954 had enough to eat. For the leaders of the Democratic Republic of Vietnam, the circulation of rice, salt, supplies, people, banknotes, and weapons had to occur within each of the state's three main regional economies (the north, center, and south), between them, and also with the surrounding colonial cities and the wider Asian region. This circulation depended, in turn, on the administration of a variety of routes, means of transportation, relays, transporters, guides, and bodyguards. These could be age-old, "traditional" routes and means of transportation, or they could be more modern ones. It did not matter. What did was making sure that things got to where they needed to go, safely, and, if at all possible, on time too. (See Map 9.)

We should remind ourselves one last time what every person manning these itineraries knew at the time: between 1945 and 1954, wartime Vietnam never resembled the country we recognize on the map today in its S-like form. Nor was there a "North Vietnam" or "South Vietnam." The Democratic Republic of Vietnam was a collection of island economies—in the south (Zone IX), in the center (zones IV and V, except for coastal city strips under French control), and the north (anchored in the nation's resistance capital at Thai Nguyen). This configuration would change in the upper half of Vietnam after the Chinese communist victory in 1950. But until then, territorial control was decentralized; exchanges ran in streams reaching out like the fingers of a hand. The administration of people, territory, and routes was continually contested. The French army threw up blockades time and again to stop their adversary's economic exchanges. As a result, the war economy, like the state running it, operated in its archipelagic form.

However, islands can be connected. Archipelagos can have an operational form: Greece and Indonesia still do. If we could view the Democratic Republic of Vietnam's routes highlighted in red from on high, say from a reconnaissance plane or, even better, with satellite infrared images taken from space, it would be possible to see how a network of land and water routes ran through a handful of liberated ports to connect our state of war in synaptic ways. Of utmost importance in the south was the government's control of much of the Ca Mau peninsula's coastline in Zone IX. A collection of trails wrapping around the tip of Ca Mau (some peeling off away from the coast) moved rice, supplies, and weapons from ingeniously camouflaged granaries, workshops, and warehouses in ports on the western side of the peninsula to areas which lacked them on the other side, and then on to lower central Vietnam's Zone V. There, hidden estuaries served as secure reception centers for small junks coming in from the south to unload. Further to the north, in upper central Vietnam, Zone IV's harbors dispatched rice, supplies, and homemade arms to Zone V. Sustained overland, river, and coastal trade occurred between Thanh Hoa province on the DRV's edge and colonial areas south of Hanoi. The republic's capital in the northern highlands had little access to the sea because of the very effective French naval surveillance of the Gulf of Tonkin. From the Thai Nguyen capital, however, the northern-based government pushed a land route westwards through the highlands, bending it around the Red River Delta's outer rim. From late 1950, following the French withdrawal from the highlands, the government pushed it further still, through Hoa Binh to Zone IV and the port of Vinh on the south side of colonial Hanoi.[34]

A variety of routes connected each core economy together on the inside. In the south, canals, a slew of waterways, not least of all the mighty Mekong and its myriad of branches, allowed the Vietnamese to move people, rice, and weapons by vessels from one zone to another. In Zone IV, an extensive canal network allowed the Vietnamese to transport food, weapons, and supplies from the port of Vinh to interior areas on the southern flank of the Red River Delta. Inland, railway workers in zones IV and V serviced sections of the French-built railroad, the Trans-Indochinese line completed in 1936, to circulate heavier things from one place to another, like Tran Dai Nghia's bazookas, by night. In the north, the government relied on water routes in the delta area, including the

Red River and its offshoots. And wherever they could, leaders used colonial-built roads to circulate goods and services.

The government's means of transportation were as varied as the geography they covered. Horses and bicycles played a particularly important role in transporting administrators and party leaders along their way in the north, including Ho Chi Minh and Vo Nguyen Giap. Elephants went to work in the south. In central Vietnam, those in charge relied on a rather rickety fleet of colonial-era cars, small trucks, and buses to carry goods and people along bumpy roads. In the deltas, economic administrators, tax collectors, and merchants moved in vessels ranging in size from small sampans to 10-ton junks. Coastal traffic circulated thanks to a wider variety of junks, some as big as 100 tons, catching seasonal monsoon winds to move up and down Vietnam's long coastline. By 1950, the French realized they were dealing with a growing number of enemy junks equipped with powerful outboard motors. This motorization of resistance vessels allowed for the transport of heavy payloads at constant or faster speeds, regardless of the winds. But in the end, collectively, smaller vessels, sampans in particular, probably moved more food, supplies, and people than the bigger boats. Harder to detect, the smaller ones crisscrossed canals few junks could enter. And if they were stopped (and they often were), the losses were proportionally smaller. As we know, the Vietnamese lost tons of priceless radio and medical equipment when the French sank the *Song Lo* in August 1949 (see Chapter 3).[35]

Ho Chi Minh's people closely monitored these routes and what they circulated as the French armed forces did their best to stop their adversary. Special troops protected convoys of sampans as they moved from one relay station in the deltas to another. Customs officials stationed across the archipelago carefully noted what left on junks, bikes, or even on the backs of human porters, and what arrived at the other end. They collected duties on what was exported and imported from one zone to another, whether into the French Indochinese federation or on to other Asian markets. The Vietnamese authorities relied on radios to organize the transport of supplies, food, medicines, and weapons within each core island, between them, and with the surrounding Asian region and the colonial cities. In May 1948, an administrator in Bien Hoa province radioed to ask the regional supervisor to send around a million *gia* of paddy (unmilled rice) there (1 *gia* equals 20 kg). In July 1949, radio intercepts revealed that forty junks were getting ready to transport rice from Zone IX up to lower central Vietnam. All of this was serious business and provides insight into the nature, paradoxical coherence, and functioning of this patchwork state in a time of guerrilla war.[36]

So too does the Vietnamese reliance on Chinese trading networks. In 1950, the French estimated that there were around 600,000 Chinese people living in southern Vietnam and 70,000 in northern Vietnam. Of those residing in the south, 450,000 lived in the Saigon-Cholon area. The majority of those in the north lived in Haiphong and, to a lesser degree, in Hanoi and along the northern border with China. In May 1947, the head of the government's economic service for the Saigon-Cholon region explained that his team had contacted "a certain number of Chinese" in order to trade in foreign currencies, buy gold, purchase arms, and import the government's surplus rice in the south to millers in the vibrant Chinatown area of Cholon. Chinese import–export houses would help them do this. He added that he had already "obtained good results" in working with several local merchants on such matters. In 1949, for example, Chinese traders were preparing to import 300,000 gia of paddy to Saigon-Cholon for the southern DRV, a part of which was to be exported abroad.[37] In his general economic plan for Saigon-Cholon in 1947, Kha Van Can, the head of the southern economy, explained that his agents were authorized "to sell products directly to Chinese traders." They would then transport them to "agents abroad." In return, Chinese traders helped with the import of much-needed goods from French-controlled zones and the surrounding Asian region into Vietnam. None of this should come as a surprise: the Chinese had historically dominated the transport of paddy from the Mekong Delta to the city. They had long taken care of the milling of rice, its processing, and organized its sale and export abroad.[38]

Besides rice, Chinese networks were instrumental in supplying pharmaceuticals too. Medicines were important to maintaining the health of the population under DRV control, civil servants, and soldiers. Vietnamese pharmacists had succeeded in producing many things in makeshift laboratories, including penicillin, but everyone agreed that Western medicines and vaccines were more effective, especially antimalarial pills like quinine, and thus in high demand until the end of the war. Despite the hyperbole, a British observer at the time put his finger on something true in a report he sent to his government: "If the French could impose a severe rationing of quinine in their area, and if they could control every ounce bought or sold, they would have a terrible weapon in their hands against the enemy. It would be one of the worst blows they could strike."[39] Thanks in part to Chinese merchants and pharmacists working in major urban centers inside and outside Vietnam, the DRV circumvented colonial efforts to deprive them of medicines, antibiotics, and vaccines. This was particularly true in Haiphong, where the sale of medicines remained uncontrolled throughout 1947. In May of that year, a Vietnamese deserter explained to his interrogators that the government was buying large quantities of medicines via Chinese dealers there. Chinese skippers then shipped them to the resistance population via a host of waterways running inland from Haiphong.[40]

Pragmatism and "Colonial Dependency"

Pragmatism drove the Vietnamese war economy until 1950 when the Chinese communists threw their weight behind Ho Chi Minh and changed the nature of the war and the Vietnamese state running it. And even then, pragmatism was never sacrificed on the altar of ideological purity. In 1947, the Communist Party's interim general secretary, Truong Chinh, published something of an official manual on the matter for cadres taking up their positions in the countryside. It was entitled *The Resistance Will Win*. He quotes Lenin and Mao Zedong favorably and speaks longingly of creating "a democratic economy"—meaning a communist one. However, he makes it clear that the wartime situation required cadres to be flexible and to avoid imposing any sort of measures that could alienate noncommunist allies and undermine the government's ability to fight. Throughout his short, crisply written text, Truong Chinh warns against any kind of Leftist-deviationism on the economic front. Yes, he reassured his fellow communists, the party was still at the helm; but, no, this was not the time to push through radical social revolutionary measures like full-blown land reform. The Vietnamese were at war. The party needed everyone on board. Victory depended on maintaining "the unity of the entire people." So did the regime's survival.[41]

Economically, the Communist Party needed the collaboration of the capitalist bourgeois, merchants, and landowners as much as it did that of peasants and the workers. Traders had the capital, contacts, and networks the government needed for exporting rice to Cholon or for importing pharmaceuticals from Haiphong. Patriotic merchants helped officials import all sorts of essential things. In exchange for their services, merchants could keep their businesses and turn a profit as long as they paid their taxes and did not serve the French (or at least not in ways that harmed the welfare of the DRV). The same was true of landowners who cooperated with the government by providing the food the state needed to feed the population, its civil servants, and soldiers. They could keep their land if they paid their taxes. In the area of the capital in Thai Nguyen province, the successful businesswoman, Nguyen Thi Nam, enthusiastically supported Ho Chi Minh's Vietnam, including the induction of two of her sons into the army. She soon became known as the "Mother of the Resistance" (Me Khang Chien). There would be no radical land reform or class warfare, not in 1947, not even as late as 1952. It came at the very end of the war, in the run-up to the Battle of Dien Bien Phu. Until then, from 1945 until 1952, the party imposed a rent reduction of 25 percent on landlords and expected cadres to respect it.[42]

Government officials stressed the importance of self-sufficiency as the guiding principle for administering the resistance economy.[43] In practice, though, the Vietnamese war economy operated in a symbiosis with the French Indochinese federation's economy. Indeed, in what may be one of the biggest paradoxes of the war, the nationalist government of the Democratic Republic of Vietnam depended on the colonial economy to operate its own. Nowhere was this form of "colonial dependency" more evident than in the national government's ability to build up its reserves in the Indochinese piaster. In 1947, now engaged in a full-scale war, officials formally prohibited people living within DRV territories from using the piaster. All transactions had to be in dong. The problem was that in order to finance imports from abroad, including the colonial cities of Saigon, Hue, Haiphong, and surrounding Asian markets, say in Thailand, the national government needed to build up its reserves in a hard, internationally recognized currency since the dong was worthless as a foreign exchange. The Indochinese piaster was not. It was tied to the French franc and guaranteed by the French government and its banks. The result was inevitable: although the Vietnamese leaders prohibited their citizens in 1947 from using the Indochinese piaster (and did so again in 1948 and yet again in 1949), the government itself meticulously built up its foreign exchange reserves in the piaster by interacting with the colonial economy.

How? Particularly important in the late 1940s was the surplus rice DRV authorities procured and stored in secure zones in the Ca Mau peninsula and then sold in Saigon-Cholon or on Asian markets in order to obtain piasters.[44] Early on, Vietnamese economic administrators in the south came up with ingenious ways for doing this. One that the French discovered went something like this: Vietnamese officials from rice-poor Zone VII west of Saigon sent Ho Chi Minh banknotes to Zone IX in the Ca Mau area. The latter's delegates then used the national tender to buy paddy from rice growers under its control (who had to accept payment in dong by law or risk arrest). From there, Chinese intermediaries would transport the paddy to Saigon-Cholon, where they sold it on behalf of the Vietnamese on the colonial market in exchange for colonial piasters. The Chinese then deposited the government's portion of the final sale to Zone VII in piasters. Because the buying price (in Ho Chi Minh notes) was so much lower than its sale price in Saigon-Cholon in Indochinese piasters, the Chinese traders realized very tidy profits, and the Vietnamese authorities procured the piasters they needed to finance their imports.[45]

The interlocking of the national and the colonial economies occurred elsewhere. In central Vietnam, the government carefully established ports of entry along the borders with the Indochinese colonial federation. Working through a series of carefully monitored "reception centers," authorized merchants carried out the government's trade in colonial markets. They exported mainly agricultural products to merchants in the French-controlled zones: rice, coffee, tea, cinnamon, sugarcane, conical hats, baskets, areca nuts, betel, bamboo, dried fish, fish sauce, and shrimp. Merchants from Zone V, for example, entered Hue to sell such goods with the connivance of the local authorities. With the piasters these DRV-approved traders obtained from selling their goods in the colonial city, they bought textiles, clothes, dishes, shoes, and other products the resistance needed. They then transported these goods and others out of French Indochina to the nearby DRV reception centers where district and provincial authorities (as well as representatives from the army) took over. Receipts were obligatory. Duties were collected. Everyone knew what was going on—and it was not autarky. It was business.

This economic intermeshing did not create huge amounts of trade or hard currency. But what it did generate was enough for the Vietnamese to buy what they needed to keep their state ticking. In Zone IV, for example, government officials allowed traders returning from colonial Vietnam to keep 25 percent of their Indochinese piasters. The remaining 75 percent, however, had to be exchanged into dong at the fixed rate (1 piaster was worth 600 dong in 1952). The government now had the Indochinese piasters whose value only appreciated against the Ho Chi Minh notes, theirs. Similar things happened along water routes. Traders left the shores of Zone V in lower central Vietnam, their junks loaded with areca nuts, tea, cinnamon, and then entered the colonial ports of Da Nang and Phan Thiet. Again, with the piasters they reaped, they bought Western medicines, sulfur, explosives, and even rice to bring back to this hungry region. These traders had permission to buy products to sell for a profit within the DRV upon their return on the condition that they exchanged a portion of their piasters into dong and, of course, paid their taxes in colonial piasters.[46] As one French officer finally summed up this colonial dependency in 1952, the Vietnamese:

> do their best to develop within their zones the production of a wide variety of goods which are not essential to their subsistence. The goal is to use them [as exports] in order to obtain the currency they need in our markets so as to buy all the products they lack [on the colonial market]. At the same time, the Vietnamese apply a tax scheme and control customs strictly so that they remain the beneficiaries of this trade [i.e. so that they ran a trade surplus]. It would not be an exaggeration to say that not only does the military budget for French Indochina constitute the economic motor of this country [French Indochina], but it also feeds a good deal of the adversary's military budget.[47]

Early Economic Warfare

All on the economic front was not about 'intermeshing', however. The outbreak of hostilities in the south in September 1945, for example, had seen Ho's officials issue orders to destroy anything of economic value that could be of use to the French. On several occasions, the authorities had approved a policy of "scorched earth tactics" including the sabotaging of colonial factories, bridges, and roads. Officials above the 16th parallel adopted a similar policy when full-scale war broke out in December 1946, leaving Hanoi, Nam Dinh, and Hue's public works and factories in shambles. In 1947, now operating overwhelmingly from the countryside, from north to south the Vietnamese began devising ways to attack the French colonial economy and to protect themselves from enemy assaults. Southerners, for example, implemented what they called a "total or comprehensive economic blockade." It consisted of the boycotting of French goods and the sabotaging of the colonial economy whenever possible. In practice, we now know, the Vietnamese blockade was anything but "total"; but it left no doubt that economic targets were as important as military ones during the Indochina War.[48]

Attacks on French rubber plantations in southern Vietnam are a case in point. Through acts of on-site sabotage of trees and machinery as well as attacks on convoys carrying rubber to Saigon, the Vietnamese sought to lower latex production and exports, thereby denying the French one of their main sources of foreign exchange (i.e., US dollars). Intimidation of workers made it harder for French plantation owners to recruit labor as easily as they had before the conflict began. One owner told a visiting journalist that his plantation produced about 50,000 tons of rubber annually, but he could easily double that number if he could find the workers he needed. French proprietors invested heavily in protecting their properties from sabotage. They installed state-of-the-art radio communications systems. They recruited Cambodian and highlander militias and veterans of the Expeditionary Corps to patrol their premises. The French armed forces provided security in the areas surrounding the plantations and escorted convoys carrying rubber by truck or train to markets in Saigon and Phnom Penh. By 1951, most rubber plantations (and probably coffee ones too) had built small airstrips to evacuate rubber by plane in small batches rather than risk losing everything to one enemy attack on a truck or train convoy. The Indochina conflict not only militarized these rubber plantations, but it also transformed them into semiautonomous zones scattered throughout the wider constellation of competing wartime states.[49]

Salt wars also broke out. In the early years of the war, especially when the French shifted their attention to fighting in the north, their salt fields in the south became immediately vulnerable to Vietnamese attack. In 1947, Vietnamese commandos attacked and killed the director of the Hon Khoi salt pit located near Nha Trang. The French counterattacked and retook the field. They immediately fortified its defenses, given that it supplied three-quarters of Indochina's total annual salt consumption. This renewed security drive at Hon Khoi included the construction of ten new military posts, seven watchtowers, and the deployment of 170 full-time, heavily armed militiamen. This military investment accurately reflected the importance of maintaining the salt monopoly for the colonial state. The French army then went on the offensive in early 1949 when it forcibly seized the DRV's salt pits in the south at Baria and Bac

Lieu, but not before the Vietnamese had flooded 35,000 tons of water into those same fields to render them unusable. To hurt the DRV's salt production elsewhere, the French air force began dropping fuel oil on enemy salt laid out to dry. The goal was to ruin it for consumption. As the high commissioner for Indochina put it, aerial attacks on the enemy's salt fields would "serve as one of the most efficient ways there is to destroy the enemy's economy indirectly." In response, Ho's officials immediately received orders to scrape off any oil slicks and, at least on some occasions, saved many of their salt fields from destruction. Meanwhile, colonial commandos sabotaged DRV salt mines or seized this essential product in surprise raids. In 1948, such operations destroyed 2,500 tons of enemy salt. Although the Vietnamese held on to most of their mines (nine in all), they lost access to a large one in Van Ly, south of Hanoi, when, in 1951, the Catholics running it finally rallied to Bao Dai's Vietnam. From that point, northern communists increased imports from Mao's China to make up the difference as French planes began using napalm against enemy salt industries.[50]

Currency was the site of yet another clash. On several occasions, the French introduced captured Vietnamese dong or counterfeited bills in order to unleash inflation upon their adversaries by increasing the supply of money in carefully selected enemy areas. The hope was that prices would spike locally and, in so doing, sap popular support for Ho Chi Minh's government in these places. As one French intelligence officer explained at the time, "We have put the notes into circulation in the hope of creating in this way a devaluation [of currency] or an increase in prices" in the DRV zones. It worked best in areas closest to French-controlled zones. For example, in Zone V in 1952, French-induced inflation got so bad that Vietnamese officials moving through the area had to stuff huge wads of banknotes into their knapsacks, sometimes weighing as much as 3 kilograms, in order to pay for food. The Vietnamese also tried to advance their terms of trade by counterfeiting the colonial piaster. In Zone IV, where the best molds, mints, and printer specialists were located, the government organized a special counterfeiting unit manned by a band of gifted printers, the security services, and underground agents in Hanoi. Leading the operation was a husband-and-wife team, Vu Duc Duong and Nguyen Thi Tam, each of whom had criminal records for counterfeiting. Apparently, it took colonial authorities three years to dismantle the operation, though I doubt the Vietnamese had the quality paper in sufficient quantities to make this work in any significant way. I doubt, too, that the Vietnamese ever counterfeited enough piasters for the French to take much notice.[51]

Rice wars broke out in the late 1940s, although they only became systematic during the second half of the Indochina War. Ho Chi Minh's officials relied on the territories they controlled to provide them with the rice they needed to feed their still rather modest number of soldiers and civil servants. But they also looked to nearby enemy zones as a source of food. The Vietnamese district and provincial authorities in colonially controlled areas close to the border of DRV territory in central Vietnam informed the French as early as 1948 that their adversary was trying to seize as much of their rice harvests in the spring and fall as they could. All were agreed that "the harvest could not fall into Viet Minh hands." Sporadic rice wars began in 1948, as both sides prepared for a protracted conflagration. In early 1949, the governor of colonial Thua Thien in central Vietnam applauded the French troops who had recently destroyed 100 tons of rice in DRV zones and "vast areas of manioc and potatoes." However, he now feared that his adversary would counterattack during the next harvest by seizing the rice in his province. To prevent that, he asked the colonial authorities to buy surplus rice from his villagers as quickly as possible and to stock it in warehouses in Hue. The governor was right: DRV officials were doing their best to buy or confiscate any surplus rice in colonial zones.[52]

As competition for rice expanded, the French riposted by imposing a series of economic blockades. Starting in January 1949, they imposed a severe one in the south to stop the flow of rice from Zone IX to the eastern side of southern Vietnam (which included Saigon and Cholon), and further up the coast to Zone V. This military blockade built on the work of General Pierre de La Tour, who had implemented an effective surveillance system of entrenched positions and watchtowers located along the major lines of communication in the south. Although the blockade apparently only lasted a year, it effectively diminished the amount of rice getting out of rice-rich Zone IX. The timing could not have been worse for the commander-in-chief of the Vietnamese armed forces in the south, General Nguyen Binh. As rice stocks dwindled during 1949, he received orders to build up his regular battalions to attack the French head on in the General Counter-offensive. When Binh's soldiers struck later that year, they did so not only to engage the French but also to break the blockade and recover rice-producing areas they badly needed to feed local populations and, above all, the growing army. The French, as we know, annihilated Nguyen Binh's counter-offensive of 1950 in the south, and there is no reason to think that the economic blockade did not contribute to it.[53] What is certain is that the success of this southern blockade would serve as a model for French military commanders, who would initiate an even more aggressive economic assault upon the DRV in the upper half of Vietnam in the early 1950s.

And lastly, the French bombed. In the early years, they bombed the cities in order to take them from Ho Chi Minh. It took years to rebuild parts of Haiphong, Hanoi, and Nam Dinh afterwards. French bombers then pursued the DRV into the countryside. Right up until the end of the conflict, colonial planes not only attacked enemy military installations and troops; they also attacked on the economic front—food production (rice mills, depots, and silos), lines of communications and infrastructure (ports, roads, canals, bridges, and dams), means of transport (locomotives, junks, and sampans), radio posts, weapons-making workshops, paper mills, textile factories, and even open markets. The French attacked Vietnamese medical facilities and government buildings. While civilians living in the borderlands learned to steer clear of colonial patrols entering their areas, those living inside the core islands of the Vietnamese archipelago state always had to beware of the French hitting them from the sky. Bombing shelters proliferated throughout Ho's Vietnam as the French expanded their bombing missions.

This was certainly the case for the area south of Hanoi, in Zone IV. In three colonial bombing raids on markets and dikes in Yen Dinh village in Thanh Hoa province in early 1950, the French killed more than 200 people, most of them women. In two aerial machine-gun attacks (*mitraillages*) on the markets of Cho Van and Cho Keo over 500 people died. The detailed bombing lists held in the French air force archives leave no doubt as to the extent of the economic targets and the devastation the bombings sowed throughout the archipelago, for civilians in particular. Here's how one witness reported a bombing sortie that occurred in Zone IV in May 1950: "Nam Dan, a town located southeast of Do Luong, was bombed by five planes in early May; more than 100 members of the population were killed. The small cottage industries located around the town were not hit but all of Nam Dan burned." The French had effectively introduced strategic bombing into their war of decolonization. It was a brutal affair, for which Vietnamese civilians paid the highest price.[54]

8

The *Levée en masse* and War Communism

Vietnamese communists were ecstatic: on 18 January 1950, Mao Ze-dong's People's Republic of China formally recognized the Democratic Republic of Vietnam led by Ho Chi Minh. Twelve days later, in Moscow, a rather reluctant Joseph Stalin followed suit and, in so doing, brought the rest of the communist bloc with him. It was a massive diplomatic victory for Vietnamese communists, to be sure. But it was one too many for the Americans. After having "lost China," President Harry S. Truman threw his country's diplomatic and military weight behind France and its Associated States in Indochina in order to stop the spread of communism any further into Asia. The Americans recognized Bao Dai's Vietnam in February 1950, followed by most of their allies across the globe. As Mao's advisers crossed into northern Vietnam to help Ho Chi Minh later that year, Truman's people established the Military Assistance Advisory Group in Indochina. The Cold War had arrived in full force in Asia. And everyone knew that behind Ho's Vietnam stood the Chinese and behind the French loomed the Americans.[1]

Ho and his party welcomed the expansion of the communist bloc to their northern shores. Their Vietnam was no longer this "Cinderella of South East Asia," as one sympathetic Indian journalist had put it in 1948, "fighting unhonoured, unwept and unsung."[2] The tables had now been turned: with the Chinese and Soviets on their side, Vietnamese communists saw themselves on the cutting edge of revolutionary change.

The modern weapons they needed to hold the line against the Americans in Southeast Asia and to take the war to the French in Indochina were on the way. Confident that history was also on their side, Ho and the communist core at the helm of the Democratic Republic of Vietnam leaned firmly towards the camp led by Stalin with Mao at his Asian side. No one forced them to do this. Like their Chinese counterparts, they chose the communist bloc of their own volition, for their own reasons.[3]

That choice, however, triggered others with far-reaching consequences. For example, on 20 January, two days after the good news from China had arrived at Thai Nguyen, Ho opened an emergency plenum of the Indochinese Communist Party to discuss what had to be done next. Of particular importance was the decision to transition immediately to conventional warfare in order to force decolonization on the French. The moment had finally come to follow the Maoist lead and shift the country and its army resolutely to the "General Counter-offensive," the third and final stage of revolutionary warfare. Time was short and the obstacles were plenty. But it could be achieved, if, Ho concluded, the "party becomes an extremely strong force capable of delivering final victory to the nation."[4]

Ho's emphasis on turning the Communist Party into this powerful force is important. For behind the decision to shift to conventional warfare was a second one: a simultaneous commitment to building a new state under the Communist Party's unique control. Not only would Beijing's military assistance allow the Vietnamese to change the course of the Indochina War by creating a professional army capable of scoring battlefield victories, but the Chinese communists would also help their Vietnamese counterparts transform the very nature of the state Ho had declared independent in 1945, so that it could become this "extremely strong force." From 1950, Vietnamese communists embraced a Maoist form of wartime communism that allowed them to fight their way to Dien Bien Phu and to create a single-party communist state at the same time. Vietnamese communists did not wait for the colonial war to end before engineering the transformation of the state. They used war to do it.

Mao's China and the Vietnamese General Counter-offensive

A Sino-Vietnamese Special Relationship

If there is a special relationship in the history of Asian communism, it is the one between the Chinese and Vietnamese comrades which began during the 1920s and not the one which the Vietnamese forged with the Cambodians and the Laotians decades later. From the start of the twentieth century, Vietnamese and Chinese revolutionary networks had intersected along a maritime arc running from southern China to Southeast Asia. Ho Chi Minh knew important Chinese communist leaders from his time in Guangzhou in the 1920s. He had helped enroll dozens of young Vietnamese to study military science and politics in places like the Huangpu Academy when he was there. In 1930, Ho got Vietnamese communism off the ground in southern China when he presided over the creation of the Vietnamese Communist Party in Hong Kong (not inside Vietnam itself because colonial surveillance was too tight there). Ho also joined Chinese revolutionaries in Bangkok and Singapore to help establish communist parties for the Thais and Malayans.[5]

Ho was himself deeply involved in these early Sino-Vietnamese connections. Like so many of his Chinese and Korean counterparts, he had navigated the revolutionary networks reaching from Paris to Guangzhou by way of Moscow. Ho discovered Mao's base in Yan'an when he passed through there in 1938 on his way back home after a long stay in Moscow. He returned a second time a few years later. During that time, he renewed his friendships with Zhou Enlai and Deng Xiaoping, both of whom he had first met in France. Chinese generals Zhu De and Ye Jianying worked with Ho in Yan'an and then in southern China during the war against the Japanese. They solicited his opinions on that war. Drawing on a text he had first prepared in Moscow, Ho lectured on the role of the peasantry in revolutionary warfare. Until he returned to Vietnam in early 1941, he served briefly in the Chinese 8th and 4th armies. He was even a member of General Ye Jianying's party network in the 4th Army.[6]

Less well known is that a handful of Vietnamese communists also followed Mao Zedong as he reoriented Chinese communism from its coastal, mainly urban configuration, to rural areas deep inside the country. As we've seen previously, one of Ho's recruits in Guangzhou, Nguyen Son, had made the Long March with Mao to Yan'an in northern China, then had joined the Chinese Red Army on the way, and finally mastered Maoist mobilization techniques so well that he trained Chinese cadres in their use before returning to Vietnam in 1945 to do the same with his comrades in Zone IV. Nguyen Duc Thuy, the man whom Ho Chi Minh had rushed to China in 1949 to help win over Mao's diplomatic support, had also navigated Sino-Vietnamese revolutionary channels during the interwar period. Fluent in Chinese, he had translated many of Mao's main political and military texts into Vietnamese during the late 1930s. And even those who had remained in Indochina, like the party's general secretary, Truong Chinh (whose name actually meant the "Long March"), and the army's commander-in-chief, Vo Nguyen Giap, could read translations of Mao's essays which had been published during the Leftist Popular Front period in French Indochina.[7]

Vietnamese communists needed no introduction to Maoist thought in 1950. Save perhaps the North Koreans, Ho and his inner circle probably knew the Great Helmsman's writings better than any other revolutionary movement in the world at the time. They certainly knew what Mao's theory of the General Counter-offensive was. Mao had developed these ideas and others in a series of lectures he delivered in Yan'an in 1938, compiled under the title *On Protracted War*. As military strategy, his theory of revolutionary warfare broke down into three main stages. They deserve our attention, if only briefly, since the Vietnamese saw them as a model to emulate, one which would transform their state and its armed forces profoundly.

The first stage in Mao's *Protracted War* theory was a guerrilla one. It reflected the military weakness of the Chinese communists as they confronted the invading Japanese forces a year into the Sino-Japanese conflict (1937–45). For Mao, guerrilla warfare would keep the resistance alive during this period as the party built up base areas through local front work, consolidated its control over people and territory wherever it could, and strengthened its regular army. Although Mao wanted the army to engage in "mobile warfare," meaning the execution of limited attacks on the Japanese, this initial stage remained a defensive one. A second, "static" phase would emerge as the Japanese, unable to defeat their elusive opponents despite their superior forces, would find themselves bogged down. As a result, the Japanese would have no choice but to consolidate their positions in areas surrounding the cities they held and rely on "puppet states" and their armies to help with "pacification." Chinese communists would use the enemy's inertia during this period to build up their regular army and territorial control in the countryside.

Unsurprisingly, their Vietnamese counterparts convening in early 1950 could easily connect Mao's first two stages (the "defensive" and the "static") to what the French were doing in Indochina: unable to score a rapid victory in late 1947 with Operation Léa, they had settled on holding the main colonial cities, controlling the delta areas around them, and accelerated their efforts to create a "puppet state." This was symbolized best in the Associated State of Vietnam led by the former emperor, Bao Dai. Formally established in mid-1949, this second Vietnam and its emerging armed forces would assist with counterinsurgency and colonial state building. During this first phase, Vietnamese communists had fought a guerrilla war, exactly as prescribed by Mao, all the while expanding their territorial control, administration, and army in archipelagic ways as the second, static period set in.

A third and final stage would emerge, Mao predicted, as the revolutionary army strengthened and the international situation changed to the aggressor's disadvantage. In China's case, Japan's woes in the Pacific War would allow the People's Liberation Army to transition from low-intensity guerrilla operations to the conventional warfare the General Counter-offensive required. Chinese regular troops, by then organized into regiments and divisions (the 8th Route and New 4th armies were formed in the late 1930s), armed and equipped with improved weapons, communications and logistical services, would lead the charge. Mao's advice was that guerrillas should maintain their operations in order to disperse enemy troops, while the main forces would attack, in pitched battle if need be, to destroy the enemy's army once and for all. If soldiers had to take up positions on the battlefront, dig trenches to protect themselves from enemy artillery fire, and go over the top to attack the enemy, then so be it. For Mao and his disciples, revolutionary war was necessarily a protracted affair. But final victory would only come when the regular army transitioned to the General Counter-offensive. This was a type of War Communism the Vietnamese could understand, because they already saw themselves as part of this revolutionary process.[8]

Theory and practice, however, are always two different things, and Mao's three stages of revolutionary warfare were no exception to this rule. Mao compiled *On Protracted War* at the start of the Sino-Japanese War, not at its close. Much of what he predicted never occurred during that global conflagration. The People's Liberation Army never truly launched a General Counter-offensive before the nuclear explosions over Japan brought an unexpectedly early end to the Second World War. Chiang Kai-shek's republican army endured the brunt of the Japanese invasion. On 15 August 1945, the day Tokyo capitulated to the Allies, Mao's army remained largely confined to base areas located in the far northern province of Yan'an and, increasingly, neighboring Manchuria, where the Soviets were pouring in to accept the Japanese surrender. Discreetly armed by Moscow, Chinese communists continued to build up their regular forces and expand their guerrilla operations as civil war broke out between Chinese republican forces and their own in 1946. But even then, Mao's regular army only truly went on the offensive in mid-1948, to finally claim victory a year later against the army led by Chiang Kai-shek.

Vietnamese communists had not applied Mao's revolutionary war theory mechanically either upon coming to power in September 1945. For one, Vietnam was not China, neither in terms of its surface area, topography, population, or the size of Ho's bases compared to those of Mao. Nor were the French carbon copies of the Japanese or Chiang Kai-shek's Republic of China. And although Mao may have used the metaphor of a "jigsaw puzzle" to describe the contours the Sino-Japanese War had imposed on his country, the Vietnamese "archipelago state" detailed in this book was something different—it was much smaller, highly decentralized, strung out in the form of islands running from north to south, hemmed in by the ocean to the east, and had fewer than 10 million people living within it as of early 1950 (Chinese communists could count their resistance population in tens of millions and mobilize accordingly).[9] While Vo Nguyen Giap had studied the Maoist gospel carefully, his General Staff had to craft guerrilla, militia, regional, and regular forces according to very specific local conditions. No matter how admiring the Vietnamese communists were of their Chinese counterparts, they had to be very careful: the French had decimated Vo Nguyen Giap's southern army when Nguyen Binh went on the offensive in 1950 without a direct supply line to China.

That did not, however, deter the communists in the north of the Democratic Republic of Vietnam. There, Mao's victory and promise to deliver military assistance, dispatch a large political-military advisory group to Vietnam, and train and outfit Ho's regiments in safe havens just across the border reassured them that this was the favorable "international event," as Mao had put it, that the Vietnamese needed for taking revolutionary warfare to the next level. By calling this emergency party plenum only two days after Mao had formally recognized their government on 18 January 1950, Vietnamese communists sought to officialize immediately that which they had already started putting in place a year earlier—their own General Counter-offensive. Indeed, the party's interim general secretary, Truong Chinh, had first announced this project in early 1949.[10] A few months later, as Mao's troops crossed the Yangzi River into southern China, the Vietnamese began creating regular battalions and revamping their General Staff, along with its communications, intelligence, and logistical services. In August 1949, the country's first modern division, the 308th, appeared. By officially approving this strategic shift to conventional warfare in early 1950, the Vietnamese communists formally committed themselves to creating a professional army. The idea was simple: attack the French head on and drive them out of Indochina just as Mao was sending Chiang Kai-shek and his troops packing to the island of Taiwan. In many ways, two conventional communist offensives took shape between 1948 and 1950, one Chinese, the other Vietnamese—three if one counts North Korea's armed invasion of South Korea in June of 1950. Meanwhile, the Americans countered these moves by ramping up their intervention along East Asia's continental rim, directly in Korea by landing troops there in 1950, and indirectly in Indochina by assisting the French in holding the line against any possible communist offensive into Southeast Asia via northern Indochina.

Conventional War and the Vietnamese Levée en masse

The question for the Vietnamese communists gathered in Thai Nguyen in late January 1950 was *how* to realize this third and final stage of revolutionary warfare on the ground in Indochina. Here, they had to confront obstacles others had encountered before them—and not just their Chinese communist counterparts. Since antiquity, whether in imperial Rome or China, running big standing armies for large-scale battles left leaders with little choice but to make increased demands on their state's populations and resources. For centuries, specific military classes (knights and samurais, for instance) and professional armies recruited locally or abroad had done the job. These soldiers all made their careers serving regimes from one end of Eurasia to the other. However, things changed in western Europe at the turn of the nineteenth century, when French revolutionaries, followed by one Napoleon Bonaparte, implemented the rather novel idea of enlisting "the people" to build massive armies capable not only of defending the fledgling republic in its hour of greatest need, but also of marching them across Europe to spread the revolutionary message and, for Napoleon, to forge a continental empire. In both cases, the French did this through the "mass mobilization" or the "levying" of the population, widely known as the *levée en masse*. Of course, French leaders and propagandists then (and others after them) cast this call-to-arms as a spontaneous event, the manifestation of deep-seated nationalism exemplified by the heroic citizen-soldier coming to the nation's defense. The victory of the French people's army over the invading Prussians at Valmy in 1792 is an obvious favorite. That nationalism was an important factor moving people to action, there can be no doubt. But the French *levée en masse* was also the result of a calculated political decision to impose conscription in order to provide the army with the people, resources, and talents it needed to carry on.[11]

We can be confident that Vietnamese communists meeting in early 1950 grasped what the leaders of the French Revolution and Napoleon's Grande Armée had discovered in the 1790s, namely that "the people" do not always rise up when foreign armies approach. They had to be moved.[12] This is why, even before convening the 1950 plenum, Vietnamese communists had already decided to do what so many others had done before them to create a "people's army"—they imposed the draft. In a landmark piece of legislation, on 4 November 1949 Ho Chi Minh decreed obligatory military service for all Vietnamese men aged between eighteen and forty-five years of age. Working via the resistance administration, the Lien Viet national front and its local associations, and the army's hierarchy, the government, guided by the Communist Party, required officials to issue military cards to all eligible males. It was essential "to make an inventory of the national resistance's resources in men and make young men aware of the honor bestowed on them to take part in the struggle for the nation." Those called up were expected to report for duty or risk legal prosecution. While the *levée en masse* was not a communist creation, it was part of the early development of Vietnamese revolutionary warfare of a conventional kind. This is how the "guerrilla tiger" of 1946 started to change its shape.[13]

Of course, the DRV authorities had mobilized people and resources from the start. In late 1945, legislation authorized the state to requisition in specific cases real estate, materials, and people (doctors and pharmacists were always in high demand). However, no full-fledged draft law was ever passed during the first half of the conflict. Military service operated on a voluntary basis. In the early days, high levels of urban-based nationalism provided the government with the bulk of its volunteers and officers, while a famine-driven wave of rural discontent at the end of the Pacific War provided scores of enlistments among peasants. The shift to the countryside with the outbreak of full-scale war in late 1946 led to increased rural participation in the Vietnamese National Army, much of it nationally driven too. But low-intensity guerrilla operations never required the creation of a large standing army or a sophisticated logistical service to supply it. "Patriotic emulation drives," widely known in Vietnamese as *phong trao thi dua*, served as the main levers through which the state exhorted people to support the war cause, but stopped short of forcibly conscripting them.[14]

All of that changed with the Chinese communist victory. Vietnamese communists might have been able to cobble together the 308th in a few months in mid-1949 by transferring regional troops and combining three or four battalions with a regiment or two in the north. But only obligatory military service—*nghia vu quan su*—could provide the sheer number of men the state now needed to create a standing army large enough to take the battle to the French over a long period of time. Army divisions would have to be replenished, as this war of a more lethal kind killed and maimed soldiers in ways guerrilla warfare did not. The military draft law was the first part of the Vietnamese *levée en masse*, the sine qua non for shifting to Mao's General Counter-offensive.

The second half came in the form of a "general mobilization" law (*tong dong vien*) signed by President Ho Chi Minh on 12 February 1950. This decree authorized the state to mobilize "all the people," men and women, their resources, and skills for the war effort. Thanks to this legislation, the state could now legally conscript civilian citizens and organize them into work teams to transport food, weapons, and supplies to this expanding and increasingly mobile army. Others received orders to build and repair roads, bridges, and dikes. The government could requisition draught animals and equipment if needed. Farmers across the land, and even those residing in enemy-controlled areas, received orders to economize on personal consumption and expand agricultural production in order to help feed the regular army and its people-powered transport and work teams. There was no debate over the military draft law or the one authorizing the mobilization of the civilian population. Like so many others before them, the Vietnamese turned these requirements into legal decrees. It was war.[15]

These laws required the communists to take the state in hand as never before, and they welcomed the chance to do it. The party's straight-talking general secretary, Truong Chinh, knew it when he made his case during the third plenum, convened specifically to discuss "the preparations for and execution of the transition to the General Counter-offensive." One of the main obstacles to achieving that goal, he lamented, was the weakness of the Communist Party's control over the state at its lower levels. Although the communists had manned the control panel of the Democratic Republic of Vietnam as best they could since 1945 from on high, at the lower levels, governance had operated in the form of a coalition. They had had no choice but to rely on thousands of noncommunist anticolonialists, many of them well educated and analytically minded, to help them run the state and its armed forces. The communists might have hoped that their "parallel hierarchies" would provide them with total control, but in reality they still did not have enough of their own people, "cadres," on the ground to run everything. Communist control was anything but totalitarian.

And that was a problem. As Truong Chinh and others speaking after him pointed out, the party's lack of complete control over the lower levels of the DRV made it difficult to organize, implement, and enforce the enrolment of the entire population in the war effort. This was particularly true in the justice, education, and security services, as well as in the Lien Viet and the myriad of patriotic associations at the district and provincial levels. Without loyal cadres in charge of these entities, the communists worried they would be unable to enforce mass mobilization locally, where it counted most. The general secretary informed his audience, too, that many noncommunists had, thanks to their better education, social standing, and networking skills, pushed back against the center's control. Some had carved out influential positions for themselves in local chapters of the nationalist fronts, administration, and even within the party. As a result, they were in a better position to protect themselves from excessive demands on their income, livestock, crops, labor, and property. Le Duc Tho, as we know from our first chapter, had flown into a rage a few months earlier when southern noncommunists had dared to tell him that they ran the Lien Viet, not the communists who had created it.[16]

It was no longer enough to urge people to contribute to the war effort, to appeal to their patriotism through emulation drives of a voluntary kind, Truong Chinh said. Nor was it acceptable to let some people shirk their responsibilities by manipulating the system. "Our state has been too soft," Truong Chinh declared. The time had come, he continued, to impose the mobilization of people, their talents, and the country's material resources by legal means. Only the use of "state power" (*chinh quyen*), he said, could guarantee this.[17]

> If we want to transition to the General Counter-offensive, then we must increase our force. If we seek to increase our force so that it becomes stronger with each day, then there is one essential matter and that is the question of general mobilization. And yet in Vietnam, the war has reached its fifth year and we still do not have a general mobilization law, but rather a collection of decrees that only partially mobilize the people.[18]

As Truong Chinh followed up a few weeks later: "Now is the time that the rich must contribute rice when the soldiers spill their blood and the poor give their labor. . . . The state is extremely humanitarian, but it is also extremely determined."[19] A few days after the plenum closed in early February 1950, Ho decreed the general mobilization of the population.[20]

With these two laws now on the books, the Vietnamese communists immediately went to work expanding the size of the regular army and organizing civilians into huge work and transport teams. The military draft law allowed the communists to forge six new divisions between 1950 and 1951, in addition to the 308th, making for seven in all. By late 1951, a conservative estimate would put the total size of this divisional army at somewhere around 150,000 regular troops (including specialist cadres in charge of expanding communications, logistics, intelligence, and medical services). Averaging around 20,000 men each by the end of the conflict, the seven divisions were: the 304th (officially established in March 1950), the 308th (August 1949), 312th (December 1950), the 316th (May 1951), the 320th (January 1951), the 325th (March 1951), and the 351st, an artillery one (March 1951). It's not necessary to be a military historian to grasp the sociopolitical implications of what the creation of this unprecedented regular army might mean. Several things stand out: the rapidity with which the Vietnamese assembled this standing army;

that its constitution depended on compulsory military service; that it was designed to fight conventional set-piece battles; that it would require ever larger amounts of food from the population in order to operate over longer distances and extended periods of time; and that its young male recruits came mainly from two core islands in the archipelago state, areas in and around Thai Nguyen province in the north and from the provinces of zones III and IV in upper central Vietnam. What is clear is that this was a new type of army engineered for a new type of war, born as much from the Chinese communist victory of 1949 as it was the Vietnamese August Revolution of 1945. The People's Army of Vietnam, or PAVN, came to life in 1950. It did not rise up from "all of Vietnam," however. It emerged from DRV territories wrapped around the Red River Delta, running from central Vietnam to the Chinese border.[21]

The operation of this unprecedented divisional army depended on the massive mobilization of the civilian population concentrated in this swath of territory running through upper Vietnam. Since 1945, guerrilla, regional, and regular troops had relied on local villages to provide the food and shelter they needed to conduct sometimes notable, but in the end mostly limited, low-intensity operations of a hit-and-run kind. Commanders working with village administrators called the shots. However, the rapid shift to conventional warfare changed all that. A division, even a regiment, now bivouacking in any given area could exhaust the food supplies of surrounding villages within days. For obvious reasons, that had to be avoided. As a result, the government had to scramble to procure, stockpile, and transport food to hungry soldiers moving across upper Indochina. The same was true for getting modern weaponry from the Chinese border to the battlefields. The organization of logistics became as important as the creation of the regular army. And the tens of thousands of civilians working in transport teams whom the government had mobilized needed to be fed too.

The communists knew this, and the man they put in charge of logistics reflected it. His name was Tran Dang Ninh. We met him earlier in our book at the head of the party's security services and internal affairs. Cool-headed and methodical to a fault, he impressed his peers when he unmasked a French secret services operation designed to sow discord within Vietnamese ranks. By 1949 he was such an important figure in the party that he traveled with Ho to Beijing to negotiate the details of Chinese communist aid. Upon his return to Thai Nguyen in early 1950, he presided over the radical upgrading of a logistical service capable of handling that assistance, getting it to the troops, and supplying them and their porters with food at the same time. He did this in close collaboration with the commander-in-chief of the army and head of the party's Central Military Commission, Vo Nguyen Giap. In fact, Ninh joined that vital committee, which was in charge of the armed forces, and its General Staff. He presided over the creation of the party's General Supply Office and ran it until his untimely death in 1955. Tran Dang Ninh weighed in on the selection, organization, and execution of every major battle the PAVN fought until the guns fell silent in mid-1954. That is how important this man was. American officers joked during the Korean War that the enemy whose identity they wished to know most was that of the one running the "G-4," the logistical section of the army. In Vietnam, we know his name.[22]

Although Ho and his team were grateful to the Chinese for sending transport trucks, everyone knew that it would be impossible to create a mechanized logistical service, at least not right away. (The outbreak of the Korean War in June 1950 delayed the large-scale delivery of trucks to the Vietnamese as the Chinese diverted what they had northwards.) As a result, in Vietnam, people and animals had to do much of the heavy lifting. This meant transporting ever-larger quantities of food to the troops—rice, fish, and salt. It entailed lugging Chinese-supplied ammunition from the border to safe places located deep inside the archipelago and then on to the battlefields which stretched from the Red River Delta to the Laotian highlands. And it meant delivering medicines and evacuating the sick and wounded from the front lines.

Under Tran Dang Ninh's leadership, logistics specialists immediately began shaping local supply committees and labor brigades for the first major battle at Cao Bang. The communist leadership conscripted hundreds of thousands of laborers (*dan cong*) into transport groups, teams of stretcher-bearers, and road crews. Work brigades repaired roads and bridges in the event of enemy bombing and sabotage. Medical teams transported the sick and wounded to field hospitals behind the lines. Others dug graves for the increasing number of fallen soldiers. For Cao

Bang and the battles which followed, the logistical service worked with the local resistance administration, security services, provincial courts, and nationalist fronts and patriotic associations to mobilize and organize people. All of this had to occur as close to the ground as possible.

The communists lost no time. Between 1950 and 1954, in DRV territories running from Zone IV northwards, people-powered work teams repaired 3,670 km of roads, created 505 km of new ones, and repaired or improved 47,000 meters of bridges.[23] When it came to specific battles, the mobilization of civilians may have only lasted a few weeks before the fighting stopped, but the levels of human mobilization achieved during those powerful spurts were mind-boggling. For the Battle of Cao Bang, which occurred only eight months after the third plenum had closed, the Vietnamese communists mobilized 121,700 people, who collectively provided over 1.7 million workdays clearing roads and delivering supplies. Three-hundred-thousand laborers made the Battle of Vinh Yen possible a few months later by clocking up an astonishing 2.8 million days of work. Two other major battles in 1951, each part of the General Counter-offensive, rounded up people in vast numbers—the Dong Trieu and the Day campaigns mobilized almost 300,000 people for a combined total of over 3.6 million days of labor. This massive mobilization of porters and road workers continued until the end of the war. In all, between 1950 and 1954, the state requisitioned over 1.5 million people, who provided a total of almost 50 million days of transport and road work. The government classified these civilian laborers as "fighter laborers" (*chien si dan cong*) and not as colonial-era "coolies." We do not know how many, mainly young, men were called up to serve in the People's Army between 1950 and 1954, but the number must have exceeded half a million out of a total DRV population of 10 million.[24]

The intensification of the war and the state's increasing demands for new recruits, laborers, and food did not necessarily meet with the spontaneous support of "the people." The landowners and the bourgeois whom Truong Chinh had singled out and insisted should make generous donations to the communist cause were not the only ones to resist state-sponsored coercion. So too did the poor peasants the party conscripted. Like the French revolutionaries in 1793 who forced the peasants to enlist in the army and, in so doing, set off riots in places like the Vendée, Vietnamese communists realized that they had to be careful not to let similar things happen on their watch. In 1950, warning bells went off in Zone IV, when the party singled out for severe criticism cadres who had used excessive force there to levy people and extract food from them. Some cadres had fired their guns into the air to force compliance from the peasants. Others had seized rice from them in order to meet their quotas.[25]

Although we do not know exactly what happened, Vietnamese citizens had clearly pushed back against the heavy-handed conscription methods the government used in this zone. Ho and Truong Chinh had to be very careful in their use of coercion. The last thing they wanted to do was trigger social unrest and possible revolts in their own lands, especially in the rice and labor basket of Zone IV. The French and their Vietnamese allies would be only too eager to exploit such a rebellion. What we do know is that the communist leadership immediately ordered the authorities in Zone IV to rein in the excessive use of force in favor of more persuasion. Ho, the father of the nation, used his moral authority to criticize local cadres for having pressed the people too hard. He offered his personal apology to the victims, promising that it would not happen again. But the president's act of contrition, what the Soviets, Chinese, and Vietnamese communists called "self-criticism" (*tu phe binh*), was a political instrument designed to smooth over problems like this in order to keep "the line" on its "correct" track. No one had any intention of backing off from the *levée en masse* in 1950. This was a turning point in the history of modern Vietnam, and the communists weren't going to blow it.[26]

1950–51: The Rise of the Single-Party Communist State

The Third Plenum of 1950: National Coalition or Communist Coup d'état?

The historic third plenum of early 1950 approved the transition to the General Counter-offensive and the conscription laws accompanying it. Equally important, leaders meeting there also discussed what the communist reconfiguration of the Democratic Republic of Vietnam would need to look like as they took the war to the French and formally rejoined the internationalist communist bloc. Although those at the top didn't reach a consensus overnight, they agreed that this new stage in the war meant that they had to take full control of the state and transform it in communist ways. They could not wait until the end of the conflict to do this; they would use the war to do it.

No one justified the Communist Party's right to run the Democratic Republic of Vietnam in wartime better than Pham Van Dong. In his address to the third plenum in early 1950, Ho's right-hand man explained clearly to his listeners that the party had to immediately consolidate its hold over the state in order to take the war to a new level in the form of the General Counter-offensive: "We must have such a state in order to align the direction of the war with our goals, in line with our war plans." If, Pham Van Dong expounded, the party wanted to fight this new kind of war and win, then it had to do nothing less than create a new kind of state, a "people's republic" (*mot nuoc cong hoa nhan dan*) similar to the one Mao Zedong had just proclaimed in China a few months earlier.[27]

To make his case, Pham Van Dong went back to the past, to the August Revolution of 1945, to explain why the Democratic Republic of Vietnam was, indeed, part of the wider communist family. He reminded everyone that on 19 August, four days after the Japanese had capitulated to the Allies, the communist-led nationalist front, the Viet Minh, had seized power in Hanoi. On that glorious day, he continued, their party overthrew the colonial regime as well as the Vietnamese monarchy the French had kept alive in the form of a protectorate. That both claims were false—the Japanese overthrew the French colonial state and Bao Dai abdicated of his own volition—mattered little. What did was that Pham Van Dong had to make two things very clear: first, that the communists had led this revolution of national liberation from the start, as the Bolsheviks had in Russia before them, and, secondly, that they had done so in the interest of the "masses" whom Dong carefully defined for his audience as "the workers and the peasants under the leadership of the working class." All of this, he argued in his speech, made it a "people's republic" just like those that had recently appeared in eastern Europe and in China. At war with the French colonialists from the start, Pham

Van Dong conceded that the Vietnamese communists had agreed to create a coalition state in the form of the Democratic Republic of Vietnam. But it was theirs: "The leadership of the Democratic Republic of Vietnam, just like the leadership of the other people's republics, was led [by the vanguard of] the working class, the Communist Party."[28]

Pham Van Dong turned to another argument to make his case—war. Since 1945, he said, the communists had led the worker and peasant masses in a resistance war against the French colonialists. "Had there not been this heroic and arduous resistance force combining the workers and the peasants, had the Communist Party not provided enlightened leadership," he argued, "then the resistance would have never been able to succeed as it has today, and who knows what would have happened to it." Stalin was right, Dong reminded his listeners: war had proven the superiority of communist statecraft. The Soviet Union had persevered against Nazism during the Second World War because of its communist core and the party's incarnation of the nation. The Democratic Republic of Vietnam was doing the same thing in its struggle against French colonialism. Only a regime led by the working class, the Communist Party, could do this, he avowed, "and not a bourgeois democratic regime."[29]

Whether or not Pham Van Dong was "right" is not the point here. What mattered was how he was constructing his argument with a view to "proving" that the Democratic Republic of Vietnam had been from its inception and would now be more than ever an authentic "people's republic" under the Communist Party's leadership, capable of joining with China and the East European communist regimes led by the Soviet Union at the table. Speaking a few days after Mao had recognized the DRV while Stalin still hemmed and hawed, Pham Van Dong made every argument he could think of to show that the Vietnam Ho Chi Minh had declared independent in 1945 had been and always would be, now more than ever, a communist-minded state like Mao's China. Although the name of the Vietnamese state remained the "Democratic Republic of Vietnam" in order not to draw the attention of the French and the Americans standing behind them, the Vietnamese were now committed to building a single-party communist state.[30]

In practice, though, in 1950 Vietnamese communists still had to compromise. The "rise" of their single-party communist state could only go so far for the time being. It had to take the French, the Americans, and their emerging Vietnamese allies lining up behind Bao Dai into account. Ho Chi Minh still needed to keep the noncommunists in his coalition on board to maintain the widest possible alliance against so many dangerous enemies. Vietnamese communists kept a close eye on how communist parties working in coalition governments in postwar Poland and Czechoslovakia, for example, had navigated similarly "complicated" situations of a coalition kind. In East Asia, Korea and China offered useful points of comparison too, especially for communist parties dealing with colonial situations in which the Americans were increasingly becoming involved.

Particularly helpful here were Mao Zedong's ideas on "New People's Democracy." This political philosophy authorized communists engaged in colonial and semicolonial wars to collaborate with patriotic bourgeois, landowning, and professional classes against their common enemy. The Chinese had used it during their struggle against the Japanese. The Vietnamese followed their lead. Once victory was achieved, Mao explained, then the communists could move in favor of the workers and peasants. Until then, "New Democracy" favored the workers and the peasants, but it kept the noncommunist bourgeoisie and landowners on board in a "democratic dictatorship" led by the party. Pham Van Dong cited Mao's ideas approvingly. The third plenum fully endorsed this principle and its ongoing shift towards the communization of the state.

This is when things became messy, as they had in other coalition-cum-communist governments in Eastern Europe and China where the communists were determined to take over one day. On the one hand, Vietnamese communists continued to reassure their noncommunist allies that they had no intention of undermining the coalition government. What counted most, they insisted, was defeating the French and the Americans. Any differences between them would be worked out once the war was over. On the other hand, the communists were lying. With the Chinese and the Soviets now standing behind them, Ho Chi

Minh and his entourage were initiating efforts to turn the Democratic Republic of Vietnam into a communist state with the workers and peasants in charge whether noncommunists liked it or not. In effect, from early 1950, Ho's Communist Party lit a slow-burning coup d'état against the coalition government and constitution the communists had accepted in 1946. "The state," Pham Van Dong had told his inner circle in early 1950, "was the instrument for realizing the party's policies." Everyone understood what he was saying: the time had come to bring forth a single-party communist state for Vietnam. This, too, was a turning point in the history of modern Vietnam.[31]

In separate speeches during the third plenum, senior party leaders elucidated how they would consolidate their hold over the state at the local levels. Another powerful party man, Hoang Quoc Viet, explained the importance of increasing the party's grip over the nationalist fronts like the Lien Viet and the myriad of patriotic associations for workers and peasants in particular. Now, more than ever, he said, these organizations would be essential to the party's ability to induct more people into its ranks from among the peasants and workers essential to building this "people's republic" from the bottom up. Through the control of the Lien Viet and the patriotic associations, the party could also educate the majority peasant population in the communist faith, as well as take control of these local instruments of state power. And, of course, the communists also needed to access people and resources at the ground level where it would count the most as the war intensified.[32]

The fronts were also essential to organizing, mobilizing, and indoctrinating the youth. Hoang Quoc Viet instructed cadres to expand rapidly youth groups at the local level. They should encourage boys to join the army and urge young adults of both sexes to join supply and work teams. As Hoang Quoc Viet told his audience: "We must realize the slogan that every young person is a soldier." In July 1950, Ho Chi Minh presided over the creation of the "Vietnamese Youth Assault Force" (*Thanh Nien Xung Phong Viet Nam*). Over the next four years, 20,000 Vietnamese young people joined it to build and repair roads and transport supplies to hungry soldiers. Later on, during the Vietnam War, another 180,000 young people would enlist in this paramilitary unit. And, as they did so, they would find themselves in the line of fire as they moved along the Ho Chi Minh Trail. This massive party-run mobilization of the young had begun in 1950, during the Indochina War.[33]

Lastly, the party plenum approved the collapsing of the Vietnamese Independence League (Viet Minh) into the Association of the United Vietnamese People (Lien Viet). The communists needed the Lien Viet's support to mobilize for war. Sober noncommunist anticolonialists in the Lien Viet knew what this was really about: the communists wanted to regain control of this nationalist front which they had created in 1946, but over which they only exercised partial control. The clash in 1949 between the party's delegate to the south, Le Duc Tho, and noncommunists in the Lien Viet was only one example of many standoffs of this kind. Indeed, in some areas, the Lien Viet had clearly become a de facto independent political institution which served as a forum for democratic debate and also as a potential check on the rise of a single-party communist state. Given that the National Assembly had not convened since 1946, the Lien Viet had effectively filled the gap in many areas. But rather than dissolving the Lien Viet and causing a potential noncommunist uproar and mass defections to Bao Dai's Vietnam, Ho's party collapsed the communist-run Viet Minh into the Lien Viet, along with their own people.[34]

It was a brilliant move. But that was not what a lot of noncommunist anticolonialists had signed up for when they joined Ho's "compromise" state in 1945–6. Republican-minded nationalists in the Lien Viet, like the chemist and member of the socialist party, Hoang Van Chi, began to leave Ho's Vietnam. Some joined Bao Dai's Vietnam, hoping the French would be lucid enough to let go of their empire, to break with 'association' so that a fully independent noncommunist Vietnam could finally emerge. It was not to be. And by refusing to decolonize in 1950 as the Dutch had done in Indonesia in 1949, albeit grudgingly, the French drove noncommunist Vietnamese anticolonialists onto the fence, abroad, or into seclusion. Paradoxically, the "French colonialists" helped the "Vietnamese communists" to consolidate the party's hold over Vietnam.[35]

The Party's Second Congress of Early 1951:
The Rise of the Single-Party State

Although the coalition state Ho presided over in 1945–6 had not been a fiction, it now started to become one. What had started out as a remarkably democratic republic now began to wither away. During the course of 1950, those at the communist center received field reports affirming the party's control over the state: new training programs for cadres, intensive administrative consolidation, expanded operations on communist front work, and increased party role in the armed forces. In early 1951, Vietnamese communists gathered again in Thai Nguyen to take part in the Indochinese Communist Party's Second Congress. The last time such an important meeting had occurred was sixteen years earlier, in 1935, in Portugueuse Macau. The outbreak of the Second World War, followed by the Indochinese one, had made organizing such a second meeting difficult. But with the Chinese communists now standing behind them and the PAVN on the move, it was time to assert officially the Communist Party's central role in leading the war and controlling the state.

In 1951, Ho Chi Minh and Truong Chinh opened the party's Second Congress. Ho laid out the party's history and its leading role in resisting colonialism since the interwar period, winning national independence in 1945, and leading the armed struggle against the French. He endorsed the transformation of the Vietnam he had declared independent in 1945 along communist lines and confidently affirmed that the Vietnamese would win the war against the French and take up their rightful place in the communist community led by Stalin and Mao. In his speech, Ho welcomed the fact that a massive communist bloc now reached from Eastern Europe to southern China with Korea and Vietnam standing on its cutting edge. He condemned American aggression against the communist camp at both ends of Eurasia. Within Asia, he criticized American hostility to Mao's China and their intervention in Taiwan, Korea, and Indochina. He deplored that the Americans had used the Marshall Plan in Europe to weaken the Soviets. Inside Vietnam, Ho recommended that its wide nationalist front be maintained in the form of the Lien Viet, but he called again for the creation of an "extremely strong" Communist Party which alone could deliver victory. This force was now, he declared, to be called the "Vietnamese Workers Party" (*Dang Lao Dong Viet Nam*).[36] Truong Chinh, now the party's official general secretary, backed him up, going into greater detail, as he had done a year earlier, on the nature of Vietnamese communism and on the Communist Party's right to control the state, the armed forces, and run the General Counter-offensive. He laid it all out in the party's new and extensive political platform hammered out and approved during the Second Congress.[37]

This historic congress adopted a slew of new measures and policies in line with the communist reconfiguration of the state already under-way. The most important was the elaboration and approval of a new political program authorizing the strengthening and the dominance of the Communist Party. During this congress, as Ho had announced, the communist leadership changed their party's name from the Indochinese Communist Party to the Vietnamese Workers Party. After having had to operate the party underground, it was now time to bring it back into the open. Ho Chi Minh and others conceded that the "dissolution" of the party in late 1945 had caused confusion. But they had no choice at the time, given the hostile forces arrayed against the "August Revolu-tion" of 1945–6 (the French, the Chinese republican occupying forces, and their powerful anticommunist Vietnamese allies, the Vietnamese Nationalist Party, the Alliance Group, and the Dai Viet).

But 1951 was not 1946. Chinese communist aid was now flowing into northern Vietnam, the People's Army of Vietnam had just scored a major border victory over the French at Cao Bang, and the entire com-munist bloc, including the mighty Soviet Union, had now united behind Ho and his party. Vietnamese communists were confident that they could pick up the communist revolution from where they had had to leave off in August 1945. The unveiling of the Vietnamese Workers Party was an accurate indication of this newly found confidence. The Second Congress affirmed that the DRV would now be based on democratic centralism, would adhere to Marxism-Leninism as an article of faith, and commit to creating an entirely communist state, like others in the bloc. Vietnamese communists proclaimed their support for the working and peasant classes, all the while reassuring noncommunist allies that they had nothing to fear (when, in fact, they most certainly did).

The leaders of the congress shifted to "Vietnam" in their party's official appellation on the grounds that the Vietnamese revolution was further advanced down the road leading to communism than that of their Laotian and Cambodian brethren. They also knew that the French, the Americans, and, especially, anticommunist Laotian and Cambodian nationalists would accuse them of practicing a form of "Red imperialism" if they held on to Indochina as a territorial framework for building a single-party communist state. But, as we shall see in Chapter 12, Ho and his disciples did not let go of Indochina in any way whatsoever.

But again, Ho and his party were careful not to go too far. They knew they had to keep their creeping confiscation of the 'coalition state' as imperceptible as possible. They were still at war with the French and, indirectly, the Americans. Inside their ranks, and especially at the lower levels, they still needed the collaboration of thousands of noncommunist anticolonialists to win. These people helped to produce food, man the state, and command the troops. Pragmatism still trumped radical social revolution. This also explains why this new type of Vietnamese revolutionary war did not include the immediate deployment of the political weapon that could change everything—full-blown land reform. If applied in its most radical form (as a forcible confiscation of land), it would have destroyed the landowning and bourgeois classes in a civil war, plain for all to see. In the third plenum in early 1950, and again at the Second Congress, the communists backed moderate land reform. They authorized and dispatched cadres into villages to categorize people into a series of different classes based on wealth and land ownership. Truong Chinh and others instructed cadres to apply property rules that were already on the books: landowners only had to reduce rents and lending rates, abolish debts to patriotic families, and redistribute French land and that of absentee Vietnamese landowners to poor peasants.[38] However, for the time being, the strengthening of the party-state did *not yet* turn on forcible land redistribution. That came later, as we shall see.[39]

When, during the third plenum, more radical-minded delegates urged Truong Chinh to launch full-scale war on the "feudal classes" instead of these half-measures, the secretary general told them to stand down. He warned them then in no uncertain terms that this was not ideological heresy, but a pragmatic strategy to get the party through the Indochina War on the winning side:

> Certain comrades suggest that we expel the landowners immediately from the state. . . . As long as the revolution requires it, we will and must elevate the landowning class. When we no longer need them, we will lower them. And when favorable conditions are realized, we will exterminate the ownership class. The party will do it energetically, but now is not the time. Revolutionary slogans only have value when they can be realized. If not, they are empty words.[40]

In sum, between early 1950 and early 1951, the third plenum and the Second Congress officialized the slow rise of the single-party communist state in modern Vietnam, the application of the *levée en masse*, the commitment to conventional warfare in the form of Mao's General Counter-offensive, the collapse of the Viet Minh into the Lien Viet (made official in early 1951), and the gradual expansion of the party's hold over the state, the army, and the society. In so doing, the Vietnamese communists lined up behind President Ho Chi Minh in 1951 had, in their minds, relaunched the revolution they had "missed" in August 1945, a communist one. This then is how the rise of the single-party communist state started—in the crucible of war, the one initiated by the *levée en masse*.

Sino-Vietnamese Mass Mobilization Techniques

From Yan'an to the Viet Bac: Mass Mobilization and the Bureaucratic Elite

There was, however, more to the "rise" than introducing the draft, passing a general mobilization law, and declaring that the Communist Party was now the vanguard of revolution and a new state.[41] The question for

Ho and his disciples was also "How?" How do you bring forth the single-party state? For answers, they looked to the communist world—the wartime experiences of the Soviet Union and Maoist China in particular. They found them in a panoply of communist techniques developed by their revolutionary big brothers: the personality cult, land reform, patriotic emulation campaigns, new hero veneration, rectification sessions, and the politicization of the armed forces. Together, these "Marxist methods" constituted the repertoire which Vietnamese communists drew upon to build their brand of wartime communism.

The global history of the creation, circulation, and adaptation of these communist mobilization techniques remains to be written. Suffice it to say here that Vietnamese communists were aware of these tools long before using them against the French and, later, the Americans. Ho Chi Minh spoke and read Russian and Chinese. He had traveled and lived in Moscow in 1924, two years after the Bolsheviks had won the Russian civil war and created the Soviet Union. He, like so many others in his entourage, would have read Lenin's collected works, including his essay on communist "emulation" methods. During his long stay in Moscow in the early 1930s, Ho's Russian was good enough for him to study at the International Lenin School for communist cadres. He would have learned about officer and cadre rectification programs, as well as the dangers of assaulting rather than mobilizing the peasant population.[42]

In China also, as we know, Ho had long worked with Chinese communists. He had witnessed at first hand the shift from urban-driven communism in coastal China in the early 1930s to Mao's peasant mobilization techniques in Yan'an during the Second World War. Like Mao, Ho and Truong Chinh realized that their Communist Party might have been born in a port city, Hong Kong, like the Chinese one in Shanghai a decade earlier, but its survival was now tied to the Vietnamese countryside, where the French had pushed the Democratic Republic of Vietnam. Thai Nguyen province was, if you will, Vietnam's Yan'an. Ho, like Mao, knew how important peasant support would be to winning the war and building a revolutionary state. He knew how Mao had used land reform to break the hold of the old order by mobilizing and politicizing the peasantry, turning them on the landowners when the time came, and then folding them into the new revolutionary order as soldiers and new bureaucrats under party control. The Chinese Communist Party's success turned on the politicization of the peasantry and its transformation into a loyal bloc of support for the regime. As an astute biographer of Mao has described this policy towards the peasant masses: "In order to politicize a social group that had until now been located outside the political realm, the [Chinese] communists mobilized. Two things went together: an activist mobilization *à la Mao* that sought to control and constrain with one that was also determined to convince and move."[43]

Taking control of the peasantry was one half of Mao's revolutionary recipe. Creating a homogenous, loyal bureaucratic class was the other. Having visited Yan'an while Mao was doing all this, Ho knew all about it. Mao had used Soviet methods for creating loyal party members and army officers, and so would he. In fact, it was Mao who had taken what was originally a Soviet political instrument and adapted it to his own need in China to create a specialty which was known as "rectification" (*zhengfeng*). Starting in Yan'an, Mao organized obligatory rectification sessions for party members and their officer counterparts. Rectification, the changing of the cadre's thinking and actions, would start at the top of the party and the army and slowly percolate its way down through a myriad of schools and training sessions. Like the Soviets, Maoists used "criticism" and "struggle sessions" led by trusted cadres to bring everyone over to the "right" or "correct" line. They had to be "rectified" or "perfected." Compliance with "the way" ensured several things. It generated loyalty from the top down and, just as importantly, it created a homogeneous bureaucratic class. All of this became the new foundation upon which a single-party state would turn in a time of war. The Great Helmsman added to this ideological mix a personality cult, inspired in large part by Stalin's model.[44]

And Ho was not alone in his familiarity with these Sino-Soviet mass mobilization techniques.[45] Since 1950, we know, 200 Chinese advisers had been sent to Vietnam, and they had introduced many more of them. It is worth considering them here in order to grasp how important they were in raising up this second Vietnam, a communist one, from its archipelagic foundation.

PLATE 1. Ho Chi Minh. Popper Photo / Getty Images.

PLATE 2. Vo Nguyen Giap. Universal History Archive / Getty Images.

PLATE 3. On the road from Nam Dinh to Thai Binh, 1954. © International Center of
Photography. Robert Capa / Magnum Photos.

PLATE 4. Women looking at dead guerrilla fighters. Howard Sochurek / Getty Images.

PLATE 5. Women praying for their men at war, 1952. © Werner Bischof / Magnum Photos.

PLATE 6. Testing a coffin, 1952. © Werner Bischof / Magnum Photos.

PLATE 7. A DRV propaganda poster with its headline reading "Wage people's war!" ECPAD.

PLATE 8. The border battle of 1950. Howard Sochurek / Getty Images.

PLATE 9. Bao Dai boarding an American warship visiting Vietnam, 1950.
Carl Mydans / Getty Images.

PLATE 10. French population in Saigon greeting the Expeditionary Corps, 1945. ECPAD.

PLATE 11. French machine-gunners at the Battle of Hanoi, early 1947. AP Photo.

PLATE 12. The Battle of Hanoi: a city in rubble. Vietnamese Revolutionary Museum.

PLATE 13. A Vietnamese child at war. Vietnamese Revolutionary Museum.

PLATE 14. Ho Chi Minh with his typewriter. AFP / Getty Images.

PLATE 15. A DRV propaganda poster, which says: "Resistance bonds are weapons to wipe out the French enemy!" ECPAD.

PLATE 16. General Raoul Salan (in center). AFP / Getty Images.

PLATE 17. General Jean de Lattre de Tassigny. Howard Sochurek / Getty Images.

PLATE 18. French bombers on a mission. Bettmann / Getty Images.

PLATE 19. Vietnamese POWs at work for the French. © Werner Bischof / Magnum Photos.

PLATE 20. Collecting rice in the Red River Delta, 1954. © International Center of Photography. Robert Capa / Magnum Photos.

PLATE 21. Patrolling the rice fields south of Hanoi, 1954. © International Center of Photography. Robert Capa / Magnum Photos.

PLATE 22. Taking a Vietnamese POW in the rice fields. Keystone / Getty Images.

PLATE 23. Léon Pignon, high commissioner of Indochina and mastermind of the Associated States of Indochina. Carl Mydans / Getty Images.

PLATE 24. Land reform in action in northern Vietnam. From Franz Fabert, *Rot Leuchtet der Song Cai* (Berlin: Kongress Verlag, 1955).

PLATE 25. General Henri Navarre (smoking a cigarette) with Colonel Gilles, 1953.
Keystone–France / Getty Images.

PLATE 26. Dien Bien Phu: Pham Van Dong, Ho Chi Minh, Truong Chinh, and Vo Nguyen Giap (standing) looking at a map of Northern Indochina. AP Photo / Vietnam News Agency.

PLATE 27. Dien Bien Phu: French troops in the trenches. Keystone–France / Getty Images.

PLATE 28. Dien Bien Phu: Vietnamese labor teams clearing a road.
Collection Jean-Claude Labbe / Getty Images.

PLATE 29. Dien Bien Phu. Vietnamese medical teams going to the front.
SeM / Getty Images.

PLATE 30. Civilians at war. From the private collection of Christophe Dutrône, with authorization from the owner.

PLATE 31. Vietnamese troops attacking at Dien Bien Phu, 1 May 1954. Getty Images.

PLATE 32. A hand placed on the Wall of Fallen Soldiers at Dien Bien Phu, 2004. Associated Press.

Patriotic Emulation Campaigns

Intimately familiar with the Soviet model of rallying the population around heros to imitate, Ho had personally introduced the "patriotic emulation" (*phong trao thi dua ai quoc*) campaigns to Vietnam in 1948. Trusted communist members fanned out across the countryside, where they organized these events to generate and maintain support and legitimacy for their beleaguered resistance state. Drawing upon personal relations, kinship ties, and local front organizations (those for farmers, women, and the young), cadres gathered villagers together to participate in these campaigns. Immediately, they identified individuals whose patriotism and industriousness as peasants, workers, soldiers, women, doctors, and merchants made them models worthy of emulation. Cadres urged everyone to imitate these people in order to eradicate illiteracy, produce more rice, step up local weapons production, give more vaccinations to the local population, and support the resistance financially. In the late 1940s, emulation campaigns served as the main mechanism through which the state provided recruits for the local militia and army and organized labor to repair bombed-out bridges, supply troops, as well as to clear new land to increase food production.[46]

The main idea was also to organize local competitions encouraging individuals, families, or villages to copy, indeed outdo, their neighbors in competitive but good-natured emulative contests. An array of prizes, medals, photographs, and certificates were awarded to stimulate participation. This might mean organizing competitions among individual villagers or having two or more villages compete against each other to produce the most rice. The winners would receive a prize in a very publicized gathering. Theoretically, such patriotic contests reached down—though not without tremendous difficulties—to people in local districts and villages, indeed, into peoples' homes, as these instructions reveal:

> If we want the village program to work, we must pay attention to the important competitive elements, which are the families in the villages and hamlets. If these families refuse to participate in the competitions, then they [the emulation competitions] will not succeed.

For these reasons, when it comes to the projects which each village must accomplish, we have created special tasks which must be executed inside each family. These tasks require the cooperation of all the people in the village. In order for each family to know its responsibilities and to acquire a line of action which will conform to the [larger, village] one, the directives for the families have to be clearly presented and readable, and displayed in a place in each house so that they can be memorized by heart by all the members of the family.[47]

In the early years, these emulation campaigns ran on patriotism, allowing the communists to mobilize the rural villages and, in so doing, to incorporate them into the party's political realm.

New Heroes and New Men

The emulation campaigns also allowed the communists to introduce "new heroes" (*anh hung moi*). New heroes referred to the "exemplary" men and women put forward and exalted by the communist leadership in the communist bloc in order to better mobilize people in specific sectors and social classes. These individuals were always first and foremost heroic and patriotic. The Soviet Union had created a heroic pantheon consisting of workers, soldiers, peasants, and heroic pilots, such as Anatoly Liapidevsky and Valentina Grizodubova. The Maoists also created a long list of heroes to emulate. At the top of that list was Dong Cunrui. This nineteen-year-old soldier in the Chinese army blew himself up in 1948 in order to destroy an enemy pillbox guarding a bridge. A few years later, during the Korean War, the Chinese communists created the Order of the Heroic Exemplar. The idea was that soldiers would always seek to emulate these virtuous role models and the leaders would use them to indoctrinate their troops in the party's line.

The Vietnamese communists followed suit. They held up the likes of Nguyen Quoc Tri for emulation as a soldier "hero" who had fought in "95 battles" and "had been wounded seven times." He was awarded the titles "Courageous Cadre" and "Fighter." Other heroes from 1952 included Ngo Gia Kham as a superlative farmer, Nguyen Thi Chien as a female fighter, and, of course, the "Hero of all Heroes," Ho Chi Minh. These were the people the communists asked their people to imitate in their daily lives. In so doing, the party increased agricultural production, recruited soldiers for the army and its supply teams, and expanded its political control.[48]

While Vietnamese communists continued to promote patriotic heroes with links to a long tradition of veneration of martyrs within Sino-Vietnamese political culture, in the 1950s, they went further, by adding the role of "new man" of a communist kind to the repertoire. (Although the term "new man" was generally used, such a person could be male *or* female.) In 1952, the party's general secretary, Truong Chinh, characterized the "new man" as follows: "This hero has a strong class sentiment. He knows how to distinguish the good from the bad, the friend from the enemy. He knows himself and has a responsible outlook towards the leadership and the masses. It is not personal interest that guides him in the war or in work production but rather the collective good." Most importantly of course, the "hero follows the party and the government's line."[49] The message was unmistakable: the "people" were to imitate the "workers" and "peasants" who were the real heroes. Patriotic emulation campaigns and new heroes—and the new Communist men they were designed to create—allowed the party to mobilize and politicize the population. As one astute scholar sums it up:

> The "new man" was a cadre, a soldier, or a meritorious peasant. The emulation of the hero was not seen only as a communist invention. For centuries, the Confucian tradition had also referred to heroic stories in its teachings as a way of educating the people. What was novel about communism was what it achieved with the method it used: a widespread and far-reaching propaganda technique and an authoritarian policy designed to mobilize the members of a collective behind the exemplary models of new and virtuous figures. This amounted to impressive ideological control. The "new man" rapidly became a successful idea for a government that was looking to root its political legitimacy among the population. Far from a philosophical abstraction,

the new heroic bureaucracy produced a contingent of men and women capable of reinforcing the structure of the state (through its administration, mass organizations, army, and so on). A study of its transformations is a study of the regime.[50]

Sino-Vietnamese Rectification

Together with patriotic emulation and new hero worship, "rectification" was the other most important Soviet-inspired Maoist method the Vietnamese communists adopted and applied to the people of their party, state, and armed forces during the early 1950s. It was the Chinese advisory group who introduced the rectification technique to their Vietnamese counterparts in Thai Nguyen. As in Yan'an during the Sino-Japanese War, the main goal of rectification (*chinh huan*) in Ho's Vietnam was the "reform" (*chinh*) and "instruction" (*huan*) of good elements in the party, state, and society. Rectification was central to shaping like-minded, reliable, and loyal cadres in the army, the party, and its mass organizations. The communists dispensed rectification via schools for the party before diffusing it throughout the state, the army, and the society. They did so through a cohort of carefully selected and devout cadres. Rectification sessions corrected, perfected, improved, and, above all, homogenized thinking along strictly approved communist lines. In these courses, the leadership inculcated the party's major themes and tenets (communist theory, land reform, emulation campaigns, new heroes, and the mass adoption of the correct "line" of thinking). Cadres, civil servants, security officers, soldiers and their commanders had no choice but to attend these rectification retreats. Once they were cut off from the outside world, party minders required them to concentrate entirely on selected readings, exercises, lectures, criticism, and self-criticism. They had to learn the "line"—they had to internalize it. Only then could they live it and apply it. As in Maoist China, the main goal of Ho's rectification campaigns was to provoke within its subject an epiphany, a conversion to the party, its family, and its core communist values. The cadre-cum-teacher was there to help, force if need be, individuals to examine and reexamine their consciences and confess their social sins through self-criticism and "struggle" sessions before they could finally be reborn as part of the wider, collective communist identity and, as loyal party subjects, spread the message themselves.[51]

Ho Chi Minh knew exactly what rectification was and just why it was so important. In the late 1940s, he had authored a primer for his trusted cadres discussing the basics of communist rectification, entitled *Changing One's Working Ways* (*Sua Doi Loi Lam Viec*). In it, the Vietnamese president provided easy-to-follow instructions for communist members and cadres, explaining how they should work and conduct themselves. Writing in 1947, as the French attacked in full force, Ho warned his party members of the dangers of individualism and the need to stay on the "line." His booklet was all about how to instill loyalty to the party and, in so doing, maintain its control. Ho personally introduced this Marxist method of political control to Vietnam.[52]

During the second half of the Indochina War, this lighter (and more optional) version of "rectification" changed and gave way to a darker, mandatory one.[53] Like full-blown land reform discussed later in this book, unthrottled rectification could spin out of control, as it had in China and the Soviet Union. The famous Vietnamese poet Xuan Dieu, who had joined the party early on as a propagandist in charge of cultural matters, found rectification a bone-chilling experience as the cadres focused on eradicating his homosexuality. As one of those present later recalled the experience:

> Xuan Dieu just sat and cried. . . . I was also silent as a clam. During those wild moments in the seductive darkness of night, I also went a bit crazy—Xuan Dieu was not by any stretch of the imagination alone in this regard. Nobody specifically mentioned these episodes [of homosexual love] but everybody raised their voices, raised their voices severely, harshly criticizing his "bourgeois thinking, his evil bourgeois thinking, which needed to be fixed." Xuan Dieu sobbed and said, "It's my homosexuality, my homosexuality," choking on his words, tears flowing, but not promising to fix anything at all.[54]

What happened to Xuan Dieu was not an isolated "incident." The awakening to the importance of adopting the communist "line" was often a full-blown psychological and, sometimes, even physical assault on the individual. In late 1950, Chinese and Vietnamese cadres in charge of the DRV's Army Officers School operating in Yunnan province in southern China imposed mandatory rectification on Vietnamese cadets training to become commanders. A study which comes from the Vietnamese internal security services indicates that instructors placed too much emphasis on "the issue of class struggle" in rectification meetings. Pressured by their Chinese advisers, they required 4,000 of their officer-cadre trainees to rectify themselves by admitting their own class shortcomings. Sessions forced cadets to "delineate the line between the enemy and our side within themselves." Interrogators pushed to find out if any of these recruits were spies for the French or anticommunist moles. Self-criticism sessions entailed extraordinary group pressure, ceaseless ideological denunciations and haranguing, all of which, "went on day and night, even during rest periods, and if results were not obtained in the barracks, then the parties were taken out into the jungle where they were attacked continuously." The instructors insisted that "whoever sincerely confesses will be forgiven, whoever is stubborn will be severely punished, and whoever makes a contribution will receive suitable commendation and rewards." Those who refused to admit their past wrongdoing and their links to the enemy were attacked as liars and ostracized. The psychological pressure was enormous. Trainees in one rectification campaign ended up "admitting" that they were working for the "enemy," or had entertained "connections with the enemy" in the past. "Some people," this study reveals, "were so upset that they could not stand it and committed suicide."

Things got so bad that communist leaders in Vietnam hustled a high-level delegation to China to find out what was going on. They feared that Sino-Vietnamese rectification was actually destroying a whole class of officers whom they badly needed to fight the French. Their investigations soon revealed that most of these "confessions" were pure fabrications designed to placate their accusers. The party applied the brakes before it was too late in that particular case, but, overall, there was no going back. Ho and his party weren't going to abandon rectification or any of the other Sino-Soviet communist tools they were using to build a new type of state. Vietnamese War Communism was now underway.

9

Of Rice and War

If we fail to consider the burden we are forcing our people to carry and if we fail to take into account our government's financial capabilities, we will be going down a risky and dangerous road: we will be recruiting and amassing a large number of troops who will not have food to eat, uniforms to wear, or weapons with which to fight. If we take too many men out of our productive labor force, our economy will not be able to keep up with our army's needs and requirements. It is then that General Rice will become more powerful than our real generals.

TRUONG CHINH, 15 APRIL 1951

The leader of the Vietnamese Workers Party issued this warning as the People's Army of Vietnam moved from the highlands into the Red River Delta.[1] The General Counter-offensive was not going well. The People's Army might have taken a large chunk of the border with China after their victory at Cao Bang a few months earlier, but each time its soldiers attacked head on in the lowlands the French repelled them in a barrage of artillery fire and napalm blasts. Unable to break the French hold on the plains, the army's commanding general, Vo Nguyen Giap, regrouped and changed tactics, pulling back the PAVN's main divisions into the highlands while sending smaller units back into the delta to fight guerrilla-style to expand the government's control there. Although Giap failed to conquer the Red River basin outright, he combined the highlands and the delta into one theater, carefully calibrating the use of both conventional and guerrilla types of warfare.

Behind this military struggle for control of upper Vietnam occurred another, closely connected clash, just as important as the first. It centered on the production and distribution of food. The leaders of the DRV needed rice to feed their rapidly expanding army, civil services, and human transport and work teams. They sent guerrillas into enemy-controlled lands to bring it out clandestinely. Of course, the French did everything in their power to stop them. They renewed pacification programs. They assigned troops to guard paddy fields during harvest time and mobilized their Vietnamese partners in the Associated State of Vietnam to help. The French also took the economic war into enemy territory. They bombed dikes, destroyed canals, and even killed livestock to deny Ho Chi Minh's people the food needed to carry on. It was an essential part of what the French called *la guerre économique*. This "economic war" played out behind every battle fought during the second half of the Indochina War, as the Vietnamese Communist Party did everything it could to feed its hungry soldiers. "Soldiers," Truong Chinh added, "are only strong when their bellies are full. That is something that we should never forget." Nor should we. But the problem for Ho Chi Minh, like Lenin during the Russian civil war, was that in order to feed the army, his human logistics teams, and civil service, the Vietnamese president had to take more from the peasantry. He had no choice.

A New Kind of War Comes to Upper Vietnam

The Consolidation of the DRV Sickle

Until October 1950, we know, the Democratic Republic of Vietnam co-existed in a delicate balancing act with the French and their Vietnamese allies in the northern half of the country. After having driven Ho Chi Minh's government out of Hanoi in early 1947, the Expeditionary Corps slowly reestablished colonial rule over the Red River lowlands. Between 1948 and early 1950, the French achieved considerable success in conquering what they called the "useful" part of the delta (*le delta utile*), the rice-rich provinces concentrated around Hanoi and Haiphong. In late

1947, to the north, the French launched Operation Léa to retake the area of Vietnam bordering China and, to the south, to secure coastal towns in central Vietnam like Dong Hoi, Hue, and Da Nang.[2]

Although the French never destroyed Ho's Vietnam, they did break it into pieces. In the north, the Democratic Republic of Vietnam operated in the form of two large islands. One was sandwiched between the French-controlled border with China and the colonial Red River Delta, with Thai Nguyen province serving as its capital. The other was situated south of French Hanoi in Thanh Hoa and Nghe An provinces, the area known as Zone IV. Each side brought in soldiers and administrators to consolidate and run their territories respectively. Where the French established pacification committees in the northern plains between Hanoi and Haiphong, the Vietnamese countered with their resistance committees. Opposed though they were, they formed two sides of the same state-building coin: one colonial, the other national.[3]

The Vietnamese victory at Cao Bang in October 1950 changed the archipelago-like configuration of the DRV in its upper half and gave new, solid territorial form to the single-party state Ho was determined to bring forth. In large part, the Vietnamese could thank their Chinese counterparts for this. Without modern weapons and help in creating the first PAVN divisions, the commander-in-chief, Vo Nguyen Giap, would have never been able to win the battle at Cao Bang and expand the government's territorial hold. Of course, the Vietnamese could congratulate themselves for being able to turn this external aid into usable military force in record time, but the communists also had the French to thank. Giap's opposite, General Marcel Carpentier, lost his nerve, and rather than counterattacking to hold the borderlands, he withdrew most of his troops to the delta for fear of being ambushed again. He also worried that the Chinese might send their own army into northern Indochina as they were doing in Korea at that very moment. In any case, by the end of the year, the French had effectively ceded the strategically important provinces of Lao Cai (to the west of Cao Bang) and Lang Son (to its east) to the Vietnamese as well as pieces of artillery and huge stocks of ammunition which had been left behind in a chaotic withdrawal. The French did manage to maintain a base in Lai Chau province on the far northwestern side of Vietnam. It was capable of harassing PAVN units moving through the area, but not much more. Its main goal was to keep as much of the Tai federation under colonial rule as possible. On the far eastern side, the navy patrolled the Gulf of Tonkin from Haiphong harbor, determined not to let the Chinese move weapons and supplies down the coast or to central Vietnam via Hainan Island.

Fearful of a Chinese invasion, the French had effectively provided their Vietnamese adversaries with the chance they needed to build a new type of army and a state to run it. Ho and his Chinese advisers seized the moment. The Vietnamese might have failed to open a maritime supply route across the Gulf of Tonkin to Hainan in 1950, but they could not believe their luck on land. Thanks to a collection of roads, rivers, and the French-built railway running from Kunming to Lao Cai since the early 1900s, Ho's Vietnam now enjoyed direct transport links to the southern Chinese provinces of Yunnan and Guangxi. For the first time since the nineteenth century, Vietnamese soldiers, administrators, and customs officials interacted with their Chinese counterparts, free of the colonizers. Perched on the end of a Eurasian communist corridor, Chinese communist aid began to pour into the DRV through its northern border. As a result, Vietnamese soldiers and administrators consolidated the DRV's hold over a large swath of territory dropping south from the Chinese border to the foothills melding into the Red River lowlands. Carpentier helped the enemy once again when he evacuated the hills on the southwestern side of the delta in Hoa Binh province. The Vietnamese immediately moved their people in as resistance committees started popping up one after another.

The form of Ho's Vietnam in its upper half changed rapidly as a result. Command of the area west of Hanoi, for example, allowed the president to connect this growing northern territory, the Viet Bac, with upper central Vietnam's Zone IV in the shape of the head of a sickle. The upper Democratic Republic of Vietnam now arced around the delta from Lang Son in the east through the capital of Thai Nguyen before running southwards through Hoa Binh to reach Zone IV south of colonial Hanoi. Rivers, forest trails, roads, and canals allowed for the circulation of weapons, troops, administrators, and food from one end to the other.

And as this expansion occurred, the fragmented configuration of this DRV crescent wrapped around the northern delta began to disappear. The French army started closing remote forts and towers (some possibly dating from the nineteenth century) they had long used for pacification in these areas, knowing Ho's regular army could now overrun them. The question now was whether the PAVN would descend from the highlands to take the Red River lowlands by a conventional attack or expand into them by other means.[4] (See Map 10.)

The French Hold on the Red River Delta

The French government realized when Cao Bang fell in October 1950 that it had to be ready to defend the northern plains around Hanoi. (The only other options were to withdraw to the south or start negotiating some form of decolonization as the Dutch were doing in Indonesia.) French intelligence services had been carefully monitoring Chinese military assistance going across the border into Ho Chi Minh's Vietnam. By late 1950, the French knew that the Vietnamese had embraced Mao Zedong's General Counter-offensive model and that they were already on their way to building a regular army to make it happen. The entry of Chinese communist troops into northern Korea at the same time as French and Vietnamese troops clashed at Cao Bang held out the real possibility that something similar could still happen in Tonkin. The Americans fully agreed. Although they were focused on fighting the communists in Korea, they counted on the French to help them hold the line in Indochina and accelerated their assistance to that end. The two fronts were connected. Committed to the Atlantic alliance, the French joined the Americans to contain the communist bloc in Asia. In so doing, they also saw the chance to keep Indochina in their empire. To make sure the French could do so in Indochina, the government in Paris hustled a new general to Vietnam and made him high commissioner there at the same time. His name was Jean de Lattre de Tassigny.

There was no questioning this Frenchman's mettle. De Lattre had seen combat at Verdun during the First World War, run counterinsurgency operations in North Africa during the interwar period, and, in 1944, led Free French troops during the liberation of southern France as the Second World War ended in Europe. He knew how to command and reveled in it. The Americans knew him from both world wars and respected him. Having served as the general inspector for the French army in the late 1940s, de Lattre was also fully aware of the army's problems in Indochina. Within weeks of his arrival in Hanoi in mid-December 1950, he had visited troops in the field, organized parades in the capital, and given speeches to reverse declining morale. He got rid of defeatist-minded officers in his ranks and recruited a team of officers who shared his ideas. He made Raoul Salan, an officer who knew northern Indochina like the back of his hand, his second-in-command, and together they went to work. Time was of the essence. (See plates 16 and 17.)

De Lattre agreed to take over in Indochina on the understanding that there would be no more debacles, no more withdrawals, and no more humiliations. He immediately swatted away suggestions that the army should withdraw from the north, "Tonkin," in order to hold onto the southern pearl of the Indochinese empire, "Cochinchina." To withdraw from the Red River basin was defeatist, he said. It would send the wrong message to the Americans fighting in Korea and jeopardize the military assistance Washington had agreed to provide. Moreover, de Lattre insisted, if Ho were to gain full control of the northern plains, he would have the food, manpower, resources, and territorial traction to turn the PAVN into a formidable fighting machine. The Tonkin delta had to remain in French hands. Finally, abandoning the north would alienate the Vietnamese who had joined the French in support of the Associated State of Vietnam created in 1949. This was unthinkable. De Lattre counted on using his dual authority as commander-in-chief of the armed forces and Indochinese high commissioner to enroll the Vietnamese on the French side of the war in a way which had never been attempted before in the history of French Indochina.

Backed by his government, de Lattre lost no time reinforcing his hold over the plains concentrated between Hanoi and Haiphong. He presided over the creation of a new string of concrete fortifications to protect the capital against attack. He reinforced existing bunkers and watchtowers to protect these rice-rich provinces against enemy infiltration. He transferred regular troops to the area from other parts of Indochina (regardless of any grumbling it caused). He stepped up the naval surveillance of the Gulf of Tonkin and Vietnam's long coastline. De Lattre improved existing airbases, built new ones, and extended runways to receive American fighter-bombers like the Hellcats, Bearcats, and especially state-of-the-art B-26s. Barbed wire sprouted up across the northern lowlands. From September 1950 onwards, de Lattre welcomed the large amounts of assistance the Americans had begun to provide him via the MAAG. Exploiting his contacts from the Second World War, he actively solicited American military aid and traveled to the United States to secure it. Since late 1950, Washington had begun supplying the Expeditionary Corps with large quantities of artillery, shells, napalm, bombers, tanks, trucks, fuel, amphibious landing crafts, and radios. The Americans also helped de Lattre finance and equip a partnering Vietnamese army. Without American aid, de Lattre and his successors in Indochina would have never been able to fight the war in the way they did.[5]

The same was true of France's enemies. Emboldened by their victory at Cao Bang and flush with Chinese military assistance and advice, the Vietnamese communists set their sights on the Red River Delta. The French had been right. De Lattre's opposite, General Vo Nguyen Giap, was convinced that he could take the Tonkin lowlands by force and lost no time in making his move. In early January 1951, he ordered regiments of the PAVN's 308th and 312th divisions to attack the delta. Leading the 308th was none other than Vuong Thua Vu, the man who had fought the Japanese in East Asia in the 1930s and commanded the Battle of Hanoi six years earlier. His units and others attacked first at Vinh Yen, an area located about 100 kilometers northwest of Hanoi, where the chalk-lined foothills meet the undulating paddy fields of the northern plains. De Lattre welcomed his adversary's willingness to come into the open. With American military aid starting to arrive, the French general was convinced he had the firepower to stop his enemy.

And he did. When PAVN troops charged enemy positions in mid-January 1951, de Lattre lit up the sky with artillery blasts and balls of fire in the form of napalm explosions. Vietnamese troops fought ferociously to take enemy positions, but a hail of machine-gun fire met each wave of young men. Giap had few, if any, anti-aircraft guns at this time, not enough to stop enemy bombers from wreaking mayhem on his troops. And while the human wave tactics he used on the battlefield in 1951 might have been new in the history of twentieth-century wars of decolonization, they did not intimidate de Lattre. He had seen them up close as a young infantryman at Verdun. De Lattre and his men held their ground, relying heavily on artillery and American napalm to back them up.[6] (See Plate 18.)

Vinh Yen was the baptism of fire for the People's Army of Vietnam. Attacks on their entrenched positions left thousands of regulars killed and wounded, hit by the very things the guerrilla soldier had always avoided—artillery shells, direct machine-gun fire, and aerial strafing. As many as 6,000 soldiers may have perished in a matter of days during the Battle of Vinh Yen before Giap called it off.[7] (If true, that approaches the number of those killed in action during the Battle of Dien Bien Phu.) Ngo Van Chieu, whom we first met as a new recruit in 1945 and then as a valiant battalion commander at Cao Bang five years later, provides us with a gripping account of what napalm looked like as it fell from the sky on him and his brothers-in-arms in early 1951:

> Be careful of the planes. They are going to drop bombs and open fire—hit the ground, hide under the bamboo. The planes dived and all hell broke loose before my eyes. Hell came in the form of a big unwieldy egg falling from the first plane . . . then a second one dropped on my right near the road where there were two machine-gunners. An enormous flame expanding over hundreds of meters, it seemed, spread terror throughout the ranks of the soldiers. Napalm: fire that falls from the sky. Another plane advanced to spray more of this fire. The bomb dropped behind us and I felt a burning wind hit my entire body. My men ran; I couldn't stop them. There was no way you could remain under this storm of fire that burned

everything in its path. Everywhere the flames were leaping. Then they [the French] let loose their artillery, mortars, and machine guns, creating a tomb of fire from what had been a small forest only ten minutes earlier.[8]

"What was that," a stunned Vietnamese soldier asked his commanding officer, "the atom bomb?" "No," Chieu told him, "Napalm."

The Americans had supplied this incendiary bomb packed with jellied petrol to the French through the port of Haiphong only weeks before the PAVN attack started in. Any reservations de Lattre or others might have had about deploying it suddenly dissipated when Giap's troops threatened to overrun colonial troops holding Vinh Yen. The French war correspondent, Lucien Bodard, was there to cover the fighting. He had moved within de Lattre's camp, knew the general, and accompanied his troops and pilots on combat missions. Anything but a fellow-traveler, he described the French use of napalm as he had witnessed it from a nearby watchtower:

And then, just below a strangely geometric ridge, a huge ball of fire the color of an orange sun rose up. It was as if it had emerged from the earth itself, though it tumbled towards the ground before unfolding like a tablecloth over one side [of the ridge]. In a matter of seconds, licked by this tongue of flames, everything was on fire, and then nothing was left except for enormous trails of oily and black smoke. It only took a minute for the "thing" to burn the entire hill and for me to understand what it was: napalm. I had just witnessed its first use in Indochina, the first harvest for this incandescent liquid. De Lattre had done it. It was the secret weapon which he had mentioned to me, which he now counted on and which he had finally dared to use. Only a few weeks earlier, the French spoke with horror of this product capable of creating the infernal flames of Gehenna, promising never to use it in Asia. They swore it on their honor. But de Lattre had no shame. On the contrary, he even instructed the censors not to cut any account of it from journalists' copy, but instead to encourage them to make the case for widespread use of this twentieth-century version of Ancient Greek fire.[9]

Bodard and Chieu provide us with the first accounts of napalm's use in a colonial war, and it was a terrible sight to behold. In another passage, Bodard cites French pilots telling him "that the flames spread faster than the Vietnamese could run, catching up and devouring hundreds of men, perhaps thousands. They saw men trying to get away before [the flames] hit them from behind. They continued to run for a few more meters, looking like human torches, before going out a few seconds later."[10] If we can believe Chieu, the DRV did not know that the Americans had delivered napalm to the French just in time for them to use it (and, if true, this was an intelligence failure with deadly consequences). Chieu's text also suggests that de Lattre had changed his mind about using napalm in early 1951 because he feared losing the delta. If so, then the Americans, and not just de Lattre, saved the French from defeat there. For the Americans, Tonkin was an important part of their greater Indo-Korean war against the Chinese.[11]

The level of violence that spread through the Red River plains and the rest of upper Vietnam from January in 1951 until the guns finally went silent in mid-1954 had no equivalent in the history of twentieth-century wars of decolonization. De Lattre's willingness to discharge large amounts of napalm to hold the line against the Vietnamese, knowing his enemy could not fight back in the same way, turned the war into a savage affair. This fire that fell from the sky was, Bodard later opined, an extension of the brutal methods that had reigned during the Second World War: "All of this to bludgeon Red Vietnam as if it were Nazi Germany—and that meant bringing down the sky on the heads of this godless Viet Minh regime like a steamroller." The only other place where this occurred after 1945 was in Korea, where the Americans also bombed on a huge scale and dropped napalm.[12]

None of this stopped the communists in their bid to drive the colonialists out. It was the price they had accepted to pay. Within weeks, Ho, Giap, and their Chinese advisers sent thousands of Vietnamese boys back into this Franco-American inferno. When PAVN troops went into battle on the night of 23–4 March 1951 in areas near Haiphong, French artillery, American-supplied B-26 aircrafts loaded with napalm, and two battleships on the coast opened up their fire.[13] Giap used his artillery as best he could, but he was badly outgunned. Without an air force and an effective anti-air defense system, his army remained woefully vulnerable to superior enemy firepower. Artillery and bombers pounded the Vietnamese general's men as they assailed fortified French positions in pitched battle. Vietnamese heroism certainly impressed their adversaries. Indeed, some in the French ranks began to speak in awe of the PAVN grunts: "We now have the proof that the Vietnamese are not just a bunch of rebels or guerrillas: they have a real army, like ours."[14] True though that was, the battlefield remained, nevertheless, asymmetrical. A Vietnamese "tiger" caught in the open like this could still be ripped apart. In mid-1951, Giap would attempt to seize a piece of the southern delta in the rice-rich provinces of Ninh Binh and Nam Dinh, but to no avail: French firepower stopped him once again. In June 1951, the communists abandoned their plans to seize the delta in set-piece battle. If Giap continued like this, he would run his army into the ground, just as his counterpart, Nguyen Binh, had done a year earlier in the Mekong Delta as part of the General Counter-offensive in the south.[15]

Giap's Second Assault on the Delta: PAVN-charged Pacification

The fact that the Democratic Republic of Vietnam failed to drive the French out of the northern delta in one massive counter-offensive during 1951 did not mean that Vietnamese strategists turned their attention away from the delta in favor of the highlands. They did not. Although Giap and his Chinese advisers did redirect the regulars of the PAVN that way later on, everyone remained equally focused on the northern delta until the end of the conflict for several reasons. Firstly, clandestine trade with the Indochinese federation (and the Associated State of Vietnam tucked inside it) allowed the Vietnamese communists to continue importing essential products they could not get from communist China in sufficient quantities (pharmaceuticals, paper, chemical products, and machine parts). Secondly, the north's lowland paddy fields produced much of the rice they needed to feed everyone who circulated throughout this upland corridor. By 1952, the PAVN consisted of seven divisions—around 150,000 men in all. The government also employed an estimated 100,000 civil servants in its rapidly expanding bureaucracy. That made for a quarter of a million people who had to be fed in order to keep the state and army operational. And that does not include the tens of thousands of porters who had to eat to work.[16] Thirdly, Giap needed people from the heavily populated delta to replenish his badly mauled regiments and to serve in his human transport service and work teams. He looked to the plains to recruit 20,000 soldiers before the end of 1951 alone. True, areas in Zone IV could help in giving him recruits and rice, but it was never enough. This DRV crescent needed continued access to the surrounding lowlands—now more than ever.[17]

What changed was the *how*. Unable to seize the northern delta in one general offensive, the Vietnamese communists changed their tactics. They decided to move in slowly, bit by bit, day by day, village by village. Methodically, they expanded government control into the lowlands by dispatching administrators, security and intelligence officials, and well-armed guerrillas, carefully targeting areas where the enemy's control was weak. They would operate by night if they could not do so during the day. This was, however, more than a simple reversion to guerrilla tactics. By ceding almost all of the borderlands with China to the DRV in late 1950, the French allowed the Vietnamese to control this highland strip hugging the delta. The Vietnamese could circulate troops, supplies, and weapons coming from China through this jungle-protected ridge largely free of sustained enemy harassment (Salan would take Hoa Binh in late 1951, only to have to give it back some two months later). This was DRV country. As a result, the Vietnamese could focus their attention on finding ways to move into the delta from a variety of perimeter points, sending out feelers and testing the enemy's ground control in order to infiltrate people into the right places at the right times. All the French could do was hope that their impressive intelligence services were keeping tabs on what was going on so that they could push back by rushing in their newly minted "mobile groups" (smaller, heavily armed task forces which could carry out specific combat operations requiring a high degree of maneuverability and mobility).

This second, indirect offensive against the delta was to work for another reason. No sooner had Giap called off his divisional attack on the delta than he began to peel off smaller, more mobile battalions in order to conduct guerrilla operations in the colonial Red River basin. He would recombine them into their original divisions for the purpose of conventional warfare when needed. Although these smaller People's Army detachments tended to avoid frontal clashes with the Expeditionary Corps' better-armed mobile groups, when they received orders to stand their ground they did so with a ferocity unknown elsewhere during the first half of the Indochina War. They could do so because they were well trained and equipped with modern arms. Moreover, they could vanish into the jungle with ease when ordered to do so, but they could also get into trouble if the French caught them in the open.[18]

In any case, from mid-1951 onwards, these PAVN combat teams operated in guerrilla formation to lead a second, sustained assault on the delta. They expanded the Democratic Republic of Vietnam's territorial hold village by village, collected rice wherever they could, and inducted young men into the army and both sexes into the government's human-powered transport and work teams. These combat teams played an important role in slowly but surely retaking villages south of colonial Hanoi. At least half-a-dozen PAVN mobile battalions operated clandestinely in the delta at that time, meaning that approximately 4,000 well-armed and trained troops were there.

Myth and Reality: De Lattre and the Colonial Levée en masse

Generals de Lattre and Salan understood what was going on as they huddled with their colonels to do what so many others had done before them: craft yet another round of colonial pacification. This time, though, they added something new. They decided it was finally time to create a Vietnamese partner army to help them in this endeavor. "Native" soldiers knew the language and would be in a better position to help colonial officials secure villages via collaboration with local leaders. Vietnamese participation in pacification would also free up the Expeditionary

Corps to go after the PAVN in the highlands. The mobilization of this second Vietnamese army deserves a detour here, for its emergence had a direct impact on the nature of the Indochina War and on the evolution of Ho Chi Minh's Vietnam. Like the American and Chinese entry into the Indochina War in 1950, the mobilization of a new Vietnamese army opened a fresh chapter in the history of the conflict and its intensification.

The reader might, understandably, ask at this point: but why did the French take so long to create a Vietnamese army to help them fight Ho's? More than anything else, colonial fear is the answer. Distrustful of Vietnamese nationalist intentions since their violent conquest of Vietnam in the nineteenth century, the French had always balked at creating an Indochinese army similar to the Indian one the British created in 1895 or the one the Americans had established for their Filipino colonial subjects in 1935. Decades earlier, some in the French army had pushed for the creation of a Vietnamese army and officer class, especially as Europe slid towards the First World War, but the political confidence was never there and settler opposition to the prospect was always ferocious. Communist or not, the Vietnamese could not be trusted to run an army of their own on the French watch. The colonial authorities had always contented themselves with operating "native units" (*tirailleurs*) under their own command and running a formidable security service as well. Even after the Second World War, resistance (within the metropolis, the colonial administration, and the settler community in particular) to creating a "native army" remained impressive. The French authorities were initially confident that the Expeditionary Corps would speedily take care of the Vietnamese "rebels" and their so-called "army." Even when it became clear that things would not be so simple, decision-makers preferred to bring in imperial troops from elsewhere in the empire, from French West and North Africa mainly, to do the fighting rather than lean on a Vietnamese army to do the job. This is why although the Associated State of Vietnam might have come to life in 1949, its national army remained colonially emasculated.[19]

For de Lattre, this would no longer do. Five years had been wasted, in his view, while, upon his arrival, the nature of the conflict had just changed dramatically. At six months in, he had already faced three powerful thrusts into the delta by a Vietnamese army whose men and officers knew how to fight and promised to continue doing so. And now Giap was sending combat teams back in to pacify villages. In order to break the PAVN's back before it was too late (because that was what the French general wanted to do before cancer would claim his life), he needed more troops—and fast. The Americans were unwilling to get involved directly. In any case, their troops were already fighting the Chinese in Korea, and the French did not want them on the ground in Tonkin. De Lattre knew from his work as inspector-general of the French army during the late 1940s that his government would be reluctant to send many soldiers directly from France: it needed them to serve in the North Atlantic Treaty Organization (NATO) and even, possibly, in a future European army (a subject under serious discussion after the start of the Korean War). The commanding general also knew that Paris did not have the political will to expand the existing military service law to force many French boys to fight in and for Indochina. This left him with only one option: to conscript the Associated State of Vietnam's population into the Indochina War.[20]

Momentum had already been building in this direction since the Cao Bang debacle, when officials in France had agreed to expand the Vietnamese army to help them hold the line against a possible communist attack. Upon his arrival in December 1950, de Lattre began transferring Vietnamese soldiers active in the Expeditionary Corps and national guard units into the Associated State's fledgling army. As high commissioner and commander-in-chief of the armed forces in Indochina, he swatted away any resistance to "arming the natives" in his ranks. Of course, the French were in charge of this new Vietnamese army (as well as its Cambodian and Laotian counterparts). They commanded this novel army through a joint General Staff and a core group of trusted Vietnamese officers. French instructors trained its soldiers and officer class in hastily built academies.

Meanwhile, like the Chinese helping Ho to assemble the PAVN in 1950, the Americans agreed to outfit the Associated State of Vietnam's troops with uniforms, guns, ammunition, artillery, and shells via the

French. They agreed that this was the best way to keep the additional troops they needed supplied. In late 1950, the Americans signed off on the creation of four divisions for the Associated State of Vietnam. This was how Washington fought on two fronts in the Asian theater of the Cold War, directly in Korea and mainly with their own troops, and indirectly in Indochina via the French Expeditionary Corps and its partner Vietnamese army. Again, for the Americans, there were not two wars, not a separate "Korean" and "Indochinese" one. There was only one, an Indo-Korean conflict.[21]

Things were more complicated on the Vietnamese side. Bao Dai, the head of state of this second Vietnam, and others in his government were favorable to creating a national army, but not necessarily within the colonial straight-jacket de Lattre proposed. The former emperor was initially reluctant to let de Lattre draft Vietnamese boys to fight what everyone knew to be a colonial war as much as an anticommunist one. De Lattre could spin his mobilization of the Vietnamese population as a nationalist crusade against communism, but Bao Dai had seen this picture before. He knew from his colonial upbringing that the new high commissioner, like so many governor-generals before him, needed him, the "native" head of state, the "monarch," "the son of heaven," to publicly rally the Vietnamese to the war cause and the general mobilization law de Lattre was quietly preparing in the wings. Indeed, Bao Dai knew that de Lattre wanted more than an army: he wanted all of the "Associated" Vietnamese involved in the war too. It took all of the general's impressive personal skills, plus General Vo Nguyen Giap's spectacular assaults on the delta during the first half of 1951, to convince Bao Dai finally that he had to choose, something he always hated to do. Unwilling to break with his colonial masters as Sultan Mohammed V was doing in Morocco and keen to keep his country out of communist hands, in a fateful decision, Vietnam's last emperor bowed to de Lattre's requests to bring his people and the Associated State into the Indochina War.[22]

This occurred for all to see on 14 July 1951 in Hanoi, the French republic's National Day. Walking side by side in downtown Hanoi, de Lattre and Bao Dai reviewed the French and Vietnamese troops as they marched through the capital with carefully orchestrated fanfare. The next day, to de Lattre's immense satisfaction, Bao Dai signed the order authorizing the general mobilization of the Associated State, its material and human resources. By the end of the month, Bao Dai's government had signed a series of decrees to this effect into law. They included, among other things, the introduction of obligatory military service for all men aged between eighteen and sixty. Vietnamese doctors, dentists, and pharmacists were called up too. The general mobilization law also allowed the French to conscript an unprecedented number of Vietnamese civilians to work in their human transport and work teams. Like the porters serving in the PAVN, tens of thousands of Vietnamese, men and women, could now be conscripted into supply teams to carry food, medicines, and ammunition for French Union troops. Others performed tasks such as digging trenches, clearing forests, and building and repairing roads. The need for labor was such that the French put thousands of their prisoners of war to work undertaking logistical tasks for the military.[23] (See Plate 19.)

This colonial mass mobilization law came a year after the national one Ho had decreed. In so doing, de Lattre expanded the impact of the war on Vietnamese society as never before, and Bao Dai let him do it. Working through their associated state, in late 1951 and early 1952 the French called up 60,000 recruits for training. Initially, the duration of this intensive training was short: two months. In June 1953, however, as the fighting entered its fiercest phase, another law established a military service of two years. By August 1953, the Associated State's regular army counted between 100,000 and 125,000 men. Half were regular soldiers organized in battalions; the other half consisted of auxiliary troops (*supplétifs*).[24]

De Lattre mobilized the Vietnamese to help him hold France's empire against those who would undo it. As the commander-in-chief confided to the officer whom he had put in charge of creating his Vietnamese army, they had to hold the imperial line: "It's in Tonkin that we are defending our positions in Africa. Everything must be subordinated to this imperative."[25] Everything, that was, short of conscripting French men from the metropolis or from among the settler populations in Algiers or Saigon to fight there. Later on, during the Vietnam War, the

American policy of "Vietnamization" constituted a phased withdrawal of American ground troops in order to bring home those "American boys" who had been conscripted to fight in Vietnam. De Lattre's fielding of a Vietnamese army, what many called the "*jaunissement*," reflected his government's *refusal* to draft "French boys" to fight there in the first place. The French preferred to use imperial troops, including those of the Associated State of Vietnam, to do the fighting.[26]

This then is why only the naive or those who admired him would have believed de Lattre when, in July 1951, he famously exhorted Vietnamese students in Saigon to be brave and to join up to fight the "Viet Minh," the DRV: "Be men! If you are communist, then join the Viet Minh. There are a lot of people on their side who fight well for a bad cause. But if you are patriots, then fight for your country because it's yours."[27] De Lattre knew this was not true—not in 1951, not even in 1954, when an armistice signed in Geneva ended the hostilities. The State of Vietnam as well as the Cambodian and Laotian ones remained part of a de facto Indochinese colonial federation. The Vietnamese lined up behind Bao Dai might have styled their army at the time as a national one. It was not. The French commanded the Vietnamese, the Laotians, and the Cambodians, just as they did the Senegalese, Algerian, or Moroccon units fighting the PAVN.[28]

More than anything else, de Lattre needed Vietnamese boots on the ground to help him with pacification in the northern delta. To this end, his team built up battalion-sized units of Vietnamese soldiers and deployed them to protect villages and their surrounding rice fields stretching from Hanoi to Haiphong. The most effective units were the Battalions du Vietnam and the battalion groups without artillery known by their Vietnamese name, the Tieu Doan Khinh Quan. General Raoul Salan continued to use these units for pacification purposes when he took command of the armed forces in early 1952 following de Lattre's death. And after him, so did Henri Navarre.

These Vietnamese units became an essential part of a new program known as the Mobile Administrative Operational Group (Groupement administratif mobile opérationnel, or GAMO). The main idea in this

latest round of pacification was much the same as it had been since Galliéni's time: once the regular forces led by the French had cleared an area
of "rebel" forces, Vietnamese administrators and troops moved in with
the colonizers to run the local administration and protect it. Mirroring
their battalion-powered PAVN adversaries, GAMO units consisted of
Vietnamese officials who specialized in health care, education, finance,
security, and, of course, administrative matters. They identified people
they could trust and sidelined those they could not. These nomadic
units operated on the administrative front lines at the village level in this
endless war of competing statecraft. But where Ho's pacification teams
sought to expand national control with communist characteristics, the
French used their GAMO units and the newly created Vietnamese
army to maintain their colonial hold under the cover of an anticommunist struggle. There was no disguising the fact that colonial pacification was the raison d'être for the mobilization of Bao Dai's army and
administration.[29]

The Return of "General Rice":
Economic Warfare in Upper Vietnam

The complexity of the Indochina War is admittedly mind-boggling.
From 1951, it was not one conflagration but a collection of several, interconnected ones—a war of colonial (re)conquest, an armed struggle for
national liberation, a civil war among the Vietnamese, a conventional
showdown between professional armies, an often vicious contest for
administrative control of the countryside, the scene of intense urban
violence at the start and unspeakable borderland atrocities throughout,
as well as the site of class warfare of a communist kind. All of this occurred in turn as the Chinese and Americans stepped in to support their
respective partners, the Vietnamese "communists" and the French "colonialists," in what was, along with Korea, the deadliest battlefield of the
Cold War and the single most destructive war of decolonization of the
twentieth century.

The Indochina conflict also became an increasingly "total war" for the Vietnamese. This occurred not only in terms of the increased levels of violence the internationalization of the conflict unleashed, it also manifested itself by the conflict's ever more "totalizing" effects on Vietnamese society. Pacification operations and the *levées en masse* decreed by Ho in 1950 and de Lattre just one year later were two examples of how the conflagration marched into people's lives. All the belligerents now sent their officials into villages to conscript young people to serve in the military, carry supplies, and join work crews. But nowhere were the totalizing effects of war more evident than in the sustained economic offensive the French operated between 1950 and 1954 to stop their adversaries from procuring the food they needed to carry on.

And this brings us back to April 1951. In that month, as we saw in the opening of this chapter, the head of the Communist Party, Truong Chinh, warned his readers that a third general was out there. He had no nationality and needed no army or conscription laws to fight. As Giap and de Lattre faced off in the delta, he walked alone. Truong Chinh called him "General Rice." While no one could actually see him, everyone knew he was out there. And all feared the deadly weapon he carried at his side—hunger. This general had taken the lives of millions across Eurasia during the Second World War. Vietnamese farmers had certainly not forgotten the famine that had killed over a million of their compatriots in 1944–5, most of them located in areas in the northern delta which the French were preparing to blockade.

However, the French saw an ally in this General Rice, one who could help them in their bid to stop the Vietnamese from feeding the standing army (both troops and civil servants) of its expanding war state. French officers referred to this project interchangeably as either the "economic war" (*la guerre économique*), or "the rice war" (*la guerre du riz*), or the "rice battle" (*la bataille du riz*). Starting in early 1951, the French systematized this economic offensive and connected it up to their war in the northern paddy fields. The goal was no longer simply to build up a loyal local administration, but also to prevent rice from getting through to

Ho's Vietnam and its hungry divisions. As one of the architects of the economic offensive put it that year: "Both sides are agreed on one thing. The battle for rice is equal in importance to the one between armies. Victory will go to those who know how to control the delta's rice grana- ries."[30] An already brutal conflagration, the Indochina War was about to get even worse.

The French Economic Offensive

Economics had always been part of the struggle between the French and the Vietnamese, and no one knew it better than Salan. He had person- ally accompanied Ho to France during the summer of 1946 as the Viet- namese president tried desperately to negotiate the prickly questions of trade, finance, and monetary policy. In November 1946, when differ- ences over sovereignty led to the violent clash in Haiphong harbor over who had the right to collect customs duties, the Vietnamese or the French, Salan was there too. And he was still there after the outbreak of full-scale war in Hanoi a month later: in 1947, he presided over Opera- tion Léa, the large-scale offensive designed to destroy Ho's government and sever its commercial ties to China. Both things failed, we know, as the Democratic Republic of Vietnam began operating from rural bases in the north, zones IV and V in central Vietnam, and rice-rich areas in the Ca Mau peninsula in the far south. Lacking the resources and man- power to be everywhere at once, the French focused on holding the Red River and Mekong deltas as each side tried to expand its territorial con- trol wherever it could.

Colonial authorities did not remain inert on the economic front, though. During the first half of the conflagration, they tried to stop their enemies from connecting up their "islands" into a functioning state and trading clandestinely with the colonial-controlled cities of Saigon and Hanoi and nearby Asian commercial hubs in Guangzhou and Bangkok. They attacked the DRV's communications, transport, cottage indus- tries, and natural resources. As we know, the French went to great lengths to block the DRV's trade in medicines, chemicals, and paper.

And they attacked Ho Chi Minh's food supplies, rice and salt in particular. However, success depended on finding officers willing to invest the time and energy into understanding all the moving parts in the enemy's economic activities. Progress also turned on the cooperation of Vietnamese partners with the intimate knowledge of the land, its languages, and local administration. As a result, colonial operations on the economic front tended to be episodic affairs. An important exception to this rule occurred during the late 1940s, when the French army effectively blocked the DRV's ability to move rice from large stockpiles on the western side of the Ca Mau peninsula to troops fighting in eastern areas in the south (as we saw in Chapter 7).

The economic assault on the Democratic Republic of Vietnam was only systematically applied from 1950 onwards, in the wake of Mao's decision to help Ho field a professional army and build a revolutionary state to run it. Inspired by the success of their southern blockade, French military officers, colonial administrators, and their Vietnamese partners began to elaborate an economic program to prevent their adversaries from feeding their soldiers and civil servants. As the communists attacked the Red River delta during the first half of 1951, the need to act increased. The French might have defeated Giap's offensive, but they realized that the Vietnamese general had moved on the delta less in order to capture Hanoi than to seize the rice fields surrounding it to feed the PAVN. The two harvests many delta areas produced annually were too hard to resist. While we do not know whether anyone on the French side had read anything in translation about Truong Chinh's General Rice, we can be sure that officers like Salan would have been familiar with Napoleon's famous warning: "An army marches on its stomach." They were determined *not* to let their adversary do so.

Based on the available documentation, the French "economic war" appears to have evolved in three overlapping phases between 1950 and 1954.[31] The first wave began in early 1950, when military authorities divided the Associated State of Vietnam into three sectors. Zone A referred to spaces where goods and services could circulate freely, located deep within the core territories of French Vietnam. The military placed

moderate restrictions on goods and services moving within an interme-
diate zone, B, located in areas which were less secure. In the borderlands, those areas where the Associated State touched up against the
Democratic Republic of Vietnam, the French created Zone C, where no
products were to circulate. The main idea behind all three categories was
to spin a layered cocoon around colonial Vietnam—a blockade similar
to the one in the Mekong Delta. They did this through the reinforce-
ment and construction of new posts, watchtowers, and blockhouses.
French military officials and their Vietnamese counterparts administered these zones at the provincial and district levels. Colonial authorities approved legislation allowing the army to control the circulation of
foodstuffs (rice, salt, and fish) and industrial inputs which the enemy
used for making weapons and explosives (machine parts, gasoline, and
chemicals). This first phase applied to all of Indochina, including the
apparent renewal of the blockade in the south. To control the country's
two rice harvests, French commanders had to collaborate closely with
their Vietnamese allies in charge of the Associated State of Vietnam at
every level. "When it comes to economic warfare," the French general
in charge of central Vietnam's rice wars wrote to his Vietnamese counterpart in 1952, "it is the perfect combination of administrative action
and military action that leads to success."[32]

As the center of gravity of the fighting moved rapidly northwards
from late 1950, so too did the French economic counter-offensive. And
as it did, a second phase emerged in the French military's desire to deny
the Vietnamese the northern delta rice they so badly needed. Salan understood that Giap's failure to take the Red River plains by force had in
no way stopped the Vietnamese from trying to find ways to get rice out
of the delta. Salan issued orders "to fight a rice war" in the delta against
the enemy using his own methods if necessary. This meant several
things, all of which remained in place until the end of the conflict: i) the
rapid deployment of troops and officials into delta villages during harvest times to protect fields from enemy penetration; ii) assisting villagers to get their paddy out of the fields and into carefully guarded silos
or nearby blockhouses as rapidly as possible; iii) carefully measuring

and inventorying harvest yields for every village to determine how much rice remained for families to meet subsistence needs; iv) guaranteeing that the colonial government would purchase surplus rice at a favorable price in colonial piasters and then store it in safe locations so that none would be left for the enemy; and, in theory, v) care was to be taken to avoid using harsh methods that could drive villagers into enemy hands. Although French troops served in the paddy fields, de Lattre and Salan increasingly relied on their Vietnamese army and local authorities to fight the rice war on the ground. Again, they knew the lay of the land, its languages, and the nitty-gritty details of local governance. Specially minted Vietnamese units known as the Armed Economic Brigades were deployed into villages to guard the rice fields during harvest time, carry paddy to secure silos, and transport any surpluses further down the line.[33] (See plates 20, 21, and 22.)

Village life during the Indochina War had never been easy in the northern delta or central Vietnam. The violence of the conventional battles during the first half of 1951 had spilled over into scores of villages. But it was the outbreak of the rice wars which ensured that the paddy fields would become very dangerous places to be for the hundreds of thousands of poor souls trying to eke out a living as the "colonialists" and the "communists" moved in on them—quite literally. As Lucien Bodard describes it, "And yet no sooner had they finished the harvest than 'the rice war' exploded, with Viet Minh and French troops coming out of nowhere to take it from them."[34] To stop enemy assaults on rice-rich areas surrounding Hanoi and Haiphong, the French unrolled barbed-wire fences and installed bamboo-piked barricades in and around thousands of northern villages. Battles over rice occurred mainly during the two harvest seasons (these usually occurred in April to May, during the fifth lunar month, and in October to November, the tenth). Attacks usually took place at night, when Vietnamese commandos tried to storm barricaded villages and overwhelm the handful of Franco-Vietnamese troops defending them and their stockpiles of food. When the French did not have their people in place, they opened up with artillery fire. Commanders often burned rice rather than leave anything behind for the other side. Watching from the sidelines, peasants wondered where they were going to get their next meal. For them, the war certainly hadn't "shifted" from the delta to the highlands.[35] They were irrevocably caught in the crossfire. How many died or were injured in the rice wars we will never know. As one French intelligence officer recognized, civilians suffered the most, caught "between the hammer and the anvil."[36]

In this second phase, in order to seal off the Red River basin from enemy penetration, colonial strategists went still further. Salan ordered the creation of a "prohibited zone," which nothing of military interest could cross. The army received the legal power it needed to stop the circulation of goods and services, including the authorization "to propose to [the Associated State's] governors any type of legal decrees on products whose transportation would seem unwarranted." Reams of documents in the archives reveal the array of outlawed products: pharmaceuticals, chemicals, paper, batteries, gasoline, and many other things. The colonial army leaned on the judicial branch to mete out harsh sentences to those caught in the act of smuggling. Significantly, the French military classified "rice" as being of "military interest"—and targeted it as such.[37]

From mid-1952, a third and final phase took the economic war to a still higher level as the April–May harvest apparently came in short for the French. Several things distinguish this final phase from its earlier ones, though they all truly combined into a crescendo, rolling through the northern delta and as far as areas around colonial Hue and Da Nang. First, Salan's entourage concluded that the lack of enforcement in the earlier phases had allowed Ho's officials to continue "importing" much of what they needed from the colonial zones, and, above all, rice. This, in turn, had allowed the Vietnamese to feed their PAVN divisions despite the fact that the Chinese communists were not providing any food aid. This was unacceptable. Next, to remedy this problem, Salan's team concluded that they had to do everything in their power to "systematize"—the new buzzword—the organization, administration, and enforcement of the economic blockade throughout "all of Indochina." The air force, navy, and special forces would help the army do this. Then, having failed to hold Hoa Binh in early 1952, Salan pushed hard to drive a wedge between the rice-rich delta and the enemy corridor hugging its perimeter, through which entire divisions were now moving into areas south of Hanoi and further still. Finally, Salan obtained the authorization to attack the DRV's own economic infrastructure in a stepped-up attempt to bring the enemy to his knees. In June 1952, he declared a "systematic economic war" (*une guerre économique systématique*) upon the Vietnamese.[38] "I think it would be easy to hurt the enemy economically by attacking their currency trading and internal exchanges," General Salan wrote. What was new in this third phase of the economic offensive was the mobilization of the navy and especially the air force. Salan and his economic team requested authorization "to bomb" the DRV's agricultural infrastructure "systematically with napalm." This is how the French in Indochina, like the Americans in Korea, reintroduced heavy bombing to East Asia only a few years after World War II had ended there.[39]

Reworking the blockade to make it airtight was the first step in this direction. Starting in June 1952, the French army began reinforcing their protective wrapping around the core of the Red River Delta. The commanding general sealed it off with soldiers and administrators, backed up by the navy and air force. In Salan's hands, this zone effectively became a separate military territory, as he described it himself: "This absolute no man's land, created in the non-controlled territory extending out from our forward posts, depends uniquely on the military authority and is not subject to the legislation of the civil authority." This buffer zone fanned out 10 kilometers or so from the Franco-Vietnamese border before meeting the edge of the Democratic Republic of Vietnam's territory. For Salan, "nothing" also meant there should be no human beings living in this strip of land. To this end, the commander-in-chief forcibly evacuated tens of thousands of people from their homes. In all, colonial authorities removed 20,000 Vietnamese from the northern and northwestern sides of the perimeter and 80,000 souls from the southwestern side. Apparently, 100,000 people lost their homes and rice fields for an indeterminate period of time.[40]

So it was that the "Salan Line" took form. The French army reserved the right to fire on any person caught in this no-man's-land. Those arrested would be treated as "prisoners of war" and anything they were transporting seized as the "spoils of war." Writing in late 1952, Salan did not mince his words: "The blockade of the delta begun in June of this year has delivered a real blow to the Viet Minh war economy. It has turned out to be an effective weapon in drying up large amounts of food supplies in the form of paddy. Therefore, it is necessary to continue with this offensive and to make it even more successful by fixing any minor problems which have been detected."[41] In September 1952, the French approved the creation of a similar "prohibited zone" between colonial and enemy rice-growing territories in the Mekong Delta. Anyone caught in it could be killed.[42] The Vietnamese communists followed what their adversaries were doing closely, translating "no-man's-land" into Vietnamese as "zone of nothing" (*khu vuc trang*)."[43] In many ways, Salan's "zone of nothing" was the precursor to the famous Morice and Challe "lines" the French army used during the Algerian War to isolate their nationalist foes.

Meanwhile, military intelligence officers went to work. They produced lists with the names of shady characters to track down—mainly merchants, transporters, and smugglers. They called on their subordinates to think outside the box. On the economic front, updating a battle order by using intelligence gathered by radio intercepts—the famous *fiches jaunes*—was not enough. To set targets effectively, intelligence officers needed information on the industries, natural resources, mines, dikes, and irrigation systems of the "Viet Minh country" in full detail. Once the maps had been prepared, the coordinates fixed, and weather permitting, pilots could then attack Ho's economic infrastructure from the air while the navy and special forces moved up rivers and canals to attack on the ground. Meanwhile, they worked with local Vietnamese governors and district chiefs to stockpile rice and protect it against enemy sabotage or exfiltration. French commanders in the fields even worked with private buyers and their transporters to get rice out of the villages as rapidly as possible. Other compromises were made as well: in 1953, colonial commanders allowed Buddhist monks living and preaching in areas around Hue to stock their own rice for consumption and use in religious ceremonies.[44]

The French intelligence services, relying on the colonial archives and scholarly studies, targeted three main rice-producing areas in this Viet Minh country for attack—Zone IV's Thanh Hoa province; Bac Giang province, located southeast of the Thai Nguyen resistance capital; and a wide strip of rice fields running from Phu Tho to Viet Tri west of there. From his time spent in Indochina between the wars, Salan must have known that the French had built hydraulic complexes in these areas to help feed the growing northern population through a double-cropping system. These networks consisted of various combinations of dikes, dams, canals, reservoirs, sluices, and silos. Starting in June 1952, the French air force began systematically bombing these irrigation systems. Salan's intelligence services tallied the attacks closely and assessed their effect on food production. On the eve of the Second World War, their reports tell us, Thanh Hoa had an estimated population of 800,000 people and produced 275,000 tons of paddy annually. Fifty-thousand hectares of rice fields in this province depended on the Bai Thuong hydraulic system to produce its two annual harvests. In July 1952, French bombers attacked it. As a result, the French reported, annual rice production for Thanh Hoa plunged to 77,000 tons, a third of what it had been before. In the Bac Giang area of the DRV, annual rice production before 1940 had peaked at about 220,000 tons, thanks to a canal system irrigating 28,000 hectares of land there. After colonial air strikes there, production fell to a third of the earlier level. Encouraged by these results, the French continued to bomb canals, dikes, and granaries elsewhere in central and northern Vietnam. As one internal memo said, the goal of destroying the enemy's irrigation system was "to destroy any hope of obtaining a harvest in rebel zones."[45]

The list of targets in this economic war was longer than we might imagine. In 1952, the French air force received authorization to "widely" and "systematically" attack and kill as much of the water buffalo and cattle population as possible (these orders are accompanied by detailed maps which show the French assault on the buffalo population, privately called Opération buffle). The goal was to deprive the enemy of a source of food and deny its farmers an important means of production for tilling their fields.[46] The air force struck deeper into people's lives by aggressively bombing the Democratic Republic of Vietnam's outdoor markets, transport system (roads, bridges, ports, and a tattered railway), natural resources (mines and salt fields), industrial capacity (weapons workshops, paper mills, and textile factories), and any remaining dams, dikes, and canals not previously destroyed or rebuilt thereafter. Sluices controlling the flow of water into agricultural fields regularly came under attack. People could taste war in their mouths when they consumed salt, which was never properly cleaned of the petrol colonial planes had dropped on it as it dried in the sun. French soldiers returning from captivity after the war confirmed that they had eaten rice tasting of oil. In fact, on taking Cao Bang in late 1950, the Vietnamese recovered rice stocks onto which departing French Union soldiers had poured diesel and stuffed with live grenades. A few weeks later Ho's troops fed this rice to prisoners of war they had taken during the same battle.[47]

Detailed histories of the DRV's war economy during the Indochina War corroborate that the French adopted a "large-scale" economic offensive from mid-1952. It turned on their colonial creation of this no-man's-land erected around the delta and a sustained air and amphibious assault on the DRV's infrastructure, most notably its rice production. According to one Vietnamese study, the enemy air force bombed twelve large-scale hydraulic systems (dams, dikes, and canals) between June and August in 1952. French planes burst the dams of water reservoirs in Zone IV—possibly the same ones the American Air force would bomb later on during their bombing campaign known as Operation Rolling Thunder in the mid-1960s.[48] Between 1952 and 1954, according to official Vietnamese studies, the colonial air force massacred "tens of thousands" of beasts of burden: in the run-up to the battle of Dien Bien Phu alone, this included the killing of 3,594 water buffalo. A French postaction report confirms that, in a single attack on 15 September 1953, bombers dropped four napalm bombs, killing 152 buffaloes.[49] The communists also allege that the colonialists used insecticides and poison against them. While the French military archives do confirm that such plans were prepared, I have found no evidence showing they implemented them. The French did, however, employ napalm in their economic assault.

What is equally important is that by April 1953 they had expanded their economic offensive southwards into Zone V, especially into rice-rich colonial areas around Hue and Da Nang which had fed the DRV's troops there for years.[50]

The consequences of this for the Vietnamese were profound. The French destruction of DRV infrastructure forced Ho to further mobilize his population to repair dikes, dams, terraces, and canals; fix roads and bridges; and clean rice and salt which the French air force had contaminated. Between 1950 and 1954, Vietnamese laborers repaired 3,670 km of road and 22,000 meters of bridges, with little or no mechanical help. To avoid colonial detection (and bombers), villagers tended to their fields at night. During the day, they turned hiding animals, gardens, and granaries into an art form. War worked women as hard as it did men. They took over in the fields when their husbands and fathers left to fight. Women would serve as human porters, road workers, and nurses between 1950 and 1954. Of the estimated 1.7 million people serving as porters during that period, half were women. Children toiled in the fields like never before in their short lives. This increased level of physical activity across all of upper Vietnam meant the burning of unprecedented amounts of calories. Fatigue spread throughout the countryside as undernourished bodies became increasingly susceptible to disease.[51]

The use of food as a weapon is by no means new. Imperial armies had practiced this form of warfare since antiquity. Blockades were common during the First World War, while the Germans and Japanese waged economic warfare during the Second to devastating effect. Chiang Kai-shek imposed blockades on his communist adversaries during China's long civil war.[52] But the French were unique in that they carried the assault into the twentieth century's wars of decolonization—with terrible consequences for the Vietnamese. By blockading the enemy's economy and trade, by bombing Ho's agricultural infrastructure, and targeting animals, the French expanded the war deeper into Vietnamese society, sending pangs of hunger into the bellies of hundreds of thousands of people. In doing so in upper Vietnam, the French collapsed the dividing line between combatants and civilians and between the home front and the battle front—the two core definitions of "total war."[53] Unsurprisingly, colonial officers involved in this economic assault were using this term by the end of the Indochina War. In 1956, one of the strongest defenders of *la guerre totale*, General Lionel-Max Chassin, commander-in-chief of the air force in Indochina during the early 1950s, told his superior that he was "convinced that had we killed all of the water buffalos, destroyed all of the rice in Indochina, we would have had the Vietnamese at our mercy whenever we wanted." Total war, he insisted, was the only solution for winning a colonial war, and economic warfare was vital to its success: "One must starve people to death." (*C'est la solution de la guerre économique: faire crever les gens de faim.*)[54]

It was a brutal war of decolonization.

Vietnamese Economic Survival

Suffice it to say that things were extraordinarily difficult on the Vietnamese side. While the communist leadership could be proud of its ability to take the war to a Western colonial power in modern battle, the slow-drip economy that had kept the DRV alive until 1950 could no longer provide the food needed to sustain its hungry army, the expanded civil service in charge of it, or the phalanx of porters supplying both. The Chinese communists had provided modern weapons, but they could spare little food for their Vietnamese brothers and sisters, at least, not yet; they were locked in battle with the Americans in Korea between October 1950 and July 1953. Mao Zedong's advisers in Vietnam diligently helped Ho on the economic front though. They provided advice, support, and models for controlling inflation, stabilizing the currency, streamlining taxes, introducing banking reform, expanding agriculture, and introducing full-scale land reform. However, the burden of implementing new economic, financial, and agricultural policies fell squarely on Vietnamese shoulders. A few examples are in order to grasp just how dire the economic situation became after 1950 and how the Vietnamese communists went about building their War Communism within the vital economic sector.

Inflation—the rise in the price of goods and services over a given period of time—had always been a problem for the DRV, but it now threatened to get out of control as the communists expanded the size of their army and state in record time. Rice was the chief concern. As paddy supplies dwindled because of French attacks and the demand for food grew, the price of rice rose precipitously. Paid in dong up to this point, civil servants struggled to buy food while peasants found it ever harder to pay their taxes in the national tender. What was worse, the official price the government imposed (the one at which the farmers had to sell their rice) was far below the (real) market one. The possibility that reluctant farmers would start providing less as the government needed more suddenly became a frightening possibility.[55]

The chronic depreciation of the national currency was a related problem. The dong had been weak since its birth in 1946. Its value only declined as the war intensified. To make matters worse, the French lowered the value of the dong further still by introducing counterfeited bills into circulation in DRV zones. They wanted to make the Vietnamese communists pay higher prices for their "colonial dependency" on the Indochinese federation which was their most important trading partner. Committed to importing essential products from French Indochina like chemicals and, increasingly, bicycles, to power their transport services, the colonial piaster remained stronger than the dong, no matter how many times the Vietnamese government revalued its national currency or tried to shift its trade towards communist China. The demand for finished textiles, medicines, and petrol coming from colonial Indochina remained high. The importation of bicycles jumped from 594 in 1952 to 7,212 in 1953. Each one of these things had to be paid for in piasters, adding further downward pressure on the dong. The colonial piaster appreciated relentlessly, rendering Vietnamese imports, clandestine or not, ever more expensive.

Peasants were not dupes. Many hoarded colonial tender and were often tempted (for reasons of survival) to sell their surplus rice to those who could pay them in piasters. Who could blame them? After all, Ho's government had also built up its own foreign currency reserves in Indochinese piasters in order to finance its imports. In the south, a chronic shortage of Ho Chi Minh bills left local authorities with no choice but to look the other way as people used the piaster, despite the risks that using the enemy's currency entailed. And Bao Dai was not the only one to resent the unilateral French decision of May 1953 to devalue the Indochinese piaster relative to the French franc. The communists relied on a strong piaster (and their reserves in it) to buy those bikes they so badly needed. By devaluating the piaster in mid-1953, the French made them a lot more expensive at the point when preparations for Dien Bien Phu were about to get underway.[56]

Nothing was more precious than food, though. The communists had not stockpiled rice in sufficient quantities in upper Vietnam during the first half of the conflict. Effective French air and naval surveillance prevented Ho from importing rice from granaries in the far south to the northern crescent. As a result, the price of rice in the Democratic Republic of Vietnam's (already agriculturally challenged) northern highlands exploded as the PAVN's divisions came to life. Le Van Hien, the minister of finances at the time, records in his diary that by June 1950 they were already having trouble finding enough rice to feed their soldiers. Shortages were such that the price of rice in this area climbed up from 3,000 dong for 100 kg of rice at the start of the year to 10,000 or even as much as 14,000 dong six months later. In his entry of 9 July, he lamented that the government lacked 25,000 tons of rice needed to feed troops following their defeat in the delta. Food was, he wrote, "beyond all others, the most important problem."[57]

Ho Chi Minh had to find ways to increase agricultural production in upper Vietnam. He personally led massive propaganda drives to exhort peasants to produce more. This included opening new ground for planting, increasing rice yields by double-cropping and using fertilizers, and urging the people to work harder and longer in the fields. Pictures showed "Uncle Ho," the father of the nation, working the land diligently like any other Vietnamese. As we know from the previous chapter, the party feted "agricultural heroes" for the population to imitate in order to increase production. Winners received rewards and prizes, and medals were never in short supply. When they were on operations, soldiers received instructions to help labor-short villages repair dikes and terraces, plant rice, or pitch in during harvest time. Austerity measures were de rigueur. The government outlawed the production of rice alcohol and flour made from it. Cadres drilled the slogan, *Tiet kiem,* into people's heads—"Economize," " Save," and "Be frugal!"[58]

Expanded food production went hand in hand with increased state control. New decrees required rice producers to measure and report their yields at harvest time and declare their stocks on a monthly basis thereafter. The same was true of other foodstuffs: meat, salt, vegetables, sugar, cattle, and poultry. Village leaders had to do the same for food produced on communal lands or any newly opened land. Cadres were dispersed into "free" and "occupied" village to take stock of food reserves well before full land reform began in late 1953. They surveyed land, inspected silos, and reported damage. They also had orders to ensure that producers, landowners, and village collectives respected the official price and, if their food supplies were requisitioned, helped to feed troops passing through. Those who refused or resisted risked severe repercussions from the police, the army, and the judicial system. When mass mobilization laws took many able-bodied Vietnamese out of the fields and incorporated them into the army or work teams, the government reserved the right to conscript special harvest units, which were to enter any given field to collect rice so that it did not rot on its stems for lack of field hands. Such was the importance of food that PAVN units broke off from their assault on the southern delta in 1951 in order to "help" villagers bring in the harvest. General de Lattre's colonial *levée en masse* in mid-1951 now competed with Ho's, as the French sent officials from the Associated State of Vietnam into the villages to recruit soldiers and porters and to collect rice. Vietnam was the site of a double mobilization, for which the Vietnamese peasants paid dearly.

Vietnamese communists knew they had to rebuild their economy, finances, and agriculture to survive. They also saw the chance to assert their party's control over the economy. They turned to their Chinese advisers to help them do both things. For one, Vietnamese communists lined up behind President Ho, and the party's general secretary, Truong Chinh, welcomed the communist techniques, models, and experiences their Chinese counterparts provided them on the economic front.[59]

The head of the advisory group's political section, Luo Guibo, had received directives from his party to assist the Vietnamese in this specific
area. As he reported back to his superiors later that year: "Financial
problems, especially as they affect food supplies and currency, are presently the most urgent problems in Vietnam. We have selected several
cadres with experience in finance, banking and grain supply work to
serve as advisers in Vietnam."[60] On personal instructions from Mao
Zedong, Luo Guibo introduced policies to the Vietnamese which his
party had used in their War Communism, including "the imposition of
grain-tax levies, the withdrawal of currency from circulation, and the
encouragement of manufacturing." Although the Vietnamese leadership
put Pham Van Dong and Le Van Hien in charge of these questions, as
the ministers of economics and finance respectively, the transformation
of the economy, like that of the army and the state, was a joint Sino-
Vietnamese project. Le Van Hien confirms this in his diary.[61]

Thanks to close assistance from the Chinese advisory team, Vietnamese communists implemented a series of major reforms with the ultimate goal of bringing the economy under direct communist control.
The new policies included the creation of the State Bank of Vietnam
(Ngan hang Quoc gia Viet Nam) in May 1951; the issuance of a new,
revalued dong later that year; the establishment of the Trading Office
(Mau dich Quoc doanh); and the streamlining of the government's tax
system in the form of an agricultural tax (*thue nong nghiep*) during the
same month. This Vietnamese War Communism in the economic realm
would accelerate over the coming years, including the adoption of full-
scale land reform in late 1953 and its continuation until 1956.

The party's new trading office was established to centralize and administer foreign trade with communist China *and* with colonial Indochina. One of its most important tasks was to erase the government's
chronic trade deficit with French Indochina, and thereby prevent the
dong's further depreciation. This new trading office explains the instructions Pham Van Dong issued to officials in 1952, which ordered them to
closely administer commerce and currency exchanges with the French
and to do everything possible to increase exports in order to improve
the balance of trade. Within the same year, the Vietnamese signed a

formal trade agreement with Beijing to administer commercial exchanges on a state-to-state basis and, in a further accord signed a year later, lifted restrictions on border trade (Chinese salt imports, of particular importance in northern Vietnam, increased). Sometime in 1953, China replaced French Indochina as the DRV's main foreign trading partner. The Trading Office oversaw this historic shift in Vietnam's foreign trade, away from the French empire and towards communist Eurasia. It occurred during the Indochina War, not after it. It was a joint Sino-Vietnamese operation.[62]

Stabilizing a national currency in wartime is a challenge for any country, and Vietnam was no exception to this rule. No matter how they sold it, leaders struggled to convince the population to trust the banknote carrying Ho's portrait. In 1951, the Vietnamese communists, acting in concert with their Chinese advisers, introduced a new dong printed on shiny Czech paper which was imported via China. In a unilateral decision, the Vietnamese government declared it to be almost ten times stronger than the old dong. While Chinese and Vietnamese sources claim the new currency was a success, French accounts are closer to the mark when they point out that the new bills met with a frosty reception among peasants and civil servants. Again, who could blame them? No matter how the communists spun it, they were unable to stop the national dong from depreciating in value relative to the piaster. In 1948, one Indochinese piaster purchased between 1.5–4 dong. By mid-1953, the ratio was 1 to 700! A pack of cigarettes cost three to five piasters instead of 20,000 dong. Although leaders could congratulate themselves for building up the government's reserves in the colonial currency, they could not control the higher prices of foodstuffs within their own lands—rice, meat, and salt. And as the price of rice in dong skyrocketed, peasants started to cut back on production. When it came to reporting how much rice they had, they started to falsify their declarations. It was a nightmare situation.[63]

This largely explains why, on 1 May 1951, two weeks after Truong Chinh warned everyone to beware of General Rice and as it became clear that the PAVN would not seize the delta in one fell swoop, the Vietnamese Communist Party decreed the streamlining of a myriad of preexisting taxes into just a few. The most important of them was the agricultural tax (*thue nong nghiep*). The imposition of the agricultural tax allowed the government to secure the rice it needed to feed the army, the civil service, the work crews, and porters. Producers had no choice but to pay this tax. Moreover, they had to pay it in kind, in quantities of rice established by the government. In theory, it was designed to be a progressive form of taxation: rich landholders paid more. The poor paid less. But *all* producers had to pay: not just inside the DRV proper, but also in the rice-rich areas of the Tonkin delta, and in and around Hue and Da Nang, where Giap had already dispatched his smaller PAVN units to collect rice for the army.[64]

From mid-1951 until the end of the war in July 1954, rice effectively replaced the dong as the national currency for the Democratic Republic of Vietnam. The National Bank and Trading Office became, in effect, state-run granaries for storing and distributing rice to the army, the civil service, workers, and rice-deficit areas. Shiny or not, the dong was worthless. Rice had a quantifiable value: the government paid salaries in it. The national budget was calculated in tons of rice. The agricultural tax—again, levied, for the most part, on rice—provided 86.2 percent of the budget for 1951, 77 percent for 1952, 71.2 percent for 1953, and 54.7 percent for 1954 (a lower number, given that the war and its ever-hungry demands ended in July of that year). Of all the taxes upon the people, this was the only one that really mattered. In all, from Zone V north to the Chinese border (including contested zones in the Tonkin delta), the agricultural tax generated 1.5 million tons of rice between 1951 and 1954. Before the Second World War, the northern delta produced an estimated *annual* production of 1.5 million tons of rice, of which 70 percent went towards feeding the population. In the best of times, this left a surplus of 360,000 tons of rice. One and a half million tons over three years rather than one was cutting it perilously short for the DRV's 10 million people, and with no possibility of importing rice from the Mekong Delta area and little from China.[65]

Vietnamese War Communism squeezed the agricultural sector and its farmers for everything they had. Like the Bolsheviks during the Russian civil war and the Maoists fighting the Japanese and Chiang Kai-shek's forces, the Vietnamese communists effectively confiscated grain and other agricultural products from the peasants in the shape of this tax. It was a terrible catch-22 for the Vietnamese. Unlike the Bolsheviks, Ho's party operated from the countryside. Its survival depended on the peasantry, not the working class. Ideologically, Ho was committed to helping the peasants (and the workers) to improve their lives and to build a communist state together. And yet as the war moved towards a crescendo in the highlands of northwestern Vietnam, the only thing the communists could do to keep their hungry army, its porters, and civil servants alive was to lean ever harder on the peasantry living in areas from lower central Vietnam to the north. In late 1952, Ho admitted that there was something terribly unjust about what was happening:

> Almost 90 percent of our people are peasants. Over 90 percent of those in our national army, regional forces, militias and guerrillas are peasants. Most of our taxpayers and those serving in our work teams are peasants. Our peasants have given the most to the resistance and have sacrificed the most for the Motherland. And yet our peasants remain among the poorest, because they lack land. The lowering of rents and usurious interest rates—something to which the peasants have the greatest right—has not yet been completely realized. It's an extremely unjust state of affairs. (*Do la mot tinh trang rat khong cong bang.*)[66]

Ho was right. And viewed from the peasants' point of view, it is easier to understand why the Vietnamese communists finally chose full-blown land reform in late 1953 at the same time as they went for broke in a faraway valley called Dien Bien Phu: they had no choice. By 1952, Ho knew that he had to give something to his people in exchange for asking them to do the impossible—even if it meant destroying the coalition government of 1946 by launching a communist class war on "the feudal-ists," the landlords who had been his patriotic allies. But would it be enough? Lenin's War Communism had driven the peasants to the brink of disaster during the Russian civil war, and later on Stalin's reforms would push millions into the same abyss. Ho Chi Minh knew this. So did Truong Chinh. They were betting on Mao's model of land reform, but would it work in Vietnam? No one could know for sure. What Ho and his disciples did know was that "General Rice" was out there, watching from the distance as the Vietnamese and the French squared off in Dien Bien Phu. The Vietnamese president also knew that, this time, General Rice had more than hunger in his arsenal. Backed by the French, he had famine too.

10

The Road to Dien Bien Phu

At Dien Bien Phu on 6 May 1954, Dr. Ton That Tung had come a long way since graduating from medical school in Hanoi in the 1930s. Here he was now, in the hills above Dien Bien Phu, working tirelessly around the clock sewing soldiers' bodies back together as the battle raged below. A brilliant surgeon by all accounts, Ton That Tung had specialized in heart and liver disorders in medical school (he would go on to perform Vietnam's first open-heart surgery in 1958). His talent was such that he broke the color line when he became the first Vietnamese doctor to practice medicine in colonial Indochina on terms commensurate with the French. Dr. Tung was also an ardent patriot. He had immediately joined Ho Chi Minh's government in September 1945. When full-scale war broke out a year later, he relocated to the maquis, presided over a wartime medical school, and helped to train modern Vietnam's first medics, nurses, and doctors. As Vietnamese artillery pounded the besieged French camp below him, Tung spoke for many when he confided to his diary that "only a few years ago, in northern Vietnam, they hunted us down mercilessly. Now they are falling to our guns like sparrows. This reversal of roles rejoices me."[1]

The road leading to this change in fortunes did not follow a straight line, however. In fact, no one in 1950 on the Vietnamese side could have imagined that the final battle would take place in the highlands. The focus still remained on the Red River Delta. Nor did anyone really grasp what they would have to do concretely to create the force that so impressed Dr. Ton That Tung as he looked down from the hills in 1954. It had all happened in the early 1950s.

The Winding Road to Dien Bien Phu

Between the Delta and the Highlands

The Vietnamese failure to take the Tonkin plains during the first half of 1951 did not mean that Ho Chi Minh and his lieutenants had simply given up on the Red River basin. They did not. From the stinging defeats of 1951, four interconnected orientations in Vietnamese strategic thinking emerged. Each reflected the degree to which the Democratic Republic of Vietnam straddled the lowlands on the one side and the highlands on the other. We have seen some of them earlier; but we need to lay them out again here, for they are essential to understanding how Dien Bien Phu became possible.

For a start, rather than favoring one zone over the other, the Vietnamese combined the Indochinese highlands and the northern lowlands into one strategic theater. They could do this thanks to the upland corridor they had consolidated after the victory at Cao Bang in late 1950. Within a few months, readers will remember, it arced along the western perimeter of the Red River Delta. It stretched from the provinces on the Chinese border via the resistance capital in Thai Nguyen to make its way to Zone IV. Viewed from above, it looked something like a half-moon wrapped around the French delta. Then, from Zone IV, a 'handle' jutted out southwards to lower central Vietnam as far as Qui Nhon in Zone V. This long, sickle-shaped territory permitted Vietnamese decision-makers working from it to look both ways at the same time—deeper into the highlands behind them and straight ahead into the lowlands at their feet. The handle, however, had colonial "chips" in it—in the areas in and around Dong Hoi, Hue, Da Nang, and Nha Trang.

Next, this new theater of war required the Vietnamese to operate an army capable of moving back and forth between the highlands and the plains. Following his defeats in the delta, in mid-1951 General Vo Nguyen

Giap withdrew his regular divisions into the upland corridor. However, rather than leaving the delta to his guerrilla forces, he immediately detached battalions from selected PAVN regiments and redeployed them in the delta to operate with local forces in new combinations. As a rule, these mobile combat teams avoided direct clashes of a conventional kind in favor of expanding territorial control indirectly—village by village, day by day. But if ordered, they could engage in combat in a way far exceeding anything local militias could manage. From 1951, the PAVN operated in regular and irregular formations, just as the French had started doing.

Then, relying on these PAVN-powered task forces, the Vietnamese made a strategic decision to reengage with the French in the delta. Starting in mid-1951, Ho's lieutenants chose to compete systematically with the French for control of the 8 million people living in the 4,000 villages wrapped around Hanoi and Haiphong.[2] Zone III, which sliced through the provinces of Nam Dinh and Thai Binh, was hotly contested. If Vo Nguyen Giap could not take the delta via conventional warfare, then he would do so gradually by expanding territorial control at the village level. Even partial control in the delta could provide springboard positions from which to attack the cities at a later date. Tactics changed, not strategy, and that remained true until the end of the war. Robert Guillain, *Le Monde*'s seasoned war correspondent, was on to this when he described the slow breakup of the delta as occurring in the form of a *carte vérole,* or a "pockmarked map." Writing as the Battle of Dien Bien Phu got underway in early 1954, he described the slow-burning territorial meltdown of the delta as equally important to anything PAVN's regular divisions were doing in the highlands:

There hangs a map of the delta in the offices of Hanoi, on which one can see the Viet Minh's zones in detail. The Viet Minh zones are in red, the white areas indicate those where the Vietnamese administration [allied with the French] has been installed. Pink is for the regions which are mixed. Anyone who has seen this map is in for a shock, as it is colored almost entirely in red. True, it is a political map, not a military one. Our mobile groups can still move through those vast red patches constituting almost one big spot; but the Viet Minh is at home there. Representatives of the [Associated State of Vietnam's] administration never risk going into the red zones. They might establish a precarious hold over the pink regions, but, even then, they turn them over to the Viet Minh during the night. Across these vast red zones a few white-and-pink corridors and islands appear—these are our roads and urban centers surrounded by the Viet Minh tide. In the end, the white, which refers to completely pacified zones, only constitutes a quarter of the map.[3]

Like so many others before and since, the French spoke of the enemy's expansion in terms of a disease: *vérole* (smallpox). But what they called the "rotting" (*pourrissement*) of the delta by Ho Chi Minh's people was really no different than what their French forebearers, Hubert Lyautey and Joseph Galliéni, had done to Ho's ancestors in the late nineteenth century with their legendary ink- or oil-spot strategy. The difference now was that the Vietnamese communists were determined to turn their own oil spots upon the French trying to protect their colonial hold on "Tonkin." What is sure is that the Vietnamese might have failed in their attempt to seize the northern delta by force in early 1951, but they had in no way given up on taking it from the French at the village level. And like the French "colonialists," the Vietnamese "communists" saw in pacification an economic, military, and state-building strategy all rolled into one.

Finally, this combined highland-delta strategy coordinating the movements of the regular army with its PAVN-powered guerrilla groups allowed Vo Nguyen Giap to *calibrate* his operations in a unique way. On the one hand, Giap could use his mobile groups in the Red River basin to gather rice and expand control at the village level, knowing that this would force the French to commit more of their own battalions to stop him. This, in turn, would relieve pressure elsewhere, so that the commander-in-chief could deploy his regular army wherever he wanted more easily. On the other hand, confident that the French would not draft their own young men to fight in Indochina and that the Americans would not send theirs, at least not with the Korean conflict on, Giap could deploy his regular divisions deep into central Vietnam or Laos, knowing that the French would have to go after them. But in order to do that, the French would have to transfer troops from the delta. It was a carefully thought-through procedure designed to keep the French moving between the delta and the highlands on the communists' terms.[4]

At the heart of all four policies were the assumptions that the French, for lack of regular troops, would be unable to hold both theaters at the same time, that Bao Dai's army would be unable to fill the gap, and that the Americans would not intervene. As it turned out, the Vietnamese were right on every count. They were also confident that they could recruit and train the soldiers they needed from anywhere in the government's sickle-shaped territory. Since late 1950, weapons, soldiers, and food increasingly circulated from one end of this corridor to the other, while agents collected rice and recruited soldiers and porters from the bordering colonial lands. In all, by mid-1951, the DRV "sickle and handle" administered upwards of 8 million people—around 2 million in the Viet Bac upland crescent, 4 million in Zone IV south of Hanoi, and 2 million in Zone V, save colonial-controlled Dong Hoi, Hue, Da Nang, Nha Trang, and surrounding colonial-held coastal strips and bases. This does not include perhaps as many as a million Vietnamese, over whom the "colonialists" and the "communists" shared sovereignty in the delta. In March 1954, as the war reached its climax, Robert Guillain was right once again when he observed that Giap could dispatch his best divisions to besiege Dien Bien Phu without imperiling his work in the colonial delta, not least of all because he had built up two independent PAVN regiments there. He had not infiltrated them into the plains, Guillain explained: "They were born there."[5]

The highland corridor running through Hoa Binh also allowed the Vietnamese to man and arm the area of the sickle's handle. In zones III and IV on the south side of Hanoi, Giap deployed the 320th division. It regularly slipped two of its regiments into the delta to help the home-grown units there. In 1953, as the French and the Vietnamese squared off in the northwest highlands, this delta force tied down 80,000 enemy troops working out of 900 village posts. The 320th also protected supply lines running from these rice-rich zones into the crescent and later to Dien Bien Phu as well. Further south, at the bottom of the handle in Zone V, the 325th division harassed French army posts outside Hue and Da Nang before moving into the central highlands at war's end. (This was the same division that was to hit American soldiers hard in a place called Ia Drang in late 1965.)[6]

In short, the upper half of Ho's Vietnam was no longer the fragmented archipelago it had been until recently. As sprawled as it remained in many areas, the Democratic Republic of Vietnam was connecting and consolidating on the inside. And its communications systems, security services, and intelligence networks contributed to this process. Although none of this necessarily permitted Giap to score immediate battle victories, it provided him and his party with options: like the "colonialists," the "communists" could fight a regular and an irregular war at one and the same time. Although the balance of military force remained asymmetrical to the end, the Vietnamese had nonetheless broken the colonial monopoly over *both* forms of warfare. This is why the French army suddenly found itself on the defensive in ways it would never be in Algeria, nor even in southern Vietnam.

Breaking the Sickle: The Battle of Hoa Binh

Vo Nguyen Giap's military opposite during much of the Indochina War, General Raoul Salan, understood what was going on. In a "testament" he penned in early 1953 for the man the government selected to replace him, Salan said that the crucial error he and de Lattre had committed after taking over in late 1950 was to have allowed the Vietnamese to create a professional army (*une véritable armée*).[7] Both men were happy to have beaten back the PAVN's conventional attacks on the northern delta during the first half of 1951, thanks in no small part to American military assistance and napalm, but they watched in something close to awe as their enemy regrouped, recalibrated, and carried on. Well-informed, Salan and his intelligence services did not remain inert, however: they accelerated their own efforts in the Tonkin delta, mobilized a Vietnamese army to help them, intensified economic warfare to include intensive bombing, and imposed a blockade around the colonial delta, as we have seen.

That said, Salan realized that these measures alone were not going to win the war for him. Drawing on his knowledge of upland Indochina during the interwar years and his command experience there since 1945, this French commander knew how important the enemy's control of Hoa Binh was to strengthening Ho's Vietnam. From one end of the DRV to the other, rice and troops moved through there. French intelligence officers referred to this interchange as the "Hoa Binh corridor."[8] It was in this context that de Lattre and Salan concluded that for their next move they had to sever the enemy's supply line before it was too late. If the PAVN dared to attack, then all the better: de Lattre and Salan would break its divisional back. In mid-November 1951, the French occupied the provincial city of Hoa Binh in the Black River valley west of Hanoi and secured the route connecting it to the colonial capital. Then Salan and de Lattre immediately reinforced their positions in the valley in preparation for an imminent attack. They unfurled barbed wire, positioned heavy artillery, brought in crack troops, and readied the air force. In the first highland clash since Cao Bang, neither French commander had the intention of getting caught in the open and repeating the debacle of a year earlier again.

The Vietnamese riposte was immediate and predictable. The territorial integrity of their war state depended on recovering that corridor. The Communist Party's directives were unequivocal: wipe out the enemy forces in Hoa Binh. Giap sent the 308th, 312th, and 304th divisions against the colonial forces hunkered down there, while the 316th and the 320th operated in partial guerrilla formation in the delta to remind the French that what they did in the highlands would cost them down below in the war for the delta. Over a three-month period, Giap mobilized over 300,000 men and women porters to supply his troops. Most of them came from the populous zones south of Hanoi, III and IV, as did the food. In mid-November, Giap sent his regulars directly into the line of fire in an attempt to overrun the enemy camp in Hoa Binh. Fighting was ferocious, occurring mainly in wave attacks in the dark of night. Each time Vietnamese regulars rushed enemy positions, they ran into heavy machine-gun fire, artillery, and aerial bombing.[9]

In the end, the Vietnamese recovered Hoa Binh, but not because they had defeated their adversary on the battlefield. Salan's men pushed the People's Army of Vietnam back each time it attacked. The problem for Salan was that his success in the highlands came at the cost of losing ground in the Red River Delta, the second front. The longer the fighting continued, the easier it was for Giap to expand his pacification efforts in the lowlands. And that is exactly what he did.[10] What was more, Salan knew that the French government would not send in any more troops and Bao Dai's army was still in no position to be of much help. Upon assuming the army's command after de Lattre's death in January 1952, Salan realized that if he continued to hold Hoa Binh, it would endanger his control over the northern plains, an unacceptable scenario. Whether he liked it or not, the preservation of the Tonkin delta took priority for political and strategic reasons. In February 1952, Salan withdrew his troops from Hoa Binh to send them after the PAVN-powered mobile units expanding the DRV's territorial control into the delta.

What happened at Hoa Binh had big implications for what the French and the Vietnamese would do next. On the French side, Salan might have held off his attackers in this clash, but he had not destroyed them. Additionally, by returning Hoa Binh to the adversary he had allowed his enemy to reestablish the territorial and military integrity of their sickle-shaped war-state. Finally, Salan's decision to withdraw confirmed the validity of Giap's strategy of engaging his PAVN regulars in the highlands while turning his local fighters upon the colonialists in the northern delta. This symbiotic relationship between the highlands and the plains did not guarantee military victory; but it diluted the French ability to claim it and bogged down Salan's men. Hoa Binh was a French victory, but it was a Pyrrhic one.

But we should not exaggerate Vietnamese success either. Although Giap might have regained control of Hoa Binh, the communists knew that they had not done this through a battlefield victory. Whatever spin Ho's propaganda machine put on it, French commanders had bested

Giap in pitched battle, again. The Vietnamese and their Chinese advisers drew at least four lessons from this: Firstly, both sides agreed that the French would not give up the Red River Delta. It was their priority—militarily and politically. Secondly, the extended duration of the Hoa Binh battle—almost three months—had come dangerously close to depleting the food supplies needed to keep the PAVN soldier in the field. Thirdly, the communists realized that if they were going to win, then they had to put their party in control of the state, the army, logistics, and the mass organizations once and for all. Lastly, Hoa Binh may have offered the Vietnamese more favorable terrain for attacking the French than fighting in the open delta, but the zone's proximity to colonial bases there allowed the adversary to supply their men by road and air and to bomb with ease. At least 3,500 Vietnamese soldiers had died trying to take Hoa Binh, and 7,000 were injured. Faced with this asymmetry, Vietnamese communists decided that if they wanted to take the battle to the French and win, then they had to move their operations into upland areas more favorable to them. There was only one way to go for the People's Army of Vietnam—westwards, deeper into the highlands. And to do this, they had to use every single instrument in the Sino-Soviet War Communism arsenal to mobilize the population for these intensive battles, which would require herculean logistical efforts over long distances.[11]

Going Deep

Sometime in the spring of 1952, Vietnamese and Chinese strategists made the historic decision to move west into the highlands—all of them. Discussions had centered on this question during the party's third plenum of early 1952 as the fighting still raged at Hoa Binh. A few months later, in July of that year, the communists made this strategic shift official by creating a new "northwestern zone" and approving battle plans a month later to make it happen. According to this plan, the People's Army of Vietnam would march west to seize new territory while administrators would move in behind them to incorporate it into the Democratic Republic of Vietnam. If the Expeditionary Corps tried to stop them, the communists would engage the enemy, expanding their positions in the delta all the while when French troops pulled troops from there in order to attack the PAVN in their upland operations (see Map 11),

This "going deep" policy effectively meant expanding the DRV's entire sickle-shape outwards to the west. This in turn dictated taking the Tai federation from the French in Lai Chau province in the far northwest in order to control the entire land border with China (except for a sliver of the frontier on the far eastern side near Haiphong.) Second, the conquest of the Tai federation and areas below it would open the way for the DRV to expand its military hold over northern Laos, including its rugged border with China. Finally, working from the sickle-handle zones, IV and V, the Vietnamese would simultaneously expand out their political and military operations into the rest of Laos and the central highlands. The Chinese communists agreed.[12]

Strategically, the Chinese and the Vietnamese designed this new policy in a bid to take control of Indochina's entire highland backbone running from the northern border with Yunnan province in China to the central highlands and southern Laos. Vietnamese soldiers and administrators were deployed into the central highlands and Laos in fits and starts and then in greater numbers when the regular army started moving in from early 1952. This fanning out into the highlands effectively turned what had until then been a mainly "Vietnamese war" into an increasingly "Indochinese one" for the first time. It also allowed the Vietnamese communists to get to work building revolutionary states of their own associated kind for their Laotian and Cambodian allies, the Pathet Lao (the Laotian Nation) and the Khmer Issarak (Free Cambodia) discussed in the following chapter. Most importantly, in the short term, this move into Indochina's uplands forced the French to fight in areas far from their lowland bases near Hanoi and their aircraft carriers operating off the coast.

Opening up Indochina's highland border with southern China was the first step. Control of the northwestern town of Nghia Lo was particularly important. Giap had already tried unsuccessfully to take this place in the fall of 1951. In 1952, he renewed his efforts with greater vigor.

Starting in the summer, he sent intelligence teams to report on colonial positions and troop strength in and around the town. By the fall, Chinese-supplied Molotova trucks and Vietnamese porters began moving supplies, weapons, and munitions westwards from the capital. These supply lines fed the 308th, 312th, and 316th divisions as its regiments began marching in that direction. On 14 October 1952, regular troops took French forward bases in northwestern Vietnam such as Tu Le, Gia Hoi, and Van Yen. Two days later, Vuong Thua Vu's 308th "iron division" overran Nghia Lo in a few hours. French Union troops led by Marcel Bigeard barely escaped to safe bases further west in Na San as the Vietnamese seized much of Son La province, on the border with Laos. As Salan informed his men: "We have taken the hit. The loss of the Nghia Lo sector is a painful one. But it is not a decisive one. . . . The game has only begun."[13]

This new game had immediate repercussions for French decision-makers inside Indochina and in Paris too. For starters, the PAVN's rapid western advance obligated the French government to commit to the defense of Laos for the first time: it was part of their Indochinese colonial state, itself part of the French Union. An attack on any member of the union compelled the French to protect it. Laos suddenly became a political and diplomatic question of great importance, and politicians in France started to pay a lot more attention. So did the Americans, worried that any armistice ending the fighting in Korea might allow the Chinese to intervene more deeply in Indochina and even strike into the heart of Southeast Asia through Laos. The highland push into the upland half of Indochina thus had the dual effect of further internationalizing the conflict and holding the French to protecting Laos, with the Americans watching from behind as they held their ground in Korea. This is how a collection of small outposts on the Vietnamese side of the Laotian border suddenly acquired increased strategic importance for all involved.

In an attempt to do something to halt Giap's western expansion, Salan decided to turn one such borderland place, Na San, into a heavily fortified camp. He concluded, correctly as it turned out, that his Vietnamese nemesis would attack him there in order to secure his march westwards. In a flurry of activity starting in October 1952, Salan transformed this small upland village into an entrenched position. Bulldozers cleared the jungle while colonial soldiers and Vietnamese workers dug trenches, laid 5,000 mines, unfurled over 1,000 tons of barbed wire, and installed heavy artillery. Engineers refurbished and extended the colonial airstrip there. Over a kilometer long, it could now handle an almost nonstop flow of landings and takeoffs. As of 23 November, Salan had 12,000 troops protecting the garrison.[14]

The French were ready when PAVN soldiers began arriving in the area on 22 November. The Vietnamese were not. Giap was clearly unaware of the extent to which his opponent had transformed Na San into a fortress. The Vietnamese commander thought this would be another Nghia Lo. What he got instead was a beefed-up "Hoa Binh," and his men paid dearly for what can only be described as a second, major intelligence failure (the first was missing the American delivery of napalm to de Lattre at Vinh Yen in late 1950). On 30 November 1952, in the black of night, Giap ordered his men to take the camp. PAVN soldiers duly attacked with legendary courage, but they immediately ran into barbed wire, mines, and a hail of machine-gun fire. French bombers attacked with impunity not just enemy troops, but the human transporters supplying them too.

Ngo Van Chieu was there, as always. This time, however, our battalion leader's luck ran out. In the heat of the battle, as bullets streaked through the air and artillery shells exploded around him, he went down: "It was a bolt of lightning, a sudden shaking, a light that emerged from the ground." Later on, as he tried to make sense of what had happened on that fateful night, he wrote in his memoir: "Then came an immense convulsion in my head, followed by the feeling of bee stings running all down my back. Then a sensation of emptiness . . . of men moving me by my feet, in the middle of hell . . . of seeing the tree hanging over me and men passing by . . . and then nothing." Silence. When he awoke, female medics were carrying him out of the valley with shrapnel still lodged in his back: "Everything I had left in me went into a final scream . . . I can't breathe . . . My God, I want to see Mai and my son, Cau, and my little daughter, Cuc. God, everything I did, I did it for the country . . . I hurt."

The medics slipped him some opium to ease the pain and then evacuated him to a field hospital where Dr. Ton That Tung's people sewed
him up.[15]

At Na San, the Vietnamese were in no position to repeat a three-
month battle on the scale of Hoa Binh. Located far from their supply
bases in Thai Nguyen and Zone IV, they would not have enough rice to
feed their troops for such a protracted siege and were already eating up
huge stocks of rice by going deep into northwestern Tai regions. Nor
did they have the artillery in sufficient quantities to protect their men,
let alone take out the enemy's airstrip. To my knowledge, Giap had no
antiaircraft guns on hand for this battle. On 7 December, only a few days
later, the commander-in-chief called off the entire attack. Instead of taking Na San, the PAVN went around it and proceeded to occupy the
small French airbase at Dien Bien Phu and the rest of Son La province,
while early in 1953 more troops marched into the provinces of Sam Neua
and Phong Saly in Laos.

For the French, Na San was another Pyrrhic victory. Although Salan
won the battle, he failed to stop his adversary from going around him,
deeper into the highlands, just as he had failed to break the DRV's sickle
at its handle in Hoa Binh. Salan withdrew his men from Na San later in
1953, worried that Giap would expand his hold on the northern delta if
he did not. The French inability to hold Hoa Binh or Na San allowed
their adversaries to fold vast stretches of the western highlands into the
Democratic Republic of Vietnam for the first time since 1945–6. It also
allowed Ho Chi Minh to create a territorial base for his Laotian allies in
this expanding highland realm bordering both his Vietnam and China.
De Lattre and Salan may have scorned their predecessors' decision to
abandon the highlands at Cao Bang in 1950, but they were clearly no
more serious than their predecessors about taking it back—and this was
despite American pressure on them to go on the offensive instead of
always playing defense.

The lessons Salan learned from all of this influenced the recommen-
dations he made to the man who replaced him in May 1953, General
Henri Navarre. In documents, including the testament mentioned

above, Salan explained to his successor how the Indochina War now operated in a symbiotic relationship between the highlands and the lowlands, with regular and irregular actions combining and adjusting in this uncanny *jeux de miroirs*. The outgoing commander-in-chief urged his replacement to concentrate on retaking the northern delta first and then going after the regular army in the highlands. Salan knew from the economic war he and de Lattre had been operating since 1950 that the Vietnamese had recruited the bulk of their people and rice needed to feed the PAVN from the plains. Take the delta from them once and for all, and the enemy army starves—or so Salan and de Lattre thought.

Ramping War Communism Up Another Notch

The Vietnamese and Chinese learned something else from Hoa Binh and Na San that would deeply affect the nature of Ho's Vietnam in the run-up to Dien Bien Phu: the Communist Party at its helm had to take control of both the state and society in an unprecedented way to be able to carry on like this. Taking charge completely was the only way, in the leadership's view, to mobilize enough people, secure the food, and organize the logistics needed to defeat the French in sustained, set-piece battle in the highlands. The time had come in 1952 for the Vietnamese to ramp up their War Communism by yet another notch.

But before I return to this important subject, I want to be very clear about Vietnamese nationalism. It was real. It burned red-hot throughout Ho Chi Minh's wartime Vietnam. It always had. It always would. Nationalism had driven tens of thousands of Vietnamese—communists and noncommunists, men and women, young and old—to fight the invading French colonial army after the Second World War, just as the same cause had moved so many people to take up arms against the Japanese and German armies coming at them from both ends of Eurasia. Nationalism, not communism, had moved Ngo Van Chieu from the moment we first met him putting on his uniform in Hanoi in 1945 to the day he was carried out of Na San on a stretcher. If I have woven this man's patriotic story deeply into the one I am telling about the First Indochina War, it is because I believe him to be symbolic of this powerful nationalist force the communists could tap into, but did not own. Similar things were true in communist China and the Soviet Union during the Second World War.

We must remember, too, the deep patriotism driving noncommunist nationalists like Nguyen Cong Luan and his father. They stayed on in Ho's Vietnam out of patriotism, despite their deep distrust of the communists. There were untold thousands like them working inside the DRV until the war's end. They were not traitors. They wanted the colonial invaders out just as much as the communists did. Some 10,000 worked in the Democratic Republic of Vietnam as members of the democratic and socialist parties, which the communists were prepared to tolerate for the time being. Countless others just kept their heads down and fought for their country, hoping things would work out later just as Ho had promised they would.

The "French colonialists" fanned the nationalist flames for the "Vietnamese communists." The sustained bombings the French unleashed from mid-1952 added raw hatred to the mix. Napalm blasts that had already started in the delta in early 1951 followed the PAVN into highlands and continued right through the battle of Dien Bien Phu, killing untold numbers of soldiers and civilians. Ngo Van Chieu almost choked on his anger and hate when his men uncovered the corpse of a calcinated baby in a napalmed town somewhere west of Nghia Lo: "What punishment awaits those who allow small children to die burned in their cradles by a fire thrown from the sky!" From one end of the DRV to the other, French planes bombed dikes, dams, canals, and animals. Talk of "total war" might have looked good to those planning it from an isolated General Staff office in Hanoi or Paris, but in applying such tactics the French drove thousands of Vietnamese into Ho's camp. And then there were those terrible "things" that happened in the borderlands. If the French rightly commemorate the horrible day in mid-1944 when the Nazis took hundreds of innocent lives in a village called Oradour-sur-Glane, the Vietnamese remember some of the terrible things that happened when the French army rolled through their villages during this conflict. The anticommunist singer and songwriter Pham Duy wrote a deeply moving ballad in the late 1940s called "The Mothers of Gio Linh" in memory of their sons killed during a French raid on this village. Enemy soldiers decapitated them and then put their heads on pikes in the middle of the village to let the people of Gio Linh know who was in charge.

And yet, no matter how powerful this ball of nationalist fire was, no matter how hotly hatred burned in Vietnamese hearts, it was not enough to win in places like Vinh Yen in the delta or Na San in the highlands. Nationalism, no matter how strong it was, conditioned outcomes, but it alone cannot explain how the Vietnamese brought down the French at Dien Bien Phu. At the time, Ho realized that the "war elephant" he had brought to life in the form of a regular army in 1950 was still not strong enough to crush the colonial force in battle. The only way to do that, Ho agreed with his Vietnamese and Chinese counterparts in Thai Nguyen, was to mobilize the entire population behind the army. This is why, as the communists went deeper still into the highlands in 1952, they simultaneously accelerated their efforts to put the party in control of "everything."

Imposing the "Party Line"

One of the main ingredients in the Sino-Vietnamese War Communism package was "rectification." Starting in 1950, as we know from an earlier chapter, Vietnamese communists, backed by the Chinese advisory group, had already begun implementing it. This method, first developed in the Soviet Union and then expanded on by Mao at Yan'an, sought to "perfect" the party center's hold over its own ranks, the armed forces, and its mass organizations.[16] Carefully indoctrinated in the basics of Marxism-Leninism and in the Vietnamese Workers Party's history and political program, the cadre class constituted the vital, vertical backbone on which the center's control turned and expanded. Once a group of "perfected" cadres had completed their coursework and exams and provided their biographies, the party center would then dispatch them to work at the lower levels of the administration (in the provinces, districts, and villages); in the army's divisions, regiments, and battalions; in mass associations like the Lien Viet; and in the state's various parts, including the security services, communications, economy, and medical offices. Cadres would interact with the state through their parallel hierarchies. This "perfected" bureaucratic class of cadres, numbering around 100,000 by 1954, would then be in a position, during wartime, to push through the establishment of the single-party state. The Soviets had done it. The Chinese had shown that it could be done in a time of war against the Japanese. The Vietnamese had to make it work against the French as well.[17]

The problem was that things were clearly not going well for the communist center in 1952. Most problematic of all was the fact that the *quality* of the cadres and party members as a whole remained poor.[18] Their training was often sketchy, their knowledge of Marxism-Leninism shallow, and their ability to face hardships disappointing. Despite claims to the contrary, the party regretted that its cadre class was sociologically "complicated": 65 percent of it was made up of the petit bourgeois. Complicated indeed because, if even only partially true, then that would mean that the leadership still had to "rectify" tens of thousands in its elite ranks. Little wonder the party center conceded that it "had not yet reformed the thinking or educated a bureaucratic class of cadres in Marxist-Leninist thought."[19]

This would no longer do, not after Hoa Binh, certainly not in the wake of Na San. The rectification of the party, the state, the army, and the mass organizations was an urgent political task. Scores of party documents repeated it. A new round of rectification got underway in May 1952, to be applied from top to bottom. President Ho Chi Minh and General Secretary Truong Chinh presided over this second round. They put powerful men in charge of the process, notably Hoang Quoc Viet, To Huu, and Le Van Luong. Ho Chi Minh did not mince his words then (or in subsequent meetings) on the importance of this "perfection" of a bureaucratic kind. In early 1953, he reminded his colleagues that too many party members and cadres remained "undisciplined" in their work. Visibly upset by the sad state of affairs, he stated that the numbers of these bad cadres were not small. To fix things, the founder of the Vietnamese Communist Party continued, the party had to "root out" the bad elements and ideas in order to establish the true line of correct thinking and action for everyone. Political and military success depended on it. This process of communization would allow the party, its state, and armed forces to become "clean, stable, and unified." It would only occur, however, in areas located from Zone IV upwards, an accurate indication as to where the core of communist power lay. The center put on hold the "rectification" process in lower central and southern Vietnam and never applied it in Laos or Cambodia. The party undoubtedly lacked the infrastructure *and* staff to administer it in these areas.[20]

Vo Nguyen Giap presided over the continued rectification of the army. He explained in 1952 that the army would further spread "proletarian ideology" throughout the army's rank and file. As elsewhere, seminars, study sessions, and discussion groups gathered thousands together to listen to communist cadres in the army called commissars explain Marxist-Leninist thought, the history of the August Revolution, and the party's political program. Together, this was the "line." Ngo Van Chieu describes in his memoirs watching Sino-Soviet propaganda films for the first time in 1952 and discussing them with his party minders. Political commissars "perfected" in the party's line themselves operated in parallel to commanding officers in the army's divisions, regiments, and battalions. The army's political section provided a host of heroes for soldiers to emulate in different areas of work: communications, truck driving, bridge-building, mine-clearing, and so on.[21]

However, although the communists had put the expansion of the party on hold in 1951 in order to increase quality over quantity, the army could not do this. The need for troops, porters, and construction workers increased proportionally as the war dragged on. Only one social group, one class, could supply these people in large enough numbers, and that was the peasantry. The 1949 military conscription law and the 1950 general mobilization decree had ensured that the army and its human logistics teams were very largely made up of peasants. Once they were inducted, the party had to politicize the peasants in order to control and motivate them. Of course, this politicization did not occur overnight, and it was often very spotty, but it happened. This is how the Vietnamese national army of 1946 became a very different animal by 1952 in the form of the People's Army of Vietnam. The PAVN obviously maintained its nationalist soul, but it also adopted a second one of a Marxist-Leninist design, the product of this War Communism.[22]

Equally important was politicizing and controlling the thousands of noncommunist civil servants working in the Democratic Republic of Vietnam. They worked in a host of state ministries, in the local administration, and in mass organizations such as national patriotic associations for intellectuals, writers, artists, women, small-scale traders, and the like. It involved a delicate balancing act. On the one hand, the communists could not push these people too hard by assaulting their individualism (although that is what Sino-Soviet "perfection" was most certainly designed to do), as Ho still needed their help in running the state and the French would have welcomed them into their colonial arms had the communists been too coercive. On the other hand, the need to favor the peasants increased every day as the war intensified. For the time being, the leadership had to maintain its alliance with the noncommunist patriots, "perfecting" liberal professionals who wanted to move into or up the communist social ladder and leaving the others alone, as long as they did their jobs and kept their heads down.[23]

The patriotic landowners posed a trickier problem. They had contributed to the war effort and supported Ho Chi Minh and his government. However, this class also possessed the land which the party wanted so badly in order to reward the peasants for giving so much. Even "rich peasants" were coming under suspicion. Although the communists held off from implementing full-blown land reform, in 1952 they started to take a harder line towards the landowning class (*dia chu*). For the first time, the party leadership targeted the landed class as "the adversaries of the revolution." It is no accident that the communists began showing the Chinese-produced film *The White-Haired Girl* (dubbed into Vietnamese in 1952) so widely. It had first played as a Maoist opera in Yan'an. This hugely popular communist musical showcased the cruelty of a

Chinese landlord and the bravery of the poor peasant woman whose life he had destroyed. Xuan Phuong, whom we met as a member of the resistance earlier on, loved the film:

> Although we knew the story inside out, we sobbed all the same every time we watched it. And when the landowner abused the peasants, some soldiers would fire at the screen. But when, suddenly, the look-outs cried "May bay!" meaning airplanes, lights went off and we all rushed to the shelters to wait out the alert. After the movie, the audience dispersed quickly and we went home, happy as could be, with the children asleep on our backs. The return trip seemed shorter because we were so busy discussing the show and talking about meeting people from the other groups again.[24]

Patriotic or not, landowners in the upper half of Vietnam catching a glimpse of this edifying Maoist film had every reason to worry that something very bad was in store for them.[25]

Revolutionary Holidays and the Cult of Ho Chi Minh

Of course, the Vietnamese communists could not and did not "rectify" the entire population in wartime.[26] Nor could they "perfect" everyone in the state, the army, and the mass organizations in such a short period of time. The party did, however, try to reach as many people as possible in "lighter" ways in order to politicize and move them. The introduction of new holidays was one such instrument. Following Sino-Soviet examples, in 1952 Vietnamese communists latched on to a host of revolutionary holidays to percolate its ideology further down into the local administration and rural society. Instructions went out in 1952 to organize celebrations locally for May 1, the International Workers' Day, the anniversary of the Russian October Revolution of 1917, the foundation of the People's Republic of China in 1949, and the establishment of the Democratic Republic of Vietnam, as well as the creation in 1950 of a new Indochinese alliance in the form of the Lien Viet, the Pathet Lao, and the Khmer Issarak. Scores of newspapers, pamphlets, pictures, posters, and radio broadcasts hammered home the message of these special days in a concerted effort to politicize, homogenize, and move the "masses" in the party's way.[27]

Since late 1945, as we know, the Vietnamese communists had been working hard to transform President Ho Chi Minh into their icon. In 1948, the party had instructed cadres to organize celebrations of Ho Chi Minh's birthday on 19 May. On that day, officials invited the population to emulate the president by doing more—planting more rice, producing more weapons, fighting more battles. We should not be surprised to discover renewed instructions in 1952 calling for the nationwide celebration of Ho Chi Minh's birthday. Vietnamese communists used Ho's birthday as a "teaching and mobilizing moment." Under close party guidance, people gathered in their villages to study President Ho, his life and teachings, so that they could follow in his way, and imitate his virtues and deeds. Newspaper articles, radio speakers, and cadres lectured on the great Vietnamese leader, issued copies of his biography and his great accomplishments, and provided portraits and pictures of him. As internal party documents confirm, this holiday and others like it served as moments needed to "reform thinking." Vietnamese communists welcomed the ritualized commemoration of this special day in order to expand their political control and mobilize people for war. They would do this for the rest of Ho's life (and well into his afterlife too) as the Vietnamese went to war against the Americans in the decades following.[28]

Proselytizing the Enemy Campaigns

In what appears to be a unique contribution to the War Communism repertoire, the Vietnamese communists developed a new form of psychological warfare. It was called *dich van* (meaning "proselytizing" or "converting the enemy to the cause"). Since the late nineteenth century, Vietnamese anticolonialists had always tried to win over their compatriots serving in the colonial army. During the Second World War the communists took it a step further. Working underground in Hanoi, the party's interim leader, Truong Chinh, his close ally, Tran Quoc Hoan, and their agents carefully targeted sympathetic French, European, and Vietnamese troops in the colonial army in a bid to win them over to the Viet Minh and then to the DRV's cause.

During the Indochina War, Vietnamese proselytizing efforts focused on the French Union armed forces. Specially trained communist cadres focused their attention on French soldiers having doubts about the legitimacy of the war they were fighting. This was especially the case for a handful of Leftists who had enrolled in the French Foreign Legion thinking they were going to fight "Japanese fascists" instead of "Vietnamese anticolonialists." Cadres also paid special attention to African troops fighting for the French. *Dich van* meant converting prisoners of war as well. French Union prisoners of war and later American ones too would get a taste of this in their camps, where often very suave political commissars, always communists, organized conversations and study sessions in order to win over promising prisoners to Ho Chi Minh's "just cause" or at least to neutralize their preconceptions about Ho and his Vietnam before releasing them. The Frenchman who, famously, had crossed over to the cause of Ho's Vietnam during the Indochina War, Georges Boudarel, got himself into trouble in the early 1990s in France for the *dich van* work he had done with French prisoners of war in the early 1950s in the Viet Bac zone.[29]

However, the Vietnamese communists probably used *dich van* most intensely on those Vietnamese working in and for the Associated State of Vietnam (and, later on, the Republic of Vietnam). In these proselytizing campaigns, the communists targeted Vietnamese soldiers, administrators, religious leaders, students, and intellectuals in the enemy state. Trusted agents infiltrated the colonial cities to proselytize among student associations, workers' unions, and within intellectual circles. The most effective agents were those who could draw upon a variety of social relationships in order to persuade, convert, and, hopefully, move people to work for the communist cause. The raising of an army for the Associated State of Vietnam and the general mobilization of the population in 1951 saw the communists ramp up their efforts by urging young men to dodge the draft or desert if they could. The importance of this kind of psychological assault was such that it became something of a specialized subgroup in the proselytizing business, known as *nguy van* ("winning over the enemy army.")[30]

Ramping Up the Patriotic Emulation Campaigns

Of all the political weapons of mass mobilization, the one Ho and his entourage preferred was the "emulation campaign." In May 1952, as another round of rectification got underway, the Vietnamese took the emulation campaigns to a new level. Whether one agrees with it or not, patriotic emulation—*thi dua ai quoc*, as it is widely known in Vietnam to this day—was an ingenious tool in the War Communism toolbox. It did not dwell on individual "shortcomings" or "sins" like the rectification campaigns did; but rather it zoomed in on the good deeds and exemplary actions of heroic individuals around whom the masses could be rallied. Like others in the communist bloc, Vietnamese communists referred to these singular individuals as "new heroes," "model fighters," and eventually as "new men" (and women). The Soviets had developed their heroic pantheon in the 1930s. By the end of the Second World War they had canonized a host of model fighters and labor heroes, the bravest of the brave, men and women of exemplary selflessness, indefectible peasants and workers, and even fearless children. The Maoists followed suit, creating their own list of heroes during the same conflict. And at the top of each emulative hierarchy stood the "hero of the heroes," Stalin and Mao.[31]

True to this Eurasian communist model, the Vietnamese erected their own pantheon of socialist heroes with President Ho perched, naturally, at the top. Each social group in this 10-million-people-strong Vietnam could find a "hero" to imitate, just as there was a Ho for everyone to adore. Selected by the party center, they represented the different groups the communists now favored in their dual struggle to defeat the invaders and build supporters for their cause. From 1952, the pantheon now included heroes to imitate for their skill in everything related which was imaginable, even executing suicide missions. Again, whether the "heroes" had truly done what they were said to have done (killed hundreds of enemy soldiers bare-handed, produced thousands of weapons, or opened vast expanses of bountiful land) does not matter. What does was the political and mobilizing function they served. All of this would go on right up to the Battle of Dien Bien Phu. It continues to this day.[32]

Significantly, the party center held up "professional heroes" for imitation for the first time in this final round of emulation. The engineer Tran Dai Nghia is a case in point. He was, as we've discovered previously, a graduate of France's Polytechnique, the equivalent of America's MIT. He had presided over the production of thousands of recoilless guns in the late 1940s and now ran the army's artillery section. The party canonized him as a hero in 1952, an exemplary man to be imitated by other bourgeois professionals. The communists accorded the same benediction to modern Vietnam's greatest surgeon, whom we met at the start of this chapter, Ton That Tung. Ho had already lionized Hoang Dao Thuy, the famous former colonial scoutmaster and communications specialist who had wired the Battle of Hanoi (and would do the same for the battlefield at Dien Bien Phu). By making "heroes" of these highly trained professionals, Ho and his closest disciples were determined to bring on board as many of the noncommunists as possible, especially those working in the sciences, as they went for broke on the battlefield in 1953–4. They also sought to homogenize everyone's thinking. And there was another message for the bourgeois in Ho's ranks—and only the naive could miss it—which was that the communists expected intellectuals and professionals to choose sides: theirs. "If you try to sit between two chairs," Ho Chi Minh warned them, "you will surely fall."[33]

In combination, patriotic emulation, the cult of personality, and rectification were powerful weapons in the Eurasian War Communism arsenal, as important as the military assistance and diplomatic recognition provided by Beijing and Moscow. What makes the Indochina War so complicated yet, at the same time, so utterly fascinating, is how the communists lined up behind Ho Chi Minh rolled nationalism, communism, and war into one vital force.[34]

The Communist Consolidation of the Security Services

In 1952, the communists also moved to take direct control of the state in sectors it deemed essential to the war effort. Nowhere was this more evident than in its appropriation of the security services. Since 1945, the communists had relied on them to control the state and keep the party at its helm, against often formidable odds. During the first half of the Indochina War, contrary to what the party would like us to believe today, the communists never exercised complete control over their own security services, and this troubled them greatly as the war entered a more intensive phase. In early 1950, Pham Van Dong warned his colleagues that the center had yet to construct a reliable and completely loyal service. Noncommunist civil servants dominated the middle and lower levels. The judicial branch remained largely independent. And there were many shortcomings on the ideological front, too. The training of security agents and judges, Pham Van Dong concluded, remained "outside of the direct leadership" of the party. As another communist official put it in May 1950, "From the day we took power until now, our party remains unable to recognize the importance of the security services. This is why this question leaves so much to be desired." [35]

This lack of control over such an important sector of the state would no longer do. The communists accelerated their efforts to command the security services from top to bottom. This included the introduction of more training courses to create a new class of communist cadres who would replace noncommunist ones. In 1952, the party also stepped up the rectification of police personnel. It also began recruiting more peasants into its security services as a way of "proletarianizing" its ranks. The peasants, the thinking went, would have a greater stake in the new communist regime and, as a result, would help push through the coming land reform.

To oversee the communization of the security services, the party center called in one of its top security experts, Tran Quoc Hoan. When war broke out in 1946, he had remained in Hanoi to operate the party's clandestine operations there. Espionage and counterespionage were his specialties. In 1951, he joined the Communist Party's most powerful branch, the Politburo. Two years later, Tran Quoc Hoan transferred out of the underground city in Hanoi to take over the DRV's security services. In his hands, policing was no longer a "simple question of practicing a specialty." It now became an ideological and political vocation operating under strict party control. Indefatigably, this man presided over the opening of training centers and a new academy to graduate a generation of police cadets of a communist kind. He ran it too. This academy alone produced over 1,000 new graduates in the early 1950s. Upon completion of their studies, cadets received important positions at the zonal, provincial, and, increasingly, the district levels. Seven became party regional members, seventeen provincial party ones, while forty-four worked at the district levels. Tran Quoc Hoan recruited more security agents from peasant and worker backgrounds, arguing that they would be the most loyal officers since the advancement of their class depended on the party's embrace of social revolution. In all, running from Zone IV to the Chinese border, Tran Quoc Hoan's officials revamped the security services for most of the DRV's sickle. The judicial branch received similar attention.[36]

The new police chief also presided over the improvement and expansion of these special administrative units called the *cap uy*. These were the party's vital chords, the strings, running horizontally between the party's administrative pillar and those in charge of the state, the army, and the mass hierarchies. They were meant to allow the party's people to influence and, hopefully, control these "parallel hierarchies." In practice, as we know, things had never worked out so neatly. For Tran Quoc Hoan, in 1952, this was no longer acceptable. If the party was to increase its control over the state at this crucial juncture in the conflict, then it had to make the *cap uy* system work. If that meant revamping them now, then so be it. And that is exactly what this powerful man did.[37]

If France's godfathers of counterinsurgency, Charles Lacheroy and David Galula, were looking for the brain behind the communists' *hiérarchies parallèles*, then they had to look no further than Tran Quoc Hoan. He penned "the manual" on *cap uy*, entitled *The Rules Guiding Interface Work* (*Le loi lam viec cua cap uy*). It was the equivalent of the one Ho had authored on the basics of party rectification, *Changing One's*

Working Ways (*Sua doi loi lam viec*). That French counterinsurgency "experts" like Lacheroy thought they found the origins of the parallel hierarchies in southern Vietnam in 1952, where (and when) the party and its hierarchies were at their weakest, demonstrates the extent to which he and his disciples preaching the gospel of French counterinsurgency theory misunderstood the nature of Vietnamese War Communism, its origins, evolution, institutions, methods, and the center in charge of it.[38]

Lastly, in 1952, the communists made the decision to detach the security services from under the control of the Ministry of the Interior by placing it in the hands of Tran Quoc Hoan and a new ministry. In 1953, as preparations for land reform and the assault on Dien Bien Phu began in earnest, he became modern Vietnam's first director of the Ministry of the Security Services.[39] Tran Quoc Hoan would remain in charge of this powerful lever of communist power for the next thirty years.[40]

11

Imperial Dust

HO CHI MINH'S ASSOCIATED STATES OF INDOCHINA

The Indochina War gave us the single-party state that rules Vietnam today, the subject of this book. It also gave us two sister states, one for Laos, the other Cambodia. This officially began in 1950, when Ho Chi Minh presided over the creation of "resistance governments" for his revolutionary partners in Laos and Cambodia. The Vietnamese did not do this in a political vacuum, though: by late 1949, the French had established their "Associated States of Indochina," consisting of Bao Dai's Vietnam, Norodom Sihanouk's Cambodia, and Sisavang Vong's Laos. As a sympathetic American communist visiting the Viet Bac in 1953 noted, the Vietnamese president's "alliance" with the Pathet Lao and Khmer Issarak was in "answer" to what the French were doing with their own associated states.[1] Indeed it was. In fact, by this time, two parallel sets of associated states had emerged from the Indochina War, one led by the "French colonialists" and the other marshaled by the "Vietnamese communists."

What Ho Chi Minh and his entourage did in Laos and Cambodia, the subject of this chapter, was not a sideshow in the larger story of the wartime making of the Democratic Republic of Vietnam. Vietnamese War Communism was a larger Indochinese project too. And that Vietnamese communists insisted on reconfiguring all of French Indochina along these lines, not just Vietnam, tells us something profound about them, their statecraft, and the states which rule Laos and Cambodia to this day. The problem is that the Vietnamese communist reconfiguration of colonial Indochina is a taboo subject in Hanoi, Vientiane, Phnom Penh, Beijing, and even Moscow. It causes painful flashbacks to the Third Indochina War and the murderous Khmer Rouge regime, whose leader, Pol Pot, almost brought down the entire Indochinese communist house on its Vietnamese communist makers. Since then, official historians, in Hanoi in particular, have tended to steer clear of "Indochina" and the federalism that held it together.

This will no longer do. While I am aware of the sensitivity of this subject, we can do better seventy years after the First Indochina War ended, and an historical approach can help us do that. This requires four things, though. First of all, it means resisting the temptation to assume that because something "bad" occurred in the late 1970s, it was already "in the making" in the early 1950s. It was never so simple. Next, it also means avoiding the tendency to reach for worn-out clichés to explain complicated things. The Vietnamese and Chinese, for example, are no more destined to be "eternal" enemies than the French and Germans are. Additionally, instead of forcing the past to fit the present, an historical approach allows us to return, if only briefly, to earlier periods of time to think about other forces that may have led the Vietnamese communists to play such a predominant role in the making of modern Laos and Cambodia. Finally, the thoughtful use of historical comparisons can help us keep things in perspective. After all, if the Vietnamese were the driving force in the making of modern-day Laos and Cambodia during the Indochina War, the Chinese were deeply involved in crafting the communist state that rules Vietnam today.

Vietnam's Imperial Pasts

There were historical precedents for Ho Chi Minh's effort to reconfigure French colonial Indochina along federal lines in the mid-twentieth century.[2] In 1922, for example, the Bolsheviks established a union of Soviet republics to administer the sprawling Russian empire they had taken over from their czarist predecessors. It was formally called the

Union of Soviet Socialist Republics. Neither Ukraine nor Georgia regained its independence from the crumbled Russian empire: each became instead associated states within this "new" Soviet federation with the Communist Party in charge. Chinese communists were no strangers to this process of imperial recuperation either. Shortly after taking power in 1949, Mao finally achieved what his noncommunist opponents had not: he stitched back together the massive Qing empire that had imploded on them all in 1911. Chinese communists maintained and ruled over former Qing protectorates in Tibet, (inner) Mongolia, and Xinjiang as "autonomous regions." For Vietnamese communists, the task was particularly daunting: not only did they have to contend with what the French had built in Indochina since the mid-nineteenth century, but they also had to deal with their own imperial dust.

Vietnam: An Imperial Creation

Like so many empires in world history, Vietnam started off in a small core area and then grew over time. The cradle of Vietnamese civilization is located in the Red River Delta, where an independent territorial state known as Co Loa emerged around the third century BCE, near today's Hanoi. Although it was a remarkably vibrant kingdom, its independence was short-lived. The Han dynasty located to the north (in what we now call China) was problematic. Rulers there had been busy building an empire on a par with what the Romans were doing in the Mediterranean. From the second century BCE, the Han Chinese seized and transformed Red River Vietnam into their southernmost province. They called it Jiaozhi. For a millennium, Jiaozhi Vietnam was part of China. To be sure, there was colonial repression in that place and resistance to it as well. There were also important exchanges. Confucianism, Chinese statecraft, and (Mahayana) Buddhism entered northern Vietnam through this imperial conduit. So did the use of chopsticks and a Vietnamese writing system based on Han ideograms. The weakening of the Chinese empire under the late Tang dynasty at the start of the tenth century saw the Vietnamese claw back their independence. Although they lost it again in the early fifteenth century when the Ming dynasty rebuilt a massive empire, this second subjugation did not last long. In 1427, the Vietnamese exited China for good, though many independent Vietnamese emperors were quite happy still to operate within its civilizational orbit.[3]

Decolonization, however, does not mean that the newly independent states will not remake themselves in imperial form. Like the Americans who left the British empire in the late eighteenth century only to create their own empire stretching across the continent and further, the Vietnamese began expanding their Red River Vietnam southwards. To this end, they often used modern Chinese weapons, statecraft, and colonial ideology of a "superior" Confucian kind (Vietnamese revolutionaries were to cast communism in uncannily similar terms when pitching it to the Laotians, Cambodians, and others in the mid-twentieth century). As their armies, administrators, and settlers moved out of the Red River basin, the Vietnamese alternated between "direct" and "indirect" forms of rule over distant, multiethnic peoples, they tested cultural assimilation, and developed their own "civilizing mission" to justify it all. By heading south, the Vietnamese vanquished the Cham people, who ruled much of today's central Vietnam, subjugated the Khmers in the lower Mekong Delta, and began to control a host of non-Vietnamese peoples living in the surrounding highlands. Whether by force, persuasion, or settlement, a Vietnamese colonial state expanded slowly but surely down the coast to the point of Ca Mau in the Gulf of Thailand. This is how modern Vietnam gradually acquired its recognizable S-like shape.

Imperial Vietnam had other forms too. At the start of the nineteenth century, after a long civil war, the leaders of the Nguyen dynasty unified Vietnam, established their capital in Hue, then pushed Vietnam's territorial expansion in more westerly directions. More of this took place during the 1830s, when an expansionist-minded emperor, Minh Mang, sent his army into the neighboring kingdom of Cambodia and incorporated it into what he called the "Greater South," the Empire of Dai Nam. The Vietnamese emperor sent Confucian-trained governors and civil servants to administer Cambodia. The court taxed Cambodians, put many of them to work building roads and canals, and encouraged both

Vietnamese and Chinese settlers to go further west. The Nguyen dynasty also expanded its territorial control into today's eastern Laos and further into the highland areas of northern and central Vietnam. By the mid-nineteenth century, Minh Mang's Dai Nam had already started to look a lot like French Indochina. (See Map 2.)

From One Empire to Another: French Indochina

What brought the French to the waters lying off Vietnam's coast was the desire, common to many before them, to get a slice of the Chinese market. The British had taken Hong Kong in 1842. In Vietnam, the French saw the chance to have something similar. Starting in the late 1850s, they attacked and turned southern Vietnam into a colony, Cochinchina, and followed it up by establishing a protectorate over Cambodia in order to control the Mekong River. They then moved northwards, to seize the rest of Vietnam by force by 1885. In 1887, the French created the Indochinese Union and, over the next two decades, filled it out by adding Laotian and more Cambodian territories. Based in Hanoi, a governor-general operated French Indochina as a federation of colonies, protectorates, and military territories. (See Map 3.)

There was continuity between the Vietnamese and French empires. For example, in order to counter Thai claims to Laotian and Cambodian territories, the French justified their colonial case by invoking nineteenth-century Nguyen imperial treaties and archives. They also did their best to realign preexisting Vietnamese imperial ambitions with theirs. No sooner had the French defeated their adversaries in 1885 than they promised them that they could become the privileged partners in France's Indochinese empire. As one of the main colonial architects of Indochina put it in 1885: "The day that this race understands that its historical ambitions can, thanks to us, come to fruition in ways that it never before imagined; when it sees that our aid allows him to take vengeance for the humiliations and defeats that he has never forgiven his neighbors; when he feels definitely superior to them and sees his domination expand with ours, only then will we be able to consider that the future of French Indochina is truly assured."[4]

Imperial intermeshing was particularly evident at the administrative level. Rather than stopping Vietnamese expansion westwards, the French simply turned to their junior partners to help them run the colonial bureaucracy in western Indochina. They had effectively divided Cambodia and Laos into two administrative halves, the first being at the federal level, in which the Vietnamese could now move unhindered. That federal bureaucracy welcomed the Vietnamese into its ranks to help with such colonial-wide matters as customs, immigration, policing, and trade. Without enough metropolitan administrators of their own available, the French trained thousands of Vietnamese bureaucrats to serve as postmen, telegraph operators, office secretaries, customs officers, and policemen in Laos and Cambodia. The French housed them, paid them, and covered their travel expenses between Hanoi and Vientiane and Saigon and Phnom Penh. The federal structure of the colonial state effectively removed preexisting royalist borders, all the while blocking the French "protected kings" from erecting national ones in their place. The second half of the administration maintained the preexisting Cambodian and Laotian monarchies in the form of protectorates, the ranks of which were largely closed to Vietnamese applicants.

Thanks to federalism, the number of Vietnamese living and working in western Indochina increased notably. In Cambodia, new roads linking it to Cochinchina saw the Vietnamese population grow there from around 80,000 in 1911 to over 140,000 in 1921. Of the sixteen Indochinese bureaucrats working in the town hall of Phnom Penh in 1913, fourteen were Vietnamese and two Cambodian. For similar reasons, the number of Vietnamese bureaucrats in Laos increased too. By the early 1930s, the Vietnamese occupied 54 percent of the posts offered at the Indochinese level of the administration. By 1937, this immigration was such that there were over 10,000 Vietnamese living in Vientiane, compared to only 9,000 Laotians. Faced with population pressures in northern and central Vietnam, colonial authorities transported Vietnamese laborers to southern Indochina to work on rubber plantations. In the 1920s, new roads allowed for the easier circulation of Vietnamese workers to toil in Laotian mines. By the eve of the Second World War, the Vietnamese dominated the ranks of the federal bureaucracy and the urban working class in Laos and Cambodia, even though they constituted only a small fraction of the total population of these two lands.[5]

The mechanisms of the Indochinese colonial federation also created tensions. For example, many Laotian and Cambodian elites (of an increasingly nationalist kind) resented how the French had allowed the Vietnamese to increase their numbers and influence within their countries. Several spoke disparagingly of the Indochinese federation as a trompe l'oeil, as Laotian Prince Phetsarath Ratanavongsa memorably put it in 1931, for a Vietnamese takeover of Laos. A few years later, a host of Cambodian nationalists attacked colonial federalism for similar reasons. Some would even ask the colonizer to sever Cambodia from Indochina and administer it as a separate colonial territory. Although the French knew that they had a problem on their hands by the 1930s, they refused to modify the shape of their Indochinese state. This was in contrast to the British, who, in 1937, under intense Burmese nationalist pressure to stop the Indians from dominating federal positions in places like Rangoon, detached the province of Burma from British India. The French should have listened to these dissonant nationalist voices coming from interwar Laos and Cambodia. Instead, they carried on, determined to run Indochina in their own way, convinced of the righteousness of their Indochinese cause, confident that things would work out for the better in the end. In fact, Vietnamese communists would come to think in remarkably similar terms.[6]

The Communist Reconfiguration of Colonial Indochina

Ho Chi Minh and the Making of Early Indochinese Communism

Leading the Indochinese communist charge was none other than Ho Chi Minh. The founder of the Vietnamese Communist Party was deeply involved in bringing communism to the whole of Southeast Asia. This extraordinary communist missionary did so in collaboration with his Chinese counterparts and Comintern agents. As we know, communism had first emerged along Eurasia's eastern edge, via port cities like Shanghai. From there, it moved southwards along a maritime arc running to Guangzhou, Hong Kong, Bangkok, and Singapore. The Comintern, created in 1919 to help communists across the globe get their parties off the ground, assisted the Chinese in establishing the Chinese Communist Party in Shanghai in 1921. In southern China, the Soviets had actually supported early efforts led by *non*communist patriots, such as Sun Yat-sen and Chiang Kai-shek, to start stitching the pieces of the shattered Qing empire back together in the form of a nation-state. The Soviets asked their communist allies in China to help, and they did through the creation of a united front. Collaboration was strongest in areas in and around the southern port city of Guangzhou, where Ho Chi Minh arrived from Moscow in 1924. He immediately went to work, enlisting young patriots from nearby Vietnam. He enrolled dozens of them in Chinese political and military academies and, together, they built up a revolutionary party. Ho also traveled to the far side of Indochina in the 1920s to recruit from Vietnamese populations living in northeastern Thai towns like Udon Thani and Nakhon Phanom.

United action in southern China came to a sudden halt in 1927, when Chiang Kai-shek turned on his communist partners and, in so doing, set off a civil war that would end in his defeat two decades later. While the outbreak of hostilities scattered Chinese and Vietnamese communists across Southeast Asia and China, the Comintern carried on with its operations clandestinely and relied on its Chinese and Vietnamese allies to help them build communist parties further down the line. Ho Chi Minh answered the call by joining the Comintern's Far Eastern Bureau. A revolutionary globetrotter like few others, Ho was an excellent choice. In addition to his French, English, and Russian, he had also mastered Chinese and knew some Thai. He had an impressive list of contacts in port cities across southern China and Southeast Asia. In a report to his superiors, Ho had suggested that Vietnamese and Chinese communists could organize their revolutionary work more effectively by relying on their respective sailors serving on ships moving between Shanghai and Singapore. Such collaboration shortly paid off. By early 1930, backed by the Chinese and the Comintern, Ho had created the

Vietnamese Communist Party in Hong Kong. He and others in the Far Eastern Bureau then traveled to Singapore, where they established the Malaya Communist Party and the Siamese (Thai) Communist Party in Bangkok. Today, visitors who stroll along the river in downtown Singapore will discover a statue of Ho Chi Minh erected in 2011 as a testament to friendly relations between Singapore and Vietnam. What is missing from the commemorative plaque, though, is any mention of communism, which was why the Comintern had sent Ho there in the first place.[7]

Ho was also among the first to bring communism to western Indochina. He did so by bending this revolutionary arc running through Bangkok to bases he had already begun to establish among the thousands of Vietnamese living in northeast Thailand. In turn, later on, Ho and his trusted lieutenants coming from this Asian revolutionary network used these places as footholds to build organizations among the Vietnamese living and working nearby in Laotian cities and mines. Ho is said to have crossed into Laos briefly, in 1930, to create the first communist cell there. If this is true, it demonstrates nicely how far this man of indomitable revolutionary spirit went to spread the communist gospel in Asia. His disciples who remained in northeast Thailand continued his work along both sides of the Mekong River throughout the Indochina War.

The problem was that the arc the Comintern was pushing into Southeast Asia relied disproportionately on Chinese and Vietnamese revolutionaries who, naturally, focused on the working classes they knew best in these areas—theirs. The colonial patterns of labor migration only reinforced this: just as the French had brought in thousands of Vietnamese to work in their offices, mines, and plantations in western Indochina, the British had also employed hundreds of thousands of Chinese emigrants to do similar things in colonial Malaya, Singapore, and Burma. The Comintern reinforced the Sino-Vietnamese tack in maritime communism further by directing its agents in the Far Eastern Bureau to rely on the working class. As a result, the Malaya Communist Party recruited heavily from the large Chinese working class in the British Straits while the Vietnamese communists relied disproportionately on their compatriots working in urban centers in Laos, Cambodia, and northeast Thailand. Even in Singapore, the man who served as the general secretary of the Malayan Communist Party until 1947, Lai Tek, was a Vietnamese from Saigon. We can be sure that Ho knew him and might well have recruited him for that job.[8]

This created a historical paradox at the core of Vietnamese communism, one that is crucial to understanding Vietnamese statecraft in Laos and Cambodia during the Indochina War. On the one hand, Ho and his associates accepted Comintern instructions in 1930 requiring them to change the name of their party from the "Vietnamese" to the "Indochinese Communist Party." They agreed that the territorial confines of their communism had to reflect the larger mission of overthrowing the French colonial state in all of Indochina. On the other hand, the urban trajectory of Vietnamese communism led them to rely disproportionately on Vietnamese living and working in Laotian, Cambodian, and northeastern Thai towns. It is not that the Laotians and Cambodians were "less revolutionary" or "less anticolonialist." They were simply not plugged into this Sino-Vietnamese communist grid running through East and Southeast Asia. Nor were they part of these colonial patterns of labor migration that had generated a continental Southeast Asian working class dominated by Vietnamese and Chinese workers.

Holding Indochina Together: Federalism of a Communist Kind

Vietnamese communists were by no means opposed to the idea of working with non-Vietnamese. In northern Vietnam, after the French crackdown on anticolonialists inside Vietnam in the early 1930s, Vietnamese radicals operated from remote areas along the Sino-Vietnamese border. This was also true during the Second World War, when Ho slipped into areas of northern Vietnam along the Chinese border where he created the Viet Minh nationalist front near Cao Bang. In these borderlands, Vietnamese communists had no choice but to work with a mosaic of ethnically diverse peoples who had been residing there for centuries. Ho needed their help to build bases, procure food and drinkable water, recruit soldiers, and navigate unfamiliar areas that had never really come under colonial control, neither French or Vietnamese. As an ethnic Nung and Tai, respectively, Chu Van Tan and Le Quang Ba helped Vo Nguyen Giap create the country's nascent army in the early 1940s and became generals in the Vietnamese armed forces during the Indochinese conflict. Le Quang Ba led the 316th division into the battle of Dien Bien Phu. Hoang Dinh Giong, an ethnic Tai, discovered Vietnamese radicalism in Hanoi (where he had studied during the 1920s), before joining Ho Chi Minh and others in southern China. His ascension was such that he attended the party's First Congress in Macau in 1935. He perished during an important mission for the party to Cambodia in 1947.

Things were different in western Indochina. Firstly, colonial surveillance before 1945 was stronger in Laos and Cambodia than it was along the rugged, northern frontier. Secondly, pagoda schools and the Buddhist temples dotting the countryside in western Indochina tended to move young Laotian and Cambodian novices in religious ways leading to Phnom Penh and Luang Prabang rather than Saigon and Hanoi. From there, Buddhist networks moved the most promising pupils on to monasteries in northeast Thailand and Bangkok rather than into the classrooms of the Huangpu Military Academy in Guangzhou. Thirdly, several future Cambodian nationalists had already emerged from areas in southern Vietnam's Mekong Delta, where Khmers still lived in large numbers. Many Cambodians still refer to these "lower areas" colonized by the Vietnamese until as late as the early nineteenth century as the Khmer Krom lands. The recovery of these "lost territories" often came up in Cambodian nationalist minds, as did the problem of French Indochina. The country's first nationalist, Son Ngoc Thanh, published a newspaper, *Nagara Vatta* (*Angkor Wat*), in which he bemoaned the Vietnamese domination of the federal bureaucracy in Cambodia. Last of all, unlike in the northern borderlands, it was always easier for Vietnamese communists to work among the large Vietnamese diaspora population in towns in western Indochina and northeast Thailand. It was only when the Indochina War broke out in 1945 that our Vietnamese communists realized that they had a major structural problem on their hands: they had few Laotian or Cambodian counterparts with whom they could build a revolutionary state in the Cambodian countryside or put in charge of a PAVN division in Laos.[9]

This did not prevent the Vietnamese communists from moving forward with their plans to recuperate the French colonial state and reconfigure it on their terms. To do so, they quickly realized that they would need federalism. As French colonial subjects, the Vietnamese knew how this "ism" worked. They could also look to what the Bolsheviks had done with it in creating the Union of Socialist Soviet Republics. Not only had Lenin held the czarist empire together in a revolutionary form, but he and his successors had also found a way through federalism, or so it seemed, to accommodate the reality of preexisting states like the Ukraine (1922) and Kazakhstan (1936). The Vietnamese were confident that they could do something like that with Laos and Cambodia too. Having resided in the Soviet Union for long periods of time during the interwar period, Ho Chi Minh and others knew the Soviet model. During the Communist Party's First Congress, held in Macau in 1935, the Vietnamese agreed that the territorial endpoint in their party's evolution would be the creation of an independent state called the "Union of the Soviet Indochinese Republics (Lien Bang Cong Hoa Xo-Viet Dong Duong)." In 1939, another party document explained that the postcolonial state would be called the "Federal Government of the Democratic Republic of Indochina (Chinh Phu Lien Bang Cong Hoa Dan Chu Dong Duong)."[10]

Although the question remained hypothetical during the 1930s, the outbreak of the Second World War forced revolutionary minds to think seriously about what they would do if their party actually came to power. What kind of state would it run? In the early years of the war, the Vietnamese tried to have it both ways. For example, when Ho Chi Minh returned to Vietnam in 1941 and presided over the creation of the "Vietnamese Independence League" or the "Viet Minh," it was, in fact, part of a larger communist-run front known as the "Indochinese Independence League (Dong Duong Doc Lap Dong Minh)." Similar nationalist fronts for Laos and Cambodia joined alongside the Viet Minh within this alliance. However, at that same meeting in 1941, the leadership apparently decided not to declare the formation of a new socialist, Soviet Indochinese republic. They put the idea on hold in favor of creating separate republics along nationalist lines, although without abandon-

ing the possibility of associating them in the form of a union of democratic republics for Vietnam, Laos, and Cambodia in the future. For the
time being, Ho focused on building up the Viet Minh, at the same time
instructing cadres elsewhere to be ready to move when the time came
in Laos and Cambodia.[11]

It did—in March 1945, when the Japanese overthrew the French in
Indochina. The collapse of French Indochina (and the realization that
the Japanese empire itself would not last much longer) forced the Vietnamese to choose. In one way, they did, when Ho declared the country's
new, independent existence as the Democratic Republic of Vietnam on
2 September 1945. In another way, they did not. In mid-1945, Truong
Chinh was still writing about an Indochinese federation, and he was not
alone in thinking that way. In fact, the party's historic orders authorizing
cadres to take power in mid-August 1945 applied not only to Vietnam,
but also to the whole of Indochina. This explains why, when the Japanese capitulated on 15 August, Vietnamese communists in Laos tried to
seize power there too. To do this, they relied on the patriotic fervor and
participation of the large Vietnamese diaspora in Laotian cities. Hundreds of young Vietnamese in Laos joined patriotic militias in those
heady days. Tran Duc Vinh, a longtime communist from northeast
Thailand, kept the center apprised of what was happening along the
Mekong, thanks to the telegraphs and telephones Vietnamese civil servants continued to operate.[12]

The leading Laotian nationalist at the time, Prince Phetsarath, could
not believe his eyes. He had been running Laos with the Japanese since
the latter had ousted the French in March 1945. With the Japanese now
on their way out, he counted on remaining in power at the head of a
fully independent Laos, whether the French liked it or not. But now the
Vietnamese seemed to be taking over. On 24 August, and again on 17
September 1945, the prince ordered them to stand down. He pleaded
with defeated Japanese authorities not to turn over administrative control to Vietnamese civil servants and even implored them to stop what
was happening by force if need be. The prince had reason to worry.
Vietnamese bureaucrats in Laos had, in fact, appropriated the administration in many places which lay along the Vietnamese border and had

even created a national salvation association in the royal capital of Luang Prabang. While we will never know exactly what these Vietnamese in Laos were thinking at the time, it is possible that, for them, long active in the federal level of the colonial administration, there wasn't anything strange about what they were doing. Surely Indochina was as much of a reality for the Laotians as it was for them?[13]

Phetsarath and other Laotian nationalists saw things very differently and let that be known. Sometime in early to mid-September, Vietnamese communists reined in their "August Revolution in Laos," as one Vietnamese historian disingenuously described it in 1975. While the exact reasons for this decision remain unclear, one of them must have been the need to remain on good terms with Phetsarath and his allies. Ho and his party simply could not afford to alienate this influential nationalist prince and risk sending him and others into the arms of the French. Phetsarath shared their opposition to the restoration of French colonial rule, and he could mobilize support among the Laotians in ways the Vietnamese could not. As a result, the communists backpedaled as fast as they could. Tran Duc Vinh even ordered Vietnamese civil servants to transfer their own positions to Laotians whenever possible in order to reassure the Laotians that the Vietnamese communists were not trying to take over—when in fact they had been.[14]

But there was still a problem, a "contradiction in terms," as a sympathetic American officer in Hanoi put it in September 1945. What was the endpoint in communist statecraft? Ho Chi Minh had just declared the independence of the Democratic Republic of Vietnam, and, although he had not said a word about his Indochinese ambitions, the Communist Party still carried that name. When the American queried Truong Chinh and others in his entourage as to whether the goal was communist Vietnam or Indochina, the party leaders hemmed and hawed, replying vaguely that in "the context of the struggle for Vietnamese independence the three nation-states' complex was interwoven in the French concept of the French Indochina 'federation.'" The terms were compatible, they said, "since the three nation states, under French rule, had developed a commonality of geographical, political, and economic interests."[15]

Despite this official doublespeak (which can be heard in Hanoi to this day), the Vietnamese had *not* abandoned their plans to reconfigure French Indochina as a communist federation. They had simply put the party's policy on hold in order to build anticolonial alliances. In private, however, the communists remained fully committed to recuperating all of French Indochina. Two years later, in August 1948, the party's general secretary, Truong Chinh, explained in detail the nature and inner workings of the coming "Indochinese revolution." He stated clearly that the end goal in terms of statecraft remained "to bring about the establishment of the 'Federation of the People's Democratic Republic of Indochina' (lam cho Dong Duong thanh mot Lien Bang Cong Hoa Dan Chu Nhan Dan)." He followed this up with: "The Indochinese federation would consist of three states: Vietnam, Laos, and Cambodia." In 2001, Vietnamese communist historians published Truong Chinh's 1948 address in their official collection of party documents. However, they censored the entire section on the Indochinese federation with a single ellipsis.[16]

Thailand and the Rise of the Asia Hands in Laos and Cambodia

From One Lao Issara to Another

Believing fervently in something like an Indochinese communist revolution does not mean that one cannot be pragmatic in going about it.[17] Ho and Truong Chinh understood that if they were going to carry on their work in Indochina after 1945, then they had to be flexible. They were in a position of weakness in late 1945 in Laos and Cambodia. As in Vietnam, they had to proceed carefully. This meant stressing anticolonialism and crafting the widest possible nationalist coalitions with Laotians and Cambodians, regardless of class or ethnicity. Phetsarath also knew that he had to swallow his nationalist pride and work with the Vietnamese to hold off their common enemy, the French. The prince had no army, no militias, and no police force. The French were on their way back, and he was not on their short list to run Laos. Sisavang Vong, the Laotian king based in Luang Prabang, was.

The Allied occupation of Indochina provided anticolonialists in Laos above the 16th parallel with a breathing space. There, the Republic of China's troops had arrived to accept the Japanese surrender in major cities like Thakhek, Vientiane, and Luang Prabang. As in areas above that line in Vietnam, the Chinese refused to let the French return to most of Laos right away, knowing that it would trigger the type of violence they spurned. As a result, until March 1946, when Chiang Kai-shek began pulling his troops out of upper Indochina, the Vietnamese did everything they could to strengthen their ties with Laotian anticolonialists. To do this, the Vietnamese targeted Laotian royalists first and foremost, and did so for several reasons. For one thing, they had few Laotian communist allies for the historical reasons discussed above. For another, Ho realized that his own Asia hands positioned along the Mekong would never be able to match the royals when it came to mobilizing the Laotian "masses." No matter how well they spoke Lao (and they did), his cadres had no real ties to the Laotian countryside where the overwhelming majority of the peasant Laotians lived (the working class was, in fact, largely based in the cities and Vietnamese). Moreover, their fervent communist faith was such that few had joined Buddhist religious networks in western Indochina or Thailand which might have allowed them to create contacts and durable alliances. Ultimately, Ho realized that Buddhist royals could help him forge the anticolonialist coalition he needed throughout Indochina. In Vietnam, lest we forget, Ho was already doing his best to win over the emperor, and it seemed to be working. In the imperial capital of Hue, Bao Dai had just abdicated and then accepted the invitation of the new Vietnamese president, Ho Chi Minh, to join the national government as special adviser.

Less well-known is the fact that travelling in the same car with Bao Dai on his journey from Hue to Hanoi was another member of a royal family, not the Vietnamese one, but the Laotian one. His name was Prince Souphanouvong, and he was a half-brother to Phetsarath. If Ho saw in Souphanouvong another potential royal through whom he could build an Indochinese coalition, the prince saw the opportunity to position himself at the top of Laotian politics through an alliance with Ho. Unlike Phetsarath, Souphanouvong was familiar with Vietnam. He had been one of the rare Laotians to have entered the federal level of the Indochinese colonial bureaucracy during the interwar years and to go east to work in Vietnam (just as so many Vietnamese had gone west to push pencils in Laos and Cambodia). Educated in an elite French high school in Hanoi and then in a top-notch engineering school in Paris, Souphanouvong returned to Indochina in the 1930s to work as an engineer in Vinh and Nha Trang. There, he met his Vietnamese wife and seems to have learned to speak Vietnamese well. Former Vietnamese classmates and work colleagues had forwarded his name to President Ho, who, in his turn, had invited him to Hanoi. Upon arriving in the Vietnamese capital in early September 1945, Bao Dai and Souphanouvong met with Ho and Vo Nguyen Giap. The Laotian prince informed an American officer in Hanoi that he was engaged in talks with the Vietnamese president to create a Vietnamese-Laotian alliance against the return of the French.[18]

Meanwhile, in Laos, Ho's officials bent over backwards to secure Prince Phetsarath's support. As happy as Ho was to have Souphanouvong on board, he knew that Phetsarath was the leading Laotian nationalist at the time and better placed in the royal family too. He had served as the viceroy of Laos before 1945, traveled the countryside from one end to the other, and was well known among the population. Ho's delegates reassured the older of the two princes that despite what had happened in Laos in late August and early September, they wanted what he wanted for Laos: national independence. The Vietnamese volunteered their militias and provided advisers to help train and outfit a Laotian armed force. Prince Phetsarath accepted. The Vietnamese even sent a telegram to the King of Laos, holed up in Luang Prabang at that point, seeking his support. Although they apparently received no reply, what Ho was doing was plain for all to see: if the Vietnamese president could win over members of Indochina's royal family, it would go far to legitimizing the Indochinese anticolonial cause and provide the Vietnamese with a powerful political instrument for mobilizing popular support in Laos and, eventually, for realizing their wider objectives in all of Indochina.[19]

The French were no fools, certainly not a chain-smoking man named Léon Pignon. A colonial administrator since the 1930s, he now served as the political advisor to the high commissioner after the Second World War. With a go-ahead from his boss, Pignon joined hands with veteran administrators he knew to build a colonial federation around Indochina's monarchs and the royalist bureaucracies undergirding them. Ho Chi Minh thus had competition for these royals from the start. The former emperor of Vietnam, Bao Dai, as we know, would leave the president's ranks in early 1946 to go into exile in southern China. From there, he opened talks with Pignon's colonial operatives and grudgingly returned to Vietnam as the head of the Associated State of Vietnam in 1949. King Sisavang Vong had already informed French agents that he would welcome the former colonizers back once the Chinese had left. The survival of his crown depended on it, and Pignon knew it.[20] (See Plate 23.)

Phetsarath was of a different mind. His antipathy for King Sisavang Vong ran deep. He had proudly proclaimed in the 1930s that it was he "who ran the show." Following the Japanese overthrow of the French in March 1945, Phetsarath wanted to lead an independent Laos on his terms. He was willing to collaborate with the Vietnamese to attain that goal; but once the French were gone, *he* would run Laos. That was enough for Ho for now. Although the Vietnamese placed most of their chips on Souphanouvong, they did their utmost to keep in Phetsarath's good graces too. When the "Provisional Government of Independent Laos" came to life in October 1945 with Phetsarath as its head of state and Souphanouvong as its minister of defense, the Vietnamese supported it enthusiastically. This included direct financial aid, the training of a "liberation army" under Souphanouvong's command, and the dispatch of advisers to help this first Laotian government, referred to widely as the Lao Issara, to stay afloat.[21]

Within just a few months, the French put this early Laotian-Vietnamese collaboration to the test. Having negotiated the withdrawal of Chinese troops from northern Indochina in late February, the high commissioner in Saigon immediately turned his attention to reconquering Laos by force. On 10 March, French troops seized Savannakhet as Vietnamese militias prepared to take a stand in Thakhek and Vientiane, the Lao Issara's only real strongholds. On 21 March 1946, the Expeditionary Corps attacked Thakhek by land and air, forcing much of the urban population to flee across the Mekong to Thailand in small boats and pirogues. Troops then assailed Vientiane. In all, some 40,000 mainly Vietnamese civilians fled to northeast Thailand, but not before colonial planes had strafed combatants and civilians crossing the river. Survivors claimed that bodies floated down the Mekong for days. Also fleeing into Thailand was the Lao Issara government, including Phetsarath and Souphanou-vong. By May, the French had retaken all of Laos, including the royal capital of Luang Prabang, and renewed their close cooperation with King Sisavang Vong, who signed a modus vivendi agreement returning Laos to the Indochinese federation and secured his throne in doing so.[22]

Luckily for the Vietnamese and the Lao Issara, Thai leaders were largely sympathetic to their cause. Thai officials resented French pressure on them to return territories they had seized in western Laos and Cambodia during the Second World War. The French wanted them back as they rebuilt their Indochinese empire. Sympathetic to Ho Chi Minh's anticolonialist struggle, Bangkok allowed the Vietnamese president's people to remain in the northeast and issued orders to local officials to help the refugees living in camps there (they were the first of many more "Indochinese refugees" to seek refuge in Thailand during thirty years of war). As a result, Vietnamese communists operated freely in Thailand as long as they remained focused on the "French colonialists" and not the "Thai feudalists." They did. The Vietnamese spent their time recruiting young men and women from the diaspora to serve in Vietnam, Laos, and Cambodia.

To put pressure on the French politically, the Thais supported the Lao Issara government, many of whose leaders had family ties to leaders in Thailand. This was particularly true of Prince Phetsarath, who could meet with Thai leaders easily. With its commanders now operating in Thailand, the Lao Issara government no longer owed as much to the Vietnamese as it had before the French reconquest of Laos. Although Souphanouvong continued to advocate close collaboration with the Vietnamese, most others in the Lao Issara did not. Phetsarath remained wary of Vietnamese intentions. He cultivated relations with the Thais, met with the Americans in Bangkok, and talked to the French when it suited him. Unlike Souphanouvong, Phetsarath kept any Vietnamese minders at a safe distance. Meanwhile, as exile dragged on, some in the Lao Issara grew tired and returned home.

Léon Pignon did his best to turn this trickle into a stream, offering amnesty and jobs to those who returned. The continued existence of the Lao Issara in Thailand was a thorn in his political side. It undermined the legitimacy of the royalist state he was cultivating in Laos. The French had just allowed the ruler of Luang Prabang to become the king of all of Laos. In exchange, the French expected Sisavang Vong to forget the past and welcome the Lao Issara's leaders back on the condition that they dissolved their pesky government-in-exile in Thailand. Upon becoming high commissioner of Indochina in 1948, Pignon crafted the Associated States of Indochina around monarchies in Laos (Sisavang Vong), Cambodia (Sihanouk), and Vietnam (Bao Dai). In July 1949, he informed his ambassador in Bangkok that:

> I accord great importance to ending this unfortunate dissidence. In addition to the fact that the return of the Laotian emigrants would constitute a success for our overall policy in Indochina and for our diplomacy, it would also reinforce the interior position of this Laos associated with France and this country could then become a useful source of stability in a time of dangerous instability. This [the end of the Lao Issara] would thus be a good thing in the spectrum of the Indochinese and international opinion as well as a political and moral victory.[23]

On 25 October 1949, Pignon scored a major success over his communist competitors when the majority of the Lao Issara's members in Thailand formally dissolved their government and returned to Laos. There were two notable exceptions though: Souphanouvong and Phetsarath. The latter wagered that his nationalist prestige and Thai connections would allow him to return to Laos at the war's end at the head of an independent Laos. Souphanouvong bet on the Vietnamese to do the exact same thing for him. In a letter to Ho Chi Minh in mid-1948, he assured the Vietnamese president that only "the frank and loyal collaboration between the Laotian and Vietnamese resistance forces would

ensure their definitive victory over the French colonialist and imperialists, the common enemy of the Indochinese peoples."[24] This was exactly
what Ho Chi Minh wanted to hear.

Communist Opposition to Colonial Association
in Laos and Cambodia

Working from their bases in Thailand, Ho Chi Minh's Asia specialists
watched all of this unfold and duly reported it back to the party center.
They knew what Léon Pignon was doing with his colonial princes and
kings and their Associated States. And they did not wait until things fell
apart in 1949 before beginning to build splinter Laotian and Cambodian
groups supporting independence. In fact, in early 1948, the party center
instructed its cadres to forge parties and armed forces for Laos and
Cambodia, allied with, and also, if possible, controlled by the Vietnamese communists. The party assigned this task to Vo Nguyen Giap. The
general realized that he had to strengthen his positions in Laos and
Cambodia to prevent the French from attacking the Democratic Republic of Vietnam from its western side; he had to have Laotian and Cambodian allies with whom he could work throughout Indochina. In 1948,
the Vietnamese began dividing Laos and Cambodia into political and
military zones as they had done a few years earlier for Vietnam. They
paired each zone in western Indochina to its counterpart in the Democratic Republic of Vietnam. Roughly speaking, the Viet Bac Zone was
in charge of northern Laos, Zone IV of central Laos, and Zone V of
lower Laos. Zone IX in the far south was paired with Cambodia in collaboration with Zone V.[25] (See Map 12.)

   To ensure careful party control over this early expansion of Vietnamese communism into Laos and Cambodia, Ho and his entourage established powerful "party affairs committees" (*ban can su*) in western Indochina, one for Laos and one for Cambodia. Vietnamese cadres in
these special administrative bodies would carry out the center's military,
political, and party operations in western Indochina. Lower, central,
northern, and western Laos would eventually possess their own party
affairs committee, all answering to the countrywide one at the top. The

same would be true for Cambodia. Given that the Vietnamese had few, if any Laotians and Cambodians in their ranks at this time, the party center naturally relied on its Asia hands from northeast Thailand to staff these party affairs committees. This process would begin in 1948 and accelerate from 1949 onwards.[26]

There was more. To help coordinate all of this, the communist leadership in Thai Nguyen established another powerful administrative body in northeast Thailand. It was called the "Center's Overseas Party Affairs Committee." In charge of it was none other than Ho Chi Minh's most trusted Asia expert of all—Hoang Van Hoan. This man had studied under the Vietnamese president in Guangzhou during the mid-1920s before following him to Thailand. Hoang Van Hoan had stayed there to spread communism along both sides of the Mekong, all the while running the maritime arc between Bangkok and Hong Kong. In all, in 1948, Hoang Van Hoan could rely on over 300 party members in Thailand to help him. At its core was a tightly knit band of communist brothers whom Hoang Van Hoan knew well and trusted. He now turned to them to create revolutionary movements in Laos and Cambodia and to man the party affairs committees in western Indochina via radio contact with the center in Thai Nguyen.[27]

Like Hoang Van Hoan, two other Asian hands joined him in building communism in western Indochina: Nguyen Chan and Nguyen Thanh Son. They, too, were from the party's Asian networks. Ho Chi Minh had first recruited and trained Nguyen Thanh Son in Guangzhou in the 1920s. After finishing his time there, Nguyen Thanh Son returned to the Mekong Delta in around 1930 and rose to the highest ranks of the party in the south. In 1948, he operated in Zone IX, along the Cambodian border. From that zone, he administered the party's Cambodian operations through a special unit created that year called the "External Affairs Committee." Nguyen Chan started his revolutionary career as a miner in Laos in the late 1920s. He may have also trained under Ho in southern China before returning to Thailand. During the 1930s he joined with Hoang Van Hoan in building communism along both sides of the Mekong River. In 1948, they joined hands with their counterparts in Zone IV to nurture a splinter Lao Issara party to life on the border with Vietnam. To supervise their Laotian operations like this, they established yet another administrative body called the "Border Affairs Office," similar to the one Nguyen Thanh Son operated for Cambodia. These three men and a handful of others were the architects of Laotian and Cambodian communism. And these "Asia hands" all answered to the man who had first brought communism (and most of them to the western side of French Indochina) in the first place—Ho Chi Minh.[28]

Hoang Van Hoan's team knew that the Lao Issara in Thailand was not fully theirs. Since late 1947, they had already begun creating a separate "Lao Issara for the East" based out of Zone IV. Nguyen Chan presided over the creation of a companion Laotian Resistance and Administrative Committee to give this alternative Lao Issara a territorial base along the border with Vietnam. Working through the Border Affairs Office, the idea was simple: grow this small splinter group into something bigger. To do this, the Vietnamese needed to bring more Laotians on board. They immediately recruited individuals like Nouhak Phoumsavanh. This young man had worked as a miner in Laos during the interwar period and as a truck driver making the journey back and forth between Vinh and Savannakhet. He spoke Vietnamese fluently and knew some of the Asia specialists, including Nguyen Chan. By 1948, Nouhak oversaw the Lao Issara for the East and its accompanying resistance administration.[29]

To the north, Vo Nguyen Giap placed his bets on another Laotian by the name of Kaysone Phomvihane. He had grown up in Vientiane as the son of a Vietnamese civil servant working at the federal level of the colonial bureaucracy. His mother was Laotian. He too spoke Vietnamese fluently. During the Second World War, Kaysone had studied law at the Indochinese University in Hanoi. According to Vo Nguyen Giap, Kaysone only came to his personal attention in 1948, when they met for the first time in the Thai Nguyen capital. When the Vietnamese general informed his Laotian guest that he wanted to move his army into the highlands bordering northern Laos, Kaysone volunteered to help. While the shift to the northwest would not begin until 1952, it was the start of a close relationship between the two men. A year later, Giap helped Kaysone start building a "liberation army," the precursor of the Laotian armed forces today. In 1949, Kaysone joined the Indochinese Communist Party.[30]

Towards a New Khmer Issarak

Getting things off the ground in Cambodia was no easier than in Laos. Early talks between Ho's officials in southern Vietnam and those of the Cambodian prime minister, Son Ngoc Thanh, did not bode well. The latter had come to power with the Japanese overthrow of the French in March 1945. Like Phetsarath, Thanh counted on building an independent Cambodia after the imminent Japanese defeat. He was open to working with Ho's newly created Vietnam; but early talks went nowhere when the Cambodian prime minister requested the return of Tra Vinh and Soc Trang provinces in southern Vietnam. He (and other Cambodian nationalists after him) wanted to recover these territories, the Khmer Krom lands, which the Vietnamese had colonized before the French came. To make matters worse, ethnic violence broke out between Vietnamese and Cambodian communities living in the lower Mekong. The French would rapidly exploit these ethnic tensions as part of their divide and rule strategy; but there were deeper antagonisms at work, legacies of Vietnam's own imperial past.[31]

The rapid French reoccupation of Cambodia only made collaboration more difficult. The British had the task of accepting the Japanese surrender in areas of Indochina located below the 16th parallel. This included all of Cambodia. In late September, they allowed the French to begin retaking lower Vietnam by force. A few weeks later, the French moved into Cambodia, arrested Son Ngoc Thanh, and whisked him away. Meanwhile, the French high commissioner in Saigon welcomed King Norodom Sihanouk's decision to sign a modus vivendi in early 1946 which returned Cambodia to the Indochinese federation. Few royals in Cambodia would seek common anticolonial cause with Ho Chi Minh during the Indochina War. That would change for Sihanouk during the Vietnam War. But until 1954, the young Cambodian king was betting on the French as the best way of protecting the monarchy. "Young and inexperienced," an official Vietnamese broadcast explained in 1950, "the monarch lacked the will to conduct himself as a patriotic king."[32]

The problem, as in Laos, was that Ho had few Cambodian allies coming from his own communist networks. There appears to have been one exception to this rule, and his name was Son Ngoc Minh. Born to a Vietnamese father and a Cambodian mother in Tra Vinh province, Son Ngoc Minh spoke Vietnamese perfectly and was a devout Buddhist. He earned his keep as a fisherman, moving up and down the Mekong from southern Vietnam to the Tonle Sap area in northwestern Cambodia. In 1936, he entered into contact with none other than Nguyen Thanh Son. Thanks to this acquaintance, Son Ngoc Minh was soon moving in Vietnamese political circles and may have joined the Indochinese Communist Party at this time. He was involved in anticolonialist politics during the Second World War and supported Son Ngoc Thanh's government in mid-1945. When the French returned in October, he fled to Vietnam's Zone IX and renewed his collaboration with Nguyen Thanh Son. He was deeply involved in running guns from Thailand back to southern Vietnam in cooperation with the Vietnamese.[33] In early 1946, the Vietnamese first gave their support to an Issarak splinter group with Son Ngoc Minh at its head. It was called the "National Committee for the Liberation of Cambodia" and advocated Cambodian independence and collaboration with the DRV. However, the difficulty was that the communists only exercised limited control over the disparate groups within it. This initial attempt at supporting a free Cambodia went nowhere.[34]

Not to be deterred, in early 1948, the Vietnamese communists unveiled their new policy to unify disparate Cambodian dissident groups into one resistance movement as they were doing for Laos. To this end, the head of the Party Affairs Committee in Thailand, Hoang Van Hoan, joined hands with Nguyen Thanh Son and others to create a second revolutionary movement for Cambodia called the "Liberation Committee for the Cambodian People." Like the Lien Viet in Vietnam, the Vietnamese designed this entity to unite "all Cambodian forces into one unique national front to fight imperialism." Through it, the Cambodians would collaborate with the Vietnamese and the Laotians against the French to secure independence for all three countries. Significantly, this time, the "new" liberation committee was designed "to serve as a provisional government." Once enough zones were liberated, "a national assembly" would convene to approve a constitution and a "definitive government."[35]

The Asia hands went to work recruiting Cambodian dissidents of all political colors, anticolonialists, bandits cum patriots, and a disgruntled prince or two. By 1948 the list included such individuals as Pok Khun, Dap Chhuon, Puth Chay, and Prince Norodom Chantaraingsey. An early anticolonialist, Pok Khun had the prestige this new entity needed to attract longstanding Khmer Issarak supporters who were still active in Thailand and western Cambodia. Dap Chhuon, a local warlord, had the armed men. To attract both, the Vietnamese made Dap Chhuon the president, with Pok Khun seconding him. Dap Chhuon also became commander-in-chief of the army (he had served under the French before).

Backed by the Vietnamese, the Cambodian liberation committee began operations in northern Cambodia in mid-1948. The Vietnamese rapidly expanded its administrative and military operations to other zones, into which they divided Cambodia. They dispatched their troops and cadres from Thailand, southern Vietnam, and Zone V to help the Cambodians generate some sort of military force. Working with their Vietnamese advisers, the Cambodians opened political schools and military academies to train cadres and officers in statecraft and military science. Operating from behind the scenes via the newly created External Affairs Office, Nguyen Thanh Son and Son Ngoc Minh introduced the basics of Sino-Vietnamese statecraft, including the establishment of local patriotic associations, front organizations, and administrative committees as well as security, economic, and even fiscal services. The Vietnamese were particularly keen on building up and financing a strong sister state in southeast and southwestern Cambodia, to take advantage of favorable trade routes with Thailand and economic control of the lucrative Cambodian pepper plantations bordering Zone IX.[36]

The problem was that the Vietnamese communists went too far and too fast in this revolutionary statecraft.[37] For one thing, the Cambodians in this committee wanted to run the show themselves, but it was plain for all to see that they did not. This was particularly true in military affairs. By 1949, warlords like Dap Chhuon and Puth Chhay increasingly resented the joint Vietnamese-Cambodian army in which their troops operated. (Moreover, they had their own reasons for building up force that had nothing to do with a communist Indochinese revolution.) Mixed military commissions and Vietnamese advisers only fueled suspicions. The heavy-handed administrative hand of Nguyen Thanh Son and Son Ngoc Minh did not help. Pok Khun confided to an American diplomat in Bangkok at the time that many Cambodians in the liberation committee were thinking of rallying to the royal government in Phnom Penh. Things got so bad in southeastern Cambodia by late 1948 that Nguyen Thanh Son admitted privately that Vietnamese-Cambodian military cooperation was badly broken. And something went terribly wrong in 1949 when Puth Chhay broke with his communist handlers in his stomping grounds in Kandal province close to the Vietnamese border. In fact, things got so bad that Puth Chhay's partisans attacked and killed 140 ethnic Vietnamese living there, leading Nguyen Thanh Son to send in Vietnamese troops to stop the bloodletting. It would not be the last time the Vietnamese would have to do this.[38]

Meanwhile, Léon Pignon was doing everything in his power to win over this volatile collection of disgruntled Cambodians. Just as he had done with the Lao Issara, the high commissioner opened an array of secrets talks with them, promising amnesty in exchange for cooperation. Pignon leaned on Sihanouk, as he had with Sisavang Vong, to let bygones be bygones: in exchange for these warlords bending the knee to their king, they would receive good positions and even their own fiefdoms. Pignon could not accept that Ho could use these groups to build a resistance government behind his back. His efforts paid off. From 1949 onwards, Dap Chhuon, Puth Chhay, Prince Chantareignsey and others pledged allegiance to King Sihanouk and the high commissioner standing behind him. An unstable constellation though it was, the Associated States of Indochina was real.

Ho Chi Minh's Associated States of Indochina
(1950–54)

The Chinese Communist Victory and Renewed
Vietnamese Internationalism

Léon Pignon's victory in rallying most of the Cambodian and Laotian groups around his Indochinese royals by late 1949 put his Vietnamese adversaries in a bind, this happening as it did just as the Chinese communists took power. Of course, the Vietnamese welcomed the Chinese communist victory. They finally had a powerful, like-minded neighbor on their northern border. In January 1950, Mao Zedong threw his weight behind Ho Chi Minh. Truong Chinh proudly proclaimed that this "revolutionary Indochina" was part of the internationalist communist family. The communists were determined to hold the Indochinese revolutionary line in Southeast Asia against the imperialist bloc led by the Americans. To that end, they would implement the General Counter-offensive to liberate all of Indochina.[39]

The problem, as Truong Chinh, Vo Nguyen Giap, and others pointed out in closed-door sessions, was that they were not yet ready to do so in Laos and Cambodia. True, since 1948, Giap had presided over efforts to build revolutionary movements and liberation armies in Laos and Cambodia. But things had not gone well. Except for a handful of men like Son Ngoc Minh, Souphanouvong, and Kaysone, the Vietnamese had hardly any Cambodian and Laotian allies with whom to work. They had no durable nationalist fronts, no resistance governments, no revolutionary parties, and no serious armies. They had a formidable communist infrastructure in the form of those expanding party affairs committees and border offices, but theirs was an overwhelmingly Vietnamese machine.[40]

In early 1950, the Vietnamese reached a turning point when it came to their Indochinese project. Ho Chi Minh, Truong Chinh, and Vo Nguyen Giap could have dialed back their attempts to bring communism to all of Laos and Cambodia. They could have focused their revolutionary sights solely on Vietnam, even if it meant sending a few divisions into Laos or Cambodia to deal with any hostile French maneuvers there. Instead, they did the opposite. They went full speed ahead in their Indochinese statecraft. With the Chinese communists now standing behind them on the northern border, the Vietnamese fervently embraced their Indochinese internationalism. The result was that in meetings in early 1950 and again during the party's Second Congress a year later, Vietnamese communists renewed their efforts to create sister states, nationalist fronts, liberation armies, and revolutionary parties for Laos and Cambodia. This then was how the Vietnamese pushed their War Communism into western Indochina.

And they did so with full Chinese backing. Some readers will object that the Chinese could not have supported this and that they must have already distrusted Vietnamese "imperial ambitions" in Indochina. I politely disagree. This is a post-1979 reading of the past, not an historical one. To my knowledge, there is no hard evidence *from the time* showing that Mao Zedong and his Chinese advisory team opposed Ho's Indochinese revolution and statecraft. Luo Guibo, the head of the Chinese advisory group and special adviser to Ho, knew what the Vietnamese were doing throughout Indochina and would have reported it back to the man who had personally dispatched him to Vietnam—Mao Zedong. Chinese communists also knew that they had helped Ho to create his own communist party for Vietnam in Hong Kong in 1930 and had then worked with him in Southeast Asia to create communist parties for Malaya and Thailand. Moreover, if Mao wanted updates on Laos, Cambodia, and Southeast Asia, then all he had to do was to ask one of Ho Chi Minh's most trusted Asia specialists, Hoang Van Hoan himself. In late 1950, Hoan left Bangkok and traveled to Beijing, where he became, in 1951, Vietnam's first ambassador to China since the nineteenth century. Hoan spoke Chinese as fluently as he did Thai. The Chinese communists knew what their Vietnamese counterparts were doing in western Indochina. In his address to the Vietnamese Second Congress held in Ho's wartime capital in early 1951, Luo Guibo fully supported the Indochinese revolution and would have only done so with Mao's personal blessing.[41]

So why did the Vietnamese communists dissolve the Indochinese Communist Party during the Second Congress in early 1951? The most important reason was that they realized that their communism, like that of the Chinese, was much more advanced along the revolutionary path than was the case in Laos and Cambodia. With Mao Zedong now standing behind them, leaders like Ho Chi Minh and Truong Chinh were ready to transform the Democratic Republic of Vietnam into a single party communist state. Their counterparts in Laos and Cambodia, like Kaysone Phoumvihane and Son Ngoc Minh, were not. They were only just entering the Southeast Asian tip of the Eurasian revolutionary arc.

There was another reason. By removing the word "Indochina," the Vietnamese also wanted to rebut nationalist and colonial propaganda accusing them of being "red imperialists." Ho knew that some Laotians and Cambodians had negative associations with the idea of sharing Indochina with the Vietnamese, communist or otherwise. In 1950, Truong Chinh bemoaned "narrow nationalism" hostile to the Vietnamese (implicitly denouncing the bloodletting which had taken place in southeastern Cambodia) and pronounced in a report that his party sincerely supported the "three nations of Vietnam, Laos, and Cambodia." [42]

However, even though the Vietnamese communists formally changed the name for their country from the Indochinese Communist Party to the Vietnamese Workers Party, this definitely didn't mean that they were forsaking their wider ambitions for the whole of Indochina. In fact, they embraced their Indochinese mission like never before. Nowhere was this more evident than at the institutional level, on the ground, where it counted most. Several things occurred. Firstly, Ho latched on to his party affairs committees in Laos and Cambodia and expanded and consolidated them during the rest of the conflict. Then, in addition, the Vietnamese paired the Laotian and Cambodian party affairs committees with their Vietnamese counterparts in the Viet Bac Zone, zones IV and V in central Vietnam, and Zone IX in the south, and they worked hard, hand in hand. The same was true for the resistance and administrative committees the Vietnamese established in Laos and Cambodia. The Border Affairs Office in Zone IV and the External Affairs Committee in Zone IX served as the administrative clearinghouses for all of this. Lastly, throughout the Indochina War, the

Politburo administered its operations in Laos and Cambodia via the Vietnamese Workers Party's Central Office for Cambodia and Laos. Powerful communists such as Nguyen Chi Thanh, Pham Van Dong, and Vo Nguyen Giap ran it for the rest of the war and well after that.

Truong Chinh went further in this institutional direction when he spoke of the need to create an Indochinese consultative chamber, one in which representatives from all three countries would meet to discuss common problems, policies, and goals, and through which their Laotian and Cambodian associates' voices could be heard. The general secretary referred to this Indochinese Assembly as the "United Indochinese National Front" or the "Vietnam-Laos-Cambodia Interdependent Committee." This embryonic Indochinese chamber came to life on paper in March 1951 as the Vietnam-Laos-Cambodia National Alliance and met for the first time in Thai Nguyen under the leadership of Ho Chi Minh in 1952. A mouthful though all of this was, taken together, this was the institutional foundation on which Ho built his Laotian and Cambodian sister states: this was Indochinese federalism of a communist kind. This is also how two sets of Associated States of Indochina came into being during the Indochina War, one run by the "French colonialists," the other by the "Vietnamese communists." The Vietnamese Politburo's Office for Cambodia and Laos was the institutional equivalent of the French Ministry for the Associated States of Indochina.[43]

The difference was that if the French could rely on Laotian and Cambodian royalist bureaucracies and civil servants going forward, the Vietnamese communists were going to have to build their sister states and parties largely from scratch. This, in turn, only worsened the Vietnamese structural domination of their Indochinese communist civil service for the simple reason that Ho did not have enough trained Laotians and Cambodians available to fill all the new posts his cadres were creating to administer western Indochina. As a result, the Politburo had no choice but to keep its Asia specialists active, to continue recruiting from the Vietnamese diaspora in western Indochina and northeast Thailand, all the while training Laotian and Cambodian cadres at full speed. Unsurprisingly, scores of party documents repeat the pressing need to train Laotian, Cambodian, and ethnic minority cadres. In Cambodia alone, between 1945 and 1954, 1,421 Vietnamese cadres, civil servants, and officers served there, working from on high in the Party Affairs Committee to policing and tax-collecting on the ground. As in Vietnam and China, War Communism in western Indochina would be a bureaucratic combat as much as a military one. But here the Vietnamese, rather than the Chinese, led the Eurasian communist charge in Laos and Cambodia.[44]

The Making of a Laotian Sister State

Following Pignon's political victories in western Indochina in 1949, Ho scrambled to create states for Laos and Cambodia that could stand alongside his Vietnam. It was an internationalist task, to be sure, but the Vietnamese would need these states to be operational if ever the General Counter-offensive expanded into western Indochina, as some suspected it might. Already, by early 1950, Vietnamese intelligence services reported that the Americans were increasingly following what was going on in Laos and Cambodia. And they were: in February that year, the Americans recognized diplomatically all three French Associated States of Indochina. Such international recognition of Pignon's states would only make it politically harder for the Vietnamese to operate in Laos and Cambodia without being accused of invading a sovereign country. Ho needed his own associated governments in western Indochina—now.

Since 1949, the communist center in Thai Nguyen had been firing off cables to its cadres in Laos, Cambodia, and Thailand, instructing them to get to work. Ho's Laotian and Cambodian partners joined hands with their Vietnamese counterparts in the party affairs committees to organize a national congress for each country. These gatherings would serve as the constituent assemblies the Vietnamese needed to get their embryonic states off the ground. Delegates would approve their respective political programs and elect a government. The Vietnamese counted on their closest Laotian and Cambodian allies to make this happen. That group can be accurately summed up as those who had not gone over to Pignon's Indochina in 1949: it included Son Ngoc Minh in Cambodia and a group of others who had already worked with the Vietnamese. In Laos, Kaysone, Nouhak, and Souphanouvong constituted the core group. These men had the chance to rise to the highest levels of power in the states the Vietnamese were putting together. Ho was not bent on creating a communist-dominated state in Laos or Cambodia as he was now doing in Vietnam. For the time being, Laotian and Cambodian sister states had to be "progressive" and allied with the Vietnamese. Nor did anyone in Ho's entourage have any problems letting a royal run the Laotian (or Cambodian) government. The party was another matter, though.

As president of the Democratic Republic of Vietnam, Ho took the lead in dealing with Prince Souphanouvong. Ho had clearly made a positive impression on the Laotian prince during their meeting in Hanoi in September 1945. Despite some earlier hesitations,[45] Souphanouvong accepted Ho Chi Minh's invitations to return to Vietnam to build a new Laotian independence movement for Laos. Shortly after the Lao Issara folded in October 1949, he was on his way to Vietnam, where he arrived in Zone IV in mid-December. Significantly, Ho's need for a royalist cover was such that he also invited Prince Phetsarath to come to Vietnam. One of Ho's top diplomats in Thailand informed Phetsarath that the Vietnamese considered him to be the "uncontested champion of Laotian independence." The prince declined the invitation for the time being, but he left his options open. (He had just turned down an offer from Léon Pignon to relocate him and his family in France.)[46]

By accepting Ho's invitation to travel to Vietnam, Souphanouvong saw the chance to build a new Laos in collaboration with the Vietnamese. From Zone IV, he traveled to the Vietnamese capital of Thai Nguyen, where he arrived in early January 1950 and stayed for about a month. It was precisely during this time that the Chinese and the Soviets recognized the Democratic Republic of Vietnam, the Americans and British recognized Pignon's Associated States of Indochina, and the Vietnamese accelerated preparations to implement the General Counteroffensive to liberate all of Indochina. Although the prince did not meet Ho at this time, it must have been an exhilarating experience for him to be in Thai Nguyen, this new Yan'an. Vo Nguyen Giap, Pham Van Dong, and Truong Chinh welcomed him warmly and gave him a tour of their resistance capital. The prince met other Laotians who had joined with the Vietnamese on the eastern side of the Annamese Cordillera, including Kaysone. They were all agreed to move fast to strengthen Laotian military forces and to create a new Lao Issara government and nationalist front allied with Ho's Vietnam and its corresponding institutions.[47]

Time was of the essence. The Laotians (and the Cambodians) had to be ready. Upon his return to Zone IV in February 1950, Souphanouvong wrote to Ho Chi Minh, reassuring the Vietnamese president that he understood: "Knowing the importance you attach to the creation of a true resistance core made up of the most capable and loyal servants to the people and the most apt to realize the union of all, we are going to work immediately."[48] Meanwhile, the Vietnamese worked via their Party Affairs Committee for Laos and operatives in Zone IV, in particular, to get a sister state for Laos going. Cadres there met in June to discuss, modify, and then finalize preparations for the establishment of a new Laotian state and political program. After months of hard work, between 13 and 15 August 1950, the Laotian People's First Congress took place in Zone IV. Delegates approved the creation of a new Lao Issara nationalist front and a Laotian resistance government. This government would work closely with its Vietnamese and Cambodian counterparts to achieve the full independence of all of Indochina. It would also join the the communist bloc. Participants considered this congress to be a constituent assembly, and a vote was held to elect the government's first cabinet. Souphanouvong became the government's first prime minister. Kaysone became minister of defense. Delegates also cabled Phetsarath to inform him that he had been elected as head of state. The prince accepted, though he deplored that such an important national event had been held in Vietnam. Phetsarath refused, however, to follow Souphanouvong to Vietnam. In the end, Phetsarath would not return to Laos until 1957, where he died a few years later.[49]

Throughout the rest of the Indochina War, Souphanouvong, Kaysone and their Laotian partners worked with the Vietnamese and their federal institutions in western Indochina to build a bureaucracy and army for the Laotian resistance government. In the north, Kaysone cooperated with Vo Nguyen Giap and the head of the Party Affairs

Committee. In Zone IV, Souphanouvong and Nouhak worked with Nguyen Chan and others in the Border Affairs Office and the Party Affairs Committee for central Laos. In both areas, the Laotians expanded their resistance and administrative committees into zones which they and the Vietnamese controlled. This included the creation of financial, economic, fiscal, and security services. In a letter to Ho Chi Minh on 21 September 1950, Souphanouvong asked the Vietnamese president "to maintain the old procedure," relying on Vo Nguyen Giap in the north and Nguyen Chan in Zone IV as his main intermediaries for crafting the resistance government. The prince informed Ho that he needed Nguyen Chan to help him in this "transitional period in the reorganization of our central services." Souphanouvong asked Ho "to 'lend' [him] Nguyen Chan for an unlimited time." We can be sure that Ho responded affirmatively. The Vietnamese president could also transfer this Asian hand easily, because Ho was institutionally at the head of a federal bureaucracy connecting western Indochina to its eastern half.[50]

The Making of a Cambodian Sister State

As in Laos, the Vietnamese scrambled to build a Cambodian sister state from the ruins of their first attempts at it in the late 1940s. In late 1949, following Pignon's establishment of the Associated States of Indochina, Nguyen Thanh Son traveled to Bangkok to discuss with Hoang Van Hoan the need to rebuild the Cambodian liberation committee fast. Upon his return to Zone IX, he convened a cadres' meeting in March 1950 to prepare for an upcoming Cambodian national congress. It would bring Cambodian (and Vietnamese) delegates together in something like a constituent assembly to officially declare the birth of a resistance government and nationalist front. The emerging Cambodian communist core was present at this March conference, not only Son Ngoc Minh, but also rising stars like Tou Samuth, Siev Heng, and Keo Muni. Joining Nguyen Thanh Son in this preparatory meeting were the two top communist leaders in southern Vietnam—Le Duc Tho and Le Duan. All were agreed to establish a new Cambodian state fast.[51]

The big event—the National Congress for a Free Cambodia—occurred in April 1950. During this meeting, over 200 Vietnamese and Cambodian delegates gathered in Zone IX with great fanfare to establish the United National Liberation Front of the Khmer Issarak and the Cambodian Central Committee for National Liberation. The latter was the debut of what the Vietnamese would shortly call the Cambodian resistance government, similar to the one that would emerge in Laos a few months later. The congress approved a new flag, national anthem, and day of independence. It affirmed the special relations binding the Cambodians to their Vietnamese and Laotian brethren and announced that Cambodia would join the communist bloc led by the Soviet Union. Son Ngoc Minh became the leader of the Khmer Issarak national front and the new Cambodian resistance government. Propaganda posters would soon show him next to Ho Chi Minh and Prince Souphanouvong at the head of this second set of associated states of Indochina (visitors to the Revolutionary Museum in Hanoi can see much of this on display).[52]

All of this was, once again, tricky, especially in Cambodia. The Vietnamese realized from their earlier experience there that they had to be careful not to play too direct a role in this revolutionary statecraft. Indirect rule was always better. In several documents, Nguyen Thanh Son pointed out that cadres had to let the Cambodians win over villages, run local administrations, and command troops. He also explained the importance of securing the support of Buddhist monks. Their monasteries, pagoda schools, and clergy could serve as powerful tools for the state-building cause. Son Ngoc Minh, a former monk himself, now joined in Buddhist festivals and courted local monks in southern Vietnam and Cambodia as his Vietnamese handlers distributed photos and tracts celebrating this new chapter of Cambodian revolutionary history.[53]

Ho and his Asia hands might have wanted the Cambodians and the Laotians to take the lead, but they all knew that neither ally had the party cadres, government civil servants, military officers, or institutional infrastructure to do this. And time was of the essence as preparations for the General Counter-offensive advanced. The Vietnamese had no choice but to continue to run their sister states, relying on their party affairs committees. Vietnamese cadres there collaborated with their counterparts across the border in zones IX and V to start training competent and loyal Cambodian civil servants to run the resistance government's ministries and the lower levels of its administration. In some cases, the Vietnamese could graft the new government's civil service on to the preexisting royalist bureaucracy in zones they controlled. In many areas though, the Vietnamese had to open a slew of cadre and officer training schools to produce the people they needed on the spot. They continued to rely on the Vietnamese diaspora to help too. The party center even transferred instructors from Vietnam to train a new bureaucratic class of Laotian and Cambodian cadres, civil servants, police and intelligence officers. Pham Ngoc Thao, one of Vietnam's best-known spies during the Vietnam War, did an administrative stint in Cambodia in the early 1950s to help his Cambodian counterparts develop their intelligence and counterespionage services—vital to any state-building project. To finance this statecraft, the Vietnamese taxed the pepper trade in nearby southeastern Cambodia. Between 1950 and 1953, it generated tax revenues to the tune of 33 million piasters.[54]

The best and the brightest in Laos and Cambodia went on to Vietnam for higher studies, some of whom graduated from the Nguyen Ai Quoc and Truong Chinh party academies in Thai Nguyen and Zone IX respectively. A graduate of the Truong Chinh Academy in late 1949, Son Ngoc Minh personally trained a communist Cambodian corps of cadres in collaboration with Nguyen Thanh Son. Le Duan, Le Duc Tho, and others personally taught Cambodian cadres the finer details of Marx and Lenin there, as well as Mao's revolutionary ideas. In 1952, two dozen Cambodian students studied in special classes on Maoism in the Truong Chinh Academy. This is how Maoism came to western Indochina. Pol Pot, the Cambodian communist who would tear his country apart in the late 1970s at the cost of 1 million lives, did not bring it. The Vietnamese did, and they did so with the blessing of the Chinese. No one among the Vietnamese and their Chinese advisers working in Thai Nguyen knew who Pol Pot was. He was not one of theirs.[55]

Pragmatic War Communism?
The "People's Parties in Laos and Cambodia"

The Vietnamese knew they had to create revolutionary parties at the head of their resistance governments. During the Second Party Congress the Vietnamese immediately issued orders to create "people's parties for Laos and Cambodia." To this end, Vietnamese cadres in western Indochina received instructions to establish a "section" of the new Vietnamese Workers Party in Laos and Cambodia to which they would belong. Working via their sections, they would then join with their Laotian and Cambodian allies to foster people's parties for Laos and Cambodia. They would do this in collaboration with the party affairs committees there.[56]

As always, the Vietnamese made exceptions for their Indochinese counterparts, whom they considered to be less advanced ideologically, less organized administratively, and whose "masses" seemed, to them, much more committed to their monarchs than the Vietnamese people were to theirs. Recruiting was less stringent, since the Vietnamese needed to increase the number of Laotian and Cambodian party members as rapidly as possible. What counted most was patriotism, reliability, and commitment to the joint Indochinese anticolonial cause. The political programs the Vietnamese elaborated for each of their partners reflected this. Efforts were always made to take into account the cultural and religious differences between western and eastern Indochina, and special care was to be taken not to denigrate the monarchy. The goal in western Indochina was to liberate the people from "French colonialism," but revolutionaries would "support the preservation of the royal family."[57]

In 1951, the Vietnamese presided over the creation of the Khmer People's Revolutionary Party, led by Son Ngoc Minh. The Laotian People's Party officially came to life in March 1955. A revolutionary boost for Laotian communism had come earlier, however, with the Chinese and Vietnamese decision in 1952 to send People's Army of Vietnam troops deep into western Indochina. The spectacular Vietnamese invasion of Laos in early 1953, discussed in Chapter 10, provided Soupha-nouvong and Kaysone with secure territories in Sam Neua and Phong Saly provinces in which they could safely craft a new Laotian adminis-tration, army, and revolutionary party. These free zones straddled the border with northwestern Vietnam *and* southern China (an accurate reflection of who had put the Laotians in power there). In 1952, Nouhak traveled to Beijing, while several hundred Vietnamese troops operating in northern Laos trained in China's Yunnan province before returning to their bases. The Chinese were on board with all of this and formally approved the Vietnamese invasion of Laos in 1953. Thanks to this Sino-Vietnamese support, the Laotians now had their own revolutionary capital in Sam Neua, at the very tip of the Eurasian arc.[58]

But as PAVN divisions went deep into the highlands running down Indochina's middle, Laos became an integral part of the northern Indo-chinese front, much as eastern Cambodia would become during the war for southern Vietnam in the 1960s. The Vietnamese dispatched hun-dreds of advisers to help their Laotian allies in Sam Neua build a revo-lutionary state, army, and party at the same time, much as the Chinese were doing for the Vietnamese in Thai Nguyen. At the end of 1950, the number of Vietnamese cadres and soldiers operating inside Laos had risen to about 8,000. In 1951, the number reached around 12,000 person-nel, then 7,809 in 1952, 7,632 in 1953, and an impressive 17,600 in 1954. (The Laotian army numbered about 2,000 men at the end of the con-flict.) Ho Chi Minh, Pham Van Dong, and their advisers reassured their Laotian counterparts that they were doing all of this for them. Their assistance was "unconditional," rooted in the "spirit of international proletarianism."[59]

However, assistance always comes with strings attached, and choices always have consequences. If Ho Chi Minh was so deeply involved in Laotian and Cambodian affairs, it is because he, his party, and their Chinese allies had made decisions in their own interest too. Militarily, if the Vietnamese were going deep into Laos in early 1953 and later that year towards Dien Bien Phu, it was because they could not take the Red River Delta from the French in one fell swoop and sought to disperse the French army in order to find a way to win. The military importance of Laos for the Vietnamese and the Chinese in the run-up to Dien Bien Phu is indisputable. They had to have a friendly government there in northern Laos. In February 1953, Ho Chi Minh personally summoned Souphanouvong and Kaysone to Thai Nguyen to discuss the future course of their cooperation. It was not the Laotians who summoned the Vietnamese. That said, in March 1953, the Vietnamese Politburo dispatched one of its own to Laos to make sure that everything would run according to their plan. His name was Nguyen Khang. As something of a proconsul, this man's job was to administer all political and military matters in Laos in coordination with the party center and the Vietnamese high command. Working closely with Souphanouvong, Kaysone, and the Asia specialists in the party affairs committees, Nguyen Khang helped get a Laotian army and state, better known today as the Pathet Lao, off the ground in Sam Neua and Phong Saly.

As it turned out, the Chinese and the Vietnamese did not have time to bring this to fruition before the war came to an unexpectedly early end. But that did not stop them from protecting their revolutionary laboratory in northern Laos. When it became clear during the Geneva Conference that the Vietnamese were going to sign a ceasefire agreement for the whole of Indochina, Vo Nguyen Giap immediately instructed Nguyen Khang to build up the Laotian army immediately, since a provision in the armistice would allow the Pathet Lao to regroup its personnel and troops in Sam Neua and Phong Saly provinces. He also instructed Nguyen Khang to stay on in Laos as the head of a special advisers group called the Doan 100. It was, in reality, the reconfiguration of the party affairs committee for Laos. It began operations on 16 July 1954. Vietnam's Nguyen Khang would remain in Sam Neua and Phong Saly to help keep Vietnam's sister state alive and well after the ink had dried on the ceasefire agreement. Joining him was the head of the 316th Division, General Chu Huy Man. Together they made sure the Pathet Lao survived the ceasefire agreement requiring the Vietnamese to withdraw. The Cambodians, led by Son Ngoc Minh, were not so fortunate. They had to disarm and dismantle their resistance state as their counterparts had to do in Vietnam below the 17th parallel. However, the

Vietnamese did manage to leave the bare bones of their communist infrastructure in place there and in southern Vietnam too.[60]

This then was how the Vietnamese brought War Communism to all of Indochina. Did Ho Chi Minh want to create "replica states" in Laos and Cambodia in the image of what Joseph Stalin had done in Eastern Europe after the Second World War?[61] Perhaps not, at least not right away. Unlike Stalin in dealing with East Germany or Poland in the late 1940s, Ho adjusted communist statecraft to local differences in western Indochina much more. He refused, for example, to apply land reform to his sister states in Laos and Cambodia. Nor did the Vietnamese ever impose military service or declare mass mobilization laws in Laos or Cambodia. Neither did they authorize the use of rectification, thought reform, or even patriotic emulation campaigns in western Indochina. Ho certainly used lighter forms from the Sino-Vietnamese playbook, such as propaganda and proselytizing the enemy campaigns, the formation of a multitude of patriotic associations and nationalist fronts, and the dispatch of thousands of "advisers" to help build states, armies, and parties for Laos and Cambodia. But there were limits to how much Sino-Vietnamese War Communism the Vietnamese would apply there. The Vietnamese and Chinese did not seek to create professional, conventional armies for their allies in Laos and Cambodia, knowing that such an undertaking would have come with huge social and political costs. The Laotians and Cambodians could rely instead on Vietnamese military power, civilian supply teams, and Ho's single-party state driving both to liberate all of western Indochina and bring communism there.[62]

But again, choices have consequences. Souphanouvong, Kaysone, and Son Ngoc Minh did not lead replica states during the Indochina War. However, their dependency on Vietnamese military power, like Bao Dai, Sisavang Vong, and Sihanouk's reliance on the French to defeat Ho's Vietnam, came at the price of their national sovereignty. None of these associated states—neither those allied with the "French colonialists" nor those supported by the "Vietnamese communists"—were fully independent when the delegates of the Republic of France and the Democratic Republic of Vietnam signed the armistice agreement in Geneva ending the First Indochina War in July 1954. Empires do not die easily. They often reconfigure themselves in new ways to carry on. This was true of the French colonial empire. It was also the case for their Vietnamese adversaries, well beyond the end of the Indochina War. Imperial dust is still to be found in Laos and Cambodia to this day—and not just the French kind.[63]

12

Dien Bien Phu

THE CHANGING OF HEAVEN AND EARTH

On 14 November 1953, President Ho Chi Minh stood before a special session of the Vietnamese Workers Party to initiate full-scale land reform. After reviewing the favorable international situation (the communist bloc was advancing, the imperialists were retreating), he then explained why the party had finally decided to take land from property owners by force and redistribute it to the peasants. He reminded his listeners of the party's slogan since first launching mass mobilization in early 1950: "Everything for the front lines, everything to win." The problem was that the general mobilization law and the military conscription law coming right before it had relied disproportionately on the peasants. They had provided the majority of the recruits. They had toiled in the fields to feed everyone. The peasants, Ho said, had given "more than anyone else to the resistance." They had certainly suffered the most. They had shouldered the brunt of the economic assault and bombing raids. The government's agricultural tax on rice only had made things worse for them, to say nothing of spiraling inflation and a weak currency. Ho's people were exhausted and they were hungry.[1]

The problem was that the Vietnamese president needed to ask more of his people yet again. As Ho closed this special party session on 23 November, the PAVN was marching on Dien Bien Phu while cadres were busy conscripting people into supply teams. Ho realized that he had to give something in return to those who had sacrificed beyond

measure. Full-scale land reform was now on the table. It would incentivize the peasantry to continue participating in the conflict. The time had
come to launch a class war.

In this our final chapter, readers will find, with a few twists, the familiar story of Dien Bien Phu summarized in its international, French, and
Vietnamese dimensions. We will follow the waves of assault Vo Nguyen
Giap launched to defeat Henri Navarre on the battlefield as negotiations
to end the conflict began in Geneva. But this will not be another battle
history, describing blow-by-blow, day-by-day details of strategy, tactics,
and combat operations, nor an in-depth analysis of the diplomacy
which ensued afterwards. Readers should be prepared to consider what
this last act in the conflict entailed for the people involved and what this
type of warfare tells us about the nature of the Democratic Republic of
Vietnam as it rose from its archipelagic matrix in the form of a single-
party communist state. Dien Bien Phu was the site of extraordinary
courage. It was also the climax of Vietnamese War Communism.

Toward Dien Bien Phu, 1953

Lessons Learned

No one knew going into 1953 that the last battle of the First Indochina
War would occur in Dien Bien Phu a year and a half later. The Vietnamese, as we know, had adopted a military strategy in 1952 which focused
on seizing as much of the Indochinese highlands as possible, without
losing sight of the Red River Delta. Although General Raoul Salan had
managed to hold on to Na San in December 1952 after easily repelling
his adversary, General Vo Nguyen Giap simply went around the camp
and invaded Laos. In April 1953, in a spectacular move designed both to
disperse the Expeditionary Corps and expand the Vietnamese government's hold over the highlands, PAVN troops seized Sam Neua and
Phong Saly and moved into the hills overlooking Luang Prabang. In the
end, the Vietnamese went no further, content to remain in Sam Neua,
install their associated state of Laos there, and widen their corridor,
which extended southwards to Zone IV and the central highlands.

Meanwhile, working from the other side of the Annamese Cordillera, Giap strengthened the 325th Division, which was stationed in Zone V, and had even dispatched parts of it into the central highlands. The Vietnamese "go deep" strategy did not necessarily guarantee victory in pitched battle, but it forced the French to keep playing defense on an Indochinese battlefield.[2]

The Vietnamese could count on sustained Chinese advice and support for the next round of fighting, as Mao Zedong's advisory team remained deeply involved in strategic planning, up to and including the Battle of Dien Bien Phu. With the war in Korea over in July 1953, the Chinese began shipping as many trucks, artillery guns, and antiaircraft systems as they could spare (while the Americans did the same for the French). Based on what they had learned at Hoa Binh and Na San, the Chinese and Vietnamese understood that to overrun any entrenched camp in the highlands in the future, they would have to achieve several things: i) bring in and deploy unprecedented amounts of carefully calibrated artillery fire on an enemy fortress; ii) destroy any airstrip it harbored with artillery barrages and use antiaircraft guns to stop planes from parachuting in troops and supplies (i.e., destroy the camp's air bridge); iii) organize a fleet of trucks to transport weapons, ammunition, food, and medicines from the Chinese border to supply bases as close to the battlefield as possible; iv) conscript tens of thousands of laborers to repair bombed-out bridges and roads along the way and carry weapons and food to the battlefield when the trucks could not; and lastly, v) ensure that enough rice, medicines, and medical personnel were on hand to keep the troops and their people-powered logistics up and running for what would likely be a drawn-out and bloody affair. This is where things stood on the battlefield in May 1953, when General Henri Navarre took over in Indochina.

The Navarre Plan

Although Navarre did not know Indochina as intimately as Salan did, the new commander-in-chief in Indochina was serious about retaking the initiative from the enemy and helping his government end this war as it entered its eighth year. Navarre went on a fact-finding mission to Indochina. He consulted officers and officials there. We know he read Salan's reports in devising his own plan for the French governments in charge at the time, the first led by René Mayer and the second, from late June 1953, by Joseph Laniel. Each statesman was ready to pursue a political solution to achieve an "honorable exit." Both expected the army to strengthen the government's negotiating hand when serious talks commenced. Without explaining what exactly that meant or providing a precise timetable for achieving it (because the talks were still in the offing), the government left it up to Navarre to come up with a strategy they could approve. (See Plate 24.)

Their new general did not disappoint. What has become known as the "Navarre plan" reflected a largely accurate understanding of the military situation in mid-1953, relying on many of the suggestions Salan had made in his own *plan d'action* a few months earlier. Navarre's project can be summed up as follows: first of all, the new commander-in-chief realized (like so many others before him) that he would get few additional troops from Paris. The government needed them as efforts got underway to create the European Defense Community to contain the Soviet threat (and the West Germans next door). As a result, Navarre built on what de Lattre had already done by further expanding the Associated State of Vietnam's army to 200,000 troops by early 1954. Next, together with this growing Vietnamese contingent of the army, the French would pacify the northern delta once and for all. This would deprive the enemy of his biggest source of rice and recruits and consolidate the Associated State's territorial control at the same time. Lastly, the Expeditionary Corps would avoid major engagements in the highlands for a year in order to secure control of the northern delta as well as to regroup and rebuild. Only during the conflict's second year, starting in the fall of 1954, would it go after the PAVN.

A final point deserves mention here for reasons that will become apparent as the Battle of Dien Bien Phu nears. Navarre decided that the Expeditionary Corps, working again with the Associated State's army, would launch a major offensive on Zone V in lower central Vietnam. This zone, the lower part of the handle in the DRV's sickle shape, was located furthest from the Chinese border. It was home to only one division and had suffered greatly from the economic blockade. Navarre's idea was to conquer this second, weaker link in the Democratic Republic of Vietnam and turn its administration over to France's Vietnamese allies, who were already in firm control of most of nearby southern Vietnam. This would grow the Associated State of Vietnam's size from the Mekong Delta up to about the 16th parallel and assuage nationalist demands from it for an increased say in military and political affairs. By taking the enemy's territorial bottom third of the country, Navarre wanted to confine Giap's remaining divisions to the sickle's head wrapped around the northern delta and, in 1954–5, to destroy it. Navarre code-named this offensive on Zone V Operation Atlante.[3]

That was the plan and it had its merits. Strangely absent, however, was any clear explanation as to what Navarre would do in the northwest if the Vietnamese continued to go deep, say into Laos again, or invaded the Tai federation in Lai Chau province—or both. There was no reason to assume that the Vietnamese would not do so, and Navarre knew it. When he asked the French government in late July if he had to defend Laos in the event of an attack, he didn't receive a clear answer until months later. This did not seem to bother Navarre as much at the time as he would claim it did later. In August 1953, he ordered the evacuation of Na San without setting up an alternative camp for his soldiers. Although the commanding general knew that any enemy attack on Laos or the Tai federation would force him to take a stand in the highlands, he preferred to wait and see which way his adversary would go before committing himself. Rather than building a defensive line from Na San to Lai Chau with Dien Bien Phu in the middle of it, he focused on the linchpin of his plan for the time being: pacifying the northern delta and preparing to take Zone V.[4]

The Highlands or the Delta?

Of course, in order to make their own military plans for 1953–4, Vietnamese and Chinese strategists wanted to know what Navarre was secretly cooking up. They had learned a few details of his projects on

30 July, when a Parisian paper leaked details of the general's recent meeting with government officials in Paris. Of particular interest was the revelation that Navarre, when pressed, had stated that he would have a hard time defending Laos in the event of an enemy attack. The Vietnamese were able to piece together more details over the next few weeks, thanks to their espionage services. Moles provided many of the specifics of Operation Atlante, confirming that Navarre's main idea was "to attack in the south and defend the north." Sometime in early September, the Chinese provided the Vietnamese with "the entire Navarre plan," which means that Chinese and Vietnamese strategists were aware of what the French were doing when devising their own campaign for 1953–4. Upon hearing his military intelligence experts sum up Navarre's strategy, Ho Chi Minh replied: "The enemy is massing his forces to occupy and hold the Tonkin lowlands, so we will force him to disperse his forces out to other sectors so that we can annihilate them."[5]

Despite the tough talk, the Vietnamese did not rush into the northwest. Nor did they abandon their interest in the delta. The highland campaigns were not as successful as official communist histories would have it: Nghia Lo and Sam Neua were victories; Hoa Binh and Na San were not. If Giap had refrained from attacking Luang Prabang in May 1953, it was because he knew Salan had another "Na San" waiting for him, and he had overextended his logistics in any case. These set-piece battles occurring across the highlands had required the mobilization of hundreds of thousands of people in order to supply and feed the army and the porters following it over these long distances. Food was always a problem. So was keeping bodies healthy. All of these things and others weighed on the minds of Vietnamese and Chinese strategists as they discussed what their next move would be.

For now, the Vietnamese and their Chinese advisers "kept two irons in the fire," as one eminent French historian of the Indochina War put it. They began preparing to renew their northwest campaign, but they tested the waters in the delta before committing. Vietnamese sources confirm that the communists were unsure what Navarre was actually doing and whether they should focus their attacks on the delta or the highlands. It is possible that some saw the lowlands as a better alternative

to the massive social mobilization a return to the highlands would require. We know that Giap had improved his position in the Red River
during the northwest campaign by pacifying an estimated 600 villages
there. We also know that logistics had been a nightmare when the army
went deep into the highlands a year earlier. Whatever the reasons, between late September and early November 1953, the commander-in-
chief activated his PAVN-powered battalions inside the delta and his
divisions circulating around it. In late October, Giap ordered the
320th to infiltrate the delta from the south side. Duly apprised by French
intelligence services, Navarre was waiting for him and responded with
massive firepower in what he called Operation Mouette. When the
fighting ended on 7 November 1953, this division had lost over 1,000
men. Those in the party thinking they could take the delta outright accepted that there was only one way left to go.[6]

By going deep into the highlands again, the Vietnamese would do
what they did best: disperse enemy forces as thinly as possible across
Indochina's entire backbone while harassing them from inside the
northern lowlands. But this time, when Navarre came out to stop Giap
by throwing up an entrenched camp as Salan had done in Na San, the
Vietnamese would be prepared to go the distance. They correctly assumed that the French general would have to take a stand to protect, if
not the Tai federation, then Laos for sure. Despite earlier reservations,
Navarre was now confident that he could handle any problem that
might come up in the highlands. If the adversary moved on him in an
unacceptable way in the northwest, then he would do as his predecessor
had done a year earlier: lift in several thousand crack troops by air, create
a heavily fortified camp, supply it through an air bridge, win, and evacuate. The increasing size of the Associated State of Vietnam's army would
allow him to maintain his pacification operations in the delta and attack
Zone V at the same time.

Where Navarre got himself into trouble was by underestimating the
ability of his enemy to learn from his mistakes. Firstly, the French
general did not think the Vietnamese capable of bringing in the heavy
artillery and antiaircraft guns needed to destroy an entrenched camp's
artillery and airstrip (but they were). Secondly, he did not believe his

enemy could organize the massive logistical system needed to supply a sustained, pitched battle in the highlands (they could). Thirdly, he hoped that the Chinese would not increase the quantity and the quality of their military aid to the Vietnamese following the armistice in Korea in July 1953 (in fact, they did). Lastly, he failed to consider how rapid diplomatic changes at the international level would require him to make adjustments on the battlefield. Any commander worth his mettle knows that the first thing to change when the fighting actually begins is the "plan."

The Changing International Context

Navarre was aware of the changes occurring at the international level since becoming commander-in-chief of the armed forces in Indochina in May 1953. Two months earlier, the leader of the internationalist communist camp since the 1920s, Joseph Stalin, had died. Although Ho Chi Minh was said to have shed tears on learning of this, not everyone in the communist bloc did. In fact, Stalin's death opened the way for a new group of Soviet leaders in the Kremlin to emerge, ones who were increasingly keen on easing Cold War tensions in Europe (in Germany and Berlin) and Asia (in Korea and Indochina). This would allow them to focus on the domestic economy and a more liberal form of communism to accompany it, a process better known as "de-Stalinization." The Chinese, led by Mao, also needed to focus on domestic issues. Having applied full-scale land reform to all of the country since 1950, they wanted to turn to their new five-year economic plan as they raced down the road to collectivization. They brought their North Korean allies on board and, with Soviet support, signed an armistice agreement ending the Korean War on 27 July 1953.

The new American president entering the White House in early 1953, Dwight D. Eisenhower, also wanted to ease international tensions in order to focus on domestic issues. He agreed to the ceasefire in Korea that kept the peninsula separated into two states at the 38th parallel, a pro-American Republic of Korea in the south, and, above that line, the Democratic People's Republic of Korea allied with the communist bloc in the north. Although the Americans and the Chinese agreed to stop their direct war in Korea, they continued to support their respective allies fighting in Indochina, the French "colonialists" and the Vietnamese "communists." If the Chinese had built up the PAVN in Vietnam to help protect their southern flank against a hostile American attack, Washington had supplied and armed the French Expeditionary Corps and the Associated State of Vietnam's army in order to stop the communists from moving into Southeast Asia at the expense of Washington's dominance over the Asia-Pacific region. Washington and Beijing were both paying attention when PAVN troops invaded Laos in early 1953.

Things started to change on the French side over the summer of 1953. As negotiations accelerated to end the war in Korea, Joseph Laniel announced in late June that, as part of his new government's mandate, he would actively pursue a negotiated settlement to the Indochina conflict. Pushing him in that direction were the stepped-up efforts by leaders in the Associated States of Vietnam and Cambodia to obtain full independence and leave the French Union. In 1953, Cambodia's Norodom Sihanouk and Vietnam's Ngo Dinh Diem went on "crusades" in France and North America to make their cases for independence and garner foreign support for it. Many in the French political class, long supportive of the war and of the Indochinese empire it was designed to preserve, began to wonder if it was really worth the continued effort if their own associated leaders wanted out so badly. Support for the Indochina War in the National Assembly was declining fast, and the French public, never really interested in the conflict anyway, favored getting out. Over the summer of 1953, for the first time really, the French government got serious about negotiations.[7]

Following the signing of the Korean armistice in July, the different parties began to talk seriously about finding a similar solution for ending the shooting in Indochina. The Soviets suggested to the French that a negotiated settlement to the Indochina conflict could be found. The French broached the subject with the Americans. The Chinese reacted favorably to a Soviet proposal in September 1953 to convene a meeting of the "Big Powers" (the USSR, USA, France, Britain, and the Soviet Union plus China) to discuss major global disputes, including the Indochina conflict. Communist bloc exchanges with Vietnamese communists also yielded important changes in strategy. In a widely broadcast interview published in the Swedish paper *Expressen* on 26 November 1953, Ho indicated his party's willingness to discuss a political solution to the war in Indochina. However, he and his Chinese advisers knew that this meant they had to score a major victory on the battlefield to strengthen their position at the negotiating table if serious talks began. Of course, Navarre would have to do the same thing for his government.

Toward the Showdown

This, then, was the backdrop against which the showdown at Dien Bien Phu rapidly emerged. The Vietnamese moved first: unable to take the delta, in early November they initiated their highland plan by moving on Lai Chau province. (The French had administered this colonial Tai island in the middle of the Vietnamese archipelago since 1945.) Around 10 November, the 316th left its base to head northwest. The French knew that their small contingent of mainly special forces teams in Lai Chau could not protect the Tai federation against a PAVN attack. Nor could their Tai partisans. In any case, Lai Chau was too close to China for comfort and too hard to supply by air. This is why Salan had already suggested the transfer of the Tai capital to Dien Bien Phu and Navarre concurred. He also agreed that Dien Bien Phu was the best choice for defending Laos. The valley had the advantage of being bigger (16km long and 9km wide). It had the required airstrip and was thought to be easier to supply by air than Na San or Lai Chau.

Located between the two points, Dien Bien Phu now acquired unprecedented importance for both sides. When the first PAVN regiments began moving towards Lai Chau in mid-November, Navarre issued orders to prepare for the airborne seizure of the valley at Dien Bien Phu. This started in the form of Operation Castor on 20 November 1953. Within days, this massive airborne intervention easily dislodged the small enemy presence there, quickly repaired the airstrip, and began turning Dien Bien Phu into another entrenched camp, bigger and better, a "super Na San" if you like. Planes brought in artillery, machine guns, ammunition, and tanks, while soldiers and laborers felled trees, dug trenches, laid minefields, and unfurled tons of barbed wire. By the end of the year, the valley was home to 12,000 French Union troops and a handful of Tai villages, most of which Giap's artillery would soon obliterate.[8]

When the Vietnamese learned that Navarre was moving on Dien Bien Phu, Giap immediately ordered his intelligence people to find out what was going on. Two questions were particularly important: "Is the enemy going to withdraw? How are they deployed?" The military intelligence service hustled scouts to the valley in search of answers. Signals teams focused on intercepting enemy radio communications to glean details on troop positions and strength. If there was ever a time for moles inside the enemy camp to provide details on the enemy's order of battle, this was it. The cartography service scrambled to provide the General Staff with an accurate map of Dien Bien Phu. The French inadvertently helped when one of their parachute drops missed its target and fell into Vietnamese hands. Among the things one excited and soon-to-be-decorated scout recovered was a detailed military map of the valley. Seasoned communist interrogators began interviewing prisoners of war who knew the area (the man who led these interrogations, Mac Lam, was later to "proselytize" American POWs to communism). Meanwhile, Giap ordered the 316th Division to change course and head for the valley. Similar orders went out to the 308th, the 312th, and the 351st. Suddenly, over half of Vietnam's professional army was on its way to Dien Bien Phu.[9]

For the Vietnamese and their Chinese advisers, Dien Bien Phu had the potential to be the showdown they were looking for as the international situation changed. Giap told his inner circle at this time that "Dien Bien Phu could be the battle." Preparations began in earnest without anyone knowing for sure whether the French would stay put or not.[10] There was room for optimism if the French remained. Supplying this valley over a sustained period of time would be easier than in Na San or areas further west like Sam Neua or Luang Prabang. The Vietnamese controlled Hoa Binh, Nghia Lo, and Tuan Giao (a hub located east of Dien Bien Phu). The French had recently evacuated Na San. The entire crescent running through Hoa Binh to Zone IV was also Ho's. If they planned and executed it carefully, the Vietnamese were confident they could supply troops, weapons, and food to Dien Bien Phu from three directions: from southern China's Yunnan province, from the western side of the DRV's crescent at Yen Bay connected to the Chinese border at Cao Bang, and from zones III and IV south of Hanoi. Thanks to their first thrust into the northwest in 1952, the Vietnamese were already hard at work building, repairing, and widening roads to move Chinese-supplied trucks to Coi Noi via Route 13 and on to Tuan Giao, thanks to Route 41. From there, thousands of porters pushing pack-bikes could transport weapons and food along 80 kilometers of trails leading to the front lines of Dien Bien Phu. Even more would carry rice in from zones III and IV thanks to route 41 connecting Hoa Binh to Tuan Giao, again, via Coi Noi. On his way to the northwest, Giap's right-hand man, Hoang Van Thai, spent a day at Na San on 30 November to study what the French had done there a year earlier.[11]

Navarre was superbly confident that he could defeat the Vietnamese in the highlands without sacrificing his control of the delta or his upcoming offensive on Zone V. On 3 December, he informed the government that he would accept the battle for the northwest at Dien Bien Phu. The fact that French leaders informed him that he would receive no more troops did nothing to change his mind. On 6 December, Navarre gave the order to evacuate Lai Chau in Operation Pollux. Well-informed of Giap's preparations, the general remained confident that he could repeat his success at Na San. If the enemy attacked at Dien Bien Phu, then all the better: he would crush the PAVN once and for all. The French slang expression for that action, *casser du Viet*, could be heard on the lips of officers and soldiers alike as they readied for the clash. René Cogny, second to Navarre and the head of the army in northern Vietnam, dared Giap to attack: "I want a clash at Dien Bien Phu. I'll do everything possible to make him eat dirt and forget about wanting to try his hand at grand strategy." Yes, Navarre could have evacuated Dien Bien Phu by air, even until late December; but he did not do so for one very simple reason: he wanted this fight.[12]

So did the Vietnamese. By the end of the month, Giap's divisions had surrounded the valley from all sides and had begun installing carefully camouflaged artillery and antiaircraft guns in the hills. The Vietnamese were confident that if they could line everything up correctly, this was a battle they could win. "Navarre had spread out his fingers," the deputy director of military intelligence at the time recalled. The Vietnamese leadership had enough information, he continued,

> to make the decision to destroy the Dien Bien Phu fortified defensive complex, turning this into the key battle of our entire 1953–1954 Winter–Spring plan. Dien Bien Phu became a battle that neither the enemy nor our side had originally anticipated in our plans . . . We were concerned that the enemy would retreat and abandon the area, while the enemy was afraid that we would not dare to attack. At this point the battle of wits entered the decisive phase.[13]

Sometime in "early January 1954," the Vietnamese Politburo officially approved the "destruction of the fortress at Dien Bien Phu." On 5 January, Giap left for the valley accompanied by the former colonial scoutmaster who would wire the battlefield for him, Hoang Dao Thuy, and his main Chinese military adviser, Wei Guoqing. No one on the Vietnamese side, however, thought this would be an easy victory. And Giap had to be very careful not to attack prematurely and destroy his best divisions. Na San was on his mind. Nowhere was this more evident than when the Vietnamese commander called off the first attack on the enemy camp in Dien Bien Phu in January 1954. Initially, the Vietnamese and their Chinese advisers had planned to hit the French camp hard and fast ("Attack swiftly to win swiftly" was the slogan). The idea was to surge through the northern and northwestern sides of the perimeter judged to be the weak spots in the enemy's defense. The goal was also to improve the government's negotiating position with a quick victory as diplomats were about to take up the Indochina question for the first time in a Great Powers meeting scheduled for 25 January in Berlin. Although Giap's troops were as keen on attacking as Navarre's were, the Vietnamese general delayed the order when some of his artillery failed to arrive on time and the enemy's perimeter turned out to be stronger than had been initially thought. Giap pushed his planned D-Day from the 20th to the 25th. In the end, to the shock of his own troops who wanted to *casser du français*, he called it off, convinced that victory was not yet sure. Giap could not risk another defeat. Wei Guoqing agreed, and so did Ho and the Politburo. Giap did all of this in real time, using the radio and telephone system Hoang Dao Thuy had installed for him. This was their "third section." It worked closely with the first and second sections, in charge of battle tactics and military intelligence. All three were essential to supplying and relaying information to the decision-makers.[14]

The good news for Giap was that Navarre launched Operation Atlante against Zone V on the same day. The Vietnamese could not believe their luck. Their intelligence services had already radioed authorities there, ordering them to prepare for such a maneuver, and they were. To disperse Navarre's forces even further and give his own men time to put the artillery into place around Dien Bien Phu, Giap ordered troops in Zone V to move in to attack in the central highlands and instructed the 308th to relocate into northern Laos. A diversionary move though it was, the thrust into Laos also served to bring back rice, secure more territories for the Pathet Lao, and make a mockery of the French claim that the engagement at Dien Bien Phu would stop the PAVN from marching in there. In mid-February, the 308th returned to Dien Bien Phu and joined a total force of 51,000 PAVN regulars now waiting in the jungles to attack the 12,000 French Union troops defending the valley below them. Meanwhile, the Vietnamese infiltrated parts of the 320th back into the Tonkin delta just as Giap had done to Salan when the latter had committed to Hoa Binh and Na San. Vietnamese operations in the Red River Delta resumed like clockwork.

This is where Navarre committed the error that would end up costing him the battle. He knew in early January that the Vietnamese were successfully bringing in artillery. He was sure that Giap was going to throw everything he had at him at Dien Bien Phu—not in the delta, not in Laos, and certainly not in Zone V's central highlands. This was all diversion. The French general also knew that there was a linkage between negotiations and the battlefield which could make Dien Bien Phu "the" battle to win, no matter what. And yet he refused to cancel Operation Atlante in order to transfer troops to help defend Dien Bien Phu. On 12 March 1954, the day before he gave the signal to attack there, Giap received a radio message from the commander of Zone V, informing him that Navarre had landed another contingent at Qui Nhon. The Vietnamese general is said to have quipped: "This is very good news; we are now certain to win."[15] Not quite, but by going ahead with Operation Atlante in lower central Vietnam, Navarre played straight into his enemy's hands in the far northwest.

Sociology of a War: Land Reform as War Communism

This, then, is where things stood on the eve of the battle of Dien Bien Phu.[16] This, too, is the point at which specialists of the Indochina War turn to tell the story of how, on 13 March 1954, Vietnamese troops attacked the enemy fortress below them and, for the next 56 days, fought tooth and nail until they overran the French camp on 7 May. As tempting as it is to follow Vietnamese troops into battle at this point in our narrative, we need to step back from the battlefield for a few pages and go back in time to ask ourselves why Ho would declare full-scale land reform in mid-November 1953. Why would he send thousands of cadres into villages to attack the established order at the very moment he was marching his troops to Dien Bien Phu for the biggest clash of the conflict? The answer is that land reform was not some sort of a socioeconomic sideshow to the Dien Bien Phu campaign, to be treated separately. The "great upheaval" as the Vietnamese communists called it, the "changing of heaven and earth" (*long troi loi dat*), was a weapon of war as well as an instrument of revolutionary statecraft. As in Mao's China, the two things went together. And that the Chinese were there to help the Vietnamese as they prepared for Dien Bien Phu and for the start of the assault on the established rural order should come as no surprise. They were doing it together as part of a shared revolutionary process reaching back to the interwar period. It is time to take a wider look at what went into Dien Bien Phu.

"The Peasant Question" and
Early Sino-Vietnamese Communism

Chinese and Vietnamese communist parties may have been born in port cities situated along China's coastline, Shanghai and Hong Kong respectively, but they did not remain centered there for long. The outbreak of the civil war in China in 1927 sent Chinese communists out of the cities and into the countryside (as well as deeper into maritime Southeast Asia). As they moved inland, leaders like Mao Zedong realized that, to succeed, he and his party would have to mobilize, politicize, and transform the majority peasant population into a source of military, economic, and political might. The working class remained concentrated in the cities. At the head of the "Chinese Soviet Republic" created in Jiangxi province between 1931 and 1934, Mao honed land reform into a weapon of revolutionary statecraft capable of mobilizing and politicizing the peasantry under his party's control. Pushed into northern China by Chiang Kai-shek's army in 1934, the leader known as the "Helmsman" turned land reform into his specialty in Yan'an during the Second World War, used it to help him secure victory throughout China in 1949, and applied it to the whole of the country during the Korean War (1950–53). Over this long period of "disruption," Mao had added land reform to other mobilization techniques his party had borrowed from the Soviet Union and wove them into a unique brand of agrarian communism.[17]

Vietnamese communists were part of this process. Circulating between the Soviet Union and China during the interwar period, Ho was as attuned to "the peasant question" as Mao. At ease in Russian and Chinese, he had followed theoretical debates on the revolutionary role of the peasantry as he helped the Comintern spread communism into Asia. In 1924, in Moscow, he was vice-president of the "Peasant International" (*Krestintern*) and penned essays on rural revolution. He discussed peasant mobilization techniques with Chinese cadres during the Second World War and even lectured on the matter in southern China. He was not alone in this endeavor. In the early 1930s, Vietnamese communists inside the country had even mirrored what the Chinese were doing in Jiangxi when they established their own "Soviets" or "revolutionary councils" in Nghe An province (which was later to become part of Zone IV).[18]

Life in the countryside had never been easy. Although the introduction of modern medicine during the colonial period had lowered mortality rates, the resulting population increase placed unprecedented pressure on the limited amount of land available in the central and northern lowlands. Colonial authorities introduced a series of hydraulic systems to alleviate the stress, as irrigation allowed several regions to produce two rice crops instead of one. It helped. So did fertilizers and migration. That said, population pressure remained high, and tens of thousands of people still tended to go hungry. As in the past, bad weather in the form of droughts or floods could spell disaster. Although a *microfundia* of small landowners increased their land holdings through predatory practices, large estates in central and northern Vietnam were rare. In the 1930s, 90 percent of the farms in upper Vietnam counted less than 1.8 hectares of land on average. The biggest landholdings were in the Mekong Delta.[19]

The Second World War revealed the fragility of this rural ecosystem. Increased population pressure, poor weather, and the stockpiling of rice by the French and the Japanese drastically reduced the amount of food available to feed the people who had produced it. By late 1944, the only way to head off famine in northern and central Vietnam was to distribute food from reserves in the south. The problem was that American bombers and submarines prevented its transportation. As a result, from December 1944 until May 1945, famine spread through upper Vietnam, killing over one million peasants before the Japanese capitulated in mid-1945. Members of the communist-led nationalist front, the Viet Minh, positioned themselves as the defenders of the rural poor and rode a wave of peasant anger to power.[20]

My point is that, like their Chinese counterparts, Vietnamese communists grasped the "peasant question" long before they took power. Thanks to a host of highly trained technicians, Ho's government did an impressive job of ending the famine before the outbreak of war with the French pushed his government out of the cities and into the countryside. However, for a long time, Ho resisted calls from within his party to redistribute land radically. Not yet. War required pragmatism: the communist hold on the government was weak and even weaker at the village level. If patriotic landlords and notables paid their taxes, respected the law, and helped where they could, then everyone could fight the colonialists in a grand alliance cutting across class lines. Communist-guided land reform began in late 1945, as we know, but it remained moderate. The government required landowners to reduce the rents they could charge for leasing fields to landless peasants by 25 percent. In theory, secondary rents, indirect taxes, and debts contracted before 1945 were cancelled. Other decrees imposed limits on the interest rates landowners and merchants could charge when loaning rice, livestock, or equipment. In areas it controlled, the government confiscated French property as well as that of "Vietnamese traitors." The communists reformed land ownership; but they did not forcibly redistribute land until late 1953. The preservation of this wide-governing coalition trumped radical social revolution for eight full years.

The real problem was that the communists had yet to create a separate bureaucratic class capable of taking over to enforce agrarian change on radical terms at the village level. At the lower levels of Ho's Vietnam since 1945, the bureaucracy had been more of a graft and a compromise than a revolutionary break with the preexisting order. This is why, as the communists moved to take control of the state and national fronts from 1950 and adopted a more radical land policy from 1952, they simultaneously accelerated efforts to produce a new communist bureaucratic class through "rectification" and "emulation." And if Ho declared class warfare in late 1953, he did so because he finally commanded an army of cadres who could lead an offensive against the "feudalists" at the village level while the People's Army fought the "imperialists" on the battlefield.[21]

Food, Famine, and the Peasant Majority

But why? Why did Ho destroy the grand alliance in 1953 by launching a class war against landowners who, on average, did not really have all that much land anyway? Why unleash chaos at the village level as the biggest battle of the Indochina War loomed on the horizon? The Vietnamese president could have waited until the end of the war before deploying his cadre class. The communists could have then easily defeated their class enemies and imposed the single-party communist state down to the grassroots level via this bureaucratic revolution of Sino-Soviet design. Why abandon pragmatism at this point?

The main reason explaining why Ho and his entourage went ahead was because they recognized that the nature of the war they had chosen to fight since 1950 was driving the peasantry into the ground. They had to do something to turn things around fast. Until 1950, Ho's guerrilla army, the "tiger," if you will, had survived on the trickle economy, wireless radios, policing, and guerrilla statecraft discussed earlier. The colonial city and regional trade provided the minimum it needed to get by and to bog down the colonial army at the same time. Troops went out on brief guerrilla operations and then returned to their villages. Civil servants tended to come from the villages where they worked. The local economy supported them all without too much trouble. In exchange, soldiers and bureaucrats chipped in to help villagers with the planting and harvest. In the archipelago state, no one needed to stockpile large quantities of food.

All that changed with the creation of a large standing army, a general mobilization law conscripting hundreds of thousands of people into supply and work teams, and a rapidly expanding civil service designed to oversee it all. By May 1954, the PAVN numbered 200,000 men operating mainly in central and northern Vietnam. The number of civil servants now living independently of their villages ballooned as the army liberated new territories which required more officials to govern them. By the war's end, over 100,000 civil servants were pushing their pencils just about everywhere (apart from Zone IX in the far south). What was worse, each conventional battle required the massive mobilization of the surrounding population. Between the battle of Cao Bang in late 1950 and that of Hoa Binh, which ended in early 1952, the party conscripted one million people for a total of 20 million workdays. The Battle of Hoa Binh alone, a three-month affair, mobilized 333,200 people.[22]

These people had to eat. Rice—its price, production, collection, and distribution—suddenly became a nightmare of a problem. A vicious circle, in fact: when the government pulled able-bodied men and women out of their fields for military operations, labor shortages rapidly appeared in the villages. Women filled in as best they could, as did children and even the elderly. But when the government drafted too many people from the same villages in the heat of the battle, it could spell disaster for those left behind. Nor was conscription evenly spread: of the 330,000 people drafted to supply the Battle of Hoa Binh, most came from Zone IV. Labor shortages and economic hardship were never far from where the PAVN "elephant" roamed.[23]

Fields started to go untended. French bombing of the agricultural infrastructure only made things worse. Villagers received orders to help their neighbors in distress, but the number of hands available to help dwindled in several areas. The party offered land to those who needed it, but many peasants did not have the strength or the equipment to farm it. Food production declined as the war intensified. But the government had no choice except to lean ever harder on the peasants. The Chinese could not come to the Vietnamese rescue, not yet. Their stockpiles went to feeding troops in Korea, and Mao was implementing a massive land reform campaign of his own.

In their rush to create a large standing army, to erect a new type of communist state to run it, and to launch a General Counter-offensive of a conventional kind, the Vietnamese communist core badly underestimated the disastrous effects this would have on the food supply and on the very population they were supposed to defend, the peasantry (who were 90 percent of the DRV's population). Unable to seize the Red River Delta and its rice fields that year, party leaders knew they had a major food crisis on their hands. As the price of rice soared and the currency tanked, they imposed an agricultural tax to be paid in rice, a national bank to stockpile it, and a commercial service to distribute it to soldiers and porters. The Soviets and the Chinese had done this in their revolutionary wars. Whether Soviet, Chinese, or Vietnamese in design, War Communism placed extraordinary pressure on the peasantry to supply food and labor at all costs.

Starting in mid-1952, the French systematized their assault on the enemy's food supply in the form of the strategic bombing of dikes, dams, canals, and the machine-gunning of beasts of burden. The French navy and air force prevented Ho from importing rice from granaries in the Mekong Delta to feed hungry mouths in central and northern Vietnam. Meanwhile, Salan blockaded the Red River Delta and sent troops into villages there and in Zone V to make sure that the enemy could not seize paddy at harvest time. And by imposing military conscription and a general mobilization law on the Associated State of Vietnam in 1951, colonial authorities only took more peasants out of their villages and, in so doing, sent more pangs of hunger deeper into rural Vietnam.

This, then, is how, for reasons connected to the changing nature of the Indochina War since 1950, the French "colonialists" and the Vietnamese "communists" triggered famine in central and northern Vietnam a couple of years later, as the Rice General looked on approvingly. This was the socioeconomic backdrop against which Dien Bien Phu occurred. In 1953, communist documents confirm that "serious and sustained manifestations of famine" had broken out in zones IV and V, contested areas in the Red River Delta, and highland areas in the northwest. Hardest hit, Zone V reported the deaths of 1,780 people due to starvation in that same year. In parts of Zone III, normally a rice-rich area in the delta, the portrait was a terrifying one. Scores of families had little to eat. Many became beggars, while others began eating off the land, scrounging for roots, grubs, anything they could get their hands on. The daily calorie intake for tens, perhaps hundreds of thousands of people in these areas plummeted. Some had become so weak that they could not even eat. People died of starvation in places such as Ninh Binh and Son Tay. Famished youths joined the army of the Associated State of Vietnam simply to find a meal. Others were tempted by the promise of a better life "on the other side." This was not what Ho wanted to hear at that point in time.[24]

The problem was that things were difficult everywhere. Salan's efforts "to starve the adversary" created food problems for those in charge of the Associated State of Vietnam too. The price of rice increased in colonial areas, and supply problems made it harder to feed hungry mouths.

In late 1952, the governor of northern Vietnam surprised Salan when he refused to classify rice as a product of "military interest" and, in doing so, somehow got it exempted from the blockade so that he could feed hungry civilians within the Associated State. General Salan's team pleaded with the governor to reconsider. When the general asked who had actually given this order, the Frenchman was shocked to learn that it had come from Bao Dai's cabinet members. Ho Chi Minh was clearly not the only one whose people were caught between the hammer and the anvil.[25]

It is only by pulling back the sociological curtain surrounding the battle history of Dien Bien Phu that we can see how exhausted and hungry much of Ho's population was by late 1953. "We must do everything we can to defeat famine," a government broadcast pleaded that year. "A grain of rice," it said, "is the equivalent of a drop of blood."[26] If Pham Van Dong warned officials in 1953 "that not one person was to be allowed to die of starvation in a Democratic Republic regime," he did so because it was already happening.[27] Things got so bad by January of that year that a peasant revolt broke out in the village of Nghia Loc in Zone IV, costing the lives of seventy villagers and seven regulars in the army. We can be sure that these people were not traitors. They were exhausted, hungry, and desperate. This revolt had occurred at the very moment Ho was explaining to his party behind closed doors why they now had to move towards full-scale land reform.[28]

The Vietnamese president knew that the nature of the war he had chosen to follow since 1950 had led him into this impasse. He also knew what had happened in Russia when Lenin pushed the peasantry too hard to feed the Red Army and the urban workers during the period of Soviet War Communism between 1918 and 1921. Ho and Truong Chinh could have pulled back at this point. They had a choice. They could have returned to the archipelago state to fight a guerrilla war like the Indonesians and the Algerians. They did not. Instead, they went all in by adopting the last weapon in the Sino-Vietnamese War Communism arsenal: full-scale land reform. Neither Stalin nor Mao imposed it. Ho embraced it because he was part of this wider communist circle and the revolutionary wars and statecraft it had generated since the early 1920s.

Sino-Vietnamese War Communism: The Luo Plan

Preparations for full-scale land reform had begun in mid-1952. The most important source of support and advice came from the Chinese advisory team headed by Luo Guibo. Since 1950, he had served as Mao's general adviser to the Vietnamese Workers Party and as the Great Helmsman's special envoy to President Ho. Luo Guibo got his revolutionary start in his home province of Fujian in the early 1930s when he helped Mao create a Soviet republic there and was deeply involved in Maoist mobilization techniques. He and his team of specialists provided Ho with detailed plans of the Chinese party's land-reform policies over the last two decades, including the one currently underway. Joining Ho in these high-level discussions were Truong Chinh, the party's general secretary, and Pham Van Dong, who oversaw economic and financial matters. Long familiar with Mao's ideas, Ho and his entourage agreed that what worked in China could work in Vietnam.[29]

In September 1952, Luo Guibo produced a blueprint for the Vietnamese to use in devising their own land reform policy over the course of the following year. It was entitled "Preliminary comments on mobilizing the masses in 1953." As the PAVN marched westwards in late 1952, he sent copies of it to Truong Chinh and Ho for their approval.[30] The main idea was that the Vietnamese could only generate the high levels of peasant support they needed to stay in the war by forcibly redistributing land. This meant taking property and equipment from the "feudalists," the landowners and notables, and giving it to the peasants. This would incentivize farmers to produce more food and to participate in the war. There was even more to it, though: this forced reordering of the social order in the countryside would allow the Communist Party to simultaneously upend the preexisting administration and expand its control at the village level. By destroying the landowning class, including merchants who got in the way, patriotic or not, the communist center could take the rural administration in hand once and for all. It would do so by moving in its own bureaucratic class, this phalanx of rectified and disciplined cadres Ho had been building offstage. The security service would follow them. Lastly, just as Mao had used the Korean War to rally his people behind the application of land reform to all of China between 1950 and 1953, Ho could do the same between 1953 and 1956. Ho would push through agrarian class warfare in patriotic guise by recasting the "feudalists" as the allies of the "imperialists." To combat the "landowners" was to defeat the "French." But why did he plan to do so until 1956? Ho did so on the assumption that the war would go beyond 1954. No one knew at the start that the war would end in July of that year. Nevertheless, the goal was the same as in China: just as Mao had used his war against the Americans in Korea to push through his land reform in the early 1950s, so too did Ho seek to use the war with the French in Indochina to launch his class war.[31]

Full-scale land reform began in the Democratic Republic of Vietnam in January 1953 in two stages. ("Full-scale" here refers to the forcible redistribution of land and related equipment and livestock from one designated class of Vietnamese to another.) The first part required cadres to enforce rent and interest reductions with greater severity and distribute any remaining "French colonialist," "Vietnamese traitor," or vacant land. No more exceptions. In so doing, the communists would finally show the peasants that they were on their side and, at the same time, they would politicize them in order to bring them under the center's control. In line with the Luo plan, the Vietnamese prepared to seize the local administration and local Lien Viet chapters. That was a good thing, Guibo said, since it would allow the party center to introduce more peasants into the mass associations and the local administration. This, in turn, would prepare the way for the second stage: the deployment of a communist bureaucratic class whose "rectified" cadres would enter the villages and, alongside their peasant allies, forcibly depose the landowning class, seize their land, and redistribute it. It was nothing less than a bureaucratic revolution of historic proportions, a communist coup d'état against the coalition state Ho had first embraced in 1946.[32]

Starting in early 1953, Ho and Truong Chinh presided over the introduction of full-scale land reform in line with the Luo plan. In a series of meetings, they explained that the Chinese had it right. Land reform would allow them to mobilize the peasantry for war, increase agricultural production, and expand the party's hold over the state and rural society. Peasants would join the army and produce more, knowing they would soon have a plot of land to call their own. They would then be more motivated to pay the agricultural tax and, as a result, more food would become available for the war effort.[33] Truong Chinh added that the "great disruption" had to occur now, rather than later, for the crucial reason that the communists were losing peasant support at a critical juncture in the war. If, he said, "the peasantry is not determined [to fight], then that is very dangerous. One should not think that the peasantry will necessarily join us in any given situation."[34] The Vietnamese general secretary was right, of course, just as his counterparts in the Soviet Union and China had discovered before him.

In April 1953, the party center went forward with the plan. In a series of legal changes approved in that month and later, Vietnamese communists assembled special land-reform teams and mobile courts to enforce the lowering of interest and leasing rates, as well as the seizing land from the "feudalists" when the time came. Ho began deploying his army of cadres into the countryside from Zone IV northwards. They started out in selected villages located in secure areas like Thai Nguyen. Backed up by the security services, cadres went into the villages which they had selected to forcibly lower rents by turning the peasants against the landlords and their allies in "struggle sessions" based on Maoist models.[35]

In July 1953, Ho Chi Minh and his entourage offered a show trial in Thai Nguyen of what their War Communism would look like. The subject of this proceeding was a well-known Vietnamese property owner named Nguyen Thi Nam. This woman had pulled herself up by her bootstraps since the 1930s. She had been a successful merchant in the emerging steel and cement industries in Haiphong before investing in a sugar plantation in Thai Nguyen. Her patriotism was impeccable: she had protected top-ranking Vietnamese communists from the French police during the colonial period. She had donated land and money to the resistance, as well as two of her sons to the army. She was widely referred to as a "Mother of the Resistance" (*Me Khang Chien*).

All of that now had to change. The communists could authorize the emulation of heroic workers, peasants, and even bourgeois professionals, but they could no longer countenance any "patriotic feudalists."[36]

Landowners, anticolonialist or not, were now an enemy class and classified as such. The Vietnamese communists deliberately chose to make an example out of Nguyen Thi Nam. They and their Chinese advisers put this woman on trial under a red banner reading: "Overthrow the despotic landlord Nguyen Thi Nam, take back the land for the peasants." Foreshadowing the "struggle" sessions which were to come a few months later, cadres placed her before hundreds of poor peasants and then led them in denunciation of this "atrocious landowner" and her list of supposed crimes. Whipped into a frenzy of hate, the crowd jeered at her, spat on her, and slapped her. At some point that summer, as the first stage of full-scale land reform began in earnest, the party leadership (all men, mind you) had her executed.[37]

The execution of Nguyen Thi Nam symbolized the end of the coalition state the communists had accepted at the start of the war. The communists would go on to execute several thousand Vietnamese before land reform ended in 1956. Cadres even practiced torture to obtain the confessions they needed to push the revolution through, while hundreds, perhaps thousands, committed suicide. By committing such acts of cruelty against innocent people whose only sin was to be of the wrong class (and that is highly debatable), Vietnamese communists sowed civil war, deep hate, and unforgettable sorrow that would drive thousands of the country's people into the enemy's arms. To claim that the father of the nation, Ho Chi Minh, was somehow a stranger to all of this is dishonest. President Ho could have said no. He had the authority and the prestige to be heard by all, including his Chinese advisers (in fact, Mao had given express orders to his men to respect any decision taken by the Vietnamese communists, above all, Ho). The president and his associates went ahead with the killings because they chose to do so.[38] (See Plate 25.)

That Vietnamese landlords did not have big properties and that the majority of the land in the DRV's upper half had *already* been distributed before radical land reform began in 1953 did not matter.[39] What did was pushing through the bureaucratic revolution, taking over the village administration, and raising up the single-party communist state from its archipelagic foundation.[40] The battle against the "French colonialists" at Dien Bien Phu and the one against "Vietnamese feudalists" in the countryside were deeply entwined.

The Battle of Dien Bien Phu

Three Waves to Victory

The Battle of Dien Bien Phu began on 13 March 1954 with a barrage of Vietnamese artillery fire.[41] Soon thereafter, thousands of PAVN troops stepped out of the jungle to fight in the open in ways Ho could never have imagined when he first told his parable of the tiger and the elephant. Battle-hardened soldiers rushed the two most vulnerable positions on the northern side of the camp, Gabrielle and Béatrice, and controlled them within a few days. On the French side, five remaining positions protected the command center in the heart of the valley. The commanding officer there was General Christian de Castries. He relied on the two officers we met at the start of our book, Pierre Langlais and Marcel Bigeard, to protect the perimeter and to counterattack. And they did so with uncommon valor. (See Map 13.)

With his first attack, the commanding general, Vo Nguyen Giap, had to achieve that which he had failed to do at Na San: destroy the enemy's airstrip and weaken the air bridge which would bring in vital supplies. On the eve of the battle, the Frenchman in charge of the camp's artillery, Captain Piroth, had bragged to Navarre that "no Viet Minh cannon will be able to fire three rounds before being destroyed by my artillery."[42] He should have held his tongue because, within a few hours of the start of the battle, the precision of the calibration and the concentration of the firepower his Vietnamese counterpart unleashed on the French fortress made it clear that this was not going to end with his adversary's swift defeat. Four days later, the Vietnamese artillery had rendered the airstrip largely unusable. As French bombers scoured the hills in search of the enemy's guns, Piroth killed himself rather than carry on.[43]

None of this signified that the French were suddenly destined to lose the battle, but it did mean that Dien Bien Phu would immediately become the site of a siege battle without precedent in any other war of decolonization in the twentieth century. Twelve-thousand French Union troops had to hold off the 51,000 PAVN regulars surrounding them from all sides. For the time being, the troops in the valley managed to hold on, thanks to supplies and soldiers the air force could still parachute in. However, this time, Giap had antiaircraft guns hidden in the hills above Dien Bien Phu. They were soon sending flak into the sky, forcing enemy planes to fly as high above them as 2,000 meters by mid-April. This, coupled with increasingly bad weather as the rainy season arrived, made it harder for them to supply the besieged camp with much accuracy.

Nowhere was the siege more evident than for those on the ground. With both sides in possession of artillery, soldiers immediately dug into the ground as exploding shells churned up the dirt into piles of rubble and created a crater-like landscape that reminded several French officers of what they had seen in the First World War. Indeed, having disrupted the French air bridge in the first attack, during the second half of March Vo Nguyen Giap focused on spinning a web of trenches around the heavily armed cluster of positions holding the fortress (Huguette, Claudine, Dominique, and Eliane). Soldiers and laborers went to work, day and night, with their pickaxes and shovels. The high command brought in specialist miners from the northeastern coalfields to dig underground tunnels as far as the enemy's bunker lines. The Vietnamese even built mine galleries not seen since the First World War. These served in trench warfare to project underground "shafts" into enemy territory and then set off explosives beneath the enemy positions. The French were not dupes and used geophones to listen for any suspicious noise coming from underneath. Giap's main goal, though, was to slowly but surely advance his web of trenches around the enemy camp as his artillery pounded it and his antiaircraft guns forced French planes to operate from ever higher altitudes as the size of their drop zones shrank. Dien Bien Phu was set-piece battle in its purest form.[44] (See plates 26, 27, 28, and 29.)

As vulnerable as the French camp was to Vietnamese artillery fire, Giap still had to order his men out of their trenches and over the top into enemy machine-gun fire and shelling. Meanwhile, French bombers moved in as close as possible to drop a host of explosives on Giap's men. Napalm rained down on the surrounding jungle as French pilots searched for the enemy's supply lines and artillery guns. Little wonder then, that even before the battle had officially started in March, Giap had sent commandos into the airfields near Hanoi and Haiphong to sabotage enemy planes, especially those American-supplied B-26s sitting on the tarmac. They destroyed a dozen fighters in all.

With their trenches in place, the Vietnamese launched their second offensive on 30 March. It was a massive attack of 12,000 men. After making considerable headway over the first two days, a ferocious counterattack led by Langlais and Bigeard pushed the assaulting force back with high casualties on both sides. The French fortress held. On 6 April, Giap called off the second attack and called up 25,000 new recruits. Meanwhile, the French air force parachuted in the last troops Navarre could spare. In all, 16,000 French Union troops fought at Dien Bien Phu.[45]

The start of the third Vietnamese attack on 26 April coincided with the opening of the Geneva Conference on Korea and Indochina. For the Vietnamese and the Chinese, the battle could not drag on any longer. Dien Bien Phu had to fall, and fast, in order to strengthen the communist negotiating position. Defeat was simply not an option. On 1 May, thousands of PAVN troops went over the top again as Giap unleashed his artillery on the camp. Thanks to the Chinese, the Vietnamese had brought in Soviet Katyusha truck-mounted multiple rocket launchers and concentrated them on the enemy fortress. These rockets are also known as Stalin's organs because of the screeching sound the shells make as they race through the air. The Soviets had used them against the Nazis during the Second World War. Giap launched them during the last few days of the battle as his men fought their way, meter by meter, trench by trench, until they finally took over the enemy fortress on the afternoon of 7 May 1954 and raised the Vietnamese flag over de Castries' bunker.[46] (See Plate 30.)

The Face of Battle[47]

Those who recall the valley floor after the guns went silent spoke of
Verdun. It could have been a scene straight out of the Second World War
too. Artillery explosions had obliterated the Tai villages that had been
there for generations and churned up the green rice fields surrounding
them into ugly craters surrounded by mounds of rubble. Although Vietnamese troops suffered many casualties storming the heavily defended
fortress, they made sure that the enemy shared their terror by unleashing their own artillery, flak, machine-gun fire, and those Stalin's organs
on them. As one of the survivors in the French camp later recalled:
"Shells rained down on us without stopping like a hailstorm on a fall
evening. Bunker after bunker, trench after trench, collapsed, burying
under them men and weapons."[48] When Dr. Ton That Tung spoke of
the pleasure he took in his people inflicting such pain on the colonizers,
we can be sure that he was referring to something like this. General de
Castries suffered some kind of psychological shock when he spoke
shortly after his capture about "going crazy" at Dien Bien Phu (and his
chief of staff had suffered a nervous breakdown before being evacuated
from the valley). On top of it all, heavy, seemingly incessant rain, which
had started in April, filled the trenches with knee-deep mud, breeding
disease and swarms of yellow flies looking for hosts. They found them
among the bodies strewn across this lunar landscape before survivors
on both sides managed to bury their dead.

Hardest to repair was the violence this type of warfare inflicted on soldiers. Artillery fire accounted for 86.3 percent of the wounds inflicted on
Vietnamese bodies at Dien Bien Phu. Of those suffering severe head and
back injuries, hundreds of them would never walk again, disabled, para-
lyzed, or worse.[49] Seventy-five percent of all French Union troop losses
were the result of artillery fire.[50] Clearly, this was not guerrilla warfare. As
Nguyen Nhu Thien recalled the hell he had witnessed at Dien Bien Phu:

> I was responsible for the transport teams evacuating the dead and
> wounded for our unit, A1. I was in a shelter some 500 meters from the
> hill [which was under attack]. I could see the bodies of our dead
> strung all over the ground, at the mercy of all kinds of enemy projec-

tiles. I couldn't hold back my tears at the scene of such violence, at the brutality of the battlefield. The evacuation became increasingly difficult because we had a limited number of porters. I had one company of porters. We waited for the rare moments of calm when we could recover our comrades on the hill. I lived among the dead. Many had to wait for days until we could bring them to the lines at the rear; often, their bodies were no longer intact. Many couldn't be identified, for we hadn't even had the time to take down the name, age, or origin of these new recruits. There are others who stayed on this hill forever, as we never succeeded in recovering their bodies.[51]

Vietnamese troops at Dien Bien Phu suffered a mortality rate (*ty le tu vong*) of 32 percent during the first wave attack, 25 percent during the second, while the third dropped to 22 percent.[52] In other words, one out of four Vietnamese boys sent over the top in the three waves died in machine-gun- and artillery-fire. Thousands more were injured. As another survivor on the French side recalled what he had seen before him:

> There were bodies of more than 500 dead Viet Minh, many of them perhaps sixteen years old or younger, sprawled in the grotesque positions inside the ravaged breastworks of Huguette 6. In the barbed wire and mine fields around the position, 300 more bodies could be counted and at least as many wounded must have been taken along by the retreating enemy. Twenty-one communist prisoners, all very young and jabbering from shock, were found among the dead and later on sent to the POW camp which Dien Bien Phu still maintained in its midst.[53]

Not everyone could take it. Many could not overcome all the physical and psychological trauma they had encountered in a few crowded hours. Others were exhausted from the endless digging to extend the trenches forward, often under enemy fire and napalm blasts. But the General Staff needed the lightly wounded back in action as quickly as possible in order to ensure that the French garrison fell.[54] A number of political cadres attached to combat units also faltered. Apparently, the French (re)capture of the position they called Eliane on 11 April sapped confidence along parts of the front line. On 29 April, as the third attack got underway, Giap sent strict orders to his political officers in which he criticized widespread manifestations of "rightist, negative thinking" among the troops, cadres, and officer corps.[55]

> All the necessary conditions are there for us to win. However, there is still one great obstacle, one extremely dangerous obstacle blocking our ability to carry out that task. That hindrance is rightist negative thinking that has seriously and insidiously infested the ranks of our cadres and committees within the party. If we do not wipe out this rightist negative thinking, then it will be extremely difficult for us to carry out our glorious victory.[56]

In sharp language designed to pull his cadre and officers together and take the fortress in one last attack, Giap singled out for severe criticism and punishment manifestations of this "rightist deviationism." This was communist doublespeak for troubling cases of insubordination, cowardice, fear of death and injury, exhaustion, and lack of morale: "Upon encountering the enemy, they refused to shoot. They had weapons but did not want to use them to destroy the enemy." This, he told his divisional commanders on 29 April, had happened in "our army."[57] To fix these problems, the party center organized three days of intensive study sessions, propaganda drives, and rectification campaigns to raise morale, assert party control, and, in so doing, return as many men to their combat positions as possible. Criticism, emulation, and rectification sessions were mandatory for soldiers and cadres.[58] Looking through their field binoculars, French officers could see commissars unleashing this on their own troops in the distance—literally, on the battlefield. Giap told his cadres and divisional commanders that there was no place for cowards in an army of the "proletarian class." They had no choice but to take out the French camp, period.[59]

For those who refused, military discipline was de rigueur. Court-martials and disciplinary actions—for the example of the others—always took place. In one instance, a military court tried a battalion leader of the 102nd regiment of the 308th Division for cowardice in battle. Only fifty years later was a veteran who had been there able to provide an alternative version of what had really happened to his comrade-in-arms on that violent April day of 1954:

> During the attack on A1, Vu Van Kha, a battalion leader in the 102nd regiment, suffered shellshock during a 120mm mortar explosion. He couldn't hear anything; he couldn't speak. I myself had experienced this before. Like him, I had been a victim of such violent explosions. I knew that in these circumstances one can still walk, but one cannot command. I told Kha to go to the rear lines. He went down the hill. Later I learned that he had been charged with abandoning his combat position and he was court-martialed. I only knew about this after the victory. Kha was severely judged for cowardice and for having deserted his position. He almost got himself executed. Later, his sentence was reduced to ten years in prison. He lost his military rank and position in the People's Army of Vietnam and was expelled from the party.[60]

But Vu Van Kha was no "rightist," nor was he a "coward." His fate was to have stared into the hard face of war and somehow survived the experience. What he saw that day we will never know. Nor would Giap or Ho, for this was a hell into which neither of them would ever go.[61]

In another instance, the party's political department court-martialed two officers who, it was alleged, had not served the interests of soldiers waiting for care in a field hospital overflowing with wounded during the battle. The trial exonerated a third person, the attending medic, Nguyen Thi Ngoc Toan. The case is known in Vietnam as "Incident T59" (T59 was the name of the medical way station where it took place). Fifty years later, Toan was to explain in an interview that she had got into trouble when she contested the court's decision to convict the two other men in her medical unit, who, she insisted, were completely innocent of negligence. The political cadres told her that they had to prosecute, explaining that "this must be done to maintain morale, the ideology of the soldiers. This is why we had to resolve the problem in this manner." Toan disagreed. In an extraordinary act of bravery, this woman looked War Communism in its (male) cadres' eyes and said no to the "line": "This is not the right solution. I no longer believe in the party."[62]

The War beyond the Valley . . .

As important as it was, there was more to this epic battle than the "valley." For the soldiers, the fighting may have started on 13 March, but for the peasants conscripted into this showdown things had begun in November 1953. From that date onwards, the communists had begun mobilizing tens of thousands of them to transport food, salt, medicines, ammunition, and weapons. The Communist Party's General Supply Office administered human and mechanical logistics under the leadership of Tran Dang Ninh. Despite the obstacles, this man of real organizational talents ensured that food, weapons, and medicines got to the front lines. Thanks to the general mobilization law of 1950 and others, he conscripted men and women into massive supply groups, organized them into work teams, and confiscated rice when he had to, as well as boats, bikes, cars, and packhorses. The supply section also had a fleet of Molotova and GMC trucks at its disposal, around 600 in all. While manpower remained important, mechanized logistics now transported most of the heavy weapons from China to Dien Bien Phu. A telephone and radio network guided it. Without this mechanization and wiring of the front and rear lines, there would have been no success. Without the people power, there would have been no victory either. Both things were required.[63]

Starting in November 1953, and even earlier in some places, work teams began repairing and widening roads running to Dien Bien Phu through the Tuan Giao interchange: from southern China's Yunnan province via Lai Chau, from Zones III and IV south of Hanoi, and from China's Guangxi province by way of Cao Bang and Thai Nguyen (see Map 14). Despite French bombing, the Vietnamese relied heavily on roads 13 and 41 to ship supplies to Dien Bien Phu. Like their counterparts fighting the Americans in Korea, each time the French destroyed a bridge or bombed out the road, thousands of workers arrived on the scene with their shovels, pickaxes, and baskets to repair them or build a new segment to keep the trucks moving and the supplies flowing. The Vietnamese navy got its baptism of fire not on the South China Sea, but when it began transporting supplies inland towards Dien Bien Phu, down rivers, streams, and canals from zones III and IV and China's Yunnan province.[64]

The Vietnamese scored a victory on the logistical front as much as they did on the battlefield. Those 600 transport trucks supplied ammunition and heavy weapons. French bombers destroyed thirty-two of them, while forty-three overturned on dangerous roads. When artillery arrived at the Tuan Giao hub, technicians there dismantled them into smaller pieces which porters, oxen, and horses lugged into the hills overlooking Dien Bien Phu. There, another group of specialists in carefully hidden places put the guns back together. French bombers circled constantly above, looking for targets. Human porters and animals also brought in rice, medicines, and supplies from nearby areas and from zones as far away as south of Hanoi. In all, 261,453 people served as human transporters. Seventy-one percent heralded from Zone IV, the Viet Bac Zone, and the northwest (a whopping 186,714 people came from Thanh Hoa province in Zone IV). Of the 21,000 pack-bikes pushed by people carrying rice and medicines, over half came from Zone IV. Many of them were of the sturdy Manufacture de Saint-Etienne design. Twelve thousand bamboo rafts and five hundred horses also contributed to this logistical victory.[65]

As always, food was as important as artillery. The communists might have initiated land reform to better control the rural administration and mobilize the peasantry, but they knew that they would not improve agricultural production in time for their operations at Dien Bien Phu. Tran Dang Ninh and his supply team had to provide enough rice, meat, and salt to feed the four divisions setting up camp around Dien Bien Phu in December 1953. The quarter of a million peasants they had conscripted had to eat too, as well as the horses and oxen. At the outset, Tran Dang Ninh's team worked on the assumption that their army would attack the enemy in Dien Bien Phu in January 1954 and win quickly.

However, the party's decision not to attack in January and to shift plans to fight a drawn-out battle sowed panic as the supply section's officials scrambled to find the additional rice to feed so many people during what ended up being a military operation of six months (from late November 1953 to early May 1954). Finding the 6,000 tons of rice needed for the January attack had been hard enough. Now they would need to double that, if not more. The PAVN "elephant" at Dien Bien Phu went through 40 to 50 tons of rice a day.[66] And once again, the communists had no choice but to lean yet again on the peasants, promising them that they would eventually get land, but requisitioning their rice and animals by force if need be in order to bring the French down at Dien Bien Phu first.

It is hard to convey how desperate the situation truly was on the food front. The People's Army had already depleted rice reserves in the northwest during its operations in the highlands in 1952–3, triggering famine in large parts of the Tai country where Dien Bien Phu was nestled. Many areas in the northwest were still experiencing famine. The party ordered each division to plant its own vegetables and raise its own animals. The government provided commanders with colonial piasters to buy rice and animals whenever they could instead of taking them by force. The 312th division organized its own fleet of bikes to bring in food locally. As always, the party restarted emulation campaigns to obtain rice and recruits from zones III and IV. In the end, the supply section obtained 25,000 tons of rice and almost 2,000 tons of meat through force, persuasion, or purchase. 16,823 tons went to the front lines. The rest fed the supply teams and the civil servants and cadres involved in this massive operation—over a quarter of a million people. (Over 3,000 cadres worked in the logistics section alone!) Zones IV and the northwest provided 65 percent of the total in rice. The northwestern zone, Lai Chau province in particular, provided 7,200 tons of rice and 250 tons of meat.[67]

The rear lines also extended northwards into Laos and China. Even before Giap had cancelled the January attack, Tran Dang Ninh had dispatched his deputy to Yunnan province in search of rice and salt. Mei Jiasheng, one of the Chinese military advisers at Dien Bien Phu, provided a letter of introduction to the provincial authorities in Yunnan. With a green light from the minister of defense in Beijing, the Chinese agreed to provide their Vietnamese allies with increased food aid. Between February and April 1954, Yunnan province provided 15 tons of salt and 1,870 tons of rice, as well as several thousand tons of grain for the 500 horses (most of which the Chinese had provided). The Chinese also provided 6,000 rafts that transported rice, salt, and animals down the Jin Shui River to Lai Chau province's Black River. Chinese peasants mobilized to transport this rice as did several hundred Chinese skippers. The French air force bombed these convoys at the border, killing 200 horses and destroying 100 tons of rice on one particularly bloody occasion. Meanwhile, the Vietnamese worked with their Laotian allies in the rice-rich areas of Sam Neua and Phong Saly to procure rice and other supplies. One-thousand, seven-hundred tons of rice arrived at the front lines from northern Laos.[68]

As the fighting unfolded in the valley, French bombers killed an untold number of civilians in work and supply teams in the surrounding hills. Hubs like Conoi and Tuan Giao came under intensive bombing. In one French raid at "KM13," on the road running from Tuan Giao to the battlefield, ninety porters died in a matter of minutes. Despite attempts to hammer them into line through emulation campaigns and heavy doses of propaganda, the communists had to accept the desertion of several civilian teams. Even an official history had to admit that these people were simply terrified of dying in a hail of fire. Of course they were. And we know that over half of the porters and work teams were made up of women. Unknown numbers were injured and killed. Trauma ran roughshod over Vietnam, regardless of gender, and would do so well into the 1970s. These, too, are some of the things the Vietnamese people carried with them long after the guns fell silent in 1954.[69] (See Plate 32.)

Glorious though the victory was, Dien Bien Phu came at a great cost for the Vietnamese. The official number of Vietnamese military casualties for the battle is 13,930, with 4,020 of that number listed as killed or missing in action. But French military intelligence estimated that the Democratic Republic of Vietnam lost around 20,000 combatants. The latter number is closer to the truth, in my view. On related fronts where fighting occurred, the casualties on the Vietnamese side totaled 15,004, including 5,833 dead. None of these statistics count the several thousand porters killed or missing in action. During the Dien Bien Phu campaign (November 1953–May 1954), one can safely assume that the DRV lost

25,000 souls in all, men and women, civilians and combatants in the area stretching from the Chinese border to Zone V.[70] Meanwhile, on another, connected battlefront, Ho Chi Minh had already marched his cadres into villages to launch class warfare on their fellow Vietnamese. Several thousand would die at the party's own hands by the time this horrifying extension of the war on the civilian front finally ended. This, once again, was Vietnamese War Communism writ large. This was its human cost. This, too, was Dien Bien Phu.

Conclusion

Readers will remember that Frantz Fanon, the Martiniquais author of the 1961 classic on revolutionary anticolonialism, *The Wretched of the Earth*, was fascinated by what the Vietnamese had achieved at Dien Bien Phu. In Fanon's view, the Vietnamese victory over the French in this remote Southeast Asian valley had demonstrated that the colonized could generate the revolutionary violence needed to force decolonization on the colonizer. But how, he asked as a member of the Algerian Front de libération nationale fighting the French in North Africa, had the Vietnamese actually done this: "'What must we do to realize a Dien Bien Phu? How do we go about doing it?'"[1] Inspired by Fanon's question and his reflection on the nature of anticolonial violence, I placed his question at the center of this book. I wanted to understand how the Vietnamese lined up behind Ho Chi Minh generated this remarkable level of force by 1954. What concretely had gone into this epic military victory?[2]

Most of those sympathetic to Ho's Vietnam reach for nationalism to explain the Vietnamese victory over the French in 1954 and then over the Americans two decades later. Capturing it best is Ho's 1946 parable of the "guerrilla tiger" fighting the "colonial elephant" against all odds— and winning. The problem with that explanation is that by 1954 the Vietnamese tiger had become something very different than what it had been going into the war. Indeed, by the end of the conflict, the Vietnamese army had grown so remarkably that it could fight like an elephant: in the open, head-on in trench warfare as artillery shells rained down around it. Surely this was the transformation that had caught Fanon's attention.

Other writers, hostile to the communist core of Ho's Vietnam, put the victory down to massive Chinese and Soviet assistance. Had the Vietnamese not received communist bloc support, they would have never possessed the modern weapons to make an "elephant" out of a "tiger," and the Vietnamese would have continued fighting a guerrilla war for independence, like the Algerians. While there is truth to both explanations, as the pages in this book have shown, neither alone provides a satisfactory answer to the question at the heart of *The Wretched of the Earth*: how exactly did the Vietnamese create that revolutionary violence, organize, and deploy it to achieve "a Dien Bien Phu?" What was the road map? What were the tools? Was there a mechanism?

In an attempt to provide an answer, I started at the beginning of the hostilities in September 1945, in order to focus on the nature of the Vietnamese state Ho crafted in war and how this entity allowed him to generate, organize, and deploy such impressive force only nine years later. In doing so, we discovered that Ho ended up administering two kinds of wartime states, one capable of holding out against the colonizer in guerrilla form like the Algerian FLN in North Africa, the other capable of generating the required military and organizational force needed to defeat a Western colonial army in set-piece battle similar to the Chinese communist one. The first state was the archipelago one. It was an operational yet territorially incomplete guerrilla regime. Based in the countryside, it was militarily weak but flexible enough to survive colonial attacks in order to still be "there" in 1950 to receive communist bloc aid and turn itself into something else. The second type of statecraft was this communist-driven, single-party state that arose from the archipelago during the second half of the conflagration thanks to the mobilization of the Vietnamese people and army, Chinese communist assistance, and Sino-Soviet mobilization techniques and state-building plans. I used the concepts of the "archipelago state" and "Vietnamese War Communism" as analytical devices to get at what really went into the making of this Vietnamese state of war.

For both types of statecraft, nationalism was important; but it was never enough to hold either together by itself. Ho and his allies relied just as much on wireless radios and human couriers; the collection, analysis, and circulation of information; the expansion of police control and the intelligence services; the movement of civil servants and their paperwork; and the administration of a war economy and clandestine commercial networks running into the French colonial cities and surrounding Asian markets. Together, these things constituted the nervous system that connected, supplied, and accorded operational coherence to what was in reality a highly fragmented and rudimentary state of war. Mastery of these things allowed the Vietnamese to "hang on." It also permitted them to be in a better position to transform foreign military, economic, and technical assistance when it began arriving from southern China in 1950. Readers will agree, I think, that if you do not have the people who can do the math to calibrate your artillery, then the shells will miss their targets when fired. If we can believe French veterans of Dien Bien Phu, Vo Nguyen Giap's artillery salvos opening this epic battle on 13 March were deadly accurate.

Of course, the Vietnamese were not the only ones in a time of decolonization to use wireless radios, create police and intelligence services, or administer a war economy and clandestine trading routes to keep their archipelago states alive. The Algerians, Indonesians, and Kenyans did similar things in their struggles against the French, Dutch, and the British, respectively.[3] I am sure there are colonially trained radio technicians like Ho's former scoutmaster, Hoang Dao Thuy, who put their communications skills in the service of nationalist causes in Africa and Asia. Where the Vietnamese communists differed was that they had access to a unique communist toolkit coming from revolutionary Eurasia, the Soviet Union and Maoist China in particular. This communist repertoire of statecraft included such things as rectification campaigns, emulation movements, new hero worship, the cult of the personality, the agricultural tax, the state trading office, and land reform. Each allowed the Communist Party to increase its central management of the state, the armed forces, and the economy. Borrowing from Lenin, I expanded the term "War Communism" to include the application of these unique tools of communist warfare and statecraft to include conflicts led by communists beyond the Soviet Union in anticolonial wars (the Chinese against the Japanese, the Vietnamese against the French) and civil ones in China, Vietnam, and Korea (East Asian communists fighting their anticommunist foes).

Like Mao in China and Kim Il-Sung in North Korea, Ho did not wait for the hostilities with the French to end before using these revolutionary tools to push through the creation of a single-party state and build the military force he needed to defeat the French colonial "elephant." The Vietnamese communists used war to do it: in fact, they ramped it up still further from 1950 onwards to create a postcolonial state very different from noncommunist nationalist movements in, say, Fanon's wartime Algeria or Sukarno's Indonesia. Of course, this Vietnamese communist state was not a carbon copy of what the Chinese and Soviets had done. The Vietnamese took Sino-Soviet models and mobilization techniques and tailored them to local circumstances and their specific needs during the struggle against the French, as we have discovered in this book. This borrowing gave rise to fascinating offshoots of War Communism as the model traveled along a Eurasian arc, taking on new shapes as it moved along its trajectory. But one thing was clear: this type of War Communism raised up the single-party communist state that would go on to fight the Americans and their Vietnamese allies to victory in 1975 from the guerrilla archipelago it had been at the start of the conflict. It rules Vietnam to this day. Nothing of the kind ever occurred in Algeria, Indonesia, or Kenya for the simple reason that communists were not in charge of the postcolonial state in those places.

However, the war Ho and his entourage led and the state they crafted to run it came at a high price for the Vietnamese people. The French, we know, inflicted terrible suffering on civilians during the Indochina War. Intensive bombing campaigns and the colonial assault on the Vietnamese food chain were two notable examples. However, the communists also worsened the plight of their own people, by conscripting males into the armed forces and members of both sexes into accompanying supply and work teams. They did so in the hundreds of thousands. On top of this, Ho initiated land reform as a tool of revolutionary war statecraft (just as Mao had done in the 1930s and was still doing in the early 1950s as his troops fought the Americans to a truce in Korea). The Vietnamese president only made things worse for the majority peasant population when he asked them to give not only their sons and daughters, but also to produce more food to feed this hungry army and those supplying it. It was a vicious circle. As during the Russian civil war of the early 1920s, Vietnamese War Communism resulted in famine in parts of Ho's Vietnam during the early 1950s, caused both by the French "colonialists" and the Vietnamese "communists." Again, this outcome did not occur during the Algerian War because the nature of the conflict in North Africa *and* the Algerian state driving it were radically different from the communist-fired ones at war in East Asia—in Ho's Vietnam, Mao's China, and Kim Il-Sung's North Korea. Even Fidel Castro's Cuban revolution never crafted a single-party communist state *during* its armed struggle (which would lead to victory in 1959). Castro built the core of his communist state *after* taking power, as well as assembling the communist troops he would send to Angola and elsewhere in Africa in the 1970s.[4]

But did the Vietnamese state that defeated the French army in battle at Dien Bien Phu in May 1954 win the war? If "win" means recovering all of the Vietnam Ho had declared independent in September 1945, then the answer can only be "no." By signing the ceasefire with the French at Geneva on 21 July 1954, the Vietnamese president and his party accepted the provisional division of Vietnam at the 17th parallel. Ho's Vietnam, the Democratic Republic of Vietnam, would take over in the territories located above that line while the French and their Vietnam-ese allies, still the Associated State of Vietnam, would do the same below it. Ho and his party accepted this political solution on the assumption that if they did not, then the Americans would intervene directly with their troops. This the communists did not want—not in 1954, at least.

So, Ho and his party rolled the political dice at Geneva. They signed the ceasefire agreement with the French on 21 July 1954, hoping that a separate declaration (duly noted but never signed by the Americans or the leaders of the Associated State of Vietnam) to hold elections two years later would allow them to recover all of the Vietnam Ho had first declared independent a decade earlier through negotiations.[5] If, however, a political solution failed, the Vietnamese reserved the right to resume the war where they had left off in July 1954, not at Dien Bien Phu, but in the central highlands, where their army had last struck in June of that year.[6] The Americans were also ready to resume their indirect war against the Vietnamese communists by "replacing" the French with a fully decolonized "State of Vietnam" (with no more colonial federalism in the form of "Association.") The French might have pulled out of the Indochina War in 1954, but the Americans and the inheritors of the Associated State of Vietnam carried on without them.[7]

Did the Soviets and Chinese communists pressure the Vietnamese to compromise at Geneva? Of course they did. But the Vietnamese had their own reasons for accepting a deal too. Ho and his party conceded, in lively internal debates in mid-July of 1954, that although they might have won an historic battle over the colonizer at Dien Bien Phu, they had not yet attained the level of military force needed to defeat the French army in all of Indochina, contrary to what Fanon had thought. In these internal party deliberations which led to the signing of the ceasefire agreement, the communist leadership admitted that their military force was still not strong enough to change the "strategic nature" of the war in fundamental ways.[8] Enough of the Vietnamese internal record is now available to confirm that, like the Chinese, the Vietnamese leadership feared that the Americans would intervene militarily if they did not compromise. And the signing of the ceasefire agreement in Korea in mid-1953 had freed up American hands in Indochina. But Ho also realized that although his army had scored an historic victory at Dien Bien Phu (and in Cao Bang and Nghia Lo before that), the PAVN had not driven the French out of Indochina by force. With the Americans standing behind them, the French armed forces remained stronger militarily.[9]

There was a third, equally important reason explaining why the Vietnamese signed the ceasefire agreement rather than carry on as they had initially intended to do on going into the 1953–4 winter offensive. In short, as their troops hoisted the national flag at Dien Bien Phu, Ho and his entourage recognized that the protracted war they had been fighting since 1945, and especially since 1950, had taken a terrible toll on their people, with the last battle of the First Indochina War serving as a particularly painful chapter in that story. By going for broke in this highland showdown, the Vietnamese had pushed their state, its army, and the population to the breaking point. As the party's mid-July resolution approving the signing of the ceasefire put it: "Yet, clearly, we must also realize that in order to fight this protracted war, the people have had to sacrifice a great deal through their contributions in manpower and resources. If the war continues indefinitely, then the people could grow weary. That could cause additional problems for us."[10]

While one would like to know more about this weariness and these potential "additional problems" as they took stock of the situation after Dien Bien Phu, the Vietnamese communists clearly recognized that their War Communism had exhausted the "people." Famine had broken out in parts of Ho's Vietnam, as well as sporadic peasant revolts. After the signing of the ceasefire in July 1954 and until around March of 1955, the French and their Vietnamese allies discovered that Ho's Trading Office was busy importing livestock and rice clandestinely from areas below the 17th parallel to feed hungry mouths above that line. "The economic situation in the north," one French intelligence officer noted in late 1954, "seems to be very critical and it would be advisable to reinforce our economic controls in our zone [below the 17th parallel] to avoid the clandestine supplying of the north."[11]

It is no stain on the glorious achievements of the Vietnamese people or their leaders to suggest here that Ho and his party agreed to end the war, at least tentatively, for the additional reason that their population was too tired to carry on. Their backs against the wall, the Vietnamese people could not give any more, as the French continued to bomb and the communists asked for ever greater amounts of manpower and food. Even the promise of land was not enough (there was not much left to divvy up in any case, except in the far south). If Ho and his disciples continued like this, they risked driving their people into the ground and pulling down the Vietnamese communist temple on their heads before it had even been completed.

Yet despite the horrific losses suffered by the Vietnamese people and armed forces during the Indochina War,[12] Ho Chi Minh had created a remarkable state of war that had allowed his Vietnam to fight and win a battle in a way which was almost unparalleled in the twentieth century. Ho might not have won the first war for Vietnam conclusively, but he had summoned the courage and resilience needed to wear the French military and political classes down. (Following Dien Bien Phu, French commanders pulled their troops back to areas around Hanoi, while the politicians turned their attention to Africa, by sending the army to Algeria to keep what was left of the empire French.) In so doing, Ho's Vietnam had prevented the colonizer from winning and forced the French to give up their colonial claim to Indochina for good. Nationalism alone cannot explain the Vietnamese victory at Dien Bien Phu in 1954. However, when Ho combined it with the revolutionary statecraft driving the Democratic Republic of Vietnam forward, both in its archipelagic and communist forms, nationalism fired a fighting machine that was very hard to shut down. To borrow a phrase from an eminent historian of the Second World War, Richard Overy, nationalism "conditioned the conduct of war, but it did not dictate the outcome of battles."[13] As always, a combination of different factors did.

Whether the Americans understood the nature of the "beast" they had before them in Vietnam in mid-1954 any better than the French did remains an open question. The Americans might not have been as blind as some have made them out to be. After all, American military and intelligence officers had seen a similar type of conflict in Korea up close. They knew that what the Chinese and the North Koreans had thrown at them in Korea went far beyond the cliché of a tiger fighting an elephant. A handful of Americans reporting on the Indochina War at the time also understood that the Vietnamese communists were capable of doing something similar to what their counterparts were doing in Korea.

The Chinese and the Soviets clearly believed their allies could fight conventional warfare. Nowhere was this more evident than in their decision to provide large amounts of modern military assistance to Ho Chi Minh's Vietnam during the final endgame of the Indochina War. In fact, between June and September of 1954, the communist bloc delivered almost 10,000 tons of modern weapons and technical equipment to Ho's Vietnam. Secretly known as Plan Z, this aid included, among other things, seventy-two 88mm antiaircraft artillery guns, forty-eight 37mm antiaircraft guns, 108 antiaircraft machine guns, and eighteen SR584 radars. The Vietnamese had already shown themselves capable of deploying such weapons during the battle of Dien Bien Phu. Never did the Algerians or Indonesians reach this level in their wars of national liberation. Did the French and the American intelligence services know about Plan Z, a clear violation of the Geneva Conference ceasefire agreements? It is hard to believe that they would have missed such an important arms shipment, including the delivery of over 500 trucks into northern Vietnam.[14]

What we do know is that French counterinsurgency "specialists" such as Charles Lacheroy, Roger Trinquier, and David Galula would march off to Algeria convinced that they understood "revolutionary warfare" better than anyone else. In my view, they understood remarkably little. Lacheroy and his acolytes spoke of Mao's "people's war," "parallel hierarchies," and "totalitarian control" of a communist kind to describe Ho's Vietnam. In Algeria, Lacheroy, Galula, and Trinquier 'theorized' about counterinsurgency methods, based on their Indochina experience, and then advertised them for use in guerrilla insurgencies elsewhere. That the Algerian nationalist movement was not communist or ever created a *standing, divisional* army like the Chinese, North Koreans, and Vietnamese posed no theoretical problems for our specialists and their acolytes. They cited Mao Zedong's texts penned at Yan'an on "revolutionary," "protracted," and "guerrilla" warfare in the late 1930s. But glaringly absent was any detailed understanding of the War Communism Mao actually *crafted over the next decade*, the methods he deployed, or the nature of the Chinese communist war state he assembled and the conventional and guerrilla army that drove it to power in 1949. To my knowledge, not one of our "French specialists," not even Bernard Fall, ever asked the question that struck Franz Fanon in *The Wretched of the Earth* as his book went to press in 1961: what kind of *state* had allowed the Vietnamese to execute a "Dien Bien Phu" and win? What combination of forces had the Vietnamese been able to harness in order to generate and then deploy such massive revolutionary violence?[15]

The answers I have tried to provide to these questions and others can help us to understand better how and why Ho Chi Minh and his communist disciples would resurrect their state of war in both its archipelago and War Communism forms and then turn each on the Americans and their Vietnamese allies with a vengeance once the French had left. Although the ceasefire agreement signed at Geneva in 1954 had held Ho to pull his people out of areas below the 17th parallel, the communists kept the bare bones of their infrastructure secretly in place in southern Vietnam, knowing they might need it one day. They would. In 1959, when it was clear that there would be no elections as promised at Geneva to unite Vietnam peacefully, the DRV's leaders resumed their war where they had left off: in the central highlands overlooking the Mekong Delta. They reactivated their Asian routes of war from Zone IV southwards and began using them to revive their archipelago state below the 17th parallel. They soon created the National Liberation Front (in the image of the Lien Viet of 1946), while PAVN troops started to make their way back into Zone V and further still. They carried modern arms with them via land and maritime routes. For Ho and his entourage, there was only one war: theirs. It had started in Saigon in 1945, and it would end there in 1975. Meanwhile, the Vietnamese restarted their War Communism in the north. The reactivation of the war in the south would allow them to mobilize the whole population behind the collectivization of communist Vietnam in the north. As in China, these things were all interconnected and had been since 1950. They would remain so until the PAVN took all of Vietnam by force in 1975. (See Map 15.)

Of course, the world has changed over the last fifty years. The Cold War has ended, and the Soviet Union is no more. But we still might keep some of the things discussed in this book in mind today, not least of all because communist *states* remain in power in Asia even if they run capitalist economies. And the states and the armed forces these Asian communists command continue to rely on many of the methods which came out of this long Eurasian arc of communist warfare at the core of this book. This is true of the Vietnamese, North Korean, and Chinese communists. Even the current leaders of Laos and Hun Sen in Cambodia are products of this same revolutionary process.[16] And contrary to what counterinsurgency specialists keep preaching in military academies to this day, the wars the Americans and their allies have been fighting in the Middle East since the end of the Cold War have *less* in common with the type of states they fought against in East Asia in the mid-twentieth century, or those with which they would be dealing if ever things lit up again in the Asia-Pacific region. This is true of the Chinese, the North Koreans, and the Vietnamese. Even Vladimir Putin's Russia is dusting off the communist instruments Lenin first developed in the Soviet Union, not least of all "emulation campaigns." Those in charge of these Eurasian states now run them on high levels of nationalism, but the mechanisms themselves derive from a specific kind of warfare, a communist one.[17]

NOTES

Abbreviations

CAOM   Centre des Archives d'Outre-mer
SDECE   Service de documentation extérieure et de contre-espionage
SHD   Service historique de la Défense

A Word about Words

1. Daniel Hémery, "L'Asie du Sud-est, 1945: Vers un nouvel impérialisme colonial?," in Charles-Robert Ageron and Marc Michel, eds., *L'Ere des décolonisations* (Paris: Karthala, 1995), pp. 65–84; and Pierre Grosser, "Une 'création continue'? L'Indochine, le Maghreb et l'Union française," *Monde(s)*, vol. 12, no. 2 (2017), pp. 71–94.

2. A brillant exception to the official line is the young scholar from Vietnam, Ninh Xuan Thao, "L'Etat du Viêt-Nam dans ses rapports avec la France (1949–1955): Une autre voie pour l'indépendance du Viêt-Nam," Ph.D. dissertation (Bordeaux: Université de Bordeaux-Montaigne, 2019).

Introduction: States of War

1. David Schoenbrun, *Vietnam: How We Got In, How to Get Out* (New York: Antheneum, 1971 [first published in 1968]), p. 25.

2. David Schoenbrun, *As France Goes* (New York: Harper & Bros., 1957), pp. 234–5.

3. Pierre Langlais, *Dien Bien Phu* (Paris: Editions France-Empire, 1963), p. 260.

4. Marcel Bigeard, *Pour une parcelle de gloire* (Paris: Editions 1, 1997 [first published in 1975]), p. 179.

5. Ferhat Abbas, *La Nuit coloniale* (Paris: René Julliard, 1962), p. 16.

6. Frantz Fanon, *Les Damnés de la terre* (Paris: Editions La Découverte & Syros, 2002 [first published in 1961]), p. 69.

7. Schoenbrun, *Vietnam: How We Got In*, p. 25.

8. Schoenbrun tells the fable of the tiger and the elephant three minutes into the "End of an Empire," *The Twentieth Century*, https://www.youtube.com/watch?v=XWY9KbIXpdI, accessed on 19 April 2019.

9. Schoenbrun, *Vietnam: How We Got In*, p. 25.

10. Michael Howard, *War in European History* (London: Oxford University Press, 2009 [updated edition]), p. 80; and Hew Strachan, "The Nation in Arms," in Geoffrey Best, ed., *The Permanent Revolution* (Chicago: University of Chicago Press, 1988), pp. 49–73, especially pp. 56–8.

11. David Marr makes this case in *Vietnam: State, War, and Revolution (1945–1946)* (Berkeley: University of California Press, 2013), as does Stein Tonnesson, *Vietnam 1946: How the War Began* (Berkeley: University of California Press, 2011).

12. On desertion in the French and American revolutionary wars, see Alan Forrest, *The Legacy of the French Revolutionary Wars: The Nation-in-Arms in French Republican Memory* (New York: Cambridge University Press, 2009); his *Conscripts and Deserters: The Army and French Society during the Revolution and Empire* (New York: Oxford University Press, 1989); Charles Neimeyer, *America Goes to War: A Social History of the Continental Army* (New York: New York University Press, 1996); and James Martin and Mark Lender, *"A Respectable Army": The Military Origins of the Republic 1763–1789*, 3rd edition (Malden: Wiley-Blackwell, 2015). As in any army, desertion occurred in Ho Chi Minh's. See Pham To, "Chi Thi cua Ban Bi Thu," 22 December 1952, *Van Kien Dang Toan Tap*, vol. 13 (1952) (Hanoi: Nha Xuat Ban Chinh Tri Quoc Gia, 2001), p. 381; and Pham Van Dong (To), "Chi Thi cua Ban Bi Thu," 25 May 1953, in *Van Kien Dang Toan Tap*, vol. 14 (1953) (Hanoi: Nha Xuat Ban Chinh Tri Quoc Gia, 2002), pp. 214–16. The history of desertion during the Vietnam Wars still awaits an historian. The social history of the armed forces in Vietnam remains to be written too.

13. See "Decree 126/SL," 4 November 1949, establishing military conscription for Vietnamese men aged between eighteen and forty-five, https://moj.gov.vn/vbpq/Lists/Vn%20bn%20 php%20lut/View_Detail.aspx?ItemID=178; and "Decree 20/SL," 12 February 1950, authorizing mass mobilization, https://thuvienphapluat.vn/van-ban/Bo-may-hanh-chinh/Sac-lenh-20-SL -quyet-dinh-tong-dong-vien-nhan-vat-tai-luc-tien-toi-Tong-phan-cong/36522/noi-dung.aspx; both documents accessed on 9 April 2020.

14. On the Associated State of Vietnam, see Ninh Xuan Thao, "L'Etat du Viêt-Nam dans ses rapports avec la France (1949–1955): Une autre voie pour l'indépendance du Viêt-Nam," Ph.D. dissertation (Bordeaux: Université de Bordeaux-Montaigne, 2019); Brett Reilly, "The Origins of the Vietnamese Civil War and the State of Vietnam," Ph.D. dissertation (Madison: University of Wisconsin at Madison, 2018); and François Guillemot, *Dai Viet: indépendance et révolution au Viet-Nam, l'échec de la troisième voie (1938–1955)* (Paris: Les Indes savantes, 2012).

15. Truong Chinh, *The Resistance Will Win* (Hanoi: Foreign Languages Publishing House, 1960 [first published in 1947 as a series of Communist Party texts in Vietnamese]), p. 64.

16. Similar states operated in wartime Indonesia and Algeria. They still do in Afghanistan and Syria as I write. They certainly did in Eurasia during the Second World War. They almost always do when war debarks in your homeland. A very rich field is developing on the question of sovereignty and war in Vietnam, from which I have drawn inspiration in my own work. See, among others, in no particular order: Christian Lentz, *Contesting Territory: Dien Bien Phu and the Making of Northwest Vietnam* (New Haven: Yale University Press, 2019); Kevin Li, "Partisan to Sovereign: The Making of the Bình Xuyên in Southern Vietnam, 1945–1948," *Journal of Vietnamese Studies*, vol. 11, nos. 3–4 (2016), pp. 140–87; Shawn McHale, *The First Indochina War: Violence, Sovereignty, and the Fracture of the South, 1945–1956* (Cambridge: Cambridge University Press, 2021); and Brett Reilly, "The Sovereign States of Vietnam, 1945–1955," *The Journal of Vietnamese Studies*, vol. 11, nos. 3–4 (2016), pp. 103–9.

17. On War Communism leading to the creation of the Soviet Union in 1922, I have relied on the following: Stephen Kotkin, *Stalin: Paradoxes of Power* (New York: Penguin Books, 2014), Chapter 8; Orlando Figes, *Peasant Russia, Civil War* (London: Phoenix Press, 2001), chapter 6; Orlando Figes, *A People's Tragedy* (New York: Penguin Books, 1996), pp. 613–19, 721–51; Nicolas Werth, *Histoire de l'Union soviétique* (Paris: Presses universitaires de France, 2008 [6th edition]), Chapter 4; and Bertrand Patenaude, "Peasants into Russians: The Utopian Essence of War Communism," *The Russian Review*, vol. 54 (October 1995), pp. 552–70. On war and statecraft, see, of course, Charles Tilly's scholarship summarized nicely in his "States, State Transformation, and War," in Jerry Bentley, ed., *The Oxford Handbook of World History* (Oxford: Oxford University Press, 2014), pp. 176–94. Most helpful for me has been the stimulating work on war and society by the likes of Michael Howard, *War in European History*, chapters 4–6; Peter Paret, *Understanding War: Essays on Clausewitz and the History of Military Power* (Princeton: Princeton University Press, 1992); and Hew Strachan, "Essay and Reflection: On Total War and Modern War," *The International History Review*, vol. 22, no. 2 (June 2000), pp. 341–70.

18. On Mao Zedong, the Korean War, and communist statecraft, see Chen Jian, *Mao's China and the Cold War* (Chapel Hill: University of North Carolina Press, 2001), Chapter 3.

19. I would like to express my gratitude here to an anonymous reader of an article I wrote years ago on wartime communications for first suggesting the term "archipelago" to describe the first state under study in this book. I am also very grateful to Talbot Imlay and Hew Strachan, who have rightly reminded us that the best ways to use terms like "archipelago," "War Communism," or, in their case, "total war" are as heuristic or analytical devices rather than imposing them as the "answers." I follow their advice. See Talbot Imlay, "Total War," *Journal of Strategic Studies*, vol. 30, no. 3 (2007), pp. 547–70; and Strachan, "Essay and Reflection," pp. 341–70. I am also grateful to Daniel Hémery, Pierre Brocheux, and the late Georges Boudarel for our conversations over the years about Vietnamese War Communism. While I define the term differently here, we all share the core idea that Vietnamese communism cannot be understood independently of the way the Indochina War helped Ho and his party to forge the single-party communist state we know today. See Daniel Hémery, "La Guerre d'Indochine," *Europe Solidaire Sans Frontières* (January 2007), http://www.europe-solidaire.org/spip.php ?article5086#outil_sommaire_1, accessed on 22 April 2020. On communist mobilization techniques and party state-building in China and Vietnam, I owe a special debt to the penetrating studies penned by Yves Chevrier, *Mao et la révolution chinoise* (Paris: Castermann, 1993); and Benoît de Tréglodé, *Héros et révolution au Vietnam* (Paris: Les Indes savantes, 2014 [revised edition]), in English translation as *Heroes and Revolution in Vietnam* (Singapore: National University of Singapore Press, 2012).

Chapter 1. The Rise of the Archipelago State

1. Le Duc Tho, "Fiche," 29 September 1949, in 10H2369, SHD, p. 1. For more on this stormy meeting, see the Vietnamese articles captured and translated by the French: "Errements du Lien Viet," *Lien Viet* (Nam Bo), no. 5 (15 July 1949); and Le Duc Tho's address of 7 July 1949 as reproduced in *Lien Viet*, no. 6 (30 July 1949); both of which are in 10H2369, and others in 10H4204 and 10H4205, SHD.

2. Philippe Devillers, *Histoire du Vietnam de 1940 à 1952* (Paris: Editions du Seuil, 1952), p. 138.

3. Bao Dai, "Tuyen Ngon Doc Lap," 24 August 1945, *Viet Nam Dan Quoc Cong Bao*, no. 1 (29 September 1945), p. 1; and Xuan Phuong, *Ao Dai* (Great Neck: New York, EMQUAD, 2004), pp. 53–4 for the citation.

4. Duong Van Mai Elliott, *The Sacred Willow* (New York: Oxford University Press, 1999), p. 115, for the stepping aside of the mandarins. That Bao Dai abdicated of his own volition, see "Note au sujet de l'ex-empereur d'Annam," 24 August 1946, 31, grouping Etats associés, Ministère des affaires étrangères, France. My thanks to Stein Tonnesson for kindly sharing a copy of this document with me.

5. Ngo Van Chieu, *Journal d'un combattant Viet-Minh* (Paris: Editions du Seuil, 1955), p. 41.

6. Vo Nguyen Giap as quoted by David G. Marr, "Ho Chi Minh's Independence Declaration," in K. W. Taylor and John K. Whitmore, eds., *Essays into Vietnamese Pasts* (Ithaca: Cornell University Press, 1995), pp. 221–31.

7. Nguyen Cong Luan, *Nationalist in the Viet Nam Wars* (Bloomington: Indiana University Press, 2012), p. 35.

8. On Ho Chi Minh's cult of personality, see Olga Dror, "Traditions and Transformations in the Formation of Ho Chi Minh's Cult," *The Journal of Asian Studies*, vol. 75, no. 2 (May 2016), pp. 433–66; and Alec Holcombe, "Rethinking Vietnamese Communism," Ph.D. dissertation (Berkeley: University of California at Berkeley, 2012). For more on Ho Chi Minh and how he is represented, see the essays penned by Benoit de Tréglodé, Daniel Hémery, Sophie-Quinn Judge, and William Duiker in Christopher Goscha and Benoit de Tréglodé, eds., *Naissance d'un Etat-Parti* (Paris: Les Indes Savantes, 2004); as well as biographies by Pierre Brocheux, *Ho Chi Minh* (Paris: Presses de Sciences Po, 2000); William Duiker, *Ho Chi Minh* (New York: Hyperion, 2000); and Martin Grossheim, *Ho Chi Minh: Der geheimnisvolle Revolutionär, Leben und Legende* (Munich: Beck, 2011).

9. It first replaced the Journal officiel de l'Indochine on 31 August 1945; see "Nghi Dinh," *Viet Nam Dan Quoc Cong Bao*, no. 1 (29 September 1945), p. 13.

10. See the long list of decrees published in the *Viet Nam Dan Quoc Cong Bao* for 1945–6. On the security service graft, see Vo Nguyen Giap's instructions dated 24 September 1945, in *Viet Nam Dan Quoc Cong Bao*, no. 2 (6 October 1945), p. 22.

11. See legislation passed in *Viet Nam Dan Quoc Cong Bao*, no. 1 (29 September 1945), pp. 7–11, for example.

12. On the court, see "Sac Lenh Chu Tich Chinh Phu Lam thoi Viet Nam Dan Chu Cong Hoa," *Viet Nam Dan Quoc Cong Bao*, no. 2 (13 September 1945), p. 20, and Ngo Van Chieu, *Journal d'un combattant viet minh*, pp. 50–51. For a long list of government-approved newspapers, see *Viet Nam Dan Quoc Cong Bao*, no. 6 (27 October 1945), pp. 59–65, among others.

13. The citation is from Merle Pribbenow's "Oral History Interview of Dinh Xuan Ba, Entrepreneur and Former Assault Youth Member," DVD 3, Hanoi, 5 June 2007, http://vietnam interviewsusc.org/?p=25, accessed on 9 April 2021.

14. "Sac Lenh so. 53," *Viet Nam Dan Quoc Cong Bao*, no. 7 (2 November 1945), p. 59. See the Indochinese colonial passports in "Saigon RGI 1–50" and "Saigon V" in the archives of the Ministère des affaires étrangères, Nantes annex. My thanks to Melissa Anderson for sharing this information with me. For scores of captured DRV identity cards, passes, and permits, see 10H3999, SHD.

15. "Nghi Dinh," *Viet Nam Dan Quoc Cong Bao*, no. 40 (5 October 1946), p. 525; and "Chi Thi cua Ban Thuong vu Trung Uong Dang ve Van De Hoa Kieu o Viet Nam," 4 December 1950, *Van Kien Dang Toan Tap*, vol. 11 (1950) (Hanoi: Nha Xuat Ban Chinh Tri Quoc Gia, 2001), pp. 544–50.

16. Oscar Salemink, *The Ethnography of Vietnam's Central Highlanders* (London: Routledge-Curzon, 2003); Philippe LeFailler, *La Rivière Noire: L'Intégration d'une marche frontière au Vietnam* (Paris: CNRS Editions, 2014); and Andrew Hardy, *Red Hills* (Copenhagen: NIAS, 2005), among others.

17. "Sac Lenh so. 175-b," 6 September 1946, *Viet Nam Dan Quoc Cong Bao*, no. 41 (12 October 1946), p. 532; "Circulaire sur les mesures préventatives contre la distribution des cartes d'identité par l'ennemi à la population," 10H2370, SHD; "Comité exécutif de résistance du Nam Bo," 9 April 1948, 10H3969, SHD. On DRV censuses, see 10H3969 and 10H3995, SHD; as well as "Chi thi," 25 September 1948, *Van Kien Dang Toan Tap*, vol. 9 (1948) (Hanoi: Nha Xuat Ban Chinh Tri Quoc Gia, 2001), pp. 351–3.

18. Bernard Fall, *Le Viet Minh: La République démocratique du Viet-Nam* (Paris: Librairie Armand Colin, 1960), pp. 76–9; and "Plan d'organisation du rouage du gouvernement," 10H4709, SHD.

19. Emmanuel Poisson makes this important point (and others) in *Mandarins et subalternes au nord du Viêt Nam, une bureaucratie à l'épreuve* (Paris: Maisonneuve & Larose, 2004).

20. Nguyen Cong Luan, *Nationalist in the Viet Nam Wars*, p. 59. The communists recognized at the time the need to make compromises, even pulling their people out of the administrative committee if they did not have the trust of the local people. "Nghi Quyet cua Toan Ky Dai Bieu Khoach Dai," 21–3 June 1946, *Van Kien Dang Toan Tap*, vol. 8 (1945–7) (Hanoi: Nha Xuat Ban Chinh Tri Quoc Gia, 2000), p. 91, for one example among many.

21. The Long March refers to the Chinese communist withdrawal to northern China from the south during 1934–5 in the face of overwhelming Chinese nationalist attacks.

22. For confirmation of the party's continued existence, see Ho Chi Minh, "Bao Cao Chinh Tri tai Dai Hoi Dai Bieu Toan Quoc Lan thu II cua Dang," no date given but early 1951, *Van Kien Dang Toan Tap*, vol. 12 (1951) (Hanoi: Nha Xuat Ban Chinh Tri Quoc Gia, 2001), p. 22; Khuong, "Chi Thi: Dang Cong San Dong Duong, so. 254/K," excerpts from central committee orders of 20 September 1948, 10H4204, SHD; Le Duc Tho, "Tinh Hinh va Nhiem Vu Moi cua Dang," 16 August 1948, *Van Kien Dang Toan Tap*, vol. 9 (1948) (Hanoi: Nha Xuat Ban Chinh Tri Quoc Gia, 2001), pp. 316–18; Truong Chinh, "Thong Cao ve Viec De Nghi Doi Ten Dang," July 1950, in *Van Kien Dang Toan Tap*, vol. 11 (1950) (Hanoi: Nha Xuat Ban Chinh Tri Quoc Gia, 2001), p. 365. The communists referred to it as the "group" or the "association," but it was the Communist Party.

23. On the failure of the Viet Minh to attract noncommunists, see Le Duc Tho, "Thong Tri," 8 August 1948, *Van Kien Dang Toan Tap*, vol. 9 (1948), pp. 158–9.

24. Truong Chinh, "Hoi Lien Hiep Quoc Dan Viet Nam Ra Doi," no date given, but clearly mid-1946, *Van Kien Dang Toan Tap*, vol. 8 (1945–7) (Hanoi: Nha Xuat Ban Chinh Tri Quoc Gia, 2000), pp. 69–71; "Nghi Quyet cua Toan Ky Dai Bieu Khoach Dai," 21–3 June 1946, *Van Kien Dang Toan Tap*, vol. 8 (1945–7), pp. 90–91; "Nghi Quyet cua Hoi Nghi Can Bo Trung Uong," 3–6 April 1947, *Van Kien Dang Toan Tap*, vol. 8 (1945–7), pp. 190–91; and Hoang Quoc Viet,

"Cung Co Khoi Dai Doan Ket de Chien Thang," no date given, but early 1951, *Van Kien Dang Toan Tap*, vol. 12 (1951), pp. 184–5.

25. Vo Nguyen Giap, "Sac Lenh no 14," 8 September 1945, *Viet Nam Dan Quoc Cong Bao*, no. 1 (29 September 1945), p. 8. For two opposing views on the nature of the national assembly, see David Marr, *Vietnam: State, War, and Revolution (1945–1946)* (Berkeley: University of California Press, 2014), Chapter 2; and Alec Holcombe's review of this book: Alec Holcombe, "The Role of the Communist Party in the Vietnamese Revolution," *Journal of Vietnamese Studies*, vol. 11, nos. 3–4 (Summer–Fall 2016), pp. 298–364; and Marr's response in the same journal, vol. 12, no. 1 (Winter 2017), pp. 155–62.

26. In July 1947, Le Duc Tho explained that the Communist Party had decided to add more noncommunists to the government so that it reflected clearly to the French and the international community the nationalist, coalition character of the government. See Le Duc Tho, "Thong Cao cua T.U. ve Viec Thay Doi Mot So Nhan Vien trong Chinh Phu," 27 July 1947, and, more generally, with no author cited, "Nghi Quyet cua Hoi Nghi Can Bo Trung Uong tu 3–4 den 6–4 1947," 3–6 April 1947, both in *Van Kien Dang Toan Tap*, vol. 8 (1945–7), pp. 248–9.

27. On electoral problems, see Nguyen Cong Luan, *Nationalist in the Viet Nam Wars*, p. 45. On the origins of Vietnamese republicanism, see my "Aux origines du républicanisme vietnamien: circulations mondiales et connexions coloniales," special issue: "Les Gauches et les colonies," *Vingtième Siècle*, no. 131 (2016/3), pp. 17–35.

28. Fall, *Le Viet Minh*, pp. 51–3; and Nguyen Cong Luan, *Nationalist in the Viet Nam Wars*, pp. 46, 48.

29. The zonal system during the war changed, repeatedly. In order to spare the reader all sorts of lengthy and complex explanations in the text, and also with the maps, I have concentrated on the main zones to which I refer frequently in the book and which, in one form or another, existed during the whole length of the war. For more on zones, see the entries for "inter-zones" in my historical dictionary online: *The Indochina War (1945–1954): An Interdisciplinary Tool*, Université du Québec à Montréal, http://indochine.uqam.ca/en/historical-dictionary.html.

30. *Tu Dien Bach Khoa Quan Su Viet Nam* (Hanoi: Nha Xuat Ban Quan Doi Nhan Dan, 1996), pp. 477–8.

31. Claire Tran Thi Lien, "Les Catholiques vietnamiens, entre la reconquête coloniale et la résistance communiste (1945–1954)," *Approches-Asie*, no. 15 (1997), pp. 169–88. For the communist take on this, see "Thuc Dan Phap va Le-Huu-Tu," in *Cuoc Khang Chien Than Thanh cua Nhan Dan Viet Nam*, vol. 3 (Hanoi: Nha Xuat Ban Su That, 1959), pp. 79–81.

32. Ninh Xuan Thao, "L'Etat du Viêt-Nam dans ses rapports avec la France (1949–1955): Une autre voie pour l'indépendance du Viêt-Nam," Ph.D. diss. (Bordeaux: Université de Bordeaux-Montaigne, 2019); Brett Reilly, "The Origins of the Vietnamese Civil War and the State of Vietnam," Ph.D. diss. (Madison: University of Wisconsin, 2018). On the British and American roles, see Mark Lawrence, *Assuming the Burden* (Berkeley: University of California Press, 2005); Fredrik Logevall, *Embers of War* (New York: Random House, 2012).

33. The Vietnamese refer to this *tâche d'huile* as *vet dau loang*, also translated as "oil slick" or "ink blots." See Truong Chinh, "Hoan Thanh Nhiem Vu Chuan Bi, Chuyen Manh Sang Tong Phan Cong," undated, but mid-January 1950, in *Van Kien Dang Toan Tap*, vol. 11 (1950), pp. 22, 37–47.

34. "Nghi Quyet cua Hoi Nghi Can Bo Trung Uong tu 3–4 den 6–4 1947," 3–6 April 1947, *Van Kien Dang Toan Tap*, vol. 8 (1945–7), p. 206.

35. "Le Problème no. 1 du Tonkin: de la pacification d'hier à celle d'aujourd'hui," *Indochine Sud-est asiatique*, no. 6 (May 1952), pp. 50–55; "Chi Thi Pha Hoi Te," 19 January 1948, *Van Kien Dang Toan Tap*, vol. 9 (1948), pp. 9–15; and above all Tran Van Thuc, "Cuoc Dau Tranh Chong Pha Hoi te o Dong Bang Bac Bo (1947–1954)," Ph.D. dissertation (Hanoi: Bo Quoc Phong, Vien Lich Su Quan Su, 2005).

36. Nguyen Cong Luan, *Nationalist in the Viet Nam Wars*, pp. 62–3.

37. Ibid., p. 82. I am unaware of any study of the prison within the Democratic Republic of Vietnam for the Indochina War. For a glimpse from a former inmate, see Nguyen Tien Lang, *Chemins de la révolte* (Paris: Amiot Dumont, 1953).

38. Tran Ngoc Chau, *Vietnam Labyrinth* (Lubbock: Texas Tech University Press, 2012), pp. 101–15.

39. Nguyen Cong Luan, *Nationalist in the Viet Nam Wars*, pp. 78–9. For a recent example from war-torn Afghanistan, see the reportage by Salma Abdelaziz, Najibullah Quraishi, and Clarissa Ward, 26 February 2019, "36 hours with the Taliban," https://edition.cnn.com /interactive/2019/02/middleeast/36-hours-with-the-taliban-intl/, accessed on 9 June 2019.

40. Nguyen Cong Luan, *Nationalist in the Viet Nam Wars*, p. 79.

41. Ibid., p. 86. Tran Ngoc Chau provides a similar account of these "neutral" zones where no single sovereignty reigned supreme. Tran Ngoc Chau, *Vietnam Labyrinth*, p. 103. Andrew X. Pham provides riveting and moving examples from his father's experiences: *The Eaves of Heaven* (New York: Three Rivers Press, 2008), pp. 220–25.

42. "Noi dau vu tham sat My Thuy khien 526 thuong dan thiet mang," *An Ninh Thu Do*, 8 April 2013, https://anninhthudo.vn/chinh-tri-xa-hoi/noi-dau-vu-tham-sat-my-thuy-khien-526 -thuong-dan-thiet-mang/493695.antd; and Dang Duc, "Vu Tham sat My Trach—Noi dau nhuc nhoi suot 66 nam," *Dan Tri*, 28 November 2013, at https://dantri.com.vn/xa-hoi/vu-tham-sat -my-trach-noi-dau-nhuc-nhoi-suot-66-nam-1371824236.htm; both accessed on 1 May 2019. For what another child saw, see "Chien Sy Dien Bien Ke Chuyen," *Dan Tri*, 5 May 2019, https:// dantri.com.vn/xa-hoi/chien-sy-dien-bien-ke-chuyen-20190504152812177.htm. Noncommunist and anticommunist Vietnamese confirm this violence against civilians. Pham, *The Eaves of Heaven*, pp. 144–53; Nguyen Cong Luan, *Nationalist in the Viet Nam Wars*, starting with Chapter 1, "A Morning of Horror" (pp. 3–10), Chapter 6, "My Dark Years in War Begin" (pp. 62–76), Chapter 7, "Between Hammer and Anvil" (pp. 77–87, p. 81 for rape), and Chapter 8, "Bloodier Battles" (pp. 104–24); Duong Van Mai Elliot, *The Sacred Willow*, pp. 148–9, 164–5; and David Chanoff and Doan Van Toai, eds., *Vietnam: A Portrait of Its People at War* (London: TPP, 2009), pp. 12–14; among others. For a DRV investigation of village rape in the borderlands, see "So. 2-B: Bao Cao cua Van Phong Ban Chap Hanh Trung Uong," 27 February 1954, *Dien Bien Phu, Van Kien Dang, Nha Nuoc* (Hanoi: Nha Xuat Ban Chinh Tri Quoc Gia, 2004), p. 172.

43. Personal email correspondence with Professor Tuong Vu, University of Oregon, on 29 July, 12 and 17 August 2020. The history of the dead during the Indochina War remains to be written, as does the history of wartime emotions. For the Vietnam War, see Heonik Kwon, *Ghosts of War in Vietnam* (New York: Cambridge University Press, 2008); and his *After the Massacre: Commemoration and Consolation in Ha My and My Lai* (Berkeley: University of California Press, 2006). On the remembrance of heroes, see Martin Grossheim, "Der Krieg und der Tod. Heldengedenken in Vietnam," *Vierteljahreshefte für Zeitgeschichte*, no. 65 (2017), pp. 545–79.

44. Ngo Van Chieu, *Journal d'un combatant Viet-Minh*, p. 134; and Nguyen Cong Luan, *Nationalist in the Viet Nam Wars*, p. 76.

45. For the number of one million, see Bernard Fall, "This Isn't Munich, It's Spain," *Ramparts* (December 1965), p. 23. Ngo Van Chieu, *Journal d'un combattant Viet-Minh*, p. 106, gives the number of half a million dead. The French specialist of the Vietnam wars, Bernard Fall, may have spoken out against the suffering the Americans had created in Vietnam by 1965, but, to my knowledge, this scholar never said a word criticizing what the French army did to the Vietnamese civilian population during the Indochina War. To provide that total number for the Indochina War dead, this scrupulous French scholar must have known that civilians were dying in massive numbers.

46. I rely on the party's internal documents for this section, in particular: Le Duc Tho, "Tinh Hinh va Nhiem Vu Moi cua Dang," 16 August 1948; and another document almost certainly by Truong Chinh, "Chung Ta Chien Dau cho Doc Lap va Dan Chu," 8–16 August 1948, both in *Van Kien Dang Toan Tap*, vol. 9 (1948), pp. 276–320 and pp. 166–249 respectively. See also 10H620, SHD.

47. "Chi Thi Gui Cac Khu Uy," 18 February 1948, in *Van Kien Dang Toan Tap*, vol. 9 (1948), pp. 60–61.

48. Duong Van Mai Elliott, *The Sacred Willow*, p. 173–4.

49. See Pierre Darcourt, *Bay Vien, le maître de Cholon* (Paris: Hachette, 1977), pp. 80–81, 106–8.

50. On China, see Roderick MacFarquhar, *The Origins of the Cultural Revolution*, vol. 1 (New York: Columbia University Press, 1974), p. 3.

51. Charles Lacheroy, *De Saint-Cyr à l'action psychologique* (Paris: Lavauzelle, 2003), pp. 10–12; and Marie-Catherine and Paul Villatoux, "Aux origines de la 'guerre révolutionnaire': le colonel Lacheroy parle," *Revue historique des armées*, no. 268 (2012), http://journals.openedition .org/rha/7512, accessed on 9 June 2019.

52. The communists admitted in 1950 that their *cap uy* or "parallel hierarchy" officials were having a hard time keeping track of what government people were doing in economic matters. See "Chi Thi cua Ban Thuong Vu ve Viec Sua Chua Quan Niem Sai Lam ve Van De Kinh Te," 30 November 1951, *Van Kien Dang Toan Tap*, vol. 11 (1950), pp. 542–3; and Le Van Hien, "May Van De Cot Yeu cua Chinh Quyen Dan Chu Nhan Dan Viet Nam," in ibid., pp. 247–9.

53. "Ban Tuyen Huan Trung Uong so. 5/TU: Thong bao ve viec D tuyen bo Giai Tan,'" 20 February 1948, Asie-Océanie, Indochine, vol. 400, Archives des Ministère des affaires étrangères, France.

54. Le Duc Tho, "Tinh Hinh va Nhiem Vu Moi cua Dang," pp. 276–81 (p. 281 for the reference to women in the party) and Truong Chinh, "Hoan Thanh Nhiem Vu Chuan Bi, Chuyen Manh Sang Tong Phan Cong," undated, but mid-January 1950, in *Van Kien Dang Toan Tap*, vol. 11 (1950), pp. 92–3.

55. Le Duc Tho, "Tinh Hinh va Nhiem Vu Moi cua Dang," pp. 290–96.

56. Ibid., p. 289.

57. Truong Chinh, "Hoan Thanh Nhiem Vu," p. 92, for the party total; and Luong, "Chi Thi Cua Ban Thuong Vu Truong Uong ve Tam Ngung Viec Ket Nap Dang Vien Moi trong Toan Quoc," 14 September 1950, *Van Kien Dang, Toan Tap*, vol. 11 (1950), pp. 481–3, for the suspension of party admissions.

58. *40 Nam Phan Dau va Truong Thanh 1949–1989* (Hanoi: Hoc Vien Khoa Hoc Xa Hoi Nguyen Ai Quoc, 1989), pp. 19–27. My thanks to Tuong Vu for sharing this information with me.

59. Le Duc Tho, "Tinh Hinh va Nhiem Vu Moi cua Dang," pp. 310–13.

60. *50 nam Truong Dang Mien Nam* (Hanoi: Nha Xuat Ban Chinh Tri Quoc Gia, 1999), pp. 10–25. The southern party academy trained 2,000 cadres by 1954 (ibid., see p. 25).

61. Le Duc Tho concedes as much in "Thong Tri cua Ban Thuong Vu Trung Uong," 8 August 1948, *Van Kien Dang Toan Tap*, vol. 9 (1948), pp. 158–9. Le Duc Tho could not believe that communists in Zone III south of Hanoi had allowed the noncommunist Pham Le Bong to preside over the Lien Viet there. The French security services were watching this carefully. See the Saigon Sûreté fédérale's report of 26 September 1949, "Activité du parti communiste indochinois en Cochinchine," in 10H4204, SHD.

Chapter 2. Building Military Force

1. Robert Guillain, *Dien Bien Phu: La Fin des illusions* (Paris: Arléa, 2004), p. 36, pp. 163–4.

2. While the party regretted its weak control over the army at its lower levels, it did everything it could to steer it from above. Le Duc Tho, "Nghi Quyet Ngay 19-2-1947," 19 February 1947, *Van Kien Dang Toan Tap*, vol. 8 (1945–7) (Hanoi: Nha Xuat Ban Chinh Tri Quoc Gia, 2000), pp. 165–6.

3. See *Lich Su Dang Bo Bo Tong Tham Muu Co Quan Bo Quoc Phong (1945–1975)*, vol. 1 (Hanoi: Nha Xuat Ban Quan Doi Nhan Dan, 2011). For the focus on guerrilla warfare, see "Nghi Quyet cua Hoi Nghi Can Bo Trung Uong tu 3–4 den 6–4 1947," 3–6 April 1947, *Van Kien Dang Toan Tap*, vol. 8 (1945–7), pp. 179–80.

4. *Lich Su Cuc Quan Huan, 1946–1996* (Hanoi: Nha Xuat Ban Quan Doi Nhan Dan, 1996), pp. 57–8.

5. The future commander of the 304th division, Hoang Minh Thao, had also studied military science at the Liuzhou Military Academy. One of the reasons Ho Chi Minh called Vo Nguyen Giap and Pham Van Dong to the Chinese border in 1940 was to enroll them in this military academy.

6. According to Nguyen Van Phai, most of the colonial troops in the Garde indochinoise crossed over to Ho Chi Minh's army in late 1945. Nguyen Van Phi, "L'Armée vietnamienne (1949–1957)," Ph.D. dissertation (Montpellier: Université Paul Valéry, 1980), pp. 41–2.

7. See my "Belated Allies: The Technical Contributions of Japanese Deserters to the Viet Minh (1945–1950)," in Marilyn Young and Robert Buzzanco, eds., *A Companion to the Vietnam War* (Oxford: Blackwell Publishers, 2002), pp. 37–64. On the Europeans, see Jacques Doyon, *Les Soldats blancs de Ho Chi Minh* (Paris: Fayard, 1973). For specific Japanese cases, see "Viec Nhap Quoc Tich Viet Nam," GF9, CAOM.

8. In their obituaries for Vo Nguyen Giap in 2013, Western media outlets spoke repeatedly of the Vietnamese general as a "Red Napoleon." For examples, simply google "Vo Nguyen Giap" and "Red Napoleon."

9. *Tuong Nguyen Son* (Hanoi: Nha Xuat Ban Ban Thong Tan, 2008, with English and Chinese translations), with extraordinary photos of Nguyen Son and his time in China. Thanks to liberal press laws during the left-wing French Popular Front period in Indochina, Vietnamese

communists could read essential Maoist writings in Vietnamese translation, such as those of
Nguyen Duc Thuy: *Phuong Phap Khang Nhat cua Hong Quan Tau* (Hanoi: no publishing house
indicated, 1938); Nguyen Van Tay, *Lam Sao cho Tau Thang Nhat* (My Tho: no publishing house
indicated, 1938); and Van Dinh (Vo Nguyen Giap), *Muon Hieu Ro Tinh Hinh Quan Su o Tau*
(Hanoi: no publishing house indicated, 1939). See also David Marr, *Vietnamese Tradition on
Trial (1925–1945)* (Berkeley: University of California Press, 1981), pp. 401–2; and Greg Lockhart,
Nation in Arms: The Origin of the People's Army of Vietnam (Sydney: Allen and Unwin, 1989),
Chapter 2 and pp. 273–4.

10. On the translation services, see *Lich Su Cuc Quan Huan, 1946–1996*, pp. 27–30. Many of
these translations can be found in the Bo Phan Khang Chien Special Collection, which features
books published by the Democratic Republic of Vietnam during the Indochina War. The Vietnamese National Library in Hanoi is home to this gold mine of information. On the revamping
of the general staff in 1949–50, see *Lich su Bo Tong Tham Muu trong Khang Chien Chong Phap
(1945–1954)* (Hanoi: Nha In Bo Tong Tham Muu, 1991), pp. 401–11.

11. David Marr, *Vietnam: State, War, and Revolution (1945–1946)* (Berkeley: University of
California Press, 2014) on northerners heading south in 1945–6; and Tran Ngoc Chau, *Vietnam
Labyrinth* (Lubbock: Texas Tech University Press, 2012), p. 14 (for the citation).

12. Ngo Van Chieu, *Journal d'un combattant Viet-Minh* (Paris: Editions du Seuil, 1955),
pp. 55, 60.

13. Tran Ngoc Chau, *Vietnam Labryinth*, p. 58.

14. *Lich su Bo Tong Tham Muu trong Khang Chien Chong Phap*, pp. 22–3. Early on, the communists had no party organization in control of the Tran Quoc Tuan Military Academy; see *Lich
Su Cuc Quan Huan, 1946–1996*, p. 11.

15. Ho Chi Minh, "Sac Lenh 71," 22 May 1946, articles 19–23, https://thuvienphapluat.vn/van
-ban/Bo-may-hanh-chinh/Sac-lenh-71-trich-luc-Sac-lenh-71-an-dinh-quy-tac-quan-doi-quoc
-gia-36000.aspx, accessed on 19 July 2019.

16. Vo Nguyen Giap, *Chien Dau trong Vong Vay* (Hanoi: Nha Xuat Ban Quan Doi Nhan Dan,
2001), pp. 30–35; *Lich su Bo Tong Tham Muu trong Khang Chien Chong Phap*, pp. 65–66, 88–90,
97, 327; "L'Armée viêtminh," *Sud-Est asiatique*, no. 18 (December 1950), p. 28; Nguyen To Uyen,
Cong Cuoc Bao Ve va Xay Dung Chinh Quyen Nhan Dan o Viet Nam trong Nhung Nam 1945–1947
(Hanoi: Nha Xuat Ban Khoa Hoc Xa Hoi, 1999), p. 166.

17. *Lich su Bo Tong Tham Muu trong Khang Chien Chong Phap*, pp. 327–9; Nguyen To Uyen,
Cong Cuoc Bao Ve, p. 166; Ngo Van Chieu, *Journal d'un combattant Viet-Minh*, p. 120.

18. *Lich Su Tai Chinh Quan Doi Nhan Dan Viet Nam (1945–1954)*, vol. 1 (Hanoi: Nha Xuat
Ban Quan Doi Nhan Dan, 1989), p. 33.

19. Lucien Bodard, *La Guerre d'Indochine* (Paris: Bernard Grasset, 1997), p. 522.

20. *Giao Su, Vien Si, Tran Dai Nghia* (Hanoi: Nha Xuat Ban Chinh Tri Quoc Gia-Su That,
2013); and Thanh Duc, *Tran Dai Nghia* (Ho Chi Minh City: Nha Xuat Ban Tre, 2015).

21. Truong Nhu Tang provides a riveting description of his meeting with Ho in Paris in
1946 in *A Vietcong Memoir* (New York: Harcourt Brace Jovanovich, Publishers, 1985),
pp. 9–17.

22. "Tran Dai Nghia—'Ong Vua' Vu Khi Viet Nam," *VN Express*, 13 September 2013, https://
vnexpress.net/khoa-hoc/tran-dai-nghia-ong-vua-vu-khi-viet-nam-2878702.html, accessed on
6 May 2019; and "Ong Vua Vu Khi Viet Nam Tran Dai Nghia, 3," *Dan Tri* (19 December 2007),

https://dantri.com.vn/phong-su-ky-su/ong-vua-vu-khi-viet-nam-tran-dai-nghia-3-1198166290
.htm, accessed on 8 May 2019.

23. For the defense industry statistics, see *Bach Khoa Tri Thuc Quoc Phong Toan Dan* (Hanoi: Nha Xuat Ban Chinh Tri Quoc Gia, 2003), p. 635. The scene with Fowler and Pyle under fire is in Graham Greene, *The Quiet American* (London: Penguin Books, 1973 [first published in 1955]), p. 108. And for a confirmation of the SKZ's actual use against such guard towers at the time, see Georges Boudarel, *Autobiographie* (Paris: Jacques Bertoin, 1991), pp. 246–7; and Bodard, *La Guerre d'Indochine*, pp. 643–4.

24. *Lich su Bo Tong Tham Muu trong Khang Chien Chong Phap*, pp. 132–5; Tran Duong, *Kinh Te Viet Nam (1945–1954)* (Hanoi: Nha Xuat Ban Hoa Hoc, 1966), pp. 197–8; "Memoire écrit par 'X' [name deleted by C. Goscha], ex-capitaine adjoint au chef du 'X' [words deleted by C. Goscha]," in "Bureau de l'Etat majeur/Viet Minh," p. 18, in 10H2353, SHD.

25. Luong, "Thong Tri cua Ban Thuong Vu Trung Uong ve Cuoc Chien Tranh Trieu Tien," 4 August 1950, *Van Kien Dang Toan Tap*, vol. 11 (1950) (Hanoi: Nha Xuat Ban Chinh Tri Quoc Gia, 2001), pp. 451–4.

26. Chen Jian, *Mao's China and the Cold War* (Chapel Hill: University of North Carolina Press, 2001), p. 126; Qiang Zhai, *China and the Vietnam Wars, 1950–1975* (Chapel Hill, University of North Carolina Press, 2000), p. 20; Le Van Thinh, "Quan He Giua Cach Mang Viet Nam va Lien Xo trong Giai Doan 1930–1954," Ph.D. dissertation (Hanoi: Hanoi University, 1999), pp. 160–61; "Memoire écrit par 'X' [name deleted by C. Goscha], ex-capitaine adjoint au chef du 'X' [words deleted by C. Goscha]," pp. 11–13; Niu Jun, "A Relook at China's Policy to Assist Vietnam in Its Resistance War against France," in Qin Yaqing and Chen Zhiruui, eds., *Future in Retrospect, China's Diplomatic History Revisited* (Singapore: World Century, 2016), p. 74; and *Su That ve Nhung Lan Xuat Quan cua Trung Quoc va Quan He Viet-Trung* (Da Nang: Nha Xuat Ban Da Nang, 1996), p. 42. Tonnage figures are from *Su That ve Nhung Lan Xuat*, pp. 21, 42 (note 1), citing documents from the army logistics archives. This assistance can be established annually as follows, according to statistics in this source: 1950: 3,983 tons; 1951: 6,086 tons; 1952: 2,160 tons; 1953: 4,400 tons; 1954: 4,892 tons. It is likely that the Soviet arms had first gone to the Chinese, who, after the Korean War ended in July 1953, rushed them to Vietnam. See also *Bach Khoa Tri Thuc Quoc Phong Toan Dan*, p. 638.

27. *Lich su Bo Tong Tham Muu trong Khang Chien Chong Phap*, pp. 324–5, 407; *Su That*, pp. 21–2; Vo Nguyen Giap, *Duong toi Dien Bien Phu*, 2nd edition (Hanoi: Nha Xuat Ban Quan Doi Nhan Dan, 2001), pp. 13–5, 23; Qiang Zhai, *China and the Vietnam Wars*, pp. 19–29; Xu Beilan and Zheng Peifei, *Chen Gun [Chen Geng] Jiangjun zhuan*, Beijing: Jiefangjun Chubanshe, 1988, p. 581; Guo Ming, ed., *Zhong-Yue guanxi yanbian sishi nian* (Nanning: Guangxi Renmin Chubanshe, 1992), p. 42, https://www.fmprc.gov.cn/mfa_eng/ziliao_665539/wjrw_665549/lrfbzjbzzl_665553/t44355.shtml, accessed on 9 April 2020. My thanks to Yuxi Liu for translating the Chinese documents for me.

28. Qian Jiang, *Zai shenmidi zhanzheng zhong—Zhongguo junshi guwentuan fu Yuenan zhengzhanji* (Zhengzhou: Hunan Renmin chubanshe, 1992), p. 58.

29. On the Vietnamese campus for training specialists in China, see Do Thi Nguyet Quang, "Qua Trinh Xay Dung va Phat Trien nen Giao Duc Viet Nam Moi tu Thang 9–1945 den Thang 7–1954," Master's thesis (Hanoi: Khoa Hoc Lich Su, 1996), pp. 105–9. On the Vietnamese military academy in China, see *Lich su Bo Tong Tham Muu trong Khang Chien Chong Phap*, pp. 324–5,

331–2, 407–8; Vo Nguyen Giap, *Duong Toi Dien Bien Phu* (Hanoi: Nha Xuat Ban Quan Doi Nhan Dan, 2001, 2nd edition), pp. 14–16; and "Note sur la collaboration sino-vietminh période du 1 septembre 1950 au 1 février 1951," 7 March 1951, 10H288, SHD. On the Chinese instructors and interpreters see Qian Jiang, *Zai shenmidi zhanzheng zhong*, p. 44. Excerpts of this document were kindly translated by Joseph Lee. The idea that the French taught the Americans how to fight "irregular" wars and insurgencies in Vietnam and elsewhere is woefully inaccurate. For an important corrective, see Elie Tenenbaum, *Partisans et centurions: Une histoire de la guerre irré-gulière au XXe siècle* (Paris: Perrin, 2018).

30. In the official Communist Party's military history of Vietnam, the entry for the People's Army of Vietnam gives 1950 as its founding date. It does not, however, provide the exact day and month on which this new people's army emerged; see *Bach Khoa Tri Thuc Quoc Phong Toan Dan* (Hanoi: Nha Xuat Ban Chinh Tri Quoc Gia, 2003), pp. 466–7. The same is true of the army's military history, *Tu Dien Bach Khoa Quan Su Viet Nam* (Hanoi: Nha Xuat Ban Quan Doi Nhan Dan, 1996), p. 664. See *Lich su Bo Tong Tham Muu trong Khang Chien Chong Phap*, p. 327, for the size of the PAVN by late 1950.

31. *Lich su Bo Tong Tham Muu trong Khang Chien Chong Phap*, pp. 23–5; see also Christopher Goscha, *Thailand and the Southeast Asian Networks of the Vietnamese Revolution* (London: Routledge, 1999), chapters 4–6, for recruits coming from Thailand.

32. *Phong Trao Nam Tien (1945–1946)* (Hanoi: Nha Xuat Ban Quan Doi Nhan Dan, 1997); and *Lich Su Bo Tham Muu Quan Khu 7 Mien Dong Nam Bo (1945–1975)* (Hanoi: Nha Xuat Ban Quan Doi Nhan Dan, 1994), pp. 22, 29–31.

33. *Lich su Bo Tong Tham Muu trong Khang Chien Chong Phap*, p. 329, for the size of the regular army in the south in 1950.

34. Ibid., p. 329; Yves Gras, *Histoire de la guerre d'Indochine* (Paris: Plon, 1979), pp. 291, 393, note 1; and Bodard, *La guerre d'Indochine*, pp. 459–64.

35. *Tu Dien Bach Khoa Quan Su Viet Nam*, pp. 102–3 (for the battles of Ben Cat and Ben Tre), p. 124 (Battle of Long Chau Hau), and p. 140 (Battle of Tra Vinh). The French received intelligence suggesting that Vo Nguyen Giap had instructed Nguyen Binh to launch the General Counter-offensive in the south: see "Bulletin de renseignement," no. 1330, 6 March 1950; and SDECE, no. 17320/PC/SG, "Renseignement," 17 September 1950; in Plan militaire, 285, grouping Haut Commissariat de l'Indochine, Centre des Archives d'Outre-mer.

36. On the southern defeat at the hands of the French, see Gras, *Histoire de la guerre d'Indochine*, pp. 291, 393; and Bodard, *La Guerre d'Indochine*, pp. 459–64. Georges Boudarel provides a firsthand account of how Le Duan, the head of the party in the south, criticized Binh for this southern failure: Boudarel, *Autobiographie*, pp. 178–9.

37. The Communist Party's secret services assassinated the two French men who had presided over their military defeat: in 1950, the Sûreté's Marcel Bazin, who had won the Battle of Saigon, and, a year later, Charles Chanson, who had broken Nguyen Binh's army in the delta.

38. Ngo Van Chieu, *Journal d'un combattant*, pp. 125–37 (citations pp. 131, 137). See also Nguyen Huy Tuong, "La Campagne des frontières," *De la reconquête française à Dien Bien Phu* (Hanoi: Fleuve Rouge, 1985), pp. 90–106. For the Battle of Cao Bang, see Gras, *Histoire de la guerre d'Indochine*, pp. 323–66; Bodard, *La Guerre d'Indochine*, pp. 531–660; and "Ngay 22/10/1950, Ket Thuc Chien Dich Le Hong Phong II," *Bao Tang Lich Su Quoc Gia*, 20 October 2012, http://baotanglichsu.vn/vi/Articles/3097/12775/ngay-22-10-1950-ket-thuc-chien-dich-le-hong-phong-ii.html, accessed on 9 April 2020.

39. That does not mean that nothing happened there! The Vietnamese communists had competition from others. See Shawn McHale, *The First Indochina War: Violence, Sovereignty and the Fracture of the South, 1945–1956* (New York: Cambridge University Press, 2021).

Chapter 3. The Asian Routes of War

1. "Prise du Bateau Song Lo," 26 September 1949; and "Note pour le Haut Commissariat," 16 October 1949; both in 10H279, SHD; "Equipage du Song Lo," 3 March 1950, "Song Lo," 10H3999, SHD; *Lich Su Nganh Duong Bien Viet Nam* (Haiphong: Tong Cuc Duong Bien, 1990), pp. 35–9; Nguyen Van Ngo, Hoi Vo Tuyen Dien Tu Viet Nam, "Nhung Nguoi Bach Khoa Da Di Xa—Thay Nguyen Nhu Kim," https://rev.org.vn/nhung-nguoi-bach-khoa-da-di-xa-thay-nguyen-nhu-kim/, accessed on 25 October 2018; and *Quan Tinh Nguyen Viet Nam o Campuchia thoi Ky 1945–1954* (Ca Mau: Nha Xuat Ban Mui Ca Mau, 1998), pp. 152–5.

2. On Chinese trading networks in the eighteenth-century civil and regional wars for Vietnam, see Dian H. Murray, *Pirates of the South China Coast, 1790–1810* (Stanford: Stanford University Press, 1987).

3. The future commander of the 308th Division, Vuong Thua Vu, first worked on the Yunnan railway during the interwar period.

4. "Demande d'importation au Vietnam à M. le Directeur des Douanes du Vietnam: Kinh Te Quoc Fong, no. 170/KTQF," dated 4 [June] 1946; "Contrat entre la RDVN, Directeur des Services Economiques et de la Défense Nationale et M. Hoang Vinh Dien," 4 June 1946; and "Demande de permis d'export-import par Trinh Van Yen," no. 168/KTQP, 6 June 1946, 13, 10H532, SHD.

5. Nguyen Thuong Dat, "Ngoai Thuong trong Thoi Ky Hinh Thanh va Xay Dung," *Tap Chi Thuong Mai*, nos. 21–2 (November 1996), pp. 11, 20; "Note sur l'organisation et le fonctionnement de l'Office du Commerce extérieur du Viet Minh," 16 September 1947 and "Information sur le trafic commercial du Viet Minh avec l'extérieur," 19 September 1947, both in 6, supplement, Conseiller Politique, CAOM; "Activités indochinoises et chinoises au Kouang Si," 31 October 1948, 10H287, SHD.

6. Nguyen Thuong Dat, "Ngoai Thuong," p. 20; "Circulaire: Commerce extérieur, service de l'importation," Phan Anh, 8 July 1947; Nguyen Duc Thuy, "La Succursale du Commerce extérieur de Cao Bang à l'Office du Commerce Extérieur de That Khe," 2 July 1947; both in "Economie Viet Minh," 6, supplement, Conseiller politique, CAOM; "Information sur le trafic commercial du Viet Minh avec l'extérieur," "Note sur l'organisation et le fonctionnement de l'Office du Commerce extérieur du Viet Minh"; and "Note [sur les] activités de l'office du commerce extérieur de Cao Bang," 15 August 1947, 34–5, Conseiller Diplomatique, Centre des Archives d'Outre-Mer; and "Tableau des Chinois ayant fait ou faisant du trafic des Viet Minh pour l'année 1947 dans la région de Cao Bang-Lang Son," 14 November 1947, "Collusion Sino-Viet Minh," 128; Conseiller Politique, CAOM.

7. King C. Chen, *Vietnam and China, 1938–1954* (Princeton: Princeton University Press, 1969), pp. 176–200; "Objet: Activité de Nguyen Duc Thuy," 17 April 1947; and "Fiche: Note [sur les] activités de l'office du commerce extérieur de Cao Bang, 338/R," 17 April 1947; both in 148, Conseiller politique, CAOM. American diplomats in Nanjing reported that while Nguyen Duc Thuy's conversations with the Guomindang (GMD, or the Chinese Nationalist Party) did not gain Chinese support, the Nanjing government would "close its eyes to arms traffic from

Kwangsi into Tonkin"; see "Nanking's A-162 June 14 to American Embassy, Paris," 12 July 1948, 851G.01/6–1448, Confidential US State Department Central Files, Internal Affairs: Indochina, 1945–1949, National Archives and Records Administration.

8. "Renseignement", 4 August 1947, "Economie Viet Minh," 6, supplement, Conseiller politique, CAOM; "BR no. 789," 16 April 1947; and "BR no. 80," 11 January 1947; both in 34–5, Conseiller diplomatique, CAOM; and "Renseignement," 4 August 1947, "Economie Viet Minh," 6, supplement, Conseiller politique, CAOM.

9. Le Van Hien, *Nhat Ky cua Mot Bo Truong* (Da Nang: Nha Xuat Ban Da Nang, 1995), vol. 2, p. 133.

10. Cited in Gilbert Bodinier, ed., *Indochine 1947* (Vincennes: SHD, 1989), pp. 286–7.

11. Raoul Salan, *Le Viet-Minh mon adversaire* (Paris: Presses de la Cité, 1971), pp. 101–18; Le Van Hien, *Nhat Ky,* vol. 1, pp. 129, 188–92; *Thong Ke cac Chien Dich trong Khang Chien Chong Phap, Khang Chien Chong My,* vol. 1 (Hanoi: Vien Lich Su Quan Su Viet Nam, 1993), p. 11; and Vo Nguyen Giap, *Chien Dau trong Vong Vay* (Hanoi: Nha Xuat Ban Quan Doi Nhan Dan, 1995), pp. 142–80.

12. "BR daté septembre 1948," 4 October 1948, "Relations entre Viet Minh et Chinois, 1948," 10H287, SHD; and Nguyen Thuong Dat, "Ngoai Thuong," p. 20.

13. Nha Thue Quan va Thue Gian Thu, "So. 130: Kiem Tra Thuoc Phien," Hanoi, 11 May 1946; "Uy Ban Hanh Chinh Bac Bo Gui ong Giam Doc So Thue Quan," no. 682/VPK, 29 June 1946; both in 16, Gouvernement de fait, CAOM; "BR no. 27," Savannakhet, 14 July 1946, 10H5636, SHD; "BRM août 1950," 5 September 1950, "Laos, 1950," 10H4303, SHD. For more on opium, see "Thuoc Phien," 34, Gouvernement de fait, CAOM; "Ruou va thuoc phien," 24, Gouvernement de fait, CAOM; and also see various documents in 16, Gouvernement de fait, CAOM.

14. Le Van Hien, *Nhat Ky,* vol. 2, p. 88; Vu Thu Hien, *Dem Giua Ban Ngay* (California: Van Nghe, 1997), p. 342; Central Intelligence Agency, "Illicit Opium Traffic Southeast Asia," 13 December 1948, p. 5, CREST, National Archives and Records Administration; and reports from the British Legation, Saigon, no. 78, 10 June 1953, FO371/106801, Public Records Office, United Kingdom. Douglas Porch assigns great importance to opium for explaining the battle of Dien Bien Phu. Douglas Porch, "Dien Bien Phu and the Opium Connection," *The Quarterly Journal of Military History,* vol. 7, no. 4 (Summer 1995), pp. 100–109.

15. For more on the Americans in the drug trade in Southeast Asia, see Alfred McCoy, *The Politics of Heroin in Southeast Asia* (New York: Harpers, 1973). The French purchasing and destruction of opium during the Indochina War was part of a bigger economic offensive discussed in Chapter 9.

16. "Société commerciale Viet Thang," 4 March 1950, 385, Service de Protection du Corps expéditionnaire, CAOM; "Bilan économique et financier Viet Minh en mai 1950," 6 June 1950, 10H3991, SHD. I rely on a large collection of captured Vietnamese documents on the Viet Thang in 385, Service de Protection du Corps Expéditionnaire. A high-ranking Vietnamese communist deeply involved in this clandestine trade also confirms that Vietnamese communists operated clandestine units in Guangzhou and Macau; see Vo Bam, *Nhung Neo Duong Khang Chien* (Hanoi: Nha Xuat Ban Quan Doi Nhan Dan, 2006), pp. 84–7.

17. "BR no. 25: Trafic maritime rebelle," 8 November 1950, p. 9, "FMEO, EM2, 1950," UUE-29, SHD; "Bulletin de renseignements," 23 October 1951, "Sud-Annam, décembre 1951," UUB-28, SHD; "Bilan économique et financier S.M. en mai 1950," 6 June 1950, p. 24, C889, SHD; "Société

commerciale Viet Thang," 4 March 1950; "Sûreté Fédérale", no. 161/IB/C (interrogation of member of the Viet Thang whose name has been withheld); and "Société commerciale Viet Thang," 19 January 1949; all in 385, Service de Protection du Corps expéditionnaire; and "BR no. 20: Mois de janvier et février 1950, Trafic maritime rebelle," 23 March 1950, p. 9, UUE-29, SHD.

18. "Bilan économique et financier Viet Minh en mai 1950"; "BR no. 24: Bilan économique et financier Viet Minh au 1 juillet 1950," 9 July 1950, p. 14, UUE-29, SHD; "Bilan économique et financier Viet Minh en mai 1950"; "Objet: Succursale de la société commerciale Viet Minh 'Viet Thang' au Khanh Hoa," p. 3, "Sud-Annam, décembre 1951," UUB-28, SHD; and "BR no. 20: Mois de janvier et février 1950, Trafic maritime rebelle," p. 9.

19. "BR no. 13: Trafic de contrebande rebelle," 20 December 1948, p. 2, "FMEO/EM/2/1948," UUE18, SHD; Central Intelligence Agency, "Illicit Opium Traffic Southeast Asia"; "BR no. 20: Mois de janvier et février 1950, Trafic maritime rebelle," p. 9; and DRV trading receipts in 12, Gouvernement de fait, CAOM, and 10H528, SHD.

20. "Rapport sur l'état actuel des relations sino-viet minh," p. 1, 13 October 1948, 34–5, Conseiller Diplomatique, CAOM; Vo Bam, *Nhung Neo Duong Khang Chien*, p. 89; Commandement en chef des forces armées en Extreme-Orient, no. 5859/FAEO/2S, "Activités économiques V.M.," intercepted cable revealing DRV smuggling of Hong Kong dollars to Bangkok, 63, 10H548, SHD.

21. "Rapport sur l'état actuel des relations sino-viet minh," p. 1; Vo Bam, *Nhung Neo Duong Khang Chien*, p. 89; "Avis de renseignements no. 10," 8 January 1948, DNEO, EM2, UUD-8, SHD; "BR no. 20: Mois de janvier et février 1950, Trafic maritime rebelle," p. 15, UUE-29, SHD; "Trafique d'armes à partir de Macao," 29 May 1950, pp. 1–7 (p. 7 for the 50 percent interception rate); "Fiche de renseignements," 24 June 1952, and "Lagune de Tam Ky," 25 April 1952, both in "Surmar Annam," UUB-28, SHD.

22. On Hainan and the South China Sea, see Bernard Estival, *La Marine française dans la guerre d'Indochine* (Nantes: Marines édition, 1998), pp. 161, 166–9; "Bulletin de renseignements," 3 November 1950, "II. Pays étrangers," C835, SHD; "BR no. 20: Mois de janvier et février 1950, Trafic maritime rebelle," p. 15; "Fiche de renseignements," 24 June 1952; "Lagune de Tam Ky"; "Trafic chinois entre la province de Nghe An et Hainan," 30 April 1950, "Relations entre Viet Minh et Chinois, 1948," 10H287, SHD; intercepted documents in 10H548, 10H549, and 10H5637, SHD. For the letter from Cao Hong Lanh, August 1948, see "Activités chinoises," 110, Conseiller Politique, CAOM.

23. I rely in this section on my *Thailand and the Southeast Asian Networks of the Vietnamese Revolution, 1885–1954* (London: Routledge, 1999), Chapter 5.

24. Ibid., Chapter 5, and Eugene Ford, *Cold War Monks: Buddhism and America's Secret Strategy in Southeast Asia* (New Haven: Yale University Press, 2017).

25. Leon Comber, "'Traitor of All Traitors'—Secret Agent *Extraordinaire*: Lai Teck, Secretary-General, Communist Party of Malaya (1939–1947)," *Journal of the Malaysian Branch of the Royal Asiatic Society*, vol. 83, no. 2 (299) (2010), pp. 1–25 and my "Towards a geo-history of Asian communism," in Geoff Wade and James Chin, eds., *China and Southeast Asia: Historical Interactions* (London: Routledge, 2018), pp. 314–35.

26. "Note d'information concernant les trafics et trafiquants au Siam au bénéfice des rebelles indochinois," pp. 1 and 7, 27 June 1950, C838, SHD; and "Aventuriers américains au Siam en 1946," SDECE/Base d'Indochine, 7 September 1948, pp. 1–9, S01, 06, UU-SUP, SHD. See also the colorful letters and reports on all sorts of traffickers and shady characters in Bangkok and

elsewhere in 91, Service de Protection du Corps Expéditionnaire, CAOM and in the "Trafics subversifs," 10H638, SHD.

27. See the French investigation in 10H279, SHD, and Bui Thi Huong, "Thuyen Truong Le Van Mot," 10 November 2008, http://antg.cand.com.vn/Tu-lieu-antg/Thuyen-truong-Le-Van -Mot---Huyen-thoai-tren-bien-dong-293001/, accessed on 11 April 2020.

28. Bazin, "Note pour le Haut Commissaire de France en Indochine," 5 November 1949, 10H279, SHD.

29. Fernand Braudel, *La Méditerranée et le monde méditerranéen à l'époque de Philippe II* (Paris: Armand Colin, 1990), p. 337.

30. Nowhere is this arc more apparent than in Hoang Van Hoan, *Giot Nuoc Trong Bien Ca* (Beijing: No publisher indicated, 1988). Hoang Van Hoan confirms Ho Chi Minh's involvement in this project from the start. Hoang Van Hoan, *Giot Nuoc*, p. 327.

31. Cited in my *Thailand and the Southeast Asian Networks*, p. 300; and "Nguoi Pho Hoi—Ky 2: Huyen Thoai Nam Them—Cao Hong Lanh", https://thanhnien.vn/van-hoa/nguoi-pho-hoi -ky-2-huyen-thoai-nam-them-cao-hong-lanh-440117.html, accessed on 11 April 2020.

32. Bui Thi Huong, "Thuyen Truong Le Van Mot."

33. Le Van Hien, *Nhat Ky*, vol. 2, pp. 230, 236–7.

34. I am relying here on the memoir of a former member of the DRV general staff who crossed over to the French: "Mémoire écrit par 'X' [name deleted by C. Goscha], ex-'X' [words deleted by C. Goscha], adjoint au chef du 'X' [words deleted by C. Goscha] de l'Etat-Major Viet Minh," and the attached "Rapport du lieutenant 'X' [name deleted by C. Goscha] sur sa mission en Baie de Halong," 10H2353, SHD. This defector had been a high-ranking member of the DRV general staff and had worked directly with Chinese advisers. The plan to create an air base failed, according to an Austrian communist working for the DRV in central Vietnam. See Pierre Sergent, *Un étrange Monsieur Frey* (Paris: Fayard, 1982), p. 301. Ho Chi Minh asked the Chinese to provide the Vietnamese with aircraft. Niu Jun, "A Relook at China's Policy to Assist Vietnam in Its Resistance War against France," in Qin Yaqing and Chen Zhiruui, eds., *Future in Retrospect, China's Diplomatic History Revisited* (Singapore: World Century, 2016), p. 71. In March 1949, the Vietnamese general staff created study sections for the navy and airforce; see *Lich Su Dang Bo Bo Tong Tham Muu Co Quan Bo Quoc Phong*, vol. 1 (Hanoi: Nha Xuat Ban Quan Doi Nhan Dan, 2011), p. 100. Intercepted telegrams confirm it in folder "Viet Minh Aviation," C888, SHD.

35. It is very possible that the three junks captured by the French were the ones mentioned in the following report: "Déclaration en date du 8 août 1950 de 'X' [name deleted by C. Goscha], commerçant domicilé près de Bong Son, capturé le 5 août 1950 par la Marine . . . se dirigeant vers Hainan," Marine, C835, SHD.

36. Vo Bam, *Nhung Neo Duong Khang Chien*, pp. 74–89. On the communist movement on Hainan Island, see Jeremy Murray, *China's Lonely Revolution: The Local Communist Movement of Hainan Island, 1926–1956* (New York: SUNY Press, 2017).

37. Naval History and Heritage Command, "By Sea, Air, and Land, Chapter 1: The Early Years, 1950–1959," https://www.history.navy.mil/research/library/online-reading-room/title -list-alphabetically/b/by-sea-air-land-marolda/chapter-1-the-early-years-1950-1959.html, accessed on 16 November 2018.

38. Vo Bam, *Nhung neo duong*, pp. 85–7; and "Bulletin de renseignement no 31, Trafic maritime rebelle," 20 August 1952, 1950, 263, 10H3999, SHD.

39. Vo Bam, *Nhung neo duong*, pp. 86–7. In November 1949, DRV radio communications indicated that the time was not yet right for sending large numbers of junks to Hainan to supply central and southern Vietnam. Although the "Naval Studies Section" may have transported men and supplies by rivers during the Battle of Dien Bien Phu, the DRV never possessed a navy during the entire Indochina War. Le Van Hien, *Nhat Ky*, vol. 2, p. 230.

40. Intercepted cable in "Bulletin de renseignements," SDECE, 3 November 1950, "Armement munitions, II. Pays étrangers," C835, SHD.

41. Pham Hung, "Uy Ban Hanh Chanh Nam Bo no 17/NM," 18 January 1952, in "Economie Viet Minh, organisation des comités no. 1," 10H3990, SHD.

42. *Phong Trao Nam Tien* (Hanoi: Nha Xuat Ban Quan Doi Nhan Dan, 1997), pp. 48–9; and *Mua Thu Roi, Ngay Ham Ba* (Hanoi: Nha Xuat Ban Chinh Tri Quoc Gia, 1996), vol. 2, part 3, pp. 330–45, 346–52. On the early coastal Ho Chi Minh Trail, see "BR no. 20: Mois de janvier et février 1950, Trafic maritime rebelle," p. 15; "Piste Ho Chi Minh," 11 November 1949, 51, 10H544, SHD; *Lich Su Bo Doi Thong Tin Lien Lac Quan khu 7–Mien Dong Nam Bo (1945–1995)* (Hanoi: Nha Xuat Ban Quan Doi Nhan Dan, 1995), p. 49; and *50 Nam Quan Doi Nhan Dan Viet Nam (Bien Nien Su Kien)* (Hanoi: Nha Xuat Ban Quan Doi Nhan Dan 1995), p. 52.

43. Nguyen Binh, "Rapport sur la Base Opérationnelle du Sud-Indochinois: Rapport établi par le Général V[iet] M[inh] NGUYEN BINH à destination au Haut-Commandement pendant son voyage à travers l'Est-Cambodge," p. 2, 10H636, SHD. Orders to begin creating a southern Indochinese base and north–south overland links began in early 1949; see "Synthèse sur la Mission Nguyen Binh," p. 2, 10H636, SHD; and Vo Nguyen Giap, *Chien Dau trong Vong Vay* (Hanoi: Nha Xuat Ban Quan Doi Nhan Dan, 1995), pp. 248, 369.

44. "Rapport sur la Base Opérationnelle du Sud-Indochinois," p. 2.

45. It was only in 1959, when the Vietnamese communists picked up where they had left off, that arms would start flowing in large quantities from the north to the south along land routes and via the sea once again. See Vo Thuan Nho, "Chi Thi cua Thuong Vu Lien Khu Uy IV," 5 July 1951, *Van Kien Dang Toan Tap*, vol. 12 (1951) (Hanoi: Nha Xuat Ban Chinh Tri Quoc Gia, 2001), pp. 758–63. On the Ho Chi Minh Trail, see John Prados, *The Blood Road: The Ho Chi Minh Trail and the Vietnam War* (Malden: Wiley-Blackwell, 2000). On the maritime Ho Chi Minh Trail, see my "The Maritime Nature of the Wars for Vietnam: (1945–75): A Geo-Historical Reflection," *War and Society*, vol. 24, no. 2 (November 2005), pp. 53–92.

Chapter 4. The City at War

1. See the images in the French propaganda newsreel in early 1947 on the Battle of Hanoi: "Les Débuts de la guerre d'Indochine: Hanoi en décembre 1946," http://fresques.ina.fr/jalons/fiche-media/InaEduoo063/les-debuts-de-la-guerre-d-indochine-hanoi-en-decembre-1946.html, accessed on 12 June 2018. The Battle of Nam Dinh was arguably the site of the most ferocious urban warfare of the Indochina War. See P. A. Léger, *Aux carrefours de la guerre* (Paris: Albin Michel, 1983), pp. 119–58; and *Nam Dinh Lich su Khang Chien Chong Thuc Dan Phap va De Quoc My (1945–1975)* (Hanoi: Nha Xuat Ban Quan Doi Nhan Dan, 1999), pp. 51–93. In 1996,

a film adaptation of the Battle of Hanoi appeared, based on Nguyen Huy Tuong's novel *Forever with the Capital* (*Song Mai voi Thu Do*). For an extract in French, see Nguyen Huy Tuong, "Barricades dans la capitale," *De la reconquête française à Dien Bien Phu, témoignages et récits* (Hanoi: Editions en langues étrangères, 1985).

2. Christopher Goscha, "This Is the End: Colonial Fear in Saigon in 1945," Congress of the French Historical Society, 24–6 April 2014, Université du Québec à Montréal, unpublished paper.

3. Germaine Krull, "Diary of Saigon Following the Allied Occupation in September 1945," unpublished work, entry for 25 September 1945. I thank David Marr for kindly providing me with a copy of this document located in the American archives.

4. For civilian losses, see Stanley Karnow, *Vietnam: A History* (New York: Viking Press, 1983), pp. 156–7. On Bidault, see Yves Gras, *Histoire de la guerre d'Indochine* (Paris: Plon, 1979), p. 147.

5. *Ha Noi Ban Hung Ca Bat tu Mua Dong 1946* (Hanoi: Ban Tuyen Giao Thanh uy Ha Noi, 2006), p. 40; and *Tong Ket 60 Ngay Dem Chien Dau Mo Dau Toan Quoc Khang Chien Chong Phap* (Hanoi: Nha Xuat Ban Quan Doi Nhan Dan, 1997), pp. 91–2.

6. On 12 (*not* 22) December 1946, the Communist Party issued instructions to cadres on how to fight a drawn-out and total war against the French (in the increasingly likely event that war would break out), "Toan Dan Khang Chien Chi Thi cua Doan the," dated 22 December 1946 and signed by the Indochinese Communist Party, Vietnamese National Archives, TBN-75, 48 (my thanks to David Marr for kindly sharing his document with me), also in *Van Kien Dang Toan Tap*, vol. 8 (1945–6) (Hanoi: Nha Xuat Ban Chinh Tri Quoc Gia, 2000), pp. 150–55.

7. *Tong Ket*, pp. 62–9, 91–2 (p. 64 for the citation "sooner or later") and Truong Chinh, "Khang Chien trong Thanh Pho," no date given, but sometime in mid- to late 1946, *Van Kien Dang Toan Tap*, vol. 8 (1945–7), pp. 454–6. Truong Chinh cites the examples of Moscow, Belgrade, and Stalingrad.

8. Ibid., pp. 75–8, 268–9; "L'Etat de siège s'étend à toute l'Indochine du Nord," *Le Monde*, no. 624 (24 December 1946), p. 1; and Trinh Vuong Hong, "Cuoc Chien Dau tai Ha Noi va Mot So Thanh Pho Thi Xa Bac Vi Tuyen 16," unpublished M.A. thesis (Hanoi: Hoc Hoc Lich Su, 1991), p. 102.

9. Ibid., pp. 70–72, 81–2, 161 (for fighting over the Dong Xuan Market), 266; *Thu do Ha Noi Lich Su Khang Chien Chong Thuc Dan Phap 1945–54* (Hanoi: Nha Xuat Ban Ha Noi, 1986), p. 18; Trinh Vuong Hong, "Cuoc Chien Dau tai Ha Noi," pp. 96–7.

10. *Tong Ket*, pp. 50–55, 82–6, 280–81 and "En Indochine: attaques et contre-attaques localisées se poursuivent," *Le Monde*, no. 654 (30 January 1947), p. 2.

11. "Vo Nguyen Giap va Hai Lan Bao Ve Thu Do," *Tienphong*, https://www.tienphong.vn/xa -hoi/dai-tuong-vo-nguyen-giap-va-hai-lan-bao-ve-thu-do-105684.tpo, accessed on 20 October 2018; *Tong Ket*, p. 92; and Vuong Thua Vu, *Truong Thanh Trong Chien Dau, Hoi Ky* (Hanoi: Nha Xuat Ban Quan Doi Nhan Dan, 1979), p. 107.

12. The Vietnamese cut the power at the electrical plant on Dinh Tien Hoang Street on the south side of the old town. Attentive tourists can still read the historical plaque there marking the beginning of full-scale war in Indochina at 20:03 p.m. on the evening of 19 December 1946.

13. Jean-Julien Fonde, *Traitez à tout prix* (Paris: Editions Robert Laffont, 1971), p. 279–80, 318; Duong Van Mai Elliott, *The Sacred Willow* (New York: Oxford University Press, 1999),

p. 135; *Tong Ket*, pp. 93–5, 228; Truong Chinh, "Khang Chien trong Thanh Pho," pp. 454–6; "Les Opérations militaires," *Le Monde*, no. 627 (27 December 1946), p. 1; "L'Etat de siège," p. 1; and Vuong Thua Vu, *Truong Thanh Trong Chien Dau*, pp. 109–10. On the battles of Hue, Nam Dinh, and Da Nang, see Trinh Vuong Hong, "Cuoc Chien Dau tai Ha Noi," unpublished M.A. thesis (Hanoi: Hoc Hoc Lich Su), pp. 104–19, and maps in his annex.

14. As cited by the French commander in the mixed military commission in Hanoi at the time, Fonde, *Traitez à tout prix*, p. 308.

15. "Les Evénements d'Indochine," *Le Monde*, no. 643 (21 January 1947), p. 2; and "Le Conflit s'étend à tout le Tonkin," *Le Monde*, no. 622 (21 December 1946), p. 1.

16. Mandaley Perkins, *Hanoi, Adieu* (Hanoi: Gioi Publishers, 2012), pp. 221–38. On the Yen Ninh massacre, see http://nhipsonghanoi.hanoimoi.com.vn/tin-tuc/Xua-va-nay/821805/thang -12-tren-pho-yen-ninh---hang-bun, accessed on 8 July 2020. A plaque commemorates the tragic event today.

17. See "Les Evénements de Hanoi du 19 décembre," *Le Monde*, no. 643 (21 January 1947), p. 2.

18. Cited by Pierre-Alban Thomas, *Combat intérieur* (Montataire: Editeur ISIS, 1998), p. 218.

19. Thomas, *Combat intérieur*, p. 213. Pierre Sergent, a paratrooper in the Indochina War (1er Bataillon étranger de parachutistes), speaks of a longtime French security agent on the northern border who, as late as 1949, "collected Viet ears in a jar of formaldehyde," in *Je ne regrette rien* (Paris: Fayard, 1972), p. 32.

20. "L'Etat de siège s'étend," p. 1.

21. On the politicization of the French army during this period, see Raoul Girardet, *La Crise militaire française (1945–1962)* (Paris: Armand Colin, 1964).

22. *Tong Ket*, pp. 104–5, 152–4, 213; Trinh Vuong Hong, "Cuoc Chien Dau tai Ha Noi," pp. 71–104; and Yves Gras, *Histoire de la guerre d'Indochine*, p. 163 for the Valluy citation.

23. Fonde, *Traitez à tout prix*, pp. 281, 334–40; *Tong Ket*, p. 234; Trinh Vuong Hong, "Cuoc Chien Dau tai Ha Noi," p. 92; Gras, *Histoire de la guerre d'Indochine*, pp. 164–5; "En Indochine," p. 2; "10,000 Chinese Trapped," *New York Times* (13 January 1947), p. 10.

24. Tran Huy Lieu, ed., *Lich Su Thu Do Ha Noi* (Hanoi: Vien Su Hoc, 1960), pp. 229–30; Vuong Thua Vu, *Truong Thanh Trong Chien Dau*, pp. 126–8; *Ha Noi Ban Hung Ca Bat Tu Mua Dong 1946*, pp. 62–3, 179, 217; Trinh Vuong Hong, "Cuoc Chien Dau tai Ha Noi," pp. 90–92; and "10,000 Chinese Trapped."

25. Thomas, *Combat intérieur*, p. 211; and, for the number of houses destroyed, see Eric Déroo and Christophe Dutrône, *Le Viet Minh* (Paris: Les Indes savantes, 2008), p. 55. The bombing of Nam Dinh was also brutal; see M. G. Lefèvre, "Indochine, 1946," *La Revue des deux mondes*, no. 24 (December 1966), pp. 509–18.

26. Elliott, *Sacred Willow*, pp. 139–40. On the Dong Xuan Market, see the memoirs of Vu Tam, *60 Ngay Dem Giu Cho Dong Xuan* (Hanoi: Nha Xuat Ban Ha Noi, 1987).

27. *Tong Ket*, p. 63; and Tran Huy Lieu, *Lich Su Thu Do Ha Noi*, pp. 231–2.

28. "Loi Keu Goi Toan Quoc Khang Chien," 19 December 1946, *Van Kien Dang Toan Tap*, vol. 8 (1945–7), pp. 160–61.

29. Tuoi Tre On-line, "'Ve Ut' Thu Do va Nhung Buc Anh Xuc Dong," 8 December 2006, https://tuoitre.vn/ve-ut-thu-do-va-nhung-buc-anh-xuc-dong-176741.htm, accessed on 13 April 2021; Nguyen Dinh Can, "Quan bao mat tran Ha Noi, Vung bi dich tam chiem," *Su Kien va Nhan Chung*, no. 190 (October 2009), pp. 38–9; "Doi Thieu Nien Quan Bao Bat Sat," *Su Kien*

va Nhan Chung, no. 14 (March 1995), p. 33; Tran Dinh Tu, Tuoi Tre On-line, "Nhung 'Gavroche' Ha Thanh," 12 December 2006, https://tuoitre.vn/nhung-gavroche-ha-thanh-177320.htm, accessed on 13 April 2021; Tran Dinh Tu, Tuoi Tre On-line, "Nhung Ve Ut Tren Chien Hao Ve Quoc," 11 December 2006, https://tuoitre.vn/nhung-ve-ut-tren-chien-hao-ve-quoc-177099.htm, accessed on 13 April 2021; Tuoi Tre On-line, "Nguoi Chep Su Ve Ut," 15 December 2006, https://tuoitre.vn/nguoi-chep-su-ve-ut-177867.htm, accessed on 13 April 2021; Tuoi Tre On-line, "Nu Ve Ut va Bau Vat 60 nam," 13 December 2006, https://tuoitre.vn/nhung-ve-ut-tren-chien-hao-ve-quoc-177099.htm, accessed on 13 April 2021; Tuoi Tre On-line, "Tieu Doi Nhi va Chien Thuat Xe Bo," 14 December 2006, https://tuoitre.vn/tieu-doi-nhi-va-chien-thuat-xe-bo-177665.htm, accessed on 13 April 2021; and Nguyen Khac Ky, Tuoi Tre On-line, "Co Dau Pho Kham Thien," 16 December 2006, https://tuoitre.vn/co-dau-pho-kham-thien-178012.htm, accessed on 13 April 2021; and Tienphong, "Ve Ut Thu Do va Nhung Buc Anh Xuc Dong," 6 December 2006, https://www.tienphong.vn/van-hoa/ve-ut-thu-do-va-nhung-buc-anh-xuc-dong-69123.tpo, accessed on 2 April 2021. In English translation, see Huong Van Ba in David Chanoff and Doan Van Toai, eds., *Vietnam: A Portrait of Its People at War* (London: TPP, 2009), pp. 29–31.

30. Phung Quan, *Thoi Tho Du Doi* (Hanoi: Nha Van Hoc, 1988). It was adapted to the screen in 2015. On his life, see https://vi.wikipedia.org/wiki/Phùng_Quán, accessed on 22 April 2020. The Vietnamese word "*du doi*" is something of a play on words here meaning "fierce" and "memorable" at the same time. A child appears holding a gun in the Battle of Hanoi in Nguyen Huy Tuong's 1961 novel, *Forever with the Capital* (*Song Mai voi Thu Do*). For an extract in French, see Nguyen Huy Tuong, "Barricades dans la capitale," *De la reconquête française à Dien Bien Phu*, pp. 48–68 (p. 68 for the child soldier).

31. On American children in the military ranks in the civil war, see William Schuette and Myrna Armstrong, "Civil War Drummer Boys: Musicians, Messengers, and Medical Assistants," *Military Medicine*, vol. 184, nos. 1–2 (January–February 2019), pp. 1–4.

32. *Cong An Thu Do, Nhung Chang Duong Lich Su, 1945–54* (Hanoi: Cong An Nhan Dan, 1990), p. 117 (for the citation). For more on the use of children during the Battle of Hanoi, see *Cong An Thu Do: Nhung Chang Duong Lich Su*, p. 117; *Lich su Bo Tong Tham Muu trong Khang Chien Chong Phap (1945–1954)* (Hanoi: Nha In Bo Tong Tham Muu, 1991), p. 132. Note 1 on that page officially confirms the use of "quite a few" (*kha nhieu*) children in the Battle of Hanoi, aged "between ten and fifteen years of age." Vuong Thua Vu, the commander of the Capital Regiment during the battle, confirms that "over one hundred children" (*hon 100 thieu nhi*) were part of the combat unit. Vuong Thua Vu, *Truong Thanh trong Chien Dau*, p. 127.

33. Xuan Phuong, *Ao Dai: My War, My Country, My Vietnam* (Great Neck: New York, EMQUAD International, Ltd., 2004), pp. 62–3.

34. Concerning Ton That Tung's library, see Do Sam and Hoang Tieu, "Tran Chien Dau Bao ve Kho Sach Qui tai Nha Bac si Ton That Tung," *Tap Chi Lich Su Quan Su*, no. 4 (1994), pp. 50–51. For the impressive number of items the Vietnamese evacuated before war broke out in Hanoi, see *Lich Su Tai Chinh Quan Doi Nhan Dan Viet Nam (1945–1954)*, vol. 1 (Hanoi: Nha Xuat Ban Quan Doi Nhan Dan, 1989), p. 40; "Etude sur l'économie viet minh," 11 December 1948, p. 12, C889, SHD; and *Tong Ket*, pp. 105–6. For the figure of 40,000 tons of machinery, see *Lich su Bo Tong Tham Muu trong Khang Chien Chong Phap (1945–1954)* (Hanoi: Nha In Bo Tong Tham Muu, 1991), p. 154.

35. The government health ministry, military medicine branch, and pharmacies relied heavily on the colonial cities and Asian markets to supply Western medicines, vaccines, anti-malarial pills, and medical equipment; see *30 Nam Phuc Vu va Xay Dung cua Nganh Quan Y Quan Doi Nhan Dan Viet Nam (1945–1975)* (Cuc Quan Y: Tong cuc Hau Can, 1976), pp. 65, 107.

36. In theory, the Indochinese Communist Party had already issued instructions to this effect to the south in late 1945; see *Lich Su Saigon Cho Lon Gia Dinh Khang Chien (1945–1975)* (Ho Chi Minh City: Nha Xuat Ban Thanh Pho Ho Chi Minh, 1994), p. 77. Truong Chinh ordered scorched earth tactics for the Battle of Hanoi: Truong Chinh, "Khang Chien trong Thanh Pho", pp. 454–6.

37. "Etude sur l'économie viet minh," p. 7.

38. Lucien Bodard, *La Guerre d'Indochine, l'enlisement* (Paris: Gallimard, 1997), pp. 187–8.

39. "Etude sur l'économie viet minh," p. 14, note 1 (for the antibiotics); Sûreté fédérale, "Renseignement," 15 July 1947, 10H534, SHD (on the Saigon pharmacists); Georges Boudarel, *Autobiographie* (Paris: Jacques Bertoins, 1991), pp. 122–35. For a detailed study, see "Circulation et transport des produits pharmaceutiques," 23 February 1953, and attached documents, 10H638, SHD.

40. Commandement des Forces terrestres du Centre Vietnam, Secteur autonome de Tourane, no. 298/SAT/2, undated, circa 1952, "V36," 10H3235, SHD.

41. Deuxième bureau, "Commandement des Forces terrestres du Centre Vietnam, Secteur de Hue," 10 October 1952, based on interviews with prisoners involved in this trade, "V36/LK V," 10H3235, SHD; Pham Van Dong's intercepted telegram "V36, LK V," 10H3235, SHD; and Do Sam and Hoang Tieu, "Tran Chien Dau Bao ve Kho Sach Qui tai Nha Bac Si Ton That Tung," pp. 50–51.

42. Fonde, *Traitez à tout prix*, p. 334; Nguyen The Bao, *Cong An Thu Do: Nhung Chang Duong Lich Su (1945–1954)* (Hanoi: Nha Xuat Ban Cong An Nhan Dan, 1990), pp. 122–4; *Lich Su Tinh Bao Cong An Nhan Dan Viet Nam (1945–1954)* (Hanoi: Cong An Nhan Dan, No year of publication), pp. 56–8; *Luc Luong Thong Tin Lien Lac Cong An Nhan Dan, Lich Su Bien Nien: 1945–1954* (Hanoi: Nha Xuat Ban Cong An Nhan Dan, 1998), pp. 55–7, 76–7, 85, and 96–7; and "Doi Thieu Nien Quan Bao Bat Sat," *Su Kien va Nhan Chung*, no. 14 (March 1995), p. 33. For Saigon, see *Luoc Su Chien Si Quyet Tu: Sai Gon Cho Lon Gia Dinh, 1945–1954* (Ho Chi Minh City: Cau Lac Bo Truyen Thong Vu Trang, 1993), pp. 59, 104–8; *Lich Su Sai Gon Cho Lon Gia Dinh Khang Chien: 1945–1975* (Ho Chi Minh City: Nha Xuat Ban Thanh Pho Ho Chi Minh, 1994), pp. 137–9.

43. Nguyen Tien Lang, *Chemins de la révolte* (Paris: Amiot Dumont, 1953), pp. 103–6.

44. William Turley, "Urbanization in War: Hanoi, 1946–1973," *Pacific Affairs*, vol. 48, no. 3 (Autumn 1975), p. 371 and *Tong Ket*, pp. 70–79.

45. Xuan Phuong, *Ao Dai*, p. 69.

46. *Tong Ket*, p. 106.

47. *Luc Luong Thong Tin Lien Lac Cong An*, p. 163.

48. *Lich Su Truyen Thong 30 Nam Thong Tin Vo Tuyen Dien Nam Bo (1945–1975)* (Hanoi: Nha Xuat Ban Buu Dien, 2003), pp. 34–7; and Boudarel, *Autobiographie*, pp. 122–35.

49. *Tu Ve Thanh Sai Gon—Cho Lon Nhung Nam Dau Khang Chien Chong Thuc Dan Phap* (Ho Chi Minh City: Hoi Cuu Chien Binh Thanh Pho Ho Chi Minh, 1995), pp. 32–3.

50. *Lich Su Tinh Bao Cong An Nhan Dan Viet Nam (1945–1954)*, pp. 55–7.

51. Nguyen Bac, *Au Coeur de la Ville Captive, souvenir d'un agent viet minh infiltré à Hanoi* (Paris: Arléa, 2004, translated by Philippe Papin), pp. 37–8.

52. Cong An Nhan Dan Viet Nam, *Lich Su Bien Nien (1945–1954)* (Hanoi: Nha Xuat Ban Cong An Nhan Dan, 1994), p. 222; *Cong An Nam Bo Trong Khang Chien Chong Thuc Dan Phap Xam Luoc* (Ho Chi Minh City: Nha Xuat Ban Cong An Nhan Dan, 1993), pp. 106–7; and *Lich Su Chien Si Quyet Tu*, pp. 97–8.

53. Cong An Nhan Dan Viet Nam, *Lich Su Bien Nien (1945–1954)*, p. 223; and *Cong An Nam Bo*, p. 129.

54. Nguyen The Bao, *Cong An Thu Do*, p. 125.

55. Tran Huy Lieu, ed., *Lich Su Thu Do*, p. 243; *Luc Luong Thong Tin Lien Lac Cong An*, p. 116; "Expériences tirées des combats des défenses, 20–24 novembre 1946, à Haiphong," 10H532, SHD; and *Lich Su Sai Gon*, p. 207.

56. For an example occurring during the Tet Offensive of 1968, see Tuyet Nguyen and Manh Tung, "Meet the Saigon Family Who Stockpiled a Secret Arsenal for the Tet Offensive," *VN Express* (2 February 2018), https://e.vnexpress.net/news/news/meet-the-saigon-family-who-stockpiled-secret-arsenal-for-tet-offensive-3707328.html, accessed on 12 June 2018.

57. Merle Pribbenow, "Oral History Interview of Dr. Nguyen Thi Ngoc Toan," Hanoi, 11 June 2007, for which, see https://www.yumpu.com/en/document/read/5742682/read-the-translation-vietnam-interviews, accessed on 31 March 2021.

58. *Luoc Su Chien Si Quyet Tu: Sai Gon Cho Lon, Gia Dinh, 1945–1954*, pp. 55–9, 100–108; Bui Kim Khoat and Hai Ha, "Gia Lam Phu Nu Di Cho Danh Up Dich," *Su Kien va Nhan Chung*, no. 54 (1998), p. 23. On the French use of these *passeuses*, see the detailed DRV intelligence report captured by the French: "Report Sent to the Security Services of Zone IV: no. C1405-B2/B7M," 2 July 1952, pp. 3–5, 10R186, SHD.

59. I base this estimate on the list of the women agents and their duties as detailed in the annex in *Luoc Su Chien Si Quyet Tu*, pp. 169–83.

60. Nguyen Bac, *Au coeur de la ville captive*, p. 20.

61. Ngo Van Chieu, *Journal d'un combattant Viet-Minh* (Paris: Editions du Seuil, 1955), p. 168.

62. Though their stories remain largely untold, women played essential roles in so many other wars in world history. For a French example, see Marie-Madeleine Fourcade, *Noah's Ark* (New York: Ballantine Books, 1975); Lynne Olson, *Madame Fourcade's Secret War* (New York: Random House, 2019), and, notably, Judy Batalion, *The Light of Days* (New York: HarperCollins, 2021).

63. "Chuyen Cua Cac Cuu Doi Vien Thieu Nhi Du Kich Mot Thoi . . . Ke Lai," *Su Kien va Nhan Chung*, no. 89 (May 2001), pp. 14–15.

64. "Le Van Tra, Viet Minh Messenger Boy," in David Chanoff and Doan Van Toai, *Vietnam: A Portrait of Its People*, p. 28. For chilling biographies of children martyrs, see *Luoc Su Chien Si Quyet Tu*, pp. 104–8.

65. The Arsenal was the dockyard servicing the French Navy's ships since the conquest of Saigon in the early 1860s.

66. FACI is the acronym of Forces, ateliers et chantiers de l'Indochine. It was a major shipbuilding and naval repair center.

67. "L'Organisation du commandement militaire rebelle dans la région de Saigon-Cholon," 20 May 1947, 10H534, SHD.

68. *Tu Ve Thanh Sai Gon-Cho Lon*, pp. 21–8; and *Lich Su Sai Gon*, pp. 95–9.

69. "Activités des organismes rebelles en Cochinchine," 21 May 1946, CP225, CAOM; *Tu Ve Thanh Sai Gon-Cho Lon*, pp. 21–8, 58–60; *Luc Luong Thong Tin Lien Lac Cong An*, pp. 85–6; and *Lich Su Sai Gon*, pp. 99–100.

70. "Renseignements," 14 February 1947, 10H532, SHD; *Tu Ve Thanh Sai Gon-Cho Lon*, pp. 26–8, 43–8, 65; *Lich Su Sai Gon*, pp. 100–101; *Luoc Su Chien Si Quyet Tu*, pp. 55–61, 104–8. Le Quang Sang, an eleven-year-old youngster, allegedly the best of the "pip-squeaks," fell into French hands while trying to pass information through enemy lines. The boy never resurfaced. "Chuyen Cua Cac Cuu Doi Vien Thieu Nhi Du Kich Mot Thoi . . . Ke Lai," *Su Kien va Nhan Chung*, no. 89 (May 2001), pp. 14–15.

71. "Renseignement," 22 March 1947, 10H532, SHD; "Interrogatoire," 15 March 1947, 10H532, SHD; and *Tu Ve Thanh Sai Gon-Cho Lon*, p. 84.

72. *Tu Ve Thanh Sai Gon-Cho Lon*, pp. 85–92; *Lich Su Sai Gon*, pp. 172–4; *Luoc Su Chien Si Quyet Tu*, pp. 84–7, 100–101, 163–5 (photos and a drawing of the attack on the Majestic Cinema). Of the 485 people listed as members of the "Soldier Death Squads" (*Chien Si Quyet Tu*) for the Saigon area during the First Indochina War, 34 percent were women. See the lists produced in the annex to *Luoc Su Chien Si Quyet Tu*, pp. 169–83.

73. Nguyen Dinh Thong, *Tieng Hat Nu Tu Tu (Vo Thi Sau Con Nguoi va Huyen Thoai)* (Hanoi: Cong An Nhan Dan, 1995); *Chuyen Muoi Phu Nu Huyen Thoai Viet Nam* (Hanoi: Van Hoc, 2004); *Nhung Guong Mat Nu Diep Bao* (Hanoi: Cong An Nhan Dan, 1997); and for Vo Thi Sau's details, see entry https://vi.wikipedia.org/wiki/Võ_Thị_Sàu, accessed on 8 October 2020.

74. Bodard, *La Guerre d'Indochine*, p. 373.

75. Cited by Fredrik Logevall, *Embers of War: The Fall of an Empire and the Making of America's Vietnam* (New York: Random House, 2012), p. xii.

Chapter 5. Wiring War

1. Cao Pha, *Nhung Ky Uc Khong Bao Gio Quen* (Hanoi: Nha Xuat Ban Quan Doi Nhan Dan, 2006), p. 97. My thanks to Merle Pribbenow for bringing this document to my attention.

2. Another Vietnamese intelligence officer present in these discussions recorded de Castries telling his captors: "My God, if the fighting had continued for a few more days, then my soldiers would have gone mad." Nguyen Ngoc Phuc, *Nha Tinh Bao va Nhung Phi Cong Tu Binh* (Hanoi: Nha Xuat Ban Quan Doi Nhan Dan, 2009), pp. 17–18.

3. Jean-Marie Mancini, "Le Réseau radioélectrique colonial français: perspectives, enjeux et réalisations," *Les Cahiers*, no. 5 (1997), pp. 39–59; René Despierres, "Le service des P.T.T. en Indochine (des origines à 1940)," *Bulletin des Amis du Vieux Hue*, vol. 31, no. 1 (1944), pp. 3–61; Le Ngoc Trac et al., *Lich Su Truyen Thong 30 Nam Thong Tin Vo Tuyen Dien Nam Bo (1945–1975)* (Hanoi: Nha Xuat Ban Buu Dien, 2003), pp. 28–33; Dang Van Than, et al., *Lich Su Nganh Buu Dien Viet Nam*, vol. 1 (Hanoi: Nganh Buu Dien Xuat Ban, 1990), pp. 81–2; "Agence radiotélégraphique de l'Indochine et du Pacifique," *Les Entreprises coloniales françaises*, http://entreprises-coloniales.fr/inde-indochine/ARIP.pdf, accessed on 12 April 2020.

4. The French assembled special files at the start of the Indochina War on Vietnamese political figures, Ho Chi Minh in particular. See the finding guide for the grouping Service de Protection du Corps expéditionnaire in the CAOM.

5. Cao Pha, *Nhung Ky Uc Khong Bao Gio Quen*, p. 59.

6. On the importance of technology and information circulation in the Comintern, see Fridrikh Firsov, et al., *Secret Cables of the Comintern, 1933–1943* (New Haven: Yale University Press, 2014).

7. For sailors in the making of early Vietnamese communism, see Didier de Fautereau, "Le Nationalisme vietnamien: Contribution des marins vietnamiens au nationalisme vietnamien (période entre les deux guerres)," M.A. thesis (Paris: Université de Paris, 1975), chapters 1–2.

8. The Revolutionary and Ho Chi Minh museums in Hanoi showcase a number of typewriters he and others used before and after coming to power in 1945.

9. Le Gian, *Nhung Ngay Song Gio, Hoi Ky* (Hanoi: Nha Xuat Ban Thanh Nien, 2003), p. 74; Nguyen Van Ngoc, *Nguoi luu day tro ve: Diep vien nhay du thanh giam doc cong an Trung bo* (Hanoi: Nha Xuat Ban Cong An Nhan Dan, 1997), pp. 190–91; and Department of the Army, Trampoline 2, *The DRVN Strategic Intelligence Service Cuc Nghien Cuu*, June 1968, pp. 10–11, in Carlisle Barracks, US Army Military History Institute Library. The British and Canadians developed the portable MKII and MKIII radio transceivers during the war, with which field agents could receive and transmit messages with superiors over long distances. To keep things technically simple, I refer here only to the MKII, but in reality the Vietnamese operated a myriad of war-era transceivers, including the MK models, RVG500s, SSR-SST sets, TM 10s, and more. So did the French.

10. Do Khac Quang, et al., *Lich Su Bo Doi Thong Tin Lien Lac, Ghi Tom Tat Theo Nam Thang*, vol. 1 (1930–1955) (Hanoi: Bo Tu Lenh Thong Tin Lien Lac, 1982), pp. 33–5; Dang Van Than, *Lich Su Nganh*, pp. 69, 81–4; *Nhung Ky Niem Sau Sac Ve Bo Truong Tran Quoc Hoan* (Hanoi: Nha Xuat Ban Cong An Nhan Dan, 2004), p. 296; and *Luc Luong Thong Tin Lien Lac Cong An Nhan Dan, Lich Su Bien Nien: 1945–1954* (Hanoi: Nha Xuat Ban Cong An Nhan Dan, 1998), pp. 29–30.

11. For the colonial scouting movement and Hoang Dao Thuy, see Brice Fossard, "Sportifs, scouts et nationalistes: itinéraire de deux jeunes Vietnamiens (1940–1945)," *Moussons*, vol. 32 (2018), pp. 93–107.

12. William Duiker, *Ho Chi Minh: A Life* (New York: Hyperion, 2000), pp. 292–306; Dixee Bartholomew-Feis, *The OSS and Ho Chi Minh* (Lawrence: University Press of Kansas, 2006), chapters 6–8; Archimedes Patti, *Why Vietnam?* (Berkeley: University of California Press, 1980); Sophie Quinn-Judge, *Ho Chi Minh: The Missing Years* (Berkeley: University of California Press, 2002), p. 204; and David Marr, *Vietnamese Tradition on Trial, 1925–1945* (Berkeley: University of California Press, 1981), p. 284. On the August Revolution and the importance of the famine in driving it, see David Marr, *Vietnam, 1945: The Quest for Power* (Berkeley: University of California Press, 1995).

13. J. Catala, "Note sur le déroulement des événements du 9 mars 1945 au 1 décembre 1945," p. 20, supplement 4, Conseiller Politique, CAOM.

14. Ibid., p. 20.

15. "When Ceylon ruled the airwaves," *The Hindu* (24 March 2012), p. 1.

16. Archimedes Patti, *Why Viet Nam?*, pp. 261–2, 315; "Note sur le déroulement," p. 20; Dang Van Than, *Lich Su Nganh*, pp. 78, 81–2, 86–8; Do Khac Quang, *Lich Su Bo Doi Thong Tin Lien Lac, Ghi Tom Tat Theo Nam Thang*, pp. 35–40; and Nguyen Chien, *Lich Su Bo Doi Thong Tin Lien Lac* (Hanoi: Nha Xuat Ban Quan Doi Nhan Dan, 1996), pp. 13–19 (note 1 on Nguyen Van Tinh).

17. Nguyen Chien, *Lich Su Bo Doi Thong Tin Lien Lac*, p. 24.

18. "Note sur le déroulement," p. 20; *Lich Su Nganh In Viet Nam*, vol. 2 (Hanoi, Cuc Xuat Ban Bo Van Hoa Thong Tin, 1992), pp. 29, 136–7.

19. See *Philatélie populaire, Revue éditée par l'Union philatélique internationale*, http://archive .is/BOMha#selection-25.0-27.53; *Aigurande, Inde*, https://www.multicollection.fr/liberation /Liberation-A-C.pdf; *Club philatélique et cartophilie de Truchtersheim*, http://wwwphilatelie -truchtersheim.e-monsite.com/album-photos/france/les-timbres-de-la-liberation/; and Del-campe.net, https://www.delcampe.net/fr/collections/timbres/france/liberation/france -timbres-de-la-liberation-12-1timbre-avec-surcharge-r-f-1-lettre-de-ffi-avec-timbre-de-petain -323836693.html, all accessed on 13 April 2020. The French experience on the monetary front in Nazi Europe strangely reflected that of their Vietnamese adversaries. See Jérôme Blanc, "Pou-voirs et monnaie durant la seconde guerre mondiale en France: la monnaie subordonnée au politique," *International Conference on War, Money and Finance, Monetary and Financial Struc-tures: The Impact of Political Unrest and Wars*, June 2008, Paris, Nanterre, France, https://halshs .archives-ouvertes.fr/halshs-00652826/document, accessed on 31 March 2019.

20. Dang Van Than, *Lich Su Nganh*, pp. 78, 81–2, 86–8; Do Khac Quang, *Lich Su Bo Doi Thong Tin Lien Lac, Ghi Tom Tat Theo Nam Thang*, 35–7; and *La Philatélie, témoin de l'histoire*, http:// www.histoire-et-philatelie.fr/pages/008_indo/521a_coexistence_armee_4.html, accessed on 13 April 2020.

21. Dang Van Than, *Lich Su Nganh*, pp. 82–90; Nguyen Chien, *Lich Su Bo Doi Thong Tin Lien Lac*, 39–40; *Bo Truong Tran Quoc Hoan*, p. 28; and Le Dinh Y et al., *Essential Matters: A History of the Cryptographic Branch of the People's Army of Viet-Nam, 1945–1975* (Fort George Meade: National Security Agency, 1994), translated by David Gaddy, p. 11.

22. For a detailed study of the DRV's communications systems during the Indochina War, see Nguyen Chien, *Lich Su Bo Doi Thong Tin Lien Lac*, pp. 10–242.

23. Do Khac Quang, *Lich Su Bo Doi Thong Tin Lien Lac, Ghi Tom Tat Theo Nam Thang*, p. 41; and Le Dinh Y, *Essential Matters*, p. 53, note 3.

24. Nguyen Chien, *Lich Su Bo Doi Thong Tin Lien Lac*, pp. 12–19, 23; Dang Van Than, *Lich Su Nganh*, pp. 88–9; and Le Ngoc Trac, *Lich su Truyen Thong 30 nam Thong Tin Vo Tuyen Dien Nam Bo (1945–1975)*, pp. 29–31; *Lich Su Bo Tong Tham Muu Trong Khang Chien Chong Phap (1945–1954)* (Hanoi: Bo Tong Tham Muu, 1991), p. 12; and Le Dinh Y, *Essential Matters*, pp. 2–3.

25. Nguyen Chien, *Lich Su Bo Doi Thong Tin Lien Lac*, p. 21.

26. Ibid., pp. 19–21.

27. *Lich su Bo Tong Tham Muu Trong Khang Chien Chong Phap*, pp. 14–15, 70–71; and Nguyen Chien, *Lich Su Bo Doi Thong Tin Lien Lac*, pp. 32–3. Scores of documents captured by the French confirm the great lengths to which the DRV went to train communications specialists. See, among others, "Interrogatoire complémentaire de 'X' [name deleted by C. Goscha] ancien radio du Viet Minh," 31 March 1952, 10H1838, SHD.

28. On the history of the Chinese typewriter, see Thomas Mullaney, *The Chinese Typewriter* (Cambridge, MA: MIT Press, 2017).

29. Phan Van Can, *Lich Su Bo Tong Tham Muu Trong Khang Chien Chong Phap*, pp. 14–15, 70–71; and Nguyen Chien, *Lich Su Bo Doi Thong Tin Lien Lac*, pp. 32–3.

30. Do Thi Nguyen Quang, "Qua Trinh Xay Dung va Phat Trien nen Giao Duc Viet Nam Moi tu Thang 9–1945 den Thang 7–1954," M.A. thesis (Hanoi: Khoa Hoc Lich Su, 1996),

pp. 74–116. Of course, the Associated State of Vietnam also used the national language in its educational system, although I am unaware of any study of this question. In areas the DRV controlled, statistics cited in the above thesis suggest that Ho's Vietnam greatly expanded the use of *quoc ngu* in highland areas whose non-Vietnamese populations had never really had to learn to read and write in Vietnamese before 1945. If true, then the affirmation or imposition of Vietnamese as the national language clearly began during the Indochina War, not after: ibid., pp. 87–8. This also means that the spread of Vietnamese into the northern highlands probably accompanied the Vietnamese military strategy of "going deep" from 1952 onwards; see Chapter 10 for further details.

31. David Marr, *State, Revolution and War in Vietnam, 1945–1947* (Berkeley: University of California Press, 2014), Chapter 6; and Central Intelligence Agency, "Indochinese Radio and Press, and Monitoring and Scrutiny Activities," March 1951, CIA Records Search Tool (CREST), National Archives and Records Administration, United States.

32. "Indochinese Radio and Press, and Monitoring and Scrutiny Activities."

33. Nguyen Chien, *Lich Su Bo Doi Thong Tin Lien Lac*, p. 30; and Central Intelligence Agency, "Viet Minh Activity in the Hanoi Area," 13 January 1950, Central Intelligence Agency, "Indochinese Radio and Press," unpaginated.

34. Robert J. Hanyok, *Spartans in Darkness: American SIGINT and the Indochina War, 1945–1975* (Fort George Meade: National Security Agency, 2002), p. 18; and the "Additional Declassified Material" version (May 2008), https://fas.org/irp/nsa/spartans/additional.pdf, accessed on 12 June 2019.

35. Nguyen Chien, *Lich Su Bo Doi Thong Tin Lien Lac*, pp. 26–8. The French knew about this because they had decrypted relevant communications.

36. *Lich Su Bo Tong Tham Muu Trong Khang Chien Chong Phap*, pp. 71–5; Do Khac Quang, *Lich Su Bo Doi Thong Tin Lien Lac, Ghi Tom Tat Theo Nam Thang*, pp. 38–40; and Le Dinh Y, et al., *Essential Matters*, p. 8.

37. *Lich Su Bo Tong Tham Muu Trong Khang Chien Chong Phap*, pp. 71–75; Nguyen Chien, *Lich Su Bo Doi Thong Tin Lien Lac*, pp. 38–40; *Lich Su Bo Doi Thong Tin Lien Lac Ghi Tom Tat Theo Nam Thang*, pp. 64–5; Le Dinh Y, *Essential Matters*, pp. 8–9; and "Rapport du Lieutenant-Colonel Vanneuil Cdt: les transmissions des FTNV relatives aux écoutes faites par le Viet Minh," 1952, 10H1838, SHD. For the war of the airwaves, see "Note de renseignement," 19 January 1952, 10H1838, SHD.

38. *Lich Su Bo Tong Tham Muu Trong Khang Chien Chong Phap*, pp. 81–2. Again, several of these radios are on display in Vietnamese museums today.

39. For a fascinating collection of personal recollections coming from a wide range of those working in this service during the Indochina War, see *Nho Ve Ban Lien Lac Dac Biet* (Hanoi: Nha Xuat ban Quan Doi Nhan Dan, 2001).

40. Dang Van Than, *Lich Su Nganh*, pp. 118–21; Nguyen Chien, *Lich Su Bo Doi Thong Tin Lien Lac*, p. 56; Le Dinh Y, *Essential Matters*, pp. 13–14; and *Lich su Bo Tong Tham Muu Trong Khang Chien Chong Phap*, pp. 108–9.

41. *Lich Su Bo Tong Tham Muu Trong Khang Chien Chong Phap*, pp. 46–8.

42. Ibid., p. 65.

43. See the intelligence report dated 25 September 1947, 10H535, SHD.

44. Nguyen Chien, *Lich Su Bo Doi Thong Tin Lien Lac*, pp. 81–2, 87, 94–5. According to a French intelligence report, thanks to its wireless radio transmissions, the DRV's southern resistance committee was in direct contact "with the radio stations of the Ministry of Defense, the Supreme Council of National Defense, the Ministry of the Interior, the Voice of Vietnam, the Viet Minh's central committee, the combined regiments 81 and 82 of Zone V, stations in Cambodia and with the government delegation in Thailand"; see "Schéma technique radio-électrique fourni par le chef de poste radio de l'Etat Major dans le sud, rallié aux Français," 10H1838, SHD; and also "Assemblée générale du Comité de résistance et exécutif du Nam Bo, 1950," pp. 38–41, 10H620, SHD.

45. I rely heavily on Dang Van Than, *Lich Su Nganh Buu Dien Viet Nam*.

46. Dang Van Than, *Lich Su Nganh Buu Dien Viet Nam*, pp. 129–43; ibid., pp. 129–43; Tran Duong, *Kinh Te Viet Nam (1945–1954)* (Hanoi: Nha Xuat Ban Khoa Hoc, 1966), p. 226.

47. Dang Van Than, *Lich Su Nganh Buu Dien Viet Nam*, pp. 139–60; and Tran Duong, *Kinh Te Viet Nam*, p. 226.

48. On tiger attacks and the fear it struck into partisans going through the jungles, see Georges Boudarel, *Autobiographie* (Paris: Jacques Bertoin, 1991), pp. 257–9.

49. Dang Van Than, *Lich Su Nganh Buu Dien Viet Nam*, pp. 134, 146–7; Tran Duong, *Kinh Te Viet Nam*, p. 226; and "Service postal: Lien Khu IV," 22 September 1953, 10R165, SHD, for a fascinating, ground-level account of the operation of the postal service in Zone IV.

50. Georges Boudarel, *Autobiographie*, pp. 268–9.

51. Boudarel provides a riveting account of the Vietnamese guide, Ngoc, who took the Frenchman's group northwards to Zone V in mid-1952. Boudarel, *Autobiographie*, pp. 264–9.

52. Dang Van Than, *Lich Su Nganh Buu Dien Viet Nam*, pp. 139–60; Dang Phong, *5 Duong Mon Ho Chi Minh* (Hanoi: Nha Xuat Ban Tri Thuc, 2008), pp. 23–9; and Nguyen Chien, *Lich Su Bo Doi Thong Tin Lien Lac*, pp. 66–7.

Chapter 6. Policing War

1. Nguyen Van Ngoc, *Nguoi Luu Day Tro Ve: Diep Vien Nhay Du Thanh Giam Doc Cong An Trung bo* (Hanoi: Nha Xuat Ban Cong An Nhan Dan, 1997), pp. 224–36. The party's most powerful security chiefs recognized the continuities between colonial and national intelligence and security services. See Mai Chi Tho, *Hoi Uc: Nhung Mau Chuyen Doi Toi*, vol. 1 (No place of publication given: Nha Xuat Ban Tre, 2001), p. 154; and Le Gian, *Nhung Ngay Song Gio, Hoi Ky* (Hanoi: Thanh Nien 2003), p. 221. Léon Sogny was one of the most important French administrators to have served in Indochina. See Louis Malleret, "Léon Louis Sogny (1880–1947)," https://www.aavh.org/?page_id=7305, accessed on 16 April 2020. On empire and intelligence, see Martin Thomas, *Empires of Intelligence: Security Services and Colonial Disorder after 1914* (Berkeley: University of California Press, 2008); Christopher Bayly, "Knowing the Country: Empire and Information in India," *Modern Asian Studies,* vol. 27, no. 1 (1993), pp. 3–43; Christopher Bayly, *Empire and Information* (Cambridge: Cambridge University Press, 1996); and Emmanuel Blanchard, et al., *Policing in Colonial Empires* (Brussels: P.I.E. Peter Lang, 2017).

2. On the colonial police services, see Patrice Morlat, *La Répression coloniale au Vietnam (1908–1940)* (Paris: Harmattan, 1990); and Melissa Anderson, "For 'the Love of Order': Race,

Violence, and the French Colonial Police in Vietnam, 1860s–1920s," Ph.D. dissertation (Madison: University of Wisconsin at Madison, 2015).

3. Andrée Viollis, *Indochine, S.O.S.* (Pantin: Les Bons Caractères, 2008 (first published in 1931)), pp. 145–6.

4. Peter Zinoman, *The Colonial Bastille: A History of Imprisonment in Vietnam (1862–1940)* (Berkeley: University of California Press, 2001).

5. On the building of the East German police state, see Norman M. Naimark, *The Russians in Germany: A History of the Soviet Zone of Occupation, 1945–1949* (Cambridge, MA: The Belknap Press of Harvard University Press, 1995), pp. 355–6.

6. Pierre Darcourt, *Bay Vien, le maître de Cholon* (Paris: Hachette, 1977), p. 95 on the term "Vietnam."

7. Cited by Daniel Hémery, *Révolutionnaires vietnamiens et pouvoir colonial en Indochine: Communistes, trotskystes, nationalistes à Saigon de 1932 à 1937* (Paris: François Maspero, 1975), p. 148.

8. On police violence, see Mai Chi Tho, *Hoi Uc*, vol. 1, pp. 66–7.

9. Le Gian, *Nhung Ngay*, chapters 6–7; Mai Chi Tho, *Hoi Uc*, vol. 1, pp. 62–4; *Dong Chi Tran Quoc Hoan* (Hanoi: Nha Xuat Ban Chinh Tri Quoc Gia, 2006), pp. 81–3; Tran Quoc Hoan, *Nhung ky niem sau sac* (Hanoi: Nha Xuat ban Cong An Nhan Dan, 2005), pp. 155–7. I rely heavily on these sources for my discussion of the security services. For Islamist use of the prison as a recruiting ground, see I. Cuthbertson, "Prisons and the Education of Terrorists," *World Policy Journal*, vol. 21, no. 3 (2004), pp. 15–22.

10. Cited in Tran Quoc Hoan, *Mot So Van De ve Xay Dung Luc Luong Cong An Nhan Dan* (Hanoi: Nha Xuat Ban Cong An Nhan Dan, 2004), pp. 143–4.

11. On the creation of the security services, see Ho Chi Minh, "Sac Lenh so 23 ngay 21 Thang 2 nam 1946 thiet lap 'Viet Nam Cong An Vu,'" Hanoi (21 February 1946), *Viet Nam Dan Quoc Cong Bao* (2 March 1946), p. 118; *Lich Su Cong An Nhan Dan Viet Nam (1945–1954), So Thao* (Hanoi: Nha Xuat Ban Cong An Nhan Dan, 1996), p. 82; Le Gian, *Nhung Ngay*, pp. 218–20, 239; *Lich Su Tinh Bao Cong An Nhan Dan Viet Nam (1945–1954)* (Hanoi: Nha Xuat Ban Cong An Nhan Dan, No year date given), pp. 32–7; *Cong An Nam Bo trong Khang Chien Chong Thuc Dan Phap Xam Luoc* (Hanoi: Nha Xuat Ban Cong An Nhan Dan, 1993), p. 47; "Les Services spéciaux Viet Min," no. 700/Y, 10 March 1951, pp. 5–6, 10H633, SHD; and "Réorganisation du Service de la sécurité publique au Nam Bo," 30 August 1952, 10H4235, SHD.

12. Le Gian, *Nhung Ngay*, p. 239; *Lich Su Cong An Nhan Dan Viet Nam (1945–1954) So Thao*, pp. 82–4; Ha Minh Quoc, "Anh Tran Dang Ninh voi 'Vu An Gian Diep H122,'" in *Tran Dang Ninh Con Nguoi va Lich Su* (Hanoi: Nha Xuat Ban Chinh Tri Quoc Gia, 1996), pp. 232–3; Dinh Xuan Lam and Do Quang Hung, *Danh Nhan Lich Su Viet Nam*, vol. 3 (Ho Chi Minh City: Nha Xuat Ban Giao Duc, 1992), pp. 45–6; and *Lich Su Tinh Bao Cong An*, pp. 33–5.

13. *Cong An Nam Bo*, p. 98.

14. *Cong An Nam Bo*, pp. 167–9; and *Lich Su Cong An Nhan Dan Viet Nam (1945–1954) So Thao*, p. 84. Cao Dang Chiem led the southern security services until 1948 and then Diep Ba until the end of the Indochina War. Pham Hung was the real leader, however.

15. "Organisation de la Sûreté Viet Minh du Nam Bo," 16 June 1954, 10H3973, SHD.

16. For more on the security services, see *Dong Chi Tran Quoc Hoan*; Tran Quoc Hoan, *Nhung Ky Niem Sau Sac ve Bo Truong Tran Quoc Hoan* (Hanoi: Nha Xuat ban Cong An Nhan Dan, 2005), pp. 88, 162–5, 344–50; Nguyen Bac, *Au coeur de la ville captive: souvenir d'un agent*

viet minh infiltré à Hanoi (Paris: Arléa, 2004), translated by Philippe Papin. This memoir first appeared in Vietnamese as *Giua Thanh Pho Bi Chiem* (Hanoi: Nha Xuat Ban Hanoi, 1994).

17. Xuan Phuong, *Ao Dai* (New York: EMQUAD, 2004), pp. 70–71.

18. Ibid., p. 90.

19. Tran Ngoc Chau, *Vietnam Labyrinth* (Lubbock: Texas Tech University Press, 2012), p. 90.

20. For more on the Vietnam Wars as civil ones, see François Guillemot, *Viet-Nam, fractures d'une nation* (Paris: La Découverte, 2018); Brett Reilly, "The Origins of the Vietnamese Civil War and the State of Vietnam," Ph.D. dissertation (Madison: University of Wisconsin at Madison, 2018); Shawn McHale, *The First Indochina War: Violence, Sovereignty, and the Fracture of the South, 1945–1956* (Cambridge: Cambridge University Press, 2021); Brett Reilly, "The Sovereign States of Vietnam, 1945–1955," *The Journal of Vietnamese Studies*, vol. 11, nos. 3–4 (2016), pp. 103–9; François Guillemot, *Dai Viêt, indépendance et révolution au Viêt-Nam. L'échec de la troisième voie (1938–1955)* (Paris: Les Indes Savantes, 2011); and Edward Miller, "The War that Dare Not Speak Its Name: The Vietnam War as a Civil War," an unpublished paper which he kindly allowed me to read. The security service's museum in downtown Hanoi leaves no doubt that the police were on the front lines of this civil war.

21. On the anticommunist parties, see Guillemot, *Dai Viêt*.

22. Le Gian, *Nhung ngay*, pp. 219–20; and *Luc Luong chong Phan Dong: Lich Su Bien Nien (1945–1954)* (Hanoi: Nha Xuat Ban Cong An Nhan Dan 1996), pp. 12–16. Le Gian provides a detailed description of his party's enemies, for which see *Nhung Ngay*, pp. 189–200. For the number of executions which occurred at this time, see David Marr, *Vietnam, 1945: The Quest for Power* (Berkeley: University of California Press, 1995), p. 519.

23. Le Gian, *Nhung Ngay*, p. 204; and *Tran Dang Ninh*, pp. 22–3.

24. *Tran Dang Ninh*, pp. 22–3.

25. The anticommunist nationalists claim that the communists set everything up. Nguyen Cong Luan, *Nationalist in the Viet Nam Wars* (Bloomington: Indiana University Press, 2012), pp. 49–52; and Guillemot, *Dai Viêt*; and his *Viet-Nam, fractures d'une nation* for the noncommunist version in detail.

26. *Lich Su Tinh Bao Cong An*, pp. 45–52; Le Gian, *Nhung Ngay*, pp. 260–70 (p. 264 for Khang's words); *Luc Luong chong Phan Dong*, pp. 49–55; *Cong An Nhan Dan Viet Nam, Lich Su Bien Nien (1945–1954)* (Hanoi: Nha Xuat Ban Cong An Nhan Dan 1994), pp. 81–5. During the Battle of Hanoi in early 1947, the French recovered the DRV's police report on the Franco-Vietnamese opposition plot to overthrow the Ho Chi Minh government. Copies are in dossier AP1, VNQDD, grouping Conseiller Politique, supplement 23, CAOM; and dossiers 342–3, 10H2963, SHD. However, I have never seen any evidence of this Franco-Dai Viet "plot" in French sources.

27. Ngo Van Chieu, *Journal d'un combattant Viet-Minh* (Paris: Editions du Seuil, 1955), pp. 84–90.

28. Miller, "The War that Dare Not Speak Its Name."

29. Quoted by Philippe Devillers, *Paris, Saigon, Hanoi: Les archives de la guerre, 1944–1947* (Paris: Gallimard, 1988), p. 334.

30. The British did this in Kenya. See Daniel Branch, *Defeating Mau Mau, Creating Kenya: Counterinsurgency, Civil War, and Decolonization* (Cambridge: Cambridge University Press, 2009). My thanks to Edward Miller for kindly bringing this book to my attention.

31. On the Cao Dai, see Jérémy Jammes, *Les Oracles du Cao Dai* (Paris: Les Indes savantes, 2014). On the Hoa Hao, see Pascal Bourdeaux, "Approches statistiques de la communauté du bouddhisme Hoa Hao (1939–1954)," in Christopher Goscha and Benoît de Tréglodé, eds., *Naissance d'un Etat parti: le Viet Nam depuis 1945* (Paris: Les Indes savantes, 2004), pp. 277–304.

32. Translation of the document: Pham Hung, Service de Gendarmerie du Nam Bo, no. 120/CAS, RDVN, Directeur de Service de gendarmerie du Nam Bo, 10 February 1947, with the official seal, 16, 10H533, SHD.

33. *Cong An Nhan Dan Viet Nam Lich Su Bien Nien*, p. 90; and Mai Chi Tho, *Hoi Uc*, vol. 1, p. 129. On the violence in the south, see Shawn McHale, "Understanding the Fanatic Mind?: The Viet Minh and Race Hatred in the First Indochina War (1945–1954)," *Journal of Vietnamese Studies*, vol. 4, no. 3 (Fall 2009), pp. 98–138; and François Guillemot, "Autopsy of a Massacre: On a Political Purge in the Early Days of the Indochina War (Nam Bo 1947)," *European Journal of East Asian Studies*, vol. 9, no 2 (2010), pp. 225–65.

34. Translation of the document: "Comité Exécutif du Nam Bo, Comité de Propagande de la Région Saigon-Cholon," no. 230, signed Hoang Minh Hai, 5 May 1947, and countersigned by the vice-president of the Executive Committee of Saigon-Cholon, 18, 10H533, SHD.

35. Required reading on this is Shawn McHale, *The First Indochina War: Violence, Sovereignty, and the Fracture of the South, 1945–1956* (Cambridge: Cambridge University Press, 2021).

36. On the Cochinchinese republic and the Associated States of Indochina as "weapons," see my *Vietnam: A New History* (New York: Basic Books, 2016), Chapter 8.

37. In the late 1940s, the respected, non-communist nationalist and member of the Dai Viet, Bui Diem, hit on the idea of convincing Bao Dai to turn on the French. He was convinced that such an action would leave the French with no choice but to give in straightaway rather than later. Bao Dai refused. See Bui Diem, *In the Jaws of History* (Bloomington: Indiana University Press, 1987), pp. 67–8. Ngo Dinh Diem could have broken with the French too, but he did not do so before 1954.

38. *Lich Su Tong Cuc Chinh Tri Quan Doi Nhan Dan Viet Nam (1944–1975)*, vol. 1 (Hanoi: Nha Xuat Ban Quan Doi Nhan Dan, 2004), pp. 41–2, 57; *Lich su Bo Tong Tham Muu trong Khang Chien chong Phap (1945–1954)* (Hanoi: Bo Tong Tham Muu, Ban Tong Ket, Bien Soan Lich Su, 1991), pp. 6–8, 46–7; *Van Kien Quan Su cua Dang*, vol. 2 (Hanoi: Nha Xuat Ban Quan Doi Nhan Dan, 1976), pp. 175–7. For more on Hoang Minh Dao, see *Chuyen Chua Biet ve Nguoi Anh Hung* (Hanoi: Nha Xuat Ban Cong An Nhan Dan, 2002); and *Khuc bi Trang Tren Song* (Hanoi: Nha Xuat Ban Cong An Nhan Dan, 2006). Nguyen Binh and Hoang Minh Dao knew each other from the Second World War.

39. See "Directives au sujet de l'organisation des SR Viet Minh," 6 August 1947, signed Vo Nguyen Giap and "Synthèse d"un document Viet Minh," dated July–August 1947, recovered by the French during the raid on Bac Kan, both in 342–3, 10H2963, SHD; and "Etude des organismes de renseignements Viet Minh," p. 4.

40. *Lich Su Tinh Bao Cong An Nhan Dan Viet Nam (1945–1954)* (Hanoi: Nha Xuat Ban Cong An Nhan Dan, no date, circa 1996), p. 59.

41. "Quan Bao Mat Tran Ha Noi trong Vung Bi Dich Tam Chiem," *Quan Doi Nhan Dan* (13 November 2009), p. 1. My thanks to Merle Pribbenow for bringing this article to my attention.

42. Nguyen The Luong (Cao Pha), *Nhung Ky Uc Khong Bao Gio Quen* (Hanoi: Nha Xuat Ban Quan Doi Nhan Dan, 2006), p. 76; and *Lich su Bo Tong Tham Muu trong Khang Chien Chong Phap*, pp. 403–4, 408–9.

43. I rely on: *Lich Su Cong An Nhan Dan Viet Nam (1945–1954) So Thao*, pp.174–5; *Cong An Thu Do* (Hanoi: Nha Xuat Ban Cong An Nhan Dan, 1990), p. 150; *Cong An Nhan Dan Viet Nam, Lich Su Bien Nien (1945–1954)*, pp. 180–82, 217–18; and Ha Minh Quoc, "Anh Tran Dang Ninh voi 'Vu An Gian Diep H122,'" pp. 232–40; Tuan Tu, "Giai Ma Vu An Mang Bi So H122," *Su Kien va Nhan Chung*, 12 August 2017, https://sknc.qdnd.vn/dieu-tra/giai-ma-vu-an-mang-bi-so-h122 -500670, accessed on 14 June 2019; and Pham Dao Ly, "Bao Cong, Tran Dang Ninh va Vu An Gian Diep," *Su Kien va Nhan Chung*, 11 June 2014, https://sknc.qdnd.vn/nhan-vat/bao-cong -tran-dang-ninh-va-vu-an-gian-diep-h122-499415, accessed on 14 June 2019. On the use of torture in the south, see *Cong An Nam Bo Trong Khang Chien Chong Thuc Dan Phap Xam Luoc* (Ho Chi Minh City: Nha Xuat Ban Cong An Nhan Dan, 1993), pp. 154–6, 198.

44. *Lich Su Cong An Nhan Dan Viet Nam (1945–1954) So Thao*, pp. 174–5; *Cong An Thu Do*, p. 150; *Cong An Nhan Dan Viet Nam, Lich Su Bien Nien*, pp. 180–82, 217–18; *Tran Dang Ninh*, pp. 232–40.

45. Pham Van Dong's report to the All-country Third Plenum of the Indochinese Communist Party, undated, but early 1950, *Van Kien Dang Toan Tap*, vol. 11 (1950) (Hanoi: Nha Xuat Ban Chinh Tri Quoc Gia, 2001), p. 185 for the quotation. See also Luong, "Chi Thi cua Ban Thuong Vu Trung Uong ve Dang Lanh Dao Cong An," 5 May 1950, in ibid., p. 327; and the captured document from the party's central committee, Le Hong Nam, "Main mise du parti communiste sur la direction de la sûreté viet minh," no. 11/CT/TV, 25 May 1950, in 801, 285, grouping Haut Commissariat de l'Indochine, Centre des Archives d'Outre-mer.

Chapter 7. Trickle Economics

1. I rely heavily here on Stein Tonnesson, *Vietnam, 1946: How the War Began* (Berkeley: University of California Press, 2010), Chapter 4; Martin Shipway, *The Road to War: France and Vietnam 1944–1947* (Providence: Berghahn Books, 1996), Chapter 9; Jean-Julien Fonde, *Traitez à tout prix* (Paris: Editions Robert Laffont, 1971), pp. 283–90; Commissariat de la République pour le Tonkin et le Nord Annam, affaires économiques, "Note sur le contrôle de l'importation et de l'exportation dans le port de Haiphong," 23 November 1946, in grouping Conseiller Politique, supplement 6, Centre des Archives d'Outre-mer, unpaginated.

2. Deeply involved in the events leading to war in 1946, Jean-Julien Fonde gives ample examples of Vietnamese telling him before, during, and after the Haiphong crisis that sovereignty was at the center of the events leading to war: Jean-Julien Fonde, *Traitez à tout prix*.

3. Tran Duong, *Kinh Te Viet Nam (1945–1954)* (Hanoi: Nha Xuat Ban Khoa Hoc, 1966), pp. 48–9; David Marr, "Beyond High Politics," in Christopher Goscha and Benoît de Tréglodé, eds., *The Birth of a Party-State, Vietnam since 1945* (Paris: Les Indes savantes, 2004), pp. 28–37.

4. Tran Duong, *Kinh Te Viet Nam*, pp. 51–5; David Marr, "Beyond High Politics," pp. 46–58; and Truong Chinh, *The Resistance Will Win* (Hanoi: Foreign Language Publishing House, 1960), first serialized internally in the party's journal in 1947, p. 55 (for the party's rebuke of local cadres for abolishing all taxes "in many places after the August uprising.") The economic reality

of taxes comes through most forcefully in decrees published in the official record for 1945 and 1946, the *Viet Nam Dan Quoc Cong Bao*.

5. See the original documents in GF16 (Gouvernement de fait), CAOM.

6. The Truong, "Nguoi Mang 32 kg Vang Ra Bac Mua Sung Dan cho Cach Mang," *Nhan Dan*, 21 July 2003, p. 1; and Tran Duong, *Kinh Te Viet Nam*, p. 50.

7. Ngo Van Chieu, *Journal d'un combattant Viet-Minh* (Paris: Editions du Seuil, 1955), p. 42.

8. "Note sur le contrôle de l'importation et de l'exportation dans le port de Haiphong," unpaginated.

9. Tran Duong, *Kinh Te Viet Nam*, pp. 56–7; Dominique Vésin, "Les ambiguïtés de la mise en place des structures étatiques dans un contexte de guerre: le cas de l'émission monétaire en République démocratique du Vietnam," *Série études et documents, Etudes indochinoises, IV* (May 1995), pp. 97–109; and Tran Quoc Du, *Dong Bac Tai Chinh Dong Bac Cu Ho, 1945–1954* (Hanoi: Nha Xuat Ban Tai Chinh, 2000), pp. 11–76.

10. Tran Duong, *Kinh Te Viet Nam*, pp. 58–60.

11. David Schoenbrun, *Vietnam: How We Got In, How to Get Out* (New York, Antheneum, 1971), p. 25.

12. Ordinances and decrees affirming the Democratic Republic of Vietnam's right to administer taxes and customs are numerous in the official government record. The decree dated 5 February 1946 and signed by the then finance minister, Pham Van Dong, is one example among many in *Viet Nam Dan Quoc Dan Bao*, no. 8 (23 February 1946), pp. 85–6.

13. Cited by Tonnesson, *Vietnam, 1946*, pp. 121–2.

14. For an alternative view focused on the French high commissioner's combined Catholicism and anticommunism, see Thomas Vaisset, "L'Amiral d'Argenlieu en Indochine, une croisade contre le communisme," *Revue historique des armées*, no. 289 (4th trimester 2017), pp. 55–68. In my view, though, Thierry d'Argenlieu's anticommunism alone cannot explain why he broke with Ho Chi Minh in 1945–6. Empire does. Like so many others in the French political class on the Right and Left, Thierry d'Argenlieu was a product of it. Like Charles de Gaulle, he was convinced that Empire was an essential component of French power, prestige, and foreign policy. My colleague and friend would agree, but my point, again, is that had Ho Chi Minh been an anticommunist opposed to the restoration of French colonial rule in September 1945–6, de Gaulle and Thierry d'Argenlieu, both Catholics, would have still gone to war with a "police action" of some kind in order to regain France's Indochinese empire just as the Dutch did against Sukarno, the noncommunist leader of the Republic of Indonesia.

15. *Lich Su Tai Chinh Quan Doi Nhan Dan Viet Nam (1945–1954)*, vol. 1 (Hanoi: Nha Xuat Ban Quan Doi Nhan Dan, 1989), p. 40.

16. It included the following provinces: Soc Trang, Bac Lieu, Can Tho, Long Xuyen, Chau Doc, and Rach Gia. See "Calcul du surplus de paddy exportable du Transbassac," October 1952, 10H638, SHD.

17. Deuxième Bureau, "Etude sur le ravitaillement V.M. dans les provinces de l'Est," p. 3, note 1, C889, SHD; "L'Economie V.M.," *Indochine Sud-est asiatique*, no. 19 (June–July 1953), p. 29; and Tran Duong, *Kinh Te Viet Nam*, p. 391.

18. *Kinh Te Viet Nam, 1945–1960* (Hanoi: Nha Xuat Ban Su That, 1960), pp. 14–15; and Tran Duong, *Kinh Te Viet Nam*, pp. 190–92. Located in the heart of Hitler's Europe during the Second

World War and deprived of Allied parachute drops and Lend Lease aid, the Polish Home Army manufactured the Błyskawica sub-machine gun. Soviet partisans made the PPSh sub-machine gun, among many other types of small arms, including grenades and explosives.

19. *Kinh Te Viet Nam, 1945–1960*, pp. 15–17; and "Etude sur l'économie viet minh," no. 0/120, pp. 8–11, 10H638, SHD.

20. Commandement des Forces terrestres en Extrême Orient, Etat-major, Deuxième Bureau, no. 3531/2, Saigon, 11 December 1948, "Fiche de renseignement," p. 53, C889, SHD. This document also reveals all sorts of other acids imported into the DRV for making explosives.

21. "Etude sur l'économie viet minh," p. 13, note 2.

22. "Activité économique de la province de Nghe Anh, Vinh," Deuxième Bureau, no. 1430/FTCV/2S, V36, 10H3235, SHD; and for the production totals, see Tran Duong, *Kinh Te Viet Nam*, pp. 192–210 (p. 193, note 16, for the total of Thanh Hoa acids and p. 197 for the figure of 7,000 tons).

23. Tran Quoc Du, *Dong Bac Tai Chinh, Dong Bac Cu Ho, 1945–1954*, pp. 17–55; Tran Duong, *Kinh Te Viet Nam*, p. 184; and *Kinh Te Viet Nam, 1945–1960*, p. 16.

24. "Renseignements sur les mines du Tonkin en zone contrôlée, synthèse," SPDN/ECG, 15 November 1953, Nord Vietnam, 10H638, SHD, among other documents in this group.

25. For more on the Mekong Delta in wartime, see Pierre Brocheux, *The Mekong Delta: Ecology, Economy and Revolution, 1860–1960* (Madison: The Center for Southeast Asian Studies, University of Wisconsin, 1995); and David Biggs, *Quagmire: Nation-Building and Nature in the Mekong Delta* (Seattle: University of Washington Press, 2010).

26. Pierre Villaret, "La Citadelle du sel," *Indochine Sud-est asiatique*, no. 9 (August 1952), pp. 26–31; and "Le Sel, monnaie forte," *Sud-est asiatique*, no. 24 (May 1951), pp. 36–40.

27. "Etude sur l'économie viet minh," pp. 7–8.

28. "Ong Chu Tich Uy Ban Hanh Chinh Luong Hoa, Kinh Te Khang Chien Nam Bo," 22 February 1947, 10H3990, SHD.

29. Nguyen Cong Luan, *Nationalist in the Viet Nam Wars* (Bloomington: Indiana University Press, 2012), p. 79.

30. Hanh Chanh Bien Hoa, Thuong vu, so. 1048, "Mat Tran Kinh Te Khang Chien," 5 July 1947, p. 32, 10H3990, SHD; "L'Economie V.M.," *Indochine Sud-est asiatique*, no. 19 (June–July 1953), p. 28; and "Etude sur l'économie viet minh," pp. 6–7.

31. "Etude sur l'économie viet minh," 11 December 1948, pp. 3, 7, C889, SHD.

32. "Etude sur l'économie viet minh," pp. 3, 7–8; and for more statistics *Kinh Te Viet Nam, 1945–1960*, pp. 17–20.

33. "Etude sur l'économie viet minh," p. 8.

34. For a fascinating account of long-standing trade between the DRV and colonial Indochina south of Hanoi, see "Echanges commerciaux entre Bui Chu et le Thanh Hoa," 25 April 1952, pp. 2–4, 10H638, SHD.

35. Claude Guigues, "Logistique viet minh," *Indochine Sud-est asiatique*, no. 16 (March 1953), p. 56; "Etude sur l'économie viet minh," pp. 22–9. For a rare photo of Ho in 1948 standing next to his horse, see the special issue on Ho Chi Minh, *Planète action* (March 1970), p. 30.

36. See Exécutif de résistance de la province de Vinh Tra, no. 63/QDT, "Décision autorisant Dang Tin, Village Song Phu de circuler sur la route Saigon, Can Tho, Sadec, Tra Vinh transportant

de marchandises," 21 October 1953; "Trafic entre la zone viet minh du sud de Ha Tien et celle de Ca Mau," 23 March 1953; and "Economie viet minh, organisation des comités no 1"; 10H3990 and 10H3999, SHD.

37. "Trafic de paddy au profit des V.M.," 21 February 1949, in 10H4905, SHD. Also see my "Le Contexte asiatique de la guerre franco-vietnamienne," Ph.D. dissertation (Paris: Ecole pratique des hautes études, 2000), especially the chapter on the overseas Chinese and chapters on southern Chinese and Southeast Asian commercial networks.

38. "Kinh Te Khang Chien Nam Bo, Khu Dac Biet Dia Phuong Saigon-Cholon," undated, but clearly 1947, 10H3991, SHD; Bo Quoc Phong, *Lich Su Quan Gioi Viet Nam Thoi Ky Khang Chien chong Thuc Dan Phap (1945–1954)* (Hanoi: Nha Xuat Ban Lao Dong, 1990), p. 110; Nguyen Khac Thu, "Comité administratif de la région de Saigon-Cholon, Service économique, no. 55/KTS, objet: Situation économique du mois de mai 1947," 1947, 10H3991, SHD; "Programme de ravitaillement," signed Kha Van Can, 14 June 1947, in 1947, 10H3991, SHD; and "BR no. 1782: Etude de terrain," dated 15 April 1951, 521/1951, 10H3998, SHD.

39. Kenneth de Courcy, "Indochina: An Approaching Decision," *Intelligence Digest, A Review of World Affairs*, no. 16 (2 May 1952), p. 19, FO959/137, Public Records Office, United Kingdom, for the citation.

40. "Fiche de renseignements: Déclaration de 'X' [name deleted by C. Goscha]," 8 November 1950, 10H2952, SHD; "Interrogatoire," 1947, 10H2952, SHD; "BR no. 2417," 6 August 1947, 10H2952, SHD. Pro-Ho Chi Minh French networks also operated on the pharmaceutical front. See Georges Boudarel, *Autobiographie* (Paris: Jacques Bertoin, 1991), pp. 98–9.

41. Truong Chinh, *The Resistance Will Win*, p. 56 on Leftist deviationism, and p. 137 for the unity of the people.

42. Tran Duong, *Kinh Te Viet Nam*, pp. 138–9.

43. Truong Chinh, *The Resistance Will Win*, pp. 49–56.

44. "Bulletin de renseignement 840," Saigon, 26 February 1951, 531, 10H3998, SHD; *Quan Tinh Nguyen Viet Nam o Campuchia Thoi Ky 1945–1954* (Cà Mau: Nha Xuat Ban Mui Cà Mau, 1998), p. 148; and "L'économie viet minh au Cambodge," no 897/2S, Phnom Penh 15 May 1953, 10H5585, SHD.

45. "Trafic de paddy au profit des V.M.," 21 February 1949, 10H4905, SHD.

46. "Etude sur l'économie viet minh," pp. 12–14; Commandement des Forces terrestres du Centre Vietnam, Secteur autonomne de Tourane, no. 298/SAT/2, no date, but during 1952; "Bulletin de renseignement no. 878," 10 October 1952; "Ravitaillement du LK V en produits français," no. 1898.FTCV/2S, V36, 10H3235, SHD; and Tran Duong, *Kinh Te Viet Nam*, pp. 235–6, 252–5.

47. "Salan au Ministre d'état chargé des relations avec les Etats associés," pp. 1–2, and "Trafics interzones et avec l'étranger," Etudes détaillées sur l'économie viet minh, 1949–1952, 10H638, SHD.

48. Uy Ban Hanh Chanh Tra Vinh, no. LL5052B, "Ong Chu Tich Uy Ban Hanh Chinh Luong Hoa: Kinh Te Khang Chien Nam Bo," 22 February 1947; Hanh Chanh Bien Hoa, Thuong vu, so. 1048, "Mat Tran Kinh Te Khang Chien," 5 July 1947, 32, 10H3990, SHD; and "Kinh Te Khang Chien Nam Bo, Khu Dac Biet Dia Phuong Saigon Cholon," 27 May 1947, 10H3991, SHD.

49. Cited in captured document: Comité exécutif du Nam Bo, Service économique, Conseil économique de résistance de l'est Nam Bo, "Discours sur le programme prononcé par le directeur du service économique Kha Van Can," 5 May 1947, 10H3991, SHD. See also "La bataille

du caoutchouc," *Indochine-Sud-est asiatique*, no. 1 (December 1951), pp. 36–41; "Etude sur l'économie viet minh," pp. 35–6; Marc Vaucel, *Planteur*, undated, but post-1975, about the life of this veteran of the Expeditionary Corps turned rubber planter, 666, Charles Meyer Papers, Cambodian National Archives; René Fabvre, "Les Plantations de caoutchouc du Vietnam," *Politique étrangère*, vol. 35, no. 4 (1970), pp. 371–403.

50. For overviews of the salt war, see "Le sel, monnaie forte," pp. 36–40; and Villaret, "La citadelle du sel," pp. 26–31. For the elaboration and details of the colonial army's assault on the DRV's salt production, including air strikes, see 10H3359, SHD, including the "Procès-verbal de la réunion du 27 décembre 1948 sur la guerre économique," p. 1. See also the tables in the annex to this document for the citation on hitting the enemy's salt mines by air with diesel. On the authorization of napalm, see "Note," no. 2/S, 20 January 1952, 10H3359, SHD; and for a napalm attack on the Degi salt field, see Deuxième Bureau, no. 52EM2, 22 September 1952, AI 4 C 865, SHD.

51. "Attitude à adopter vis à vis des stocks de billets Ho Chi Minh," no. 823/ZS62, no date; "Note à l'attention du colonel commandant le zone Sud, objet monnaie Ho Chi Minh," 1026/FTCVN/2S; undated, both in V36, LKV, 10H3235, SHD; Tran Quoc Du, *Dong Bac Tai Chinh Dong Bac cu Ho*, pp. 75–100 (for an overview); and documents in 10H638, SHD. On the counterfeiters, see Tran Quoc Du, *Dong Bac Tai Chinh Dong Bac cu Ho*, pp. 42–3. On carrying huge wads of banknotes, see Boudarel, *Autobiographie*, pp. 296–8.

52. "Le chef de la province de Thua Thien au gouverneur du Centre Vietnam," Hue, 16 March 1949, signed Phan Dinh Tap, 10H3461, SHD; and "Note de service: bataille du riz," no. 262/SSN, 25 April 1948, 10H3648, SHD. For the early rice wars in central Vietnam, see various documents in es 10H3461 and 10H3648, SHD.

53. On the southern blockade, see the documentation in 10H638, SHD; and for an overview: Pierre Cellier, "Le Viet minh dans l'impasse: un grain de riz = une goutte de sang," *Indochine Sud-est asiatique*, no. 1 (December 1951), p. 24.

54. "Généralités sur l'action du bombardement," a collection of after-action reports for early 1950, pp. 2–5, in CAEO Deuxième Bureau, IV; and Forces françaises, 12) Action de l'aviation française: chasse et bombardements, Commandement de l'Air en Extrême-Orient, no. 850/GATAC.N/3/2, both in AI 4 C865, SHD; and Air Extrême Orient, "Repertoire dossiers d"objectifs," 1950, in AI 4 C861, SHD. For French-intercepted Vietnamese reports on the colonial bombing of a DRV medical school in Zone III, south of Hanoi, on the bombing of Yen Dinh, and on the bombing of Nam Dan, see SDECE, "Bombardement de l'école de médecine V.N.," 2 February 1950; SDECE, "Raids de l'aviation française sur la province de Thanh Hoa," 7 June 1950; and Deuxième Bureau, "Renseignement," 27 July 1950; all in AI 4 C 865–2, SHD. (It also contains dozens of Vietnamese cables reporting on the French bombing of markets.) The history of bombing during the Indochina War awaits an historian.

Chapter 8. The *Levée en masse* and War Communism

1. See my "Decolonization and American Intervention in Asia: From Japan to Vietnam," in David Engermann, Max Friedman, and Melani McAlister, eds., *The Cambridge History of American Foreign Policy*, vol. 4 (New York: Cambridge University Press, 2021).

2. *The Mail*, 23 May 1948, cited by Ton That Thien, *India and South East Asia, 1947–1960: A Study of India's Policy towards the South East Asian Countries in the Period 1947–1960* (Geneva: Librairie Droz, 1963), p. 149.

3. For more on this revolutionary moment and diplomacy more generally, see chapters in Christopher Goscha and Christian Ostermann, eds., *Connecting Histories: Decolonization and the Cold War in Southeast Asia, 1945–1962* (Stanford: Stanford University Press, 2009); and Tuong Vu, *Vietnam's Communist Revolution: The Power and Limits of Ideology* (Cambridge: Cambridge University Press, 2017).

4. Ho Chi Minh, "Thu Gui Hoi Nghi Toan Quoc cua Dang," 20 January 1950, in *Van Kien Dang Toan Tap*, vol. 11 (1950) (Hanoi: Nha Xuat Ban Chinh Tri Quoc Gia, 2001), p. 17.

5. See my "Towards a Geo-history of Asian Communism," in Geoff Wade and James Chin, eds., *China and Southeast Asia: Historical Interactions* (London: Routledge, 2018), pp. 314–35.

6. "Ho Chi Minh as Commander Hu Guang in China," Dtinews (4 December 2010), http://dtinews.vn/en/news/024/6308/ho-chi-minh-as-commander-hu-guang-in-china.html, accessed on 12 December 2019; and Wong How Man, "Ho Chi Minh's Chinese Connections and Poems," *China Exploration and Research Society*, undated, http://www.cers.org.hk/index.php/en/preserving-culture/culture-and-history/181-ho-chi-minhs-chinese-connections-and-poems, accessed on 4 June 2020.

7. David Marr, *Vietnamese Tradition on Trial (1925–1945)* (Berkeley: University of California Press, 1981), p. 328 (notes 4, 5, and 6) and p. 401 (note 88). The publication of "The Peasant Question" by Vo Nguyen Giap and Truong Chinh in late 1937 dovetailed nicely with the ruralization of Chinese communism under Mao Zedong. Vo Nguyen Giap penned essays on the Sino-Japanese war during the Popular Front period. See, for example: Vo Nguyen Giap (Van Dinh), *Muon Hieu Ro Tinh Hinh Quan Su o Tau* (Hanoi: unknown publisher, 1939).

8. Mao's essays are well worth reading, including his "On Protracted War" (sections 35–50), https://www.marxists.org/reference/archive/mao/selected-works/vol.-2/mswv2_09.htm, accessed on 2 July 2019.

9. Tran Duong, *Kinh Te Viet Nam (1945–1954)* (Hanoi: Nha Xuat Ban Khoa Hoc, 1966), p. 391, for the number of 10 million.

10. Truong Chinh, "Tich Cuc Cam Cu va Chuan Bi Tong Phan Cong," 14–18 February 1949, in *Van Kien Dang Toan Tap*, vol. 10 (1949) (Hanoi: Nha Xuat Ban Chinh Tri Quoc Gia, 2001), pp. 25–67.

11. I have drawn inspiration in this section from the works of Michael Howard, *War in European History* (Oxford: Oxford University Press, 2009, updated version), chapters 4–6; and Peter Paret, *Understanding War: Essays on Clausewitz and the History of Military Power* (Princeton: Princeton University Press, 1992). The proclamation of the French military levy (draft) is well worth reading: "Concerning a Levy of 300,000 Men and the Method to be Used in Effecting Same," 24 February 1793, as is the mass mobilization law: "Decree Establishing the Levy *en masse*," 23 August 1793, both in John Stewart, *A Documentary Survey of the French Revolution* (New York: The Macmillan Company, 1951), pp. 402–8, pp. 472–4, respectively. For Napoleon's use of the draft, see "The First General Conscription Law," 5 September 1798, in ibid., pp. 729–39.

12. See Alan Forrest, *The Legacy of the French Revolutionary Wars: The Nation-in-Arms in French Republican Memory* (New York: Cambridge University Press, 2009); also his *Conscripts*

and Deserters: The Army and French Society during the Revolution and Empire (New York: Oxford University Press, 1989); and his "L'Armée de l'an II: La levée en masse et la création d'un mythe républicain," *Annales historiques de la Révolution française*, no. 335 (January/March 2004), pp. 111–30.

13. "Sac Lenh so 126/SL," dated 4 November 1949, https://moj.gov.vn/vbpq/Lists/Vn%20 bn%20php%20lut/View_Detail.aspx?ItemID=178, accessed on 23 April 2020.

14. On conscription, see Ban Khoa Hoc Hau Can, *Cong Tac Hau Can Chien Dich Dien Bien Phu, Dong Xuan 1953–1954* (Hanoi: Tong Cuc Hau Can, 1979), pp. 350–59. On patriotic volunteering for military service in the early years, see David Marr, *Vietnam 1945: The Quest for Power* (Berkeley: University of California Press, 1995).

15. "Sac Lenh so 20-SL," 12 February 1950, https://thuvienphapluat.vn/van-ban/Bo-may -hanh-chinh/Sac-lenh-20-SL-quyet-dinh-tong-dong-vien-nhan-vat-tai-luc-tien-toi-Tong-phan -cong/36522/noi-dung.aspx, accessed on 23 April 2020. See also Tran Duong, *Kinh Te Viet Nam*, pp. 122–3; and *Cong Tac Hau Can Chien Dich Dien Bien Phu*, pp. 350–59. For a photograph of the original mass mobilization decree, see *Lich Su Quoc Hoi Viet Nam, 1946–1960* (Hanoi: Nha Xuat Ban Chinh Tri Quoc Gia, 2000), p. 137. Hardly an accident, in early April 1960, Ho Chi Minh signed a new obligatory military service law, as the war threatened to resume where it had left off before the armistice signed in Geneva in 1954. See "Sac Lenh so 11/SL," 15 April 1960, https:// thuvienphapluat.vn/van-ban/Bo-may-hanh-chinh/Luat-nghia-vu-quan-su-1960-11-SL-36858 .aspx, accessed on 23 April 2020.

16. Truong Chinh, "Hoan Thanh Nhiem Vu Chuan Bi Chuyen Manh Sang Tong Phan Cong," early 1950, in *Van Kien Dang Toan Tap*, vol. 11 (1950), pp. 23, 28, 36–7, 62–3, and especially 85–100.

17. Truong Chinh, "Hoan Thanh Nhiem Vu Chuan Bi," pp. 63–4.

18. Ibid., p. 62.

19. Cited in Tran Duong, *Kinh Te Viet Nam*, p. 123.

20. "Decree SL/20," 12 February 1950. That the communists rammed it through, see *Van Kien Dang Toan Tap*, vol. 11 (1950), pp. 187, 212–13. On coercion, see ibid., p. 324 ("bat buoc tham gia theo dung sac lenh tong dong vien.")

21. *Bach Khoa Tri Thuc Quoc Phong Toan Dan* (Hanoi: Nha Xuat Ban Chinh Tri Quoc Gia, 2003), pp. 466, 626.

22. Tran Duong, *Kinh Te Viet Nam*, p. 113. On Tran Dang Ninh's role, see "Tran Dang Ninh, Mot Tam Guong Sang Ngoi Pham Chat Cach Mang," *Nhan Dan* (18 September 2010), https:// nhandan.com.vn/vanhoa/item/17809002-.html, accessed on 29 July 2019; and Bich Trang, "Tong Cuc Truong Tran Dang Ninh trong Ky Uc Nguoi o Lai," *Su Kien va Nhan Chung* (11 July 2017), https://sknc.qdnd.vn/chuyen-tuong-linh/tong-cuc-truong-tran-dang-ninh-trong-ky-uc-nguoi-o -lai-500641, accessed on 29 July 2019. On the G-4 mystery in Korea, see Robert Futrell, *The United States Air Force in Korea 1950–1953* (New York: Duell, Sloan, and Pearce, 1961), p. 308.

23. Tran Duong, *Kinh Te Viet Nam*, p. 217; Luong, "Thong Tri cua Ban Thuong Vu Trung Uong ve Viec Kien Toan Bo May Chi Dao Quan Su Trung Uong," 28 June 1950, *Van Kien Dang Toan Tap*, vol. 11, pp. 346–7; and see p. 324 for Tran Dang Ninh's plan.

24. Tran Duong, *Kinh Te Viet Nam*, p. 245; and *Cong Tac Hau Can Chien Dich Dien Bien Phu*, pp. 356–9.

25. Le Van Luong, "Chi Thi cua Ban Thuong Vu Trung Uong ve Viec Kiem Thao de Su Doi Nen Nep Van Dong Dan theo Ho Chu Tich," 22 July 1950, *Van Kien Dang Toan Tap*, vol. 11

(1950), pp. 432–3; and "Thu Gui Dong Bao Lien Khu 4, Nho Uy Ban Khang Chien Hanh Chinh Lien Khu Huyen," undated, but clearly mid-1950, *Van Kien Dang Toan Tap*, vol. 11 (1950), pp. 438–9.

26. For Ho Chi Minh and Pham Van Dong's letters, see 65, 10H549, SHD. Ho Chi Minh ordered his letter of apology to be read (rather than published in any paper) in all the villages of Zone IV.

27. Pham Van Dong, "Phai Kien Toan Chinh Quyen Cong Hoa Nhan Dan De Tong Phan Cong va Kien Thiet Che Do Dan Chu Nhan Dan Viet Nam," undated, but early 1950, *Van Kien Dang Toan Tap*, vol. 11 (1950), pp. 179–96 (p. 186 for the first citation, p. 187 for the second on "the people's republic.") Though it is undated, the editors of this collection of party documents identify it as given during the third plenum of early 1950.

28. Pham Van Dong, "Phai Kien Toan Chinh Quyen Cong Hoa Nhan Dan De Tong Phan Cong va Kien Thiet Che Do Dan Chu Nhan Dan Viet Nam," pp. 179–83.

29. Ibid., p. 180.

30. Ibid., pp. 179–96.

31. Ibid., p. 183–96 (p. 193 for the citation). See also Le Van Hien in *Van Kien Dang Toan Tap*, no date given, but early 1951, vol. 12 (1951) (Hanoi: Nha Xuat Ban Chinh Tri Quoc Gia, 2001), pp. 121–5.

32. Hoang Quoc Viet, "Cong Tac Mat Tran Va Dan Van Trong Nam Chuyen Manh Sang Tong Phan Cong" and "Nghi Quyet cua Hoi Nghi Toan Quoc Lan Thu Ba ve Viec Chuyen Manh Sang Tong Phan Cong (21 January–3 February 1950); both in *Van Kien Dang Toan Tap*, vol. 11 (1950), pp. 154–78 and 197–219, respectively.

33. Hoang Quoc Viet, "Cong Tac Mat Tran Va Dan Van Trong Nam Chuyen Manh Sang Tong Phan," p. 165 for the citation. For the numbers, see *Bach Khoa Tri Thuc Quoc Phong Toan Dan* (Hanoi: Nha Xuat Ban Chinh Tri Quoc Gia, 2003), p. 631. Also see François Guillemot, "Death and Suffering at First Hand: Youth Shock Brigades during the Vietnam War (1950–1975)," *Journal of Vietnamese Studies*, vol. 4, no. 3 (2009), pp. 17–60.

34. Hoang Quoc Viet, "Cong Tac Mat Tran Va Dan Van Trong Nam Chuyen Manh Sang Tong Phan," pp. 168–9.

35. See the memoirs of Hoang Van Chi, *From Colonialism to Communism: A Case History of North Vietnam* (London: Pall Mall, 1964).

36. Ho Chi Minh, "Bao Cao Chinh Tri tai Dai Hoi Dai Bieu Toan Quoc Lan Thu II cua Dang" (Hanoi: Nha Xuat Ban Chinh Tri Quoc Gia, 2001), vol. 12 (1951), pp. 12–39 (p. 39 for "extremely strong.")

37. Truong Chinh, "Hoan Thanh Giai Phong Dan Toc, Phat Trien Dan Chu Nhan Dan, Tien Toi Chu Nghia Xa Hoi," no date given, but early 1951, *Van Kien Dang Toan Tap*, vol. 12 (1951), pp. 40–175.

38. Ibid., pp. 131–5.

39. On the need to control land reform, see Truong Chinh, "Chinh Sach Ruong Dat Cua Dang Va Van De Dieu Tra Nong Thon," 10 February 1950, *Van Kien Dang Toan Tap*, vol. 11 (1950), pp. 229–42.

40. French captured text of Truong Chinh's "conclusion générale" during the plenum of early 1950, in "Conclusions de la présidence du congrès et du comité central au sujet des délibérations du congrès [plenum]," 10H620, SHD.

41. I owe a great debt here to the pioneering work of Yves Chevrier on Maoist China and Benoît de Tréglodé on Ho Chi Minh's Vietnam: Yves Chevrier, *Mao et la révolution chinoise* (Paris: Castermann, 1993); and Benoît de Tréglodé, *Héros et révolution au Vietnam* (Paris: Les Indes savantes, 2014 (revised edition)), and in English translation as *Heroes and Revolution in Vietnam* (Singapore: National University of Singapore Press, 2012). I am also indebted to the outstanding work of two young scholars in the United States on similar themes: Alex Thai Vo, "From Anticolonialism to Mobilizing Socialist Transformation in the Democratic Republic of Vietnam, 1945–1960," Ph.D. dissertation (Ithaca: Cornell University, 2019); and Alec Holcombe, *Mass Mobilization in the Democratic Republic of Vietnam, 1945–1960* (Honolulu: University of Hawai'i Press, 2020).

42. On Soviet practices, see Brigitte Studer, "L'Etre perfectible: la formation du cadre stalinien par le 'travail sur soi,'" *Genèse*, vol. 51 (June 2003), pp. 92–113; and V. I. Lenin, "How to Organize Competition?," written in late 1917 and published in *Pravda*, no. 17 (20 January 1929), in V. I. Lenin, *Collected Works* (Moscow: Progress Publishers, 1964), vol. 26, pp. 404–15.

43. Chevrier, *Mao et la révoluton chinoise*, pp. 93–4. On Maoism during this time, I rely here on Rana Mitter, *China's War with Japan, 1937–1945* (London: Penguin Books, 2013); and Chevrier, *Mao et la révoluton chinoise*.

44. Studer, "L'Etre perfectible," pp. 92–113; and V. I. Lenin, "How to Organise Competition?," pp. 404–15.

45. This is based on my notes from the finding guide and consultation of scores of publications in the special "resistance collection" held in the annex of the Vietnamese National Library in Hanoi: the Bo Phan Khang Chien (1945–54). This collection is a gold mine of information, especially for the second half of the Indochina War. See my handwritten notes for selections from this collection on-line at https://cgoscha.uqam.ca/documents/.

46. On the emulation campaigns, see Tréglodé's *Héros et révolution au Vietnam*. See also Tran Duong, *Kinh Te Viet Nam*, pp. 342–70. On the Soviet origins of communist competition campaigns, see Anne Applebaum, *Iron Curtain: The Crushing of Eastern Europe, 1944–1956* (Toronto: Signal, 2012), Chapter 13, pp. 316–27 in particular. For the Maoist version, see Govind Kelkar, "The Role of Labour Heroes in the Yenan Period," *China Report*, vol. 13, no. 4 (1977), pp. 52–66.

47. Comité de résistance administratif de la LKI, no. 8/TD, RDV, "Instructions sur l'élaboration de programme de compétitions patriotiques pour l'échelon de village," p. 6, in 10H2941, SHD.

48. See Tréglodé, *Héros et Révolution*; *Kinh te*, pp. 367–9; Yinghong Cheng, *Creating the "New Man": From Enlightenment Ideals to Socialist Realities* (Honolulu: University of Hawai'i Press, 2009); and Mary Sheridan, "The Emulation of Heroes," *The China Quarterly*, no. 33 (January–March 1968), pp. 47–72. The party's complete documents, *Van Kien Dang Toan Tap* and the *Resistance Collection (Bo phan khang chien)*, held in the National Library of Vietnam in Hanoi, provide rich documentation on emulation drives and new hero campaigns.

49. Tréglodé, *Héros et Révolution*, p. 69.

50. Ibid., p. 65.

51. The scholarship on Chinese rectification is immense. See, among others, Ritter, *China's War*, Chapter 15; Vidya Prakash Dutt, "The Rectification Campaign in China," *International Studies*, vol. 1, no. 1 (July 1959), pp. 28–50; Yinghong Cheng, *Creating the "New Man"*; Peter J. Seybolt,

"Terror and Conformity: Counterespionage Campaigns, Rectification, and Mass Movements," *Modern China*, vol. 12, no. 1 (January 1986), pp. 39–73. For the Soviet Union, see Studer, "L'Etre perfectible," pp. 92–113. For Vietnam, see Georges Boudarel, "L'Idéocratie importée au Vietnam avec le maoïsme," *La Bureaucratie au Vietnam* (Paris: L'Harmattan, 1983), pp. 31–106; and especially Holcombe, *Mass Mobilization*.

52. X.Y.Z. (Ho Chi Minh), *Su Doi Loi Lam Viec* (Hanoi: Nha Xuat Ban Su That, 1947), http://kllct.dlu.edu.vn/Resources/Docs/SubDomain/kllct/Sửa%20đổi%20lối%20làm%20việc.pdf, accessed on 23 April 2020.

53. Truong Chinh, "Hoan Thanh Giai Phong Dan Toc," p. 102.

54. Cited by Lai Nguyen Ai and Alec Holcombe, "The Heart and Mind of the Poet Xuan Dieu: 1954–1958," *Journal of Vietnamese Studies*, vol. 5, no. 2 (Summer 2010), p. 11.

Chapter 9. Of Rice and War

1. Truong Chinh, "Phuong Cham Chien Luoc Hien Nay," *Nhan Dan*, no. 4 (15 April 1951), in *Cuoc Khang Chien Than Thanh cua Nhan Dan Viet Nam*, vol. 3 (Hanoi: Nha Xuat Ban Su That, 1959), p. 26.

2. Pierre Cellier, "Le Viet minh dans l'impasse: un grain de riz = une goutte de sang," *Indochine Sud-est asiatique*, no. 1 (December 1951), p. 24.

3. In mid-1947, the French launched their first concerted postwar pacification effort in the northern delta, called the Comité Provisoire de Gestion administrative et d'action sociale. "Le problème no. 1 du Tonkin: de la pacification d'hier à celle d'aujourd'hui," *Indochine Sud-est Asiatique*, no. 6 (May 1952), pp. 50–55. On the intersection between French pacification and the Vietnamese revolutionary statecraft, see also Shawn McHale, *The First Indochina War: Violence, Sovereignty, and the Fracture of the South, 1945–1956* (Cambridge: Cambridge University Press, 2021), Chapter 8.

4. Vietnamese and French sources confirm the creation of this corridor. Tran Duong, *Kinh Te Viet Nam (1945–1954)* (Hanoi: Nha Xuat Ban Khoa Hoc, 1966), p. 121. The French intelligence officers called it the "couloir de Hoa Binh." Deuxième Bureau, "Etude sur l'économie viet minh," p. 7, 8 March 1952, 10H638, SHD. On the closing of colonial towers unable to hold out against the DRV's force, see "Note de service," no. 1134/CFTCV/3/8, 16 May 1952, pp. 2–3, 10H3646, SHD.

5. Yves Gras, *Histoire de la guerre d'Indochine* (Paris: Plon, 1979), p. 445, for American aid and the date of late 1950; Robert Aeschelmann, "Métamorphose des ailes françaises en Indochine," *Sud-est Asiatique*, no. 27 (August 1951), pp. 10–16. On American advice and support during the Indochina War, see Ronald Spector's *The United States Army in Vietnam*. vol. 1: *Advice and Support: The Early Years, 1941–1960* (Washington, DC: Center of Military History, U.S. Army, 1983). On America's indirect war in Vietnam from 1950, see my "Decolonization and American Intervention in Asia: From Japan to Vietnam," in David Engermann, Max Friedman, and Melani McAlister, eds., *Cambridge History of America and the World*, vol. 4 (New York: Cambridge University Press, 2021); Fredrik Logevall, *Embers of War* (New York: Random House, 2012).

6. On the delta battles, see Gras, *Histoire de la guerre d'Indochine*, p. 379; and the "Bombes au napalm" in AI 4 C 865, SHD.

7. Gras, *Histoire de la guerre d'Indochine*, p. 379.

8. Ngo Van Chieu, *Journal d'un combattant Viet-Minh* (Paris: Editions du Seuil, 1955), pp. 154–5.

9. Lucien Bodard, *La Guerre d'Indochine* (Paris: Grasset, 1997), p. 823.

10. Ibid., p. 823. For the history of napalm, see Robert Neer, *Napalm: An American Biography* (Cambridge, MA: Harvard University Press, 2015); and see http://www.napalmbiography.com, accessed on 20 April 2021. For another interesting view of one of the first times napalm was used in the conflict, see this YouTube link https://www.youtube.com/watch?app=desktop&v=rfzHg9wEXV0&feature=share&fbclid=IwAR3Ec6_ML1i0YxcsqOh0aGn12JbJofTgbjnMlXO WJkVmQYx9bhWVdeBR0sQ, accessed on 4 May 2021.

11. Ngo Van Chieu, *Journal d'un combattant Viet-Minh*, p. 156. In February 1951, Ho Chi Minh's security services in Hanoi reported that the Americans had supplied de Lattre with napalm from Korea and authorized him to use it in order to avoid defeat in the northern delta. Intercepted cable, SDECE, 5 March 1951, "Cong An Hanoi a Cong An Central" and accompanying DRV documents in AI 4 C 865, SHD. The DRV Ministry of Defense reported the French use of napalm on 21 November 1950. Deuxième Bureau, no. 0070/FAEO/2S, AI 4 C 865–2, SHD. However, the first concerted French napalm assaults occurred on 15 and 17 January 1951. Deuxième Bureau, "Etude sur les résultats des bombardements," p. 3, 20 January 1950, in AI 4 C 865–2, SHD.

12. Bodard, *La Guerre d'Indochine*, p. 983.

13. On the American planes sent to Indochina by 1951, see Aeschelmann, "Métamorphose des ailes françaises en Indochine," pp. 10–16; and Spector, *The United States Army in Vietnam*, vol. 1, chapters 7–9.

14. Bodard, *La Guerre d'Indochine*, p. 835.

15. Gras, *Histoire de la guerre d'Indochine*, p. 402.

16. "L'Economie V.M.," *Indochine Sud-est asiatique*, no. 19 (June–July 1953), p. 29.

17. On rice and recruits, see Gras, *Histoire de la guerre d'Indochine*, pp. 412, 462. For Giap on the need to operate in the lowlands, see Vo Nguyen Giap, "May Net Chinh ve Tinh Hinh va Nhiem Vu Quan Su Hien Nay," address to the third party plenum in April 1952, *Van Kien Dang Toan Tap*, vol. 13 (1952) (Hanoi: Nha Xuat Ban Chinh Tri Quoc Gia, 2001), pp. 111–13.

18. Robert Guillain, *Dien Bien Phu: la fin des illusions* (Paris: Arléa, 2004), pp. 116–19; and Gras, *Histoire de la guerre d'Indochine*, pp. 420–21. The French unleashed massive amounts of firepower against units they isolated in ways the Americans would repeat during the Vietnam War. Yves Gras referred to the French attack on the 98th batallion in the delta as a "veritable slaughter" (*un véritable hallali*). Gras, *Histoire de la guerre d'Indochine*, pp. 458–9.

19. No one puts the French settler distrust of a Vietnamese army better than Albert de Pouvourville in November 1912, reproduced in *Le Figaro* (2 December 2012), https://www.lefigaro.fr/mon-figaro/2012/11/02/10001-20121102ARTFIG00458-les-officiers-de-notre-armee-jaune.php, accessed on 23 April 2020. For an excellent analysis of the Associated State of Vietnam's army see Ivan Cadeau, "De la politique de jaunissement," *Pensée militaire* (May 2019), https://www.penseemiliterre.fr/de-la-politique-de-jaunissement-des-effectifs-du-corps-expeditionnaire-francais-d-extreme-orient-1-2_114101_1013077.html, accessed on 23 April 2020.

20. Faced with a dwindling number of available imperial troops as decolonization moved from Asia to Africa in the 1950s, French leaders finally sent metropolitan conscripts to Algeria

to preserve what was left of the empire. Revealingly, the French refused to create an Algerian Army.

21. General Georges Spillman describes in detail how he presided over the creation of this new Vietnamese army. Georges Spillman, *Souvenirs d'un colonialiste* (Paris: Presses de la Cité, 1968), pp. 238–40, 278–92 (p. 279 for confirmation of the American approval of four divisions for the colonial army). On American advice and support, see Spector, *The United States Army in Vietnam*, vol. 1.

22. On the colonial instrumentalization of Bao Dai, see Spillman, *Souvenirs d'un colonialiste*, pp. 238–40 including the photo section. On French attempts to use colonial monarchy in Vietnam, see my "Colonial Monarchy and Decolonisation in the French Empire: Bao Dai, Norodom Sihanouk and Mohammed V," in Robert Aldrich and Cindy McCreery, eds., *Monarchies and Decolonisation in Asia* (Manchester: Manchester University Press, 2020), pp. 152–74.

23. Nguyen Van Phu, "L'Armée vietnamienne (1949–1957): contribution à l'étude d'un cas de formation d'armée nationale," Ph.D. dissertation (Montpellier: Université Paul Valéry, 1980), pp. 89–97; and for the mobilization law, p. 106 (notes 3–9); and Gras, *Histoire de la guerre d'Indochine*, pp. 357–8, 390, 443–5.

24. Spillman, *Souvenirs d'un colonialiste*, pp. 269–70, 278–81; Nguyen Van Phu, "L'Armée vietnamienne (1949–1957)," p. 90; and Gras, *Histoire de la guerre d'Indochine*, pp. 444–6. On desertion, see Nguyen Van Phu, "L'Armée vietnamienne (1949–1957)," p. 90. On the French use of the colonial army during the Second World War, see Eric Jenning, *Free French Africa in World War II: The African Resistance* (Cambridge: Cambridge University Press, 2015).

25. Spillman, *Souvenirs d'un colonialiste*, p. 288.

26. On the Force noire, see Pap Ndiaye, "Les Soldats noirs de la République," *L'Histoire*, no. 337 (December 2008), https://www.lhistoire.fr/les-soldats-noirs-de-la-république, accessed on 18 February 2020. On the Armée jaune, see Mireille Le Van Ho, "Le Général Pennequin et le projet d'armée jaune (1911–1915)," *Outre-Mers*, no. 279 (1988), pp. 145–67. On the French government's opposition to sending French conscripts to fight in Indochina in 1951, see Eric Mechoulan, "Jules Moch et la défense de l'Europe," *Révue historique des Armées* (September 2000), no. 220, pp. 89–97. Whether he was bluffing or not, on 7 July 1954 Pierre Mendès France threatened to draft French boys to fight in Indochina in 1954 if the negotiations broke down at Geneva. See Pierre Mendès France's speech to the National Assembly on 22 July 1954, http://www2.assemblee-nationale.fr/decouvrir-l-assemblee/histoire/grands-discours -parlementaires/pierre-mendes-france-22-juillet-1954, accessed on 3 October 2020.

27. General de Lattre de Tassigny, "Discours prononcé à Saigon le 11 juillet 1951, à la distribution des prix du Lycée Chasseloup-Labuat," annex 1, in Jean Ferrandi, *Les Officiers français face au Viet Minh, 1945–1954* (Paris: Fayard, 1966), pp. 269–70.

28. None of the "Associated States of Indochina" achieved complete, legal independence before the end of the Indochina War. Contrary to what many have written (including this author), the Cambodians and the Laotians did not secure full independence in 1953 either. The French remained in control of all military operations in eastern Cambodia, and Cambodia remained part of the French Union until September 1955. Gras, *Histoire de la guerre d'Indochine*, pp. 507–11. Members of the Associated States of Indochina carried passports with the words "French Union" printed on them. For examples, see Saigon, RGI, 1 à 50, archives du Ministère des affaires étrangères, Nantes annex.

29. For the GAMO and the *Tieu Doan Khinh Quan*, see Gras, *Histoire de la guerre d'Indochine*, pp. 460–62; Jean-Marc Le Page, "Le Tonkin, laboratoire de la 'pacification' en Indochine?," *Revue historique des Armées*, no. 248 (2007), pp. 116–25; André Dulac, *Nos guerres perdues* (Paris: Fayard, 1969), pp. 47–51; and Nguyen Van Phu, "L'Armée vietnamienne (1949–1957)," pp. 48–66, 109 (note 54), 121–31. For the Vietnamese communist explanation of their pacification methods, see Vo Nguyen Giap, "May Van De Cu The ve Chien Tranh Du Kich," *Cuoc Khang Chien Than Thanh cua Nhan Dan Viet Nam*, vol. 2 (Hanoi: Nha Xuat Ban Su That, 1959), pp. 143–7.

30. Deuxième Bureau, "La Question du riz, question vitale pour le Nord Vietnam," p. 1 for the citation, 23 July 1952; and Salan's explanation of his economic offensive to the Minister of the Associated States, undated but based on the attached note possibly early 1951, both in 10H638, SHD.

31. My discussion of the systematic French economic war relies on the following documents: "Fiche: possibilités d'action en matière économique," January 1951; EMIFT, "Guerre économique," 6 January 1951; "Etudes sur la répression des trafics au Tonkin," 29 August 1952; Deuxième Bureau, no. 1015/EMTCC/2, 30 May 1951; Deuxième Bureau, "Comment faire entrer la guerre économique dans les réalités," 7 May 1952 (approved by Salan in margin); Deuxième Bureau, no. 0/120EMIFT, 2S, undated; "Salan au Ministre d'Etat chargé des relations avec les Etats associés," January 1951; and Salan, "Blocus du delta"; all in 10H638 and 10H2377, SHD. For central Vietnam's economic battles, I rely on documents in 10H1312, 10H3166, and 10H3359, SHD.

32. "Général LeBlanc à son 'Excellence' [unidentified]," 9 June 1952, 10H3166, SHD and see also: "Note de service: bataille du riz," pp. 1–2, 30 March 1953, no. 600/ST/PAC-SC, 10H3359, SHD.

33. Salan is cited in "Fiche: possibilités d'action en matière économique," January 1951, 10H638, SHD. For a fascinating DRV action plan for fighting the rice war in the villages, see the captured document "Bao Ve Mua, Fat Trien [sic] Du Kich Chien Tranh," 5 April 1953, pp. 1–6, in Deuxième Bureau, "Note, no. 378/SQT/2," 19 April 1953, A-09-8, 10H3631, SHD; and Etat du Vietnam, "Compte rendu, no. 350/QB2.M," 5 May 1951, 10H3461, SHD. For an explanation of what controlling the harvest meant for the colonial authorities, see "Contrôle du riz," 2 April 1953, no. 338/SQT/2.SC; and "Bataille du riz," 30 March 1953; both in 10H3166, SHD.

34. Bodard, *La Guerre d'Indochine*, p. 483.

35. Gras, *Histoire de la guerre d'Indochine*, pp. 420–21, 450–51. For rare photos of French troops fighting the food war in the rice fields, see Pierre Cellier, "Le Viet Minh dans l'impasse: un grain de riz = une goutte de sang," *Indochine Sud-est asiatique*, no. 1 (December 1951), p. 23.

36. "La Question du riz, question vitale, pour le Nord Vietnam," p. 4 (for the citation), 23 July 1952, 10H638, SHD; and for the shelling of rice fields, see "Note de service," 2 April 1953, no. 585/SH3, 10H3359, SHD.

37. They also treated it as a "military objective" and "war material." See "Note de service," no. 87/3B, undated, p. 1; and "Note," no. 335/PAO.CVN, 27 April 1953, p. 2; both in 10H3359, SHD; "Colonel de St. Martin au chef du province du Quang Nam," 20 April 1953, no. 326/SAT/3/SC, p. 1; and "Protection des greniers de riz," General LeBlanc, 16 April 1953, p. 1; both in Pacification, 10H3166, SHD.

38. "Comment faire entrer la guerre économique dans les réalités," pp. 1–3 (citation p. 3), 10H638, SHD.

39. "Salan au Ministre d'Etat chargé des Relations avec les Etats associés," undated, p. 2 (for the quotation) and attached note, p. 2, 10H638, SHD.

40. Raoul Salan, "Le Blocus," annex, in 10H638, undated but probably late 1952, p. 6.

41. "Etudes sur la répression des trafics au Tonkin," 29 August 1952, pp. 2–4; Raoul Salan, "Projet," sent to the commanding general of French Ground Forces in Northern Vietnam and the Commissioner for Tonkin, dated November 1951 (a question mark in the margin suggests that the date was perhaps 1952: a typing error?); "Notes sur la protection de la récolte du 5ème mois," no. 2375 FTNV 2 and no. 2470/FTNV, 2, 9, and 14 May 1952; both in 10H638, SHD; and Général des armées de Linarès au Commissaire de la République, Nord Vietnam, "Analyse sur l'économie viet minh," 6 July 1952, 10H638, SHD.

42. "Procès-verbal succinct de la réunion du 9.9.1952," and attached documents from the French high commissioner's office, 10H638, SHD.

43. Chu Truong Lap, "Khu Vuc Trang cua Giac," in *Cuoc Khang Chien Than Thanh cua Nhan Dan Viet Nam*, vol. 3 (Hanoi: Nha Xuat Ban Su That, 1959), pp. 95–6, dated 16 August 1951.

44. Deuxième Bureau, "Etude sur l'économie viet minh," p. 1 (for "pays viet minh"), 8 March 1952; "Etudes sur la répression des trafics au Tonkin," 29 August 1952, pp. 2–4; "Notes sur la protection de la récolte du 5ème mois"; and "Analyse sur l'économie viet minh," all in 10H638, SHD. For the rice wars in lower central Vietnam, near Hue and Da Nang, see scores of reports in 10H3166. For the use of private merchants for evacuating rice and according exceptions to the Buddhist clergy, see "Protection de la récolte," 20 September 1953, 10H3166, SHD.

45. Deuxième Bureau, "L'économie viet minh, Indochine du Nord," pp. 9–10, May 1953, 10H638, confirmed in part by L. M. Chassin, *Aviation indochine* (Paris: Amiot Dumont, 1954), pp. 151–2; and "Note de service," 6 July 1950, no. 1564/FTCVP/3S, 10H3359, SHD, for the quotation on the rebel zones. Bombing of the irrigation systems continued in 1953. See "Reprise de l'action contre les grands réseaux d'irrigation," no. 318/AIR.EO:2B, 10 January 1953, pp. 1–6, and related documents in AI 4 C 861, SHD.

46. "Note de service: Destruction des buffles," 23 February 1952, p. 2 (for "massively"); and "Directives relatives à la campagne de destruction systématique des troupeaux de buffles," 27 February 1952, p. 1–3; both in 10H3359, SHD. In the classic history of the Vietnamese war economy, the authors provide photos of the French bombing of dikes, dams, and canals. See Tran Duong, *Kinh Te Viet Nam*, photo inset between pp. 136 and 137. The French intentionally ordered the killing of buffalos in order to damage the peasants' ability to farm their fields. See "Directives relatives à la campagne de destruction systématique des troupeaux de buffles," 27 February 1952, pp. 1–3, 10H3359, SHD.

47. "Liste des photographies aériennnes les plus remarquables sur les résultats de l'action aérienne depuis le 1 janiver 1952," 21 October 1952, AI 4 C 865, SHD; "Etude sur l'économie viet minh," EMIFT/Deuxième Bureau, 8 March 1952, 10H638, SHD; and Le Van Hien, *Nhat Ky cua Mot Bo Truong*, vol. 2 (Danang: Nha Xuat Ban Da Nang, 1995), pp. 391–2. On the taste of rice, see Captain Morichère, "Les Opérations du groupement de supplétifs de Cao Bang dans le repli de cette place au Nord Tonkin en octobre 1950," p. 19 for the citation, in the private papers of Captain Morichère, GR 1 KT 1154, SHD. My thanks to Ivan Cadeau for sharing this document with me. For the things the French targeted in their strategic air war, including markets, see the long lists in Air Extrême Orient, "Repertoire, dossier d"objectifs" and accompanying photos in AI 4 C861, SHD. For more on bombing in Zone V, see Hang Hing Quang, "A Long Road Trav-

eled" (personal memoir, 2020), http://stephenshenfield.net/places/east-asia/vietnam/214
-memoirs-of-han-hing-quang-a-long-road-traveled, accessed on 10 November 2020.

48. Tran Duong, *Kinh Te Viet Nam*, pp. 151–2. For American bombing attacks on this same
area, see *Daily Report: Foreign Radio Broadcasts*, no. 110, 8 June 1966, p. JJJ1.

49. For number of water buffalo killed in the run-up to the Battle of Dien Bien Phu, see *Kinh
Te Viet Nam, 1945–1960* (Hanoi, Nha Xuat Ban Su That, 1960), p. 24. For the tens of thousands
killed during the Indochina War, see Tran Duong, *Kinh Te Viet Nam*, pp. 151–2.

50. Tran Duong, *Kinh Te Viet Nam*, pp. 151–2; and Pham Van Dong, "Bao Cao Kinh Te Tai
Chinh," no date, but early 1953, *Van Kien Dang Toan Tap*, vol. 14 (1953) (Hanoi: Nha Xuat Ban
Chinh Tri Quoc Gia, 2001), p. 97. For the exact water-buffalo number, *Kinh Te Viet Nam, 1945–
1960*, p. 24. For the French after-action report, see "Bulletin de renseignement," no. 1692, p. 1,
entry 1, 3 October 1953, AI 4 C 865, SHD. On the use of poison, see documents dated late 1952 in
10H839, SHD. On the rice wars and their effects in central and lower central Vietnam, see documents in 10H3359 and 10H3166, SHD, especially "Récolte du riz du 3ème mois lunaire," 19
March 1953, no. 147/SQT/3/S, pp. 1–3; "Général LeBlanc à son Excellence," 9 June 1952; and
"Blocus économique," 9 January 1953, Colonel Gautier, pp. 1–6. Colonel Gautier and General
LeBlanc led the rice wars in central Vietnam while Salan presided over the northern
offensive.

51. *Kinh Te Viet Nam, 1945–1960*, pp. 25–6, 42; and Ban Khoa Hoc Hau Can, *Cong Tac Hau
Can Chien Dich Dien Bien Phu, Dong Xuan 1953–1954* (Hanoi: Tong Cuc Hau Can, 1979),
pp. 354–7. The latter source claims that over half of the porters during the battle of Cao Bang in
1950 were women and that that majority remained the case for subsequent battles. For a glimpse
of peasant children at work, see Georges Boudarel, *Autobiographie* (Paris: Jacques Bertoin,
1991), p. 257.

52. Lizzie Colingham, *Taste of War: World War II and the Battle for Food* (London: Penguin
Books, 2013).

53. On total war, see Hew Strachan, "Essay and Reflection: On Total War and Modern War,"
The International History Review, vol. 22, no. 2 (June 2000), especially pp. 353–5.

54. "Chassin au Conseil supérieur des forces armées," 20 January 1956, AI 02 E2753, SHD.
My thanks to Paul Villatoux for kindly sharing this document with me. See also Chassin, *Aviation Indochine*, pp. 239–40.

55. On the chronic problem of printing money, see Dang Phong, *Lich Su Kinh Te Vietnam,
1946–2000*, vol. 1 (Hanoi: Nha Xuat Ban Khoa Hoc Xa Hoi, 1960), pp. 374–5; Tran Duong, *Kinh
Te Viet Nam*, pp. 325–6; *Kinh Te Viet Nam, 1945–1960*, pp. 18–19. Between 1946 and 1950, the DRV
printed money nineteen times, increasing the money in circulation from 606 million dong to
11,600 million. *Kinh Te Viet Nam, 1945–1960*, p. 18.

56. *Kinh Te Viet Nam, 1945–1960*, p. 20. On bicycle imports, Dang Phong, *Lich Su Kinh Te
Viet Nam 1945–2000*, vol. 1, pp. 346–7.

57. Le Van Hien, *Nhat Ky*, vol. 2, pp. 239, 252.

58. Tran Duong, *Kinh Te Viet Nam*, p. 48.

59. *Kinh Te Viet Nam, 1945–1960*, p. 21.

60. Luo Guibo, "A Glorious Model of Proletarian Internationalism: Mao Zedong and Helping Vietnam Resist France," translated and online at http://digitalarchive.wilsoncenter.org
/document/120359, accessed on 18 February 2020.

61. Luo Guibo, "A Glorious Model of Proletarian Internationalism"; and Le Van Hien, *Nhat Ky*, vol. 2, pp. 375–432. Le Van Hien wrote repeatedly in his memoirs of his work with Chinese advisors, in particular a certain "Trieu" and "Tiet Ngoc" as well as the main advisor, Luo Guibo.

62. See Dang Phong, *Lich Su Kinh Te Viet Nam*, pp. 348–50; *Kinh Te Viet Nam, 1945–1960*, pp. 39–40; Pham Van Dong, "Chi Thi Cua Ban bi Thu," November 1952; "Nghi Quyet cua Bo Chinh Tri," 17 April 1952; and Truong Chinh (Than), "Chi Thi cua Ban Chap Hanh Trung Uong," 8 June 1952; all in *Van Kien Dang Toan Tap*, vol. 13 (1952), pp. 357–60, pp. 54–7, and pp. 204–7 respectively. That the French pushed the Vietnamese the Chinese way, see Ming Guo, ed., *Zhong Yue Guan Xi Yan Bian Si Shi Nian* (Guangxi: Guangxi Ren Min Chu Ban She, 1992), p. 54 (excerpts translated by Yuxi Liu).

63. "L'Economie V.M.," *Indochine Sud-est asiatique*, no. 19 (June–July 1953), pp. 31–2; and "L'Economie viet minh, Indochine du Nord," p. 12. On false declarations, see "Rapport sur la récolte de riz du 3ème mois," 31 May 1952, no. 537/SAT/3/2, p. 2, 10H3166, SHD, based on intercepted Vietnamese documents.

64. Ho Chi Minh, "Sac Lenh no. 13-SL," dated 1 May 1951, https://thuvienphapluat.vn/van-ban /Thue-Phi-Le-Phi/Sac-lenh-13-SL-cai-cach-che-do-dam-phu-bai-bo-quy-cong-luong-thue-dien -tho-v-v-bai-bo-mua-thoc-dinh-gia-dat-thue-nong-nghiep-mua-bang-thoc/36646/noi-dung.aspx, and followed up by a second decree in July 1951, https://thuvienphapluat.vn/van-ban/Thue-Phi -Le-Phi/Sac-lenh-40-SL-ban-hanh-dieu-le-tam-thoi-thue-nong-nghiep-36668.aspx, accessed on 17 February 2020. For a general account, see Tran Duong, *Kinh Te Viet Nam*, pp. 123–5; and François Houtard and Geneviève Lemercinier, *Hai Van: Life in a Vietnamese Commune* (London: Zed Books, 1984), pp. 10–11. For an excellent definition of the *Mau Dich Quoc Danh* or the Trading Office, see https://vn24h.info/mau-dich-la-gi/, accessed on 10 February 2020.

65. Tran Duong, *Kinh Te Viet Nam*, pp. 323–40, especially p. 335, for percentages of rice in the annual budget, and p. 332 for total production levels. See also Dang Phong, *Lich Su Kinh Te Viet Nam*, vol. 1, p. 378. For the total estimates, "La Question du riz, question vitale pour le Nord Vietnam," 23 July 1952, 10H638, SHD.

66. Cited in *Kinh Te Viet Nam, 1945–1960*, p. 23. Cited also in French translation in "L'Economie V.M.," *Indochine Sud-est asiatique*, no. 19 (June–July 1953), p. 29 (see the caption in the lower photo). I translated this excerpt into English from the Vietnamese original.

Chapter 10. The Road to Dien Bien Phu

1. Ton That Tung, *Reminiscences of a Vietnamese Surgeon* (Hanoi: Foreign Language Publishing House, 1980), p. 48. See also Thomas Helling and Daniel Azoulay, "Ton That Tung's Livers," *Annals of Surgery*, vol. 259, no. 6 (June 2014), pp. 1245–52.

2. Yves Gras, *Histoire de la guerre d'Indochine* (Paris: Plon, 1979), pp. 446–7 and p. 447, note 1.

3. Robet Guillain, *Dien Bien Phu, la fin des illusions* (Paris: Arléa, 2004), pp. 114–15.

4. Gras, *Histoire de la guerre d'Indochine*, pp. 446–7; and Guillain, *Dien Bien Phu*, p. 116 for the estimation of French control in March 1954.

5. Guillain, *Dien Bien Phu*, pp. 113–25, p. 122 for the citation.

6. Gras, *Histoire de la guerre d'Indochine*, pp. 420–21, 492–3, 500. On the size of the PAVN's regiments in the delta, see Gras, *Histoire de la guerre d'Indochine*, pp. 456–62; and Guillain, *Dien Bien Phu*, pp. 121–5.

7. Philippe Schillinger, "Le 'Testament' du général Salan ou pourquoi Dien Bien Phu?" *Revue historique des Armées*, no. 4 (1989), pp. 60–66; and Gras, *Histoire de la guerre d'Indochine*, pp. 500–501.

8. Deuxième Bureau, "Etude sur l'économie viet minh," p. 7 ("le couloir de Hoa Binh,") 8 March 1952, 10H638, SHD.

9. Gras, *Histoire de la guerre d'Indochine*, pp. 425–7, 429–62.

10. See "Chi Thi cua Ban Chap Hanh Trung Uong Dang," 20 January 1952, in *Van Kien Dang Toan Tap*, vol. 13 (1952) (Hanoi: Nha Xuat Ban Chinh Tri Quoc Gia, 2001), pp. 4–10; Le Van Luong, "Chi Thi cua Ban Bi Thu," 26 January 1952, in ibid., pp. 15–23; and Truong Chinh, "Bao Cao cua Tong Bi Thu Truong Chinh tai Hoi Nghi Lan Thu Tu," January 1953, *Van Kien Dang Toan Tap*, vol. 14 (1953) (Hanoi: Nha Xuat Ban Chinh Tri Quoc Gia, 2001), p. 58.

11. Gras, *Histoire de la guerre d'Indochine*, p. 454.

12. Truong Chinh, "Nghi Quyet cua Ban Bi Thu," 17 July 1952; and Truong Chinh, "Chi Thi cua Ban Chap Hanh Trung Uong," no date given, but mid-1952, *Van Kien Dang Toan Tap*, vol. 13 (1952), pp. 210–13 and 304–6, respectively.

13. On Nghia Lo, see Gras, *Histoire de la guerre d'Indochine*, pp. 474–9 (pp. 478–9 for the Salan quote).

14. On the Battle of Nasan, see Gras, *Histoire de la guerre d'Indochine*, pp. 483–8; and Jean Maurier, "Nasan: Echec à Giap," *Historia*, hors-série 25 (1972), p. 46 for the citation.

15. Ngo Van Chieu, *Journal d'un combattant Viet-Minh* (Paris: Editions du Seuil, 1955), pp. 219–20.

16. See Brigitte Stüder, "L'Etre perfectible: la formation du cadre stalinien par le 'travail sur soi,'" *Genèse*, vol. 51 (June 2003), pp. 92–113; her "Liquidate the Errors or Liquidate the Person? Stalinist Party Practices as Techniques of the Self," in Brigitte Studer and Heiko Haumann, *Stalinist Subjects* (Zurich: Chronos, 2006); and Claude Pennetier and Bernard Pudal, eds., *Le Sujet communiste: identités militantes et laboratoires du "moi"* (Rennes, Presses universitaires de Rennes, 2014, published online in 2019), https://books.openedition.org/pur/50557, accessed on 29 May 2020.

17. According to Bertrand de Hartingh, the number of cadres grew from 3,000 in late 1945 to 100,000 by 1956. *Entre le peuple et la nation: La République démocratique du Viet Nam de 1953 à 1957* (Paris: Ecole française d'Extrême Orient, 2003), p. 152. On Soviet rectification, see Brigitte Studer, "L'Etre perfectible," pp. 92–113. For scores of captured Vietnamese communist study materials, see 10H3978, 10H3979, and 10H3980, SHD.

18. "Bao Cao ve May Nhiem Vu Cong Tac Noi," no date but identified in the text as the third plenum of 1952, *Van Kien Dang Toan Tap*, vol. 13 (1952), p. 95, note 1.

19. Le Van Luong, "Van De Chinh Dang," no date given, but mid-1952, *Van Kien Dang Toan Tap*, vol. 13 (1952), p. 102, for the 65 percent statistic. On the new round of party rectification in 1952, see this document and the following: "Nghi Quyet Tinh Hinh va Nhiem Vu," in ibid., pp. 167–8; "Thong Cao Hoi Nghi Ban Chap Hanh Trung Uong Dang Lao Dong Viet Nam Lan Thu Ba," in ibid., pp. 169–73, among others.

20. Le Van Luong, "Van De Chinh Dang," *Van Kien Dang Toan Tap*, vol. 13 (1952), pp. 101–6; and Ho Chi Minh, "Bai Noi tai Lop Chinh Huan Dau Tien cua Trung Uong," 11 May 1952, *Van Kien Dang Toan Tap*, vol. 13 (1952), pp. 184–6; and, especially, Ho Chi Minh, "Bai Noi trong Buoi Khai Mac Lop Chinh Huan Can Bo Dang, Dan, Chinh o Co Quan Trung Uong," 6 February 1953,

Van Kien Dang Toan Tap, vol. 14 (1953), pp. 148–60 (p. 154 for the citation, "If you sit between two chairs.")

21. Ngo Van Chieu, *Journal d'un combattant Viet-Minh*, pp. 206–8. For the list of heroes to emulate in the army, see *Le Tuyen Duong cac Anh Hung Quan Doi Nhan Dan Viet Nam* (Hanoi: Ton Cuc Chinh Tri Bo Tong Tu Lenh Xuat Ban, 1955), p. 19 for the list. For one confirmation among scores that rectification continued up to and including Dien Bien Phu: "Bao Cao cua Van Phong Ban Chap Hanh Trung Uong," so. 2-B, 27 February 1954, *Dien Bien Phu, Van Kien Dang, Nha Nuoc* (Hanoi: Nha Xuat Ban Chinh Tri Quoc Gia, 2004), pp. 154–83.

22. Vo Nguyen Giap, "May Net ve Tinh Hinh va Nhiem Vu Quan Su Hien Nay," third plenum of April 1952, in *Van Kien Dang Toan Tap*, vol. 13 (1952), pp. 113–17; and Than (Truong Chinh), "Nghi Quyet cua Ban Chap Hanh Trung Uong ve To Chuc Dang trong Bo Doi Chu Luc," *Van Kien Dang Toan Tap*, vol. 13 (1952), pp. 189–94.

23. Ho Chi Minh, "Bai Noi trong Buoi Khai Mac Lop Chinh Huan," 6 February 1953, in *Van Kien Dang Toan Tap*, vol. 14 (1953), pp. 148–60.

24. Xuan Phuong, *Ao Dai: My War, My Country, My Vietnam* (Great Neck, New York: EMQUAD International, Ltd., 2004), p. 128.

25. Truong Chinh, "Mat Tran Dan Toc Thong Nhat va Van De Dai Doan Ket," undated, April 1952, pp. 76–82; author's name not indicated, but almost certainly Truong Chinh, "Hoi Nghi Trung Uong Lan Thu Ba," 22–8 April 1952, pp. 65–75; both in *Van Kien Dang Toan Tap*, vol. 13 (1952), pp. 76–82; and "Nhan Dan Dan Chu Chuyen Chinh o Viet Nam va Van De Cong Nong Thuc Te Tham Gia Chinh Quyen," undated, but April 1952, *Van Kien Dang Toan Tap*, vol. 13 (1952), pp. 83–9. For more on *The White-Haired Girl*, see Chris Buckley, "'White-Haired Girl,' Opera Created Under Mao, Returns to Stage," *New York Times* (10 November 2015), https://sinosphere.blogs.nytimes.com/2015/11/10/white-haired-girl-opera-created-under-mao-returns-to-stage/, accessed on 28 May 2020.

26. I rely heavily on Olga Dror, "Establishing Ho Chi Minh's Cult: Vietnamese Traditions and Their Transformation," *The Journal of Asian Studies*, vol. 75, no. 2 (May 2016), pp. 433–66.

27. Le Van Luong, "Chi Thi Cua Ban Bi Thu, To Chuc Ky Niem ngay 3–3," 14 February 1952, *Van Kien Dang Toan Tap*, vol. 13 (1952), pp. 28–32; and Le Van Luong, "Chi Thi cua Ban Bi Thu, ve Ky Niem ngay 1–5," 18 April 1952, *Dang Toan Tap*, vol. 13 (1952), pp. 58–61; among others. For the wider communist context in which the Vietnamese were operating, see Anne Applebaum, *Iron Curtain: The Crushing of Eastern Europe, 1944–1956* (Toronto: Signal, 2012). For a fascinating essay on the politics of communist medal making in North Korea, see Martin Weiser, "Chests Full of Brass: A DPRK Political History in Orders, Medals, Prizes, and Titles," Sino-NK (8 January 2016), https://sinonk.com/2016/01/08/chests-full-of-brass-a-dprk-political-history-in-orders-medals-prizes-and-titles/, accessed on 28 September 2020. For an example of Ho's portrait in a peasant house in the early 1950s, see Joseph Starobin, *Eyewitness in Indo-China* (New York: Cameron and Khan, 1954), p. 77.

28. Le Van Luong, "Chi Thi ve Ngay Sinh Nhat Ho Chu Tich (ngay 19.5)," 2 April 1948, *Van Kien Dang Toan Tap*, vol. 10 (1949) (Hanoi: Nha Xuat Ban Chinh Tri Quoc Gia, 2001), pp. 89–94; Le Van Luong, "Chi Thi Cua Ban Bi Thu ve Viec Ky Niem Ngay 19–5," 19 April 1952, *Van Kien Dang Toan Tap*, vol. 13 (1952), pp. 62–4. For other holidays, see Truong Chinh, "Chi Thi Cua Ban Chap Hanh Trung Uong ve Viec Ky Niem Ngay 19–8 va Ngay 2–9 Nam Nay," 30 July 1952, *Van Kien Dang Toan Tap*, vol. 13 (1952), pp. 216–20; and Truong Chinh, "Chi Thi cua

Ban Bi Thu ve Hoan Nghenh Dai Hoi Lan Thu 19 cua Dang Cong San (Bonsovich) Lien Xo (5–10) va Ky Niem Cach Mang Thang Muoi Lan Thu 35 (7–11)," 4 October 1952, *Van Kien Dang Toan Tap*, vol. 13 (1952), pp. 312–15.

29. See Jacques Doyon, *Les Soldats blancs de Ho Chi Minh* (Paris: Fayard, 1973); and Georges Boudarel, *Autobiographie* (Paris: Jacques Bertoin, 1991). For an American account, see Winston Groom and Duncan Spencer, *Conversations with the Enemy* (New York: G. P. Putnam's Sons, 1983).

30. On Dich Van, see *Cong Tac Dich Van Trong Dai Doi* (Viet Bac: Chinh Tri Cuc Xuat Ban, undated but late 1940s); Van Tien Dung, *Cong Tac Dich Van* (Viet Bac: Chinh Tri Cuc Xuat Ban, 1948); *Day Manh Cong Tac Nguy Van va Au Phi Van* (Viet Bac: Cuc Dich Van, 1952); and *Cong Tac Van Dong Nguy Binh va May Y Kien ve viec Pha Tuyen Mo* (Viet Bac: Cuc Dich Van, 1951). For some extraordinary original Vietnamese documents on *dich van*, see 10R 193, SHD. For an insider account, see Nguyen Bac, *Au Coeur de la Ville captive, souvenir d'un agent viet minh infiltré à Hanoi* (Paris: Arléa, 2004, translated by Philippe Papin from the original Vietnamese version, *Giua Thanh Pho Bi Chiem*, 1994).

31. For the East European context, see Applebaum, *Iron Curtain*, Chapter 13 ("Homo Sovieticus,") pp. 300–330. For China, see Rachel Funari and Bernard Mees, "Socialist Emulation in China: Worker Heroes Yesterday and Today, *Labor History*, vol. 54, no. 3 (2013), pp. 240–55.

32. No one explains this better than Ho Chi Minh, "Bai Noi Tai Dai Hoi Cac Chien Si Thi Dua va Can Bo Guong Mau Toan Quoc," 1 May 1952, *Van Kien Dang Toan Tap*, vol. 14 (1953, pp. 174–83. For a list of communist saints for Vietnamese soldiers to imitate in their daily lives, see *Le Tuyen Duong cac Anh Hung Quan Doi Nhan Viet Nam*. For a document showing how the local party chapter in central Vietnam put forward a heroine, Nguyen Thi Chien, for imitation, see the captured documents in: "Le Comité commandement des troupes provinciales à combatants exemplaires des unités de guérilleros des villes et districts," 1 January 1953, A-09–8, 10H3631, SHD.

33. Ho Chi Minh, "Bai Noi Tai Dai Hoi Cac Chien Si Thi Dua va Can Bo Guong Mau Toan Quoc," 1 May 1952, p. 181 for the first quote; and Ho Chi Minh, "Bai Noi trong Buoi Khai Mac Lop Chinh Huan Can Bo Dang, Dan, Chinh o Co Quan Trung Uong," 6 February 1953, *Van Kien Dang Toan Tap*, vol. 14 (1953), p. 154 for the second citation. On the emulation of Tran Dai Nghia, see *Cuu Quoc*, no. 2048 (4 April 1952), p. 1. Ho Chi Minh singled out Tran Dai Nghia as the perfect professional/intellectual to emulate. See Ho Chi Minh, "Bai Noi trong Buoi Khai Mac Lop Chinh Huan Can Bo Dang, Dan, Chinh o Co Quan Trung Uong," 6 February 1953, *Van Kien Dang Toan Tap*, vol. 14 (1953), pp. 151–2.

34. As always, Ngo Van Chieu, *Journal d'un combatant Viet-Minh*, p. 184, provides a glimpse into what emulation meant for the soldiers at the time, free of the communist spin.

35. Pham Van Dong, "Phai Kien Toan Chinh Quyen Cong Hoa Nhan Dan De Tong Phan Cong va Kien Thiet Che Do Dan Chu Nhan Dan Viet Nam," undated, but early 1950, *Van Kien Dang Toan Tap*, vol. 11 (1950) (Hanoi: Nha Xuat Ban Chinh Tri Quoc Gia), pp. 184–5 (undated but early 1950) for the first citation; and for the second: Bureau permanent du Comité central du parti communiste, no 11/CT/TV, "Instructions," dated 25 May 1950, captured document in 801, 285, grouping Haut Commissariat de l'Indochine, Centre des Archives d'Outre-mer. The communist security services were particularly weak in southern Vietnam. See documents in 285.

36. *Dong Chi Tran Quoc Hoan* (Hanoi: Nha Xuat Ban Chinh Tri Quoc Gia, 2006), pp. 311–21; *Dong chi Tran Quoc Hoan voi Cong An Nhan Dan Viet Nam* (Hanoi: Nha Xuat Ban Cong An Nhan Dan, 2004), pp. 68–9, 85–6, 222–4, 309–11.

37. Ibid.

38. Charles Lacheroy, "Une arme du Viet Minh: les hiérarchies parallèles," Conference delivered at Bien Hoa, November 1952, in Charles Lacheroy, *De Saint-Cyr à l'action psychologique* (Paris: Lavauzelle, 2003), p. 11.

39. This section relies heavily on the information provided by several security officers of the time in *Dong chi Tran Quoc Hoan*, pp. 214–15; and "Réorganisation du service de la sécurité publique au Nam Bo, 30 août 1952," 11 February 1953, 10H4235, SHD.

40. *Cong An Nhan Dan Viet Nam, Lich Su Bien Nien (1945–1954)* (Hanoi: Nha Xuat Ban Cong An Nhan Dan, 1994), pp. 357–62; and *Luc Luong Chong Phan Dong: Lich Su Bien Nien (1945–1954)* (Hanoi: Nha Xuat Ban Cong An Nhan Dan, 1996), pp. 205–6. For more on Tran Quoc Hoan and the security services, see Martin Grossheim, "Fraternal Support: The East German 'Stasi' and the Democratic Republic of Vietnam during the Vietnam War," Cold War International History Project (September 2014), working paper 71, https://www.wilsoncenter .org/sites/default//media/documents/publication/CWIHP_Working_Paper_71_East _German_Stasi_Vietnam_War.pdf, accessed on 28 September 2020.

Chapter 11. Imperial Dust: Ho Chi Minh's Associated States of Indochina

1. Joseph Starobin, *Eyewitness in Indo-China* (New York: Cameron and Kahn, 1954), pp. 50, 61–3.

2. Jane Burbank and Frederick Cooper's *Empires in World History* (Princeton: Princeton University Press, 2010).

3. Liam Kelley, *Beyond the Bronze Pillars* (Honolulu: University of Hawai'i Press, 2005); and Alexander Woodside, *Vietnam and the Chinese Model* (Cambridge, MA: Harvard University Press, 1988).

4. Jules Harmand as cited in Christopher Goscha, *Going Indochinese* (Honolulu: University of Hawai'i Press/Nordic Institute of Asian Studies, 2012), p. 23.

5. Ibid., pp. 30–32.

6. On Laotian and Cambodian hostility for the Indochinese federation and the Vietnamese moving within it, see Goscha, *Going Indochinese*, pp. 91–117. For the Burmese break with British India, see Jessica Hendrick, "Burma Divorces India: les relations difficiles entre Birmans et Indiens en Birmanie coloniale," M.A. thesis (Montreal: Université du Québec à Montréal, 2017).

7. Ho Chi Minh, "Bao Cao Gui Quoc Te Cong San," February 1930, in *Lich Su Quan He Dac Biet Viet Nam-Lao, Lao-Viet Nam, Van Kien*, vol. 1 (1930–1945) (Hanoi: Nha Xuat Ban Chinh Tri Quoc Gia, 2011), p. 91.

8. Leon Comber, "'Traitor of All Traitors'—Secret Agent 'Extraordinaire': Lai Teck, Secretary-General, Communist Party of Malaya (1939–1947)," *Journal of the Malaysian Branch of the Royal Asiatic Society*, vol. 83, no. 2 (299) (December 2010), pp. 1–25; and my "Towards a Connected History of Asian Communism," in Geoff Wade and James K. Chin, eds., *China and Southeast Asia, Historical Interactions* (London: Routledge, 2018), Chapter 14.

9. On Cambodian nationalism in the 1930s, see David Chandler, *A History of Cambodia* (Boulder: Westview Press, 1983), pp. 160–65; and Shawn McHale, *The First Indochina War: Violence, Sovereignty and the Fracture of the South, 1945–1956* (New York: Cambridge University Press, 2021), Chapter 4.

10. Goscha, *Going Indochinese*, p. 88.

11. Hollis Hebbel, "The Special Relationship in Indochina," in Joseph Zasloff, ed., *Postwar Indochina* (Washington: Foreign Service Institute, 1988), p. 110; and Goscha, *Going Indochinese*, p. 89.

12. On the Indochinese-wide nature of the party's instructions for taking power, see Stein Tonnesson, *The Vietnamese Revolution of 1945* (London: SAGE, 1991), pp. 336–7, 377; and my "Le Contexte asiatique de la guerre franco-vietnamienne (d'août 1945 à mai 1954)" (Paris: Ecole Pratique des Hautes Etudes, 2000), pp. 73–6, https://cgoscha.uqam.ca/wp-content/uploads/sites/28/2020/10/Thèse-Christopher-Goscha-compressé.pdf, accessed on 21 April 2021.

13. Benedict Anderson, *Imagined Communities* (London: Verso, 2006, revised edition), pp. 113–40.

14. On the "August Revolution in Laos," see Tran Xuan Cau, "Cach Mang Thang Tam Lao Nam 1945," *Nghien Cuu Lich Su*, no. 163 (July–August 1975), pp. 28–46; and Goscha, "Le Contexte asiatique," pp. 73–89, citing Vietnamese sources from the time.

15. Archimedes Patti, *Why Viet Nam?* (Berkeley: University of California Press, 1982), pp. 567–8, note 2.

16. For the original, uncensored version, see Truong Chinh, "Trich Ban Bao Cao 'Chung Ta Chien Dau cho Doc Lap va Dan Chu' cua TRUONG CHINH tai Hoi Nghi Can Bo Lan Thu V (8–16 thang 8 nam 1948)" (My Tho: Tu Sach Giai Phong, 18 November 1949), pp. 34–5, original in 10H3978, SHD. Compare this original one online at www.cgoscha.uqam.ca with the censored version of 2001: *Van Kien Dang Toan Tap*, vol. 9 (1948) (Hanoi: Nha Xuat Ban Chinh Tri Quoc Gia, 2001), p. 209.

17. The following section owes much to the work of Steve Heder, *Cambodian Communism and the Vietnamese Model* (Bangkok: White Lotus, 2004); Ben Kiernan, *How Pol Pot Came to Power: Colonialism, Nationalism, and Communism in Cambodia, 1930–1975* (New Haven: Yale University Press, 2004); David Chandler, *A History of Cambodia* (Boulder: Westview Press, 1983); Jean Deuve, *Le Royaume du Laos* (Paris: L'Harmattan, 2003); Jean Deuve, *Le Laos 1945–1949: Contribution à l'histoire du mouvement Lao Issala* (Montpellier: Université Paul Valéry, n.d.); and exchanges with Martin Rathie, an independent scholar in Laos, who kindly shared his thoughts with me. See his forthcoming essay, "From Messengers to Mentors: The Western Cadres Committee."

18. Goscha, "Le Contexte asiatique," p. 91, note 96.

19. Ibid., pp. 90–91.

20. "Léon Pignon, l'homme-clé de la solution Bao Dai et de l'implication des États-Unis dans la Guerre d'Indochine," *Outre-mers*, nos. 364–5 (December 2009), pp. 277–313.

21. On Phetsarath, see Christopher Goscha and Soren Ivarsson, "Prince Phetsarath (1890–1959): Nationalism and Royalty in the Making of Modern Laos," *Journal of Southeast Asian Studies*, vol. 38, no. 1 (2007), pp. 55–81.

22. Matthew Wheeler, "The Tailor of Nakhon Phanom," *ICWA Letters* (March 2004), http://www.icwa.org/wp-content/uploads/2015/10/MZW-11.pdf, accessed on 24 October 2020.

23. "Pignon à Léon Marchal," 9 July 1949, signed Léon Pignon, "Dissolution du Lao Issara," 119, grouping Conseiller Politique, Centre des Archives d'Outre-mer.

24. Souphanouvong, "Lettre à S.E. Ho Chi Minh," 17 May 1948, reproduced in the annex, p. 1, of Do Dinh Hang, "Quan He Viet Nam-Lao-Campuchia trong Thoi Ky Khang Chien Chong Phap, 1945–1954," M.A. thesis (Hanoi: Truong Dai Hoc Tong Hop Ha Noi, 1993).

25. On Vietnamese military operations and state-making in Laos and Cambodia, I rely heavily on the following, extraordinarily detailed studies: *Tu Lieu Lich Su Quan Tinh Nguyen Viet Nam o Campuchia (1945–1954)* (Cà Mau: Nha Xuat Ban Mui Cà Mau, 2000); and *Lich Su Quan He Dac Biet Viet Nam- Lao, Lao-Viet Nam, 1930–1975, Bien Nien Su Kien*, vol. 1 (1930–1975) (Hanoi: Nha Xuat Ban Chinh Tri Quoc Gia, 2011), especially pp. 187–271 on the creation of political, military, and party zones.

26. For the full Vietnamese documentation of this, see the studies in Ibid.

27. See Hoang Van Hoan's detailed memoirs: Hoang Van Hoan, *Giot Nuoc Trong Bien Ca* (Beijing, 1980), sections 2 and 5, http://www.talawas.org/talaDB/showFile.php?res=5548&rb =08, accessed on 7 December 2020.

28. Goscha, "Le Contexte asiatique," pp. 110–12, 126–8. On Nguyen Thanh Son, see https://vi .wikipedia.org/wiki/Nguyễn_Thanh_Sơn_(nhà_cách_mạng), accessed on 25 April 2021.

29. Goscha, "Le Contexte asiatique," pp. 118–19; and personal correspondence with Martin Rathie.

30. Goscha, "Le Contexte asiatique," pp 114–19; and *Dai Tuong Chu Huy Man, Thoi Soi Dong* (Hanoi: Nha Xuat Ban Quan Doi Nhan Dan, 2004), pp. 219–20. For Giap's account of his early collaboration with Kaysone Phoumvihane, see Vo Nguyen Giap, *Chien Dau trong Vong Vay* (Hanoi: Nha Xuat Ban Quan Doi Nhan Dan, 2001), pp. 291–3.

31. McHale, *The First Indochina War*, Chapter 4; and Goscha, "Le Contexte asiatique," pp. 232–3.

32. "Extrait du bulletin des écoutes Viet Minh," no. 901, dated 20 June 1950, "Message du délégué du gouvernement du Vietnam à l'occasion de la fête de l'unification du Cambodge libre," p. 4, 107, Service du Protection du Corps Expéditionnaire, CAOM. To view Sihanouk's reception of the French High Commissioner Georges Thierry d'Argenlieu, see https://www.ina .fr/video/AFE85001366, accessed on 19 November 2020.

33. Goscha, "Le Contexte asiatique," pp. 235; *Quan Tinh Nguyen Viet Nam o Campuchia*, pp. 66–70; Lt. Colonel Caan, "Le Communisme en Indochine," p. 45, no. 719/DGD, 1 May 1954, in Asie-Océane, Indochine, vol. 309, Ministère des affaires étrangères, France; and an online history of the communist party for Tra Vinh province at https://tuyengiao.travinh.gov.vn/1458 /39703/72995/619944/phong-trao-khmer-yeu-nuoc/chuong-i-cac-chi-bo-dang-cong-san-ra -doi-lanh-dao-phong-trao-dau-tranh-cach-mang-cua-dong-bao-kh, accessed on 28 December 2020. My thanks to Martin Rathie for sharing this reference.

34. Goscha, "Le Contexte asiatique," pp. 235–9; and *Quan Tinh Nguyen Viet Nam o Campuchia*, pp. 56–8.

35. *Quan Tinh Nguyen Viet Nam o Campuchia*, pp. 72–129; "Organisation des rebelles indochinois au Siam," February 1948, Book III, Annex II, "Formation du Comité de Libération du Peuple Khmer," p. 1, and the translation of its "Programme du Comité de libération du people khmer," in "Renseignements," 8 March 1948, all in 10H536, SHD; and Goscha, "Le Contexte asiatique," pp. 245–54. That this Cambodian Liberation Committee was a Vietnamese com-

munist creation, see Truong Chinh, "Hoan Thanh Nhiem Vu Chuan Bi, Chuyen Manh Sang Tong Phan Cong," report to the 1950 plenum, in *Van Kien Dang Toan Tap*, vol. 11 (1950) (Hanoi: Nha Xuat Ban Chinh Tri Quoc Gia, 2001), p. 27; and documents in C882, SHD.

36. For full documentation of these efforts, Goscha, "Le Contexte asiatique," pp. 240–62.

37. For a detailed description of this state building, see *Quan Tinh Nguyen Viet Nam o Campuchia*, pp. 72–129.

38. Goscha, "Le Contexte asiatique," pp. 254–7; and *Quan Tinh Nguyen Viet Nam o Campuchia*, pp. 74–6, 85–6.

39. Truong Chinh, "Hoan Thanh Nhiem Vu Chuan Bi," *Van Kien Dang Toan Tap*, vol. 11 (1950), pp. 100–103; his "Hoan Thanh Giai Phong Dan Toc, Phat Trien Dan Chu Nhan Dan, Tien Toi Chu Nghia Xa Hoi," no date given, but early 1951, *Van Kien Dang Toan Tap*, vol. 12 (1951) (Hanoi: Nha Xuat Ban Chinh Tri Quoc Gia, 2001), pp. 99–100; and Vo Nguyen Giap, "Nhiem Vu Quan Su Truoc Mat Chuyen Sang Tong Phan Cong" (original, 1950, in my possession), pp. 40–42, 85.

40. Truong Chinh, "Hoan Thanh Nhiem Vu Chuan Bi Chuyen Mang Sang Tong Phan Cong" (northern Vietnam: Sinh Hoat Noi Bo Xuat Ban, 1950, original copy, uncensored version in my possession), pp. 37–40.

41. Luo Guibo (La Quy Ba), "Dien Van cua Dai Bieu Dang Cong San Trung Quoc," no date given, but February 1951, in *Van Kien Dang Toan Tap*, vol. 12 (1951), pp. 637–9.

42. Truong Chinh, "Hoan Thanh Giai Phong Dan Toc, Phat Trien Dan Chu Nhan Dan, Tien Toi Chu Nghia Xa Hoi," pp. 111, 148–9; and Truong Chinh, "Hoan Thanh Nhiem Vu Chuan Bi, Chuyen Manh Sang Tong Phan Cong," a report to the 1950 plenum, in *Van Kien Dang Toan Tap*, vol. 11 (1950), p. 101 on "narrow nationalism."

43. "Nghi Quyet cua Hoi Nghi Trung Uong Lan Thu Nhat," March 1951, *Van Kien Dang Toan Tap*, vol. 12 (1951), pp. 515–17 (on creating parties for Laos and Cambodia) and p. 520 on the Laotian Cambodian office in the Politburo; *Lich Su Quan He Dac Biet Viet Nam-Lao, Lao-Vietnam, 1930–2007, Bien Nien Su Kien*, vol. 1, pp. 259–60, on the party's infrastructure from the top down. On the Vietnam-Laos-Cambodia Interdependent Committee, see Truong Chinh, "Hoan Thanh Nhiem Vu Chuan Bi Chuyen Mang Sang Tong Phan Cong," p. 65; *Lich Su Quan He Dac Biet, Bie Nien Su Kien*, vol. 1, pp. 281–2; and Goscha, "Le Contexte asiatique," pp. 197–9. For an extraordinary description of the Politburo's office for Laos and Cambodia, see https://vi .wikipedia.org/wiki/Trưởng_ban_Đối_ngoại_Trung_ương_Đảng_Cộng_sản_Việt_Nam, accessed on 28 December 2020.

44. See the exhaustive list in *Quan Tinh Nguyen Viet Nam o Campuchia*, pp. 252–300.

45. Goscha, "Le Contexte asiatique," pp. 138–46.

46. Ibid., pp. 150–53

47. "Quyet Nghi cua Ban Thuong Vu Trung Uong," meeting of 15–16 January 1950, *Van Kien Dang Toan Tap*, vol. 11 (1950), pp. 11–12.

48. Souphanouvong, "Lettre à M. le Président Ho Chi Minh," 6 February 1950, no. 192/PTN, in Do Dinh Hang, "Quan He Viet Nam-Lao-Campuchia," annex, p. 9.

49. Gouvernement de résistance, no. 1/PG, Souphanouvong, "Le Premier Ministre, Président du conseil (laotien) à M. le Premier Ministre, président du Conseil de la République démocratique du Vietnam (Ho Chi Minh)," 23 August 1950; and his letter to Ho Chi Minh, no. 10/PG, 2 September 1950; both in Do Dinh Hang, "Quan He Viet Nam-Lao-Campuchia,"

annex, pp. 1–3; Goscha, "Le Contexte asiatique," pp. 183–6; Caan, "Le Communisme en Indo-chine," pp. 46–7 on the Laotian congress.

50. Soupanouvong, "Lettre au Premier ministre, président du Conseil (Ho Chi Minh)," no. 16/PG, 21 September 1950, in Do Dinh Hang, "Quan He Viet Nam-Lao-Campuchia," annex, p. 13. For fascinating Vietnamese accounts of their bureaucratic tasks in Laos during the Indo-china War, see *Quan Tinh Nguyen Viet Nam Tren Truong Chien Truong Ha Lao-Dong Bac Cam-puchia (1948–1954)* (Hanoi: Nha Xuat Ban Quan Doi Nhan Dan, 1998); and Vietnamese docu-ments cited in Goscha, "Le Contexte asiatique," pp. 193–6.

51. *Quan Tinh Nguyen Viet Nam o Campuchia*, pp. 129–35.

52. Ibid., pp. 138–43; Truong Chinh, "Hoan Thanh Nhiem Vu Chuan Bi Chuyen Manh Sang Tong Phan Cong" (report to the third party plenum, 21 January to 3 February 1950) (northern Vietnam: Sinh Hoat Noi Bo Xuat Ban, 1950), pp. 37–40, 55 (on a resistance government for Cambodia), 63–65; and Goscha, "Le Contexte asiatique," pp. 283–7.

53. Goscha, "Le Contexte asiatique," pp. 277–300.

54. *Quan Tinh Nguyen Viet Nam o Campuchia*, p. 148; and Goscha, "Le contexte asiatique," pp. 267–9, 289–92.

55. On Cambodians in the Truong Chinh Academy in zone IX, see Goscha, "Le Contexte asiatique," pp. 289–92. On his arrival in the maquis in 1953, Pol Pot's first assignment was a "people's job working in a base" (*duoc giao cho di lam cong tac quan chung o co so*). *Quan Tinh Nguyen Viet Nam o Campuchia*, p. 219. It must have been a menial job at the start.

56. "Nghi Quyet cua Hoi Nghi Trung Uong Lan Thu Nhat," March 1951, *Van Kien Dang Toan Tap*, vol. 12 (1951), pp. 515–17; and "Hoi Nghi Lan Thu Nhat Trung Uong Dang Lao Dong Viet Nam," in *Lich Su Quan He Dac Biet, Bien Nien Su Kien*, pp. 259–60.

57. Goscha, "Le Contexte asiatique," pp. 274.

58. Soupanouvong, "Chu tich Mat Tran Neo Lao Itsala kinh gui Ong Nhouhack [sic]," 16 December 1952, in Do Dinh Hang, "Quan He Viet Nam-Lao-Campuchia," annex, pp. 6–7; Gos-cha, "Le Contexte asiatique," pp. 198–9; *Quan Tinh Nguyen Viet Nam o Campuchia*, pp. 163–7; and "Doan 82 Quan Tinh Nguyen Viet Nam To Chuc Vu Trang Tuyen Truyen Xay Dang Co So Giup Lao," in *Lich Su Quan He Dac Biet, Bien Nien Su Kien*, p. 276. On the Chinese approval of the Vietnamese invasion of Laos, see *Lich Su Bo Tong Tham Muu trong Khang Chien Chong Phap (1945–1954)* (Hanoi: Bo Tong Tham Muu, 1991), pp. 665, 680. On the Laotian People's Party in 1953, see *Lich Su Bo Tong Tham Muu trong Khang Chien Chong Phap*, pp. 644, 680. On its official appearance, see *Dai Tuong Chu Huy Man, Thoi Soi Dong* (Hanoi: Nha Xuat Ban Quan Doi Nhan Dan, 2004), pp. 231–4.

59. For the statistics, see Pham Sang, "Ho Chi Minh voi Cach Mang Giai Phong Dan Toc Lao," M.A. thesis (Hanoi: Vien Nghien Cuu Chu Nghia Mac-Lenin va Tu Tuong Ho Chi Minh, 1991), appendix 1, pp. 164–7; and Goscha, "Le Contexte asiatique," pp. 195–6. On "unconditional" aid, see "Dong Chi Pham Van Dong Noi Chuyen tai Hoi Nghi Can Bo Viet-Lao," 3 October 1952; and "Ban Can Su Lao De Nghi voi Trung Uong Dang Lao Dong Viet Nam," 5 May 1953; both in *Lich Su Quan He Dac Biet, Bien Nien Su Kien*, pp. 282–3, and 302–3 respectively.

60. On Chu Huy Man's role in the Doan 100 in Laos, see *Dai Tuong Chu Huy Man*, pp. 204–31. On Nguyen Khang, see "Trung Uong Dang Lao Dong Viet Nam Cu Dong Chi Nguyen Khang Phu Trach Cong Tac Giup Lao," and "Thanh Lap Doan 100 Co Van Quan Su Viet Nam Giup Cach Mang Lao," both in *Lich Su Quan He Dac Biet, Bien Nien Su Kien*, pp. 328–40. On

state-building in Sam Neua and Phong Saly, see ibid., pp. 293–330; *Lich Su Quan Tinh Nguyen Viet Nam trong Cuoc Khang Chien Chong Thuc Dan Phap tai Lao (1945–1954)* (Hanoi: Nha Xuat Ban Quan Doi Nhan Dan, 2002), pp. 285–7; Goscha, "Le Contexte asiatique," pp. 191–201. On Ho's summons, see Ho Chi Minh, "Kinh gui Hoang Than Souphanouvong," 3 February 1953, in Do Dinh Hang, "Quan He Viet Nam-Lao-Campuchia," annex, unpaginated. For those who stayed in Cambodia, see *Dong Chi Pham Van Xo* (Hanoi: Nha Xuat Ban Chinh Tri Quoc Gia, 2006), pp. 159–60.

61. This is the term Tony Judt uses to describe the process in eastern Europe in *Postwar: A History of Europe since 1945* (London: Penguin Books, 2005), p. 167. My thanks to Jane Burbank for bringing this concept to my attention.

62. Not only did Vietnamese troops liberate Sam Neua and Phong Saly for their Laotian partners, Vietnamese porters from zones III and IV did all the supplying. In the first Vietnamese invasion of Laos, 35,000 porters entered Laos, putting in over one million combined work hours. *Lich Su Bo Tong Tham Muu trong Khang Chien Chong Phap*, pp. 673–4.

63. Postcolonial scholars are so Eurocentric in their approach to imperialism that they miss a whole range of non-Western empires and their colonial vestiges. Anyone interested in the extraordinary role the Vietnamese played in the making of modern Laos should consult the multi-volume collection of party documents, memoirs, and chronologies in the very official *History of the Special Relations between Vietnam and Laos and Laos and Vietnam: Lich Su Quan He Dac Biet Viet Nam Lao, Lao Viet Nam*, published in Hanoi in 2011–12 and covering the period 1930–2012. Many documents come from the party and defense archives.

Chapter 12. Dien Bien Phu: The Changing of Heaven and Earth

1. Ho Chi Minh, "Bao Cao cua Chu Tich Ho Chi Minh," 14–23 November 1953, *Van Kien Dang Toan Tap*, vol. 14 (1953) (Hanoi: Nha Xuat Ban Chinh Tri Quoc Gia, 2001), pp. 369–83 (p. 376 for the citation).

2. Yves Gras, *Histoire de la guerre d'Indochine* (Paris: Plon, 1979), pp. 494–9.

3. Gras, *Histoire de la guerre d'Indochine*, pp. 511–15; Philippe Schillinger, "Le 'Testament' du général Salan ou pourquoi Dien Bien Phu?," *Revue historique des armées*, no. 4 (1989), pp. 60–66; and Michel Grintchenko, *L'Opération Atlante: Les dernières illusions de la France en Indochine* (Paris: Economica, 2008).

4. Gras, *Histoire de la guerre d'Indochine*, pp. 513–14.

5. Cao Pha, "Dinh Cao Chien Cong Tinh Bao Thoi Chong Phap," *Su Kien va Nhan Chung* (21 October 2005), p. 1 for the citation; Nguyen The Luong (Cao Pha), *Nhung Ky Uc Khong Bao Gio Quen* (Hanoi: Nha Xuat Ban Quan Doi Nhan Dan, 2006), pp. 85–6; and Qiang Zhai, *China and the Vietnam Wars, 1950–1975* (Chapel Hill: University of North Carolina Press, 2000), p. 45. Qiang Zhai and Nguyen The Luong confirm that the Chinese provided the Navarre Plan.

6. Gras, *Histoire de la guerre d'Indochine*, pp. 518–20 (p. 520 for the citation about having two irons in the fire); Robert Guillain, *Dien Bien Phu, la fin des illusions* (Paris: Arléa, 2004), p. 119 for the loss of the 600 villages; and *Lich Su Bo Tong Tham Muu trong Khang Chien Chong Phap (1945–1954)* (Hanoi: Nha In Bo Tong Tham Muu, 1991), p. 714. On the final decision to focus on the highlands and not the delta, see Hoang Minh Phuong, "Hoi Uc ve Chien Dich Dien Bien

Phu," Dien Dan, https://www.diendan.org/tai-lieu/tai-lieu/hoi-uc-ve-chien-dich-111ien-bien -phu-1, accessed on 31 July 2020.

7. Edward Miller, "Vision, Power, and Agency: The Ascent of Ngo Dinh Diem, 1945–54," *Journal of Southeast Asian Studies*, vol. 35, no. 3 (October 2004), pp. 433–58; and Christopher Goscha, "Colonial Monarchy and Decolonisation in the French Empire: Bao Dai, Norodom Sihanouk and Mohammed V," in Robert Aldrich and Cindy McCreery, eds., *Monarchies and Decolonisation in Asia* (Manchester: Manchester University Press, 2020), pp. 152–74.

8. Gras, *Histoire de la guerre d'Indochine*, pp. 520–23.

9. For the Vietnamese side, see *Lich Su Bo Tong Tham Muu Trong Khang Chien Chong Phap*, pp. 720–32, 734–6.

10. *Lich Su Bo Tong Tham Muu Trong Khang Chien Chong Phap*, pp. 714, 719–24 (p. 723 for Giap's words), and pp. 727–9 on the Politburo's final decisions.

11. *Lich Su Bo Tong Tham Muu Trong Khang Chien Chong Phap*, p. 732.

12. Gras, *Histoire de la guerre d'Indochine*, p. 528–9 (for the Cogny citation); and Guillain, *Dien Bien Phu*, pp. 148–9 on the phrase *casser du Viet*; albeit writing after the events, Joseph Laniel claims that Navarre told one of his emissaries to Vietnam on the eve of the Battle of Dien Bien Phu that this would be "the destruction of the Viet Minh's regular army." Joseph Laniel, *Le Drame indochinois* (Paris: Plon, 1957), pp. 41–4 (citation on p. 43). For Navarre's strong belief in "entrenched camps" on the eve of Dien Bien Phu, see his "Directives pour la défense des espaces," 8 March 1954, 10H3645, SHD.

13. Cao Pha, "Dinh Cao Chien Cong Tinh Bao Thoi Chong Phap," *Su Kien va Nhan Chung* (21 October 2005), p. 1.

14. Nguyen Chien, *Lich Su Bo Doi Thong Tin Lien Lac, 1945–1954* (Hanoi: Nha Xuat Ban Quan Doi Nhan Dan, 1996), pp. 104–5, 218.

15. Cited in ibid., p. 218.

16. For the land reform, I rely on the party documents for 1952–3 in *Van Kien Dang Toan Tap*, vols. 13–14 (1952–3) and the studies penned by the following: Olivier Tessier, "Le 'Grand Boulversement': regards croisés sur la réforme agraire en République démocratique du Viet Nam," *Bulletin de l'Ecole française d'Extrême-Orient*, nos. 95–6 (2008–9), pp. 74–134; Bertrand de Hartingh, "L'adoption de la réforme agraire par la République démocratique du Vietnam: pragmatisme ou idéologie?" *Autrepart*, no. 3 (1997), pp. 5–24; Alex-Thai Vo, "Nguyen Thi Nam and the Land Reform in North Vietnam, 1953," *Journal of Vietnamese Studies*, vol. 10, no. 1 (2015), pp. 1–62; Luo Guibo, "Preliminary Comments on Mobilizing the Masses, 1953," *Sojourn*, vol. 31, no. 3 (November 2016, translated and commentary provided by Alex-Thai Vo), pp. 983–1018; Alec Holcombe, *Mass Mobilization in the Democratic Republic of Vietnam, 1945–1960* (Honolulu: University of Hawai'i Press, 2020); and Edwin Moise, *Land Reform in China and North Vietnam: Consolidating the Revolution at the Village Level* (Chapel Hill: The University of North Carolina Press, 2012 [first published in 1983]).

17. I rely on Yves Chevrier, *Mao et la révolution chinoise* (Florence: Casterman, 1993).

18. Pierre Brocheux provides an insightful analysis in "Les Communistes et les paysans dans la révolution vietnamienne," in Pierre Brocheux, ed., *Histoire de l'Asie du sud-est, révoltes, réformes, révolutions* (Lille: Presse Universitaires de Lille, 1981), pp. 247–76.

19. Tessier, "Le 'Grand Boulversement,'" pp. 75–6.

20. See David Marr, *Vietnam, 1945: The Quest for Power* (Berkeley: The University of California Press, 1995), p. 104, as to how peasant hunger "lifted" the Viet Minh to victory in August 1945.

21. On the state of this army of cadres in early 1954, see "Bao Cao cua Van Phong Ban Chap Hanh Trung Uong," So 2-B, 27 February 1954, *Dien Bien Phu, Van Kien Dang, Nha Nuoc* (Hanoi: Nha Xuat Ban Quan Doi Nhan Dan, 2004), pp. 179–83.

22. Tran Duong, *Kinh Te Viet Nam (1945–1954)* (Hanoi: Nha Xuat Ban Khoa Hoc, 1966), the chart on p. 358. According to Bertrand de Hartingh, by 1956 the DRV employed 100,000 cadres and 131,195 civil servants, making for a total of 231,195 employees for 1956. Bertrand de Hartingh, *Entre le peuple et la nation: La République démocratique du Viet Nam de 1953 à 1957* (Paris: Ecole française d'Extrême-Orient, 2003), p. 152. My estimate of "over 100,000" for 1954 is a conservative one.

23. *Kinh Te Viet Nam*, p. 358. The party center instructed officials to be very careful about how they conscripted people at the local level. See To (Pham Van Dong), "Chi Thi cua Ban Bi Thu," 9 January 1953, *Van Kien Dang Toan Tap*, vol. 14 (1953), pp. 7–9.

24. "Bao Cao cua Van Phong Ban Chap Hanh Trung Uong," 27 February 1954, *Dien Bien Phu, Van kien Dang, Nha Nuoc*, p. 170 (Zone V deaths); Pham Van Dong (To), "Chi Thi cua Ban Bi Thu ve Phong Doi va Cuu Doi," 12 May 1953, *Van Kien Dang Toan Tap*, vol. 14 (1953), pp. 207–13 (p. 207 for the citation about sustained famine); "Chi Thi cua Lien Khu Uy III," 7 May 1953, in ibid., pp. 630–36 (p. 630, for deaths in Ninh Binh and Son Tay, p. 635 for Pham Van Dong's words); and Dang Tran, "Chi Thi Cua Lien Khu Uy V ve Day Manh Cong Tac Cuu, Chong Doi," 8 February 1953, ibid., pp. 683–7. French-intercepted DRV telegrams confirmed nineteen deaths in Zone IV in early 1953. See SDECE, "Renseignement," 10 March 1953, 10R165, SHD. Alec Holcombe and Christian Lentz have also underlined the importance of famine, and I draw on their excellent work in this section. See Alec Holcombe, *Mass Mobilization in the Democratic Republic of Vietnam, 1945–1960*; and Christian Lentz, *Contesting Territory: Dien Bien Phu and the Making of Northwest Vietnam* (New Haven: Yale University Press, 2019).

25. Raoul Salan, "Guerre économique," 4 January 1953 and attached documents in 10H638, SHD. Later in 1953 the French army rejected requests to soften legal restrictions on the circulation of medicines, although some exceptions occurred on an individual basis. See "Cogny à M. le Gouverneur du Nord Vietnam," no. 5012/FTNV/2, 24 August 1953, and attached documents in 10H2377, SHD.

26. For the "grain of rice" citation, see Pierre Cellier, "Le Viet minh dans l'impasse: un grain de riz = une goutte de sang," *Indochine Sud-est asiatique*, no. 1 (December 1951), pp. 25–6.

27. For Pham Van Dong's words, see "Chi Thi cua Lien Khu Uy III," 7 May 1953, *Van Kien Dang Toan Tap*, vol. 14 (1953), p. 635. See also Pham Van Dong (To), "Chi Thi cua Ban Bi Thu ve Phong Doi va Cuu Doi," 12 May 1953, in ibid., pp. 207–13; and Dang Tran, "Chi Thi cua Lien Khu Uy V," 8 February 1953, in ibid., pp. 683–7.

28. André Clermont, "L'Economie V.M.," *Indochine Sud-est asiatique*, no. 19 (June–July 1953), p. 29 for the revolt.

29. Ministry of Foreign Affairs of the People's Republic of China, entry for Luo Guibo, https://www.fmprc.gov.cn/mfa_eng/ziliao_665539/wjrw_665549/lrfbzjbzzl_665553/t44355.shtml, accessed on 26 June 2020.

30. Luo Guibo, "Preliminary Comments on Mobilizing the Masses, 1953," pp. 983–1018.

31. Chen Jian, *Mao's China and the Cold War* (Chapel Hill: The University of North Carolina Press, 2001), Chapter 3. A Vietnamese General Staff history states that as late as December 1953, "There was no one who knew that there would be negotiations." *Lich Su Bo Tong Tham Muu Trong Khang Chien Chong Phap*, p. 729.

32. Luo Guibo, "Preliminary Comments," pp. 1002–3 for the quotation, p. 1004 for the *cap uy*. On the stages of land reform culminating in the radical, forced distribution of land, see Tessier, "Le 'Grand Bouleversement,'" p. 74.

33. Ho Chi Minh, "Bao Cao tai Hoi Nghi Lan Thu Tu Ban Chap Hanh Trung Uong Dang Khoa II," 25 January 1953, *Van Kien Dang Toan Tap*, vol. 14 (1953), pp. 14–29, in particular pp. 23–6.

34. Truong Chinh, "Bao Cao cua Tong Bi Thu Truong Chinh tai Hoi Nghi Lan Thu Tu," January 1953, *Van Kien Dang Toan Tap*, vol. 14 (1953), pp. 30–83 (p. 48 for the citation).

35. Tessier, "Le 'Grand Boulversement,'" pp. 88–94.

36. Truong Chinh, "Chi Thi cua Bo Chinh Tri," 13 July 1953, *Van Kien Dang Toan Tap*, vol. 14 (1953), pp. 258–61.

37. See Alex-Thai D. Vo, "Nguyen Thi Nam and the Land Reform in North Vietnam, 1953," pp. 1–62; Tessier, "Le 'Grand Boulversement,'" pp. 92–107 (p. 103 on Nguyen Thi Nam's execution), pp. 109–110 (for other cases); Nguyen Minh Can, "Xin dung quen," *Radio Free Asia* (22–3 May 2006), https://www.rfa.org/vietnamese/binhluan/Land_Reform_P2_NMCan-20060522 .html, accessed on 28 August 2020.

38. See Alec Holcombe, "The Complete Collection of Party Documents: Listening to the Party's Official Internal Voice," *Journal of Vietnamese Studies*, vol. 5, no. 2 (2010), pp. 225–42 (pp. 231–5 on the killing); Tessier, "Le 'Grand Boulversement,'" pp. 99–106 (p. 102 on torture) and pp. 104–5 (on the massive party errors of classification); and Tuong Vu, "Triumphs or Tragedies," *Journal of Southeast Asian Studies*, vol. 45, no. 2 (June 2014), p. 253. On Mao Zedong's deep esteem for Ho Chi Minh and instructions to respect Ho's point of view, see Luo Guibo, "A Glorious Model of Proletarian Internationalism," points 4, 6, and 7 at the Digital Archive of the Wilson Center: https://digitalarchive.wilsoncenter.org/document/120359.pdf?v=7a799c4f09 9e81719e1f58d46935fd87, accessed on 31 August 2020.

39. According to Olivier Tessier, the party had already distributed almost 480,000 hectares of land by 1953, almost 60 percent of all the land (810,000 hectares) that would change hands between 1945 and 1957. Tessier, "Le 'Grand Boulversement,'" p. 80. That number presumably refers only to the upper half of Vietnam above the 17th parallel, over which the communists took full control after the ceasefire of July 1954.

40. Pham Van Dong put it more or less this way in authorizing the party to show itself to the people as policy. Pham Van Dong, "Thong Tri cua Ban Bi Thu," 16 July 1953, *Van Kien Dang Toan Tap*, vol. 14 (1953), pp. 262–3.

41. On Dien Bien Phu, I rely on *Lich Su Bo Tong Tham Muu Trong Khang Chien Chong Phap*, 693–853; documents in *Dien Bien Phu, Van Kien Dang, Nha Nuoc*; Gras, *Histoire de la guerre d'Indochine*, pp. 543–57; Pierre Rocolle, *Pourquoi Dien Bien Phu?* (Paris: Flammarion, 1968); and Bernard Fall, *The Siege of Dien Bien Phu: Hell in a Very Small Place* (Philadelphia: Lippincott, 1967).

42. Fall, *Hell in a Very Small Place*, p. 100.

43. Ibid., p. 100.

44. Ibid., pp. 237–8.

45. Gras, *Histoire de la guerre d'Indochine*, p. 555.

46. Ngoc An, "Tieu Doan Hoa Tien 224," *Tap Chi Lich Su Quan Su*, no. 4 (July–August 1997), p. 58. For an online glimpse of this firepower, see https://www.youtube.com/watch?v=VduZuCsqLoo, accessed on 9 July 2020.

47. I borrow this from John Keegan's classic, *The Face of Battle* (London: Jonathan Cape, 1976).

48. Cited by Fall, *Hell in a Very Small Place*, p. 137.

49. *Lich Su Quan Y Quan Doi Nhan Dan Viet Nam*, vol. 1 (Hanoi: Tong Cuc Hau Can Xuat Ban, 1991), pp. 473, 471–8.

50. Fall, *Hell in a Very Small Place*, p. 207.

51. *Dien Bien Phu vu d'en face, paroles de bo doi* (Paris: Nouveau Monde Editions, 2010), pp. 179–80.

52. *Lich Su Quan Y*, p. 487.

53. Fall, *Hell in A Very Small Place*, p. 221.

54. *Lich Su Quan Y*, pp. 477, 479; *30 Nam Phu Vu Va Xay Dung cua Nganh Quan Y Quan Doi Nhan Dan Viet Nam, 1945–1975* (Hanoi: Cuc Quan Y Tong Cuc Hau, 1976), p. 193; and Rocolle, *Pourquoi Dien Bien Phu?*, p. 469, note 228.

55. "Nghi Quyet cua Bo Chinh Tri Ngay 29.4.1954 Doi Voi Mat Tran Dien Bien Phu," *Van Kien Quan Su cua Dang, 1951–54*, vol. 3 (Hanoi: Nha Xuat Ban Quan Doi Nhan Dan, 1977), p. 602; and in Vo Nguyen Giap, "Bao Cao Ket Luan cua Bi Thu Tong Quan Uy tai Hoi Nghi cac Bi Thu Dai Doan Uy," *Mot So Van Kien Chi Dao Chien Cuoc Dong Xuan 1953–1954 va Chien Dich Dien Bien Phu* (Hanoi: Nha Xuat Ban Quan Doi Nhan Dan, 2004), pp. 543–78.

56. "Bao Cao cua Dong Chi Van o Hoi Nghi cac Bi Thu Dai Doan Uy va Cac Dong Chi Phu Trach cac Tong Cuc Mat Tran Dien Bien Phu," *Dien Bien Phu, Van Kien Dang, Nha Nuoc*, 26 April 1954, pp. 741–2 (for the citation); "Nghi Quyet cua Bo Chinh Tri," 19 April 1954; and "Truong Chinh Gui Dong Chi Vo Nguyen Giap," 21 April 1954; both in *Nhung Tai Lieu Chi Dao cac Chien Dich cua Trung Uong Dang, Tong Quan Uy va Bo Tong Tu Lenh*, vol. 4 (Hanoi: Bo Tong Tham Muu Xuat Ban, 1963); see pp. 232–6 for more on what happened in mid-April in Giap's ranks.

57. "Bao Cao Ket Luan cua Dai Tuong Vo Nguyen Giap tai Hoi Nghi Tong Ket Chien Dich Dien Bien Phu," 28 July 1954, in *Dien Bien Phu, Van Kien Dang, Nha Nuoc*, pp. 742–3; and especially Vo Nguyen Giap, "Bao Cao Ket Luan," in *Mot So Van Kien Chi Dao Chien Cuoc Dong Xuan 1953–1954*, pp. 550–51.

58. On the use of punishment and discipline for the example of others during the battle, see "Bao Cao Ket Luan," in *Mot So Van Kien Chi Dao Chien Cuoc Dong Xuan 1953–1954*, pp. 557–72; *Dien Bien Phu, Van Kien Dang, Nha Nuoc*, pp. 795–6; *Lich su 60 nam Toa An Quan Su Viet Nam, 1945–2000* (Hanoi: Nha Xuat Ban Quan Doi Nhan Dan, 2005), pp. 113, 118–19.

59. On just how bad things were, see Vo Nguyen Giap, "Mot So Van Kien Chi Dao Chien Cuoc Dong Xuan 1953–1954," pp. 544–80 (p. 550 for the "proletarian army"); and Rocolle, *Pourquoi Dien Bien Phu?*, p. 469, note 228, p. 483 for French officers watching what was going on through binoculars.

60. *Dien Bien Phu vu d'en face*, pp. 180–81.

61. This history of trauma during the thirty years of war in Vietnam still awaits an historian.

62. For the T59 incident, "viec T59," see *Lich Su Quan Y*, p. 473; and Merle Pribbenow's interview with Nguyen Thi Ngoc Toan in 2007, https://www.yumpu.com/en/document/read /5742682/read-the-translation-vietnam-interviews, accessed on 2 October 2020.

63. *Lich Su Tai Chinh Quan Doi Nhan Dan Viet Nam tap 1 (1945–1954)* (Hanoi: Nha Xuat Ban Quan Doi Nhan Dan, 1989), pp. 121–2; and Ban Khoa Hoc Hau Can, *Cong Tac Hau Can Chien Dich Dien Bien Phu, Dong Xuan 1953–1954* (Hanoi: Tong Cuc Hau Can, 1979), pp. 38–41, 60–94, 354–7, especially pp. 522–49. According to the latter source, mechanized logistics accounted for 85 percent of the transport to the battlefield. The rest was done by bikes and human porterage; see ibid., p. 94.

64. *Cong Tac Hau Can Chien Dich Dien Bien Phu Dong Xuan 1953–1954*, p. 566.

65. Figures in ibid., pp. 554, 565; and *Dien Bien Phu, Van Kien Dang, Nha Nuoc*, pp. 862–3. On the Vietnamese use of Manufacture de Saint-Etienne bicycles, see Xuan Phuong, *Ao Dai: My War, My Country, My Vietnam* (Great Neck, New York: EMQUAD International, Ltd., 2004), p. 132. For unclear reasons, most of the bikes came from or through Thanh Hoa province in Zone IV; see *Lich Su Bo Tong Tham Muu Trong Khang Chien Chong Phap*, p. 614; and *Cong Tac Hau Can Chien Dich Dien Bien Phu Dong Xuan*, p. 272. I can only hypothesize that Zones III and IV relied so heavily on bikes because they had no trucks or only a few. On average, each refitted bike could haul between 100 and 200 kilograms of rice. By the end of the Battle of Dien Bien Phu that number reached a whopping 300 kilograms. Dao Phuong, "Les Bicyclettes de Dien Bien Phu," in *De la reconquête française à Dien Bien Phu* (Hanoi: Fleuve Rouge, 1985), p. 272; and *Dien Bien Phu, Van Kien Dang, Nha Nuoc*, pp. 864, 878–80.

66. Christian Lentz examines the question of famine in his excellent *Contesting Territory: Dien Bien Phu and the Making of Northwest Vietnam*.

67. *Lich Su Tai Chinh Quan Doi Nhan Dan Viet Nam tap 1*, pp. 123–8 (p. 124 for the citation on famine in the northwest); *Cong Tac Hau Can Chien Dich Dien Bien Phu Dong Xuan*, pp. 20–22, 34–45, 71–94, 131–5; and *Dien Bien Phu vu d'en face*, pp. 103–4, 112. For the requisitioning of rice, see the captured letter from the head of the supply office for the 325th division to his superior, 29 January 1953, A-09-8, 10H3631, SHD.

68. On China and food assistance, see Jiang Qian, *Yuenan Mizhan, 1950–1954, Zhongguo Yuanyue Zhanzheng Jishi* (Sichuan: Renmin Chubanshe, 2015), Chapter 28. My thanks to Yuxi Liu for kindly translating sections of this book. On rice from Laos, see *Lich Su Bo Tong Tham Muu Trong Khang Chien Chong Phap*, p. 75, 646; and *Cong Tac Hau Can Chien Dich Dien Bien Phu Dong Xuan*, p. 554, for the figure of 1,700 tons of rice from Laos and also SDECE, no. 2771/ PC/QP, March 1954; no. 2766/PC/GF, April 1954; and no. 2612/PC/GF, March 1954, all in 10H660, SHD. The French reported that a revolt broke out against rice requisitions for Dien Bien Phu in China's Mengla county jutting into northern Laos west of Dien Bien Phu. SDECE, "Aide au Vietnam par la Chine," no. 2237/PC/NA, 10H660, SHD. If so, the social shockwaves the Dien Bien Phu epicenter created profoundly affected non-Vietnamese peoples in the highlands of Indonesia as well as those living in southern China too.

69. Ban Khoa Hoc Hau Can, *Cong Tac Hau Can Chien Dich Dien Bien Phu, Dong Xuan 1953–1954* (Hanoi: Tong Cuc Hau Can, 1979), pp. 23, 40–43, 60–71, 111–12, 125, 143–53, 272–3 (p. 60 on the majority of women porters, p. 269 on pregnant women, p. 111 on desertion, p. 125

on tonnage of bombs, p. 143 on fear of dying). For more on women in wartime, see François Guillemot, *Des Vietnamiennes dans la guerre civile, 1945–1975* (Paris: Les Indes savantes, 2014).

70. *Lich su Bo Tong Tham Muu trong Khang Chien chong Phap*, p. 799; Rocolle, *Dien Bien Phu*, pp. 553–4; and "Le Viet-Minh et la campagne de Dien Bien Phu," p. 8 and annex no. 4, 15 June 1954, C2130, SHD.

Conclusion

1. Frantz Fanon, *Les Damnés de la terre* (Paris: Editions La Découverte & Syros, 2002 (first published in 1961)), p. 69.

2. For a Vietnamese communist critique of Fanon's understanding of "armed struggle" and "revolution" in 1963, see Nguyen Nghe (Nguyen Khac Vien), "Frantz Fanon et les problèmes de l'indépendance," *La Pensée*, no. 107 (1963), pp. 23–36. For an English translation of this text: https://www.viewpointmag.com/2018/02/01/frantz-fanon-problems-problems-independence -1963/, accessed on 9 October 2020.

3. James Smith, "Njama's Supper: The Consumption and Use of Literary Potency by Mau Mau Insurgents in Colonial Kenya," *Comparative Studies in Society and History*, vol. 40, no. 3 (July 1998), pp. 524–48.

4. Richard Fagen, "Mass Mobilization in Cuba: The Symbolism of Struggle," *Journal of International Affairs*, vol. 20, no. 2 (1966), pp. 254–71. In the late 1950s, the Vietnamese communists agreed to an Algerian request to train military cadres. Instead of sending Vietnamese advisors to North Africa to do this, though, the Vietnamese preferred to train a handful of Algerian soldiers who had crossed over to Ho's side during the Indochina War. I doubt much came of this. *Bien Nien Su Kien: Bo Tong Tham Muu trong Khang Chien Chong My, Cuu Quoc*, vol. 1 (Hanoi: Nha Xuat Ban Quan Doi Nhan Dan, 2003), pp. 282–9.

5. Both Ho Chi Minh and Truong Chinh were on the same page in Politburo meetings leading up to the ceasefire agreement in Geneva. Each emphasized that it was best to stop the war with the French now, rather than risk going to war against the Americans. See Ho Chi Minh, "Bao Cao tai Hoi Nghi Lan thu Sau cua Ban Chap Hanh Trung Uong Dang (Khoa II)," 15 July 1954, *Van Kien Dang Toan Tap*, vol. 15 (1954) (Hanoi: Nha Xuat Ban Chinh Tri Quoc Gia, 2001), pp. 162–72; and Truong Chinh, "De Hoan Thanh Nhiem Vu va Day Manh Cong Tac Truoc Mat," 15–17 July 1954, in ibid., pp. 173–222. On the DRV and the Geneva agreements, see the excellent work of Pierre Asselin, "The Democratic Republic of Vietnam and the 1954 Geneva Conference: A Revisionist Critique," *Cold War History*, vol. 11, no. 2 (2011), pp. 155–95; and his "Choosing Peace: Hanoi and the Geneva Agreement on Vietnam, 1954–55," *Journal of Cold War Studies*, vol. 9, no. 2 (2007), pp. 95–126. In French, see my *Vietnam: Un état né de la guerre* (Paris: Armand Colin, 2011), chapters 9 and 10.

6. A high-level Communist Party document captured by the French in Saigon after the ceasefire confirmed that the Vietnamese communists reserved the right to resume their war if a political solution favorable to the DRV was not reached. See "Document viet minh récupéré le 29 Novembre 1954 à Rach Hoc Thom: Situation nouvelle—nouvelle mission," in Deuxième Bureau, no. 10747/2, p. 6 (on the party promise to resume war if needed at a later date), in D 09–1, Economie-Trafic, 10H3631, SHD.

7. See my "Decolonization and American Intervention in Asia: From Japan to Vietnam," in David Engerman, Max Friedman, and Melani McAlister, eds., *Cambridge History of America and the World*, vol. 4 (New York: Cambridge University Press, 2021).

8. "Nghi Quyet cua Hoi Nghi Ban Chap Hanh Trung Uong Lan thu Sau Mo Rong," 15–17 July 1954, *Van Kien Dang Toan Tap*, vol. 15 (1954), p. 223.

9. Vo Nguyen Giap, "Bao Cao cua Dai Tuong Tong Tu Lenh tai Hoi Dong Chinh Phu ve Chien Dich Dien Bien Phu," undated but sometime before the signing of the ceasefire, in *Dien Bien Phu, Van Kien Dang, Nha Nuoc* (Hanoi: Nha Xuat Ban Chinh Tri Quoc Gia, 2004), p. 814 ("nhung chua phai la manh hon dich").

10. "Nghi Quyet cua Hoi Nghi Ban Chap Hanh Trung Uong Lan thu Sau Mo Rong," 15–17 July 1954, in *Van Kien Dang, Toan Tap*, vol. 15 (1954), p. 224. In the Vietnamese original: "Nhung chung ta cung can nhan ro do chien tranh truong ky, nhan dan ta phai dong gop suc nguoi, suc cua cung nang. Neu chien tranh keo dai thi co the sinh ra nhung hien tuong met moi va kho khan cua chung ta co thi nhieu hon."

11. Deuxième Bureau, no 56/1/Dinard/2, 3 November 1954, in 10H3631, SHD. Bad weather in September and October 1954 had only made things worse in Zone IV. And, contrary to earlier years, in 1953 the French and their Vietnamese allies successfully seized most of their rice harvests before their adversaries could do so. See documents in 10H3166, SHD.

12. Bernard Fall, "This Isn't Munich, It's Spain," *Ramparts* (December 1965), p. 23. Although the French rightfully deplored the high rate of death in the DRV's prisoner-of-war camps, they did not push their adversary to provide detailed lists of the dead, for they knew that then they would have to provide the lists of those who had died in colonial camps. The total number of Vietnamese prisoners of war who "died or were executed" (*décédés ou exécutés*) in French camps or prisons exceeded 9,000. Worse still, the French could only account for 2,080 tombs for this total of dead prisoners. Internal records revealed a high level of French executions of Vietnamese prisoners in 1952 and 1953. "Beaufort à M. le général d'armées," Hanoi, 11 March 1955, in Robert Bonnafous, "Les Prisonniers français dans les camps viet minh, 1945–1954," Ph.D. dissertation (Montpellier: Université Paul Valéry, 1985), pp. 292–3.

13. Richard Overy, "Who Really Won the Arms Race?," *Times Literary Supplement* (13 November 1998), p. 5.

14. *Lich Su Nganh Ky Thuat Quan Doi Nhan Dan Viet Nam (1954–1975)*, vol. 2 (Hanoi: Nha Xuat Ban Quan Doi Nhan Dan, 2004), pp. 13–14. On breaking the Geneva ceasefire agreement, see *Hoi Ky Tran Kinh Chi* (Ho Chi Minh City: Saigon Books/Nha Xuat Ban Hong Duc, 2017), pp. 133–4. My thanks to Merle Pribbenow for kindly sharing these two references with me.

15. The French "counterinsurgency" canon is vast. For a start, see Roger Trinquier, *Modern Warfare: A French View of Counterinsurgency* (New York: Frederick A. Praeger, 1964, translated from the French original of 1961). Bernard Fall penned the preface for Trinquier's book. Galula never served in Indochina. Lacheroy did not know Vietnam much better. He only arrived in 1952 and then served only in the south, which was hardly touched by War Communism. That Marcel Bigeard and Pierre Langlais, both veterans of the battle of Dien Bien Phu, held counterinsurgency specialists in low esteem should come as no surprise.

16. See Hun Sen's Ph.D. dissertation on the nature of the Cambodian revolution: Hun Sen, "Tinh Dac Thu cua Qua Trinh Cach Mang Campuchia," Ph.D. dissertation (Hanoi: Khoa Triet

Hoc, 1991). On the Vietnamese role in the creation of Laos' security services, see Le Quang Manh, "Qua Trinh Hop Tac Lao-Viet Nam trong Dao Tao, Boi Duong Can Bo An Ninh cua Lao tu Nam 1962 den Nam 2012," Ph.D. dissertation (Hanoi: Hoc Vien Khoa Hoc Xa Hoi Viet Nam, 2017).

17. "Patriotic Mobilisation in Russia," *International Crisis Group, Europe Report*, no. 251 (4 July 2018), https://d2071andvipowj.cloudfront.net/251-patriotic-mobilisation-in-russia.pdf; John Dotson, "The CCP's Renewed Focus on Ideological Indoctrination, Part 1: The 2019 Guidelines for 'Patriotic Education,'" *Jamestown Foundation* (19 December 2019), https://jamestown.org/program/the-ccps-renewed-focus-on-ideological-indoctrination-part-1-the-2019-guidelines-for-patriotic-education/, accessed on 9 October 2020; and Suisheng Zhao, "A State-Led Nationalism: The Patriotic Education Campaign in Post-Tiananmen China," *Communist and Post-Communist Studies* vol. 31, no. 3 (1998), pp. 287–302. For those who read Vietnamese, google "thi dua" or "thi dua ai quoc" to see what I mean. The methods the Chinese Communist Party deploys in dealing with Hong Kong and Xinjiang are revealing as to what is still inside the communist toolkit. See Anna Fifield, "China Thinks 'Patriotic Education' Built a Loyal Generation. But in Hong Kong? Not So Fast," *Washington Post* (29 November 2019), https://www.washingtonpost.com/world/china-thinks-patriotic-education-built-a-loyal-generation-but-in-hong-kong-not-so-fast/2019/11/28/80f4d586-0c2c-11ea-8054-289aef6e38a3_story.html; and Anna Fifield, "China Celebrates 'Very Happy Lives' in Xinjiang, After Detaining 1 Million Uighurs," *Washington Post* (30 July 2019), https://www.washingtonpost.com/world/china-celebratesvery-happy-lives-in-xinjiang-after-detaining-a-million-uighurs/2019/07/30/0e07b12a-b280-11e9-acc8-1d847bacca73_story.html; both accessed on 9 October 2020.

INDEX